The Definitive Guide to Pylons

James Gardner

Apress®

The Definitive Guide to Pylons

Copyright © 2009 by James Gardner

ISBN-10 (pbk): 1-59059-934-9

ISBN-13 (pbk): 978-1-59059-934-1

ISBN-13 (electronic): 978-1-4302-0534-0

Printed and bound in the United States of America 9 8 7 6 5 4 3 2 1

Trademarked names may appear in this book. Rather than use a trademark symbol with every occurrence of a trademarked name, we use the names only in an editorial fashion and to the benefit of the trademark owner, with no intention of infringement of the trademark.

Lead Editors: Steve Anglin, Matt Wade
Technical Reviewer: Michael Orr
Editorial Board: Clay Andres, Steve Anglin, Mark Beckner, Ewan Buckingham, Tony Campbell,
    Gary Cornell, Jonathan Gennick, Michelle Lowman, Matthew Moodie, Jeffrey Pepper,
    Frank Pohlmann, Ben Renow-Clarke, Dominic Shakeshaft, Matt Wade, Tom Welsh
Project Manager: Beth Christmas
Copy Editor: Kim Wimpsett
Associate Production Director: Kari Brooks-Copony
Production Editor: Katie Stence
Compositor: Linda Weidemann, Wolf Creek Press
Proofreader: Lisa Hamilton
Indexer: Becky Hornyak
Artist: April Milne
Cover Designer: Kurt Krames
Manufacturing Director: Tom Debolski

Distributed to the book trade worldwide by Springer-Verlag New York, Inc., 233 Spring Street, 6th Floor, New York, NY 10013. Phone 1-800-SPRINGER, fax 201-348-4505, e-mail orders-ny@springer-sbm.com, or visit http://www.springeronline.com.

For information on translations, please contact Apress directly at 2855 Telegraph Avenue, Suite 600, Berkeley, CA 94705. Phone 510-549-5930, fax 510-549-5939, e-mail info@apress.com, or visit http://www.apress.com.

Apress and friends of ED books may be purchased in bulk for academic, corporate, or promotional use. eBook versions and licenses are also available for most titles. For more information, reference our Special Bulk Sales–eBook Licensing web page at http://www.apress.com/info/bulksales.

The information in this book is distributed on an "as is" basis, without warranty. Although every precaution has been taken in the preparation of this work, neither the author(s) nor Apress shall have any liability to any person or entity with respect to any loss or damage caused or alleged to be caused directly or indirectly by the information contained in this work.

The source code for this book is available to readers at http://www.apress.com.

Dedicated to my brother, Ian,
and my parents, John and Maggie,
whom I love very much.

Contents at a Glance

PART 1 ■ ■ ■ Getting Started

PART 2 ■ ■ ■ Advanced Pylons

PART 3 ■■■ Expert Pylons

Contents

PART 1 ■ ■ ■ Getting Started

PART 2 ■ ■ ■ Advanced Pylons

CHAPTER 13   Documentation 263

CHAPTER 14   SimpleSite Tutorial Part 2 279

PART 3 ■ ■ ■ Expert Pylons

About the Author

 **JAMES GARDNER** is an Oxford University graduate in physics; cofounder of the Pylons web framework; and founder of 3aims Ltd, a knowledge interaction technology consultancy based in London. The majority of his professional experience has been in the development and support of R&D systems for three different National Health Service organizations in the United Kingdom, and he also coded the popular "What Should I Read Next?" book recommendation service.

James has been writing computer programs since he was a small boy when he first got his hands on a Sinclair ZX Spectrum and was very proud to show his grandmother the flashing colored shapes he had managed to get to appear on a black background on the TV. The excitement and satisfaction of being able to create something extraordinary from a series of carefully ordered characters in a file and a little bit of logical thinking has never left him.

James is heavily involved in open source software, and in addition to his involvement in Pylons, he wrote the Python web modules AuthKit and FormBuild and has a keen interest in authentication and single sign-on systems such as OpenID. He is an advocate of building web applications with the Web Server Gateway Interface APIs that you'll learn about in this book.

While not traveling to London or Oxford, James enjoys nothing more than discussing ideas with challenging and like-minded individuals or sitting down with a cup of tea, a pile of blank paper, a pen, and an Internet connection to think about better ways to solve complex problems using web technology.

In his spare time, James enjoys everything to do with the outdoors from cycling to climbing and from astronomy to scuba diving. In fact, he recently went on a dive trip to the Farne Islands off the coast of Northumbria in the United Kingdom where he thoroughly enjoyed having his equipment nibbled by inquisitive seals. James is lucky enough to have traveled widely and enjoys meeting new people and learning about the different ways people see the world.

James' company's web site is at `http://3aims.com`, and he maintains a personal blog documenting his experiments with Python and Linux, amongst other things, at `http://jimmyg.org`.

About the Technical Reviewer

MICHAEL ORR is one of the Pylons developers and has been writing Python web applications on several frameworks for the past ten years. Michael is the release manager for the WebHelpers component in Pylons. Previously he was the editor of Linux Gazette, a web-based ezine. Mike lives in Seattle, and his other interests include MMA fight sports, languages, and vegetarian cooking.

Acknowledgments

Thanks must go primarily to Ben Bangert and Philip Jenvey for their work on Pylons. Ben in particular is the rock of the Pylons community and should take huge credit for its success. Thanks also go to Ian Bicking who is responsible for Paste, FormEncode, and other Pylons-related projects and who was kind enough to let me use a couple of examples from the FormEncode documentation in the book. Thanks to Mike Bayer for his work on SQLAlchemy and Mako and for reading the SQLAlchemy chapter alpha online and giving his comments at an early stage. Thanks also to Graham Higgins for all his help, particularly when the idea of writing a book was first being discussed.

Thanks to all the visitors to the http://pylonsbook.com site who read the online alpha and gave comments. The following people in particular provided detailed feedback for which I am especially grateful: Chris AtLee, Christine Simms, Harri Vartiainen, Henry Miller, Mike Coyle, Nick Daly, and Krzysiek Tomaszewski. This Pylons book wouldn't be what it is without all your efforts, and I apologize if not all of your suggestions made it into the final text.

I'd like to thank Apress for sharing the vision for this book and allowing me to release it under an open source license so that it can be improved and built upon by the Pylons community, and I'd like to thank everyone at Apress who helped me with this book for their time and energy.

Thanks too have to go to Mike Orr, the technical reviewer. He did an excellent job of reviewing the first draft and pushed me toward making this book more about Pylons and less about the tools and techniques I use in my own web development projects, and that can only be a good thing for you, the reader.

I'd also like to thank some less obvious people. Thanks to all the people who work at the Hub in Islington, London, on social enterprise projects. Thanks to Luke, Stephen, Chris, Tom, Holly, Maria, Fred, and everyone else I've discussed this book with. You've been an inspiration and enormously fun to share a workspace with.

Thanks to Richard Noble for giving me the space and support I needed to work on the book when we were both keen to start our new business venture together and for being great company when I was working on the book.

Finally, I'd like to thank Beth Christmas, the project manager for this book. She, more than anyone else, can take credit for this book ever reaching the publishing stage. I haven't made her life easy, but she was always there to support me when I needed support and push me when I needed pushing. I appreciate her efforts enormously and hope they are repaid to some small extent by you all knowing how grateful I am to her.

Source Code and Updates

This book contains many source code examples as well as the code for a complete hierarchical wiki application called SimpleSite. All the source code is available to download from the Apress web site at `http://www.apress.com` or from `http://pylonsbook.com`. The source code includes a `README.txt` file that outlines what each example demonstrates. The examples were all tested in early November 2008 with Pylons 0.9.7 and SQLAlchemy 0.5 release candidates.

This book is released under the GNU Free Documentation License (the same license used by Wikipedia), so I have also been able to publish the text online. You can find the online versions of the chapters at `http://pylonsbook.com`.

The Pylons community is always dynamic and constantly improving, so if you find a problem in the text or source code with the version of Pylons you are using, I encourage you to report it via the `http://pylonsbook.com` web site so that the online chapters can be updated. It is my hope that, with your help and the help of the Pylons community, this book will continue to be a useful resource for a long time to come. If you are interested in contributing to the online version of this book or in helping me review the updates or contributions that other readers send in, I'd love to hear from you. My address is `feedback@pylonsbook.com`.

I very much hope you enjoy the book and find it a useful resource to help you learn and fully understand Pylons. I'm sure you'll find working with Pylons very liberating, and I look forward to meeting you online if you choose to take part in the Pylons community to share your thoughts and ideas.

PART 1

■ ■ ■

Getting Started

CHAPTER 1

■■■

Introducing Pylons

This book is about Pylons, an exciting, modern web development framework that puts the developer firmly in control and makes building complex web applications as easy as possible.

Pylons has grown hugely in popularity in recent years because of its careful balance of powerful development features and its modular internal architecture, which help developers to quickly create sophisticated web applications without hiding what is really going on behind the scenes. Pylons gives you the power you need to efficiently create web sites and web applications while also being flexible enough to allow you to do things differently when you really need to. Best of all, Pylons is an open source project with a great community behind it to offer help and support when you need it.

The first part of this book will give you all the knowledge you need to start using Pylons' default configuration to build high-quality production web sites. In Part 2, you'll learn about some of Pylons' more advanced features, such as Unicode and internationalization support, Ajax, and URL routing, before moving on to Part 3 to learn about expert topics such as the Web Server Gateway Interface, authentication and authorization, deployment, and logging.

Each chapter will serve as a complete guide to each of the topics covered and will contain links to areas you can go for further information. Throughout the book, I will also be taking you through how to develop a simple web site application called SimpleSite so that you can see how the principles described in each of the chapters apply in a real Pylons application.

The Old Way: CGI Scripts

In the past, developers typically wrote web applications as a series of simple scripts, each of which would be responsible for accessing the database for the data it needed and generating HTML to produce the pages it output. Each individual script was quick to write and easy for an experienced developer viewing the code for the first time to understand, because everything relevant to the generation of a particular page would be in one script. Developers had direct access via SQL to the database they were using and had the power and flexibility to write their code in whichever way was appropriate for their needs.

Here's a simple example of the way CGI scripts used to be written:

```
#!/usr/bin/env python

# Get the configuration for the script
import ConfigParser
config = ConfigParser.ConfigParser()
config.read('/path/to/config.ini')
```

```python
# If debugging is enabled, set up the cgitb module
if config.get('general', 'debug') == 'on':
    import cgitb; cgitb.enable()

# Begin the non-configuration-dependent imports
import cgi
import MySQLdb
import os

# Output the HTTP headers
print "Content-type: text/html\n\n"

# Output the head of the HTML page
print "<html><head><title>Example</title></head>"
print "<body><h1>Example</h1><p>Here are the comments:</p>"

# Get the ID from the URL based on the QUERY_STRING environment
# variable using the cgi module
fields = cgi.FieldStorage()
page = int(fields['page'].value)

# Fetch data from the database
connection = MySQLdb.connect(
    db=config.get('database', 'database'),
    user=config.get('database', 'user'),
    passwd=config.get('database', 'password'),
    host=config.get('database', 'host')
)
cursor = connection.cursor()
cursor.execute("SELECT id, data FROM comment WHERE page=%s", (page,))
results = cursor.fetchall()
cursor.close()
connection.close()

# Output the comments
for id, data in results:
    print "<p>Commment #%s: %s</p>"%(id, cgi.escape(data))

# Output the rest of the HTML page
print "</body></html>"
```

This script would display a list of comments when a URL such as /cgi-bin/test.cgi?page=1 was entered. You would also need a config file, which looked something like this:

```
[general]
debug = off

[database]
database = dbname
host = localhost
user = james
password = somepassword
```

The CGI script code isn't as elegant as it could be, but it does have some benefits. Let's look at the pros and cons. First, here are the pros:

- Someone who understands HTTP and SQL will probably be able to understand most of this code because it uses standard web development techniques.

- Coding in this manner gives the developer a huge amount of power because they have control over every aspect of the HTTP response and can write SQL queries that are as complex as they like.

Now, here are some of the cons:

- Every script in the site needs the same code to load the config file and to handle the errors.

- Writing database access code is very repetitive, and the data structures from the database don't necessarily represent the objects your application wants to deal with.

- CGI scripts can be slow because the whole Python interpreter as well as the modules the script uses need to be loaded into memory on each request.

- Designers will find it difficult to change the theme of the site because the HTML-generating code is interspersed with Python code.

There are also some more subtle problems with creating a whole application as a series of scripts:

- Code is frequently duplicated in multiple scripts so over time the code can become difficult to maintain as developers change the database or the code in certain files but aren't aware that other scripts also rely on the way the database or code used to work.

- It can be difficult to understand how the whole application is structured because each script can behave fairly autonomously.

- URLs in the form `/cgi-bin/path/to/script.cgi?controller=page&action=view&id=3` do not readily reflect the structure of your web application and are not as natural to a user as a URL such as `/page/view/3`.

The Pylons Way

To address these problems, Pylons (as well as other popular frameworks such as Django, Turbo-Gears, and Ruby on Rails) use two main techniques:

- A Model View Controller (MVC) architecture

- Convention over configuration

Pylons also puts particular emphasis on loose coupling and clean separation. You'll learn about each of these ideas in the following sections.

Model View Controller Architecture

The *Model View Controller* architecture is a result of the recognition that, at their heart, most web applications:

- Store and retrieve data in a way that is natural to the programming language involved (the model)

- Represent the data in various ways, most commonly as HTML pages (the view)

- Execute logic code to manipulate the data and control how it is interacted with (the controllers)

In Pylons, each of these components is kept separate. Requests are dispatched to a *controller*, which is an ordinary Python class with methods called *actions* that handle the application logic. The controller then interacts with the model classes to fetch data from the database. Once all the necessary information has been gathered, the controller passes the key information to a *view template* where an HTML representation of the data is generated and returned to the user's browser. The user then interacts with the view to create a new request, and the process starts again. The model and controller don't contain code for generating HTML, and the view templates shouldn't interact directly with the model.

This architecture is useful because it not only reflects what happens in most web applications, but it also keeps your application easy to maintain because you always know where the code handling a particular aspect of your application can be found. For example, Pylons uses a templating language called Mako to help you generate HTML and recommends the object-relational mapper SQLAlchemy to help you with your model. You'll learn much more about models, controllers, and view templates in the following chapters.

■**Caution** Those of you coming to Pylons from Django might be accustomed to Django's approach to the MVC architecture, which it refers to as MTV (which stands for model/template/view). Although conceptually quite similar to Pylons' traditional approach to MVC, there are two key terminology differences:

Django's template is equivalent to Pylons' view.

Django's view is equivalent to Pylons' controller.

The model is treated similarly in Django and Pylons. You can find a discussion of Django's reasons for its terminology on the Django web site at `http://tinyurl.com/3mwwhf`.

Convention Over Configuration

A lot of the complexity of web development can be removed by assuming that the developer wants to do the most obvious thing. For example, almost every time a user requests a page from your site, you will want to return a simple HTML page. Sometimes you may want to return an image or perhaps stream some custom binary data, but most of the time, a simple HTML page is all that's required.

With this in mind, the Pylons developers designed Pylons to automatically *assume* data you return is HTML *unless* you specify otherwise. This means that for the common cases you don't have to *configure* the Content-type because the *convention* is that it will be text/html unless you want to do things differently.

Loose Coupling and Clean Separation

Web frameworks such as Django and Ruby on Rails have become extremely popular in recent years because they provide a structure that allows you to quickly create good-looking web sites by defining the way the data is structured. The tools they provide then work on that data either to automatically generate code (scaffold in the case of Ruby on Rails) or to create form interfaces at runtime (as is the case with Django).

Although these frameworks maintain a clean separation between the model, view, and controller layers of code, they aren't loosely coupled in the way that Pylons is because the ability of the application as a whole to work relies heavily on the glue code found in the framework itself. Although it can be easy to write a simple application with these frameworks, it can also be harder to customize their behavior later in a project because doing so frequently involves understanding how the code provided by the framework itself works before you can change its behavior. To make the framework itself easy to use, the framework code sometimes has to be quite complex, and as a result, customization can sometimes be rather difficult.

Pylons, on the other hand, is much more loosely coupled. Because it doesn't provide tools to automatically generate a nearly finished site for you from the definition of the model, it doesn't need complicated glue code holding everything together. Instead, it provides sensible low-level APIs and methodologies that allow you to quickly and easily glue together the component parts you choose to use for yourself.

This loosely coupled approach doesn't mean you have to code absolutely everything for yourself either. Pylons uses convention over configuration and assumes you will want to use a standard setup when you create a new project. If you don't want a standard setup, it is easy to customize the way Pylons works. For example, by default Pylons uses a templating framework called Mako to help you generate the templates for your views, but you are under no obligation to use it. By customizing your Pylons project, you can easily use any of the other major Python templating languages including Genshi, Jinja, or even TAL or Breve.

Other Features

In addition to handling a model, views, and controllers, modern web frameworks also have to provide tools to facilitate each of the following processes:

- Mapping the URL a user visits to the code to be run
- Reading data such as form posts that are sent via HTTP
- Validating and repopulating forms
- Dealing with user accounts
- Storing session information, perhaps using a cookie

They also often provide the following:

- A server component to run the application
- Automatic documentation generation tools
- Systems for packaging, distribution, and deployment
- Testing tools
- Internationalization tools and Unicode support

- Interactive debugging tools
- Logging facilities

Pylons is no exception and provides tools and methodologies for handling all of these things. You'll learn about each of them during the course of the book.

The Python Language

Python is a fantastic language for a huge range of programming problems. It is easy to learn and yet powerful and expressive enough to handle all manner of tasks. It is also great for web programming (there are good reasons it is one of the three official languages at Google). Perhaps its key benefit is that Python has a great deal of support across all popular platforms including BSD, Linux, Mac OS X, and Windows, as well as a huge range of software libraries already available for it, so the majority of the time you will be able to find a suitable tool for the task you are trying to achieve without having to write it yourself.

If you haven't yet learned Python, now would be a good time to read the Python Tutorial at `http://docs.python.org/tut/tut.html`, which will give you all the knowledge you need to get started developing applications with Pylons.

Another good source of information for learning Python is Mark Pilgrim's book *Dive Into Python* published in 2004. It is freely available online at `http://www.diveintopython.org/toc/index.html` and goes into a bit more detail about Python.

Python 3.0

Python 3.0 is a new version of the Python programming language that is currently in alpha release (as of this writing). Unlike recent upgrades to the Python programming language, Python 3.0 will not be fully backward compatible with previous versions, so it is likely that code written for Pylons at the moment will not automatically work with Python 3.0.

Luckily, this isn't a problem you need to be too worried about for three reasons:

- The changes in Python 3.0 are fairly small, so it is going to be fairly easy to upgrade your code.
- The Python language team will continue to release 2.*x* versions of Python after the 3.0 release.
- A tool will be available to automatically translate Python source files from 2.*x* to 3.*x*, and it will handle the vast majority of the conversions necessary. If you are interested, the current development version is at `http://svn.python.org/projects/sandbox/trunk/2to3/`.

Once there is enough demand for a Python 3.0 version of Pylons and enough of the Pylons dependencies have been updated, the Pylons team plans to release a pair of feature-identical Pylons versions, one for Python 2.6 and one for Python 3.0, in line with the Python community's current recommendation.

Python 2.6 includes a feature to print warning messages about any code that is not compatible with Python 3.0, so you will be able to run your code on Pylons for Python 2.6 to find out where any problems might be and then, after making changes or running the 2to3 refactor tool, you will be able to run your code on Pylons for Python 3.0.

The Pylons Community

A key benefit of choosing Pylons is that there is a thriving and helpful community built around it. Getting active in the Pylons community is easy, and we're always looking to increase community participation.

Besides the official documentation, there is also a Pylons Cookbook that contains user-contributed documentation as part of the Pylons wiki. The community always welcomes new contributions to the Cookbook or comments on existing articles, and if you register on the wiki, you can even export to PDF by clicking the PDF icon in the top right of the pages to take them on the road with you.

Pylons wiki: `http://wiki.pylonshq.com/`

Official documentation: `http://wiki.pylonshq.com/display/pylonsdocs/`

Cookbook: `http://wiki.pylonshq.com/display/pylonscookbook/`

For more direct help, the Pylons Discuss mailing list on Google Groups is always active, and usually quite a few people on the Pylons freenode channel on IRC are happy to help too.

IRC: `#pylons` on `irc.freenode.net`

Mailing list: `http://groups.google.com/pylons-discuss`

Pylons Components

Unlike other web frameworks where each component has been custom built for the framework and then tightly integrated into its other components. Pylons is more like a collection of very carefully chosen third-party software. Rather than starting from scratch on each of the components making up Pylons, the developers instead worked with existing software teams to develop standards and APIs that would allow their software to work with Pylons.

This approach turns out to be hugely useful and has three core benefits:

- The APIs and methodologies that allow Pylons to work with one class of component—say, templating languages—also mean that when newer and better software comes along, it is a simple task to use the same APIs and methodologies to allow Pylons to work with the new software.

- From the individual software project's point of view, the APIs that have been developed to allow the software to work with Pylons also mean the software is much easier to integrate into other frameworks since the required APIs already exist.

- Because many of the components weren't initially designed just to be used in Pylons, it also means you are much more likely to be able to use them in ways you wouldn't normally expect web framework components to be used. For example, FormEncode is also an excellent general-purpose conversion library, and SQLAlchemy is used in many projects entirely unrelated to the Web. This means that as your applications grow or if your requirements change, Pylons is much more likely to be able to keep pace.

One of the problems for newcomers to Pylons is that it can be difficult to know how all the components fit together, particularly because the individual projects' documentation isn't necessarily web-focused. That's where this book comes in.

What's Coming Up

Over the next 20 chapters, you'll learn everything you need to know to create a simple web site with a navigation hierarchy, editable sections and pages, a comment system, and tags support. The application will serve as a very good starting point for any Pylons-based web site you create.

The book is divided into three parts: "Getting Started," "Advanced Pylons," and "Expert Pylons." In the first part, you'll learn the following:

- How to install Pylons on Linux, Mac, or Windows in a way that doesn't interfere with other software on your system

- How to use project templates to create customizable project skeletons to get you up and running quickly

- The basics of HTTP and how Pylons' request and response objects make working with it much easier

- The basics of the Pylons architecture and what each of the Pylons globals is for

- How to use Pylons' industry-leading interactive debugger, as well as email reporting tools

- How to create view templates with Mako including how to take advantage of features such as inheritance to apply consistent themes across multiple pages as well as how to use components to generate common structures such as navigational elements

- How to create forms using the Pylons helpers and how to validate and repopulate them as necessary using FormEncode and HTML Fill

- How to deal with file uploads and repeating validation structures involving one-to-many mappings in your model

- The various software options for your model, whether it be an XML database, an Amazon S3 store, or a traditional relational database management system

- How you can use SQLAlchemy to model your database, saving you time and effort

At the end of Part 1, you'll also get started with the example application called SimpleSite so that you see how the techniques you've learned apply in a real application.

Once you've mastered the basics, you'll move on to Part 2 to take a look at some of the more advanced features and techniques that can be used in Pylons applications. These include the following:

- How to use Routes to allow complex mappings between the URLs your application handles and the code that powers them as well as best practices for URL design and how URLs can be used as simple state stores

- What Unicode is and how to use it throughout your Pylons application

- How to write a Pylons application that supports multiple languages and displays non-Western characters such as Japanese or Arabic

- The YUI library and how it can be used to simplify your client-side CSS and layouts

- The basics of the JavaScript language including the areas where it differs from Python

- How to use Ajax and animation to improve your web applications

- How to write effective unit and functional tests

- How to use docstrings and reStructuredText to quickly and easily write good documentation for your Pylons project

You'll then return to the SimpleSite example and add a navigation hierarchy, CSS, and JavaScript to the example application as well use some advanced SQLAlchemy features such as inheritance.

Once you've mastered these techniques, you'll learn all about Pylons' internal structure and how you can easily use a specification called the Web Server Gateway Interface to extend or change the way Pylons itself works. in Part 3, you'll cover the following:

- The Web Server Gateway Interface specification and the details of how to program various types of Web Server Gateway Interface components

- A bit about the history of Pylons and how it influences the design methodology

- How Pylons uses the PasteDeploy package and egg entry points to allow easy customization of middleware and applications in configuration files

- How Pylons uses the egg format and `setuptools` to allow easy packaging and distribution of Pylons applications and dependencies on the Python Package Index

- How to use AuthKit to implement authentication and authorization appropriate to your application's needs

- The principles of various ways web applications can be written including multithreaded, multiprocess, and asynchronous web applications and why most deployment options for Pylons are multithreaded

- How to deploy a Pylons application using Apache or Nginx proxying to a Paster server, how to use `mod_wsgi` to embed a Pylons applications in an Apache server, and where to learn about the many other ways to deploy Pylons applications

- How to use Python's powerful logging system with a Pylons application

You'll then take a final look at the SimpleSite application and see how to turn the project back into a project template so that other people can use it as a starting point for their own applications.

By the end of the book you should have a thorough understanding of how to use Pylons as well as a good knowledge of the technologies Pylons uses and the underlying reasons for their inclusion in the Pylons framework so that you are empowered to make your own choices about which components to use in your own Pylons applications.

Pylons is a framework that is designed to work with you and not to enforce its view of the world on your project. This book will give you the skills you need to use Pylons' default options but also to know when to break the rules.

Summary

This chapter gave you a broad understating of some of the design philosophies of Pylons and what makes it slightly different from other frameworks you might have used.

There's clearly a lot to learn, so let's get started!

■ ■ ■

# CHAPTER 2

Installing Pylons

Pylons is written in the Python language and is designed to run on any platform that supports a modern version of Python. It can therefore be used on Windows, Mac OS X, Linux, BSD, and many other platforms. Because Python is an interpreted language, Pylons applications you write for one platform will be able to run on other platforms without any modification.

You can install Pylons in quite a few different ways depending on your needs, but the three main tools most Pylons developers use are as follows:

- A virtual Python environment
- The easy_install program
- The Python Package Index

In this chapter, you'll look at what a virtual Python environment is before turning your attention to the Python Package Index and the easy_install program. Once you have a thorough understanding of the install processes used by Pylons, you'll turn your attention to Python itself and look at any subtleties you need to be aware of on your particular platform, including how to install packages that include C and C++ extensions.

Note If you don't have a copy of Python installed yet, you might want to jump ahead to the platform-specific notes later in this chapter to learn how to install a recent version of Python such as 2.5 or 2.6 on your platform. However, since almost all platforms apart from Windows already come with a recent version of Python, you'll probably be able to create a virtual Python environment straightaway.

Quick Start to Installation for the Impatient

Pylons is actually very easy to install. If you are not so interested in the details but just want to get up and running with a Pylons installation on Linux as quickly as possible, the following steps show you how. You'll find steps specific to Windows and Mac OS X later in the chapter.

1. Download the `virtualenv.py` script from `http://pylonsbook.com/virtualenv.py`.

2. Create a virtual Python environment in a directory called `env` so that packages you install for Pylons do not affect any other programs using Python on your system:

   ```
   python virtualenv.py --no-site-packages env
   ```

3. Windows users would use `Scripts` instead of bin in the above command but full details are explained later in the Windows-specific instructions. Use the `easy_install` program (which was automatically installed into your virtual Python environment by the previous command) to install Pylons:

   ```
   env/bin/easy_install "Pylons==0.9.7"
   ```

Once the installation has finished, you should always use the programs in `env/bin` rather than the scripts in your system Python installation. For example, where examples in the book specify something like this:

```
$ paster serve --reload development.ini
```

you would actually need to type the following to have the command run from your virtual Python environment:

```
$ env/bin/paster serve --reload development.ini
```

If you don't quite understand the implications of the setup described here, please read the rest of the chapter for the full details.

Installation in Detail

Now that you've seen the commands used to install Pylons, let's take a detailed look at the installation process and what the commands actually do. In the following sections, you'll learn about how packages are stored in a format known as an *egg*, how Easy Install searches online to find the packages you require, and how to install and work with a virtual Python environment.

Using the Python Package Index

You can download all Python packages from a special part of the Python web site known as the Python Package Index (PyPI) at `http://pypi.python.org`. As well as providing the packages, the Python Package Index also contains information about each package such as the author, the project's home page, and a description of the project. Python packages can contain Python source code, configuration files, data files, C or C++ extensions, and metadata about the package.

In Part 3 of the book, you'll learn how you can package up your Pylons applications and automatically upload them to PyPI, but for the moment you need to know only that PyPI is the main place where you can find Python software.

Setting Up a Virtual Python Environment

A *virtual Python environment* is an isolated Python installation set up in such a way that the libraries it contains do not affect programs outside it, making it a good choice for experimenting with new packages or deploying different programs with conflicting library requirements. You can also create a virtual Python environment and install software to it without requiring root or administrator privileges, making it a very useful technique for installing Pylons in a shared environment. *It is highly recommended you install Pylons this way if it's your first time using it.*

A number of tools are available in the Python community for creating a virtual Python environment, but the two most popular are Buildout and `virtualenv.py`. Buildout is popular in the Zope community because it has a lot of features that help you manage all aspects of a deployment, but it can be rather complicated. `virtualenv.py` is a lighter solution designed to handle just the creation of a virtual Python environment, which makes it perfect for most use cases involving Pylons.

To create a virtual Python environment, you need the `virtualenv.py` bootstrapping script. The current version of this script at the time of writing this book is available at `http://pylonsbook.com/virtualenv.py`, and many Linux distributions provide a `python-virtualenv` package, but you will probably want to use the most recent version instead. To obtain the latest version, visit the Python Package Index, and search for `virtualenv`. Download the `.tar.gz` version of the software, and extract the `virtualenv.py` file from the distribution.

You can do so with commands similar to the following, but be sure to update them for the version you want to download:

```
$ wget http://pypi.python.org/packages/source/v/virtualenv/virtualenv-1.1.tar.gz
$ tar zxfv virtualenv-1.1.tar.gz
$ cp  virtualenv-1.1/virtualenv.py ./
```

You can now remove the old files if you like:

```
$ rm -r virtualenv-1.1
$ rm virtualenv-1.1.tar.gz
```

Windows users will need to download the file manually because `wget` is not available, and they will need to use a tool such as 7-zip from `http://www.7-zip.org` to extract the files. Mac users and some Linux users will need to use `curl -O` instead of `wget` to download the file.

■ Note If you are using a system that already has the `easy_install` program installed, you could instead install `virtualenv` automatically like this:

```
$ easy_install "virtualenv==1.1"
```

The `virtualenv.py` script will then be available in your Python installation's `bin` or `Scripts` directory.

Whichever way you choose to obtain the `virtualenv.py` script, you can now use it to create an isolated virtual Python environment to keep your Pylons libraries separate from other libraries on your system.

You are now ready to create a virtual Python environment. Here's how it looks on Windows:

```
C:\>C:\Python25\python.exe "C:\Documents and Settings\Administrator\Desktop\virt
ualenv-1.1\virtualenv.py" C:\env
New python executable in C:\env\Scripts\python.exe
Installing setuptools..............................done.
```

Windows users shouldn't create the virtual Python environment in a path with a space. Otherwise, you may see an error similar to this:

```
ValueError: The executable 'C:\\Documents and Settings\\Administrator\\Desktop\\
env\\Scripts\\python.exe' contains a space, and in order to handle this issue
you must have the win32api module installed
```

As the error suggests, installing the `win32api` module from `http://sourceforge.net/project/showfiles.php?group_id=78018` fixes this issue.

On Linux platforms, you should ensure you have the `python-dev` package for your Python version installed; otherwise, the `virtualenv.py` script might complain about include files.

It is also worth noting for advanced users that a virtual Python environment is not necessarily compatible with a customized `distutils.cfg` file.

Working with Easy Install

Now that the virtual Python environment is set up, you can turn your attention to easy_install, which is a Python program that automatically fetches packages from PyPI as well as any dependencies it has. It then installs them to the same Python environment where the easy_install program is installed.

The easy_install program is actually part of a module called setuptools and is installed automatically by the virtualenv.py script you just ran.

Tip If you did not use a virtual Python environment, you can still use easy_install. Download the ez_setup.py file from http://peak.telecommunity.com/dist/ez_setup.py, and then run this command:

```
$ python ez_setup.py
```

You can find full documentation for Easy Install at http://peak.telecommunity.com/DevCenter/EasyInstall, and although it is a powerful tool with many options for advanced users, its basic use is very straightforward. To give you a flavor of the common ways to use it, I will run through some examples.

To install the latest version of the PasteDeploy package used by Pylons and its dependencies, you would simply run this command:

```
$ easy_install PasteDeploy
```

When you run this command, Easy Install will visit the Python Package Index and the Pylons download page to find the most appropriate version of each of the required packages and install them each in turn. The PasteDeploy package doesn't have any dependencies, but if it did, Easy Install would search the Python Package Index for the most appropriate versions of the dependent packages and automatically download them too.

If you are using a virtual Python environment, you have to add the path to the virtual environment's bin directory before the easy_install command. If you installed your virtual Python environment to the env directory as described earlier, the command would be as follows:

```
$ env/bin/easy_install PasteDeploy
```

On Windows, commands such as easy_install are often real Windows applications, so you can add the .exe extension to them if you prefer. A virtual Python environment on Windows installs programs to the Scripts directory rather than to the bin directory, so on Windows the command would be as follows:

```
$ env/Scripts/easy_install.exe PasteDeploy
```

Caution The rest of the chapters in the book assume you will always add the correct path to your virtual Python environment scripts and the .exe extension if it is necessary on your platform.

You can install virtually all packages on the Python Package Index in the same way as you installed the PasteDeploy package here, simply by specifying the package name as the argument to the easy_install command.

Installing Pylons

Now that you know how to use `easy_install` on your platform, it is time to install Pylons.

Pylons consists of lots of different packages that all need to be installed for Pylons to work. Pylons itself is distributed under the open source license listed in the preface of the book. All its dependencies are also open source too, but if you are concerned about the details of the licenses, you should check each package.

Rather than leaving you to install each package separately, Pylons uses the Easy Install system you've just learned about to download and install all its dependencies automatically.

At a command prompt, run this command to install Pylons 0.9.7 and its dependencies:

```
$ easy_install "Pylons==0.9.7"
```

At the end of the process, you should have the latest version of Pylons and all its dependencies installed and ready to use.

Tip If you are a Windows user and are using Python 2.3, you will also need to install a package called `subprocess`, which you can download from `http://www.pylonshq.com/download/subprocess-0.1-20041012.win32-py2.3.exe`. Python 2.4 (and newer) users already have this package.

Incidentally, Pylons may not support Python 2.3 for very much longer because of its lack of decorator support, so you would be wise to upgrade to a more recent version like Python 2.5 or 2.6.

If you want to make sure you have the latest version of Pylons, you can use this command:

```
$ easy_install -U Pylons
```

This will install the latest version if it is not already present or upgrade Pylons to the latest version if an old version has already been installed.

If you are using a virtual Python environment, you will see that the `pylons` module has been installed into the virtual environment:

```
C:\>C:\env\Scripts\python.exe
Python 2.5.1 (r251:54863, Apr 18 2007, 08:51:08) [MSC v.1310 32 bit (Intel)] on
win32
Type "help", "copyright", "credits" or "license" for more information.
>>> import pylons
>>>
```

However, if you try to do the same with the system Python executable, you'll get an error because the virtual Python installation has isolated the packages from the main system Python as expected:

```
C:\>C:\Python25\python.exe
Python 2.5.1 (r251:54863, Apr 18 2007, 08:51:08) [MSC v.1310 32 bit (Intel)] on
win32
Type "help", "copyright", "credits" or "license" for more information.
>>> import pylons
Traceback (most recent call last):
  File "<stdin>", line 1, in <module>
ImportError: No module named pylons
>>>
```

Now that you have successfully installed Pylons and all its dependencies, you are able to move on to Chapter 3, but if you really want a thorough understanding, read on!

Understanding Eggs

Most new Python software including Pylons and all its dependencies are distributed as *eggs*. Eggs, a new package format, have many extra features over the old `distutils` packages, including the addition of dependency information used by the `easy_install` program installed with your virtual Python environment.

■**Tip** If you haven't come across the egg format before, you can think of eggs as being similar to `.jar` files in Java or `.gem` files in Ruby.

Python eggs are simply ZIP files of Python modules with a few metadata files added, and if you rename them to `.zip`, you can explore their contents. Module ZIP files have been supported in Python since version 2.3, so using a ZIP file instead of a directory structure is nothing new.

In Part 3 of the book, you'll look at how you can create your own egg files from a Pylons application, and I'll discuss more advanced features of eggs such as *entry points*.

Advanced Topics

You've now seen how to set up a virtual Python environment and how to use Easy Install to automatically install Python packages such as Pylons from eggs on the Python Package Index. Before you move on to learning about platform-specific issues, I'll cover a few advanced topics that are worth being aware of to help get the most from your installation.

Activating and Deactivating a Virtual Python Environment

If you are working regularly with the files in a `virtualenv` virtual Python environment, it can become tedious to have to type the `path/to/env/bin/` part in front of every script you want to execute. You can solve this problem by *activating* the environment in which you are currently working. This puts the virtual Python environment executables first in your `PATH` environment variable so that you can run them without typing the full path to the virtual Python environment.

Here's how to do it on Windows:

```
C:\Test>..\env\Scripts\activate.bat
(env) C:\Test>python
Python 2.5 (r25:51908, Sep 19 2006, 09:52:17) [MSC v.1310 32 bit (Intel)] on win32
Type "help", "copyright", "credits" or "license" for more information.
>>> import pylons
>>>
```

Once you've activated a virtual Python environment with `activate.bat`, the scripts in the virtual Python environment take precedence over the normal system ones. In the previous example, you can see that entering `python` actually runs the version in your virtual Python environment where Pylons is installed, not the main system Python. The same is true for the other available scripts.

You can deactivate it by typing `deactivate.bat`, and things go back to normal:

```
(env) C:\Test>..\env\Scripts\deactivate.bat
C:\Test>
```

On Linux and Mac OS X, you activate the environment using a Bash script like this:

```
$ source env/bin/activate
```

This script works in Bash and zsh and probably most other Bourne-compatible shells. It will not work on csh or tcsh. If it doesn't work in your non-Bash shell, you'll have to modify it to conform to your shell's syntax. Don't forget the word source! That makes it execute in the current shell rather than starting a new process so that it can modify the current shell's PATH and other variables. After a shell is activated, notice that the prompt changes to (env) to remind you which environment you're in. This is handy if you end up working in multiple virtual environments in different windows.

If you want to deactivate a shell, you would enter this command on Linux and Mac OS X:

```
deactivate
```

The paths will then return to normal, and the prompt will disappear.

Caution There is one potential problem to keep in mind with activate/deactivate. The shell keeps the path of each command in memory so it doesn't have to look it up again when the command is reexecuted. This bypasses activate's changes to the environment, so activate and deactivate try to clear this cache, but sometimes they fail. The result is that you type the command name and get the "wrong" one. To make 100 percent sure you're getting the right command, run which python (or which easy_install, and so on) to see the full path of the command that would have executed. If it's the wrong one, execute it once by typing the full path, and it will update the memory cache to use that version of the command.

If in doubt, it is probably worth using the executables directly without the activate/deactivate magic.

Setting Virtualenv Options

The virtualenv.py script has two interesting command-line options that you can use when creating your virtual Python environment:

- --no-site-packages: Don't make the global site-packages directory accessible in the virtual environment.
- --clear: Delete any previous install of this virtualenv and start from scratch.

The examples so far have used the --no-site-packages option, but you can leave this option out if you prefer your virtual Python environment to also have access to all the packages already installed into the system Python environment.

Choosing Package Versions with Easy Install

Easy Install allows you to be very specific about the version of a particular piece of software you want to install. Let's use the PasteDeploy package again as an example.

To install the latest version of the PasteDeploy package used by Pylons and its dependencies, you would simply run this command, as you've already seen:

```
$ easy_install PasteDeploy
```

To install the PasteDeploy package version 1.7, you would use this:

```
$ easy_install "PasteDeploy==1.7"
```

You can also have more complicated version requirements. For example, to install a version of the PasteDeploy package between 1.5 and 1.7 inclusive, you could do this:

```
$ easy_install "PasteDeploy>=1.5,<=1.7"
```

You can also use Easy Install to upgrade packages. You use the `easy_install` command in a similar way but specify the `-U` flag to tell Easy Install to upgrade the package. Notice how you can still specify version requirements even when upgrading:

```
$ easy_install -U "PasteDeploy>=1.5,<=1.7"
```

Of course, you can also use Easy Install to directly install eggs that exist on your local system. For example, to install the Python 2.5 egg for the PasteDeploy package, you could issue this command:

```
$ easy_install PasteDeploy-1.7-py2.5.egg
```

You can use Easy Install to install source distributions that were created with the old `distutils` module that forms part of the Python distribution and that Easy Install is designed to replace:

```
$ easy_install PasteDeploy-1.5.tar.gz
```

In this case, Easy Install first creates the `.egg` file from the source distribution and then installs it. Easy Install is also equally happy taking URLs as arguments as well as package names or paths to local files on the filesystem.

Tip Easy Install works by maintaining a file in your Python installation's `lib/site-packages` directory called `easy_install.pth`. Python looks in `.pth` files when it is starting up and adds any module ZIP files or paths specified to its internal `sys.path`. Easy Install simply maintains the `easy_install.pth` file so that Python can find the packages you have installed with Easy Install.

If you ever want to remove a package, the easiest way is to remove its entry from the `easy_install.pth` file. You shouldn't ever need to remove a package, though, because Easy Install will always use the last one you installed by default.

One really useful option for use with `easy_install` is `--always-unzip`. This forces Easy Install to extract all files from the egg packages so that you can browse their source files on the filesystem to see how the packages they contain actually work. That's very handy if you are an inquisitive developer!

Installing with a Proxy Server

If you try to install Pylons using `easy_install` and get a message such as `error: Download error: (10060, 'Operation timed out')`, it might be because your computer is behind an HTTP proxy and so `easy_install` cannot download the files it needs.

For `easy_install` to be able to download the files, you need to tell it where the proxy is. You can do this by setting the `HTTP_PROXY` environment variable. On Linux, you would type this:

```
$ export HTTP_PROXY="http://yourproxy.com:port"
```

or if you need proxy authentication, you would type this:

```
$ export HTTP_PROXY="http://user:password@yourproxy.com:port"
```

On Windows you would set the following:

```
> set HTTP_PROXY=http://your.proxy.com:yourPort
```

You should then be able to run `easy_install Pylons` again, and this time the program will be able to find the files. See the next section for installing Pylons offline if you still have difficulties.

Troubleshooting Easy Install

On rare occasions, the Python Package Index goes down but it is still possible to install Pylons and its dependencies in these circumstances by specifying Pylons' local package directory for installation instead. You can do so like this:

```
$ easy_install -f http://pylonshq.com/download/ Pylons
```

This command tells Easy Install to first check the Pylons web site before going to PyPI. If it finds links to everything it needs on the specified page, it won't have to go to PyPI at all.

▪Note If you're using an older version of Pylons, you can get the packages that went with it at the time it was released by specifying the version desired and the Pylons version-specific download site:

```
$ easy_install -f http://pylonshq.com/download/0.9.6.2/ "Pylons==0.9.6.2"
```

You can use the same technique to install any of Pylons' dependencies too. The -f option here tells Easy Install to search the URL specified as well as the Python Package Index when looking for packages.

If you can't connect to the Internet at all, you will need to install Pylons offline. Download all of Pylons' dependencies, and place them in a directory called downloads. Then use Easy Install to install the software from the directory using this command:

```
$ easy_install -f downloads/ "Pylons==0.9.7"
```

Occasionally Easy Install fails to find a package it is looking for on the Python Package Index. If this situation occurs, you should first ensure you have the latest version of setuptools by issuing this command (the -U flag means upgrade, as you saw earlier):

```
$ easy_install -U setuptools
```

You will need to do this in Ubuntu 7.04, for example, if you obtained Easy Install via the python-setuptools*.deb file rather than as part of your virtual Python environment setup because the version in the .deb file is too old for Pylons and its dependencies.

After upgrading, try to install Pylons again, and if one of the dependencies still fails, you will need to manually install that dependency first before attempting the Pylons installation once again.

Another error message you may occasionally encounter when using Easy Install is a pkg_resources.ExtractionError error that reads as follows:

```
Can't extract file(s) to egg cache The following error occurred while
trying to extract file(s) to the Python egg cache: [Errno 13] Permission
denied: '/var/www/.python-eggs' The Python egg cache directory is currently set
to: /var/www/.python-eggs Perhaps your account does not have write access to
this directory? You can change the cache directory by setting the
PYTHON_EGG_CACHE environment variable to point to an accessible directory.
```

As the error message suggests, an egg containing a module being imported by pkg_resources (another module installed with setuptools and easy_install) needs to have its contents extracted before the module can be used, but the running script doesn't have permission to extract the egg to the default location. You can change the place the eggs are extracted to by setting the environment variable PYTHON_EGG_CACHE to somewhere the application has permission to write to. One way of doing this is as follows:

```
import os
os.environ['PYTHON_EGG_CACHE'] = '/tmp'
```

You would need to add this line before the module import that is failing, and you would usually use a more appropriate location than /tmp.

If you are still having problems, you'll need to look online or contact the Pylons mailing list at pylons-discuss@googlegroups.com. Two good places to start are the Easy Install documentation at http://peak.telecommunity.com/DevCenter/EasyInstall and the TurboGears install troubleshooting guide at http://docs.turbogears.org/1.0/InstallTroubleshooting. TurboGears 1.0 uses the same install system as Pylons, so the problems encountered are often similar.

Working on the Bleeding Edge

If you want to use the development version of Pylons—or even contribute to Pylons development—you can install the bleeding-edge latest version directly from the Pylons Mercurial at http://pylonshq.com/hg.

Mercurial is a popular open source revision control system written in Python that many projects including Pylons are choosing instead of Subversion because of its distributed nature and more powerful feature set. Mercurial is documented in detail in the Mercurial Book at http://hgbook.red-bean.com/hgbook.html, but if you just want to get started quickly, you will find this guide on the Pylons wiki very useful: http://wiki.pylonshq.com/display/pylonscookbook/Mercurial+for+Subversion+Users.

Once Mercurial is installed, you will need to clone the development versions of Pylons and all its dependencies. It can be quite a time-consuming process to track down all the repositories and clone the source files, so the Pylons developers created a go-pylons.py script to set up a virtual Python environment and automate the process.

Download the program for Pylons 0.9.7 from http://www.pylonshq.com/download/0.9.7/go-pylons.py, and then run this command:

```
$ python go-pylons.py --no-site-packages devenv
```

The script whirs away and sets up a development virtual Python environment. The go-pylons.py script is being improved all the time and might not always be used only to install development packages. It is likely a future version might also be capable of installing a release version of Pylons.

■**Caution** Although the Pylons development team always tries to ensure the code in the Pylons trunk is functioning and up-to-date, there is no guarantee it will be stable. If you choose to use the development version instead of the official release, you should be aware that Pylons may not behave as you expect and is more likely to contain some bugs as new features are introduced.

Platform-Specific Notes

Pylons works with all versions of Python since 2.3, but it is recommended that you use Python 2.4 or newer because some of the third-party packages you are likely to use when developing a Pylons application are less likely to support the older versions. Python 2.5 or 2.6 are ideal.

The following sections describe how to install Python on Linux/BSD, Windows, and Mac OS X platforms. They also go into some detail about other tools and software you are likely to need on your platform as well as any extra steps you need to take or platform-specific issues you need to know.

■Note Python supports the use of C or C++ extensions to facilitate integration with other libraries or to speed up certain sections of code. Although you are unlikely to ever need to write your own extensions when developing a Pylons application, you may find some third-party packages, particularly database drivers, do contain extensions.

Unlike pure Python packages, packages containing extensions need to be compiled for each platform on which they are run. Most of the time a binary version of a particular package will already exist for your platform (particularly if you run Windows), but if not, the extension may need to be compiled. The compilation step will happen automatically, but in order for it to work, you will need to set up a suitable development environment. The installation sections for Linux/BSD and Mac OS X platforms will describe how to do this.

Linux and BSD

Most modern Linux and BSD platforms include Python as part of their standard installation. You can find out which version of Python you have on your platform by typing python at a prompt and reading the information that is displayed. If the python command loads an old version of Python, you might find that the command python2.5 or python2.4 loads more recent versions.

If your platform doesn't have a recent version of Python, you will need to install a binary version in whichever way is appropriate for your platform. For example, on Debian you would use the apt-get command, on Fedora or Red Hat you would use RPM, and on FreeBSD you would use the packages system.

Compiling Python directly from source is also straightforward, and you're free to do so if you prefer. First download the source distribution from http://www.python.org/download/source/, and then extract all the files. One of the extracted files is a README file, which includes build instructions for various platforms. You should follow the instructions for your particular platform.

If you want to be able to compile Python packages with C or C++ extensions, you will also need to install a build environment that includes the same version of the GNU Compiler Collection (GCC) as Python and its dependencies were compiled with. Some platforms also require you to install a python-dev package as well.

For example, to set up Debian 4.0 to be able to compile Python extensions, you would need to install these development packages:

```
$ sudo apt-get install python-dev libc6-dev
```

Sometimes particular packages need to be compiled with a version of GCC older than the default on the platform. On Debian you can install GCC 2.95 with this command:

```
$ sudo apt-get install gcc-2.95
```

To use this older version, you would set the CC environment variable before trying to build a package. The way you do this depends on your shell, but for Bash, you would run this command:

```
$ export CC=/usr/bin/gcc-2.95
```

Once the required version of GCC has been set up, Easy Install should be able to automatically compile any dependencies from the same shell. If you need to open another shell, you will need to check the CC variable is still set and set it again if necessary:

```
$ echo $CC
/usr/bin/gcc-2.95
```

Mac OS X

Python 2.5 comes preinstalled on Mac OS X Leopard complete with Easy Install, so Leopard users can get started creating a virtual Python environment and installing Pylons straightaway.

Older versions of Mac OS X also include Python, but the version included is sometimes either one or two years old because of Apple's release cycle. The overwhelming recommendation of the "MacPython" community is for users of old versions of Mac OS X to upgrade Python by downloading and installing a newer version. Visit http://www.python.org/download/mac/ for more details.

■**Caution** It is worth being aware that if you install packages to /Library/Python/2.5/site-packages and then use virtualenv to install Pylons to a local directory, any applications you run from the local directory won't be able to find those in the /Library/... path, so it is always best to install everything locally.

If you encounter this problem, you can fix it by running Easy Install from your virtual Python environment for each of the packages that appear to be missing. Easy Install will then find them and add them to virtual Python environment's easy-install.pth file.

Windows

If you are using Windows 95, 98, NT, 2000, ME, XP, 2003 Server, or Vista, you can download the Python installer from http://python.org/download/. Once you have downloaded the correct version for your platform (which will usually be the x86 version), you simply double-click the installer file and follow the installation instructions (see Figure 2-1).

Figure 2-1. *The Python 2.5 Installer running on Windows XP*

■Note To use the installer, the Windows system must support Microsoft Installer (MSI) 2.0. Just save the installer file to your local machine, and then run it to find out whether your machine supports MSI. Windows XP and newer already have MSI, but many older machines will already have MSI installed too.

If your machine does not have the Microsoft Installer, you can download it:

Windows 95, 98, and ME platforms use this version: `http://www.microsoft.com/downloads/details.aspx?FamilyID=cebbacd8-c094-4255-b702-de3bb768148f&displaylang=en`.

Windows NT 4.0 and 2000 use this version: `http://www.microsoft.com/downloads/details.aspx?FamilyID=4b6140f9-2d36-4977-8fa1-6f8a0f5dca8f&DisplayLang=en`.

On Windows, any scripts that are installed by Easy Install will be put in the `Scripts` directory of your Python installation. By default neither this directory nor your main Python executable are on your `PATH`, so you will not be able to run Python itself or any Python scripts from a command prompt unless you first navigate to the correct directory or specify the full path each time.

To fix this and save yourself a lot of typing in the future, you should add some directories to your `PATH` environment variable. Luckily, this is straightforward to do, so the examples in this book will assume you have set up your path correctly.

Of course, if you are using a virtual Python environment, you should specify the `Scripts` directory within the virtual Python environment rather than the system Python, or you could activate your virtual Python environment instead as described earlier in the chapter.

If you are using Windows 2000 or Windows XP, you can do the following:

1. From the desktop or Start menu, right-click My Computer, and click Properties.

2. In the System Properties window, click the Advanced tab.

3. In the Advanced section, click the Environment Variables button.

4. Finally, in the Environment Variables window, highlight the path variable in the Systems Variable section, and click Edit (see Figure 2-2). Add the text `C:\Python25\;C:\Python25\Scripts` to the end of the path. Each different directory should be separated by a semicolon, so the end of your path might look something like this:

   ```
   C:\Program Files;C:\WINDOWS;C:\WINDOWS\System32➥
   ;C:\Python25\;C:\Python25\Scripts
   ```

5. You might need to restart your computer for the change to take effect.

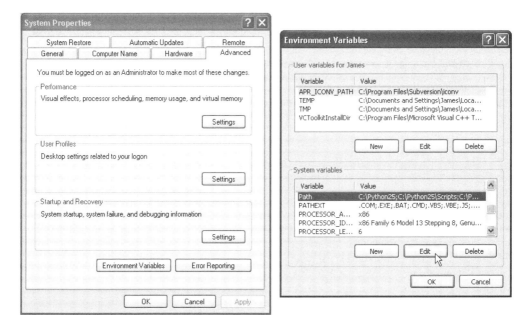

Figure 2-2. *Configuring your* PATH *on Windows XP*

To test your installation has worked and your path is configured correctly, you should select Start ➤ Run and enter the text cmd in the input field. When you click OK, a Windows command prompt will load. You can then run Python by typing python at the prompt. You should see something similar to what is shown in Figure 2-3.

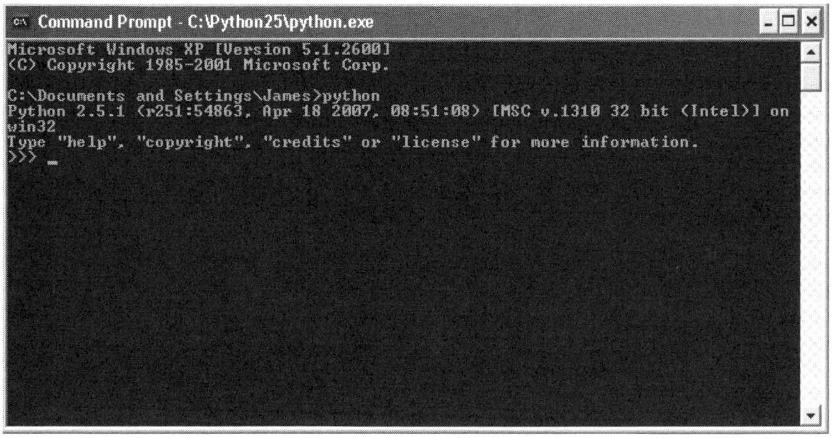

```
Command Prompt - C:\Python25\python.exe

Microsoft Windows XP [Version 5.1.2600]
(C) Copyright 1985-2001 Microsoft Corp.

C:\Documents and Settings\James>python
Python 2.5.1 (r251:54863, Apr 18 2007, 08:51:08) [MSC v.1310 32 bit (Intel)] on
win32
Type "help", "copyright", "credits" or "license" for more information.
>>> _
```

Figure 2-3. *Windows command prompt running Python*

If so, the installation has worked. To exit the Python interactive interpreter, you can press Ctrl+Z followed immediately by pressing the Enter key.

■**Tip** When you develop Pylons applications, you will find you frequently need access to a Windows command prompt. It can quickly become quite tedious to load a command prompt from the Run option on the Start menu and then manually navigate to the directory containing your Pylons application. To make life easier, Microsoft has released an extension called the Open Command Window Here PowerToy, which allows you to right-click a directory and load a command prompt at that location by choosing Open Command Window Here from the menu. You can download the extension from `http://www.microsoft.com/windowsxp/downloads/powertoys/xppower-toys.mspx`.

There are two slight complications to be aware of when developing Python applications on Windows. The first is that paths on Windows use the \ character as a path separator rather than the / character used on the Linux and Mac OS X platforms. The \ character is treated as an escape character in strings within Python source code, so you cannot use Windows paths in source code strings without first escaping the \ characters. You can do this by adding an extra \ character before each \ in the string. For example, a Windows path might be written like this:

```
my_path = "C:\\Documents and Settings\\James\\Desktop\\Pylons"
```

Luckily, Python also treats / characters in paths on the Windows platform as path separators, so you can also write the same path like this:

```
my_path = "C:/Documents and Settings/James/Desktop/Pylons"
```

■**Note** Rather than writing different versions of commands for Windows, Linux, and Mac OS X platforms throughout this book, I will instead assume you have set up the `C:\Python25\Scripts` directory to be on your PATH. Also, I will write any paths using / characters rather than \ characters, so please be aware that you may have to interpret these slightly differently on Windows.

The second slight complication is the way Windows treats line-end characters. On Unix-like platforms, the newline character \n is treated as the line end, whereas on Windows the characters \r\n are used. If you have ever loaded a file in Notepad and wondered why it shows an entire paragraph as one long line, it is likely that the file was written on a Unix-like platform and Notepad simply didn't understand the line-end characters.

Luckily, Python understands line-end issues and will work equally well regardless of the line-end characters used, but not all software does. It is generally easiest to stick to one type of line-end character. If you are going to deploy your software on a Unix-like platform, you should strongly consider writing all your Python source files with Unix-style line ends even if you are using Windows. Although FTP software frequently tries to translate Windows line ends to Unix-style line ends, you can save yourself the complication by simply using Unix line ends to start with.

Tip Python comes with a built-in editor called IDLE for editing Python source files that you can read about at `http://www.python.org/idle/doc/idle2.html`. IDLE is a very powerful IDE, but unfortunately it doesn't have an option for choosing which line-end characters to use.

One free editor that does allow you to choose which line ends to use is called SciTE and can be downloaded from `http://scintilla.sourceforge.net/SciTEDownload.html`. You can choose your line-end characters from the menu by selecting Options ➤ Line End Characters. The options are CR+LF, CR, and LF (see Figure 2-4). LF stands for Line Feed and is the Unix line-end character written \n in Python strings, and CR stands for carriage return. Windows uses carriage returns and line feeds represented as \r\n in Python strings. If you want to convert from one type of line end to another, you can use the Convert Line End Characters option in the Options menu.

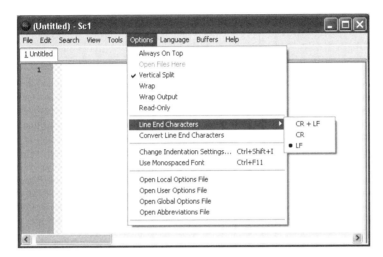

Figure 2-4. *SciTE line endings menu*

Summary

You should now have a very good understanding of all the different tools and techniques used for setting up Python and Pylons, and you should have a virtual Python environment set up and ready to go. With everything in place, it's time to move on to the next chapter and get started learning Pylons.

CHAPTER 3

■ ■ ■

Exploring Pylons

Now that you have seen how to set up a Python environment and have used Easy Install to install Pylons and its dependencies, it is time to create your first Pylons project. In time-honored tradition, I'll start with an example that outputs the words Hello world! to the web browser.

In this chapter, you'll also learn the basics of the Hypertext Transfer Protocol, learn about Pylons' request and response objects, and begin learning how Pylons works and about the other objects Pylons sets up for you.

Exploring Pylons' Dependencies

As you learned in Chapter 1, Pylons is more like a collection of very carefully chosen separate components than a tightly integrated framework, but it can often be difficult to work out exactly how each of the components fits together. You'll learn this over the course of the book, but let's take a quick look at the packages that were installed along with Pylons so that you can get an idea of the big picture.

If you followed the installation instructions from the previous chapter, take a look at the lib/python2.5/site-packages directory in your virtual Python environment. You will see all of Pylons' dependencies as well as the easy-install.pth and setuptools.pth files, which Easy Install uses to keep track of the installed eggs. If you've installed other packages too, you will also see them.

The following list contains the components relevant to Pylons 0.9.7. Of course, the version numbers might change slightly over time and future versions of Pylons might have slightly different dependencies, but the following list is correct at the time of this writing:

Beaker-0.9.5-py2.5.egg: Beaker is a piece of software used internally by Pylons to implement its caching and session functionality. The Pylons session global described later in the chapter uses Beaker, as does Pylons' caching functionality described in the Pylons Cookbook at http://wiki.pylonshq.com/display/pylonsdocs/Caching+in+Templates+and+Controllers, but you would never normally interact with Beaker yourself directly.

decorator-2.2.0-py2.5.egg: This is a simple tool used by Pylons to create the @validate and @jsonify decorators. You'll learn about @validate in Chapter 6, and you'll learn about @jsonify in Chapter 15. Once again, you won't normally use decorator in your own programs because you'll usually use the decorators provided by Pylons.

FormEncode-1.0.1-py2.5.egg: FormEncode is a library for validating form submissions from web sites. Although Pylons doesn't use it internally, Pylons users work with it so often that it is considered an essential part of Pylons. The FormEncode package also includes a module named formencode.htmlfill that can be used to populate a string containing HTML fields with values and error messages. Together FormEncode and HTML Fill make an ideal tool set for handling forms in a Pylons application. Chapter 6 is dedicated to explaining how to use FormEncode and HTML Fill in a Pylons application.

`Mako-0.2.0-py2.5.egg`: Mako is one of the three template languages that Pylons 0.9.7 supports out of the box. The others are Genshi (an XML template language) and Jinja (based on Django's template system). You have to install Genshi and Jinja separately if you want to use them, whereas Mako is included in the default Pylons installation because it is the recommended template language to use. Using Mako to generate your views is described in detail in Chapter 5.

`nose-0.10.3-py2.5.egg`: This provides tools to help you write and run automated unit tests. Testing is described in Chapter 12.

`Paste-1.6-py2.5.egg`, `PasteDeploy-1.3.2-py2.5.egg`, and `PasteScript-1.6.3-py2.5.egg`: Paste comes in three packages for the benefit of framework developers who require only one part of its functionality. Pylons uses all three packages for a wide variety of things throughout the framework, but once again, as a Pylons application developer, you won't normally directly interact with the Paste components yourself.

Over time, the functionality in the Paste modules has been split up into custom packages. For example, the `paste.wsgiwrappers` module, which provided the `pylons.request` and `pylons.response` objects in Pylons 0.9.6, is now replaced by WebOb, which provides the Pylons 0.9.7 versions of those Pylons objects. The `paste.eval_exception` module, which provided the 0.9.6 error handling, is replaced by WebError in Pylons 0.9.7, and even the `paste.auth` functionality has been built upon and improved in AuthKit, which you'll learn about in Chapter 18. Don't be surprised if future versions of Pylons include even more projects spun out from their roots in Paste.

Despite the gradual shift to separate packages, Pylons still relies on Paste for its configuration files, registry manager, development HTTP server, project template creation, test fixtures, error documents, and more. The various parts of Paste are described throughout the book as they are encountered.

`Pylons-0.9.7-py2.5.egg`: This is where everything needed to glue together the other components of Pylons is found. Pylons itself is relatively small, so if you are the curious type, feel free to look at its code to get a feel for how everything works.

`Routes-1.9-py2.5.egg`: Pylons uses a system called Routes that allows you to map a URL to a set of variables usually including `controller` and `action`. These variables are then used to determine which Pylons controller class and method should be used to handle the request. At the same time, Routes allows you to specify a set of variables and have a URL generated from them so that you never need to hard-code URLs into your application. I'll introduce Routes in this chapter, but you will learn the details of all of Route's powerful features in Chapter 9.

`setuptools-0.6c8-py2.5.egg`: This contains the methods used by the `easy_install` script to provide all of its features and allow the use of egg files.

`simplejson-1.8.1-py2.5-linux-x86_64.egg`: This package converts data back and forth between JSON and Python formats and is used by the `@jsonify` decorator mentioned earlier. Pylons application developers also occasionally use `simplejson` directly in their controllers.

`Tempita-0.2-py2.5.egg`: Tempita is a small template language that is a dependency of Paste. It is used only behind the scenes for simple variable substitutions when you create a new Pylons project directory with the `paster create` command described later in this chapter.

`WebError-0.8-py2.5.egg`: WebError provides Pylons' powerful interactive debugging and traceback functionality described in Chapter 4.

`WebHelpers-0.6-py2.5.egg`: WebHelpers is a collection of stand-alone functions and classes that provide useful functionality such as generating common HTML tags and form fields, handling multiple pages of results, and doing much more.

`WebOb-0.9.2-py2.5.egg`: This provides the new `pylons.request` and `pylons.response` objects in Pylons 0.9.7.

You might have noticed that SQLAlchemy, a database toolkit you'll learn about in Chapter 7, and AuthKit, a toolkit you'll learn about in Chapter 18, are not included in the list of packages installed automatically with Pylons. This is because Pylons can be used perfectly well without them, and although most users will choose to install them, some developers will want to choose alternatives instead.

Installing Pylons also installs some scripts. If you look in your virtual Python environment's `bin` directory (or the `Scripts` directory on Windows), you will see the following:

`activate` (or `activate.bat` on Windows): This is an optional script described in Chapter 2 for activating a virtual Python environment to make the other scripts available automatically on the current shell or command prompt without having to type the full path to the virtual Python environment.

`nosetests`: This is a script used for running your Pylons tests; it is provided by the `nose` package, which was mentioned earlier and will be described in Chapter 12.

`python`: This is the Python executable you should use for all work within the virtual Python environment.

`easy_install`: This is the Easy Install program for installing software into your virtual environment described in Chapter 2. `mako-render`: This is a simple script installed with Mako that takes a single file containing Mako template markup as an argument and outputs the rendered template to the standard output on your console. This isn't very useful for Pylons development.

`paster`: This is a very useful script that uses the Paste Script package and has a number of subcommands including `paster create` and `paster serve`, which you'll see later in this chapter, that are for creating a new Pylons project and serving a Pylons application, respectively. You'll also see `paster make-config` and `paster setup-app`, which are for handling the creation of a config file from a distributed Pylons project and for setting it up. These are advanced features you'll learn about in the SimpleSite tutorial throughout the book.

Your `bin` (or `Scripts`) directory might also see a file such as `easy_install-2.5`, which is simply a Python 2.5 version of the `easy_install` script, or a `python2.5` script, which is a Python 2.5 version of the `python` script if you are using multiple versions of Python on your system. You should generally use the `easy_install` and `python` versions because they match the version of Python you used when you ran the `python virtual_python.py env` command in Chapter 2.

Don't worry if you don't understand everything I've mentioned in this section; it will all become clear as you get more familiar with Pylons.

Creating a Pylons Project

Now that you've seen a quick overview of all the Pylons components, it's time to create your first Pylons project.

Let's get started by using Paste's `paster create` command to automatically generate a Pylons project directory structure for you. You are completely free to create all the files and directories yourself if you prefer, but the Pylons project template provides a useful starting point that most people prefer to use.

> ■**Caution** In Pylons terminology, there are two different types of template, and it is important not to get con-
> fused between the two. *View templates* are text files that contain a mixture of Python and HTML and are used to
> generate HTML fragments to return to the browser as the view component of the MVC architecture. Any template
> written with Mako is a view template. *Project templates* are sets of files and directories that are used by the
> paster create command to generate a complete project directory structure to use as a basis for a new Pylons
> application.

Create a new project named HelloWorld based on the Pylons default project template with this
command:

```
$ paster create --template=pylons HelloWorld
```

The --template option tells the paster create command which project template to use to create the HelloWorld project. You will also see examples using -t instead of --template, but both have
the same effect:

```
$ paster create -t pylons HelloWorld
```

> ■**Note** If you have problems running the previous paster create command, it is likely you have forgotten to
> include the full path to the paster script (or the paster.exe executable in the case of Windows). You might see
> a message such as paster: command not found or 'paster' is not recognized as an internal or
> external command, operable program or batch file.
>   Remember that if you are using a virtual Python environment, you will need to type the full path to the exe-
> cutable (for example, env/bin/paster or C:\env\Scritps\paster) or modify your PATH as described in
> Chapter 2, either directly or by using the activate or activate.bat script. The examples in this book assume
> you have read Chapter 2 and will type whatever is appropriate for your installation.

The project template used in the previous paster create command is called pylons, which
is the default for Pylons. You can always see which project templates are available with the
--list-templates option shown here, but bear in mind that because Paste is a general-purpose
library, not all the templates available will be for generating Pylons projects. In Chapter 19, you'll
learn how to create your own Pylons project template to add to this list:

```
$ paster create --list-templates
Available templates:
  basic_package:   A basic setuptools-enabled package
  paste_deploy:    A web application deployed through paste.deploy
  pylons:          Pylons application template
  pylons_minimal:  Pylons minimal application template
```

Advanced users might like to experiment with the pylons_minimal application template, which
leaves you to do more configuration yourself.

Now let's return to the HelloWorld example. Once you have run the paster create
--template=pylons HelloWorld command, you will be asked some questions about how you want
your project set up. You can choose which view template language you want to use for the project
and whether you want SQLAlchemy support built in. For this example, choose the defaults of
Mako for the view template language and no SQLAlchemy support since you haven't installed
SQLAlchemy yet anyway. Just press Enter at each of the prompts, and the script will quickly generate your new project.

Serving a Pylons Application

Now that you have a sample project application, it is a good idea to run it with a web server to see what the default project provides; however, before you can serve the Pylons application you've just created, you need to learn about configuration files.

Configuration Files

Configuration files enable you to set up the same Pylons application on different servers with different settings and for different purposes without having to change the source code for the project.

The project template you have used creates two configuration files for you in the HelloWorld directory, one named development.ini and one named test.ini. The development.ini file contains settings to run the Pylons application in a development environment such as your local workstation, whereas the test.ini file contains the settings you want to use when testing the application. You create a new configuration file called production.ini when you are ready to serve the application file in production.

The following code is the top part of the development.ini file generated as part of the application template. There is also some logging configuration, which you'll learn about in Chapter 20.

```
#
# helloworld - Pylons development environment configuration
#
# The %(here)s variable will be replaced with the parent directory of this file
#
[DEFAULT]
debug = true
# Uncomment and replace with the address which should receive any error reports
#email_to = you@yourdomain.com
smtp_server = localhost
error_email_from = paste@localhost

[server:main]
use = egg:Paste#http
host = 127.0.0.1
port = 5000

[app:main]
use = egg:helloworld
full_stack = true
cache_dir = %(here)s/data
beaker.session.key = helloworld
beaker.session.secret = somesecret
# If you'd like to fine-tune the individual locations of the cache data dirs
# for the Cache data, or the Session saves, un-comment the desired settings
# here:
#beaker.cache.data_dir = %(here)s/data/cache
#beaker.session.data_dir = %(here)s/data/sessions

# WARNING: *THE LINE BELOW MUST BE UNCOMMENTED ON A PRODUCTION ENVIRONMENT*
# Debug mode will enable the interactive debugging tool, allowing ANYONE to
# execute malicious code after an exception is raised.
#set debug = false
```

As you can see, the configuration file is in three parts. The [DEFAULT] section contains global configuration options that can be overridden in other sections. The [server:main] part contains information for the server used to serve the Pylons application, and the [app:main] section contains configuration options for the Pylons application. All the option values can contain the string %(here)s, which gets replaced with the location of the config file, enabling you to easily specify relative paths.

Let's discuss the options available:

debug: This can be true or false. If true, the Pylons interactive debugger is enabled to allow you to track down problems, as you'll learn about in the next chapter. You should always disable the interactive debugger in production environments by setting debug to false.

email_to, smtp_server, error_email_from: These options specify where error reports should be sent if the interactive debugger is disabled, but they could potentially be used by third-party components too since they are specified in the [DEFAULT] section and are therefore available to all components using the configuration file.

host, port: These specify the IP address and port the server should listen on for requests. Only the server uses them.

full_stack: You can set this to false to disable Pylons interactive debugging, error report support, and error documents support, but you'll usually leave this set to true.

cache_dir: This is the directory where components can store information on the filesystem. Session information from Beaker and cached view templates from Mako are stored in this directory. You can manually override where Beaker stores its session information with the beaker.cache.data_dir and beaker.session.data_dir options, but you won't usually need to do so.

beaker.session.key: This should be something unique to your application so that other applications using Beaker can't access your application's data.

beaker.session.secret: This is a random string of letters and numbers used to make the cookie value representing the session harder to guess to reduce the risk of a malicious user trying to gain access to someone else's session information. You should always change this to something other than somesecret if you are using Pylons session functionality.

The Paste HTTP Server

To run your application for development purposes, it is recommended you use the Paste HTTP server from the Paste package that was installed as one of Pylons' dependencies. The Paste HTTP server does for Pylons applications what Apache does for PHP and other languages; it listens for HTTP requests and dispatches them to the running application, returning the result via HTTP to the user's browser.

The Paste HTTP server has two features that make it more suitable for Pylons development than most web servers:

- It can be made to automatically reload when you change the source code.
- It understands the configuration files used by Pylons, so they can be used directly. As you'll see in Chapter 19, other servers require the assistance of the Paste Deploy package to turn a Pylons config file into an application.

You can start the server with your development configuration with this command:

```
$ cd HelloWorld
$ paster serve --reload development.ini
Starting subprocess with file monitor
Starting server in PID 17586.
serving on 127.0.0.1:5000 view at http://127.0.0.1:5000
```

If you are Windows user, you may be prompted to unblock Python on port 5000 depending on your firewall settings.

The `--reload` option puts the Paste HTTP server into a very useful mode where the server carefully monitors all Python modules used by your application as well as the `development.ini` configuration file. If any of them change, the server is automatically reloaded so that you can immediately test your changes. This is useful during development because it saves you from having to manually stop and start the server every time you make a change.

To stop the server, you can press Ctrl+C (or Ctrl+D if you're running Windows), but don't stop it yet. If you visit `http://127.0.0.1:5000/` in your web browser when the server is running, you will see the welcome page shown in Figure 3-1.

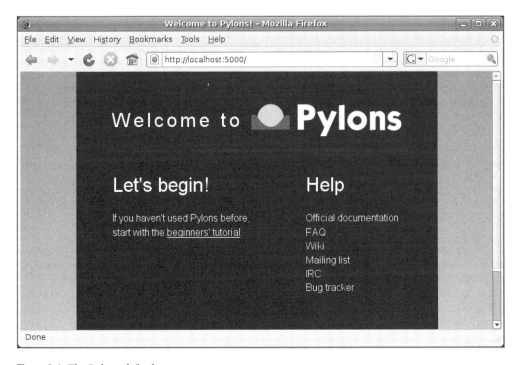

Figure 3-1. *The Pylons default page*

Static Files

Now that the server is running, try creating a new file named `hello.html` in the `HelloWorld/helloworld/public` directory with the following content:

```
<html>
    <body>
        Hello world!
    </body>
</html>
```

If you visit `http://127.0.0.1:5000/hello.html`, you will see the `Hello world!` message.

A Pylons project's `public` folder is a bit like an `htdocs` directory in Apache. Any files in the `public` directory are treated as static files and are served treating the URL as the path to the file to serve. If the URL represents a directory and that directory contains an `index.html` file, it will be served instead; however, for security reasons, Pylons does not provide a directory index facility, so if no `index.html` file is present in a directory, a "404 File Not Found" response is returned.

Pylons automatically provides E-Tag caching for static files in the `public` directory. This allows browsers that support E-Tag caching to check to see whether a file has changed since the last time they fetched it. If it hasn't changed, the browser won't download the file a second time.

A Word About IP Addresses, Hosts, and Security

The numbers `127.0.0.1` in the URL you have been using to test your `HelloWorld` application represent the IP address on which the Paste HTTP server is serving the Pylons application. The IP address `127.0.0.1` is a special IP address that references your own computer. This means your Pylons application can be accessed only from the computer on which you are running the Paste HTTP server. This is actually very important because, as you will learn in the next chapter, Pylons comes with a powerful interactive debugging tool that is enabled by default when using the `development.ini` configuration file. If people could access your running development instance and an error occurred, they might be able to use the interactive debugger to enter malicious commands, so this is why as of Pylons 0.9.7 the default configuration file instructs the Paste HTTP server to bind to `127.0.0.1` so it answers requests only from the local computer.

If you want to test how the application works from a different computer, you can change the IP address the Paste HTTP server uses by editing the `host` option in the `[server:main]` section of the `development.ini` file. You can also change the port on which the server runs by changing the `port` variable. If you don't want `:5000` in your URLs, you should set the server to run on port 80. Browsers will connect to port 80 by default for HTTP requests if no port is specified in the URL. Most production systems run on port 80 for this reason, but for development it is fine to run your application on port 5000.

The IP address `0.0.0.0` is also worth knowing about. Setting the `host` option to `0.0.0.0` will cause the Paste HTTP server to respond to requests on all IP addresses on your server. This is the setting normally used in production configurations when the Pylons interactive debugger has been disabled.

Servers frequently have hostnames mapped to particular IP addresses, and you can specify a server's hostname instead of the IP address if you prefer. It is a convention on most platforms that the hostname localhost will refer to the IP address `127.0.0.1`, so for the majority of the time, you can use localhost rather than the IP address `127.0.0.1`. With the Paste HTTP server still running, try visiting `http://localhost:5000/hello.html`; chances are you will still see the same `Hello World!` message you did before.

Exploring a Pylons Project's Directory Structure

Now that you've seen a simple Pylons application serving static files from the `public` directory, I'll take the opportunity to show you the rest of the files and directories that the `paster create` command generated for you from the default `pylons` application template.

The main `HelloWorld` directory contains the following files and directories:

`docs`: This directory is where you can keep documentation for your project. Pylons applications are often documented in a language called reStructuredText. The reStructuredText files can then be converted to HTML using tools such as Sphinx. Both reStructuredText and Sphinx are discussed in Chapter 13.

`helloworld`: This is the main application directory, but its name depends on the package name you gave as the argument to the `paster create` command when the project was generated. Pylons applications are usually given a package name in CamelCase, but the application directory itself is the lowercase version of the package name. In this case, you specified the package name as `HelloWorld`, so the main Pylons application directory is named `helloworld`. If you were to write `import helloworld`, it would be this directory's files that are imported. I'll return to this directory in a moment to explore the subdirectories it contains.

`HelloWorld.egg-info`: This is a special directory that contains metadata about your project in a format that is used by `setuptools` when you treat the application as an egg.

`development.ini` and `test.ini`: These are the configuration files I discussed in the previous section.

`ez_setup.py`: Your Pylons application relies on some features provided by the `setuptools` module, but not every Python installation comes with the `setuptools` module already installed, because it isn't an official part of the Python distribution. The `ez_setup.py` file is therefore included to automatically install `setuptools` if someone without it tries to install your Pylons application.

`MANIFEST.in`: Your Pylons application contains various files that aren't Python modules such as the templates and static files. These files are included in a Python package only if they are specified in a `MANIFEST.in` file. The `MANIFEST.in` file in your project's directory forces these files to be included.

`README.txt`: Having a `README` file in a project's root directory is standard practice, so this file is simply there for you to describe your project to anyone looking at its source code. You can customize it as you see fit.

`setup.cfg` and `setup.py`: The `setup.py` and `setup.cfg` files control various aspects of how your Pylons application is packaged when you distribute it. They also contain metadata about the project. You'll see them being used as you read the SimpleSite tutorial chapters.

You may also notice a `data` directory that contains cached session and template information. It is created the first time you run a Pylons application that needs it to be present. The location of this directory can be configured with the `cache_dir` option you saw a moment ago when I discussed configuration file options.

Now let's take a look at the main Pylons application directory. As mentioned a moment ago, this will have a name based on the package name, so it will be different in each Pylons project. In this case, it is called `helloworld` and contains the following files and directories:

`config`: The `config` directory is where most Pylons functionality is exposed to your application for you to customize.

`controllers`: The `controllers` directory is where your application controllers are written. Controllers are the core of your application. They allow you to handle requests, load or save data from your model, and pass information to your view templates for rendering; they are also responsible for returning information to the browser. You'll create your first controller in the next section.

lib: The lib directory is where you can put Python code that is used between different controllers, third-party code, or any other code that doesn't fit in well elsewhere.

model: The model directory is for your model objects; if you're using an object-relational mapper such as SQLAlchemy, this is where your tables, classes, and relations should be defined. You'll look at using SQLAlchemy as a model in Chapter 7.

public: You've already seen the public directory. It is similar to the htdocs directory in Apache and is where you put all your HTML, images, JavaScript, CSS, and other static files.

templates: The templates directory is where view templates are stored.

tests: The tests directory is where you can put automated unit tests for your application.

__init__.py: The __init__.py file is present so that the helloworld directory can be imported as a Python module within the egg.

websetup.py: The websetup.py contains any code that should be executed when an end user has installed your Pylons application and needs to initialize it. It frequently contains code to create the database tables required by your application, for example. We'll discuss this in Chapter 8.

Creating a Controller and Modifying the Routes

It's now time to learn how to generate the message dynamically using a Pylons *controller*. Controllers are the basic building blocks of Pylons applications. They contain all the programming logic and can be thought of as mini-applications. Controllers are implemented as Python classes. Each method of the class is known in Pylons as an *action*. On each request Pylons routes the HTTP information to a particular controller action based on the URL that was requested. The action should return a response, which Pylons passes back to the server and on to the browser.

Let's see this in practice by creating a controller. Once again you can use a paster command to help you get started quickly:

```
$ paster controller hello
```

This command creates a skeleton controllers/hello.py file for you as well as a helloworld/ tests/functional/test_hello.py file that is used for running some of the functional tests of the controller discussed in Chapter 12. If you are using the Subversion revision control system to manage the source files in a Pylons project, the paster controller command will also automatically add both files to your working copy.

Modify the index() action of the HelloController to look like this:

```
class HelloController(BaseController):
    def index(self):
        return 'Hello from the index() action!'
```

Let's test this code. With the server still running, visit http://127.0.0.1:5000/hello/index, and you should be greeted with the Hello from the index() action! message.

Let's look closely at that URL. If you have used ASP, PHP, or CGI scripts, you'll know that the URL the user visits directly represents the path on the filesystem of the script the server should execute. Pylons is much more flexible than this; it uses a system called Routes to map sets of URLs to particular controllers. This means your URLs don't always have to directly represent the controllers that handle them. By default, Routes is set up so that the first URL fragment after the hostname and port represents the controller and the second part represents the action. In this case, /hello/index means use the index action of the hello controller, and so the URL you just visited results in the index() method of HelloController being called to display the response.

One very common requirement is the ability to map the root URL http://localhost:5000/ to a controller action. After all, you wouldn't want to be limited to having a static file as the root URL. To do this, you need to add a line to the routes configuration. Add a new line to the top of the main route map in helloworld/config/routing.py just after the # CUSTOM ROUTES HERE comment so that the routes are defined like this:

```
# CUSTOM ROUTES HERE

map.connect('/', controller='hello', action='index')
map.connect('/{controller}/{action}')
map.connect('/{controller}/{action}/{id}')
```

This tells Routes that the root URL / should be mapped to the index action of HelloController. Otherwise, Routes should look for URLs in the form /controller/action/, and /controller/action/id. This, along with other details of Routes, is described in detail in Chapter 9.

Since you have made changes to a Python file used by the project, you would need to restart the server for the changes to be picked up. Because you started the server with the --reload option, though, this will happen automatically.

If you visit http://127.0.0.1:5000/ again, you will notice that the static welcome page is still there. This is because Pylons looks in the public directory for files to serve before attempting to match a controller. Because the public/index.html file still exists, Pylons serves that file.

If you delete the public/index.html file, you should see the Hello from the index() action! message you were expecting.

Understanding How HTTP Works

At this point it is worth taking a step back from Pylons to understand what is actually going on to display the Hello from the index() action! message.

At its heart, web development is all about the Hypertext Transfer Protocol (HTTP). Any web page you visit that starts with http:// is using HTTP to communicate between the browser and the server. Other protocols are used on the Internet too, such as the File Transfer Protocol (FTP), but for creating data-driven web sites with Pylons, HTTP is the only one you need to understand.

▓**Note** If you're new to web development, it is important not to get confused between HTTP and HTML. HTTP is the protocol with which the browser communicates with a server, whereas HTML is a markup language used to create web pages.

To understand exactly what is going on when you create a web page, it is useful to be able to see the HTTP information being sent back and forth between a web browser and a Pylons application. One good tool for doing this is the LiveHTTPHeaders extension for the Firefox web browser, which you can download from http://livehttpheaders.mozdev.org/. Once you have installed it, you can select View ➤ Sidebar ➤ LiveHTTPHeaders from the menu to load the extension in the sidebar, and it will display all the HTTP information sent and received on each request.

■**Tip** You can download the Firefox web browser from `http://mozilla.com/products/firefox`. It will run on the Windows, Mac OS X, Linux, and BSD platforms. It is particularly useful for web development because of the extensions available that give you fuller access to the processes going on within the web browser.

Another particularly useful extension is the Web Developer toolbar available from `https://addons.mozilla.org/en-US/firefox/addon/60`, which offers facilities for managing cookies and style sheets as well as for outlining block-level elements and tables.

Firefox also has powerful extensions such as Firebug, which in addition to its JavaScript and DOM manipulation facilities allows you to analyze page load times. I will discuss Firebug in Chapter 15 when I cover Ajax.

When you request a page, the browser sends an HTTP request to the server. When the server receives that request, it will calculate an HTTP response. Depending on the request, it may retrieve information from a database or read a file from the filesystem to prepare the response.

HTTP supports different types of requests. You are probably already familiar with the GET method used to retrieve information from a URL and the POST method used primarily to send form data, but there are other less well-known methods such as HEAD, OPTIONS, PUT, DELETE, TRACE, and CONNECT.

Figure 3-2 shows a simple HTTP GET request where you can see the HTTP information sent when visiting `http://127.0.0.1:5000/`.

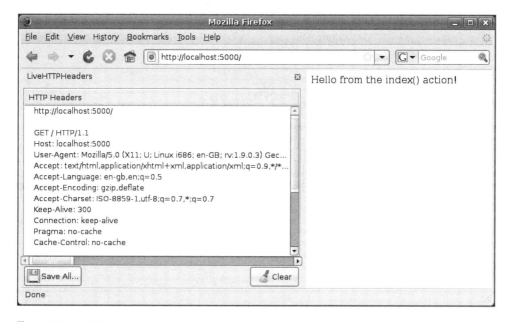

Figure 3-2. *An HTTP request in LiveHTTPHeaders*

Figure 3-3 shows the response returned.

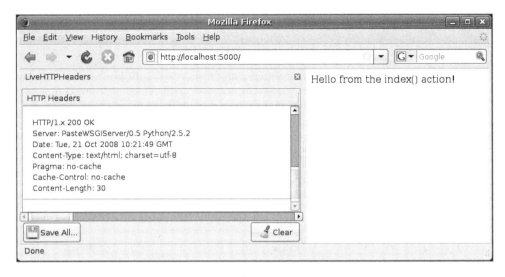

Figure 3-3. *An HTTP response in LiveHTTPHeaders*

As you can see, the browser sends quite a lot of information to the server. The application then processes this information and performs any necessary operations before returning a status and any HTTP headers it wants to send back. Of particular note is the Content-type header that tells the browser what sort of content is going to be sent (in this case text/html). Finally, the application returns the content that will be displayed by the browser (in this case the HTML that makes up the page). The server may add extra HTTP headers or perform other modifications before the response is returned.

In this example, the HTTP status code is 200, which means everything went fine and no error occurred. The application and server can use many other status codes to tell the browser what happened while processing the request. Table 3-1 describes some of the most commonly used codes.

Table 3-1. *Commonly Used HTTP Status Codes*

Status Code	Description
200 OK	The request has succeeded.
401 Unauthorized	The request requires user authentication.
403 Forbidden	The server won't let the user access what was requested, perhaps because the user doesn't have the appropriate permissions.
404 Not Found	The server has not found anything matching the request URI.
500 Internal Server Error	The server encountered an unexpected condition that prevented it from fulfilling the request.

For the vast majority of web development situations, the areas of the protocol I have discussed are all you need to know, but if you are interested in the details of HTTP, you can find the full specification at http://www.w3.org/Protocols/rfc2616/rfc2616.txt, including an explanation of all the request methods and status codes.

Exploring the Environment

Information about the HTTP request as well other information is presented to your Pylons application through environment variables. These are a set of dynamic values set by the web server on each request. Exactly which variables are set depends on the web server, the browser, and the action the user is trying to perform. Once Pylons receives these variables from the environment, they are passed to the Pylons `request` object for use in your controllers. You wouldn't usually access environment variables directly, but it is useful to know where the Pylons `request` object gets its information from.

If you have ever written CGI scripts or used PHP, you will most likely be familiar with using environment variables already, in which case many of the variables mentioned in this section will be familiar. It is worth remembering, though, that Pylons controllers aren't executed in the same way as CGI or PHP scripts, so consequently some of these variables have slightly different meanings in the Pylons context.

The following variable is set for all requests and are not request specific:

`SERVER_NAME`: The server's hostname, DNS alias, or IP address as it would appear in self-referencing URLs.

The following are specific to the request:

`SERVER_PORT`: This is the number of the port to which the request was sent.

`SERVER_PROTOCOL`: This is the name and revision of the protocol used in the request. Usually it is `HTTP/1.1`.

`REQUEST_METHOD`: This is the method with which the request was made, such as GET, HEAD, POST, and so on.

`REMOTE_HOST`: This is the hostname making the request (set only if the server has this information).

`REMOTE_ADDR`: This is the IP address of the remote host making the request.

`REMOTE_USER`: This is the username of an authenticated user but is set only if a user is signed in.

`AUTH_TYPE`: If the server supports user authentication, this is the authentication method used to validate the user.

`CONTENT_TYPE`: If the request was an HTTP POST or PUT, then there could be content sent by the client. This is the content type of the data.

`CONTENT_LENGTH`: If a `CONTENT_TYPE` is specified, this is the length of that content.

`QUERY_STRING`: This is the part of the URL after a ?, such as `foo1=bar1&foo2=bar2`.

`SCRIPT_NAME` and `PATH_INFO`: In a Pylons application, `SCRIPT_NAME` is the part of the URL before the URL the Pylons application would treat as its site root, and `PATH_INFO` is the part of the URL after it. If you are serving the application, normally `SCRIPT_NAME` will be `''` and `PATH_INFO` will be the part of the URL before the query string. If you were to mount the Pylons application at, say, `/myapp`, then `SCRIPT_NAME` would be `/myapp` and `PATH_INFO` would be the part of the URL after it and before the query string.

In addition to these environment variables, any HTTP headers that are sent in the request and not dealt with by previous environment variables are also included after being prefixed with `HTTP_` and having any - characters replaced with _ characters. Since these are set by the user's browser, they warrant more suspicion than the previous environment variables. Here are some of the more familiar ones as examples:

HTTP_HOST: This is the hostname and domain name portion of the URL, such as www.pylonshq.com.

HTTP_COOKIE: This is the content of the client's cookie(s).

HTTP_USER_AGENT: This is the user-agent string to identify the browser type and version.

Although you would normally access these variables through the more convenient request object, Pylons is all about giving power to the developer, so you can still access environment variables directly in your controllers if you choose. They are available as the request.environ dictionary. You'll see how to use the request object in a few moments.

In addition to the CGI-style variables listed earlier, the server running your Pylons application also adds extra information to the environment called *WSGI variables*, which can sometimes be useful to know about for use in your Pylons application.

■**Tip** WSGI stands for the Web Server Gateway Interface, and although you don't need to know anything about it to develop Pylons applications, it is actually a very powerful API on which much of Pylons is based, so I'll cover it in detail in Chapters 16 and 17.

Here are the WSGI variables you will also find in the Pylons request.environ dictionary:

wsgi.version: This is a tuple, (1,0), representing WSGI version 1.0.

wsgi.url_scheme: This is a string representing the "scheme" portion of the URL at which the application is being invoked. Normally, this will have the value http or https, as appropriate.

wsgi.input: This is an input stream (a file-like object) from which the HTTP request body can be read for PUT and POST requests.

wsgi.errors: This is a text mode output stream (a file-like object) to which error output can be written. Applications should use \n as a line ending and assume it will be converted to the correct line ending. For many servers, wsgi.errors will be the server's main error log.

wsgi.multithread: This evaluates to true if the application object can be simultaneously invoked by another thread in the same process; it evaluates to false otherwise. It typically takes the value 0 or 1.

wsgi.multiprocess: This evaluates to true if an equivalent application object can be simultaneously invoked by another process, and it evaluates to false otherwise. It typically takes the value 0 or 1.

wsgi.run_once: This evaluates to true if the server or gateway expects that the application will be invoked only this one time during the life of its containing process. Normally, this will be true only if your Pylons application is being run from a CGI script.

Once again, you will rarely need to access WSGI variables directly because the components in Pylons that add them also present a clean API for their use, but it is useful to know they are there.

To see all the environment variables that Pylons sets up for you, add another action called environ() to the HelloController you created earlier so that it looks like this:

```
class HelloController(BaseController):

    def index(self):
        return 'Hello from the index() action!'
```

```
def environ(self):
    result = '<html><body><h1>Environ</h1>'
    for key, value in request.environ.items():
        result += '%s: %r <br />'%(key, value)
    result += '</body></html>'
    return result
```

If you visit http://127.0.0.1:5000/hello/environ, you will see all the keys and values displayed, including the WSGI variables and the traditional CGI-style environment variables.

Understanding the Pylons Request and Response

Now that you have learned about the fundamentals of HTTP and the environment, let's return to learning about Pylons, specifically, the request and response objects.

The request and response objects together represent all the information Pylons receives about the HTTP request and all the information Pylons is going to send in the response. Let's start by looking at the request object.

Request

The Pylons request object is actually a subclass of the webob.Request class provided by the WebOb package, which was automatically installed as one of Pylons' dependencies. A new instance of the class is created on each request based on the HTTP information Pylons receives via the environment. The object is available as the pylons.request object and is automatically imported at the top of any controllers you create with the paster controller command.

You can look at the API reference on the WebOb web site at http://pythonpaste.org/webob/ for full details of the Webob.Request object's API and on the Pylons web site at http://docs.pylonshq.com/modules/controllers_util.html#pylons.controllers.util.Request for details of the subclass, but there are a few methods and attributes that are particularly worth mentioning now:

request.environ: You've already seen this when I discussed the environment. It is a dictionary that contains CGI-style environment variables, WSGI variables, and request header information, but it is not normally used directly. Instead, other attributes of the request global are used to obtain Python representations of the information it contains.

request.headers: This is a dictionary representing all the HTTP request headers. The dictionary is case insensitive.

request.method: This is the HTTP method used to request the URL; typically, it is GET or POST but could be PUT, DELETE, or others.

request.GET: This is a dictionary-like object with all the variables in the query string.

request.POST: This is a dictionary-like object with all the variables in the request body. This has variables only if the request was a POST and it is a form submission.

request.params: This is a dictionary-like object with a combination of everything in request.GET and request.POST. You will generally use request.params rather than request.GET or request.POST, although they all share the same API. I'll cover request.params more closely in a minute because it is the main object you will use to deal with form submissions.

request.body: This is a file-like object representing the body of a POST request.

request.cookies: This is a dictionary containing the cookies present.

request.url: This is the full request URL, with the query string, such as http://localhost/app-root/doc?article_id=10. There are also other attributes and methods for obtaining different parts of the URL and even for generating URLs relative to the current URL.

The request object also has attributes for most of the common HTTP request headers, such as request.accept_language, request.content_length, and request.user_agent. These properties expose the parsed form of each header for whatever parsing makes sense. For instance, request.if_modified_since returns a datetime object (or None if the header was not provided).

Although the request object has plenty of useful attributes and methods, the one you are likely to use the most is request.params. This contains a MultiDict object representing all the GET and POST parameters of the request. Of course, you can access the GET and POST parameters separately via the request.GET and request.POST attributes, but most of the time you are unlikely to be trying to obtain GET and POST parameters at once, so you can just use request.params that combines the data from each.

Note A MultiDict object is a dictionary-like object defined in the WebOb package that allows multiple values with the same key.

The request.params object can be treated in a number of ways. Imagine you've visited the URL http://localhost:5000/hello/index?a=1&a=2; you could then use the request.params object in the following ways:

```
>>> request.params
MultiDict([('a', '1'), ('a', '2')])
>>> request.params['a']
'1'
>>> request.params.get('a', 'Not present')
'1'
>>> request.params.get('b', 'Not present')
'Not present'
>>> request.params.getall('a')
['1','2']
```

Caution If you are used to programming with Python's cgi module, the way request.params works might surprise you because if the request has two parameters with the same name, as is the case with our example variable a, using request.params['a'] and request.get('a') returns only the first value rather than returning a list. Also, the methods described return the actual value, not an object whose .value attribute contains the value of the parameter.

There is also one other method, request.params.getone(), which returns just one value for the parameter it is getting. In this case, calling request.params.getone('a') raises an error because there is more than one value for a:

```
>>> request.params.getone('a')
Traceback (most recent call last):
...
    raise KeyError('Multiple values match %r: %r' % (key, v))
KeyError: "Multiple values match 'a': ['1', '2']"
```

To avoid problems obtaining just one value for a parameter when you expected many or obtaining many when you expected just one, you are encouraged to use the request.params.getone() and request.params.getall() methods in your own code rather than the dictionary-like interface.

Response

Now that you've looked in detail at the `request` object, you can turn your attention to the `response` object. You have actually been implicitly using the `response` object already if you've been following the examples in this chapter. Any time you return a string from a controller action, Pylons automatically writes it to the `response` object for you. Pylons then uses the `response` object to generate the HTTP information it returns to the browser, so any changes you make to the `response` object affect the HTTP response returned. Let's look at the `response` object in more detail.

The `response` object is also a subclass of `webob.Response`, and once again you can find full details on the WebOb web site and the Pylons documentation web site at the same URLs as mentioned for the `request` object, but there are some features worth drawing your attention to here.

The `response` object has three fundamental parts:

`response.status`: This is the response code plus message, like `'200 OK'`. To set the code without the reason, use `response.status_int = 200`.

`response.headerlist`: This is a list of all the headers, like `[('Content-Type', 'text/html')]`. There's a case-insensitive dictionary-like object in `response.headers` that also allows you to access these headers as well as add your own.

`response.app_iter`: This is an iterable (such as a list or generator) that will produce the content of the response. You rarely need to access this in a Pylons application, though, because Pylons automatically uses this to produce the content of the response for you.

Everything else derives from this underlying state. Here are the highlights:

`response.content_type`: This is the content type not including the `charset` parameter.

`response.set_cookie(key, value, max_age=None, path='/', domain=None, secure=None, httponly=False, version=None, comment=None)`: This sets a cookie. The keyword arguments control the various cookie parameters. The `max_age` argument is the length for the cookie to live in seconds (you can also use a `datetime.timedelta` object). The `Expires` key will also be set based on the value of `max_age`.

`response.delete_cookie(key, path='/', domain=None)`: This deletes a cookie from the client. This sets `max_age` to `0` and the cookie value to `''`.

Looking at the `HelloWorld` example from earlier in the chapter, you might have noticed that although the `Content-type` header sent to the browser was `text/html`, the message you returned was actually plain text, so the `Content-type` header should have been set to `text/plain`. Now that you have learned about the `response` object, you can correct this. Update the `index()` action of the hello controller so that it uses this response:

```
def index(self):
    response.content_type = 'text/plain'
    return 'Hello from the index() action!'
```

The server will reload when you save the change, and you can test the example again by visiting `http://localhost:5000/`. This time, the browser treats the message as plain text instead of HTML. If you are using the Firefox browser, you may notice it uses a different font to display the message this time.

Understanding Pylons Globals

The `request` and `response` objects you learned about in the previous section are referred to as Pylons *globals* because Pylons takes great care behind the scenes to make sure they can be used throughout your application including in your project's controllers and its templates. In this section, I'll cover all the other Pylons globals you can use in your application. Let's start by looking at the objects made available by default in your controllers.

If you look at the `controllers/hello.py` file in the `HelloWorld` project I've been using as an example, you will see the following imports at the top:

```
from pylons import request, response, session, tmpl_context as c
from pylons.controllers.util import abort, redirect_to
```

These lines are for importing the core Pylons globals, but in addition to these globals, there are also some other imports Pylons developers can add to their controllers to import optional Pylons globals:

```
import helloworld.lib.helpers as h
from helloworld.lib import app_globals
from pylons import config
```

You've already learned about the `request` and `response` globals, and I'll cover `h`, `app_globals`, and the template context object `c` in detail in the following sections, so let's just concentrate on `session`, `abort`, `redirect_to`, and `config` for the time being:

`abort(status_code=None, detail="", headers=None, comment=None)`: Occasionally you might want to immediately stop execution of the request and return a response bypassing the normal flow of execution of your application. You can do this with the `abort()` function, which is used like this:

```
def test_abort(self):
    username = request.environ.get('REMOTE_USER')
    if not username:
        abort(401)
    else:
        return"Hello %s"%username
```

In this example, if no `REMOTE_USER` environment variable is set, it means that no user has signed in, so the request is immediately aborted and returns a 401 status code (the correct HTTP status code for when a user has not been authenticated and is therefore not authorized to see a particular resource).

The function also allows you to add some text to form part of the status as well as any extra headers that should be set. If you use a 300 status code, the `detail` option should be the location to redirect to, but you would be better using the `redirect_to()` function in such circumstances.

Internally, the `abort()` function uses WebOb HTTPExceptions, which you'll learn about in Chapter 17.

`config`: This contains configuration information about the running application. It is described at `http://docs.pylonshq.com/modules/configuration.html`.

`redirect_to(*args, **kwargs)`: This function takes the same arguments as the `url_for()` function you will learn about in the next section. It allows you to specify a URL to redirect to by stating the routing variables that you want the URL to produce once it is called.

It is also possible to specify the HTTP status code you want to use with the `_code` argument.

For example:

```
redirect_to(controller='hello', action='other_action', _code=303)
```

`session`: This is a proxy to the Beaker session object that can be used as a session store with various back ends. By default, the session information is stored in your project's `data` directory, and cookies are used to keep track of the sessions. You'll learn how to use sessions in Chapter 8 when you implement a flash message system.

In Chapter 11, you will also learn about four more Pylons globals named `translator`, `ungettext()`, `_()`, and `N_()`, but these are too advanced for now.

Helpers

Helper functions (or *helpers* as they are known) are a concept borrowed from Ruby on Rails and are simply useful functions that you will find yourself using over and over again to perform common tasks such as generating form fields or creating links. Helper functions are all kept in the `lib/helpers.py` module in your project directory structure, but you must manually import them into your controllers if you want to use them. Since helpers are used frequently, it is common to import them using the shortened module name `h` rather than the full name `helpers` to save on typing:

```
import helloworld.lib.helpers as h
```

One of the most useful helpers is `h.url_for()`, which is a function that comes from the Routes package to help you generate URLs. You've already seen how the Routes system maps a URL to a particular controller action. Well, the `h.url_for()` helper does the reverse, mapping a controller and action to a URL. For example, to generate a URL for the `environ` action of the `hello` controller, you would use the following code:

```
h.url_for(controller='hello', action='environ')
```

In Pylons it is generally considered bad practice to ever write a URL manually in your code because at some point in the future you might want to change your URL structure, or your Pylons application might be mounted at a different URL. By using `h.url_for()` to generate your URLs, you avoid these problems since the correct URL is always generated automatically.

The Routes system is actually extremely powerful, and you will see some of the details of the way it works in Chapter 9. One aspect worth mentioning now is that you can also specify extra variables in your route maps. For example, if you wanted URLs in the format `/calendar/view/2007/06/15`, you might set up a map that treats `calendar` as the controller and `view` as the action and then assigns `2007` to a variable `year`, `06` to a variable `month`, and `15` to a variable called `day`. When Pylons called your controller action, it would pass in `year`, `month`, and `day` as the parameters, so your action would look like this:

```
def view(self, year, month, day):
    return "This is the page for %s/%s/%s"%(year, month, day)
```

In this way, the URL itself can contain important information about what the page should display, and this both saves you having to pass such variables around your application as hidden fields and means your URL structure much better matches what is actually going on in your application.

You can use many other useful helpers to make your programming easier, but one of the great things about Pylons is that you can easily add your own too. Adding a new helper to the `h` object is as simple as importing a new function into your project's `lib/helpers.py` module or defining a new object in it. As an example, let's refactor the code you wrote earlier to print the environment into a useful helper. At the end of your project's `lib/helpers.py` file, add the following function:

```
def format_environ(environ):
    result = []
    keys = environ.keys()
    keys.sort()
    for key in keys:
        result.append("%s: %r"%(key, environ[key]))
    return '\n'.join(result)
```

Then after importing the helpers as h, you can update your action to look like this:

```
def environ(self):
    response.content_type = 'text/plain'
    return h.format_environ(request.environ)
```

Tip In this case, the helper function needed access to the environment that formed part of the request, so if you are a keen object-oriented programmer and had wanted to refactor the environment formatting code, you might have been tempted to add a private method to the controller rather than create a helper function that needs the request information passed in. Generally speaking, it is a lot better to add useful code that you intend to use a lot as a simple helper object than to add methods to controller classes because then they can easily be accessed throughout your Pylons application rather than just in controller actions.

You'll see more of the built-in Pylons helpers when I cover form handling in Chapter 6.

Context Object

When you develop a real Pylons application, you will quickly find you need to pass request-specific information to different parts of your code. For example, you might need to set some variables to be used in a template or in a form validator.

Because Pylons is designed to work in a multithreaded environment, it is important that this information is passed around your application in a thread-safe way so that variables associated with one request don't get confused with variables from any other requests that are being executed at the same time.

Pylons provides the context object tmpl_context for precisely this purpose, and again, since it is used so frequently, it is imported by default into your controllers as the c object. The c object is a StackedObjectProxy that always returns the correct data for the current request.

You can assign attributes to the c object like this, and they will be available throughout the application:

```
c.my_data = 'Important data'
```

You can choose any attribute name you want to assign variables to as long as they don't start with the _ character and are a valid Python name. They will then be available throughout your templates and application code and will always contain the correct data for the thread that is handling a particular request.

As was mentioned in the discussion about helpers, the Routes system Pylons uses allows you to use parts of the URL as variables in your application. Since you frequently need to access these variables in templates and other areas of your code, Pylons automatically sets up the c object to have any of the Routes variables that your action specified attached to it. You could therefore modify the helpers example from earlier to look like this, and it would still work in the same way:

```
def view(self, year, month, day):
    return "This is the page for %s/%s/%s"%(c.year, c.month, c.day)
```

There is one more important aspect to learn about the c variable that you might not expect at first. If you access an attribute that doesn't exist, the value returned will be the empty string ' ' rather than an AttributeError being raised as you might expect. This enables you to write code such as this without needing to test each part of the statement to check that the attribute exists:

```
data = c.some_value or c.some_other_value or "Not specified"
```

This code will set data to be c.some_value if it exists and otherwise c.some_other_value if that exists; if neither exist, the value will be set to "Not specified".

This style of code can be useful occasionally, but if you are not used to writing code like this, I strongly recommend you stick to explicitly testing values of attributes you are not sure about to avoid the risk of errors. You can do this with the Python functions hasattr() and getattr(), which are used like this:

```
if hasattr(c, "foo"):
    x = c.foo
else:
    x = 'default'
y = getattr(c, "bar", "default")
```

To use the strict version of the c global, edit your project's config/environment.py file, and add the following line just before the lines to customize your templating options:

```
config['pylons.strict_c'] = True
# Customize templating options via this variable
```

With the strict_c option enabled, c will raise an AttributeError as you would expect. It is strongly recommended you set the strict_c option if you are a Pylons beginner.

■**Caution** If you come across an error you can't quite understand when performing some operation on an attribute of c, it is possible that you have forgotten to specify the attribute and that the empty string is being returned instead. Trying to perform an operation on the string when you expected it to be a different object may be what is causing the error.

App Globals Object

Sometimes you might want information to be available to all controllers and not be reset on each request. For example, you might want to set up a database connection pool when the application is loaded rather than creating a connection on each request. You can achieve this with the app_globals object.

■**Note** In previous versions of Pylons, the app_globals global was simply named g. New Pylons applications should use the full name app_globals instead.

The app_globals variable is actually just an instance of your Globals class in your application's lib/app_globals.py file. It gets set up in the config/environment.py file of your project.

Any attributes set to self in the __init__() method of the Globals class will be available as attributes of app_globals throughout your Pylons application. Any attributes set on app_globals during one request will remain changed for all subsequent requests, so you have to be very careful not to accidentally change any global data by mistake.

Here is a simple counter example that demonstrates how the `app_globals` object works. First modify your `lib/app_globals.py` Globals class so that the `__init__.py` method looks like this:

```
def __init__(self):
    self.visits = 0
```

You will now be able to access the `visits` attribute as `app_globals.visits` in your controllers. First import the global from Pylons:

```
from pylons import app_globals
```

Next add a new action to the end of the `HelloController`:

```
def app_globals_test(self):
    app_globals.visits += 1
    return "You are visitor number %s." % app_globals.visits
```

If you restart the Paste HTTP server and visit `http://localhost:5000/hello/app_globals_test`, you should see the message `You are visitor number 1`. If you visit the page again, the message will be changed to `You are visitor number 2`. On each subsequent request, the counter will increase.

If you restart the server, you will see that the value of `app_globals.visits` is reset to 0 because a new instance of the `helloworld.lib.app_globals.Globals` class is created when the server starts.

■**Caution** Because the `app_globals` object is persistent across requests, it can be modified by any thread. This means it is possible that a value attached to `app_globals` might be different at the start of a request than at the end if another thread has changed its value in between. This doesn't matter in our example, but it is something to be aware of if you aren't used to working in multithreaded environments.

Configuring Pylons

You configure Pylons applications in two places. The first is the configuration file you saw earlier in the chapter when you looked at the `HelloWorld` project's `development.ini` file. The configuration file is where any per-instance configuration options should be put. For example, the port and hostname might vary between a production deployment of your Pylons application and a development installation, so these are options that are set in the configuration file.

Any configuration that should affect the whole application and should not be customizable on a per-instance basis is set in Python code in one of the files in your project's `config` directory. These are the following:

`middleware.py`: This is where the Pylons application is constructed and where you can change the Pylons middleware stack itself. Middleware is considered an advanced topic and is dealt with in Part 3 of the book.

`routing.py`: This is where you define your application's routes. You saw a simple example earlier in the chapter and will look at routing in much more detail in Chapter 9.

`environment.py`: This is where you configure most of Pylons' internal options, although you generally don't need to because the defaults are very sensible. One time when you might need to set some options in this file is if you want to use a different templating language to the Pylons default, which is Mako. You'll learn about this in Chapter 5.

Once you have configured your application, whether in the configuration file or the `config/environment.py` file, you will want to be able to access that configuration in your Pylons application. All configuration is contained in the `config` global, which can be imported into a controller like this:

`from pylons import config`. The `config` object has a number of attributes representing different aspects of Pylons configuration. These are described in detail at `http://docs.pylonshq.com/modules/configuration.html`, but these are two that you are likely to use frequently:

`config.app_conf`: This is a dictionary of all the application options set in the `[app:main]` part of the config file being used including any custom options used by your application. For example, to access the location of the cache directory, you could use `config.app_conf['cache_dir']`.

`config.global_conf`: This is very similar to `config.app_conf`, but rather than providing a dictionary interface to the `[app:main]` section of the config file, this attribute represents the global options specified in the `[DEFAULT]` section.

There are also attributes for the package name, default character set, paths to look for templates, and more. See the documentation for full details.

Controller Imports

In addition to the Pylons globals I've described, there are a number of other useful objects that Pylons provides for you to use in your controllers. Each of these objects is described in detail in the Pylons module documentation, which you can browse online at `http://docs.pylonshq.com/modules/index.html`, but they are worth mentioning here so that you are aware of them.

First let's look at the available decorators:

`pylons.decorators.jsonify(func)`: Given a function that will return content, this decorator will turn the result into JSON, with a content type of `text/javascript`, and output it.

`pylons.decorators.validate(...)`: This validates input either for a FormEncode schema or for individual validators. This is discussed in detail in Chapter 6.

`pylons.decorators.secure.authenticate_form(func)`: This decorator uses an authorization token stored in the client's session for prevention of certain cross-site request forgery (CSRF) attacks.

`pylons.decorators.secure.https(*redirect_args, **redirect_kwargs)`: This decorator redirects to the SSL version of a page if not currently using HTTPS.

`pylons.decorators.rest.dispatch_on(**method_map)`: This dispatches to alternate controller methods based on the HTTP method.

`pylons.decorators.rest.restrict(*methods)`: This restricts access to the function depending on the HTTP method. You'll see it used in Chapter 8.

`pylons.decorators.cache.beaker_cache(...)`: This cache decorator utilizes Beaker. This caches the action or other function that returns a "pickleable" object as a result.

Pylons also provides two different types of controllers:

`pylons.controllers.core.WSGIController`: This is the controller that your project's `BaseController` is inherited from and is the only controller you will use in this book.

`pylons.controllers.xmlrpc.XMLRPCController`: This controller handles XML-RPC responses and complies with the XML-RPC specification as well as the XML-RPC Introspection specification. It is useful if you want to build XML-RPC web services in Pylons.

Finally, it is worth mentioning three more objects you are likely to use a lot in your controllers, but each of these has their own chapter and will be dealt with later in the book:

`render`: This is used for rendering templates and is discussed in Chapter 5.

`model`: This is used for the model component of your application and is discussed in Chapter 7.

`log`: This is used to output log messages.

In its simplest form, you can simply write `log.error('Log this message')` in a controller, and the message will be logged to the console of the Paste HTTP server. Logging is described in detail in Chapter 20.

Summary

This chapter covered quite a lot of ground, including using static files, understanding HTTP and the environment, using the `request` and `response` objects, and understanding the basics of Routes. In the next chapter, you'll take a detailed look at how to track down problems when they occur and how to handle them so that the user is presented with an appropriate error message. After that, you'll be ready to get properly stuck into Pylons development, so you'll learn how to use templates before looking at how forms are handled.

■■■

# CHAPTER 4

Tracking Down and Handling Problems

One of the factors that most affects how quickly you can develop an application is your ability to track down and fix problems. Pylons provides three sets of tools to help you in this regard:

- A world-class web-based interactive debugger
- A console-based interactive testing shell
- A powerful set of logging tools

You'll learn about the interactive debugger in this chapter, but I'll leave the discussion of the interactive shell until Chapter 12 and the discussion of logging until Chapter 20.

You'll also learn about how to present a page to the user when an error occurs using Pylons' error documents support.

It is also worth remembering that the `--reload` option from the Paste HTTP server described in the previous chapter can also help speed up the debugging process. When the `--reload` option is used, the server keeps track of all the Python files your application uses, and if any of them should change, the server gets automatically restarted so that you can test your changes straightaway.

Using the Pylons Interactive Debugger

When you create a new Pylons application and keep the `full_stack` config option set to its default value of `true`, Pylons will include a special component called the `ErrorHandler` middleware in your application. You'll learn more about how the `ErrorHandler` middleware actually works in Chapter 17, but you don't need to know the details of how the `ErrorHandler` middleware works in order to use the Pylons interactive debugger.

If an exception occurs when debug mode is set to `true` in the config file, the `ErrorHandler` middleware catches the exception and triggers the Pylons interactive debugger, which is a web page that provides various means of debugging the application, including an interactive Ajax-based Python console (see Figure 4-1).

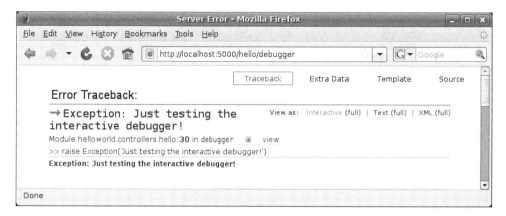

Figure 4-1. *The Pylons interactive debugger*

The interactive debugger screen has four main tabs, three of which are particularly useful:

Traceback tab: This tab provides the raw exception trace and allows you to see the local variables at each part in the traceback. If you click >>, you will be able to see the source code around the area where the code was called. Clicking + next to a particular part of the traceback will open an interactive Ajax Python prompt, which allows you to enter Python commands to debug the application at that point in the call stack. It also provides a view of all the local variables at that point in the stack. You can, of course, open many interactive Ajax Python prompts at different parts of the traceback to debug different parts of the call stack.

Extra Data tab: This tab displays the CGI environment and WSGI variables at the time of the exception as well as information about the global and application-level configuration options that are set in your `development.ini` config file.

Template tab: If the exception occurred while rendering a Mako template, this tab will be displayed by default and will contain Mako's HTML representation of what went wrong. This can often be a lot more useful than the main traceback information because the syntax error that occurred can be displayed visually, enabling you to go straight to the template code to correct the error. If the exception that triggered the interactive debugger was not triggered in a template, the Template tab will be empty.

Let's modify the `HelloWorld` application created in the previous chapter to re-create the exception shown in Figure 4-1. Add another action to the `HelloController`:

```
def debugger(self):
    value = "Some value"
    raise Exception('Just testing the interactive debugger!')
```

If you visit `http://localhost:5000/hello/debugger`, an exception will occur, and this will trigger the interactive debugger.

Try clicking the >> link by the words raise Exception, and you will see a representation of the code near where the error occurred. If you click the + icon after the word debugger on the previous line, you will be shown the local variables list and the interactive Ajax Python prompt. Try entering the following line:

```
print value
```

You should see the value Some value displayed, just like you would in a normal Python prompt (see Figure 4-2). Try entering some other Python commands, and you will see the prompt behaves exactly as a normal prompt. You can even use the up and down arrow keys to scroll through the command history.

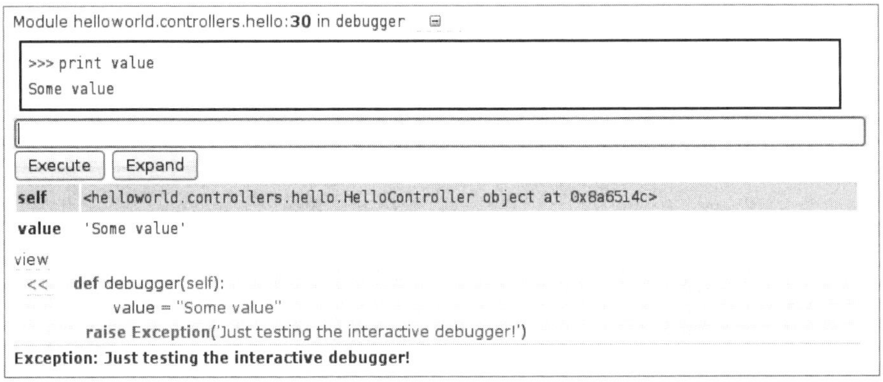

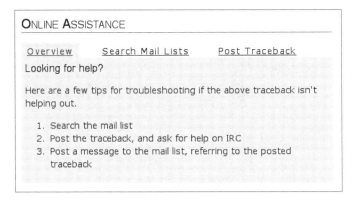

Figure 4-2. *The interactive debugger in use*

A new feature of the interactive debugger in Pylons 0.9.7 is the Online Assistance box shown in Figure 4-3. Clicking Search Mail Lists will present a search box with the exception prepopulated to allow you to search the Pylons mailing list for the error that occurred. You can also search related mailing lists such as the Python, Mako, and SQLAlchemy lists.

ONLINE ASSISTANCE
_____

Overview   Search Mail Lists   Post Traceback

Looking for help?

Here are a few tips for troubleshooting if the above traceback isn't helping out.

1. Search the mail list
2. Post the traceback, and ask for help on IRC
3. Post a message to the mail list, referring to the posted traceback

Figure 4-3. *The online assistance tools*

If you can't find a discussion of the error that has occurred, you can post the complete trace-back online. You can then send an e-mail to the mailing list referencing your traceback post or talk to other Pylons users directly in the IRC channel.

■**Caution** When posting traceback information online, be sure to check that you don't post any private information such as usernames and passwords. All the information you post is publically accessible.

Occasionally it is even handy to deliberately put an exception into your code like this during development to act a bit like a breakpoint and allow you to see what is happening at that point in the code.

You can even use the interactive debugger to debug Ajax requests. Every time an error occurs, the interactive debugger will log an error message containing a URL at which the error traceback can be accessed. You simply need to visit that URL in a web browser to be able to interactively debug that particular request. Each request that results in an error is given a slightly different URL so that you can be sure you are debugging the correct request.

In addition to printing the debug URL to the error log, an HTTP header named X-Debug-URL containing the debug URL will also be added to the HTTP response headers, so you can read the URL from there too. In Figure 4-4, you can see that the exception just raised will also be available to debug at `http://localhost:5000/_debug/view/1217245745`. The number at the end of the URL will be different on each request, though.

Since the interactive debugger is accessed at the URL /_debug, it is important that you don't design any URLs into your application to start with /_debug, or the interactive debugger is likely to interfere with them.

Figure 4-4. *The HTTP response including an* X-Debug-URL *header*

Production Use

If you haven't realized it already, leaving the interactive debugger enabled in production environments represents a major security risk because in the same way that you can enter any Python command you like in order to track down a potential problem when an exception occurs, a malicious visitor to your web site could use the same tool to enter malicious Python commands to do damage to your system or, worse, to use your system to launch attacks on other people's systems.

For this reason, it is important you disable the interactive debugger when running a Pylons application in any environment where a page containing the interactive debugger might be shown to someone other than yourself if an error occurs.

To disable debugging, uncomment the following line in the [app:main] section of your development.ini file:

```
#set debug = false
```

so that it reads as follows:

```
set debug = false
```

You have been warned!

■**Caution** Do not leave the interactive debugger enabled on production systems.

E-mail Options

Once you have disabled the interactive debugger for production use, you will be able to set up your application to send error reports to your e-mail address should an exception occur. The error reports will contain the full traceback as well as the information that would normally appear on the Extra Data tab.

To enable Pylons' error reporting, you need to ensure you have disabled interactive debugging as described earlier, but you also need to set your e-mail address in the email_to variable in the [DEFAULT] section at the top of the config file. The e-mail will be sent via SMTP, so you must also specify an SMTP server you have access to and choose an e-mail address that the e-mail should appear to come from:

```
[DEFAULT]
debug = true
# Uncomment and replace with the address which should receive any error reports
email_to = feedback@pylonsbook.com
smtp_server = smtp.pylonsbook.com
error_email_from = server.error@pylonsbook.com
```

The error reports look something like Figure 4-5 and will help you identify the problem that caused the exception.

If an error report is sent, a 500 Internal Server Error response is displayed using Pylons error documents support. You'll learn how to customize error documents in Chapter 19, when you put the finishing touches on SimpleSite, the example application you will develop throughout the book.

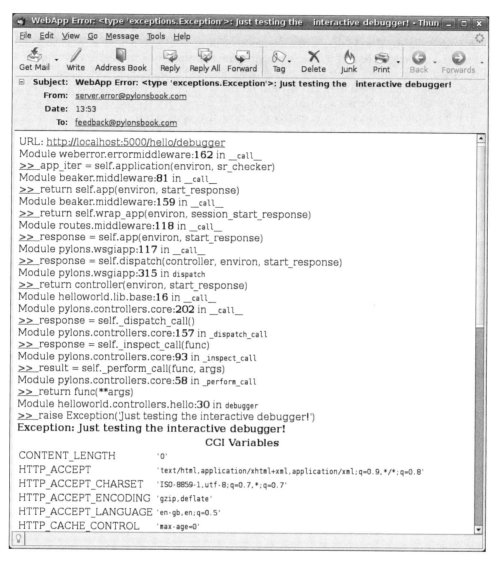

Figure 4-5. *An e-mail error report*

Summary

Now that you know how to use the interactive debugger, you can move on and start looking at individual topics involved in Pylons development. If you are following along with the examples in the book, feel free to explore the traceback any time an exception occurs. The interactive debugger is a very useful tool that will help you track down problems quickly as well as give you better insight into what is going on beneath the surface of your Pylons application.

CHAPTER 5

■ ■ ■

Using View Templates

Real web applications require the generation of a lot of HTML pages. In the HelloWorld example from Chapter 3, you saw how to generate a string in Python code and return it from a controller action to the user's browser to produce some visible output.

If you tried to generate a whole web application with lots of different HTML pages by generating strings in Python code, it would quickly become rather cumbersome because the Python language was not specifically designed to make it easy to generate HTML. Instead, it is often helpful to use a *templating system*.

Rather than writing Python code containing HTML strings, templating systems typically allow you to write HTML directly and embed Python code in your HTML when you need to do so. Since most of your template is likely to be HTML rather than Python, this is often a lot quicker. Templating languages typically also offer simple constructs for substituting variables or repeating certain sections of HTML.

Here is a simple template written using Pylons' default templating language, Mako. It simply prints a personalized greeting:

```
<html>
<head>
    <title>Greetings</title>
</head>
<body>
    <h1>Greetings</h1>
    <p>Hello ${name}!</p>
</body>
</html>
```

As you can see, most of the template consists of HTML. Areas of the template that represent Python expressions that add to the content of the template are written inside ${}. In this example, the value of name would replace the ${name} text when the template was rendered.

Let's see how to use this template in Pylons. Throughout this chapter, you'll create a new Pylons application that demonstrates various features of Mako, and by the end of the chapter, you will have created a complete set of templates you can use in your own Pylons application.

Start by creating a new project. Once again, you will be asked some questions; you can choose the defaults:

```
$ paster create --template=pylons TemplateDemo
Selected and implied templates:
  Pylons#pylons  Pylons application template
```

```
Variables:
  egg:      TemplateDemo
  package:  templatedemo
  project:  TemplateDemo
Enter template_engine (mako/genshi/jinja/etc: Template language) ['mako']:
Enter sqlalchemy (True/False: Include SQLAlchemy 0.4 configuration) [False]:
Enter google_app_engine (True/False: Setup default appropriate for Google App Engine)
[False]:
Creating template pylons
Creating directory ./TemplateDemo
  Recursing into +package+
    Creating ./TemplateDemo/templatedemo/
    Copying __init__.py_tmpl to ./TemplateDemo/templatedemo/__init__.py
    Recursing into config
    ... etc
```

Remember that the `--template` option in the previous command refers to *project* templates used to create a project directory structure for you, whereas this chapter is about *view* templates used to help render the HTML for a view.

Pylons projects store view templates in the project's `templates` directory, but if you want to store them somewhere else, you can configure where Pylons should tell Mako to look to find your view templates by editing your project's `config/environment.py` file. By default, it looks like this:

```
# Create the Mako TemplateLookup, with the default autoescaping
config['pylons.app_globals'].mako_lookup = TemplateLookup(
    directories=paths['templates'],
    ...
)
```

You can replace `paths['templates']` with a list of the places that Mako should search for view templates. Mako searches the directories in order.

Now that the project has been created, let's test the greeting example you saw earlier. Save the greeting template in the `TemplateDemo/templatedemo/templates/` directory as `greeting.html`.

You'll also need a controller to test the template. Create a new controller in your `TemplateDemo` project named `greeting`:

```
$ cd TemplateDemo
$ paster controller greeting
```

Update the `index()` action of the `greeting` controller so that it looks like this:

```
def index(self):
    name = 'Pylons Developer'
    return render('/greeting.html', extra_vars={'name': name})
```

The `render()` function is imported at the top of the controller from your project's `lib/base.py` file. Within that file you'll find the import below so the render() function in your controller is really just an alias for Pylons' `render_mako()` function:

```
from pylons.templating import render_mako as render
```

You'll look at how to use other templating languages later in the chapter. Also notice that the template paths have to start with a slash (/). This requirement was introduced in Pylons 0.9.6.

If you start the server with the `paster serve --reload development.ini` command and visit `http://localhost:5000/greeting/index`, you should see the `Hello Pylons Developer!` greeting in your browser (see Figure 5-1).

Figure 5-1. *The output produced by the* `greeting.html` *template*

Using the Template Context c Global

Although passing the `name` argument directly as an extra argument to `render()` works perfectly well, it is usually considered a better practice to assign template variables to Pylons via the template context global c, which you learned about in Chapter 3. Here is the updated controller:

```
def index(self):
    c.name = 'Pylons Developer'
    return render('/greeting.html')
```

Before you can use the c global, it needs importing into your controller:

```
from pylons import tmpl_context as c
```

You might prefer to assign template variables to c rather than pass them in directly as arguments to `render()` for two reasons:

- There is less chance you will accidentally assign a variable that has the same name as either one of the Pylons globals or one of the global names set up by Mako.

- If a particular variable is useful in a template, there is a good chance it will be useful elsewhere in your application too. Since the c object is a Pylons global, you can also use objects assigned as attributes of c elsewhere in your application during a request.

Here's the updated `greeting.html` template:

```
<html>
<head>
    <title>Greetings</title>
</head>
<body>
    <h1>Greetings</h1>
    <p>Hello ${c.name}!</p>
</body>
</html>
```

Notice that this time the call to `render()` doesn't include the c global explicitly. Pylons automatically passes this and other globals to Mako anyway, so you don't need to do so yourself.

If you test this updated example, you will see the same output as before.

■**Caution** Be careful when setting c attributes that begin with an underscore (_) character. c and other global variables are really a StackedObjectProxy, which reserve the attribute names _current_obj, _push_object, and _pop_object for their internal methods.

You'll learn about how these objects actually work under the hood in Chapter 17.

The c global is reset on each request so that you don't need to worry about a controller still having old values set from a previous request.

One issue you learned about in Chapter 3 is that the c object doesn't raise an AttributeError when you attempt to access an attribute that doesn't exist and instead returns an empty string. This behavior is confusing for new Pylons developers (as well as more experienced ones), so it is recommended you disable it by specifying the strict_c option in config/environment.py. Add a new line after the Pylons configuration options:

```
# CONFIGURATION OPTIONS HERE (note: all config options will override
# any Pylons config options)
config['pylons.strict_c'] = True
```

The template context global c makes it easy to pass information around your application, but it is available only during a request. As a result, you should be very careful about creating libraries that explicitly rely on it; otherwise, your code might quickly become quite tangled.

As an example, imagine you had assigned the variables name and age to the c object and then created a function that performed some simple formatting. You might be tempted to write it like this:

```
from pylons import c

def format_age():
    return "Name: %s, Age: %s"%(c.name, c.age)
```

Although this works perfectly well, it is bad practice—your function can be used only when Pylons is processing an HTTP request because this is the only time the c global is available. It is much better to write your function like this:

```
def format_age(name, age):
    return "Name: %s, Age: %s"%(name, age)
```

and then to use it like format_age(c.name, c.age) so that the function itself does not rely on the presence of the c global. This will make it much more obvious how your code works and will make refactoring later much easier.

For the same reason, it is better to avoid using other Pylons globals such as request and response where possible. Being explicit is usually a good idea.

Basic Template Syntax

Now that you've seen how a very simple template works, it is time to look in more detail at the template syntax you'll frequently use when working with Mako templates.

If you'd like to follow along with any of the examples in this section, create a new template called basic.html, and then create a new action in the controller to render it, because you will return to the greeting.html example later in the chapter so shouldn't change that template now.

```
def basic(self):
    return render('/basic.html')
```

Let's get started. You've already seen basic expression substitution using the ${} construct. You can use any valid Python expression that would be suitable as a function argument within the brackets. Here is an example:

```
The value of 3 + 5 is: ${3 + 5}
A string representation of 3 to the power 4 is ${pow(3, 4)}
```

You can add comments to your templates by starting a line with the ## characters. A single # is used quite a lot in templates for CSS selectors and output for various programming languages, so it was decided ## should be used for comments rather than adopting the Python comment format of a single # character.

Make sure the ## characters are at the very start of the line with no whitespace. For example:

```
## This is a comment which will not be rendered
This will be rendered ## and so will this.
```

You can also use multiline comments using <%doc> tags. For example:

```
<%doc>
    This is a multiline comment which will not be rendered. This style of
    comment is particularly useful for documentation as well as situations where
    you want to comment out a large region of your template temporarily during
    testing.
</%doc>
```

Related to the <%doc> tag is the <%text> tag, which simply outputs verbatim whatever text is specified without treating it as Mako markup. This is very handy for documenting Mako. For example, the following:

```
<%text>
    This is some Mako syntax which will not be executed: ${variable}
    Neither will this <%doc>be treated as a comment</%doc>
</%text>
```

produces the unchanged output, as you would expect:

```
This is some Mako syntax which will not be executed: ${variable}
Neither will this <%doc>be treated as a comment</%doc>
```

You might need to view the HTML source code to see that this is indeed the output produced because some web browsers, including Internet Explorer, don't handle tags containing % characters such as the <%doc> and </%doc> tags in this example.

Mako also supports the full range of control structures supported by Python, including if, elif, else, while, and for. These structures are very useful in templates. For example, to control which information is displayed, you might use an if statement:

```
% if c.name == 'Pylons Developer':
    Welcome Pylons Developer
% else:
    Welcome guest
% endif
```

These statements work in the same way they would in Python, including the need for a colon (:) at the end of the line. The only difference is that because templates don't have to conform to the strict indentation rules that Python source code follows, you have to specify the point at which the control structure ends. In this case, you used an % endif line, but if you were using a while loop, for example, you would use % endwhile.

You can, of course, combine control structures too. For example, you might want to generate an HTML list from a data structure that looks like this:

```
c.links = [
    ('James','http://jimmyg.org'),
    ('Ben','http://groovie.org'),
    ('Philip',''),
]
```

The template might look like this:

```
<ul>
% for item in c.links:
    <li>\
% if item[1]:
    <a href="${item[1]}">${item[0]}</a>\
% else:
    ${item[0]}\
% endif
    </li>
% endfor
</ul>
```

This would generate a list that looked like this:

```
<ul>
    <li><a href="http://jimmyg.org">James</a></li>
    <li><a href="http://groovie.org">Ben</a></li>
    <li>Philip</li>
</ul>
```

Notice how the variable item specified in the for loop can still be used as an expression in the ${} construct even though it is generated in a loop and was not directly passed into the template as a namespace argument.

Also, if the bottom % endif statement was not in line with the % if statement, the template would have worked equally well. Mako doesn't require the same indentation that Python does, although it is usually good practice to properly structure your templates anyway.

The final thing to point out about this example is that it has made extensive use of the \ character, which, when placed at the end of a line, consumes the newline character that follows it to prevent Mako from adding a line break at the end of the line.

Sometimes it is useful to be able to directly write Python code in templates. This can be done with Python blocks, although as has already been described, Python code is really best kept to the controllers where possible to provide a clean interface between your controllers and view. You can use a Python block like this:

```
<%
    title = 'Pylons Developer'
    names = [x[0] for x in c.links]
%>
```

Any variables you declare in Python blocks are then available to be used in control statements or in ${} constructs. For example, this code:

```
% for i, value in enumerate(names):
${i+1}. ${value} <br />
% endfor
```

produces the following output:

```
1. James
2. Ben
3. Philip
```

Any code within Python blocks must be properly indented in the same way normal source code is. The block itself can have any level of indentation. For example, although this code looks messy, it is perfectly valid:

```
Your title is ${title}
    <%
        # This block can have any indentation as long as the Python
        #  code within it is properly indented
        if title == 'Pylons Developer':
            msg = 'You must program in Python!'
        else:
            msg = ''
     %>
An optional message: ${msg}
```

The code within these blocks is executed each time the template is rendered.

Because you can put Python expressions in a line containing a Mako control structure such as % if, you might be tempted to think you can write any expression after a % sign, for example, like this:

```
## The line below is NOT allowed:
% a = 3
```

Instead, any expressions should be written in blocks.

A variation of the <% %> block places the Python code within it at the top of the cached Python file Mako generates, making it very useful for import statements. Notice the ! character after the start of the first bracket in the following example:

```
<%!
    import datetime
%>
```

This is called a *module-level block*, and when used in the context of a multithreaded Pylons application, the code it contains is executed only the first time a template is executed. Module-level blocks, as the name suggests, are good places for putting module imports, in this case, to make the datetime module available throughout the template. Module-level blocks don't have access to the usual Mako environment and cannot be used for outputting content. We'll discuss module-level blocks again when you learn how Mako caches templates later in the chapter.

■**Tip** So far, all the templates have been designed to generate HTML, but of course you can use templates to generate any sort of text-based file, be it an e-mail, a rich-text document, a configuration file, or a file format specific to your application.

Default Pylons Template Variables

The template context global c is not the only object Pylons passes to Mako for you automatically via the render() function. In addition, the following are set up by default:

`tmpl_context` and its alias `c`: This is the template context object you have already seen. Although it is usually accessed as `c`, you can also access it within templates as `tmpl_context`.

`config`: This is the Pylons `config` global described in Chapter 3.

`app_globals` and its alias `g`: This is the project application globals object you learned about in Chapter 3, usually accessed as `g` but available as `app_globals` in templates.

`h`: This is the project `helpers` module. In this case, this is `templatedemo.lib.helpers`, which is the place you should put all your helper functions. Again, these are described in Chapter 3.

`request`: This is the Pylons request object for this request.

`response`: This is the Pylons response object for this request.

`session`: This is the Pylons session object (unless sessions are removed).

`translator`, `ungettext()`, `()`, and `N_()`: These are objects to help you with internationalization. You will learn about these in Chapter 11, so you don't need to worry about them now.

As an example, to add the current URL to the `greeting.html` template you have been using, you might use the `h` object and update the template like this:

```
<html>
<head>
    <title>Greetings</title>
</head>
<body>
    <h1>Greetings</h1>

    <p>Hello ${c.name}! You are visiting ${h.url_for()}</p>
</body>
</html>
```

You also need to import the `url_for()` function into the `templatedemo/lib/helpers.py` file with this import:

```
from routes import url_for
```

Later in the chapter when you look at custom `render()` functions, you will see how you can customize which variables are used by default. For more information about template variables, see `http://docs.pylonshq.com/views.html#default-template-variables`.

Mako Runtime Built-Ins

In addition to the Pylons default template variables that the Pylons `render()` global sets up for you, it is worth being aware that Mako sets up a number of runtime built-ins for you. I'll mention most of these in the course of this chapter, but for full information about each, you should consult the Mako documentation at `http://www.makotemplates.org/docs/documentation.html#runtime_builtins`.

Here's a quick summary so that you can make sure you don't accidentally use any of these as names of your own variables in templates:

context: This context is the central object that is created when a template is first executed and is responsible for handling all communication with the outside world. It includes the output buffer and a dictionary of the variables that can be freely referenced within a template; this includes the other Mako runtime built-ins, the Pylons default variables, and any extra variables passed by the extra_variables argument to render(). As such, the context object is very important. You can learn more about it at http://www.makotemplates.org/docs/documentation. html#runtime.

local, self, parent, and next: These are all namespaces and have particular meanings in the context of template inheritance chains. You'll look at these later in the chapter.

capture: This is a function that calls a given def and captures its resulting content into a string, which is returned. A *def* is Mako terminology for a reusable block of template code wrapped in a <%def> tag that behaves a bit like a function in Python. You'll learn about defs and the capture() function later in the chapter.

caller: This is a "mini" namespace created when using the <%call> tag to define a "def call with content." You don't deal with caller in this book, but it is well documented at http://www. makotemplates.org/docs/documentation.html#defs_defswithcontent if you are interested.

UNDEFINED: This is an instance of mako.runtime.Undefined that raises an exception when its __str__() method is called. It is used when you use a variable in a template without assigning it a value. If you see an UNDEFINED, it is likely that you mistyped a variable name or forgot to pass a particular variable to a template.

pageargs: This dictionary can be specified with the <%page> tag and tells templates the arguments that the body() def takes. You'll look at the body() def and its use in template inheritance chains later in the book, but for details of pageargs, consult the Mako documentation at http://www.makotemplates.org/docs/documentation.html#namespaces_body.

Three very useful methods of the context object are get(), keys(), and write(). Here's an example demonstrating how they are each used:

```
<html>
<body>
<%
    context.write('<p>Here is an example:</p>')
%>
<p>
% for key in context.keys():
The key is <tt>${key}</tt>, the value is ${str(context.get(key))}. <br />
% endfor
</p>
</body>
</html>
```

Create a new template called context.html, and add a new action to the controller to test it like this:

```
def context(self):
    return render('/context.html')
```

If you visit http://localhost:5000/greeting/context, a long list of output is produced, including all the variables that can be used in templates. The source starts like this:

```
<html>
<body>
<p>Here is an example:</p>
<p>
The key is <tt>all</tt>, the value is &lt;built-in function all&gt;. <br />
The key is <tt>help</tt>, the value is Type help() for interactive help, or ➥
help(object) for help about object.. <br />
The key is <tt>vars</tt>, the value is &lt;built-in function vars&gt;. <br />
The key is <tt>SyntaxError</tt>, the value is &lt;type ➥
'exceptions.SyntaxError'&gt;. <br />
The key is <tt>session</tt>, the value is {}. <br />
The key is <tt>unicode</tt>, the value is &lt;type 'unicode'&gt;. <br />
The key is <tt>sorted</tt>, the value is &lt;built-in function sorted&gt;. <br />
...
```

The two important things to realize are that writing output with `context.write()` has the same effect as using `${}` and that any variables that can be used in a template can be accessed with `context.get()`.

Separation of Logic and View

The greeting example you have been using so far is rather artificial because you could have just put your name directly into the template. Real web applications respond to data from various sources, so let's make our example slightly more realistic by retrieving the name of the visitor from the query string on each request. If no query string is present, you'll just use `Visitor` as the name.

```
def index(self):
    c.name = request.params.get('name', 'Visitor')
    return render('/greeting.html')
```

If you were now to visit `http://localhost:5000/greeting/index?name=Pylons+Developer`, you would see the same greeting as the first example.

This is a much more realistic example. Here the controller does some processing based on some logic and then passes relevant information to the template to display. In this setup, the template represents a *view* of the data in the Model View Controller architecture, and in line with this architecture, it is generally considered best practice to keep logic code in your controller and use Python only in your template to assist with rendering the information passed by the controller.

Some templating languages take the separation of logic code and view code to extremes and actively prohibit any sort of data processing in the template. Although this might be good practice, it can be sometimes be terribly frustrating when you want to do something simple if the templating language prevents you from doing it. Mako takes the view that the developer knows best and therefore provides some powerful templating tools and the ability to embed Python code in the template. It is then up to you as a developer to decide how much to use the tools Mako provides.

Here is the same example written slightly differently just to demonstrate that you can put simple logic in templates if you really need to do so. Here's the action:

```
def index(self):
    return render('/greeting.html')
```

and here's the new template:

```
<html>
<head>
    <title>Greetings</title>
</head>
```

```
<body>
    <h1>Greetings</h1>
    <p>Hello ${request.params.get('name', 'Visitor')}!</p>
</body>
</html>
```

Security Considerations and WebHelpers

One point to watch out for when you are using any data from the Web in a template is that a malicious user might put HTML characters in the data. If, for example, you visit the URL http://localhost:5000/greeting/index?name=Ja%3Cb%3Em%3C%2Fb%3Ees, the value of request.params ['name'] would be James, and if Mako didn't apply any special escaping, this value would be rendered, resulting in the m being made bold in the HTML rendered by the browser.

In itself this might not seem like a big problem, but actually it opens your web application up to so-called cross-site scripting (XSS) attacks. For example, a malicious user could insert JavaScript into your page to replace some of your own content to trick the user of the page into giving away information or visiting a site they didn't intend to because they thought the content on the page was generated by you.

This is a real risk for many websites today, so it is well worth being aware of. Pylons protects you from making this mistake by automatically escaping all values rendered by Mako. If you look at your project's config/environment.py again, you will see that the full configuration for Mako looks like this:

```
# Create the Mako TemplateLookup, with the default autoescaping
config['pylons.app_globals'].mako_lookup = TemplateLookup(
    directories=paths['templates'],
    module_directory=os.path.join(app_conf['cache_dir'], 'templates'),
    input_encoding='utf-8', output_encoding='utf-8',
    imports=['from webhelpers.html import escape'],
    default_filters=['escape'])
```

The last argument, default_filters, means that all output is filtered through the webhelpers.html.escape function, which automatically applies HTML escaping to make the content safe.

Of course, sometimes you want to pass data to Mako and have it treated as HTML. To do this, you have to wrap the content in a webhelpers.html.literal() object. A literal is a special type derived from Python's built-in unicode type. When the escape() function finds a literal, it doesn't escape it.

To demonstrate these features, update the greeting.html template so it looks like this:

```
<html>
<head>
    <title>Greetings</title>
</head>
<body>
    <h1>Greetings</h1>

    <p>${c.greeting} ${c.name}!</p>
</body>
</html>
```

Rather than using the `webhelpers.html.literal` object directly, most Pylons developers prefer to import it into their project's `lib/helpers.py` file so that it can be accessed as `h.literal` in controllers.

Update the `lib/helpers.py` file to include this import:

```
"""Helper functions

Consists of functions to typically be used within templates, but also
available to Controllers. This module is available to both as 'h'.
"""
# Import helpers as desired, or define your own, ie:
# from webhelpers.html.tags import checkbox, password

from webhelpers.html import literal
```

Now import the `helpers` module into your controller as `h` by adding this at the top of `controllers/greeting.py`:

```
import templatedemo.lib.helpers as h
```

Finally, change the `index()` action of the controller to look like this:

```
def index(self):
    c.greeting = h.literal('<b>Welcome</b>')
    c.name = request.params.get('name', 'Visitor')
    return render('/greeting.html')
```

Now visit `http://localhost:5000/greeting/index?name=Ja%3Cb%3Em%3C%2Fb%3Ees`, and you will see that the HTML wrapped in `literal()` is rendered as an HTML literal, whereas the data passed to Mako from the `request` object is correctly escaped and the < and > characters are rendered correctly.

Writing Your Own Helpers

As of WebHelpers 0.6, all the HTML helper functions automatically return `literal()` objects, described earlier, so that their return values are treated as HTML. If you have created your own helper functions for a previous version of Pylons and try to use them with a Pylons 0.9.7 application, you will probably be surprised to find that all the output is escaped. You can solve this problem by modifying the helper functions to return an HTML `literal` object instead of a Python `unicode` or `str` object.

When writing or upgrading helper functions to use HTML literals, you should be careful that you don't accidentally introduce security holes. For example, consider this function:

```
from webhelpers.html import literal

def emphasize(value):
    return literal('<em>'+value+'</em>')
```

Imagine you used this in your greeting action like this:

```
c.name = emphasize(request.params.get('name', 'Visitor'))
```

You have introduced a security hole because the `Ja<b>m</b>es` string is concatenated with the `<em>` and `</em>` strings in the `emphasize()` helper, and the whole string `<em>Ja<b>m</b>es</em>` is marked as a literal. The `<b>` and `</b>` tags now pass through the `escape()` function and through to the HTML document. This is not the behavior you want. Instead, the `emphasize()` function should be written like the following so the value itself isn't accidentally marked as an HTML literal:

```
def emphasize(value):
    return literal('<em>') + value + literal('</em>')
```

To avoid the problem, WebHelpers 0.6 introduced an `HTML` object that can be used for generating HTML fragments in a safe way. Here is the `emphasize` helper written using the `HTML` object:

```
def emphasize(value):
    return HTML.em(value)
```

You can also nest HTML objects; the following would also wrap the value in a `<span>` tag:

```
def emphasize(value):
    return HTML.span(HTML.em(value))
```

You can also add HTML attributes as keyword arguments to `HTML`. Where an attribute name is a reserved word in Python, you should add _ to the end of the argument. For example, here is a `<span>` tag with an `id` attribute of `first` and a `class` attribute of `highlight`:

```
def emphasize(value):
    return HTML.span(HTML.em(value), id='first', class_='highlight')
```

Calling `emphasize('Ja<b>m</b>es')` would return a `literal` object representing the Unicode string `u'<span id="id" class="highlight"><em>Ja&lt;m&gt;es</em></span>'` with the HTML characters from the argument correctly escaped.

See the WebHelpers documentation for more information at `http://docs.pylonshq.com/thirdparty/webhelpers/html/html.html`.

Applying Filters in Templates

The `escape()` function set up as a default filter in `config/environment.py` is applied to all Mako output, but you can also apply filers to specific Mako output by using Mako's | operator within a `${}` expression in a template.

The built-in escape functions are as follows:

u: This produces URL escaping, provided by `urllib.quote_plus(string.encode('utf-8'))`.

h: This produces HTML escaping, provided by `cgi.escape(string, True)`. Note that this is *not* the same as the `helpers` module object h, which is also available in templates. Mako knows when you are using h as a filter and when it is supposed to refer to your project's `helpers` module.

x: This produces XML escaping.

`trim`: This produces whitespace trimming, provided by `string.strip()`.

`entity`: This produces HTML entity references for applicable strings, derived from the `htmlentitydefs` module in the standard library.

`unicode`: This produces a Python Unicode string (this function is applied by default).

`decode.<some encoding>`: This decodes input into a Python Unicode string with the specified encoding.

n: This disables all default filtering; only filters specified in the local expression tag will be applied.

You can also use the `escape` function because Mako is configured by the following line to automatically import into all templates:

```
imports=['from webhelpers.html import escape'],
```

Here's an example of how filtering works:

```
${ c.test | trim,entity }
```

If c.test had the value u" It will cost £5 ", the spaces would be stripped by trim, the £ sign would be converted to the HTML entity £, and the output would simply be It will cost £5.

If you have an HTML string that is *not* wrapped in literal() but that *shouldn't* be escaped, you can disable the default escape filter with n. For example, if c.test contained the Unicode string u'Hello', you could have this passed through *unescaped* like this:

```
${ c.test | n}
```

Structuring Template Code

The ability to substitute variables, control program flow, and execute small snippets of Python are all very useful, but what gives templates their real value is the ability to define template blocks and call them from other templates to produce complex page layouts with as little duplication of effort as possible. In the following sections, you'll learn about some of the ways Mako allows you to do this.

Using <%def> Blocks

A *def* block is rather like a Python function in that each def block has a name, can accept arguments, and can be called. As an example, let's update the list-generating code you used earlier to be a reusable def block:

```
<%
    items = [
        ('James', 'http://jimmyg.org'),
        ('Ben', 'http://groovie.org'),
        ('Philip', ''),
    ]
%>

${navigation_links('James', items)}

<%def name="navigation_links(selected, links)">
    <%def name="link(label, url)">
        % if url:
            <a href="${url}">${label}</a>
        % else:
            ${label}
        % endif
    </%def>

    <ul>
    % for item in links:
        <li>\
    % if item[0] == selected:
        <b>${link(item[0], item[1])}</b>\
    % else:
        ${link(item[0], item[1])}\
```

```
    % endif
        </li>
    % endfor
    </ul>
</%def>
```

There's quite a lot going on in this example, so let's take it piece by piece. You can see you have two functions. The first is called `navigation_links()` and takes two arguments: `selected` is the label of the currently selected navigation link, and `links` is the list of links.

Within the `navigation_links()` function, there is another function called `link()` that generates an HTML link if a URL is associated with the navigation link.

Finally, there is a definition of the links defined in Python block at the top and some code to call the `navigation_links()` function at the bottom. Save this template code as `navigation.html`. You can then test it by adding a new action to the controller:

```
def navigation(self):
    return render('/navigation.html')
```

The template generates the following HTML source:

```
<ul>
    <li>        <b>
        <a href="http://jimmyg.org">James</a>
</b>        </li>
    <li>
        <a href="http://groovie.org">Ben</a>

        </li>
    <li>
        Philip
        </li>
</ul>
```

The extra whitespace is because you have concentrated on making your template look neat rather than concentrating on the HTML output. To remove all the whitespace, your HTML statements would have to begin at the start of the line because by default Mako does not strip out whitespace.

Notice that you have controlled some of the line endings, though. Leaving a trailing \ character at the end of the line tells Mako not to insert a line end character, so you can see there is no line end after the `</b>` tag even though there is some whitespace, which comes from the following line in the template before the `</li>` tag.

Defs in Mako behave very similarly to functions in Python and have access to their parent scope. This means you would be able to use the `selected` and `links` variables within the `link()` def.

You might also have noticed that the `navigation_links()` function was called before its definition. All top-level functions are loaded into memory before the main body of the template is rendered, so this is perfectly acceptable too.

The `link()` def is called from within `navigation_links()`. Just like in Python, the `link()` function would not be callable from outside `navigation_links()` because it is local to the `navigation_links()` scope.

The Mako Cache

It can sometimes be difficult to remember exactly what rules apply to defs, particularly when you get involved with more complex examples such as the inheritance chains you'll see later in the chapter. Luckily, there is an easy way to find out what is going on behind the scenes.

Mako works by compiling the templates you write into ordinary Python code the very first time it is executed or any time it is executed after it has been changed. Any subsequent times the template is rendered, the Python file is simply executed, and the output is returned.

Mako caches these templates according to the value of the cache_dir variable in your project's development.ini file. By default, this is set to the value %(here)s/data. The %(here)s value gets replaced with the location of the development.ini file, so Mako will cache the files in your project's data/templates directory by default.

Let's have a look at the cached template for the navigation.html template you've just created. Its cached counterpart is in TemplateDemo/data/templates/navigation.html.py. Let's look at each part of the file in turn starting with the top:

```
from mako import runtime, filters, cache
UNDEFINED = runtime.UNDEFINED
__M_dict_builtin = dict
__M_locals_builtin = locals
_magic_number = 4
_modified_time = 1219507190.1808441

_template_filename='/Users/james/TemplateDemo/templatedemo/templates/➥
navigation.html'
_template_uri='/navigation.html'
_template_cache=cache.Cache(__name__, _modified_time)
_source_encoding='utf-8'
from webhelpers.html import escape
_exports = ['navigation_links']
```

Here Mako defines various variables related to your template. You can see the import of the escape function that was specified as an argument to the TemplateLookup in your project's config/environment.py file. If you had defined any module-level blocks, their contents would also be placed in this part of the cache.

Next is the render_body() function that represents the main body of each template:

```
def render_body(context,**pageargs):
    context.caller_stack._push_frame()
    try:
        __M_locals = __M_dict_builtin(pageargs=pageargs)
        def navigation_links(selected,links):
            return render_navigation_links(context.locals_(__M_locals)➥
,selected,links)
        __M_writer = context.writer()
        # SOURCE LINE 1

        items = [
            ('James', 'http://jimmyg.org'),
            ('Ben', 'http://groovie.org'),
            ('Philip', ''),
        ]


        __M_locals.update(__M_dict_builtin([(__M_key, __M_locals_builtin()➥
[__M_key]) for __M_key in ['items'] if __M_key in __M_locals_builtin()]))
        # SOURCE LINE 7
        __M_writer(u'\n\n')
        # SOURCE LINE 9
        __M_writer(escape(navigation_links('James', items)))
        __M_writer(u'    \n\n')
```

```
        # SOURCE LINE 31
        __M_writer(u'\n\n\n\n')
        return ''
    finally:
        context.caller_stack._pop_frame()
```

In this case, you can see the items list being defined and the call to navigation_links() being made. This in turn calls the render_navigation_links() function, which is rather long, so I won't repeat it here.

Each part of the cached template is simply normal Python code even though some of the variables start with __M_ to avoid the risk of naming conflicts. You can also see the escape() function being used, so it is clear which variables are escaped and which aren't.

If you look carefully at the render_body() method, you'll notice context.caller_stack.push_frame() is called at the start of the rendering and context.caller_stack.pop_frame() is called at the end. These two calls help Mako keep track of where it is in the inheritance chains you will learn about later in the chapter.

Although you would never use the cached Mako templates directly, it is helpful to realize they are there. If you ever run into difficulties, looking at the cached version can sometimes shed light on a problem.

Capturing Output

Something to be aware of when calling defs is that their output is rendered straight to the context output buffer—it isn't actually returned.

If you look at the cached template example again, it should be clear why. Each line of source template is wrapped in an __M_writer() call, which has the effect of calling context.write(). If you want to actually capture the output of a def to a variable rather than to the output buffer, you have to use capture().

For example, consider this:

```
<%def name="add(num1, num2)">
${num1+num2}
</%def>

<%def name="display(num1, num2, result)">
The result of ${num1} + ${num2} is ${result}
</%def>

${display(1, 2, add(1,2))}
```

Running this example produces the following HTML source (although you won't see the line breaks in a web browser):

```
3

The result of 1 + 2 is None
```

What happens here is that the output of the add() def is written to the output buffer, not captured and passed to the display() def. The add() def actually returns None, which is the value returned by ordinary Python functions if no value is explicitly returned. Instead, you want to capture the output from the add() def. You can do this by modifying the line that calls it to look like this:

```
${display(1, 2, capture(add, 1, 2))}
```

The `capture` function is one of Mako's built-in template variables. It takes the def to capture as the first argument and the values to pass to the def as the subsequent arguments. The new output is as follows:

```
The result of 1 + 2 is 3
```

If you are interested, you can read more about Mako's output buffering in the Mako documentation.

Namespaces

In a real web application, it is likely that most of the pages will need navigation links, so it would be useful if you could import the `navigation_links()` function you have just created into other templates. You can do this using the `<%namespace>` tag.

Update the `greeting.html` template so that it imports and uses the `navigation_links()` function from the template you just created.

```
<%namespace name="nav" file="/navigation.html" />

<html>
<head>
    <title>Greetings</title>
</head>
<body>
    <h1>Greetings</h1>

    ${nav.navigation_links('Ben', links=[
        ( not )'James','http://jimmyg.org'),
        ('Ben','http://groovie.org'),
        ('Philip',''),
    ])}

    <p>${c.greeting} ${c.name}!</p>
</body>
</html>
```

The `<%namespace>` tag takes a `file` argument to specify the template you want to import and a `name` argument to specify the namespace under which the defs should be imported.

You can then use the `nav` namespace to generate navigation links in the greetings template.

Sometimes it is useful to have the components imported directly into the local namespace rather than a namespace of their own. This is possible too using this alternative syntax:

```
<%namespace file="navigation.html" import="navigation_links" />

${navigation_links('James', type='list', links=[
    ['James','http://jimmyg.org'],
    ['Ben','http://groovie.org'],
    ['Philip',''],
])}
```

When the `import` attribute is used, the `name` attribute is optional.

You can also just use `import="*"` to import everything from another template or `import="component1, component2"` to specify specific components you want to import. The names imported by the `import` attribute take precedence over any names that exist within the current context.

Namespaces can also import regular Python functions from modules as long as they accept an argument named `context` as their first argument. As an example, a module file `my/module.py` might contain the following callable:

```
def write_greeting(context):
    context.write("hello world")
```

A template can then use this module as follows:

```
<%namespace name="my" module="my.module" />

${my.write_greeting()}
```

Note that the `context` argument is not needed in the call. When Mako generates the cached Python version, it creates a locally scoped callable, which is responsible for passing the `context` object in for you.

The body() Def

There is one other important `<%def>` you will need to know about called the `body()` def. The `body()` def represents the whole of the body of the template, that is, any template code not wrapped in its own def. For example, if you had a template that looked like this, the `12:00pm` line would be in the `body()` def.

```
<%def name="test()">Hello World!</%def>

12:00pm
```

You can see this in action by using this template in another one. Imagine the previous template was saved as `greeting_and_time.html`. You could create another template like this to use its functionality under the namespace `other`:

```
<%namespace name="other" file="/greeting_and_time.html" />

The greeting is ${other.test()}
The time is ${other.body()}
```

Notice how the calling body method is effectively just like a normal `<%def>` but without the opening and closing `<%def>` tags needing to be specified. The output is as you would expect:

```
The greeting is Hello World!
The time is 12:00pm
```

Being able to access the body of a template is really useful when you are using template chains in an inheritance structure. Let's look at this in the next section.

Template Inheritance Chains

The real value of templating languages isn't so much that they help you mix and match Python and plain text in a more efficient manner but that so much of their functionality can be reused effectively in other pages. You've already seen how you can create reusable components using `<%def>` blocks and then import them into other templates using the `<%namespace>` tag, but Mako also provides facilities to enable you to structure your templates so that derived templates can inherit functionality from a base template.

Simple Inheritance

Using a template chain in Mako is best explained with an example. The following is a base template named base.html, which defines some HTML and a footer but also has two defs, self.title() and self.body(). Save this template as base.html in templatedemo/templates:

```
<html>
    <head>
        <title>${self.title()}</title>
    </head>
    <body>
        ${self.body()}
        <div class="footer">
            <p>This is a simple page footer</p>
        </div>
    </body>
</html>
```

Let's modify the greeting example to use this template. Let's ignore the namespace code you added earlier in the chapter for the minute and just concentrate on inheriting the base template. Here's how it looks:

```
<%inherit file="/base.html"/>\
<%def name="title()">Greetings</%def>
<h1>Greetings</h1>

<p>${c.greeting} ${c.name}!</p>
```

Save this new version of greeting.html. The index() action of the greeting controller should still look like this:

```
def index(self):
    c.greeting = h.literal('<b>Welcome</b>')
    c.name = request.params.get('name', 'Visitor')
    return render('/greeting.html')
```

If you visit http://localhost:5000/greeting/index in your browser again, you will see the following HTML rendered:

```
<html>
    <head>
        <title>Greetings</title>
    </head>
    <body>

<h1>Greetings</h1>

<p><b>Welcome</b> Visitor!</p>

        <div class="footer">
            <p>This is a simple page footer</p>
        </div>
    </body>
</html>
```

Let's think about what is going on to produce this HTML. Because greeting.html inherits from the base.html control for rendering passes directly to the base.html body() def. The <html> line is rendered first, followed by all the other characters until ${self.title()} is called.

In the context of rendering a normal template, self would refer to the template itself, but in the context of an inheritance chain like this one, self always refers to the template at the bottom of the inheritance chain, which is always the template that was originally specified in the call to render(), in this case, greeting.html. This means that although you are rendering the base.html body() def, ${self.title()} refers to the title() def in greeting.html. This renders the Greeting text, which appears in the page title.

Once the title is rendered, control passes back to the base.html template, and more HTML is rendered until ${self.body()} is reached. Once again, self refers to greeting.html, so the body() def of greeting.html is rendered. Finally, control passes back to base.html to render the footer, and the whole page is rendered.

As you can imagine, being able to structure your templates like this is really useful because it means you can now create multiple templates based on base.html without having to duplicate its content in each child template. By using defs in the way you used title(), you can create regions that can be replaced in child templates. These don't just have to contain static text; they can also contain navigation elements, CSS, JavaScript, section headings, or any other content you like. When you start the SimpleSite tutorial, you'll use inheritance chains to create a full-featured site.

■**Caution** If you are following the Mako documentation, you should be aware that Mako describes the template at the top of the chain (base.html in our example) as being the bottom-most template and the template at the bottom as being the top-most template, so you need to be aware of the slightly confusing terminology.

In the previous example, you used the self namespace to effectively mean "use the def from the template furthest down the inheritance chain." Mako also provides two related namespaces called next and parent, which are especially useful if you have more than two templates involved in an inheritance chain.

Next Namespace

Imagine the greeting template you've been using is actually part of the user administration section of a site. This site might also need some section links to allow the user to navigate around the section, but if these links were put in the base.html template, they would appear on all pages in the site, not just in the user administration section. You could put the links in the greeting.html template, but then you would also have to duplicate them in other templates in the same section. You could do this by keeping the links in a namespace and simply calling the def in each template rather than duplicating the code each time, but Mako provides a better solution.

It turns out that you aren't limited to two templates in an inheritance chain; you can have as many templates as you like. Rather than inheriting the greeting.html template from the base.html template, let's create a new template specifically for the user administration section; call it section. html, and save this file in the templatedemo/templates directory with the following content (there is a deliberate mistake in this template, though, so you might want to read on first):

```
<%inherit file="/base.html"/>
<%namespace file="/navigation.html" import="navigation_links" />
```

```
${navigation_links('Admin Home', links=[
    ('Admin Home', '/admin'),
    ('Settings', '/admin/settings'),
    ('Sign Out', '/admin/signout'),
])}
```

```
${self.body()}
```

```
<%def name="title()">User Administration</%def>
```

Notice that this template inherits from base.html and that you are still using the navigation.html template you created earlier to do the hard work of creating the links.

For the greeting.html template to use this template, you need to change its <%inherit> tag to look like this:

```
<%inherit file="/section.html"/>\
```

If you refresh the browser, you will see that the content hasn't changed! This might surprise you, so let's think about what's happened. You call render() to render greeting.html, and control is passed to the section.html body() def, but this template is inherited from base.html, so control passes to the base.html body() def. Once again, HTML is rendered until ${self.title()} is reached. Remember that self refers to the *last* template in the chain, in this case, greeting.html, so it is the greeting.html title() def and body() def that are rendered, not the ones in section.html.

To solve this problem, you need to use Mako's next namespace. next is similar to self but refers to the next template in the chain, not the last one. To use next, you'll need to change all the references to ${self.title()} and ${self.body()} in base.html and section.html to use ${next.title()} and ${next.body()}, respectively.

Once you've updated the templates, they behave as you expect. When ${next.title()} is reached, the title() def from section.html is rendered. Control is passed back to base.html until ${next.body()} is reached; then the body() def of section.html is rendered, producing the navigation links. When ${next body()} is reached in section.html, the body() def from greeting is rendered. When it is finished, control passes back to section.html and then back to base.html to finish off the rendering.

Figure 5-2 shows the result.

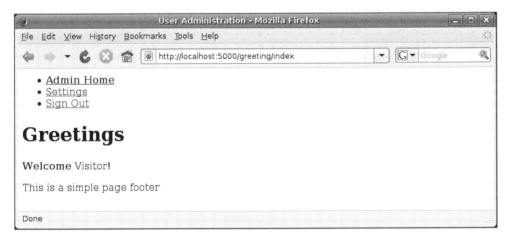

Figure 5-2. *Greeting produced with a template inheritance chain*

If the `section.html` template didn't have a `title()` def, the call to `${next.title()}` in `base.html` would have rendered the `title()` def in `greeting.html` instead.

Middle templates such as `section.html` are normally used for sections of the site in this way with base templates such as `base.html` containing content that applies to every page and child templates such as `greeting.html` containing only page-specific information. Of course, if you have a large site, it might make sense to have more than one middle template so that you can implement subsections or different page layouts within a section. The inheritance technique is very flexible.

Parent Namespace

In the same way that the `next` namespace allows you to refer to a def in the namespace of the child template immediately below it, Mako also provides a `parent` namespace that allows a child template to refer to a def in the parent template immediately above it. This is useful if you want a child template to be able to control where in a parent template its content is inserted.

■**Note** Using the `parent` namespace might remind you of using `super` in a derived class to access a method in a base class in a normal Python inheritance structure. The two are similar, but in Python there is no equivalent to the `next` namespace; that is, you cannot access a child method from a parent class.

Let's change the way the `title()` def works so that `greeting.html` can decide whether to include the content from the `section.html` body() def. The first thing you need to do is change `base.html` so that it calls `${self.title()}` rather than `${next.title()}`. This means that when the title is rendered, control for rendering the def will pass to `greeting.html`, bypassing `section.html`.

```
<html>
    <head>
        <title>${self.title()}</title>
        ...
```

If you tested the example, you will see that the page title now displays `Greetings` again. Now let's change `greeting.html` so that the title also includes the section title. You'd like the title to read "User Administration > Greetings." Update the `title()` def in `greeting.html` to look like this:

```
<%def name="title()">${parent.title()} &gt; Greetings</%def>
```

Now when control for rendering the `title()` def passes from `base.html` to `greeting.html`, the `greeting.html` `title()` def calls its parent template `title()` def where the `User Administration` string is rendered as expected.

Using the `parent` namespace in this way is particularly useful when working with sections containing JavaScript or CSS, because you'll often find that it is useful to be able to control whether the JavaScript and CSS for the child template is rendered before or after that of the parent.

In summary, the rule of thumb is that if the base template should have control of where the child content should be placed, use `next`. If the child template needs control of where its own content is placed, use `parent`.

Behind the Scenes

Now that you have a good idea of how to use Mako templates within Pylons, you can turn your attention to how Pylons links the `render()` function you call to the template engine code as well as how it adds default variables. Once you understand the basic principles, you'll look at how to use the alternative template languages Pylons supports, as well as how to add support for your own template languages.

If you intend to use only Mako in your Pylons applications and are not interested in understanding what is going on behind the scenes, you might prefer to jump ahead to the next chapter to begin learning about forms.

Let's start by looking at the definition of the `pylons.templating.render_mako()` function that you imported as `render()` in the greeting controller. It looks something like this:

```
def render_mako(template_name, extra_vars=None, cache_key=None,
                cache_type=None, cache_expire=None):
    def render_template():
        globs = extra_vars or {}
        globs.update(pylons_globals())
        template = globs['app_globals'].mako_lookup.get_template(template_name)
        return template.render(**globs)

    return cached_template(template_name, render_template, cache_key=cache_key,
                           cache_type=cache_type, cache_expire=cache_expire)
```

The first thing you should notice is that the function supports caching with a call to `cached_template()`. You'll look at the caching options in a minute, but let's start by looking at what happens in the `render_template()` function.

First, a dictionary is set up called `globs`, which contains any values you specified in the `extra_vars` keyword. This dictionary is then updated with all the Pylons globals that I described earlier in the "Default Pylons Template Variables" section. These are returned automatically by the `pylons_globals()` function.

One of the globals returned is the `app_globals` object, which you'll remember from Chapter 3, is an instance of your project's `templatedemo.lib.app_globals.Globals` class. This class has an attribute called `mako_lookup`, but if you look at your project's `templatedemo/lib/app_globals.py` file, you'll see that `mako_lookup` isn't defined there. It is actually added dynamically when the application is first loaded by the configuration code in `config/environment.py`. Here are the relevant lines. You'll recall that you looked at the options to `TemplateLookup` earlier in the chapter:

```
def load_environment(global_conf, app_conf):
    ...
    config['pylons.app_globals'] = app_globals.Globals()
    ...
    config['pylons.app_globals'].mako_lookup = TemplateLookup(...)
    ...
```

Once the template has been returned, the final act of the `render_template()` function is to return the rendered template, passing in the variables you have specified as keyword arguments.

As you can see, although it takes a careful look through the code, the templating setup is actually easy to understand. This is typical of the way most of Pylons works. With a little digging through the source code, you can usually work out what is going on and customize the behavior you want in your own Pylons application.

Tip Don't be afraid to look at the Pylons source code. It is available online at `http://pylonshq.com/hg`.

Caching

Sometimes it is useful to be able to cache template calls to speed up performance. As you've seen, the render_mako() function has a number of options to support this, each of which defaults to None if it is not specified:

cache_key: This is the key to cache this copy of the template under.

cache_type: This is the cache type. Valid options are dbm, file, memory, database, or memcached.

cache_expire: This is the time in seconds to cache this template with this cache_key. Or use never to designate that the cache should never expire.

These options are then used, along with the template name, to cache the result of the call to the render_template() function I've just described. The caching functionality comes from the Beaker package and is described in detail at http://docs.pylonshq.com/caching.html. Pylons also supports sophisticated caching options to cache other types of data and supports other types of caching, but these are beyond the scope of the book; have a look at the previously mentioned link for the full information.

To test the caching, let's modify the base.html template to add the current date and time to the footer of every page. Change the template to look like this:

```
<%!
    import datetime
%>
<html>
    <head>
        <title>${self.title()}</title>
    </head>
    <body>
        ${next.body()}
        <div class="footer">
            <p>Page generated at ${str(datetime.datetime.now())}</p>
        </div>
    </body>
</html>
```

When you visit http://localhost:5000/greeting/index this time, the footer will show the exact time the page was generated. For example:

```
Page generated at 2008-08-24 15:40:10.568216
```

Now modify the controller to add some caching:

```
def index(self):
    c.greeting = h.literal('<b>Welcome</b>')
    c.name = request.params.get('name', 'Visitor')
    return render('/greeting.html', cache_expire=5)
```

Now the first time you visit the page, the current time will be displayed, but every subsequent visit will result in the page being returned from the cache until five seconds have passed. After five seconds, a new page will be rendered with a new date and time, but once again, this new page will be returned from the cache only after five seconds have passed.

If no cache_type is specified, the default used is dbm, which stores the cached pages in a simple database within your cache directory. Have a look at data/cache, and you will see the data folders present where the cache has been stored on disk. If you don't specify a cache_key, the key default is used. Specifying never as the cache_expire argument will mean the cache won't expire. Obviously, though, if you are using the memory cache type, restarting the server will cause the cache to be emptied.

Alternative Template Languages

As well as supporting Mako, Pylons supports these template languages out of the box:

Jinja 1 (http://jinja.pocoo.org/): This describes itself as a state-of-the-art, general-purpose template engine. It was originally inspired by Django's template syntax.

Genshi (http://genshi.edgewall.org/): This is an XML templating language designed to make generating valid XHTML and XML straightforward. Genshi is very popular with Pylons programmers and is used as the default templating language in TurboGears.

All three template engines are very different, but they each have one thing in common: they are all written as improvements to existing template engines. Genshi is the formal successor of Kid, Mako replaced Myghty, and Jinja was inspired by Django templates. This means all three are well-thought-out and production-ready template systems. They all use Unicode internally and have an API that is easy to use with Pylons.

Deciding between them is really a matter of preference. If you are primarily writing an application that outputs XML or XHTML, then you might find Genshi useful because it guarantees that your output is well formed. On the other hand, Mako and Jinja are much faster than Genshi and allow much more flexibility in the output they produce. Genshi requires a completely different syntax for text-based output, but if you are writing a predominantly XHTML-based application, this may not be a problem. All three handle the escaping of data correctly with Pylons thanks to the use of the HTML literals I described earlier.

If you are fairly new to templating languages and are trying to pick a templating language to use with Pylons, Mako is a good choice, and that is why it was chosen to be the default templating language for Pylons. Of course, Pylons doesn't restrict you to using a single templating language. If you think it would be helpful in your application, you can use multiple templating languages at the same time. You'll see how to do this later in the chapter.

To use an alternative template language, you will need to first install it:

```
$ easy_install Genshi
$ easy_install Jinja
```

If you want to use one of the alternative templating languages in your project but don't need Mako support, the easiest thing to do is to specify the templating language you want when you run the `paster create` command. For example, to get a Genshi project, you might do this, specifying `genshi` when prompted:

```
$ paster create --template=pylons GenshiTemplateDemo
Selected and implied templates:
  Pylons#pylons  Pylons application template

Variables:
  egg:      GenshiTemplateDemo
  package:  genshitemplatedemo
  project:  GenshiTemplateDemo
Enter template_engine (mako/genshi/jinja/etc: Template language) ['mako']: genshi
...
```

This will set up `config/environment.py` with the following lines:

```
# Create the Genshi TemplateLoader
config['pylons.app_globals'].genshi_loader = TemplateLoader(
    paths['templates'], auto_reload=True)
```

Then in your `lib/base.py` file, rather than importing the `render_mako()` function, you would import `render_genshi()` like this:

```
from pylons.templating import render_genshi as render
```

Genshi doesn't generate output directly; instead, it generates a stream of nodes. Genshi streams can be serialized using one of four methods: `xml`, `xhtml`, `html`, or `text`. The `render_genshi()` function takes an extra argument named `method` that you can use to specify the output method. It defaults to `xhtml`, but you can choose a different value if you want a different type of output.

You can follow a similar process to set up a project to work exclusively with Jinja, specifying `jinja` when prompted by `paster create` and using the `render_jinja()` function in your controllers.

Multiple Template Languages

As was mentioned a moment ago, nothing is stopping you from using more than one templating language in your Pylons application. This requires a little more work because you must add the template lookup code to `config/environment.py` yourself. This isn't difficult, though.

Let's modify the `TemplateDemo` example you've been using to add Jinja support too. First install Jinja:

```
$ easy_install "Jinja==1.2"
```

Now open `config/environment.py`, and change the end of the `load_environment()` function to look like this:

```
# CONFIGURATION OPTIONS HERE (note: all config options will override
# any Pylons config options)

# Import the jinja components we need
from jinja import ChoiceLoader, Environment, FileSystemLoader

# Create the Jinja Environment
config['pylons.app_globals'].jinja_env = Environment(loader=ChoiceLoader(
        [FileSystemLoader(path) for path in paths['templates']]))

# Jinja's unable to request c's attributes without strict_c
config['pylons.strict_c'] = True
```

Jinja will look in the same location as Mako for its files. If you wanted to keep the templates for each in different directories, you could specify different paths for each.

Let's create a simple Jinja template:

```
<!DOCTYPE HTML PUBLIC "-//W3C//DTD HTML 4.01//EN">
<html lang="en">
<head>
    <title>Jinja Greeting</title>
</head>
<body>
    <h1>Jinja Greeting</h1>
    {{ c.greeting }}
</body>
</html>
```

Save this in the `templates` directory as `jinja.html`. Now you need a new action in the greeting controller:

```
def jinja(self):
    c.greeting = 'Hi from Jinja!'
    return render_jinja('/jinja.html')
```

You'll need to import the Jinja render function:

```
from pylons.templating import render_jinja
```

If you test the example, you'll see the `Hi from Jinja!` greeting.

Working with Your Own Templating Language

One of the great benefits of choosing a web framework based on Python is the sheer breadth of software available for you to use, including a large number of templating languages. If you've come from a background of Cheetah, Tal, Stan, Myghty, Kid, Breve, or any of the other templating languages available, you can easily integrate them into your Pylons application. The integration requires two steps:

1. Create a template lookup object attached to the `app_globals` object in `config/environment.py`.

2. Create a render function, using the `pylons_globals()` and `cached_template()` functions if necessary, and use the template lookup attached to `app_globals` to render the template.

Use the `render_mako()` function and `config/environment.py` listings from earlier in this chapter as a basis for your own code. If you need a further example, the Pylons documentation includes an example of how to integrate Kid via a custom `render()` function. You can read it at `http://docs.pylonshq.com/views.html#custom-render-functions`.

Note Previous versions of Pylons implemented template plug-in support via the TurboGears Buffet API. This API is deprecated in Pylons 0.9.7, although you can still use the API for legacy purposes if you need. See `http://docs.pylonshq.com/modules/templating.html#legacy-buffet-templating-plugin-and-render-functions` for more information.

Summary

This chapter was a fairly in-depth guide to the main aspects of templating in Pylons. You learned how to pass variables to templates via the template context variable `c`, how to avoid security problems through automatic escaping, and how to use HTML literals. You also learned the main features of Mako, from its template syntax to its inheritance chains, and you saw how to use its `next` and `parent` namespaces. You also learned all about what goes on behind the scenes to make templating in Pylons work from the Mako cache to the `render()` function setup.

There has clearly been a lot to take in. Don't worry if you didn't understand every detail on the first read. You'll be using Mako templates throughout the book, particularly in the SimpleSite tutorial chapters, so you'll get plenty of practice working with them to build real applications.

Next up you will learn how to create forms with Pylons, how to validate their content, and how to present error messages to the user if they enter invalid data.

■ ■ ■

Working with Forms and Validators

Form handling is one of those areas that at first glance appears very simple but in real applications can quickly become rather complicated. There are generally two approaches to dealing with forms. The first is to code all your forms, validation, and logic manually to give you complete control over how your forms work. The alternative approach is to use a form framework where ready-made classes exist for each of the field types you might want to use. The form framework then automates the generation of HTML, the validation of data, and the display of error messages for you.

At first glance, it might appear that a form framework would save you a lot of time, but in reality, form frameworks are rarely flexible enough to deal with all the situations you might want to develop, and in the long run you can sometimes find yourself spending more time creating custom fields for your form framework than it would have taken if you had coded all your forms manually.

Because of this, Pylons encourages you to do a lot of the work of generating forms yourself, but it does provide four sets of tools to make form handling as painless as possible:

- Form helpers to generate the HTML for common field types

- Validators to validate form data and convert between HTML and Python representations of particular data types

- HTML Fill to take an HTML form and automatically populate it with values and error messages for redisplaying the form data

- The `@validate` decorator to automate the process of validating a form and redisplaying it if it contains invalid data

These four tools can help make handling forms much simpler without in any way constraining your creativity as a developer. Pylons does support an alternative approach with a tool, called ToscaWidgets, although it won't be covered in this chapter. ToscaWidgets is a full form framework developed from the original widgets code in TurboGears that automates every aspect of form handling. ToscaWidgets is still officially in prerelease, but if you are interested in its approach, you should visit `http://toscawidgets.org` to find out more. The majority of developers prefer the flexibility of the approach you'll use in this chapter.

The Basics

When a user submits a form on a web site, the data is submitted to the URL specified in the `action` attribute of the `<form>` tag. The data can be submitted either via HTTP GET or POST as specified by the `method` attribute of the `<form>` tag. If your form doesn't specify an `action`, then it's submitted to the current URL, but generally you'll want to specify an `action` attribute.

This is a simple form coded in HTML and without any Pylons-specific features:

```
<form name="test" method="get" action="/formtest/submit">
Email Address: <input type="text" name="email" />
              <input type="submit" name="submit" value="Submit" />
</form>
```

If your form contains a file upload field such as `<input type="file" name="myfile" />`, you will also need to specify an `enctype="multipart/form-data"` attribute, and you have to choose the `post` method.

Many people put the value of the `method` attribute in uppercase. If your HTML page uses XHTML, the `method` attribute value is supposed to be lowercase, which is why in this example it is specified as `method="get"`, not `method="GET"`, as many examples will show.

Later in the chapter, you'll see how you can improve this example by using the `h.url_for()` helper in the form action and by using Pylons' field helpers to generate most of the HTML for the form automatically. First, though, let's create a new Pylons project to test this example as it stands:

```
$ paster create --template=pylons FormDemo
```

Accept the default options by pressing Enter to choose Mako as the template engine and no SQLAlchemy or Google App Engine support.

Once the project has been created, let's create a simple template in `FormDemo/formdemo/templates/base.html` to use as a basis for the examples in this chapter:

```
<html>
<head>
<title>FormDemo</title>
</head>
<body>
${next.body()}
</body>
</html>
```

Create a new template called `simpleform.html` with the following content to test the example form:

```
<%inherit file="/base.html" />
<h1>Enter Your Email Address</h1>

<form name="test" method="get" action="/formtest/submit">
Email Address: <input type="text" name="email" />
              <input type="submit" name="submit" value="Submit" />
</form>
```

You'll remember from the previous chapter that the `<%inherit>` tag allows the body of a template to be inserted into a parent template.

Now create a new controller called `formtest`:

```
$ cd FormDemo
$ paster controller formtest
```

Add two actions to the controller that look like this:

```
def form(self):
    return render('/simpleform.html')

def submit(self):
    return 'Your email is: %s' % request.params['email']
```

Start the server:

```
$ paster serve --reload development.ini
```

Visit `http://localhost:5000/formtest/form`, and you will see the form. In this case, the generated HTML looks like this:

```
<html>
<head>
<title>FormDemo</title>
</head>
<body>

<h1>Enter Your Email Address</h1>

<form name="test" method="get" action="/formtest/submit">
Email Address: <input type="text" name="email" />
               <input type="submit" name="submit" value="Submit" />
</form>

</body>
</html>
```

Try entering the e-mail address `test@example.com` and clicking Submit. The URL should change to `http://localhost:5000/formtest/submit?email=test%40example.com&submit=Submit`, and you should see the text `Your email is: test@example.com`.

Pylons has parsed and decoded the query string and set up the `request.params` object you saw in Chapter 3. As you'll recall, this object behaves a bit like a dictionary where the keys are the names of the fields in the form, and their corresponding values are Unicode strings, with all the characters in the query string properly decoded ready for you to use. If you have two fields with the same name in the form, then using the dictionary interface will return the first string. You can get all the strings returned as a list by using the `.getall()` method. If you expect only one value and want to enforce this, you should use `.getone()`, which raises an error if more than one value with the same name is submitted. By default, if a field is submitted without a value, the dictionary interface returns an empty string. This means that using `.get(key, default)` on `request.params` will return a default only if the value was not present in the form.

POST vs. GET

Forms can be submitted using either GET or POST HTTP methods depending on the value you set for the `method` attribute of the `<form>` tag. The GET method results in the form data being sent to the server via the URL query string, and the POST method sends the data as part of the HTTP body. Figure 6-1 and Figure 6-2 show the LiveHTTPHeaders information for both types of requests.

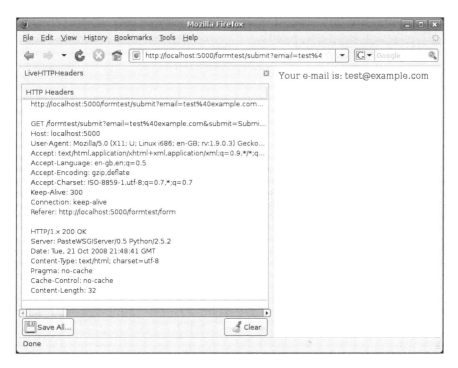

Figure 6-1. *A GET request in LiveHTTPHeaders*

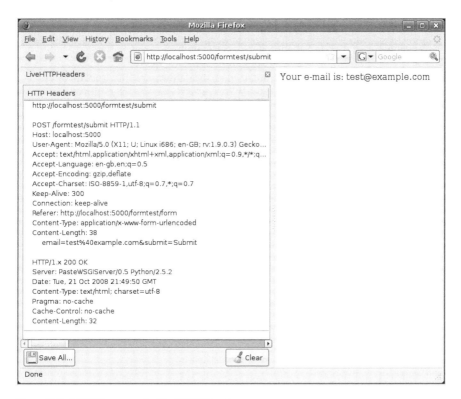

Figure 6-2. *A POST request in LiveHTTPHeaders*

As you can see, the request method (in the first line of both figures) is different in each. You'll also see that the POST request has the e-mail address sent as extra content in the body rather than as part of the URL. It is possible to send very large amounts of data in the request body, but most browsers and servers can cope only with URLs that are less than 1,024 characters in length. This is why if you are using a file upload field, you should use the POST method, because the data is then sent in the body of the request.

You can test the POST method by editing the `simpleform.html` template so that the method is changed to `post`. If you rerun the example, you will see the same message is displayed as before, but the URL displayed in the browser after you submit the form is simply `http://localhost:5000/formtest/submit` without the query string. If you are writing forms that contain password fields, you should usually use POST to prevent the password from being visible to anyone who might be looking at the user's screen. If you are ever in any doubt as to which method to use in a particular circumstance, it is normally safer to use POST.

Regardless of whether the form data is submitted as a GET or a POST request, Pylons still makes the values available in your controllers using the same interface through `request.params`.

You might be wondering how Pylons copes if you submit a form with a POST method to a URL containing a query string. The answer is that both sets of values get merged into the `request.params` object. Occasionally you might want to access the query string data separately from the POST data, so Pylons also provides two other `MultiDict` objects that behave in the same way as `request.params` to allow you to do just that. They are accessed as `request.GET` and `request.POST`, respectively.

The Resubmitted Data Problem

When writing form-based applications, you will occasionally find that users will press Refresh immediately after submitting a form. This has the effect of repeating whatever actions were performed the first time the form was submitted, but this might not always be the behavior your users expect.

If your form was submitted with a POST, most browsers will display a message to the user asking them whether they want to resubmit the data (see Figure 6-3). This will not happen with a GET, so POST is preferable to GET in those circumstances.

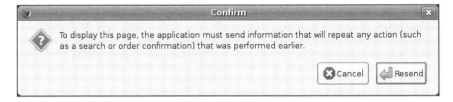

Figure 6-3. *The dialog box displayed by Firefox when you click Refresh on a page where POST data has been submitted*

Of course, the best way to solve this issue is to structure your code in such a way that if the user refreshes the page, the data isn't resubmitted. Here's one way of achieving this with an HTTP redirect:

```
# in the controller

def form(self):
    return render('/simpleform.html')
```

```
def submit(self):
    # Code to perform some action based on the form data
    # ...
    h.redirect_to(controller='formtest', action='result')

def result(self):
    return 'Your data was successfully submitted.'
```

This code requires the use of the `redirect_to()` helper. Add the following import to the project's `lib/helpers.py` file:

```
from pylons.controllers.util import redirect_to
```

Then in the controller, import the `helpers` module by adding this line at the top:

```
import formdemo.lib.helpers as h
```

Now you can test the controller. In this case, once the form is submitted, the data is saved, and an HTTP redirect occurs so that the browser redirects to `http://localhost:5000/hello/result`. If the user then refreshes the page, it simply redisplays the message rather than reperforming the action.

One issue with this approach is that if you want to display some of the submitted data, you will need to load it again in the `result()` action because the request that calls that action doesn't contain any of the submitted data. In Chapter 8, I'll cover how these sorts of messages can be displayed by storing information in a session store.

Building Forms with Helpers

Forms can also be created with Pylons' built-in helpers. You've already seen the helpers in Chapter 3 and learned about how they escape data to avoid security problems in Chapter 5; in this section, you'll learn how to use the HTML helpers to create forms.

■**Note** The WebHelpers package from which the Pylons helpers are imported changed significantly in version 0.6. All the old helpers from Rails were deprecated in favor of the new-style literal approach documented in Chapter 5. All the JavaScript integration with Prototype and Script.aculo.us was also removed because the majority of developers preferred to use their own JavaScript framework. You'll learn more about Pylons integration with JavaScript frameworks in Chapter 15.

Let's update the form you've been working on to use some of the HTML form helpers. Change the `simpleform.html` file to look like this:

```
<%inherit file="/base.html" />
<h1>Enter Your E-mail Address</h1>

${h.form(h.url_for(controller='formtest', action='submit'), method='get')}
Email Address: ${h.text('email')}
               ${h.submit('submit', 'Submit')}
${h.end_form()}
```

You can see that you are using the form(), url_for(), text(), and submit() helpers. The url_for() helper actually comes from Routes, but the other helpers come from the webhelpers.html.tags module. You'll need to add all these helpers to your sample project's lib/helpers.py file too in order for this example to work:

```
from routes import url_for
from webhelpers.html.tags import *
```

The built-in form helpers simply generate fragments of HTML to help you build forms. There are no built-in checks to ensure that you have closed an open form tag, so it is up to you to ensure that you produce valid HTML. Of course, this is actually very useful because it gives you a lot of flexibility. For example, you are free to mix and match HTML and helpers in whichever way you see fit, or you could even define the start of a form in one template and the end of a form in another without the helpers getting in your way. The helpers do correctly escape any string or Unicode values you pass them, but they don't modify any values that have already been escaped with `literal()`.

It is worth becoming familiar with the form helpers available because using them can save a lot of time (particularly with more complex fields such as selects), and they will also ensure all your data is properly escaped. The HTML helpers are well documented at `http://docs.pylonshq.com/thirdparty/webhelpers/html/html.html#webhelpers-html-tags`, so you can always refer to the documentation for the details of how a particular helper works.

Let's take a look at the definition of the `text()` helper as an example:

```
text(name, value=None, **attrs)
```

This creates a standard text field. `value` is a string, the content of the text field. The following are the options:

> `disabled`: If set to `True`, the user will not be able to use this input.

> `size`: This is the number of visible characters that will fit in the input.

> `maxlength`: This is the maximum number of characters that the browser will allow the user to enter.

The remaining keyword options are standard HTML options for the tag.

All form helpers start with a `name` argument, which should be a string representing the name of the field, and they also have an `**attrs` argument. In Python, `**` is a notation that means that any extra keyword arguments passed to the function should be put in a dictionary called `attrs` where the keys are the parameter names and the values are their corresponding values.

Any extra parameters you pass to any of these helpers are treated as extra attributes to be added to the HTML tag generated. Here's an example where you specify an attribute that isn't part of the HTML specification to an `<input>` field. Again, the helpers won't flag this as an error; it is up to you to decide what is right for your application and be responsible for the attributes you set.

```
>>> h.text('test', 'Welcome', myattribute='myvalue')
'<input type="text" value="Welcome" myattribute="myvalue" />'
```

One common use for this functionality is to specify the CSS class the field should have. The problem is that `class` is a reserved word in Python, so to specify the `class` attribute, you need to pass in the parameter `class_` with a trailing `_` character.

```
>>> h.text('test', 'Welcome', class_='wide')
'<input type="text" value="Welcome" class="wide" />'
```

The `text()` helper has a special behavior for the attributes `disabled`, `size`, and `maxlength`. All the single value field helpers behave in a similar way. They are `checkbox()`, `file()`, `hidden()`, `image()`, `password()`, `radio()`, `submit()`, and `textarea()`.

There is also a `select()` helper, and it behaves slightly differently. If you look at the documentation for `select()`, you'll see it is defined like this:

```
select(name, selected_values, options, **attrs)
```

Instead of taking a value, it has a selected_values argument and an options argument:

selected_values: A string or list of strings or integers giving the value(s) that should be prese-lected.

options: An iterable of (value, label) pairs. The value is what is returned to the application if this option is chosen; the label is what is shown in the form. You can also pass an iterable of strings, in which case the labels will be identical to the values.

If you are used to the select() helper from an earlier version of WebHelpers, you might expect to be able to use options_for_select(). This has been deprecated and is not available in Pylons 0.9.7. Instead, you just pass in the list of tuples directly via options. You'll also notice that the order of items in the tuple is reversed. options_for_select() expects arguments in the form (label, value), but this isn't how most Python objects are generated.

The following shows select() in action:

```
>>> select("currency", "$", [["$", "Dollar"], ["DKK", "Kroner"]])
literal(u'<select name="currency">\n<option selected="selected" value="$">➥
Dollar</option>\n➥
<option value="DKK">Kroner</option>\n</select>')
>>> select("cc", "MasterCard", [ "VISA", "MasterCard" ], id="cc", class_="blue")
literal(u'<select class="blue" id="cc" name="cc">\n➥
<option value="VISA">VISA</option>\n<option selected="selected"➥
value="MasterCard">MasterCard</option>\n</select>')
>>> select("cc", ["VISA", "Discover"], [ "VISA", "MasterCard", "Discover" ])
literal(u'<select name="cc">\n➥
<option selected="selected" value="VISA">VISA</option>\n➥
<option value="MasterCard">MasterCard</option>\n➥
<option selected="selected" value="Discover">Discover</option>\n</select>')
```

Uploading Files

File upload fields are created by using the file input field type. The file() helper provides a short-cut for creating these form fields:

```
${h.file('myfile')}
```

To use the file field, you need to import it into the project's lib/helpers.py file:

```
from webhelpers.html.tags import file
```

The HTML form must have its enctype attribute set to multipart/form-data to enable the browser to upload the file. The form helper's multipart keyword argument provides a shortcut for setting the appropriate enctype value. You don't need to explicitly mark the form to use a POST because the helper automatically sets the method attribute to post when you specify the enctype for a file upload.

Let's add a new controller to the form named upload:

```
$ paster controller upload
```

Change the index() action so it looks like this:

```
def index(self):
    return render('/uploadform.html')
```

Then add this new template to the `templates` directory as `uploadform.html`:

```
<%inherit file="/base.html" />
<h1>Upload a File</h1>


${h.form(h.url_for(controller='upload', action='upload'), multipart=True)}
Upload file:      ${h.file('myfile')} <br />
Description:      ${h.text('description')} <br />
                  ${h.submit('submit', 'Submit')}
${h.end_form()}
```

If you visit `http://localhost:5000/upload/index`, you should see the form.

Now let's think about how to handle the upload. When a file upload has succeeded, the `request.POST` (or `request.params`) `MultiDict` will contain a `cgi.FieldStorage` object as the value of the field.

`FieldStorage` objects have three important attributes for file uploads:

`filename`: This is the name of the file uploaded as it appeared on the uploader's filesystem.

`file`: This is a Python `tempfile` object from which the file can be read. For example:

```
data = request.params['myfile'].file.read()
```

`value`: This is the content of the uploaded file, eagerly read directly from the file object.

The easiest way to gain access to the file's data is via the `value` attribute, which returns the entire contents of the file:

```
def upload(self):
    myfile = request.POST['myfile']
    return "Successfully uploaded: %s, size: %i, description: %s" % (
        myfile.filename,
        len(myfile.value),
        request.POST['description']
    )
```

However, reading the entire contents of the file into memory is undesirable, especially for large file uploads. A common means of handling file uploads is to store the file somewhere on the filesystem. The `FieldStorage` instance already reads the file onto the filesystem; however, it's to a nonpermanent location, via a Python `tempfile` object.

Here's an example that uses `shutil.copyfileobj` to perform an efficient copy of the temp file's data to a permanent location specified by the `permanent_store` variable in the config file:

```
def upload(self):
    myfile = request.POST['myfile']
    permanent_file = open(
        os.path.join(
            config['app_conf']['permanent_store'],
            myfile.filename.replace(os.sep, '_')
        ),
        'wb'
    )
    shutil.copyfileobj(myfile.file, permanent_file)
    myfile.file.close()
    permanent_file.close()
```

```
    return 'Successfully uploaded: %s, description: %s' % (
        myfile.filename,
        request.POST['description']
    )
```

For this example to work, you'll need to add some imports at the top of the file:

```
import os
from pylons import config
import shutil
```

You'll also need to edit the development.ini config file and add this to the end of the [app:main] section:

```
permanent_store = %(here)s/data/uploads
```

You'll remember from the discussion of config files in Chapter 3 that %(here)s is replaced with the location of the config file, so this example would upload files to the project's data directory used as a cache for templates and sessions. You'll need to create the uploads directory within the data directory because it won't exist yet.

▧Caution This basic example allows any file uploaded to overwrite any file in the permanent_store directory to which your web application has permissions.

Also note the use of myfile.filename.replace(os.sep, '_') to ensure that the file name doesn't start with a / character. This is a simple security measure to help prevent specially crafted file names resulting in other files on your system being overwritten. You should always be suspicious of all data coming from a user's web browser and take appropriate steps to try to ensure that the data is safe.

Now that you can handle files being uploaded to the server, you might also want to provide a way for your users to download those files again.

First you'll need to import the mimetypes module to guess the content type of the file, so you should add the following import to the top of your controller:

```
from mimetypes import guess_type
```

You can then provide the download with an action like this:

```
def download(self):
    requested_filename = request.params['requested_filename']
    filename = os.path.join(
        config['app_conf']['permanent_store'],
        requested_filename.replace(os.sep, '_')
    )
    if not os.path.exists(filename):
        return 'No such file'
    permanent_file = open(filename, 'rb')
    data = permanent_file.read()
    permanent_file.close()
    response.content_type = guess_type(filename)[0] or 'text/plain'
    return data
```

You can test this by uploading a text file called somefile and then visiting the URL http://localhost:5000/upload/download?requested_filename=somefile. The example so far will correctly send the file to the browser, but the browser will try to display it if it is a type it recognizes such as a JPEG or a PNG file. If you want to force the browser to download the file as an attachment, you can add another HTTP header to the response like this just before you return the data:

```
response.headers['Content-Disposition'] = 'attachment; filename="%s"'%(
    requested_filename
)
```

This time the browser will treat the file as an attachment and prompt the user to ask how the file should be handled (see Figure 6-4).

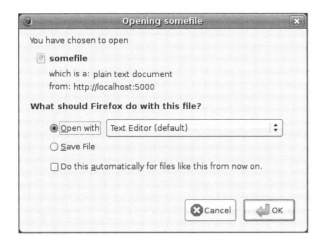

Figure 6-4. *The Firefox attachment download dialog box*

Notice how in this example because the name given for the file name in the Content-Disposition HTTP header was somefile, the browser automatically tried to name the file somefile on the user's computer.

▪Caution Internet Explorer 6 has trouble downloading certain files as attachments over sites using a secure connection (see http://support.microsoft.com/default.aspx?scid=kb;en-us;812935).

If you are writing a secure application that will be accessed by users with Internet Explorer, you should also add the following headers to the response to correct the problem:

```
response.headers['Content-Length'] = len(data)
response.headers['Pragma'] =  'public'
response.headers['Cache-Control'] = 'max-age=0'
```

Note that this an issue with Internet Explorer 6, not with Pylons!

Handling Forms Manually

In the initial example in this chapter, I described how to create a simple form that enables a user to enter their e-mail address and to redisplay the value that was entered in a Pylons application. In most situations, it is important to be able to validate the information the user has entered. If you were asking for an e-mail address with an intention to use it to contact someone, it is important the e-mail address is a real address, so you would want to run some basic checks to ensure the e-mail wasn't obviously entered incorrectly. For example, the e-mail address should contain two strings separated by an @ character, and the domain name portion should contain a . character that should be followed by at least two characters representing the top-level domain. There are even more checks you could make, including ensuring the domain portion of the e-mail was a real domain name, but this probably isn't necessary for most situations.

If a user did enter an invalid e-mail, you would need to redisplay the form together with the e-mail address entered and an error message explaining what was wrong so that the user could correct their mistake. Let's create a controller to demonstrate this process manually. Later in the chapter, you'll learn how the Pylons tools make this process a lot simpler.

Let's update the `formtest` controller from earlier in the chapter to demonstrate this. Update the `submit()` action to look like this, and remove the `result()` action:

```
def submit(self):
    c.email_msg = ''
    email = request.params.get('email')
    if not email:
        c.email_msg = "Please enter a value"
    elif '@' not in email:
        c.email_msg = "An email address must contain at least one '@' character."
    else:
        domain = email.split('@')[1]
        if '.' not in domain:
            c.email_msg = "An email address domain must contain "
            c.email_msg += "at least one '.' character."
        if not domain.split('.')[-1]:
            c.email_msg = "Please specify a domain type after the '.' character"
    if c.email_msg:
        c.email_value = email
        return render('/simpleform.html')
    return 'Your email is: %s' % request.params['email']
```

Update the `simpleform.html` template to look like this:

```
<%inherit file="/base.html" />
<h1>Enter Your E-mail Address</h1>

${h.form(h.url_for(controller='formtest', action='submit'), method='get')}
% if c.email_msg:
    <span class="error-message">${c.email_msg}</span><br />
% endif
E-mail Address: ${h.text('email', value=c.email_value)}
                ${h.submit('submit', 'Submit')}
${h.end_form()}
</form>
```

You've used the Pylons' helpers to generate the fields in this example; remember, you are free to use the helpers or to code your own HTML.

If you visit `http://localhost:5000/formtest/form`, you will see that it achieves the desired result. If a user enters an invalid e-mail address, it will result in the form being redisplayed to show the error with the incorrect value still present in the text field ready to be corrected.

To make the error show up better, it would be sensible to add some Cascading Style Sheets (CSS) so that the error appears in red. The `<head>` of the page is defined in the `base.html` template, so you better add the CSS there.

Edit `base.html` so that you include the following line in the `<head>` section:

```
<link rel="stylesheet" type="text/css"
    href="${h.url_for('/style/style.css')}" />
```

Then create a `style` directory in your project's `public` directory, and create a file called `style.css` with the following content:

```
span.error-message {
    font-weight: bold;
    color: #f00;
}
```

You should find that all the error messages now appear in red, which will make the error much more obvious to your users (see Figure 6-5).

Figure 6-5. *The error message highlighted in red*

Although the approach you've used here to manually validate the form works perfectly well, it would quickly become very complex if you were to also write code to handle many other types of fields in the same way. Luckily, Pylons comes with tools to make the processes you have just used much simpler.

Introducing FormEncode

The recommended tool for validating forms in Pylons is FormEncode. FormEncode has two parts:

- A set of *validators* used together to create *schemas*, which convert form data back and forth between Python objects and their corresponding form values
- A tool called HTML Fill that takes an HTML form and parses it for form fields, filling in values and error messages as it goes from Python objects

Pylons provides a `@validate` decorator, which can make the process of validating form data and redisplaying the form if necessary very easy, but in order to really understand what is going on during the validation process, I'll first explain the process in full.

For each form you create, you also create a validation schema. Here is the validation schema for the form you've been using so far. The example also includes a date field so I can later demonstrate how you can use schemas to convert data from one type to another as well as just validate input.

```
import formencode

class EmailForm(formencode.Schema):
    allow_extra_fields = True
    filter_extra_fields = True
    email = formencode.validators.Email(not_empty=True)
    date = formencode.validators.DateConverter(not_empty=True)
```

Although the form now has three fields—an e-mail text field, a date validator, and a submit button—you are interested only in validating the e-mail address and the date. If extra fields are submitted, FormEncode's default behavior is to consider the form invalid, so you specify `allow_extra_fields = True` so that the value of the submit button is not validated. Since you don't want to use the value of the submit button, you also specify `filter_extra_fields = True` so that the value is ignored completely.

The third line specifies that the e-mail field should be validated with an `Email()` validator. In creating the validator, you also specify `not_empty=True` so that the e-mail field will require input. The final line specifies your date field and also that this particular date field should not be empty either.

Table 6-1 outlines the options that can be used in a schema in addition to the validators themselves.

Table 6-1. *Additional Options That Can Be Used in a FormEncode Schema*

Attribute Name	Default Value	Description
pre_validators	[]	These validators will be applied before the schema.
chained_validators	[]	These validators will be applied after the schema.
allow_extra_fields	False	If True, then it is not an error when keys that aren't associated with a validator are present.
filter_extra_fields	False	If True, then keys that aren't associated with a validator are removed.
if_key_missing	NoDefault	If this is given, then any keys that aren't available but are expected will be replaced with this value (and then validated). This does not override a present .if_missing attribute on validators. NoDefault is a special FormEncode class to mean that no default values have been specified and therefore missing keys shouldn't take a default value.
ignore_key_missing	False	If True, then missing keys will be missing in the result, if the validator doesn't have .if_missing on it already.

It is usually best to keep form schemas together so that you have a single place you can go to update them. It's also convenient for inheritance since you can make new form schemas that build on existing ones. If you put your forms in a `model/form.py` file, you can easily use them throughout your controllers. However, if you are creating a schema that is going to be used in only one controller, it is often more convenient to keep the schema with the controller. This is what you'll do here. Add the `EmailForm` schema to the top of the controller.

Now that you have added the schema, you need to be able to use it in your controller to validate the submitted form data that comes in via `request.params` and to convert the validated values from the format in which they are submitted to Python objects that can be used in the controller.

This is very straightforward because each `Schema` base class (and therefore the `EmailForm` class) has a `to_python()` method to handle the validation and conversion. If any of the validators fail to be able to convert the data, they raise a special exception type called a `formencode.Invalid` exception, which contains information about why the validation and conversion failed. Let's see it in practice. Be sure you've added the `EmailForm` schema and `import formencode` line to the top of the controller file, and then update the `submit()` action to look like this:

```
def submit(self):
    schema = EmailForm()
    try:
        form_result = schema.to_python(dict(request.params))
    except formencode.Invalid, error:
        response.content_type = 'text/plain'
        return 'Invalid: '+unicode(error)
    else:
        return 'Your email is: %s'%form_result.get('email')
```

You'll also need to update the `simpleform.html` template to add the date field:

```
<%inherit file="/base.html" />
<h1>Enter Your E-mail Address</h1>

${h.form(h.url_for(controller='formtest', action='submit'), method='get')}
<p>E-mail Address: ${h.text('email')}</p>
<p>Date:          ${h.text('date')}</p>
<p>               ${h.submit('submit', 'Submit')}</p>
${h.end_form()}
</form>
```

This new template is much simpler, but you'll notice that it doesn't contain any logic for setting the value of the e-mail field or displaying an error message. This will be handled separately using HTML Fill, which I'll discuss later in the chapter.

If the values entered in the form are valid, the schema's `to_python()` method returns a dictionary of the validated and coerced data, in this case assigned to `form_result`. This means you can guarantee that the `form_result` dictionary contains values that are valid and correct Python objects for the data types desired.

In this case, the e-mail address is a string, so `request.params['email']` happens to be the same as `form_result['email']`, but for the date field, `request.params['date']` is a string in the form `"mm/dd/yyyy"`, whereas `form_result['date']` is a Python `datetime.date` object representing the date the user entered. For even more complex data types, this ability of FormEncode to coerce data becomes very valuable.

Try entering some dates and e-mail addresses, both valid and invalid, and see the error messages FormEncode produces. As an example, if you entered the e-mail address `james.example.com` and the date `01/40/2008`, you would get the following errors:

```
Invalid: date: That month only has 31 days
email: An email address must contain a single @
```

Now try entering some valid data such as `james@example.com` and `01/15/2006` and change the end of the `submit()` action to look like this:

```
...
else:
    raise Exception(form_result)
    return 'Your email is: %s'%form_result.get('email')
```

From the exception that occurs, you can see that form_result actually contains the following:

{'date': datetime.date(2006, 1, 15), 'email': u'james@example.com'}

As you can see, FormEncode has done more than simply validate the data; it has also converted it to the appropriate Python type so that you can easily work with it. The DateConverter validator has converted the text entered in the form into a Python date object, and the Email validator has returned a Unicode string. This is useful if you want to convert Python objects from your database to display in a table as part of your web application, for example. It is also used by HTML Fill to automatically repopulate form data if your form contains errors.

Here are some of the most frequently used FormEncode validators. For the full list, see the Available Validators documentation on the FormEncode web site:

MaxLength: The submitted value is invalid if it is longer than the maxLength argument. It uses len(), so it can work for strings, lists, or anything with length.

MinLength: The submitted value is invalid if it is shorter than the minLength argument. It uses len(), so it can work for strings, lists, or anything with length.

Regex: The submitted value is invalid if it doesn't match the regular expression regex. This is useful for matching phone numbers or postal codes, for example.

PlainText: This validator ensures that the field contains only letters, numbers, underscores, and hyphens. It subclasses Regex.

DateConverter: This validates and converts a date represented as a string, such as mm/yy, dd/mm/yy, dd-mm-yy, and so on. By using the month_style argument you can support mm/dd/yyyy or dd/mm/yyyy. Only these two general styles are supported.

TimeConverter: This converts times in the format HH:MM:SSampm to (h, m, s). Seconds are optional.

StringBool: This converts a string such as "true" or "0" to a boolean.

Int: This converts a value to an integer.

Number: This converts a value to a float or integer. It tries to convert it to an integer if no information is lost.

String: This converts things to string but treats empty things as the empty string.

UnicodeString: This converts things to Unicode strings. This is a specialization of the String class.

URL: This validates a URL, either http:// or https://. If check_exists is True, then you'll actually make a request for the page.

Email: This validates an e-mail address with the facility to check that the domain entered actually exists.

OneOf: This tests that the value is one of the members of a given list. This is particularly useful when validating an option from a select field because you can use it to check that the value submitted was one of the original values.

FieldsMatch: This tests that the given fields match, that is, are identical. It is useful for password+confirmation fields. Pass the list of field names in as field_names.

ForEach: Use this to apply a validator/converter to each item in a list.

All: This class is like an and operator for validators. All validators must work, and the results are passed in turn through all validators for conversion.

Any: This class is like an or operator for validators. The first validator/converter that validates the value will be used.

It can sometimes be difficult to work out the arguments that each validator will accept. The best way to find out is to look at the example usage for each type of validator on the FormEncode site. In addition to these arguments, validators also accept common arguments to configure their error messages and behavior. You'll learn about these next.

Configuring Validators

Each of the validators will have a number of messages as well as a number of configuration options. Here are some examples of the sorts of messages available; these are for the `ConfirmType` validator:

```
badType: "The input must be a string (not a %(type)s: %(value)r)"

empty: "Please enter a value"

inSubclass: "%(object)r is not a subclass of one of the types %(subclassList)s"

inType: "%(object)r must be one of the types %(typeList)s"

noneType: "The input must be a string (not None)"

subclass: "%(object)r is not a subclass of %(subclass)s"

type: "%(object)r must be of the type %(type)s"
```

To override the default value for an error message, you pass a `msgs` argument to the validator's constuctor. For example:

```
name = String(msgs={'empty':'Please enter a name'})
```

In each of these examples, constructs such as `%(object)r` and `%(type)s` are standard Python string-formatting terms. They are replaced by a string representation of the value to which they are referring. Terms ending in `s` result in the object being converted to a string with `str()`, and terms ending in `r` result in the objects being converted to a string with the `repr()` function that displays a Python representation of the value. You can use these same terms in your own custom messages if you like.

You don't need to specify messages for every error; FormEncode will use its defaults for any you don't specify. Messages often take arguments, such as the number of characters, the invalid portion of the field, and so on. These are always substituted as a dictionary (by name). So, you will use placeholders like `%(key)s` for each substitution. This way you can reorder or even ignore placeholders in your new message.

Later you'll see how to create your own validator. When you are creating a validator, for maximum flexibility you should use the `message` function:

```
messages = {
    'key': 'my message (with a %(substitution)s)',
    }

def validate_python(self, value, state):
    raise Invalid(self.message('key', substitution='apples'),
                  value, state)
```

Most validators support the following options (including your own validators, if you subclass from `FancyValidator`):

if_empty: If set, then this value will be returned if the input evaluates to `false` (an empty list, empty string, `None`, and so on), but not a `0` or `False` objects. This applies only to `.to_python()`.

not_empty: If `True`, then if an empty value is given, this raises an error (both with `.to_python()` and also `.from_python()` if `.validate_python` is `True`).

strip: If True and the input is a string, strip it (occurs before empty tests).

if_invalid: If set, then this validator will raise Invalid during .to_python(); instead, return this value.

if_invalid_python: If set, when the Python value (converted with .from_python()) is invalid, this value will be returned.

accept_python: If True (the default), then .validate_python() and .validate_other() will not be called when .from_python() is used.

The values of the configuration options are stored as class attributes. As an example, look at the DateConverter you used earlier. It is documented at http://formencode.org/class-formencode.validators.DateConverter.html, where you can see that the class has a number of attributes including month_style, which defaults to mm/dd/yyyy. There are two ways to set these attributes. The first is to pass the name of the attribute as an argument to the validator's constructor when you create it. You've already seen an example of this technique when you passed not_empty=True to the DateConverter and EmailValidator validators in your schema.

The other way to configure a validator is by using inheritance. You can create a new validator derived from the old one but with different default values for the attributes. As an example, here is a UKDateConverter, which uses the U.K. format for the date by default:

```
class UKDateConverter(DateConverter):
    month_style = 'dd/mm/yyyy'
```

You could then update your schema to look like this:

```
class EmailForm(formencode.Schema):
    allow_extra_fields = True
    filter_extra_fields = True
    email = formencode.validators.Email(not_empty=True)
    date = UKDateConverter(not_empty=True)
```

You'll learn more about creating your own validators later in this chapter.

Using HTML Fill

Now that you have learned how to use FormEncode to validate and coerce data, you will still need to display error messages along with a repopulated form should the user have entered any invalid data.

This is from the HTML Fill documentation:

> htmlfill *is a library to fill out forms, both with default values and error messages. It's like a template library, but more limited, and it can be used with the output from other templates. It has no prerequesites and can be used without any other parts of FormEncode.*

The basic usage looks something like this:

```
>>> from formencode import htmlfill
>>> form = '<input type="text" name="fname">'
>>> defaults = {'fname': 'Joe'}
>>> htmlfill.render(form, defaults)
'<input type="text" name="fname" value="Joe">'
```

The parser looks for HTML input elements (including select and textarea) and fills in the defaults. HTML Fill is therefore very useful in processing forms because you can return the form to the user with the values they entered, in addition to errors.

Let's update the controller to use HTML Fill. Change the submit() action to look like this:

```
def submit(self):
    schema = EmailForm()
    try:
        c.form_result = schema.to_python(dict(request.params))
    except formencode.Invalid, error:
        c.form_result = error.value
        c.form_errors = error.error_dict or {}
        html = render('/simpleform.html')
        return htmlfill.render(
            html,
            defaults=c.form_result,
            errors=c.form_errors
        )
    else:
        return 'Your email is: %s and the date selected was %r.' % (
            c.form_result['email'],
            c.form_result['date'],
        )
```

You'll also need to import HTML Fill. Add this import to the top of the controller:

```
from formencode import htmlfill
```

In this example, when an error occurs, you use Pylons' render() function to render the HTML of the original form as it was before the user submitted it. You then pass the HTML, as well as the form result values and the error messages dictionary, into HTML Fill's render() method. HTML Fill then parses the HTML, adding any error messages and field values for you automatically. The filled HTML is then returned so that the user can correct the errors as before.

Notice that you don't need the template code for the error messages and that none of the fields have values specified directly. HTML Fill populates the fields with the correct values and inserts any error messages automatically.

Tip Being able to use plain HTML in this manner is actually very useful because it means any designers working on your project are able to use visual tools such as Dreamweaver (or the open source Nvu program based on Mozilla project code) and HTML Fill will still work perfectly, whereas these tools are not designed to visually display fields generated in templates with the helper functions. The decision as to whether you should use the field helpers or code HTML fields directly will depend largely on whether you want to use such tools.

If you run the example, you will see that the result is very similar to what was generated when you handled the form manually earlier in the chapter. The HTML generated for the error messages is slightly different, though. It includes some comments added by HTML Fill.

This is the generated HTML:

```
<html>
<head>
<title>FormDemo</title>
<link rel="stylesheet" type="text/css"
    href="/style/style.css" />
</head>
<body>

<h1>Enter Your E-mail Address</h1>
```

```
<form action="/formtest/submit" method="get">
<p>E-mail Address: <!-- for: email -->
<span class="error-message">An email address must contain a single @</span><br />
<input name="email" type="text" class="error" value="test_example.com" /></p>

<p>Date:           <!-- for: date -->
<span class="error-message">That month only has 31 days</span><br />
<input name="date" type="text" class="error" value="1/40/2008" /></p>
<p>               <input name="submit" type="submit" value="Submit" /></p>
</form>
</form>


</body>
</html>
```

Error Message Formatting

The error message formatting might not be quite what you were after, so HTML Fill defines two special tags that can be used to customize how the error messages are displayed:

> `<form:error name="field_name" format="formatter">`: This tag is eliminated completely if there is no error for the named field. Otherwise, the error is passed through the given formatter (`"default"` if no `format` attribute is given).

> `<form:iferror name="field_name">...</form:iferror>`: If the named field doesn't have an error, everything between the tags will be eliminated. Use `name="not field_name"` to invert the behavior (in other words, include text only if there are no errors for the field).

Formatters are functions that take the error text as a single argument and return a string that is inserted into the template. Formatters are specified as arguments to the `htmlfill.render()` function, which I will describe next. The default formatter returns the following:

```
<span class="error-message">(message)</span><br>
```

where (`message`) is replaced with the error message concerned. Most of the time it is best to use a formatter because the second form displays the static HTML you've specified, not the actual error message generated.

If any errors are generated for fields that don't exist, they are added at the top of the form.

Render Arguments

HTML Fill's `render()` function has the following arguments that you can use to customize how the form is rendered:

```
def render(form, defaults=None, errors=None, use_all_keys=False,
     error_formatters=None, add_attributes=None,
     auto_insert_errors=True, auto_error_formatter=None,
     text_as_default=False, listener=None)
```

It is important to note that HTML Fill's `render()` function has nothing to do with the `render()` function you've been using to render templates; it is just unfortunate that both have the same name.

The example so far has used the `form`, `defaults` and `errors` arguments, but other options can be useful too:

use_all_keys: If this is True, if there are any extra fields from defaults or errors that couldn't be used in the form, it will be an error.

error_formatters: This is a dictionary of formatter names to one-argument functions that format an error into HTML. Some default formatters are provided if you don't provide this.

add_attributes: This is a dictionary of field names to a dictionary of attribute name/values. If the name starts with +, then the value will be appended to any existing attribute (for example, {'+class': ' important'}).

auto_insert_errors: If this is True (the default), then any errors for which <form:error> tags can't be found will be put just above the associated input field, or at the top of the form if no field can be found.

auto_error_formatter: This is used to create the HTML that goes above the fields. By default, it wraps the error message in a span and adds a <br>.

text_as_default: If this is True (the default is False), then <input type=unknown> will be treated as text inputs.

listener: This can be an object that watches fields pass; the only one currently is in formencode.htmlfill_schemabuilder.SchemaBuilder.

Doing Validation the Quick Way

Now that you've seen in detail how to use FormEncode and HTML Fill, you'll be pleased to know that Pylons provides an even simpler way of using the same functionality that is suitable for the majority of use cases you are likely to encounter.

You can use it like this:

```
def form(self):
    return render('/simpleform.html')

@validate(schema=EmailForm(), form='form', post_only=False, on_get=True)
def submit(self):
    return 'Your email is: %s and the date selected was %r.' % (
        self.form_result['email'],
        self.form_result['date'],
    )
```

You'll need to import the @validate decorator at the top of the controller:

```
from pylons.decorators import validate
```

What this says is that if the data submitted to the submit() action contains any errors, then the request should be rerun as a GET request to the form() action. The result of calling the form() action is then passed through HTML Fill to render the errors and repopulate the form with the values that were submitted.

■**Note** Python 2.3 doesn't support decorators, so rather than using the @validate() syntax, you need to put email = validate(schema=EmailForm(), form='form', post_only=False, on_get=True)(email) after the e-mail function's declaration.

By default, if you don't specify `post_only=False` and `on_get=True` to the `@validate` decorator, validation would occur only on POST requests, so you would need to alter your form definition so that the method is a POST:

```
<% h.form(h.url_for(action='submit'), method='post') %>
```

Caution If you do this, calling an action wrapped by `@validate` using a GET request will bypass the validation and call the action anyway. You need to make sure this doesn't pose a security risk in your application. You could prevent this by testing whether a GET or a POST is being used in the body of the action. The request method can be determined using `request.method`.

You can customize the way HTML Fill is called by passing any of the arguments accepted by `htmlfill.render()` as keyword arguments to `validate()`. For example, to specify a custom error formatter, you can do this:

```
from formencode import htmlfill

def custom_formatter(error):
    return '<span class="custom-message">%s</span><br />\n' % (
        htmlfill.html_quote(error)
    )
```

Update the `submit()` action to look like this:

```
@validate(schema=EmailForm(), form='form', post_only=False, on_get=True,
    auto_error_formatter=custom_formatter)
def submit(self):
    return 'Your email is: %s and the date selected was %r.' % (
        self.form_result['email'],
        self.form_result['date'],
    )
```

With this in place, the error messages will be wrapped in `<span class="custom-message">` tags. If you run the example, you will notice that the error messages are no longer highlighted in red because there is no style set up for the new error class.

You can pass other options to the HTML Fill `render()` function in the same way via the `@validate` decorator.

The `@validate` decorator is documented at `http://docs.pylonshq.com/modules/decorators.html#module-pylons.decorators`.

Using Custom Validators

FormEncode comes with a useful set of validators, but you can also easily create your own. One common reason for wanting to do this is if you are populating a select field with values from a database and you want to ensure the value submitted is one of the values in the database.

For this example, imagine you have a function called `get_option_values()` that interacts with a database every time it is called and returns a list of valid integers.

Here's a potential implementation:

```
class ValidOption(formencode.validators.FancyValidator):

    def validate_python(self, value, state):
        valid_values = get_option_values()
        if value not in valid_values:
            raise formencode.Invalid("Invalid value", value, state)
```

When the validator is used in a schema and checked, an error message will be displayed if the value submitted isn't one of the options returned by get_option_values().

You might use it like this:

```
class EmailForm(formencode.Schema):
    allow_extra_fields = True
    filter_extra_fields = True
    email = formencode.validators.Email(not_empty=True)
    date = formencode.validators.DateConverter(not_empty=True)
    option = ValidOption()
```

Let's have a look at the implementation in more detail. Notice that the validate_python() method also takes a state argument. It's used for very little in the validation system but provides a mechanism for passing information from Pylons to any custom validators you write. The c global is used in Pylons for storing per-request state information, so it makes sense to also use it as the state argument to your validators, although you are free to use other objects if you prefer.

As an example, let's imagine that get_option_values() relied on a database connection that was set up on each request. You couldn't pass the connection as an argument to ValidOption because the connection wouldn't exist at the point Python created the schema. The connection exists only during the request, so you would attach it to the c global during the request and pass the c global as the state argument when instantiating the schema. Here's how the start of the submit() action might look from the full FormEncode and HTML Fill example earlier:

```
def submit(self):
    # Imagine we have a connection object now:
    c.connection = connection
    schema = EmailForm(state=c)
    ... same as before
```

You could now update the example like this:

```
class ValidOption(formencode.validators.FancyValidator):

    def validate_python(self, value, c):
        valid_values = get_option_values(c.connection)
        if value not in valid_values:
            raise formencode.Invalid("Invalid value", value, c)
```

In this way, the validator can use request-specific information even though it is defined before the request starts.

The previous implementation uses the validate_python() method, which simply raises an exception if it needs to do so. This is useful in this example because the conversion needs to be done by the validator when converting to and from Python. This won't be the case for all the validators you create, though. The _to_python() and _from_python() methods are provided for you to implement any conversion code to convert to or from Python, respectively.

The validate_python() method is called *after* _to_python() so that the value argument will be a normal Python object by the time it comes to being validated. validate_python() is called *before* _from_python(). Both _to_python() and _from_python() take the same arguments as validate_python().

You'll remember from earlier in the chapter that validators can be customized when you instantiate them in a schema. At the moment, the validator you've created always displays the message Invalid value. Let's update the validator to allow it to be customized:

```
class ValidOption(formencode.validators.FancyValidator):

    messages = {
        'invalid': 'Invalid value',
    }

    def validate_python(self, value, c):
        valid_values = get_option_values(c.connection)
        if value not in valid_values:
            raise formencode.Invalid(
                self.message("invalid", c),
                value,
                c
            )
```

You can also include values in the message itself like this:

```
class ValidOption(formencode.validators.FancyValidator):

    messages = {
        'invalid': 'Invalid value %(invalid)s',
    }

    def validate_python(self, value, c):
        valid_values = get_option_values(c.connection)
        if value not in valid_values:
            raise formencode.Invalid(
                self.message("invalid", c, invalid=value),
                value,
                c
            )
```

The message string specified gets interpolated with a dictionary made from the keyword arguments you pass to the self.message() function. This system is designed to make the messages easy to format for different environments or replaceable for different languages.

You'll also notice that you use a special exception class, formencode.Invalid, to raise an error. This is the same exception class you catch in the controller action and use to obtain the values to pass to htmlfill.render(). Besides the string error message, Invalid exceptions have a few other instance variables:

value: This is the input to the validator that failed.

state: This is the associated state.

msg: This is the error message (str(exc) returns this).

error_list: If the exception happened in a ForEach (list) validator, then this will contain a list of Invalid exceptions. Each item from the list will have an entry, either None for no error or an exception.

error_dict: If the exception happened in a Schema (dictionary) validator, then this will contain Invalid exceptions for each failing field.

.unpack_errors(): This method returns a set of lists and dictionaries containing strings for each error. It's an unpacking of error_list, error_dict, and msg. If you get an Invalid exception from a Schema, you probably want to call this method on the exception object.

If you are interested in writing your own validators, it is useful to see the source code for the FancyValidator class. It is in the formencode.api module and explains all the options and methods validators have. There are other types of validators too such as compound validators and chained validators. Generally speaking, the best way to implement your own validator is to look at the source code of an existing validator that behaves in a similar manner and implement your own validator in the same way.

Solving the Repeating Fields Problem

In real-world examples, you rarely just need a form that can be populated from a flat dictionary structure. Forms that contain subforms or repeating sets of fields are actually very common.

Let's imagine a situation where you are writing a form to allow a researcher to add information about a research project they are conducting. They might need to provide the following information:

- The title of the study
- When it is going to start and end
- The contact details of the people who are participating

Contact details consist of the following information:

- Title
- First name
- Surname
- Role in the project

Let's also imagine that a research project requires at least one person to be added and also that there can be only one person with the role of chief investigator.

You can easily provide a form to enter the study title, start date, and end date, but providing a form to allow an unknown number of people's contact details to be entered is slightly trickier. You can take one of two approaches:

- Design the form in a wizard format. The user enters the title, start date, and end date on the first screen and clicks Submit. The data is saved, and the second screen is displayed, allowing the user to add the contact details of the first person. Once they have submitted the form, they are asked whether they want to add another person. This continues until they have added all the necessary data.

- Display a single form containing the title, start date, and end date as before but with a button to allow the user to add fields to add a person. When the user clicks the Add New Person button, a set of fields to enter the first person are shown. The user can submit the form or click the Add New Person button again to add another set of fields. Finally, once they have completed the whole form containing the study and person data, they click Save, and the data is validated and saved in one go.

The advantage of the first approach is that at any one time you are dealing with only one set of fields that can be submitted as simple name/value pairs, so the data structure is very straightforward. The disadvantage is that at each step in the wizard you need to store the data that has already been submitted, and this has its own problems. Imagine, for example, you save the study information in the first step but the user changes their mind and never completes the second step of adding a person. One of the requirements was that studies should have at least one person associated with them, but now you have saved a study that doesn't have any people. Say, instead, that the user does add a person and gives them a role of chief investigator. Now let's imagine they add another person and give them a role of chief investigator too. You can't have more than one chief investigator, so the validation code will display an error explaining the problem. Imagine, though, that the user really does want the second person to be the chief investigator and made a mistake in giving the first person the chief investigator role. The user has no choice but to start the form again.

Obviously, all the problems with the wizard approach can be solved. You can store the data in a temporary location or a session store and save it properly only at the end of the wizard, or you can provide Back buttons so the user can go back through the wizard and make changes, but it can be a surprising amount of work to program the logic and validation code for this sort of workflow.

The major advantage of the second approach is that all the required data is stored client-side throughout the submission and validation cycles, which means your Pylons controller needs to store the data only once, after all the input has been validated. This can greatly reduce the complexity of your controller logic. FormEncode provides the necessary tools to help you with this.

Creating the Form

The first thing you need to do is define the schema. Here's what the main study schema might look like:

```
class Study(Schema)
    title = String(not_empty=True)
    start_date = DateConverter()
    end_date = DateConverter()
    people = ForEach(Person())
```

As you can see, the schema has `title`, `start_date`, and `end_date` fields, which use ordinary validators as you would expect, but there is also a `people` field that takes a `ForEach()` validator. The `ForEach()` validator takes a single argument, which is another validator or schema it should validate. In this case, you want it to validate people, so you've specified an instance of a `Person` schema. The `Person` schema looks like this:

```
class Person(Schema):
    title = String()
    firstname = String(not_empty=True)
    surname = String(not_empty=True)
    role = OneOf(['1', '2', '3'])
```

The `role` field will be a select drop-down that takes the values in Table 6-2.

Table 6-2. *Possible Values for Role*

Name	Value
Chief investigator	1
Assistant	2
Student	3

The OneOf validator checks that the value submitted for the role is one of the values specified.

Now turn your attention to the template defs to produce the fields. You'll create a working example as you go through this chapter, so let's create a project for it (accept the default values when prompted):

```
$ paster create --template=pylons FormExample
$ cd FormExample
$ paster controller study
```

Create two directories named base and derived in the templates directory, and add a base/index.html file that looks like this:

```
<html>
<head>
<title>FormsExample</title>
<style type="text/css">
span.error-message{
    font-weight: bold;
    color: #c00;
}
</style>
</head>
<body>
${next.body()}
</body>
</html>
```

Then create a new template called derived/form.html with the following content:

```
<%inherit file="/base/index.html" />

<%def name="study()">
    <fieldset><legend>Study</legend>

        <label for="title">Title</label><br />
        ${h.text(name="title", id="title")}<br />

        <label for="start_date">Start Date</label><br />
        ${h.text(name="start_date", id="startdate")}<br />

        <label for="end_date">End Date</label><br />
        ${h.text(name="end_date", id="enddate")}<br />
    </fieldset><br />
        % for id in range(c.number_of_people):
            ${person(id=id)}
        % endfor
</%def>

<%def name="person(id)">
    <fieldset><legend>Person</legend>

        <label for="person-${id}.title">Title</label><br />
        ${h.text(name="person-%s.title"%(id), id="person-%s.title"%(id))}<br />
```

```
        <label for="person-${id}.firstname">First Name</label><br />
        ${h.text(
            name="person-%s.firstname"%(id),
            id="person-%s.firstname"%(id
        ))}<br />

        <label for="person-${id}.surname">Surname</label><br />
        ${h.text(name="person-%s.surname"%(id), id="person-%s.surname"%(id))}<br />

        <label for="person-${id}.role">Role</label><br />
        ${h.select(
            "person-%s.role"%(id),
            [],
            [
                ['1', 'Chief Investigator'],
                ['2', 'Assistant'],
                ['3', 'Student'],
            ],
            id="person-%s.role"%(id),
        )}<br />

        ${h.submit(name="action", value="Remove %s"%(id))}

    </fieldset><br />
</%def>

<h1>Create a Study</h1>

${h.form(h.url_for(controller='study', action='process'))}
${study()}
${h.submit(name="action", value="Save")}
${h.submit(name="action", value="Add New Person")}
${h.end_form()}
```

Rendering this template would result in the study() def being called, and this in turn would call the person() def to create a set of fields for the number of people specified in c.number_of_people, which you will set in the controller in a minute.

▨Tip The template you've created uses <fieldset> and <label> HTML tags to create the form rather than creating a layout with tables or other HTML structures. This is considered best practice because the for attributes of the <label> tags clearly associate the text of the label with the field itself so that people who use screen readers will still be able to fill in your form. Using this technique also makes your forms much easier to style using CSS.

The Study schema expects nested data structures, but HTML forms produce flat structures with keys (field names) and their associated values. To solve this problem, FormEncode provides a NestedVariables class in the nestedvariables module that provides a way of converting nested data structures to and from a flat set of field names. To do this, it uses keys with "." for nested dictionaries and "-int" for (ordered) lists. A structure like this:

```
{
    'people': [
        {'fname': "John", 'lname': "Doe"},
        {'fname': "Jane", 'lname': 'Brown'},
        "Tim Smith"
    ],
    'action': {
        None: "save",
        'option': "overwrite",
        'confirm': "yes"
    },
}
```

can therefore be mapped to form fields with the names and values in Table 6-3.

Table 6-3. *Field Names Used in the Example and Their Corresponding Values*

Names	Value
people-0.fname	John
people-0.lname	Doe
people-1.fname	Jane
people-1.lname	Brown
people-2	Tim Smith
action	save
action.option	overwrite
action.confirm	yes

Notice how the value save is associated directly with action rather than action.None. This is so that if the dictionary contained a key "None" and a key None, they could both be handled correctly.

Returning to the example, notice how in the person def you just created the field names that make up each person follow this naming convention so that FormEncode can automatically convert the values submitted from the HTML form into the nested data structure the Study schema requires.

To make this conversion happen automatically, you need to add a NestedVariables prevalidator to the Study schema so it looks like this:

```
class Study(Schema):
    pre_validators = [NestedVariables()]
    title = String(not_empty=True)
    start_date = DateConverter()
    end_date = DateConverter()
    person = ForEach(Person())
```

Prevalidators are validators that are run on the values before the values are passed to each of the other validators for validation and conversion. Schemas also take a chained_validators attribute, which you'll see later is for performing validation on the whole form after the prevalidators and individual field validators have been run.

The form also includes buttons for adding new people and removing ones the user added by mistake. These fields aren't part of the schema and don't need to be included in the validated and converted output, so you can also add the attributes `allow_extra_fields=True` and `filter_extra_fields=True` to the Study schema.

At this stage, you can start adding content including the finished schemas to the `study` controller you created earlier. At the top of the file after `log` is set up, add the following:

```
from formencode.schema import Schema
from formencode.validators import Invalid, FancyValidator
from formencode.validators import Int, DateConverter, String, OneOf
from formencode import variabledecode
from formencode import htmlfill
from formencode.foreach import ForEach
from formencode.api import NoDefault

class Person(Schema):
    title = String()
    firstname = String(not_empty=True)
    surname = String(not_empty=True)
    role = OneOf(['1', '2', '3'])

class Study(Schema):
    allow_extra_fields = True
    filter_extra_fields = True
    pre_validators = [variabledecode.NestedVariables()]
    title = String(not_empty=True)
    start_date = DateConverter()
    end_date = DateConverter()
    person = ForEach(Person())
```

One of the requirements was that a study should have at least one person. The `ForEach` validator you are using to validate people takes the same `not_empty` argument that validators such as `String` take, so you might think that adding `not_empty=True` to the validator constructor would be all you had to do. Unfortunately, this isn't the case; the `ForEach` validator is set up to return the value `[]` if the field is missing, so FormEncode doesn't notice the problem. There are two ways to fix this depending on what you want to achieve:

- Use `not_empty=True`, but always specify a hidden field such as `<input type="hidden" name="person" value="" />` so that a value is always submitted and FormEncode is forced to validate the field. When the value `""` is received, the `not_empty=True` argument means the standard empty message `Please enter a value` gets displayed and the user is aware of the problem. When people are added, the hidden field still gets submitted, but `variabledecode` overwrites the value with the decoded people values, so everything works as it should.

- Use `if_missing=NoDefault` to tell FormEncode not to return an empty list, `[]`, if no people are submitted (which is the default behavior). Instead, because there is no default, the `Study` schema will display its `missing` message `Missing value`.

You can also customize the `Missing value` message using the second approach like this:

```
ForEach(
    Person(),
    if_missing=NoDefault,
    messages={'missing':'Please add a person'}
)
```

Another requirement is that there should be only one chief investigator. You can check this condition by creating a custom validator to check for the presence of the one chief investigator. You could implement this as a normal validator, but here you are going to implement it as a chained validator. Chained validators are slightly different from normal validators because they are checked only once all the individual fields have been validated. They are usually used when a validation rule depends on more than one field.

Ordinary validators are passed the raw unconverted value from the field they are validating. Chained validators are passed the validated and converted dictionary of data generated after all the other validators have been run.

Here's what the validator looks like:

```
from formencode.validators import FancyValidator

class OneChiefInvestigator(FancyValidator):

    messages = {
        'too_many_cis':"Only one Chief Investigator is allowed, not %(number)s"
    }

    def validate_python(self, values, c):
        chief_investigators_found = 0
        for person in values['person']:
            if person['role'] == u'1':
                chief_investigators_found += 1
        if chief_investigators_found > 1:
            raise Invalid(
                self.message("too_many_cis", c, number=chief_investigators_found),
                values,
                c
            )
```

Add this validator to the schema like this:

```
class Study(Schema):
    ...
    chained_validators = [OneChiefInvestigator()]
```

The schema and templates are now in place, so turn your attention to the controller code that will tie everything together. The first thing to notice is that the user will expect very different behavior depending on the button that is clicked. There are buttons to do the following:

- Save the form

- Add a new set of person fields

- Remove a particular set of person fields

To rerender the form after any of these actions, you need to calculate the number of people so that the form is regenerated with the correct number of sets of person fields. Here's a function to do that:

```
def number_of_people(values):
    people_count = 0
    for key in values.keys():
        if key.startswith('person-') and key.endswith('title'):
            people_count += 1
    return people_count
```

You'll also need a function to render the template and fill it with the correct values and error messages:

```
def render_form(values=None, errors=None, number_of_people=0):
    c.number_of_people = number_of_people
    html = render('/derived/form.html')
    return htmlfill.render(html, defaults=values, errors=errors)
```

You can add these two functions beneath the schema definitions in your controller.

All the buttons have the same name, action, so the process() action you'll create can determine which button has been pressed by looking at the value of the action URL parameter.

Here is the complete code including the schemas, validators, and controller:

```
import logging

from pylons import request, response, session, tmpl_context as c
from pylons.controllers.util import abort, redirect_to

from formexample.lib.base import BaseController, render
#from formexample import model

log = logging.getLogger(__name__)
from formencode.schema import Schema
from formencode.validators import Invalid, FancyValidator
from formencode.validators import Int, DateConverter, String, one_of
from formencode import variabledecode
from formencode import htmlfill
from formencode.foreach import ForEach
from formencode.api import NoDefault

class OneChiefInvestigator(FancyValidator):

    messages = {
        'too_many_cis':"Only one Chief Investigator is allowed, not %(number)s"
    }

    def validate_python(self, values, c):
        chief_investigators_found = 0
        for person in values['person']:
            if person['role'] == u'1':
                chief_investigators_found += 1
        if chief_investigators_found > 1:
            raise Invalid(
                self.message("too_many_cis", c, number=chief_investigators_found),
                values,
                c
            )

class Person(Schema):
    title = String()
    firstname = String(not_empty=True)
    surname = String(not_empty=True)
    role = OneOf(['1', '2', '3'])
```

```
class Study(Schema):
    allow_extra_fields = True
    filter_extra_fields = True
    pre_validators = [variabledecode.NestedVariables()]
    title = String(not_empty=True)
    start_date = DateConverter()
    end_date = DateConverter()
    person = ForEach(
        Person(),
        if_missing=NoDefault,
        messages={'missing':'Please add a person'}
    )
    chained_validators = [OneChiefInvestigator()]

def render_form(values=None, errors=None, number_of_people=0):
    c.number_of_people = number_of_people
    html = render('/derived/form.html')
    return htmlfill.render(html, defaults=values, errors=errors)

def number_of_people(values):
    people_count = 0
    for key in values.keys():
        if key.startswith('person-') and key.endswith('title'):
            people_count += 1
    return people_count

class StudyController(BaseController):

    def index(self):
        return render_form()

    def process(self):
        action = request.params.getone('action')
        values = dict(request.params)
        # Don't use the values field for repopulation
        del values['action']
        if action == 'Add New Person':
            # Render the form with one extra set of person fields
            return render_form(
                values=values,
                number_of_people = number_of_people(values) + 1
            )
        elif action.startswith('Remove'):
            # Get the ID of the set of person fields to remove
            id = int(action.split(' ')[-1])
            # Create a new set of values without those fields
            new_values = {}
            for k, v in values.items():
                if not k.startswith('person-'+str(id)+'.'):
                    new_values[k] = v
            # Render the form with the new values
            return render_form(
                values=new_values,
                number_of_people = number_of_people(new_values)
            )
```

```
    elif action=='Save':
        # Assume we are trying to save the form
        schema = Study()
        try:
            result = schema.to_python(dict(request.params), c)
        except Invalid, e:
            return render_form(
                values=values,
                errors=variabledecode.variable_encode(
                    e.unpack_errors() or {},
                    add_repetitions=False
                ),
                number_of_people=number_of_people(values)
            )
        else:
            # You would save the data here before redirecting
            # values will be a Python nested data structure
            # which shouldn't need any further conversion.

            # In this case we just display the result
            return str(result)
else:
    raise Exception('Invalid action %s'%action)
```

Since this is a new project, you'll need to add some helpers to the lib/helpers.py file before this example will work. Add these lines:

```
from webhelpers.html.tags import *
from routes import url_for
```

To test this example, start the development server with the paster serve --reload development.ini command, and visit http://localhost:5000/study/index.

If the Add New Person button is clicked, the form is rerendered with its submitted values and an extra set of person fields. No validation takes place at this stage, so the values redisplayed are the same as those entered.

If the user clicks one of the Remove Person buttons, the ID of the set of person fields to be removed is obtained from the button value, and that set of fields is manually removed from the dictionary of values that is used to repopulate the form when it is rendered.

If the action isn't recognized, it is assumed the user clicked the Save button. The Study schema is used to validate and convert the data. The NestedVariables prevalidator converts the flat HTML form data into a nested data structure. Each of the fields in turn is then checked against its validator. In the case of person, this means each of the sets of person fields is itself validated against the Person schema. If there are no errors, the OneChiefInvestigator chained validator is run to ensure there is only one chief investigator.

If any of the validation checks fail, the form errors are encoded into a flat data structure using the variabledecode.encode() function so that each of the keys associated with the errors can be understood by htmlfill.render() and redisplayed next to the fields to which they refer.

Finally, if all the validation checks pass, the schema.to_python() method returns the decoded, validated, and converted values ready for your program to handle the data in whichever way it sees fit. Ordinarily, this would most likely be to save the data to a database before using h.redirect_to() to redirect the user to a page confirming the data had been saved. This example simply prints a message and displays the converted data structure.

Figure 6-6 shows the example during validation and with only one set of person fields added.

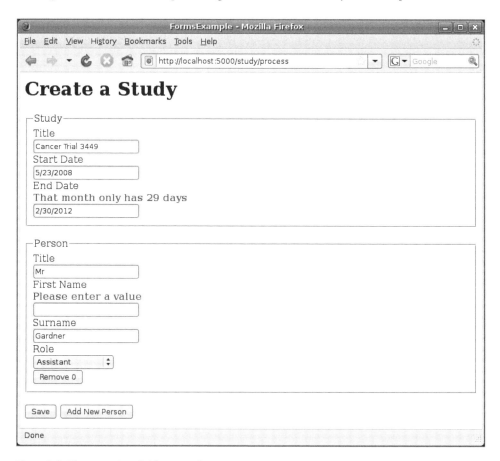

Figure 6-6. *The repeating fields example in action*

If you were to add some valid data, the result would be structured as shown here (although I've added some whitespace for clarity):

```
{
    'person': [
        {'surname': u'Gardner', 'role': u'2', 'firstname': u'James', 'title': u'Mr'}
    ],
    'start_date': datetime.date(2008, 5, 23),
    'end_date': datetime.date(2012, 2, 3),
    'title': u'Cancer Trial 3449'
}
```

Summary

Form handling can be a complex area, but in this chapter you learned the key principles involved in creating HTML forms, populating fields, validating complex data structures, and displaying error messages. By dealing with these processes individually, Pylons gives you the flexibility to create any sorts of forms your application needs.

In Chapter 15, you'll revisit forms and see how you can use Ajax to make certain aspects of form handling slicker.

■ ■ ■

# CHAPTER 7

Introducing the Model and SQLAlchemy

When people think about a model layer, they often immediately think of using a relational database management system (RDBMS) such as PostgreSQL or MySQL. In fact, there are many different ways to store your data in a Pylons application, so there are many different ways to model that data. It is important to decide on the correct approach for your particular needs. Some approaches might include these:

- Storing data in files in the filesystem
- Storing data via a web service such as Amazon S3
- Storing data in an object database
- Storing data in an XML database
- Storing data in an RDBMS

Pylons supports all of these approaches, but each has its advantages and disadvantages. If you are heavily relying on XML data, then an XML database makes sense. If you want to be able to manipulate and store Python objects that don't need to be indexed quickly, an object database might suit your needs. If you are storing lots of binary data such as photographs or videos that don't need to be searchable, you might store them in a third-party storage solution such as Amazon S3. And if you have large amounts of related data that needs to be quickly indexed, an RDBMS might be best.

In this chapter, I'll cover these different approaches to storing information and then give you an in-depth look at how to use RDBMSs with SQLAlchemy in Pylons.

Storing Data in the Filesystem

There isn't a great deal of point in storing data types such as photos, videos, and other binary data in a database because they take up a lot of space, which will slow down queries. It is much better to store binary data on the filesystem and store only key properties such as the filename or the creation date in a database.

You might be tempted to store your application's data in your project's data directory since it is already present and can be customized in your application's config file. The disadvantage is that because it is already used to store temporary session, cache, and template information, other Pylons developers working on your project might be used to deleting it when they want to clear this temporary information. To avoid this problem, it is better to keep the data directory for cached information and to add a new directory for your user's data. Let's call ours attachments, but the location will be customizable in the config file too.

You could write code like this to load one of the files in this directory:

```
import os
from pylons import config

def load_file(filename):
    path = os.path.join(config['app_conf']['attachments'], filename)
    fp = open(path, 'rb')
    data = fp.read()
    fp.close()
    return data
```

You can save a file to the directory with a function like this:

```
def save_file(filename, data):
    path = os.path.join(config['app_conf']['attachments'], filename)
    fp = open(path, 'wb')
    fp.write(data)
    fp.close()
```

You can list all the files like this:

```
def list_files():
    path = os.path.join(config['app_conf']['attachments'])
    return os.listdir(path)
```

For this example, you'll need to add a new variable in your project config file's [app:main] section:

```
# You could customize this to specify something like /var/lib/myapp/attachments
# if you prefer
attachments = %(here)s/attachments
```

Each Pylons project has a model directory, which is where code for interacting with the application's data should be stored so you can define the previous functions in model/__init__.py, for example.

You can get information about a particular file like this:

```
path = os.path.join(config['app_conf']['attachments'], filename)
size = os.path.getsize(path)
```

The os.path module documented at http://docs.python.org/lib/module-os.path.html has other similar methods for accessing other information about files such as getmtime(path), which returns the modification time.

For additional filesystem information, see the os.stat() function, which returns an object whose attributes correspond to the members of the stat structure, namely, st_mode (protection bits), st_ino (inode number), st_dev (device), st_nlink (number of hard links), st_uid (user ID of owner), st_gid (group ID of owner), st_size (size of file, in bytes), st_atime (time of most recent access), st_mtime (time of most recent content modification), and st_ctime (platform dependent; time of most recent metadata change on Unix or the time of creation on Windows). It can be used in two ways, as described in the module documentation at http://docs.python.org/lib/os-file-dir.html:

```
>>> import os
>>> statinfo = os.stat('somefile.txt')
>>> statinfo
(33188, 422511L, 769L, 1, 1032, 100, 926L, 1105022698,1105022732, 1105022732)
>>> statinfo.st_size
926L
>>> statinfo[7]
1105022698
```

You might want to turn the access and modification times into Python datetime objects and then format them in a different way:

```
>>> import datetime, time
>>> modified = datetime.datetime.fromtimestamp(statinfo[7])
>>> modified
datetime.datetime(2005, 1, 6, 14, 44, 58)
>>> modified.strftime("%Y-%m-%dT%H:%M:%S")
'2005-01-06T14:44:58'
```

It is sometimes useful to express in words when something happens. You can do so like this using the time_ago_in_words() function included with WebHelpers:

```
>>> from webhelpers.date import time_ago_in_words
>>> time_ago_in_words(modified)
'over 2 years'
```

It is also useful to express a file size in human-readable terms. Here's a helper that does just that, which you can add to your project's lib/helpers.py file and use as h.size_to_human():

```
def size_to_human(size, unit=1024, round=True):
    unit_name = 'bytes'
    size=int(size)
    if size > unit:
        size = size/float(unit)
        unit_name = 'KB'
    if size > unit:
        size = size/float(unit)
        unit_name = 'MB'
    if size > unit:
        size = size/float(unit)
        unit_name = 'GB'
    size = str(size)
    if round:
        if len(size)>4:
            size = "%d" % float(size)
    return size+' '+unit_name
```

Here is some further reading on filesystem use:

- http://docs.python.org/lib/bltin-file-objects.html

- http://docs.python.org/lib/os-file-dir.html

- http://docs.python.org/lib/module-shutil.html

The shutil module's copytree() function can be particularly useful on occasion.

Storing Data in Amazon S3

If you are building a web application to store very large amounts of information, it is possible that you might prefer to use a third-party storage service to look after your data rather than using your own hard disk space. Amazon S3 is one such service, but there are many others, including CacheFly. The basic principle of these services is that you pay for the bandwidth and storage used. If you have a startup and can't predict in advance how popular it will be, you may struggle to predict how many servers you will need for storage. By using a third-party service, the storage problem is largely solved because you can just order more storage without needing to buy any more machines.

Amazon S3 works via an XML web services API, but a number of Python libraries provide a Python interface to these services. Here's how you would upload and retrieve a file from Amazon S3 using a package called `boto` from `http://code.google.com/b/boto`:

```
from boto.s3.connection import S3Connection
from boto.s3.key import Key
conn = S3Connection('<aws access key>', '<aws secret key>')
bucket = conn.create_bucket('pylonsbook')
k = Key(bucket)
k.key = 'foobar'
k.set_contents_from_filename('foo.png')
k.get_contents_to_filename('bar.png')
```

In S3, bucket names are not unique to individual users, so you will have to find a bucket name that hasn't yet been used rather than using `pylonsbook`. You can install `boto` using Easy Install like this:

```
$ easy_install "boto==1.4c"
```

Once the file is uploaded, your users will be able to access it directly without you needing to download it again every time it is requested, because it has a publicly accessible URL. You can visit a file uploaded with the previous code at `http://s3.amazonaws.com/pylonsbook/foobar`.

Amazon S3 also allows you to store metadata about files you upload. As long as you don't need to be able to search this metadata, you might find Amazon S3 provides all the tools you need for your particular application. Here's how you would set some metadata associated with the file:

```
k.set_metadata('meta1', 'This is the first metadata value')
k.set_metadata('meta2', 'This is the second metadata value')
```

This code associates two metadata key/value pairs with the key `k`. To retrieve those values later, you'd use this code:

```
>>> k.get_metadata('meta1')
'This is the first metadata value'
>>> k.get_metadata('meta2')
'This is the second metadata value'
```

Tip To test this example, you would need to sign up for an Amazon web services account and replace the example values `<aws access key>` and `<aws secret key>` with your real Amazon keys. You will be charged for any data you store on Amazon, although for a simple test like this, the charge is very low. Just remember to delete your data if you don't want to be continually charged for its storage each month.

Exploring Database Approaches

Storing data structures in files or via third-party storage solutions clearly isn't the right approach for all data storage needs. Often the key requirement is to be able to search or select related sets of information. In that case, a database is a sensible way to go.

I'll discuss the different types of databases you can use in your Pylons application.

Object Databases

If most of the data in your Pylons applications is in the form of classes, one very sensible way of storing that data is in an *object database*. An object database looks like a Python dictionary that is automatically saved to disk. You can store strings, numbers, dates, class instances, or even nested dictionaries and lists to create arbitrarily deep data structures. Compared to a regular Python dictionary, you have to call a few extra commands to open the database and commit changes, but reading/setting values works exactly like the normal Python operations. This avoids the complexity of converting a Python data structure to a non-Python medium (XML or RDBMS tables), and it allows you to quickly prototype a model because you can easily change and extend it.

Two object databases are available for Python: Durus and ZODB. Durus is smaller and simpler, while ZODB is the database used in large Zope applications. Durus is recommended only for databases with fewer than 1 million records.

Durus and ZODB can store only "pickleable" data types, in other words, those that can be serialized with Python's `pickle` module. This includes all the standard data types including lists and dictionaries and instances of classes defined at the top level of their module. It does not include objects tied to external resources (an open file object or a database connection) or classes defined inside another class or inside a function. The Python standard library lists exactly which types can be pickled; see `http://docs.python.org/lib/node317.html`. Some users choose to store only built-in Python types (for example, dicts instead of class instances) to guarantee the data can always be unpickled on any Python system.

Both Durus and ZODB have a "persistent" class. Any object subclassing this will be saved and loaded separately rather than with its parent object.

The main disadvantage of object databases is that all searching is done in Python code, in `for` loops you write, while an RDBMS such as PostgreSQL has heavily optimized C routines for searching very quickly and with low memory overhead. Depending on the nature of your data and the types of searches you do, an RDBMS may or may not have a significant performance advantage. If you are considering using an object database, you should weigh this against the programming convenience of using the familiar and flexible Python types an object database provides.

Some users unfamiliar with object databases wonder how stable they are. Of course, this is a question you should ask about any database engine before trusting your data to it. Durus and ZODB use an append-only strategy with a simple filesystem layout to minimize the possibility of errors. Rather than overwriting objects, new versions are simply appended to the end of the file, and the old versions are abandoned. Backing up the data is a simple matter of copying the file. If the latest transaction at the end of the file gets corrupted or incompletely written, Durus and ZODB will simply truncate the file to return to the state that existed before the last transaction. Periodically the administrator runs a "pack" operation to rewrite the file without the abandoned sections, shrinking the file size.

Since the majority of Pylons developers use an RDBMS for their model, documentation on using ZODB or Durus is very thin. If an object database is an approach you'd like to consider, then these links might help:

Durus: `http://www.mems-exchange.org/software/durus/`, `http://sluggo.scrapping.cc/python/pylons/pylons-durus.html`

ZODB: `http://pypi.python.org/pypi/ZODB3`, `http://en.wikipedia.org/wiki/ZODB` (links to tutorials)

XML Databases

XML databases use XML documents as the unit of data they store and manipulate. If your Pylons application uses a lot of XML, it might make sense to store that information directly as XML in an

XML database rather than storing it in another type of database. The following are the advantages of this approach:

- You don't need to do any conversion between the data store and the document format your application uses.

- You can use query languages such as XPath and XQuery to quickly perform searches on documents in an optimized way.

Two XML databases you can use with Pylons are eXist and Berkeley DB XML:

eXist XML database (`http://exist.sourceforge.net/`): The eXist server is written in Java but has XML-RPC and REST-style HTTP APIs that can be used from a Pylons application. Some parts of the main `pylonshq.com` web site currently use an eXist back end.

Oracle Berkeley DB XML (`http://www.oracle.com/database/berkeley-db/xml/index.html`): This is an open source, embeddable XML database with XQuery-based access to documents stored in containers. DB XML has a Python binding that could be used to integrate it into a Pylons application. One thing to be aware of with DB XML is that the license would require that your Pylons application be released under the source license too unless you bought a commercial license from Oracle.

Relational Database Management Systems

Despite the advantages of object databases and XML databases for certain situations, the vast majority of people choose to use an RDBMS for the data persistence layer of their applications. Most of the time when people refer to a database, they mean an RDBMS such as MySQL, PostgreSQL, and many others. In the relational model, data and relationships can be represented in tables, rows, and columns that are defined and manipulated using a special language called Structured Query Language (SQL; pronounced "sequel").

RDBMSs can be used in small, personal applications or in huge, multinational projects. Although the basic principles of how to use an RDBMS remain broadly the same in both cases, you will need a much greater understanding of how relational database management systems actually work in order to use them effectively in larger-scale projects because issues such as replication, failover, and partitioning become more important. These topics are beyond the scope of this book, but if you are interested, plenty of information is available online and in specialist books.

Object-Relational Mappers

Object-relational mappers (ORMs) are tools that map the data structures in your database, namely, the rows in each table to objects in your Pylons application. As you manipulate the objects in the application, they automatically generate the SQL necessary to manipulate the underlying data.

Using an object-relational mapper has a number of advantages:

- They make it much easier and more convenient to work with the underlying data.

- Your Pylons application will work on any of the database engines supported by the object-relational mapper you use.

- They usually deal with some of the complications such as connection pools and thread safety for you.

- They're often easier to learn for newcomers than learning SQL.

Although object-relational mappers have major advantages, they are not without their weaknesses:

- By abstracting away the SQL, you generally have less control over the database than you would have had. Tools such as SQLAlchemy make up for this by also providing you with raw SQL access for the occasions when it is needed.

- If you don't understand how object-relational mappers work, it is easy to write inefficient code that requires many SQL statements to be executed. (Careful reading of this chapter should prevent that problem, though.)

- Object-relational mappers can sometimes contain quite complex code that is necessary to make the interfaces they expose so easy to use. This means that if you run into a problem, it can be hard to track it down in the source code. By choosing a popular ORM such as SQLAlchemy, the chances are that there are a very few bugs, and any you find are likely to be dealt with quickly by the community.

Overall then, the benefits of object-relational mappers outweigh their disadvantages for the vast majority of Pylons developers.

Quite a few object-relational mappers are available for Python:

- SQLAlchemy (http://sqlalchemy.org) is a modern object-relational mapper and Python SQL toolkit with powerful features, excellent documentation and support, and a full-featured API. It provides a full suite of well-known enterprise-level persistence patterns, is designed for efficient and high-performing database access and exposes a simple and Pythonic API.

- Storm (https://storm.canonical.com/) is a new object-relational mapper from Canonical, the company behind Ubuntu Linux. It is simpler than SQLAlchemy with thorough unit tests. Storm is particularly designed to feel very natural to Python programmers and exposes multiple databases as stores in a clean and easy-to-use fashion.

- SQLObject (http://sqlobject.org) is a popular object-relational mapper for providing an object interface to your database, with tables as classes, rows as instances, and columns as attributes. SQLObject is fairly old now, and although it is still used in TurboGears 1 and some other older frameworks, most users now choose SQLAlchemy instead.

By far the most popular tool for use as a model in a Pylons application is SQLAlchemy, and with good reason. It is a very powerful tool that handles the vast majority of cases you are ever likely to need, has a large and helpful community behind it, and has extensive and accurate documentation. That's not to say it is always the right tool for the job, and as you've seen so far in this chapter, Pylons is flexible enough to work with many different tools as a model. For the majority of cases, SQLAlchemy is a really good choice.

Setting Up SQLAlchemy

In this section, you'll look at everything you need to install and set up in order to use SQLAlchemy.

SQLAlchemy relies on various DB-API 2.0 drivers to handle the actual connections to the RDBMS software. Before you can use SQLAlchemy in earnest, you need to download and install the DB-API 2.0 driver for the RDBMS software you want to use. Not all RDBMSs have a Python DB-API 2.0 driver, and not all Python DB-API drivers can be used with SQLAlchemy.

Table 7-1 outlines the major RDBMSs used by Pylons developers and the Python driver you need in order to be able to use them from Pylons. Other drivers are available for these RDBMSs, but at the time of writing, these are the drivers supported by SQLAlchemy.

It is worth noting that if you are using Python 2.5 or newer, you don't need to install `pysqlite`, because it is already included as part of the Python standard library.

Table 7-1. *Popular RDBMSs and the Corresponding DB-API Drivers*

RDBMS Engine	Python DB-API 2.0 Driver
PostgreSQL `http://postgreql.org`	`psycopg2` `http://initd.org/projects/psycopg2`
MySQL `http://mysql.org`	`MySQLdb` module packaged as `mysql-python` `http://sourceforge.net/projects/mysql-python`
SQLite `http://sqlite.org`	`pysqlite` `http://initd.org/tracker/pysqlite`
Oracle `http://www.oracle.com/technology/products/database/oracle10g/index.html`	`cx_Oracle` `http://www.python.net/crew/atuining/cx_Oracle/`
Microsoft SQL Server `http://microsoft.com/sql/default.aspx`	`pyodbc` (recommended), `adodbapi`, or `pymssql` `http://pyodbc.sourceforge.net/`
Firebird `http://www.firebirdsql.org/`	`kinterbasdb` `http://kinterbasdb.sourceforge.net/`
Informix `http://www.ibm.com/software/data/informix/`	`informixdb` `http://informixdb.sourceforge.net/`

If you are just looking to get started quickly, SQLite is a good choice. You can download the latest SQLite 3 binary for your platform from `http://www.sqlite.org/download.html`. Once you have installed it, you will be able to run the `sqlite3` command to get an interactive prompt:

```
$ sqlite3
SQLite version 3.4.0
Enter ".help" for instructions
sqlite>
```

You can type `.help` for help or `.quit` to quit.

I'll use SQLite for the examples because it is so easy to set up, but you could equally well use any of the systems in Table 7-1. SQLite also has the advantage that the Python modules it needs are already included with Python 2.5 and newer.

Installing the DB-API Driver

Once you have installed, configured, and started the RDBMS you want to use, you need to install the appropriate DB-API 2.0 driver. In the case of SQLite, this is very easy because the software is automatically included with Python 2.5 or newer. If you are using Python 2.4 or older, you will need to install the driver in the same way you would for any RDBMS.

The driver you will need for your RDBMS is listed in Table 7-1 along with the URL where you can obtain it. Most Pylons-related software is available on the Python Package Index and can be installed with the `easy_install` command, but if you are not running on Windows, it is usually necessary to have a build environment set up with the Python development package and appropriate client library for the RDBMS you want to use already installed so that `easy_install` can compile the C or C++ libraries it needs to compile. For example, with MySQL, you might run this:

```
$ easy_install mysql-python
```

This would download the source for the `MySQLdb` module (this is a rare example when the package name is significantly different from the module name) and compile it. To compile it successfully, you will need the client library. For example, on Debian Etch, you would need to install the `libmysqlclient15-dev` package and the `python-dev` package.

Most commonly used software that isn't on the Python Package Index will be available through your platform's software repository. For example, versions of `MySQLdb` are available for Windows that you can install with its installer, and `MySQLdb` is available through the repositories for Debian, Ubuntu, Fedora, and other platforms. Mac OS X users can typically download a binary for the version of their operating system too.

If you are compiling a driver from source, it is always a good idea to read the software's `README` or `INSTALL` files and to follow the instructions carefully. Bear in mind that you might need to use an older compiler than the one that comes with your platform.

Although installing a Python database driver sounds like it might be difficult, in practice it is normally easy because you can usually find a binary version.

If you are following along using SQLite and are using Python 2.4 or older, let's install `pysqlite2`:

```
$ easy_install pysqlite
```

This installs the `pysqlite2` module to use in your application, but note that the package name is `pysqlite` even though you need to import `pysqlite2` to use the module.

Installing SQLAlchemy

Installing SQLAlchemy is easy. You simply specify the version you require with Easy Install, and it will be downloaded and installed for you. At the time of this writing, the latest version is 0.5, so the examples in this book are likely to work with any version above 0.5 and below 0.6. It is always wise to read the release notes for each new version, though:

```
$ easy_install "SQLAlchemy>=0.5,<=0.5.99"
```

If you want to ensure that your application uses only the version of SQLAlchemy you tested your application on, you should specify the version explicitly:

```
$ easy_install "SQLAlchemy==0.5.0"
```

Creating a Database

Now that you have the RDBMS software up and running, an appropriate DB-API driver, and SQLAlchemy itself, you will want to create a database.

Creating a database on the command line with SQLite is a simply a matter of connecting to it. The database is created if it doesn't already exist:

```
$ sqlite3 test.db
```

You don't actually need to create a database on the command line with SQLlite because a database will automatically be created for you when you connect from SQLAlchemy.

With other databases, things are a little more complex. PostgreSQL uses the `createdb` command, and MySQL uses a `CREATE DATABASE` SQL statement. Refer to your RDBMS documentation for the correct approach.

With everything in place, let's take a look at SQLAlchemy's architecture.

Exploring SQLAlchemy's Architecture

SQLAlchemy's architecture contains a complete set of APIs, each representing one aspect of what is actually going on. Conceptually you can think of these APIs in three layers, each building on top of the previous one:

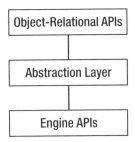

The abstraction layer consists of the SQL Expression API and the Metadata and Type APIs, which help isolate your Python code from the details of the underlying database engine. SQLAlchemy also includes a Declarative API, which you'll learn about later in this chapter.

You'll learn about each of these components in this chapter and see many of the key ways in which they are used.

Engine API

The lowest-level API you are likely to use is the Engine API. This represents a low-level abstraction of a database engine, allowing you to use the same API to create connections to different RDBMSs for sending SQL statements and for retrieving results.

In this section, I'll show an example of how you might use an engine to directly execute some SQL. Let's test this example using SQLite. Create a file called engine_test.py with the following content:

```
from sqlalchemy.engine import import create_engine

engine = create_engine('sqlite:///:memory:')
connection = engine.connect()
connection.execute(
    """
    CREATE TABLE users (
        username VARCHAR PRIMARY KEY,
        password VARCHAR NOT NULL
    );
    """
)
connection.execute(
    """
    INSERT INTO users (username, password) VALUES (?, ?);
    """,
    "foo", "bar"
)
result = connection.execute("select username from users")
for row in result:
    print "username:", row['username']
connection.close()
```

To work with an engine, you need to have a connection to it. The connection in the example is an instance of a SQLAlchemy Connection object, and result is a SQLAlchemy ResultProxy object (very much like a DB-API cursor) that allows you to iterate over the results of the statement you have executed.

If you run this example, you'll see the following output:

```
username: foo
```

When using `create_engine()`, you can specify different data source names (DSNs) to connect to different databases. For example, with SQLite, you can use `sqlite:///relative/path` to specify a file relative to the current working directory. You can use `sqlite:////absolute/path` to specify an absolute path. SQLite also has a memory mode that doesn't use the filesystem at all and loses all its information when the program exits. This can be very useful for testing. To use it, specify `sqlite:///:memory:` as the argument to `create_engine()`. The `create_engine()` function can also be used in a similar way with other RDBMSs. For example, to connect to the database `my_database` on a MySQL server at `some.domain.com` with the username `foo` and the password `bar`, you could use `mysql://foo:bar@some.domain.com/my_database`.

You'll also notice that the values you inserted were passed as separate arguments to `connection.execute()` rather than as part of the SQL string. This is so that the values can be automatically encoded to the correct SQL types, which helps avoid the risk of *SQL injection attacks*, something you'll learn more about later in the chapter.

Notice also that you were able to access the username column using dictionary-like access to the `row` object. This is a feature of the SQLAlchemy `ResultProxy` object that was returned.

SQLAlchemy engines have a number of features over and above the Python DB-API connections you might be used to, not least the ability to automatically use pools of connections. Here's a representation of the structure:

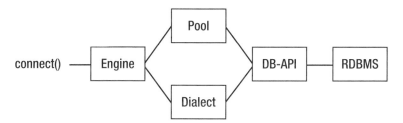

Let's look at each part of this diagram. You've already seen how to use a connection to execute SQL statements and retrieve results, and you've seen how to create an engine object to represent the particular database you want to connect to within the underlying RDBMS. You also know that SQLAlchemy uses the underlying DB-API 2.0 driver behind the scenes to communicate with the RDBMS, so let's look at dialects and pools.

Instances of `Dialect` objects tell SQLAlchemy how to deal with the subtleties of the different implementations of the DB-API 2.0 drivers to make some of SQLAlchemy's internal code a little simpler, but you wouldn't usually interact with them directly.

Pools, on the other hand, are more interesting. Aside from SQLite, most RDBMSs run as servers that the client connects to over a network. Each request that comes to the server and that needs to interact with a database will need its own database connection. Creating a connection can often be quite a costly exercise, and if you have a lot of requests, you will need to open and close lots of connections, which could impact the performance of your application. One solution to this problem is to have SQLAlchemy manage a pool of connections for you. When Pylons loads, SQLAlchemy can make a number of DB-API 2.0 connections to the underlying RDBMS and keep them open. When your application calls `engine.connect()` to obtain a connection, SQLAlchemy can return one of the connections from the pool rather than creating a new one. When you close the SQLAlchemy connection, it can return the DB-API connection to the pool ready to be used again the next time you call `engine.connect()`. This enables you to write your Pylons application in the same way you would if you were creating and closing lots of connections but have SQLAlchemy reuse connections from its internal pool.

You can configure pool options as arguments to the `create_engine()` function:

`pool_size`: The number of connections to keep open inside the connection pool.

`pool_recycle`: The length of time to keep connections open before recycling them. If not specified, the connections will stay open forever. This should be specified for MySQL in particular because servers typically close connections after eight hours, resulting in a "MySQL server has gone away" error.

`pool_timeout`: The number of seconds to wait before giving up on getting a connection from the pool.

Connection pools can quickly become quite complex, so if you are interested in using them, you should read the SQLAlchemy documentation for further information:

- `http://www.sqlalchemy.org/docs/05/dbengine.html#dbengine_options`
- `http://www.sqlalchemy.org/docs/05/pooling.html`

In the following sections, you'll learn about other APIs you can use with SQLAlchemy including the Metadata, SQL Expression, and Object-Relational APIs. These APIs abstract away the engine and connections so that you don't need to work with them directly. Behind the scenes, they will all use connections and engines to perform their work, so it is useful to understand how they work and, in particular, to know how to create engines with the appropriate options.

The flipside of this is that SQLAlchemy engines will work without any of the other SQLAlchemy infrastructure being in place so that even if you want to work directly with SQL rather than using the rest of SQLAlchemy's powerful feature set, it makes sense to use an SQLAlchemy connection rather than a DB-API connection so that you get all of SQLAlchemy's other benefits such as connection pools and result proxies.

You can find full information about engines and connections as well as threading implications in the excellent SQLAlchemy engine documentation at `http://www.sqlalchemy.org/docs/05/dbengine.html`.

Metadata and Type APIs

Now that you've seen how the Engine API has abstracted how SQL queries are executed and how results are returned, you can turn your attention to how SQLAlchemy abstracts the tables and other schema-level objects of the database itself. It does this with database *metadata*.

To represent the various different data types that table columns can store, SQLAlchemy uses its *types system*. Together the types system and metadata can completely describe the database schema in an RDBMS-independent manner.

The following is part of a table to store information about a page. Add this code to a new file called `metadata_test.py`.

```
from sqlalchemy import schema, types

metadata = schema.MetaData()

page_table = schema.Table('page', metadata,
    schema.Column('id', types.Integer, primary_key=True),
    schema.Column('name', types.Unicode(255), default=u''),
    schema.Column('title', types.Unicode(255), default=u'Untitled Page'),
    schema.Column('content', types.Text(), default=u''),
)
```

Here you've created a `metadata` object from `schema.MetaData`, which will hold all the information about the tables, columns, types, foreign keys, indexes, and sequences that make up the database structure. You'll see more about how these are used later in the chapter.

You've then created a `schema.Table` object to describe the `page` table and passed it the `metadata` object. This is so that the table object can add information about the table to the `metadata` object. SQLAlchemy is then able to access the table information via the `metadata` object. Add the following to the end of the `metadata_test.py` file too:

```
for t in metadata.sorted_tables
    print "Table name: ", t.name
    print "t is page_table: ", t is page_table
```

If you run this example, you will see the following output:

```
$ python metadata_test.py
Table name:  page
t is page_table: True
```

As you can see, the `metadata` object contains information about the tables, and the table object assigned to `t` in this example is the same as the `page_table` object.

Each of the columns that makes up the tables has its own type. SQLAlchemy supports the following built-in types:

- `String`
- `Unicode`
- `Text/UnicodeText`
- `Numeric`
- `Float`
- `Datetime/Date/Time`
- `Interval`
- `Binary`
- `Boolean`

In addition to the types listed here, there is a `PickleType` that is based on SQLAlchemy's `Binary` type. `PickleType` uses Python's `pickle.dumps()` to "pickle" objects being saved to the database, and it uses `pickle.loads()` to unpickle objects being retrieved. It therefore allows you to store any pickleable Python object as a serialized binary field. The same rules about which Python objects can be pickled apply whether you are using the `PickleType` field with SQLAlchemy or whether you are using an object database such as Durus or ZODB. Have a look at the Python documentation at `http://docs.python.org/lib/node317.html` for more information.

SQLAlchemy also supports some dialect-specific types to handle columns that occur only in particular databases. You can even create your own types if you need to do so. For full information, look at the SQLAlchemy types documentation at http://www.sqlalchemy.org/docs/05/types.html.

You can get information about the columns used in a table via the table's .columns attribute. Add the following to the end of the metadata_test.py example:

```
for column in page_table.columns:
    print "Column Table name: ", column.type
```

If you run it again, you'll see this output including the column information:

```
$ python metadata_test.py
Table name:  page
t is page_table: True
Column:  Integer()
Column:  Unicode(length=255)
Column:  Unicode(length=255)
Column:  Text(length=None, convert_unicode=False, assert_unicode=None)
```

At this stage, the metadata is just information; it doesn't relate to any properties of a real database. To connect the metadata to a real database, you need to bind the metadata object to an engine.

Add the following to the end of the metadata_test.py example:

```
from sqlalchemy.engine import create_engine

engine = create_engine('sqlite:///:memory:')
metadata.bind = engine
```

At this point, the metadata is connected to the database via the engine. Once again, I've chosen to use an in-memory SQLite database for the example, but you are free to use different parameters to create_engine() if you prefer.

■Tip It is worth being aware that you can have SQLAlchemy automatically convert all string types to handle Unicode automatically if you set up the engine like this:

```
create_engine('sqlite:///:memory:', convert_unicode=True)
```

In this book, you will instead use the Unicode type explicitly when you want to work with Unicode strings, but some Pylons developers prefer to take this shortcut.

SQLAlchemy now has enough information to allow you to start manipulating the database with the SQL Expression API, but the metadata object has a few more tricks. If the tables described by the metadata don't actually exist in the database, the metadata object can be used to create them. Add this line to the end of the metadata_test.py file:

```
metadata.create_all(checkfirst=True)
```

The checkfirst=True argument means it will create the table only if it doesn't already exist.

You'll notice that you didn't need a connection in order to create the tables. This is because the metadata object creates and closes a connection automatically from the engine.

If tables exist in the database that have not yet been defined in the metadata object, you can have SQLAlchemy automatically reflect the information like this:

```
comment_table = schema.Table('comment', metadata, autoload=True)
```

There are plenty of other things you can do to specify information about the schema. The following are all supported:

- Overriding some of the metadata for columns obtained by reflection
- Specifying the schema name for databases that support the concept of multiple schemas
- Cascading updates and deletes for databases supporting them
- Handling database-specific options such as MySQL's table back ends including `InnoDB` or `MyISAM`
- Default values
- Dropping tables
- Adding constraints, indexes, sequences, and more

These are all described in detail at `http://www.sqlalchemy.org/docs/05/metadata.html`.

SQL Expression API

Once you have set up all the database metadata, SQLAlchemy has all the information it needs for you to be able to use its SQL Expression API.

The SQL Expression API enables you to build SQL queries programmatically using Python objects and operators. This can take a lot of the pain out of SQL because you don't have to worry about converting Python values to safe SQL strings.

Let's create a new file called `sqlexpression_test.py` and add the following to it:

```
from metadata_test import engine, page_table
```

You can now use the `page` table to perform simple operations. Here's how you might perform a simple insert operation. Add the following to `sqlexpression_test.py` too:

```
print "\nSQL Expression Example\n"

connection = engine.connect()

ins = page_table.insert(
    values=dict(name=u'test', title=u'Test Page', content=u'Some content!')
)
print ins
result = connection.execute(ins)
print result

connection.close()
```

If you run this example, the output from `metadata_test.py` will be displayed first because you imported that file; then it will be followed by the output from `sqlexpression_test.py`, which looks like this:

```
SQL Expression Example

INSERT INTO page (name, title, content) VALUES (?, ?, ?)
<sqlalchemy.engine.base.ResultProxy object at 0x58c3f0>
```

The `ins` object automatically generates the correct SQL to insert the values specified, and an instance of a `ResultProxy` object (which you saw in the Engine API description) is returned to allow you to iterate over the results. Since this is an insert statement, there won't be any interesting values returned.

As an alternative, you could have written the same code like this:

```
print "\nSQL Expression Example\n"

ins = page_table.insert(
    values=dict(name=u'test', title=u'Test Page', content=u'Some content!')
)
print ins
result = ins.execute()
print result
```

In this case, the opening/closing of the connection is handled by the metadata object associated with the page_table object. It is usually better to execute SQL Expression objects like ins via connection.execute() so that you always know precisely which connection is being used. This becomes particularly important when you are using the Object-Relational API within Pylons with a scoped session when you probably want to use the connection used by the session rather than letting the metadata object create a connection for you. You'll see how this works in Chapter 8.

Note Because you are still using a SQLite in-memory database, each time this code is run, the database is created, the table is created, and the data is inserted. Once the code is executed, everything is lost so that when the code is run again, no errors occur. If you were to use a permanent database, you would need to drop the page table before rerunning the code.

SQL Injection Attacks

The most important point about the sqlexpression_test.py code is that SQLAlchemy handles any type conversion of the values you specified to insert() using its types system. This is important because if you build the SQL strings yourself using values that a user has submitted, there is a chance you might not perform the conversions quite correctly. This can expose your application to a particular type of attack called a *SQL injection attack*.

As an example, consider this action:

```
# This is really BAD, don't do it!
def create(self):
    name = request.params['name']
    title = request.params['title']
    sql = "INSERT INTO page (name, title) VALUES ('%s', '%s')" % (name, title)
    connection.execute(sql)
    return "Page added"
```

If the user submits the values NewPage for the name variable and New Page for the title, everything works perfectly well. An attacker might instead submit the values NewPage and New Page'); DROP TABLE page; --. At first sight this just looks very odd, but consider the SQL string your application now builds; it actually looks like this:

```
INSERT INTO page (name, title) VALUES ('NewPage', 'NewPage'); DROP TABLE page; --')
```

In SQL, -- comments out the rest of the line, so the following statements would be executed without a syntax error, dropping the page table and removing all its data:

```
INSERT INTO page (name, title) VALUES ('NewPage', 'NewPage');
DROP TABLE page;
```

This clearly isn't what you wanted, which is why it is so important to let SQLAlchemy handle conversions for you using the SQL Expression API rather than writing SQL strings yourself, because the variables would have been correctly escaped and the page would just have had a very odd-looking title.

Selecting Results

Here's a simple select statement that explicitly uses the connection object from the engine. Add it to the end of the `sqlexpression_test.py` file before the `connection.close()` line:

```
print "\nSelecting Results\n"

from sqlalchemy.sql import select

s = select([page_table])
result = connection.execute(s)
for row in result:
    print row
```

Before you test this example, it is useful to know about SQLAlchemy's `echo` option, which tells the `engine` object to log all the SQL it executes to `sys.stdout` so you can see what SQLAlchemy is doing behind the scenes. Edit `metadata_test.py`, and add `echo=True` to the `create_engine()` function so it looks like this:

```
engine = create_engine('sqlite:///:memory:', echo=True)
```

Now when you run the example, you'll be able to see the SQL `SELECT` statement SQLAlchemy will actually use without needing to manually add `print` statements. This can be useful when running test scripts to try different aspects of SQLAlchemy's functionality but shouldn't be enabled when you are using Pylons, because depending on the server and logging configuration you are using, it might result in messages going either to the error log or being sent to the browser. Instead, you can use Pylons' logging system to log SQLAlchemy messages in a much more structured way. This is described in Chapter 20.

If you run this example now, you will see the following at the end of the output:

```
Selecting Results

2008-09-04 16:01:22,294 INFO sqlalchemy.engine.base.Engine.0x..90➥
SELECT page.id, page.name, page.title, page.content
FROM page
2008-09-04 16:01:22,294 INFO sqlalchemy.engine.base.Engine.0x..90 []
(1, u'test', u'Test Page',  u'Some content!')
```

As you can see, this results in the SQL statement `SELECT page.id, page.name, page.title, page.content FROM page` being executed.

You can also specify `WHERE` clauses using a similar construct. For example, to specify pages that have an `id` greater than 1, you would write this:

```
s = select([page_table], page_table.columns.id>1)
result = connection.execute(s)
print result.fetchall()
```

You'll remember from the the "Metadata and Type APIs" section earlier in the chapter that table objects have a `.columns` attribute. The object returned contains a `Column` instance for each column in the table and these can be accessed as attributes based on the column name. In the example the id column can therefore be accessed as `page_table.columns.id`. SQLAlchemy knows how the standard Python operators should interact with the column objects to generate the appropriate SQL.

If you added this to the example, the extra output printed as a result of setting `echo=True` would be as follows:

```
2008-09-04 16:16:10,891 INFO sqlalchemy.engine.base.Engine.0x..b0➥
SELECT page.id, page.name, page.title, page.content
FROM page
WHERE page.id > ?
2008-09-04 16:16:10,891 INFO sqlalchemy.engine.base.Engine.0x..b0 [1]
[]
```

As you can see, the SQL `WHERE page.id > ?` has been added to the query, and the `[1]` shows that the value 1 will be substituted into the query in place of the `?` character to execute the correct query.

Once again, a `ResultProxy` object is returned, but this time you use its `fetchall()` method to return all the results in one go. Since there is only one page and its `id` is not greater than 1, there are no results, so an empty list is returned. The `ResultProxy` object also has `fetchone()` and `fetchmany()`, which are similar to their DB-API 2.0 counterparts.

If you have a complex `WHERE` clause, it can be cumbersome to keep typing `page_table.columns`, so SQLAlchemy also allows you to write `page_table.c`. The `.c` attribute is just an alias to the same object you access using `.columns` but is shorter to type.

SQLAlchemy overloads most of the Python operators for use in `WHERE` clauses so that they behave the way you would expect when used in SQL. You've seen how to use `>` in the previous example, but the operators `==`, `<`, `<=`, `>=`, and `!=` have similar results.

SQLAlchemy also provides operators for `AND`, `OR`, and `NOT` in the form of the Python operators `&`, `|`, and `!`. If you use these, you have to be careful to correctly add parentheses to all the expressions you are operating on because Python operator precedence is slightly different from that of SQL. Here's an example:

```
s = select([page_table], (page_table.c.id<=10) & (page_table.c.name.like(u't%')))
```

Notice that you were able to use a `LIKE` clause too as a method of the `name` column.

If you don't want to use the `&`, `|`, and `!` operators, SQLAlchemy also provides `and_()`, `or_()`, and `not_()` functions that you can use instead:

```
from sqlalchemy.sql import and_, or_, not_
s = select([page_table], and_(page_table.c.id<=10, page_table.c.name.like(u't%')))
result = connection.execute(s)
print result.fetchall()
```

This has the same effect. If you add this to the end of the `sqlexpression_test.py` file before `connection.close()` and run the program, the corresponding output is as follows:

```
2008-09-04 16:34:27,014 INFO sqlalchemy.engine.base.Engine.0x..b0➥
SELECT page.id, page.name, page.title, page.content
FROM page
WHERE page.id <= ? AND page.name LIKE ?
2008-09-04 16:34:27,015 INFO sqlalchemy.engine.base.Engine.0x..b0 [10, u'%t']
[(1, u'test', u'Test Page', u'Some content!')]
```

As you can see, the `WHERE` clause has been generated correctly, and this time the values 10 and t% replace the two question marks in the SQL query. This time the query results in the row being returned again.

One operator that behaves slightly differently from the others is the `+` operator. If `+` is operating on two strings, it generates the appropriate SQL for concatenation. If it operates on two integers, it produces the SQL to add them together:

```
>>> print page_table.c.name + user_table.c.title
page.name || user.title
>>> print page_table.c.id + comment_table.c.id
page.id + comment.id
```

The SQL builder assembles chunks of SQL, and printing them displays the SQL. Notice that it has correctly added the || operator, which causes the strings to be concatenated in most RDBMSs. MySQL is slightly different, though. It requires strings to be concatenated with the concat() function. SQLAlchemy even does the right thing with MySQL. On MySQL you get this:

```
>>> print page_table.c.name + user_table.c.title
concat(page.name, user.title)
```

Once you have generated a select object, you can still add extra clauses to it. For example, if you wanted to add an ORDER_BY clause, you could write this:

```
s = select([page_table], and_(page_table.c.id<=10, page_table.c.name.like(u't%')))
s = s.order_by(page_table.c.title.desc(), page_table.c.id)
```

This would run the same query as before but order by title descending and then by id.

You can write update statements like this:

```
print "\nUpdating Results\n"

from sqlalchemy import update

u = update(page_table, page_table.c.title==u'New Title')
connection.execute(u, title=u"Updated Title")
```

If you add the previous to the sqlexpressions_test.py file before connection.close() and execute it again, the corresponding UPDATE statement looks like this:

```
Updating Results

2008-09-04 17:00:58,673 INFO sqlalchemy.engine.base.Engine.0x..d0➥
UPDATE page SET title=? WHERE page.title = ?
2008-09-04 17:00:58,673 INFO sqlalchemy.engine.base.Engine.0x..d0➥
[u'Updated Title', u'New Title']
2008-09-04 17:00:58,674 INFO sqlalchemy.engine.base.Engine.0x..d0 COMMIT
```

Notice that SQLAlchemy automatically sent a COMMIT message to save the changes.

Finally, let's look at deleting rows. The pattern should be getting very familiar now. You can write delete statements like this:

```
print "\nDeleting Row\n"

from sqlalchemy import delete

d = delete(page_table, page_table.c.id==1)
connection.execute(d)
```

If you add the previous to the sqlexpressions_test.py file before connection.close() and execute it again, the corresponding DELETE statement looks like this:

Deleting Row

```
2008-09-04 17:04:34,460 INFO sqlalchemy.engine.base.Engine.0x..f0➥
DELETE FROM page WHERE page.id = ?
2008-09-04 17:04:34,460 INFO sqlalchemy.engine.base.Engine.0x..f0➥
[1]
2008-09-04 17:04:34,461 INFO sqlalchemy.engine.base.Engine.0x..f0➥
COMMIT
```

The important thing to note about all these examples is that the code you write with the SQL Expression API will have the same effect on any of the RDBMSs that SQLAlchemy supports without you having to change any of your code. The only thing you need to change is the URI string to the create_engine() function. This automatic abstraction is a huge advantage if you are trying to write Pylons applications to work on multiple database back ends.

This has been a taste of the SQL Expression API, but there is a lot more too. It is extremely powerful, allowing you to do complex joins, aliases, group bys, functions, unions, other set operations and more, all through natural-feeling Python code based on information defined through the metadata in your tables and columns.

Once again, the SQLAlchemy documentation is the best place to go to learn about all the features: http://www.sqlalchemy.org/docs/05/sqlexpression.html

Exploring the Object-Relational API

The highest-level API SQLAlchemy provides is the Object-Relational API, which is the one you will spend the majority of your time using in your Pylons applications. The API allows you to work directly with Python objects without needing to think too much about the SQL that would normally be required to work with them.

Before you learn about the details of how the API works, I'll cover some key concepts about relational databases.

Object-Relational Principles

As you learned earlier in the chapter, object-relational mappers (ORMs) map rows from tables in relational databases to the objects used in your Pylons application.

The difficulty is that Python objects don't always easily map to rows in tables. Before you look at SQLAlchemy's Object-Relational API, let's take a few moments for a very quick overview of the core ideas of relational databases that you need to know to use SQLAlchemy effectively.

Let's consider a wiki application that allows the creation of pages, has a comments system, and allows pages to be tagged. Each of the items mentioned in the previous sentence are known as *entities* in relational database terminology. They are the main things that exist in the real world. Ordinarily, each entity in the real world is represented by a table in the database, and each row in the table represents one instance of the entity. In our example, you would therefore need three tables: page, comment, and tag.

Each row in each of the tables must have something unique about it that differentiates it from other rows in the table. In the case of wiki pages, this might be the page title or the URL of the page. A unique identifier of this type is called the *primary key* of the table. In the case of a wiki, you might choose to the use the page title as the primary key if each page title is different. This could cause a problem if the page title was able to change. To avoid this problem, all modern databases can assign an ID to a row automatically when the row is inserted into the table. By using an automatically assigned ID, you can be sure that all rows in a table have a different ID and that if any of the other properties change, the record will still be able to be accessed via a primary key lookup.

If you are designing a database structure for use with SQLAlchemy, it is a good idea to add an id column to each table as a primary key. The rest of the examples in this book will use this approach.

Once the primary entities have been represented in tables with each row having a primary key, you need to think about how the different entities are related. There are three common ways they might be related:

One to one: Data items in two tables both represent the same entity; it is just that you have chosen to store the fields in different tables. Most of the time, you will avoid one-to-one relationships because they are an indication that you might not have properly understood the key entities in your data structure.

One to many: One entity has zero or more instances of another entity associated with it.

Many to many: Zero or more instances of one entity are associated with zero or more instances of another entity.

Thinking about entities and mappings can be a bit abstract, so I'll show a wiki comments system as a concrete example.

Each wiki page can have lots of different comments, but the same comment won't appear on more than one page. This means there is a one-to-many mapping between pages and comments.

The best way to represent a one-to-many mapping is by adding what is known as a *foreign key* to the comments table to store the id of the page to which the comment has been added. An appropriate name for the column to hold the foreign key might be pageid. This means that to find all the comments on, say, page 5, you would select all the comments in the comments table where pageid is 5.

So far so good. Now let's think about the tags that are a little more complicated. Once again, pages can have multiple tags, but this time the same tag can also be used on multiple pages. You have a many-to-many relationship. This time the relationship can't be modeled by adding a foreign key to the tag table because although this would allow you to work out the tags used on a particular page, it wouldn't allow you to work out which pages used a particular tag unless you had duplicate tags in the tags table.

Creating duplicates of primary entities is often bad practice, so the only way to model the relationship between tags and pages is with a third table. We'll call it pagetag. The pagetag table will have three columns, a foreign key to the page table, a foreign key to the tag table, and a primary key of its own. Here's an example of the data the tables might contain:

page table

```
+-----+------------------+------------+---------------+
| id  | content          | posted     | title         |
+-----+------------------+------------+---------------+
| 1   | When I was...    | 2007-05-08 | The Other Day |
| 2   | Databases are... | 2007-07-13 | Databases     |
+-----+------------------+------------+---------------+
```

tag table

```
+-----+------------+------------+
| id  | name       | created    |
+-----+------------+------------+
| 1   | databases  | 2007-07-13 |
| 2   | life       | 2007-03-10 |
| 3   | fun        | 2007-04-28 |
| 4   | news       | 2008-03-30 |
+-----+------------+------------+
```

```
pagetag table
+-----+-------+----------+
| id  | tagid | pageid   |
+-----+-------+----------+
| 1   | 1     | 2        |
| 2   | 2     | 1        |
| 3   | 3     | 1        |
| 4   | 3     | 2        |
+-----+-------+----------+
```

In this example, the tags databases and fun are associated with page 2, and life and fun are associated with page 1. Looking at the same data from the tags perspective, you can see that the fun tag is used on two pages, whereas the others are only associated with one page each. You can also see that the news tag hasn't been used on any pages yet.

To find out the tag names associated with page 2, you would use a SQL JOIN to find all the rows in the pagetag table with a pageid of 2 and then use the corresponding tagid to look up the name of the tag from the tag ID.

Writing SQL joins of this type isn't complicated, but it can be time-consuming. Wouldn't it be nice if you could just have a page object and get the tag names like this?

```
for tag in page.tags:
    print tag.name
```

This is precisely what you can do with SQLAlchemy's Object-Relational API. In the next sections, you'll look at how to set up the table, class, and mapper objects necessary to make this sort of API access possible.

More Metadata

The first step toward setting up the Object-Relational API is to describe the database metadata. The Object-Relational API and the SQL expression language described earlier both use the same metadata. After all, both need to know how the database is structured in order to work. Let's see how you would model the tables described earlier for the wiki system. Save the following in a file called model.py:

```
import datetime
from sqlalchemy import schema, types

metadata = schema.MetaData()

def now():
    return datetime.datetime.now()

page_table = schema.Table('page', metadata,
    schema.Column('id', types.Integer,
        schema.Sequence('page_seq_id', optional=True), primary_key=True),
    schema.Column('content', types.Text(), nullable=False),
    schema.Column('posted', types.DateTime(), default=now),
    schema.Column('title', types.Unicode(255), default=u'Untitled Page'),
    schema.Column('heading', types.Unicode(255)),
)
```

```
comment_table = schema.Table('comment', metadata,
    schema.Column('id', types.Integer,
        schema.Sequence('comment_seq_id', optional=True), primary_key=True),
    schema.Column('pageid', types.Integer,
        schema.ForeignKey('page.id'), nullable=False),
    schema.Column('content', types.Text(), default=u''),
    schema.Column('name', types.Unicode(255)),
    schema.Column('email', types.Unicode(255), nullable=False),
    schema.Column('created', types.TIMESTAMP(), default=now()),
)

pagetag_table = schema.Table('pagetag', metadata,
    schema.Column('id', types.Integer,
        schema.Sequence('pagetag_seq_id', optional=True), primary_key=True),
    schema.Column('pageid', types.Integer, schema.ForeignKey('page.id')),
    schema.Column('tagid', types.Integer, schema.ForeignKey('tag.id')),
)

tag_table = schema.Table('tag', metadata,
    schema.Column('id', types.Integer,
        schema.Sequence('tag_seq_id', optional=True), primary_key=True),
    schema.Column('name', types.Unicode(20), nullable=False, unique=True),
)
```

There are some features in this example you haven't seen before:

- The comment and pagetag tables use schema.ForeignKey() so that SQLAlchemy knows how the tables are related. Notice that the foreign keys are represented by a string in the format table.column

- The content column in the page table and the name column in the tag table are specified as nullable=false, which means SQLAlchemy will raise an exception if rows are inserted without values for those columns.

- The id columns are all specified with primary_key=True so that SQLAlchemy knows to treat those columns as primary keys.

- The primary key columns also specify an optional Sequence object. This allows SQLAlchemy to use sequences on databases that support them such as PostgreSQL and Oracle but to use autoincrementing fields on databases such as MySQL. If you haven't come across sequences before, they are a bit like separate tables that keep track of the next available ID for a table. You don't need to know about sequences to use SQLAlchemy; they are an advanced feature that SQLAlchemy can use if it is available, but your objects will behave in the same way whether or not sequences are used. See http://www.sqlalchemy.org/docs/05/documentation.html#metadata_defaults_sequences for more information.

- The DateTime columns all have a default value of now. This means that if a value isn't specified when a row is inserted, SQLAlchemy will call the now() function to generate a default value. The now() function is defined at the top and in turn uses the datetime module to get the current time. In this example, you could just have specified datetime.datetime.now as the default, but in other circumstances you will have to define your own function, so the example is written the way it is to demonstrate this.

- The tag table's name column uses unique=True to enforce the constraint that no two tags should have the same name.

It is worth noting that although database-level constraints are useful to ensure data integrity, your Pylons application should be validating data it passes to the database using FormEncode to ensure it doesn't break any database-level constraints. After all, an Internal Server Error page resulting from an exception raised by SQLAlchemy or the underlying engine won't help your users know what was wrong. You'll learn how to combine FormEncode and SQLAlchemy in a Pylons application in the next chapter.

Classes and Mappers

Now that you have defined the table structures, turn your attention to the classes and mappers. Here's what the Page class looks like; add it to the end of the model.py file:

```
class Page(object):
    pass
```

Similar classes would need to be created for comments and tags; add them to the end of model.py too:

```
class Comment(object):
    pass

class Tag(object):
    pass
```

■**Tip** Although I've chosen to create the classes you need without any extra methods, one popular way of setting up the classes is to have an __init__() method that takes arguments for each of the required fields in the table and sets them as class attributes. This setup helps you remember to always set all the required attributes because you can't create objects without them.

You might also like to add a customized __repr__() method to each of your classes that includes representations of key attributes such as the primary key. This can make it clearer which objects you are looking at if you interact with your model from the command line or via the Pylons interactive shell, which you'll see used for testing in Chapter 12 and used to interact with your model in Chapter 19.

So far, the Page class is still just a class and has nothing to do with the page table. To map the class to the table, you use a *mapper*. A simple mapper for Page might look like this (you'll need a more complex one, though):

```
orm.mapper(Page, page_table)
```

The mapper() function creates a new Mapper object and stores it away for future reference. It also adds the column names of the page table as attributes of the Page class so that class attributes correspond to table column names. SQLAlchemy keeps track of any changes to those attributes so the database can be automatically updated.

The Page class actually has a relationship to the comments table as well as the page table because pages can have multiple comments. You can specify this relationship like this:

```
orm.mapper(Page, page_table, properties={
    'comments':orm.relation(Comment, backref='page')
})
```

This tells SQLAlchemy that the Page class is mapped to the page_table table but that page objects should have an extra property called comments, which should return all the Comment objects related to that page when you read its .comments property. The relation() function also takes a backref argument, which means that all comment objects should also have a property named page that returns the page object to which a particular comment is related.

By using this single definition, you have therefore been able to define the relationship between pages and comments and also specify the properties on each, which will return instances of the other.

In fact, pages are related to tags as well as to comments, so you need a slightly more sophisticated call to orm.mapper().

Add this import to the top of the model.py file:

```
from sqlalchemy import orm
```

Add this version of the mapper code to the end of model.py:

```
orm.mapper(Page, page_table, properties={
    'comments':orm.relation(Comment, backref='page'),
    'tags':orm.relation(Tag, secondary=pagetag_table)
})
```

This is the same as the previous example but also specifies a tags property to relate the page to the tag objects associated with it. This call to relation() specifies a *secondary table*, pagetag_table, to be used to handle the many-to-many relationship between pages and tags. Once again, SQLAlchemy can work out the details from the metadata definitions of the tables and columns. All many-to-many relations should have the secondary argument to specify how the tables are related.

Now that you've mapped the Page class, let's look at the mappers for Tag and Comment. They look like this and are the last lines you'll need to add to model.py:

```
orm.mapper(Comment, comment_table)
orm.mapper(Tag, tag_table)
```

The mapper for Comment doesn't need the page property specified because the mapper for Page has already specified it via the backref. The mapper for Tag doesn't need to have the relation to Page specified because SQLAlchemy can already work it out via the secondary argument.

In this example, the Comment and Tag mappers actually need to be specified before the mapper for Page because the classes are used in the properties of the Page mapper. You sometimes have to think quite carefully about the order mappers are defined in order to be able to specify all the relationships correctly in Python code.

One point to note is that this setup doesn't provide a way to get a list of pages that share one tag because you haven't specified a backref on the tags property in the Page mapper, but you can always use a query if you need that information. When designing your mappers, there is a trade-off between adding relational structure to express an important structure or to simplify accessing data that is frequently used vs. the simplicity of using queries for things that might only occasionally be used.

Once again, SQLAlchemy has many more features than can be described here including lazy and eager loading, mapping to joins, and more. The SQLAlchemy documentation is very good and has all the details.

Tip When you are thinking about naming table columns, it is a strongly recommended that you don't start any of the column names with _. SQLAlchemy adds certain objects to mapped class instances, and each of these starts with _, so you won't want to create names that conflict with SQLAlchemy objects.

Understanding the Session

There is one problem I haven't discussed yet, and that is how SQLAlchemy manages objects in memory. After all, it wouldn't be efficient for it to contact the database every time you accessed an attribute of an object. SQLAlchemy handles this problem by keeping track of objects in memory in what it calls a *session*.

■**Caution** The SQLAlchemy session is completely unrelated to the Beaker session, which provides session management between requests using a cookie. It's unfortunate that two different pieces of software chose the term *session* to mean completely different things.

SQLAlchemy provides different configuration options for the session depending on the type of application you are writing. You can read all about the various options in the SQLAlchemy documentation, but in this section you'll use the same configuration options used by Pylons. You'll also use the model.py you've just created.

Create a new file called object_test.py in the same directory as model.py, and add the following content:

```
import model
from sqlalchemy import orm
from sqlalchemy import create_engine

# Create an engine and create all the tables we need
engine = create_engine('sqlite:///:memory:', echo=True)
model.metadata.bind = engine
model.metadata.create_all()

# Set up the session
sm = orm.sessionmaker(bind=engine, autoflush=True, autocommit=False,
    expire_on_commit=True)
session = orm.scoped_session(sm)
```

Let's look at this in detail. First you have a number of imports including the model module you created earlier. Next you create an engine as you've done before using the echo=True argument so that the SQL being generated behind the scenes gets output to the console (remember that you shouldn't use this argument in a Pylons application and instead should use the logging technique described in Chapter 20). Finally, you get into the interesting part and create the session itself.

In this example, the session is created in two parts. First you use a sessionmaker() function to return an object for building the particular type of session you want. To understand what the options mean, you need to know a little terminology. In SQLAlchemy, *flushing* is the process of updating the database with the changes made to the objects you have been working with, and *committing* is the process of sending a COMMIT statement to the database to make those flushes permanent. If you were to *roll back* some changes after they had been flushed but before the changes were committed, then the changes would be lost. With these definitions in mind, let's look at the arguments.

Let's look at the arguments being used:

bind=engine: This ensures that the session is bound to the same engine to which the metadata object is bound. The session will automatically create the connections it needs.

autoflush=True: If you commit your changes to the database before they have been flushed, this option tells SQLAlchemy to flush them for you before the commit goes ahead. This ensures changes aren't lost because you forgot to flush them.

`autocommit=False`: This tells SQLAlchemy to wrap all changes between commits in a transaction so that the commit and rollback behavior just described works correctly in RDBMSs that support this feature. If you specified `autocommit=True`, SQLAlchemy would automatically commit any changes after each flush, which normally isn't what you want. If a problem happens halfway through a Pylons request, it is usually important that all uncommitted changes made up to that point are not saved so that the database isn't left in a half-changed state. If you've used SQLAlchemy in earlier versions of Pylons such as 0.9.6, you may have noticed that the argument `transactional=True` was used. `autocommit=False` in SQLAlchemy 0.5 is the same as `transactional=True` in earlier versions, so the two arguments do the same thing.

`expire_on_commit=True`: This happens to be the default value anyway, but it means that all instances attached to the session will be fully expired after each commit so that all attribute/object access subsequent to a completed transaction will load from the most recent database state.

The second part of the session creation code is the call to `scoped_session()`. As you've already learned, Pylons is a multithreaded framework. If you were to use an ordinary SQLAlchemy session in Pylons, different requests would change the session at the same time, which would result in some users seeing other people's data, other users not seeing data they'd entered, and frequent application crashes. The `scoped_session()` object ensures that a different session is used for each thread so that every request can have its own access to the database. Although you don't need this to run the test examples in this chapter, you will need to understand it to work with SQLAlchemy in a Pylons application, so it is worth learning the details now.

Exploring the Session

Now that you've seen how the session is configured, let's run through some examples of how it is used and see the effects the configuration options chosen actually have. For this part of the chapter, I'll use an interactive Python prompt to execute commands so that you can see when SQLAlchemy actually generates the SQL. Start a prompt in the same directory where you've been writing the modules:

```
$ python
Python 2.5.1 (r251:54863, Apr 15 2008, 22:57:26)
[GCC 4.0.1 (Apple Inc. build 5465)] on darwin
Type "help", "copyright", "credits" or "license" for more information.
>>>
```

Now import the `session` object from the `object_test` module you just created:

```
>>> from object_test import session
```

A load of output will fly by as SQLAlchemy sets up the tables. Now let's start by importing the `model` module and creating a new page:

```
>>> import model
>>> test_page = model.Page()
>>> test_page.title = u'Test Page'
>>> test_page.content = u'Test content'
>>> test_page.title
u'Test Page'
```

The first step toward persisting the `test_page` object is adding it to the session so that SQLAlchemy is aware of it:

```
>>> session.add(test_page)
```

If you were creating lots of pages at once, you could use session.add_all([test_page1, test_page2, test_page3]) instead. SQLAlchemy 0.4 used session.save() instead but session.add() is the correct method to use for SQLAlchemy 0.5 and above.

At this stage, objects added to the session are still *pending*, and no SQL has been issued or echoed to the console. Let's see what happens when you access the test_page object's .id attribute:

```
>>> print test_page.id
None
```

As you can see, it returns None. You'll remember from the table definition that id is the page table's primary key column and that an id value is automatically assigned by the underlying RDBMS when the row is created. At this stage, although test_page has been added to the session, its data hasn't been sent to the underlying RDBMS. You can force this to happen by *flushing* the session. Once the session has been flushed, the SQL is sent, and SQLAlchemy finds out the id of the page:

```
>>> session.flush()
2008-09-04 20:53:55,191 INFO sqlalchemy.engine.base.Engine.0x..90 BEGIN
2008-09-04 20:53:55,193 INFO sqlalchemy.engine.base.Engine.0x..90➥
INSERT INTO page (content, posted, title, heading) VALUES (?, ?, ?, ?)
2008-09-04 20:53:55,194 INFO sqlalchemy.engine.base.Engine.0x..90➥
[u'Test content', '2008-09-04 20:53:55.193033', u'Test Page', None]
```

As you can see, SQLAlchemy has now sent the INSERT statement to the SQLite database, but the interesting thing is that it also sent the SQL keyword BEGIN before it sent the INSERT statement. This starts a transaction within the RDBMS so that any changes can still be rolled back until they are committed. It also means that the changes won't yet be visible to other users.

■**Caution** Some RDBMSs don't support transactions and therefore cannot roll back data or hide it from other users after it has been flushed. MySQL's default MyISAM tables don't support transactions, so if you need this functionality, you should use InnoDB tables instead. If you are using MySQL, you can specify this by adding mysql_engine='InnoDB' to your Table classes. See http://www.sqlalchemy.org/docs/05/documentation.html#metadata_tables_options for more information.

Let's see whether the test_page has an id now that the test page has been flushed:

```
>>> test_page.id
1
```

As you can see, id has now been assigned. Notice that SQLAlchemy didn't need to query the database again to tell you. Now let's commit the changes:

```
>>> session.commit()
2008-09-04 20:54:13,189 INFO sqlalchemy.engine.base.Engine.0x..90 COMMIT
```

SQLAlchemy sends the COMMIT statement that permanently commits the flushed changes and ends the transaction.

Let's access the test page's id again and see what happens:

```
>>> test_page.id
2008-09-04 21:08:19,024 INFO sqlalchemy.engine.base.Engine.0x..30 BEGIN
2008-09-04 21:08:19,027 INFO sqlalchemy.engine.base.Engine.0x..30
SELECT page.id AS page_id, page.content AS page_content, page.posted➥
AS page_posted, page.title AS page_title, page.heading AS page_heading
FROM page
WHERE page.id = ?
2008-09-04 21:08:19,027 INFO sqlalchemy.engine.base.Engine.0x..30 [1]
1
```

This time, SQLAlchemy reads the data from the database again. This might surprise you, but if you look back at the session creation code, you'll recall that the expire_on_commit option was set to True, causing SQLAlchemy to automatically expire all objects attached to the session. Notice that SQLAlchemy actually fetched all the attributes, not just the id. If you access the id or any of the page's other attributes, they will now be loaded from the session without access to the database:

```
>>> test_page.id
1
>>> test_page.title
u'Test Page'
```

The default values for the columns will also have been applied, so you can now also access the page's posted attribute:

```
>>> test_page.posted
datetime.datetime(2008, 9, 4, 21, 3, 34, 975799)
```

Let's now delete this object:

```
>>> session.delete(test_page)
```

Once again, no SQL is sent until you flush the session:

```
>>> session.flush()
008-09-04 21:39:13,247 INFO sqlalchemy.engine.base.Engine.0x..30 SELECT ➥
comment.id AS comment_id, comment.pageid AS comment_pageid,➥
comment.content AS comment_content, comment.name AS comment_name,➥
comment.email AS comment_email, comment.created AS comment_created➥
FROM comment
WHERE ? = comment.pageid
2008-09-04 21:39:13,248 INFO sqlalchemy.engine.base.Engine.0x..30 [1]
2008-09-04 21:39:13,255 INFO sqlalchemy.engine.base.Engine.0x..30➥
SELECT tag.id AS tag_id, tag.name AS tag_name
FROM tag, pagetag
WHERE ? = pagetag.pageid AND tag.id = pagetag.tagid
2008-09-04 21:39:13,255 INFO sqlalchemy.engine.base.Engine.0x..30 [1]
2008-09-04 21:39:13,258 INFO sqlalchemy.engine.base.Engine.0x..30
DELETE FROM page WHERE page.id = ?
2008-09-04 21:39:13,258 INFO sqlalchemy.engine.base.Engine.0x..30 [1]
```

As you can see, quite a few SQL statements are sent. SQLAlchemy is checking to ensure that there aren't any comments or tags associated with the page you are deleting.

At this stage, you could commit the changes, but this time let's try a rollback:

```
>>> session.rollback()
2008-09-04 21:41:42,989 INFO sqlalchemy.engine.base.Engine.0x..30 ROLLBACK
```

SQLAlchemy sends a ROLLBACK statement, causing the RDBMS to undo the changes. It is now as if the delete never happened. Once again, you can try to access the test page's id. Once again, SQLAlchemy fetches the data from the database because the old session was automatically expired after the rollback:

```
>>> test_page.id
2008-09-04 21:40:30,281 INFO sqlalchemy.engine.base.Engine.0x...55cc ➥
BEGIN
2008-09-04 21:40:30,282 INFO sqlalchemy.engine.base.Engine.0x...55cc ➥
SELECT page.id AS page_id, page.content AS page_content, page.posted AS ➥
page_posted, page.title AS page_title, page.heading AS page_heading
```

```
FROM page
WHERE page.id = ?
2008-09-04 21:40:30,283 INFO sqlalchemy.engine.base.Engine.0x...55cc [1]
1
```

As you can see, the page clearly still exists, so the rollback was successful. Of course, if you exit the Python interactive prompt, all the data will be lost because you are still using an in-memory database, so don't be surprised if the row is not there if you fire up another Python interactive shell.

You should now have a good understanding of the inner working of the session in the same configuration as you would find in a Pylons application, but there is one complication you haven't yet dealt with. How do you use the SQL Expression API in the same transaction as a particular session?

Start a new Python interactive prompt, and type the following to set up the tables and session and create a test_page object as before:

```
>>> from object_test import session
>>> import model
>>> test_page = model.Page()
>>> test_page.title = u'Test Page'
>>> test_page.content = u'Test content'
>>> session.add(test_page)
>>> session.flush()
2008-09-04 21:59:29,852 INFO sqlalchemy.engine.base.Engine.0x..30 BEGIN
2008-09-04 21:59:29,854 INFO sqlalchemy.engine.base.Engine.0x..30
INSERT INTO page (content, posted, title, heading) VALUES (?, ?, ?, ?)
2008-09-04 21:59:29,855 INFO sqlalchemy.engine.base.Engine.0x..30
[u'Test content', '2008-09-04 21:59:29.854464', u'Test Page', None]
```

I've already discussed all the output from this code, so I'll just say that at this point a transaction has been started and the test page has been flushed to the database within that transaction.

Now let's write a SQL expression to select that row from the database, even though the changes haven't been committed. The only way you can do this is if you make sure you use the same transaction as the session. The session has an execute() method for precisely this purpose. Let's see it in action:

```
>>> from sqlalchemy.sql import select
>>> s = select([model.page_table])
>>> result = session.execute(s)
2008-09-04 21:59:29,868 INFO sqlalchemy.engine.base.Engine.0x..30
SELECT page.id, page.content, page.posted, page.title, page.heading
FROM page
2008-09-04 21:59:29,868 INFO sqlalchemy.engine.base.Engine.0x..30 []
>>> result.fetchall()
[(1, u'Test content', datetime.datetime(2008, 9, 4, 21, 59, 29, 854464), ➥
u'Test Page', None)]
```

Using session.execute() ensures that the same connection (and hence the same transaction) is used by both the session and the SQL expression object s. For this reason, it is always best to use session.execute() when working with SQL expressions in Pylons rather than creating a separate connection via the engine metadata.

Now that you've seen how to create objects and how to use the session to save their data to their corresponding tables, it's time to look at how to query the database to get data back out using the Object-Relational API instead of the SQL Expression API. Commit the page that has just been flushed, and you will continue the example as you look at queries:

```
>>> session.commit()
```

In a Pylons application, if you don't call session.commit(), any changes you make will be discarded at the end of the request.

Queries

All SQLAlchemy Object-Relational API queries are performed with query objects that are created from the session. The simplest way to create and use a query object is like this:

```
>>> page_q = session.query(model.Page)
>>> for page in page_q:
...     print page.title
...
2008-09-04 22:13:03,885 INFO sqlalchemy.engine.base.Engine.0x..30➥
SELECT page.id AS page_id, page.content AS page_content, page.posted➥
AS page_posted, page.title AS page_title, page.heading AS page_heading
FROM page
2008-09-04 22:13:03,885 INFO sqlalchemy.engine.base.Engine.0x..30 []
Test Page
```

In this example, you have iterated over every page in the database, and SQLAlchemy has created a page object for each so that you can access its `.id` attribute and print its title. You can see the SQL used and that the title of the test page, being the only page in the database at the moment, is correctly printed.

Let's take a closer look at some of the properties of the query object. You can use the same query object more than once, so let's use its `all()` method to get all the pages in one go as a list of Page objects:

```
>>> page_q.all()
[<model.Page object at 0x72670>]
```

Query objects also have a `one()` method that returns just one object, raising an exception if there are zero or more than one results. Another useful method on query objects is `first()`, which returns the first result or None if there are no results, again the log output isn't included:

```
>>> page = page_q.first()
>>> page.title
u'Test Page'
```

Query objects also allow you to set a `LIMIT` and `OFFSET` by treating the query object as a list that can be sliced. For example, to retrieve results only from 2 to 5, you would write this:

```
>>> page_q[2:5]
2008-09-04 22:23:49,556 INFO sqlalchemy.engine.base.Engine.0x..30
SELECT page.id AS page_id, page.content AS page_content, page.posted➥
AS page_posted, page.title AS page_title, page.heading AS page_heading
FROM page
 LIMIT 3 OFFSET 2
2008-09-04 22:23:49,556 INFO sqlalchemy.engine.base.Engine.0x..30 []
[]
```

Of course, you have only one page, so this returns an empty list, but you can see from the logged SQL that `LIMIT` and `OFFSET` were applied correctly.

Most of the time, you will want to be more specific about the results you return. SQLAlchemy allows you to do this in a number of ways. First, if you know the primary key of the row you are looking for, you can use the page query's `get()` method:

```
>>> page_q.get(1)
<model.Page object at 0x72670>
```

Notice this time that SQLAlchemy didn't need to send any SQL to retrieve this object because it was already in the session from the queries you have already run. Query objects also have `filter()` and `filter_by()` methods. Both are similar, but `filter()` takes an expression of the type you saw earlier, whereas `filter_by()` takes keyword arguments representing attributes on the class you are querying. Their use is best demonstrated with examples:

```
>>> titles1 = [page.title for page in page_q.filter(model.Page.id==1)]
2008-09-04 22:40:24,236 INFO sqlalchemy.engine.base.Engine.0x..30 SELECT ➥
page.id AS page_id, page.content AS page_content, page.posted AS page_➥
posted, page.title AS page_title, page.heading AS page_heading
FROM page
WHERE page.id = ?
2008-09-04 22:40:24,236 INFO sqlalchemy.engine.base.Engine.0x..30 [1]
>>> titles2 = [page.title for page in page_q.filter_by(id=1)]
2008-09-04 22:40:40,098 INFO sqlalchemy.engine.base.Engine.0x..30 SELECT ➥
page.id AS page_id, page.content AS page_content, page.posted AS page_posted, ➥
page.title AS page_title, page.heading AS page_heading
FROM page
WHERE page.id = ?
2008-09-04 22:40:40,101 INFO sqlalchemy.engine.base.Engine.0x..30 [1]
>>> titles1 == titles2
True
```

The same results are obtained whether the filter() or filter_by() syntax is used.

■**Tip** You might not have seen the notation used in the previous example to generate both the title lists. It is called a *list comprehension* and is a handy way of quickly iterating over an object to produce a new list.

It is also possible to use table columns as an argument to filter() rather than object attributes. Here's an example:

```
>>> filtered_page_q = page_q.filter(model.page_table.c.title.like(u'%page%'))
>>> page = filtered_page_q.first()
2008-09-04 23:23:33,128 INFO sqlalchemy.engine.base.Engine.0x..30 SELECT ➥
page.id AS page_id, page.content AS page_content, page.posted AS page_➥
posted, page.title AS page_title, page.heading AS page_heading
FROM page
WHERE page.title LIKE ?
 LIMIT 1 OFFSET 0
2008-09-04 23:23:33,136 INFO sqlalchemy.engine.base.Engine.0x..30 [u'%page%']
>>> page.title
u'Test Page'
```

Notice that the return value from filter() or filter_by() is another query object, so you can further manipulate the results or apply more filters. You can also create more complex expressions using AND, OR, and NOT:

```
>>> from sqlalchemy.sql import and_
>>> page = page_q.filter(and_(model.Page.title.like(u'%page%'), ➥
model.page_table.c.id==1)).first()
2008-09-04 23:24:51,196 INFO sqlalchemy.engine.base.Engine.0x..30 ➥
SELECT page.id AS page_id, ➥
page.content AS page_content, page.posted AS page_posted, page.title ➥
AS page_title, page.heading AS page_heading
FROM page
WHERE page.title LIKE ? AND page.id = ?
 LIMIT 1 OFFSET 0
2008-09-04 23:24:51,196 INFO sqlalchemy.engine.base.Engine.0x..30 [u'%page%', 1]
>>> page.title
u'Test Page'
```

Notice that you can use either attributes of the class or columns of the table in the query. Using this technique you can even use SQL strings, bind parameters, or complex statements built using the SQLAlchemy expression language `select()` function. See the SQLAlchemy documentation for details.

Working with Objects

The great thing about using the SQLAlchemy Object-Relational API is that you get actual Python objects returned from the queries rather than values. Any changes you make to the objects are then automatically reflected in the underlying database when you commit changes to the session. This means that working with the database becomes just like working with ordinary Python objects.

Let's start by changing the title of the `page` object you've just selected:

```
>>> page.title = u'New Title'
>>> session.commit()
2008-09-04 23:27:13,893 INFO sqlalchemy.engine.base.Engine.0x..30 ➡
UPDATE page SET title=? WHERE page.id = ?
2008-09-04 23:27:13,893 INFO sqlalchemy.engine.base.Engine.0x..30 [u'New Title', 1]
2008-09-04 23:27:13,896 INFO sqlalchemy.engine.base.Engine.0x..30 COMMIT
```

As you can see, SQLAlchemy automatically generated an `UPDATE` statement to update the column and then committed the change.

Now let's think about how you could add a comment to the page. One approach would be to insert a new row into the `comment` table using the SQL Expression API, ensuring that the `pageid` field contained the value 1 so that the comment was associated with the correct page via a foreign key. This would work perfectly well, but the Object-Relational API provides a better approach:

```
>>> comment1=model.Comment()
>>> comment1.name = u'James'
>>> comment1.email = u"james@example.com"
>>> comment1.content = u'This page needs a bit more detail ;-)'
>>> comment2=model.Comment()
>>> comment2.name = u'Mike'
>>> comment2.email = u'mike@example.com'
>>> page.comments.append(comment1)
>>> page.comments.append(comment2)
>>> session.commit()
2008-09-04 23:38:52,900 INFO sqlalchemy.engine.base.Engine.0x..30 ➡
INSERT INTO comment (pageid, content, name, email, created) VALUES ➡
(?, ?, ?, ?, ?)
2008-09-04 23:38:52,901 INFO sqlalchemy.engine.base.Engine.0x..30 [1, u'This ➡
page needs a bit more detail ;-)', u'James', u'james@example.com', '2008-09-04 ➡
22:12:24.775929']
2008-09-04 23:38:52,903 INFO sqlalchemy.engine.base.Engine.0x..30 INSERT INTO ➡
comment (pageid, content, name, email, created) VALUES (?, ?, ?, ?, ?)
2008-09-04 23:38:52,904 INFO sqlalchemy.engine.base.Engine.0x..30 [1, u'', ➡
u'Mike', u'mike@example.com', '2008-09-04 22:12:24.775929']
2008-09-04 23:38:52,907 INFO sqlalchemy.engine.base.Engine.0x..30 COMMIT
```

You have created the comment objects in a similar way as you created the `test_page` object earlier in the chapter, assigning various attributes appropriate values. The interesting thing here is that rather than having to manually set the `.pageid` attribute on each of the columns with the `id` of the page, you simply appended the comments to the page's `.comments` attribute. Really, the comments should have been added to the session with `session.add_all([comment1, comment2])`, but SQLAlchemy was smart enough to realize that if they had been appended to an object that was already in the session, then they needed to be added too. When `session.commit()` was called, the `autoflush=True` option to the session caused the session to be flushed, and the SQL for the two required `INSERT` statements to be sent to the database before being committed.

This behavior is possible only because of the relationships that were defined when the tables and mappers were created in the `model.py` file earlier in the chapter. If you recall, the mapper for the page table looks like this:

```
orm.mapper(Page, page_table, properties={
    'comments':orm.relation(Comment, backref='page'),
    'tags':orm.relation(Tag, secondary=pagetag_table)
})
```

Notice that you specified a backref called `page` on the `Comments` class. This means you should be able to access the page object from a comment's `.page` attribute as well as accessing a list of comments from a page's `.comments` attribute. Let's see:

```
>>> comment_q = session.query(model.Comment)
>>> comment = comment_q.get(2)
2008-09-04 23:53:21,084 INFO sqlalchemy.engine.base.Engine.0x..30 BEGIN
2008-09-04 23:53:21,085 INFO sqlalchemy.engine.base.Engine.0x..30 SELECT ➥
comment.id AS comment_id, comment.pageid AS comment_pageid, comment.content ➥
 AS comment_content, comment.name AS comment_name, comment.email AS comment_➥
email, comment.created AS comment_created
FROM comment
WHERE comment.id = ?
2008-09-04 23:53:21,086 INFO sqlalchemy.engine.base.Engine.0x..30 [2]
>>> page = comment.page
2008-09-04 23:53:28,047 INFO sqlalchemy.engine.base.Engine.0x..30 ➥
SELECT page.id AS page_id, page.content AS page_content, page.posted ➥
AS page_posted, page.title AS page_title, page.heading AS page_heading
FROM page
WHERE page.id = ?
2008-09-04 23:53:28,048 INFO sqlalchemy.engine.base.Engine.0x..30 [1]
>>> page
<model.Page object at 0x72670>
>>> page.id
1
>>> page.title
u'New Title'
```

As you can see, it is the same page with the updated title. You'll see a lot more of the Object-Relational API as you read the SimpleSite tutorial chapters. As well as seeing how SQLAlchemy works in the context of a Pylons application, you'll see how to work with tags as an example of a many-to-many relationship, how to use `ORDER BY` clauses with query objects, and how to hook SQLAlchemy up to FormEncode to validate data.

Declarative API

SQLAlchemy 0.5 also has a Declarative API that offers a higher-level API to allow you to define *on one go* the same classes, tables, and mappers you added to your `model.py` file earlier in the chapter. For many applications, this is the only style of configuration needed.

Let's rewrite the `model.py` file using the Declarative API:

```python
import datetime
from sqlalchemy import schema, types, orm

metadata = schema.MetaData()

def now():
    return datetime.datetime.now()

from sqlalchemy.ext.declarative import declarative_base

# Assign the same metadata object we created earlier.
Base = declarative_base(metadata=metadata)

# We still need the pagetag table because we don't want to explicitly define a
# Pagetag class but still
# need to specify the table in the relation between pages and tags.
pagetag_table = schema.Table('pagetag', metadata,
    schema.Column('id', types.Integer,
        schema.Sequence('pagetag_seq_id', optional=True), primary_key=True),
    schema.Column('pageid', types.Integer, schema.ForeignKey('page.id')),
    schema.Column('tagid', types.Integer, schema.ForeignKey('tag.id')),
)

class Page(Base):
    __tablename__ = 'page'

    id = schema.Column(types.Integer,
        schema.Sequence('page_seq_id', optional=True), primary_key=True)
    content = schema.Column(types.Text(), nullable=False)
    posted = schema.Column(types.DateTime(), default=now)
    title = schema.Column(types.Unicode(255), default=u'Untitled Page')
    heading = schema.Column(types.Unicode(255))
    comments = orm.relation("Comment", backref="page")
    tags = orm.relation("Tag", secondary=pagetag_table)

class Comment(Base):
    __tablename__ = 'comment'

    id = schema.Column(types.Integer,
        schema.Sequence('comment_seq_id', optional=True), primary_key=True)
    pageid = schema.Column(types.Integer,
        schema.ForeignKey('page.id'), nullable=False)
    content = schema.Column(types.Text(), default=u'')
    name = schema.Column(types.Unicode(255))
    email = schema.Column(types.Unicode(255), nullable=False)
    created = schema.Column(types.TIMESTAMP(), default=now())

class Tag(Base):
    __tablename__ = 'tag'

    id = schema.Column(types.Integer,
        schema.Sequence('tag_seq_id', optional=True), primary_key=True)
    name = schema.Column(types.Unicode(20), nullable=False, unique=True)

page_table = Page.__table__
```

As you can see, this example uses many of the same principles you've already learned about but in a more compact form. The table name has to be specified via a `__tablename__` attribute, but SQLAlchemy can infer the column names from the attribute names you've specified. When setting up the relationships, you can pass a string to `relation()` rather than a class because you might need to map a relationship before the class has been defined.

Classes that are mapped explicitly using `mapper()` can interact freely with declarative classes, and table definitions created explicitly can be used too, as you can see with the `pagetag` table in the previous example.

Declarative classes get access to the underlying `metadata` object, and hence the underlying engine, because they are inherited from `Base`, and `Base` has access to `metadata` because it is passed as an argument to the `declarative_base()` function.

The underlying `Table` object created by the `declarative_base()` version of each of these classes is accessible via the class's `__table__` attribute, as you can see from the last line in the example.

If you save the updated `model.py`, you will find that all the examples using the `object_test` module still work in the same way, even with the new model.

Although the Declarative API can be more approachable to newcomers, most Pylons developers at the moment still choose to use the more explicit APIs you saw earlier, which is the approach you'll follow for the rest of the book. If you are interested in using the Declarative API, you should read the SQLAlchemy documentation at `http://www.sqlalchemy.org/docs/05/plugins.html#plugins_declarative`.

Maintaining Performance

SQLAlchemy is a well-designed package, and although it isn't ever going to be as fast as using the DB-API 2.0 directly, it should perform extremely well as long as you use it correctly.

One thing you should avoid at all costs is writing a query like this:

```
for page in session.query(model.Page):
    if page.id == 1:
        print page.title
```

This would select every page from the database and create a new `page` object from the `Page` class for each row in the table, just so that you can find the page with an `id` of 1. Since there is only one page in the database, this code isn't too bad, but if you had 10,000 pages, that is 10,000 objects that need to be created and checked in Python rather than in the underlying RDBMS.

Iterating over results as Python objects is obviously a very inefficient way of searching through data in a table, because each row has to be loaded into memory as a Python object. SQL databases are designed to be very fast at performing complex queries, so it is much better to use one of SQLAlchemy's filter methods to generate the SQL necessary to make the underlying database do all the hard work, or in this case, you can just use the `get()` method you saw earlier, which might not even have to contact the database if the page is already in memory in the session:

```
page = session.query(model.Page).get(1)
```

The final thing to remember is that the Object-Relational API isn't always the best tool for the job. If you are updating or deleting multiple rows at once, for example, you are much better off using the SQL Expression API to allow SQLAlchemy to build a SQL statement that the underlying RDBMS can use to change the rows using its efficient C code. Remember that you can always mix and match the Object-Relational API code and the SQL Expression API code within the same transaction using the session's `execute()` method. For example, to update a set of rows in one go, you might write the following:

```
from sqlalchemy.sql import update
u = update(model.page_table, model.page_table.c.title==u'New Title')
session.execute(u, params={'title': u"Updated Title"})
```

Summary

So, that was a whistle-stop tour of SQLAlchemy's architecture. You'll be using SQLAlchemy through-out the book, and it will all become much clearer as you use it. In the next chapter, you'll begin creating a real application, and you'll see how to use SQLAlchemy's Object-Relational API to per-form queries on the database.

If you haven't quite understood everything yet, it really is worth returning to this chapter and reading it again once you've read the rest of the book just to make sure everything is clear. A good understanding of SQLAlchemy will really help you write effective code in Pylons.

CHAPTER 8

■ ■ ■

Starting the SimpleSite Tutorial

■**Note** You can download the source code for this chapter from `http://www.apress.com`.

You've now learned about many of the most important components of an application. The previous chapters have been fairly detailed, so don't worry if you haven't understood everything you've read or if you've skipped over one or two sections. Once you have used Pylons a little more, you will appreciate having all the information on a particular topic in one place, even if it seems a lot to take in on the first reading.

In this chapter, I'll recap many of the important points as I show how to create a simple web site from scratch so that you can see how all the components you've learned about in the preceding chapters fit together. The example will be created in a way that will also make it a really good basis for your own Pylons projects.

You'll use SQLAlchemy to store the individual pages in the site in such a way that users can add, edit, or remove them so that the application behaves like a simple wiki. Each of the pages will also support comments and tags, so you can use some of the knowledge gained in the previous chapter to help you create the application. You'll also use FormEncode and HTML Fill to handle the forms.

Later in the book you'll return to SimpleSite and add authentication and authorization facilities, and you'll add a navigation hierarchy so that pages can be grouped into sections at different URLs. You'll implement some JavaScript to animate messages and use some Ajax to populate one of the form fields. The application will also have a navigation hierarchy so that you can see how to create navigation components such as breadcrumbs, tabs, and navigation menus using Mako.

Figure 8-1 shows what the finished application will look like after the SimpleSite tutorial chapters (this chapter, Chapter 14, part of Chapter 15, and Chapter 19).

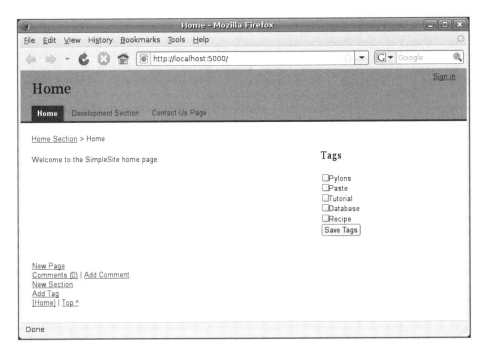

Figure 8-1. *The finished wiki with a customized front page*

Getting Started with SimpleSite

The first thing you need to do is create a new Pylons project called SimpleSite. You'll remember from Chapter 3 that the command to do this is as follows:

```
$ paster create --template=pylons SimpleSite
```

You'll use Mako and SQLAlchemy in this chapter, so in particular note that you need to answer True to the SQLAlchemy question so that SQLAlchemy support is included for you:

```
Selected and implied templates:
  Pylons#pylons  Pylons application template

Variables:
  egg:      SimpleSite
  package:  simplesite
  project:  SimpleSite
Enter template_engine (mako/genshi/jinja/etc: Template language) ['mako']:
Enter sqlalchemy (True/False: Include SQLAlchemy 0.4 configuration) [False]: True
Creating template pylons
```

All these options are configurable later, but it is easier to have Pylons configure them for you when you create the project.

Once the application template has been created, start the server, and see what you have:

```
$ cd SimpleSite
$ paster serve --reload development.ini
```

Note Notice that the server is started with the `--reload` switch. You'll remember that this means any changes you make to the code will cause the server to restart so that your changes are immediately available for you to test in the web browser.

If you visit `http://127.0.0.1:5000`, you will see the standard Pylons introduction page served from the application's `public/index.html` file as before.

Pylons looks for resources in the order applications are specified in the cascade object in `config/middleware.py`. You'll learn more about the cascade object in Chapter 17, but it causes static files such as the introduction page to be served in preference to content generated by your Pylons controllers for the same URL. You will want the SimpleSite controllers to handle the site's home page, so remove the welcome page HTML file:

```
$ cd simplesite
$ rm public/index.html
```

If you now refresh the page, the Pylons built-in error document support will kick in and display a 404 Not Found page to tell you that the URL requested could not be matched by Pylons.

You'll now customize the controller so that it can display pages. Each of the pages is going to have its own ID, which the controller will obtain from the URL. Here are some example URLs that the controller will handle:

```
/page/view/1
/page/view/2
... etc
/page/view/10
```

You'll also recall that Pylons comes with a routing system named Routes, which you saw in Chapter 3 and will learn about in detail in the next chapter. The default Routes setup analyzes the URL requested by the browser to find the controller, action, and ID. This means that to handle the URLs, you simply need a controller named `page` that has an action named `view` and that takes a parameter named `id`.

Let's create the page controller. Once again, Pylons comes with a tool to help with this in the form of a plug-in to Paste. You create the controller like this (notice that the command doesn't include the `create` part, which is used when creating a project template):

```
$ paster controller page
Creating /Users/james/Desktop/SimpleSite/simplesite/controllers/page.py
Creating /Users/james/Desktop/SimpleSite/simplesite/tests/functional/test_page.py
```

This creates two files—one for any tests you are going to add for this controller (see Chapter 12) and the other for the controller itself. The command would also add these files to Subversion automatically if your Pylons application were already being managed in a Subversion repository.

The `controllers/page.py` file that is added looks like this:

```
import logging

from pylons import request, response, session, tmpl_context as c
from pylons.controllers.util import abort, redirect_to

from simplesite.lib.base import BaseController, render
#import simplesite.model as model

log = logging.getLogger(__name__)

class PageController(BaseController):
```

```
def index(self):
    # Return a rendered template
    #   return render('/template.mako')
    # or, Return a response
    return 'Hello World'
```

This is a skeleton controller that you'll customize to handle pages. The first few lines import some of the useful objects described in Chapter 3 so that they are ready for you to use. The controller itself has one action named index(), which simply returns a Hello World message.

Replace the index() action with a view() action that looks like this:

```
def view(self, id):
    return "Page goes here"
```

The Paste HTTP server should reload when you save the change (as long as you used the --reload option), so you can now visit the URL http://localhost:5000/page/view/1. You should see the message Page goes here.

The page isn't very exciting so far and isn't even HTML, so now I'll cover how to create some templates to generate real HTML pages.

Exploring the Template Structure

Most web sites have the following features:

- Header and footer regions
- Sign-in and sign-out regions
- Top-level navigation tabs
- Second-level navigation tabs
- A page heading
- Breadcrumbs
- Content
- A head region for extra CSS and JavaScript

The SimpleSite application will need all these features too, so the template structure needs to be able to provide them.

You'll remember from Chapter 5 that Pylons uses the Mako templating language by default, although as is the case with most aspects of Pylons, you are free to deviate from the default if you prefer. This is particularly useful if you are building a Pylons application to integrate with legacy code, but since you are creating a new application here, you are going to use Mako.

Because you are going to need a few templates that will all look similar, you can take advantage of Mako's inheritance chain features you learned about in Chapter 5 and use a single base template for all the different pages. You'll also need to create some derived templates and some templates containing the navigation components.

You'll structure these templates as follows:

templates/base: All the base templates.

templates/derived: All the templates that are derived from any of the base templates. There is likely to be a subdirectory for every controller you create. Since Pylons has already created an error controller, you'll create a subdirectory for it, and you'll need a subdirectory for the page controller templates too.

templates/derived/error: Templates for the error controller to render error documents.

templates/component: Any components that are used in multiple templates.

This structure is useful because it keeps templates that serve different purposes in different directories. If you are following along by creating the application yourself, you should create these directories now.

Let's start by creating the base template. Save the following template as `templates/base/index.html`:

```
## -*- coding: utf-8 -*-

<!DOCTYPE HTML PUBLIC "-//W3C//DTD HTML 4.01//EN"
"http://www.w3.org/TR/html4/strict.dtd">
<html>
<head>
    <title>${self.title()}</title>
    ${self.head()}
</head>
<body>
    ${self.header()}
    ${self.tabs()}
    ${self.menu()}
    ${self.heading()}
    ${self.breadcrumbs()}
    ${next.body()}
    ${self.footer()}
</body>
</html>

<%def name="title()">SimpleSite</%def>
<%def name="head()"></%def>
<%def name="header()"><a name="top"></a></%def>
<%def name="tabs()"></%def>
<%def name="menu()"></%def>
<%def name="heading()"><h1>${c.heading or 'No Title'}</h1></%def>
<%def name="breadcrumbs()"></%def>
<%def name="footer()"><p><a href="#top">Top ^</a></p></%def>
```

This template should be fairly self-explanatory. It is a simple HTML document with eight defs defined. Each of the calls to `${self.somedef()}` will execute the def using either the definition in this base template or the definition in the template that inherits from it. The `${next.body()}` call will be replaced with the body of the template that inherits this one.

You'll also see that the `header()` and `footer()` defs already contain some HTML, allowing the user to quickly click to the top of the page. The `title()` def contains some code that will set the title to SimpleSite, and the `heading()` def will obtain its content from the value of `c.heading` or will just use `'No title'` if no heading has been set.

`## -*- coding: utf-8 -*-` has been added at the top of the file so that Unicode characters can be used when the template is saved as UTF-8 (you'll learn more about Unicode in Chapter 10).

■Note If you prefer using the `strict_c` option to ensure that accessing an attribute of the template context global raises an exception if that attribute doesn't exist, you should change the content of the `heading` def to look like this:

```
<h1>${hasattr(c, 'heading') and c.heading or 'No Title'}</h1>
```

This ensures that the `heading` attribute exists before testing its value.

Now that the base template is in place, you can start creating the templates for the web site content. Create a new template in the templates/derived/page directory called view.html. This will be the template used by the page controller's view action. Add the following content to it:

```
<%inherit file="/base/index.html"/>
```

```
${c.content}
```

You'll now need to update the view() action in the controller to use this template:

```
def view(self, id):
    c.title = 'Greetings'
    c.heading = 'Sample Page'
    c.content = "This is page %s"%id
    return render('/derived/page/view.html')
```

Now when you visit http://localhost:5000/page/view/1, you should see the page shown in Figure 8-2.

Figure 8-2. *A basic page being rendered from a template*

Using SQLAlchemy in Pylons

Now that you have the project's templates and controller set up, you need to start thinking about the model. As you'll recall from Chapter 1, Pylons is set up to use a Model View Controller architecture, and SQLAlchemy is what is most often used as the model. Chapter 7 explained SQLAlchemy in detail, but now you'll see how to apply that theory to a real Pylons project. If you haven't already done so you'll need to install SQLAlchemy 0.5 which is the version used in this book. You can do so with this command:

```
$ easy_install "SQLAlchemy>=0.5,<=0.5.99"
```

Let's begin by setting up the *engine*. Open your project's config/environment.py file, and after from pylons import config, you'll see the following:

```
from sqlalchemy import engine_from_config
```

You learned about engines in Chapter 7 when you created one directly. Pylons uses the engine_from_config() function to create an engine from configuration options in your project's config file instead. It looks for any options starting with sqlalchemy. in the [app:main] section of your development.ini config file and creates the engine based on these options. This means that all you need to do to configure SQLAlchemy is set the correct options in the config file.

Configuring the Engine

The main configuration option you need is `sqlalchemy.url`. This specifies the data source name (DSN) for your database and takes the format `engine://username:password@host:port/database?foo=bar`, where `foo=bar` sets an engine-specific argument named `foo` with the value `bar`. Once again, this is the same setting you learned about in Chapter 7 during the discussion of engines.

For SQLite, you might use an option like this to specify a database in the same directory as the config file:

```
sqlalchemy.url = sqlite:///%(here)s/databasefile.sqlite
```

Here `databasefile.sqlite` is the SQLite database file, and `%(here)s` represents the directory containing the `development.ini` file. If you're using an absolute path, use four slashes after the colon: `sqlite:////var/lib/myapp/databasefile.sqlite`. The example has three slashes because the value of `%(here)s` always starts with a slash on Unix-like platforms. Windows users should use four slashes because `%(here)s` on Windows starts with the drive letter.

For MySQL, you might use these options:

```
sqlalchemy.url = mysql://username:password@host:port/database
sqlalchemy.pool_recycle = 3600
```

Enter your username, your password, the host, the port number (usually 3306), and the name of your database.

It's important to set the `pool_recycle` option for MySQL to prevent "MySQL server has gone away" errors. This is because MySQL automatically closes idle database connections without informing the application. Setting the connection lifetime to 3600 seconds (1 hour) ensures that the connections will be expired and re-created before MySQL notices they're idle. `pool_recycle` is one of many engine options SQLAlchemy supports. Some of the others are listed at `http://www.sqlalchemy.org/docs/05/dbengine.html#dbengine_options` and are used in the same way, prefixing the option name with `sqlalchemy.`.

For PostgreSQL, your DSN will usually look like this:

```
sqlalchemy.url = postgres://username:password@host:port/database
```

The options are the same as for MySQL, but you don't generally need to use the `pool_recycle` option with PostgreSQL.

By default, Pylons sets up the DSN `sqlalchemy.url = sqlite:///%(here)s/development.db`, so if you don't change it, this is what will be used. Whichever DSN you use, you still need to make sure you have installed SQLAlchemy along with the appropriate DB-API driver you want to use; otherwise, SQLAlchemy won't be able to connect to the database. Again, see Chapter 7 for more information.

Creating the Model

Once you have configured the engine, it is time to configure the model. This is easy to do; you simply add all your classes, tables, and mappers to the end of `model/__init__.py`. The SimpleSite application will use the structures you worked through in the previous chapter, so I won't discuss them in detail here.

Change `model.__init__.py` to look like this:

```
"""The application's model objects"""
import sqlalchemy as sa
from sqlalchemy import orm

from simplesite.model import meta

# Add these two imports:
import datetime
from sqlalchemy import schema, types

def init_model(engine):
    """Call me before using any of the tables or classes in the model"""
    ## Reflected tables must be defined and mapped here
    #global reflected_table
    #reflected_table = sa.Table("Reflected", meta.metadata, autoload=True,
    #                             autoload_with=engine)
    #orm.mapper(Reflected, reflected_table)

    # We are using SQLAlchemy 0.5 so transactional=True is replaced by
    # autocommit=False
    sm = orm.sessionmaker(autoflush=True, autocommit=False, bind=engine)

    meta.engine = engine
    meta.Session = orm.scoped_session(sm)

# Replace the rest of the file with the model objects we created in
# chapter 7

def now():
    return datetime.datetime.now()

page_table = schema.Table('page', meta.metadata,
    schema.Column('id', types.Integer,
        schema.Sequence('page_seq_id', optional=True), primary_key=True),
    schema.Column('content', types.Text(), nullable=False),
    schema.Column('posted', types.DateTime(), default=now),
    schema.Column('title', types.Unicode(255), default=u'Untitled Page'),
    schema.Column('heading', types.Unicode(255)),
)

comment_table = schema.Table('comment', meta.metadata,
    schema.Column('id', types.Integer,
        schema.Sequence('comment_seq_id', optional=True), primary_key=True),
    schema.Column('pageid', types.Integer,
        schema.ForeignKey('page.id'), nullable=False),
    schema.Column('content', types.Text(), default=u''),
    schema.Column('name', types.Unicode(255)),
    schema.Column('email', types.Unicode(255), nullable=False),
    schema.Column('created', types.TIMESTAMP(), default=now()),
)

pagetag_table = schema.Table('pagetag', meta.metadata,
    schema.Column('id', types.Integer,
        schema.Sequence('pagetag_seq_id', optional=True), primary_key=True),
    schema.Column('pageid', types.Integer, schema.ForeignKey('page.id')),
    schema.Column('tagid', types.Integer, schema.ForeignKey('tag.id')),
)
```

```
tag_table = schema.Table('tag', meta.metadata,
    schema.Column('id', types.Integer,
        schema.Sequence('tag_seq_id', optional=True), primary_key=True),
    schema.Column('name', types.Unicode(20), nullable=False, unique=True),
)

class Page(object):
    pass

class Comment(object):
    pass

class Tag(object):
    pass

orm.mapper(Comment, comment_table)
orm.mapper(Tag, tag_table)
orm.mapper(Page, page_table, properties={
    'comments':orm.relation(Comment, backref='page'),
    'tags':orm.relation(Tag, secondary=pagetag_table)
})
```

As I mentioned, this will look very familiar because it is a similar setup to the one you used in the previous chapter. There are some points to note about this code, though:

- The MetaData object Pylons uses is defined in model/meta.py so is accessed here as meta.metadata, whereas in the previous chapter the examples just used metadata.

- Pylons generated the init_model() function when the project was created. It gets called after the engine has been created each time your application starts from config/environment.py to connect the model to the database.

■**Caution** Pylons generates a project to use SQLAlchemy 0.4, but many users will want to use the newer SQLAlchemy 0.5 described in Chapter 7. They are very similar, but the transactional=True argument to orm. sessionmaker() in init_model() is deprecated. Instead, you should specify autocommit=False. This has the same behavior but will not generate a deprecation warning.

Creating the Database Tables

Pylons has a built-in facility to allow users who download your application to easily set it up. The process is described in detail in the later SimpleSite tutorial chapters (Chapters 14 and 19), but you'll use it here too so that you can easily set up the tables you need.

The idea is that users of your application can simply run paster setup-app development.ini to have the database tables and any initial data created for them automatically. You can set up this facility through your project's websetup.py file.

The default websetup.py file for a SQLAlchemy project looks like this:

```
"""Setup the SimpleSite application"""
import logging

from simplesite.config.environment import load_environment

log = logging.getLogger(__name__)

def setup_app(command, conf, vars):
    """Place any commands to setup simplesite here"""
    load_environment(conf.global_conf, conf.local_conf)

    # Load the models
    from simplesite.model import meta
    meta.metadata.bind = meta.engine

    # Create the tables if they aren't there already
    meta.metadata.create_all(checkfirst=True)
```

When the `paster setup-app` command is run, Pylons calls the `setup_app()` function and loads the Pylons environment, setting up a SQLAlchemy engine as it does so. It then binds the engine to the metadata and calls `metadata.create_all(checkfirst=True)` to create any tables that don't already exist.

Binding the metadata in this way connects the engine to the `metadata` object used by the classes, tables, and mappers in the model. You can think of it as a shortcut to set up the model without the complexity of a session.

You'll now customize the default code so that it also adds a home page to the database. Add the following to the end of the `setup_app()` function:

```
log.info("Adding homepage...")
page = model.Page()
page.title=u'Home Page'
page.content = u'Welcome to the SimpleSite home page.'
meta.Session.add(page)
meta.Session.commit()
log.info("Successfully set up.")
```

You'll also need to add this import at the top:

```
from simplesite import model
```

▪Note The recommended way of adding an object to the SQLAlchemy session in SQLAlchemy 0.4 was to call the session's `save()` method. The session in SQLAlchemy 0.5 provides the `add()` method instead. Since this book covers SQLAlchemy 0.5, the examples will use the `add()` method.

To test this functionality, you should first make SimpleSite available in your virtual Python environment. Rather than installing SimpleSite as you would install a normal Python package, you can instead use a special feature of the `setuptools` package used by Easy Install called *development mode*. This has the effect of making other Python packages treat your Pylons project's source directory as if it were an installed Python egg even though it is actually just a directory structure in the filesystem.

It works by adding a `SimpleSite.egg-link` file to your virtual Python installation's site-packages directory containing the path to the application. It also adds an entry to the `easy_install.pth` file so that the project is added to the Python path. This is very handy because it means that any changes you make to the SimpleSite project are instantly available without you having to create and install the package every time you make a change. Set up your project in development mode by entering this command:

```
$ python setup.py develop
```

If you haven't specified `sqlalchemy.url` in your `development.ini` config file, you should do so now. Then you are ready to run the `paster setup-app` command to set up your tables:

```
$ paster setup-app development.ini
```

If all goes well, you should see quite a lot of log output produced, ending with the following lines and the message that everything was successfully set up:

```
12:37:36,429 INFO  [simplesite.websetup] Adding homepage...
12:37:36,446 INFO  [sqlalchemy.engine.base.Engine.0x..70] BEGIN
12:37:36,449 INFO  [sqlalchemy.engine.base.Engine.0x..70]➥
INSERT INTO page (content, posted, title, heading) VALUES (?, ?, ?, ?)
12:37:36,449 INFO  [sqlalchemy.engine.base.Engine.0x..70]➥
[u'Welcome to the SimpleSite home page.', '2008-09-12 12:37:36.449094',➥
 u'Home Page', None]
12:37:36,453 INFO  [sqlalchemy.engine.base.Engine.0x..70] COMMIT
12:37:36,460 INFO  [simplesite.websetup] Successfully set up.
```

Querying Data

Now that the home page data is in SQLAlchemy, you need to update the `view()` action to use it. You'll recall that you query SQLAlchemy using a *query* object. Here's how:

```
def view(self, id):
    page_q = model.meta.Session.query(model.Page)
    c.page = page_q.get(int(id))
    return render('/derived/page/view.html')
```

Notice that since the heading is optional, you are using the title as the heading if the heading is empty.

To use this, you need to uncomment the following line at the top of the controller file:

```
#import simplesite.model as model
```

Now add some more imports the controller will need:

```
import simplesite.model.meta as meta
import simplesite.lib.helpers as h
```

Finally, you'll need to update the `templates/derived/page/view.html` template to use the `page` object:

```
<%inherit file="/base/index.html"/>

<%def name="title()">${c.page.title}</%def>
<%def name="heading()"><h1>${c.page.heading or c.page.title}</h1></%def>

${c.page.content}
```

The new heading def will display the heading if there is one and the title if no heading has been set.

Visit `http://localhost:5000/page/view/1` again, and you should see the data loaded from the database (Figure 8-3). You'll need to restart the server if you stopped it to run `paster setup-app`.

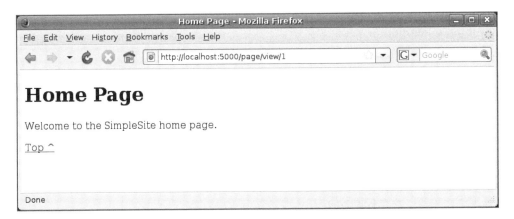

Figure 8-3. *A basic page being rendered with data from the database*

■Caution Generally speaking, it is a good idea to try to keep your model and templates as separate as possible. You should always perform all model operations in your controller and never in a template. This is so that you, and other people working on your project, always know where changes to your model are happening so that code is easy to maintain.

To avoid the risk of a lazy programmer performing operations on the model from within a template, you might prefer not to pass model objects directly to the controller and instead pass the useful attributes. In this case, rather than passing c.page, you might instead pass c.title, c.content, and other useful attributes rather than the whole object. In this book, I'll be strict about only using model objects for read-only access in templates, so it is OK to pass them in directly.

Understanding the Role of the Base Controller

Every Pylons project has a base controller in the project's lib/base.py file. All your project's controllers are by default derived from the BaseController class, so this means that if you want to change the behavior of all the controllers in your project, you can make changes to the base controller. Of course, if you want to derive your controllers directly from pylons.controllers. WSGIController, you are free to do so too.

The SimpleSite base controller looks like this:

```
"""The base Controller API

Provides the BaseController class for subclassing.
"""
from pylons.controllers import WSGIController
from pylons.templating import render_mako as render

from simplesite.model import meta

class BaseController(WSGIController):
```

```
def __call__(self, environ, start_response):
    """Invoke the Controller"""
    # WSGIController.__call__ dispatches to the Controller method
    # the request is routed to. This routing information is
    # available in environ['pylons.routes_dict']
    try:
        return WSGIController.__call__(self, environ, start_response)
    finally:
        meta.Session.remove()
```

All the individual controllers that you create with the `paster controller` command also import the `render()` function from this file, so if you want to change the templating language for all your controllers, you can change the `render()` import in this file, and all the other controllers will automatically use the new function. Of course, you will have to set up the templating language in your project's `config/environment.py` file too. This was described in Chapter 5.

Using a SQLAlchemy Session in Pylons

You've learned about SQLAlchemy sessions in some detail in Chapter 7, but now let's take a brief look at how sessions are used in Pylons.

The relevant lines to set up the session are found in your `model/__init__.py` file's `init_model()` function and look like this:

```
sm = orm.sessionmaker(autoflush=True, autocommit=False, bind=engine)

meta.engine = engine
meta.Session = orm.scoped_session(sm)
```

The `meta.Session` class created here acts as a thread-safe wrapper around ordinary SQLAlchemy session objects so that data from one Pylons request doesn't get mixed up with data from other requests in a multithreaded environment. Calling `meta.Session()` returns the thread's actual session object, but you wouldn't normally need to access it in this way because when you call the class's `meta.Session.query()` method, it will automatically return a query object from the correct hidden session object. You can then use the query object as normal to fetch data from the database.

Since a new session is created for each request, it is important that sessions that are no longer needed are removed. Because you chose to use a SQLAlchemy setup when you created the project, Pylons has added a line to remove any SQLAlchemy session at the end of the `BaseController` class's `__call__()` method:

```
meta.Session.remove()
```

This simply removes the session once your controller has returned the data for the response.

Updating the Controller to Support Editing Pages

To quickly recap, you've set up the model, configured the database engine, set up the templates, and written an action to view pages based on their IDs. Next, you need to write the application logic and create the forms to enable a user to create, list, add, edit, and delete pages.

You'll need the following actions:

`view(self, id)`: Displays a page

`new(self)`: Displays a form to create a new page

create(self): Saves the information submitted from new() and redirects to view()

edit(self, id): Displays a form for editing the page id

save(self, id): Saves the page id and redirects to view()

list(self): Lists all pages

delete(self, id): Deletes a page

This structure forms a good basis for a large number of the cases you are likely to program with a relational database.

view()

The existing view() method correctly displays a page but currently raises an error if you try to display a page that doesn't exist. This is because page_q.get() returns None when the page doesn't exist so that c.page is set to None. This causes an exception in the template when c.page.title is accessed.

Also, if a URL cannot be found, the HTTP specification says that a 404 page should be returned. You can use the abort() function to immediately stop the request and trigger the Pylons error documents middleware to display a 404 Not Found page. You should also display a 404 page if the user doesn't specify a page ID. Here's what the updated code looks like. Notice that the action arguments have been changed so that id is now optional.

```
def view(self, id=None):
    if id is None:
        abort(404)
    page_q = meta.Session.query(model.Page)
    c.page = page_q.get(int(id))
    if c.page is None:
        abort(404)
    return render('/derived/page/view.html')
```

■**Tip** When you are testing a condition that involves None in Python, you should use the is operator rather than the == operator.

new()

You also need a template for pages that don't already exist. It needs to display a form and submit it to the create() action to create the page. Most of the functionality to display the form will take place in the templates. Here's what the action looks like; add this to the controller:

```
def new(self):
    return render('/derived/page/new.html')
```

Thinking ahead, the edit() action will also display a form, and it is likely to have many of the same fields. You'll therefore implement the fields in one template where they can be shared and create the form itself in another.

First let's create the fields in templates/derived/page/fields.html. Here's what the file looks like:

```
${h.field(
    "Heading",
    h.text(name='heading'),
    required=False,
)}
${h.field(
    "Title",
    h.text(name='title'),
    required=True,
    field_desc = "Used as the heading too if you didn't specify one above"
)}
${h.field(
    "Content",
    h.textarea(name='content', rows=7, cols=40),
    required=True,
    field_desc = 'The text that will make up the body of the page'
)}
```

Remember that h is simply another name for your project's simplesite.lib.helpers module and that it is available in both the templates and the controllers. In this case, you're using a helper called field() that generates the HTML for a row in a table containing a label for a field and the field itself. It also allows you to specify field_desc, which is a line of text that appears immediately below the HMTL field, or label_desc, which is for text appearing immediately below the label. Specifying required=True adds an asterisk (*) to the start of the label, but it doesn't affect how the controller handles whether fields are actually required.

To use the field helper, you need to first import it into the helpers module. You'll also use form_start() and form_end(), so let's import them at the same time. At the top of lib/helpers.py, add the following:

```
from formbuild.helpers import field
from formbuild import start_with_layout as form_start, end_with_layout as form_end
from webhelpers.html.tags import *
```

Notice that you are using a package called FormBuild here. You could equally well code all your field structures in HTML, but FormBuild will help create a structure for you. FormBuild actually contains some extra functionality too, but you will use it only for its field(), start_with_layout(), and end_with_layout() helpers in the book. At some point in the future, these helpers are likely to be added to the Pylons WebHelpers package. Install FormBuild like this:

```
$ easy_install "FormBuild>=2.0,<2.99"
```

You should also add it as a dependency to your project by editing the setup.py file and adding FormBuild to the end of the install_requires argument, and updating the SQLAlchemy line to look like this:

```
install_requires=[
    "Pylons>=0.9.7",
    "SQLAlchemy>=0.5,<=0.5.99",
    "Mako",
    "FormBuild>=2.0,<2.99",
],
```

Next you need the form itself. Like the view.html page, this can be based on the /base/ index.html page using Mako's template inheritance. Here's how /derived/page/new.html looks:

```
<%inherit file="/base/index.html" />
<%namespace file="fields.html" name="fields" import="*"/>

<%def name="heading()">
    <h1 class="main">Create a New Page</h1>
</%def>

${h.form_start(h.url_for(controller='page', action='create'), method="post")}
    ${fields.body()}
    ${h.field(field=h.submit(value="Create Page", name='submit'))}
${h.form_end()}
```

This template imports the defs in the `fields.html` file into the `fields` namespace. It then calls its `body()` def to render the form fields. `h.form_start()` and `h.form_end()` create the HTML `<form>` tags as well as the `<table>` tags needed to wrap the rows generated by each call to `h.field()`.

You'll also need to add the `url_for()` helper to `lib/helpers.py`. This is a function from Routes that you'll learn about in Chapter 9. For the time being, it is enough to know that it takes a controller, action, and ID and will generate a URL that, when visited, will result in the controller and action being called with the ID you specified. Routes is highly customizable and is one of the central components Pylons provides to make building sophisticated web applications easier. Add this line to the `import` statements in `lib/helpers.py`:

```
from routes import url_for
```

You can now test the form by visiting `http://localhost:5000/page/new`.

When the user clicks the Create Page button, the information they enter is submitted to the `create()` action, so you need to write that next.

create()

The `create()` action needs to perform the following tasks:

- Validate the form
- Redisplay it with error messages if any data is invalid
- Add the valid data to the database
- Redirect the user to the newly created page

Let's start by creating a FormEncode schema to validate the data submitted. You need to import `formencode` at the top of the page controller and then import `htmlfill`, which will be used by the `edit()` method later in the chapter:

```
import formencode
from formencode import htmlfill
```

Next define the schema, which looks like this:

```
class NewPageForm(formencode.Schema):
    allow_extra_fields = True
    filter_extra_fields = True
    content = formencode.validators.String(
        not_empty=True,
        messages={
            'empty':'Please enter some content for the page.'
        }
    )
    heading = formencode.validators.String()
    title = formencode.validators.String(not_empty=True)
```

Setting the `allow_extra_fields` and `filter_extra_fields` options to `True` means that FormEncode won't raise `Invalid` exceptions for fields such as the Create Page button, which aren't listed in the schema, but will filter them out so that they don't affect the results.

You'll notice that `title` and `content` are required fields because they have `not_empty=True` specified. You'll also notice that the `content` field has a customized error message so that if no text is entered, the error `Please enter some content for the page.` will be displayed. Notice also that although you specified `not_empty=True` in the `formencode.validators.String` validator, the key corresponding to the message is the string `'empty'`. This might catch you out if you expected the key to be `'not_empty'`.

To handle the validation and redisplay of the form if there are any errors, you'll use the `@validate` decorator you learned about in Chapter 4. This requires another import:

```
from pylons.decorators import validate
```

You want it to redisplay the result of calling the `new()` action if an error occurs, so this is how you use it:

```
@validate(schema=NewPageForm(), form='new')
def create(self):
    ...
```

Calling an action wrapped by `@validate` using a GET request will bypass the validation and call the action anyway. You need to make sure this doesn't pose a security risk in your application. You could prevent this by testing whether a GET or a POST is being used in the body of the action. You can determine the request method using `request.method`, or Pylons provides another decorator called `@restrict` that you can use.

Let's use the new decorator and add the body of the action to create the page:

```
@restrict('POST')
@validate(schema=NewPageForm(), form='new')
def create(self):
    # Add the new page to the database
    page = model.Page()
    for k, v in self.form_result.items():
        setattr(page, k, v)
    meta.Session.add(page)
    meta.Session.commit()
    # Issue an HTTP redirect
    response.status_int = 302
    response.headers['location'] = h.url_for(controller='page',
        action='view', id=page.id)
    return "Moved temporarily"
```

You'll also need another import:

```
from pylons.decorators.rest import restrict
```

If the data entered is valid, it will be available in the action as the dictionary `self.form_result`. Here you're using a trick where you can iterate over the dictionary and set one of the page attributes for each of the values in the schema. Finally, you save the page to the session and then commit the changes to the database. You don't need to explicitly call `meta.Session.flush()` because the Pylons session is set to automatically flush changes when you call `meta.Session.commit()` (this was the `autoflush=True` argument to `sessionmaker()` in the model). Once the page has been flushed and committed, SQLAlchemy assigns it an id, so you use this to redirect the browser to the `view()` action for the new page using an HTTP redirect.

Issuing an HTTP redirect to the view() action is preferable to simply returning the page because if a user clicks Refresh, it is the view() action that is called again, not the create() action. This avoids the possibility that the user will accidentally add two identical pages by mistake by resubmitting the form.

This can cause other problems; for example, how do you pass information obtained during the call to create() to the view() action called next? Because the two pages are generated in two separate HTTP requests, you need to use a session to store information that can be used across the requests. You'll learn about this later in the chapter.

This is a good point to test your new application. If the server isn't already running, start it with the paster serve --reload development.ini command. Visit http://localhost:5000/page/new, and you should see the form. If you try to submit the form without adding any information, you will see that the validation system repopulates the form with errors.

The errors don't show up too well, so let's add some styles. Create the directory public/css, and add the following as main.css:

```
span.error-message, span.required {
    font-weight: bold;
    color: #f00;
}
```

You want to be able to use this style sheet in all the templates, so update the head() def of the /templates/base/index.html base template so that it looks like this:

```
<%def name="head()">
    ${h.stylesheet_link(h.url_for('/css/main.css'))}
</%def>
```

Once again, you'll need to import the stylesheet_link() helper into your lib/helpers.py file:

```
from webhelpers.html.tags import stylesheet_link
```

The helper takes any number of URLs as input and generates link tags for each. Any keyword arguments are added as attributes to each tag. For example:

```
>>> print stylesheet_link('style.css', 'main.css', media="print")
<link href="/stylesheets/style.css" media="print" rel="stylesheet"
    type="text/css" />
<link href="/stylesheets/main.css" media="print" rel="stylesheet"
    type="text/css" />
```

You should find that all the error messages appear in red, which will make any mistakes much more obvious to your users (see Figure 8-4). Why not go ahead and create a test page? If you enter any characters such as <, >, or &, you will find they are correctly escaped by Mako because they haven't been created as HTML literals. This means you can be confident that users of your application can't embed HTML into the page that could pose a cross-site scripting (XSS) attack risk, as explained in Chapter 4.

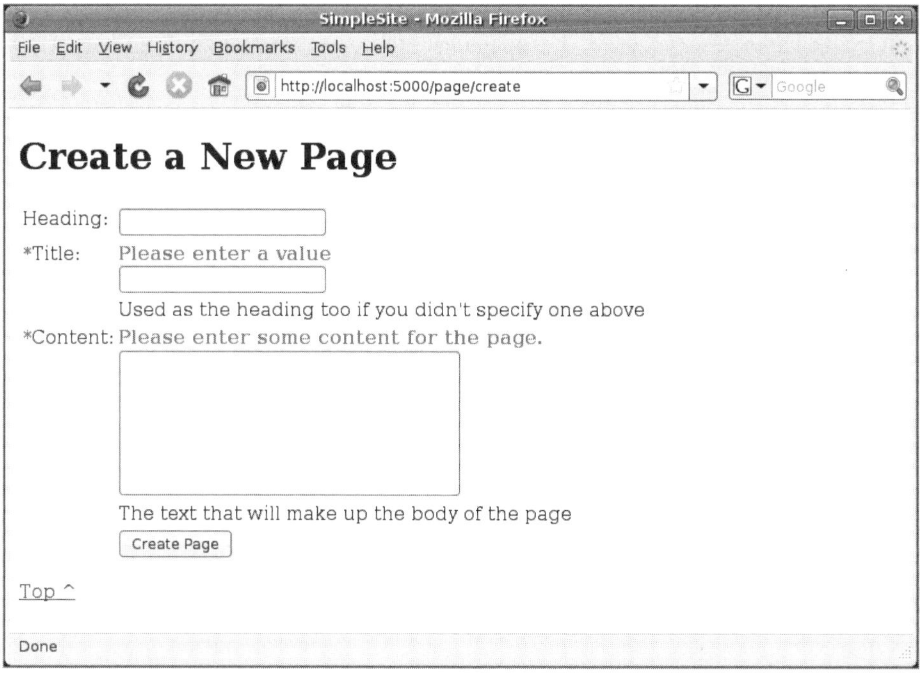

Figure 8-4. *The error message in red*

If you save the page with valid data, you'll see you are correctly redirected to the page you have created at the URL `http://localhost:5000/page/view/2`.

edit() and save()

Now that you've implemented the code to create new pages, let's look at the very similar code required to edit them. Once again, you'll have an action to display the form (in this case `edit()`) and an action to handle saving the code (in this case `save()`). The `edit()` action will need to load the data for the page from the model and then populate the form with the page information. Here's what it looks like:

```
def edit(self, id=None):
    if id is None:
        abort(404)
    page_q = meta.Session.query(model.Page)
    page = page_q.filter_by(id=id).first()
    if page is None:
        abort(404)
    values = {
        'title': page.title,
        'heading': page.heading,
        'content': page.content
    }
    return htmlfill.render(render('/derived/page/edit.html'), values)
```

Notice how this example uses FormEncode's `htmlfill` module to populate the form fields with the values obtained from the `page` object. The call to `render('/derived/page/edit.html')` generates the HTML, and the call to `htmlfill.render()` populates the values.

The `/derived/page/edit.html` template can also use the same fields you used in the `new.html` template. It looks very similar:

```
<%inherit file="/base/index.html" />
<%namespace file="fields.html" name="fields" import="*"/>

<%def name="heading()">
    <h1 class="main">Editing ${c.title}</h1>
</%def>

<p>Editing the source code for the ${c.title} page:</p>

${h.form_start(h.url_for(controller='page', action='save',
    id=request.urlvars['id']), method="post")}
    ${fields.body()}
    ${h.field(field=h.submit(value="Save Changes", name='submit'))}
${h.form_end()}
```

The only difference is that the form action points to `save` instead of `new`.

The `save()` action is also slightly different from the `create()` action because it has to update attributes on an existing page object. Here's how it looks:

```
@restrict('POST')
@validate(schema=NewPageForm(), form='edit')
def save(self, id=None):
    page_q = meta.Session.query(model.Page)
    page = page_q.filter_by(id=id).first()
    if page is None:
        abort(404)
    for k,v in self.form_result.items():
        if getattr(page, k) != v:
            setattr(page, k, v)
    meta.Session.commit()
    # Issue an HTTP redirect
    response.status_int = 302
    response.headers['location'] = h.url_for(controller='page', action='view',
        id=page.id)
    return "Moved temporarily"
```

Notice how this time attributes of the page are set only if they have changed. Remember when using FormEncode in this way, when the form is valid, the converted results get saved as the `self.form_result` dictionary, so you should get the submitted content from there rather than from `request.params`. Also, in this instance, the FormEncode schema for creating a new page is the same as the one needed for editing a page, so you are using `NewSchemaForm` again in the `@validate` decorator. Often you will need to use a second schema, though.

Why not try editing a page? For example, to edit the home page, you could visit `http://localhost:5000/page/edit/1`.

list()

Add the list() action:

```
def list(self):
    c.pages = meta.Session.query(model.Page).all()
    return render('/derived/page/list.html')
```

The list() action simply gets all the pages from the database and displays them. Notice the way you use the template context object c to pass the page data to the template. Create a new file named templates/derived/page/list.html to display the list of pages:

```
<%inherit file="/base/index.html" />

<%def name="heading()">
    <h1 class="main">Page List</h1>
</%def>

<ul id="titles">
% for page in c.pages:
<li>
    ${page.title} [${h.link_to('visit', h.url_for(controller='page', action='view',
        id=page.id))}]
</li>
% endfor
</ul>
```

The h.link_to() helper is a tool for generating a hyperlink, of course you can also write the <a> tag out yourself if you prefer. To use it add the following import to the end of lib/helpers.py:

```
from webhelpers.html.tags import link_to
```

If you visit http://127.0.0.1:5000/page/list, you should see the full titles list, and you should be able to visit each page.

delete()

Users of the application might want to be able to delete a page, so let's add a delete() action.

Add the following action to the page controller:

```
def delete(self, id=None):
    if id is None:
        abort(404)
    page_q = meta.Session.query(model.Page)
    page = page_q.filter_by(id=id).first()
    if page is None:
        abort(404)
    meta.Session.delete(page)
    meta.Session.commit()
    return render('/derived/page/deleted.html')
```

This page searches for the page to be deleted and aborts with a 404 Not Found HTTP status if the page doesn't exist. Otherwise, the page is deleted using the Session object, and the changes are committed.

Add the templates/derived/page/deleted.html template with the following content to display a message that the page has been deleted:

```
<%inherit file="/base/index.html" />

<%def name="heading()">
    <h1 class="main">Page Deleted</h1>
</%def>

<p>This page has been deleted.</p>
```

Later in the chapter you'll see how you can use a session and a *flash message* to display a simple message like this on a different page rather than needing to create a template for it.

At this point, you have a very simple (yet perfectly functional) web site for creating pages and editing their content. There is clearly more that could be done, though, so now it's time to turn your attention to other aspects of the SimpleSite application you are creating.

Updating the Footer

Now that the basic structure of the controller is in place, the users of SimpleSite will need a quick and easy way of adding, editing, and deleting the pages without having to enter the appropriate URLs in the browser address bar.

Modify the derived/page/view.html template so that it includes some links in the page footer:

```
<%inherit file="/base/index.html"/>

<%def name="title()">${c.page.title}</%def>
<%def name="heading()"><h1>${c.page.heading or c.page.title}</h1></%def>

${c.page.content}

<%def name="footer()">
## Then add our page links
<p>
  <a href="${h.url_for(controller='page', action='list', id=None)}">All Pages</a>
| <a href="${h.url_for(controller='page', action='new', id=None)}">New Page</a>
| <a href="${h.url_for(controller='page', action='edit',
        id=c.page.id)}">Edit Page</a>
| <a href="${h.url_for(controller='page', action='delete',
        id=c.page.id)}">Delete Page</a>
</p>
## Include the parent footer too
${parent.footer()}
</%def>
```

Notice that the h.url_for() call for both a new page and to list all pages has id=None specified. You'll learn about Routes in Chapter 9, but for now you simply need to know that by default Routes automatically fills in values for routing variables based on the ones that were used to route the request to the current controller and action. This is not a recommended behavior, and you'll learn how to change it in Chapter 9. The new() and list() actions don't take an id, but unless you specify id=None, Routes fills in the id of the current page.

If you view a page, you will now see the links you need are present.

Using Pagination

If you want to display large numbers of items, it isn't always appropriate to display them all at once. Instead, you should split the data into smaller chunks known as *pages* (not to be confused with the web site pages I've been talking about) and show each page of data one at a time. This is called *pagination*, and providing an interface for the user to page through the results is the job of a *paginator*.

As an example, imagine what would happen if lots of people started adding pages to the site. You could quickly get, say, 27 pages, which might be too many to display comfortably in a single list. Instead, you could use a paginator to display the web site pages ten at a time in each page in the paginator. The first page of results would show web site pages 1–10, the second would show 11–20, and the last would display 21–27.

The user also needs some way of navigating through the different pages of results. The Pylons WebHelpers come with a `webhelpers.paginate` module to make pagination easier, and it provides two solutions to allow the user to navigate the pages of data. The first is called a *pager*, and it produces an interface like the one shown here. The single arrows take you backward or forward one page of results at a time, and the double arrows take you straight to the first or last page.

```
<< < 11-20 of 27 > >>
```

The second navigation tool is called the *navigator* and produces an interface that looks like this:

```
[1] [2] [3]
```

This allows you to click directly on the page of results you want to view.

Let's update the `list()` action to use the paginator. First import the paginator module into the page controller:

```
import webhelpers.paginate as paginate
```

Then update the `list()` action to look like this:

```python
def list(self):
    records = meta.Session.query(model.Page)
    c.paginator = paginate.Page(
        records,
        page=int(request.params.get('page', 1)),
        items_per_page = 10,
    )
    return render('/derived/page/list.html')
```

There is also a subtlety in this example which you could easily miss. The `paginate.Page` class has built-in support for SQLAlchemy so in this case, rather than simply providing the paginator with a standard list of Python objects, we are passing in an SQLAlchemy query object. This allows the paginator to only select the records it needs from the database for the page of results it is displaying.

It is unfortunate that the records you are paginating here are pages when the word *page* is also used to describe a set of records displayed by the paginator. In this case, the `page` variable retrieved using `request.params` is referring to the paginator page, not the `id` of a page record.

The `list.html` template also needs updating to use the paginator. Here's what it looks like:

```
<%inherit file="/base/index.html" />

<%def name="heading()"><h1>Page List</h1></%def>

<%def name="buildrow(page, odd=True)">
    %if odd:
        <tr class="odd">
    %else:
        <tr class="even">
```

```
    % endif
        <td valign="top">
            ${h.link_to(
                page.id,
                h.url_for(
                    controller=u'page',
                    action='view',
                    id=unicode(page.id)
                )
            )}
        </td>
        <td valign="top">
            ${page.title}
        </td>
        <td valign="top">${page.posted.strftime('%c')}</td>
        </tr>
</%def>

% if len(c.paginator):
<p>${ c.paginator.pager('$link_first $link_previous $first_item to $last_item of➥
$item_count $link_next $link_last') }</p>
<table class="paginator"><tr><th>Page ID</th><th>Page Title</th><th>Posted</th></tr>
<% counter=0 %>
% for item in c.paginator:
    ${buildrow(item, counter%2)}
    <% counter += 1 %>
% endfor
</table>
<p>${ c.paginator.pager('~2~') }</p>
% else:
<p>
    No pages have yet been created.
    <a href="${h.url_for(controller='page', action='new')}">Add one</a>.
</p>
% endif
```

As you can see, the paginator is set up at the bottom of the template, but for each record the
`buildrow()` def is called to generate a representation of the page.

When you click any of the navigation components in the paginator, a new request is made to
the `list()` action with the ID of the paginator page. This is sent via the query string and passed as
the page argument to `paginate.Page` to generate the next set of results.

The nice thing about the Pylons paginator implementation is that it can be used to page any
type of information, whether comments in a blog, rows in a table, or entries in an address book.
This is because the rendering of each item in the page can be handled in your template so that you
have complete control over the visual appearance of your data.

To test the paginator, you might need to create a few extra pages and try setting the
`items_per_page` option to `paginate.Page()` to a low number such as 2 so that you don't have to
create too many extra pages.

Here are the variables you can use as arguments to `.pager()` in the template:

`$first_page`: Number of first reachable page

`$last_page`: Number of last reachable page

`$current_page`: Number of currently selected page

`$page_count`: Number of reachable pages

$items_per_page: Maximum number of items per page

$first_item: Index of first item on the current page

$last_item: Index of last item on the current page

$item_count: Total number of items

$link_first: Link to first page (unless this is the first page)

$link_last: Link to last page (unless this is the last page)

$link_previous: Link to previous page (unless this is the first page)

$link_next: Link to next page (unless this is the last page)

Because these variables look a bit like Mako variables, you might be tempted to think you can put other template markup in the format string to .pager(), but in fact you can use only these variables.

Figure 8-5 shows a page generated with the paginator-enhanced code.

Figure 8-5. *The paginator in action*

Formatting Dates and Times

To get the date to display in the way it does in the paginator column, you made use of the fact that Python datetime.datetime objects have a strftime() method that turns a date to a string based on the arguments specified. You used %c, which tells the strftime() method to use the locale's appropriate date and time representation. The display format is highly customizable, though, and takes the options documented in Table 8-1.

Table 8-1. *Python Date and Time Formatting Directives*

Directive	Meaning	Notes
%a	Locale's abbreviated weekday name.	
%A	Locale's full weekday name.	
%b	Locale's abbreviated month name.	
%B	Locale's full month name.	
%c	Locale's appropriate date and time representation.	
%d	Day of the month as a decimal number [01,31].	
%H	Hour (24-hour clock) as a decimal number [00,23].	
%I	Hour (12-hour clock) as a decimal number [01,12].	
%j	Day of the year as a decimal number [001,366].	
%m	Month as a decimal number [01,12].	
%M	Minute as a decimal number [00,59].	
%p	Locale's equivalent of either a.m. or p.m.	
%S	Second as a decimal number [00,61].	The range really is 0 to 61; this accounts for leap seconds and the (very rare) double leap seconds.
%U	Week number of the year (with Sunday as the first day of the week) as a decimal number [00,53]. All days in a new year preceding the first Sunday are considered to be in week 0.	
%w	Weekday as a decimal number [0(Sunday),6].	
%W	Week number of the year (with Monday as the first day of the week) as a decimal number [00,53]. All days in a new year preceding the first Monday are considered to be in week 0.	
%x	Locale's appropriate date representation.	
%X	Locale's appropriate time representation.	
%y	Year without century as a decimal number [00,99].	
%Y	Year with century as a decimal number.	
%Z	Time zone name (no characters if no time zone exists).	
%%	A literal % character.	

Using Sessions and a Flash Message

One of the problems with the setup you have so far is that no notification is displayed to confirm that changes have been successfully saved after you've edited a page. As was hinted at earlier in the chapter, you can solve this problem by using Pylons' session-handling facilities to display a *flash message*.

Session handling is actually provided in Pylons by the Beaker package set up as middleware, and it can be configured in your development.ini file. By default, session information is stored in a sessions directory within the directory specified by the cache_dir option. This means that by default sessions are stored in your project's data/sessions directory.

Start by importing the session object into the page controller:

```
from pylons import session
```

The session object exposes a dictionary-like interface that allows you to attach any Python object that can be pickled (see http://docs.python.org/lib/module-pickle.html) as a value against a named key. After a call to session.save(), the session information is saved, and a cookie is automatically set. On subsequent requests, the Beaker middleware can read the session cookie, and you can then access the value against the named key.

In the save() action, you simply need to add the following lines before the redirect at the end of the action:

```
session['flash'] = 'Page successfully updated.'
session.save()
```

Now the message will be saved to the flash key. Then in the base template, you'll need some code to look up the flash key and display the message if one exists. Add the following to the end of templates/base/index.html:

```
<%def name="flash()">
    % if session.has_key('flash'):
    <div id="flash"><p>${session.get('flash')}</p></div>
    <%
        del session['flash']
        session.save()
    %>
    % endif
</%def>
```

Now add this in the same template before the call to ${next.body()}:

```
${self.flash()}
```

Let's also add some style so the message is properly highlighted. Add this to the public/css/main.css file:

```
#flash {
    background: #ffc;
    padding: 5px;
    border: 1px dotted #000;
    margin-bottom: 20px;
}
#flash p { margin: 0px; padding: 0px; }
```

Now when the save() action is called, the message is saved in the session so that when the browser is redirected to the view() page, the message can be read back and displayed on the screen.

Give it a go by editing and saving a page (see Figure 8-6).

Figure 8-6. *The flash message in action*

You can find more information about Pylons sessions at `http://docs.pylonshq.com/sessions.html`.

Summary

That's it! You have created a very simple working web page editor. Now, although the site so far does everything you set out for it to do and forms a very good basis for any application you might create yourself, you'll probably agree it isn't overly exciting. In the rest of the book, you'll change that by adding a comment system, a tagging facility, a navigation hierarchy, a hint of Ajax, and a set of navigation widgets. By the end of the book, you'll have a template project that will serve very well as a basis for many of your own projects, and you will understand many of the key principles you will need to write your own Pylons applications.

PART 2

■ ■ ■

Advanced Pylons

# CHAPTER 9

URLs, Routing, and Dispatch

All web applications and frameworks need some mechanism for mapping the URL that a user enters in the browser to the code that should be executed when the server receives the request. Different languages and frameworks take different approaches to this. In PHP- or CGI-based systems, the URL represents a path on the hard disk to the file that should be executed. In Zope, URLs are treated as paths in an object hierarchy, and in Django, URLs are matched to code based on regular expressions.

Pylons doesn't use any of these approaches. Instead, it uses a very powerful and flexible system called Routes, which is an improved version of the Ruby on Rails routing system. Routes allows you to quickly and easily specify how groups of similar URLs map to your controllers; in turn, this allows you to create whatever URL structure you prefer for your application. Unlike other lookup systems, the URL is completely decoupled from the code that handles it. This also makes it easier to change your URL structure if you need to do so.

You've already seen Routes in action in previous chapters. For example, in Chapter 3 you saw a route that looked like this:

```
map.connect('/{controller}/{action}/{id}')
```

Each of the labels between curly brackets represents dynamic parts of a route. When a route is matched, the corresponding URL parts are matched, and their values are assigned to routing variables corresponding to the labels of the dynamic parts within the curly brackets. In this way, the one route can be used to match a large range of URLs.

You can also use Routes to generate URLs with `h.url_for()`. To do this, you need to import the Routes `url_for()` function into your project's `lib/helpers.py` file:

```
from routes import url_for
```

Here's an example of how to use `h.url_for()`, which results in the URL `/page/view/1` being generated:

```
h.url_for(controller='page', action='view', id=1)
```

As you can see, the arguments to `h.url_for()` correspond to the routing variable names used when defining the route.

When a user visits this URL, the same route used for generating the URL will also be used for matching it. In this case, the URL generated by the earlier call to `h.url_for()` will also generate the routing variables `controller='page'`, `action='view'`, and `id=1` when the URL is visited, and this results in the page controller's `view()` action being called with the ID 1.

You can also give individual routes a name by specifying a string as the first argument to `map.connect()`. This reduces the amount of typing you have to do when generating URLs. For example, you might define this route:

```
map.connect('blog_entry', '/blog/view/{id}')
```

You could then generate a URL to the entry with ID 1 like this:

```
h.url_for('blog_entry', id=1)
```

Now that you have a rough feel for how Routes works, let's dive in straightaway and look at how Routes is set up and used in Pylons and how Pylons uses information from Routes to dispatch requests.

■**Caution** One problem with Routes is that because it was originally ported from the Ruby on Rails implementation, it still contains a number of features that you might have used when developing a Pylons 0.9.6 project that are no longer considered good practice. In the section "Unnecessary Routes Features" later in this chapter, I'll explain why these features are no longer recommended. It is likely they will be removed in a future version of Routes, so it is important you avoid using them.

Pylons Routing in Detail

At its heart Routes is all about two things: analyzing a URL to produce a list of variables and being able to re-generate that URL from the same variables. These variables are known as *routing variables*, and they are used by Pylons to determine which controller action should be called and the arguments it should be called with. The URL matching is done by comparing the URL to a series of strings known as *route paths*, which, together with a set of options, define how a particular set of URLs can be turned into routing variables and back to URLs again. The route paths and options together are known as a *route*, and a set of routes is known as a *route map*.

Let's see how these concepts are applied in a Pylons application. You can find your project's route map in its config/routing.py file. Let's use the SimpleSite route map as an example. It looks like this:

```
def make_map():
    """Create, configure and return the routes Mapper"""
    map = Mapper(directory=config['pylons.paths']['controllers'],
                 always_scan=config['debug'])
    map.minimization = False

    # The ErrorController route (handles 404/500 error pages); it should
    # likely stay at the top, ensuring it can always be resolved
    map.connect('/error/{action}', controller='error')
    map.connect('/error/{action}/{id}', controller='error')

    # CUSTOM ROUTES HERE

    map.connect('/{controller}/{action}')
    map.connect('/{controller}/{action}/{id}')

    return map
```

Here you can see that the make_map() function is responsible for creating a route map object called map and returning it. The routes are added to the map via the map.connect() function, which takes a route path such as '/{controller}/{action}/{id}' and some optional arguments called the *route options*. Each of the labels for the dynamic parts between the { and } characters specify the positions of routing variables that are matched against any value in the corresponding position within a URL. When a URL is entered, Pylons tries to match it by calling `map.match(url)`. Routes then searches each of the routes in the route map from top to bottom until it finds a route that matches the URL. Because matching is done from top to bottom, you are always advised to put your custom routes below the ones that Pylons provides to ensure you don't accidentally interfere with the default behavior of Pylons. More generally speaking, you should always put your most general routes at the bottom of the route map so that they don't accidentally get matched before a more specific route lower down in the route map.

To demonstrate the behavior of the route map as it stands, let's consider some example URLs and the routing variables that are produced when the URL is matched. Let's start with the site root URL, which is /:

```
URL:    /
Result: None
```

As you can see, there are no routes with just one / character in them, so the URL / is not currently matched. If you visited this URL, you would see the `index.html` file served from your project's `public` directory or a 404 Not Found error page. You'll add a route to handle the root URL in the second part of the SimpleSite tutorial in Chapter 14.

```
URL:    /page/view/1
Result: {'action': 'view', 'controller': 'page', 'id': '1'}
```

As you already know from having tested the SimpleSite application in Chapter 8, this URL is matched by the last route in the route map and results in a page being displayed. The URL fragment `page` is matched to {`controller`}, `view` is matched to {`action`}, and 1 is matched to {`id`}.

Now consider the URL /error/img:

```
URL:    /error/img/logo.png
Result: {'action': 'img', 'controller': 'error', 'id': 'logo.png'}
```

This is matched by the second route, `map.connect('/error/{action}', controller='error')`, because the first part of the URL begins with /error/. The img part is matched to {`action`}, and `logo.png` is matched to {`id`}. Notice that the route path doesn't contain a {`controller`} part, though, so you might wonder how the `controller` routing variable gets assigned a value. You'll see in the route map that the error route definition also takes a default argument of `controller='error'`. This means that if the route is matched, the `controller` routing variable will be automatically added to the results with a value of `'error'`. You'll learn about how Pylons uses this route in its internal handling of error documents in Chapter 19.

So far, this should all seem fairly intuitive; URLs are matched against static text or dynamic parts representing routing variables in the route path, and default values can be added when needed. Let's try another example:

```
URL:    /section/view/1
Result: None
```

This time the URL isn't matched even though at first glance it looks like it should be. To understand why, you need to know a little bit more about how Routes works.

The `Mapper` object takes a number of arguments, including the following:

`controller_scan`: This takes a function that will be used to return a list of valid controllers during URL matching. If the `directory` argument is also specified, it will be passed into the function when it is called.

`directory`: This is passed into `controller_scan` for the directory to scan. It should be an absolute path if using the default `controller_scan` function.

`always_scan`: This specifies whether the `controller_scan` function should be run during every URL match. This is typically a good idea during development so the server won't need to be restarted when a controller is added, but you might want to disable it on production systems to avoid the small overhead of the check. After all, you are unlikely to have specified routes to controllers that don't exist in production code.

`explicit`: This has a default value of `False`, but when it is set to `True`, some of the features of Routes such as route memory and implicit defaults are disabled. You'll learn about these features and why you should usually set this option to `True` in the "Unnecessary Routes Features" section.

Pylons uses the Routes default `controller_scan()` function, which will scan the directory specified by the `directory` argument to check for controllers. If a particular route matches a URL but the controller resulting from the match doesn't exist, the route will be ignored, and the next route will be tried. In this case, the `directory` argument is set to `config['pylons.paths']['controllers']`, which contains the path to your project's `controllers` directory. Since no `section` controller exists yet, the route in the previous example didn't match. For production use, you don't need to have Routes scan the controller directory on each match because the controllers aren't likely to change, so the `always_scan` variable is automatically set to the same value as the value of the `debug` option in the config file, enabling the scan in development mode and disabling it in production mode.

■Note You are very unlikely to want to customize the `controller_scan()` function in your own application, but I've mentioned it here so that you are aware of its behavior when you see it crop up in some of the examples in this chapter.

By carefully defining routes and specifying their order in the *route map*, it is possible to quickly and easily map quite complex URL structures into simple sets of routing variables that can be used in your application. Before you go on to look at the details of how to write your own routes, let's take a brief look at how Pylons uses the routing variables to call a particular controller action.

Pylons Dispatch

Once a URL has been matched against a route and the controller has been verified to exist, Pylons checks to see whether it can find the action.

Pylons is set up so that any controller methods that start with an _ character are not considered actions at all and cannot be called as a result of a URL dispatch. If the action specified in the routing variables doesn't exist or it starts with an _ character, then the check fails. In debug mode for development, this raises an exception to explain the mistake; in production mode, it simply results in a 404 Not Found error page being displayed.

If the controller and action both exist, then Pylons looks for a `__before__()` method attached to the controller class. If the method exists, it is executed. The `__before__()` method can therefore be used to set up per-request objects or perform other processing to be carried out before each action in the controller is called.

Next, Pylons inspects the action to see what arguments it takes and calls it in such a way that any arguments that have the same names as the routing variables are called with the value of the routing variable as the argument. Here are some examples:

```
# No routing variables used in the action
def no_routing_variables(self):
    return 'No routing variables used'
```

```
# Populate the ``id`` with the value of the ``id`` routing variable
def id_present(self, id):
    return 'The id is %s' % id
```

Tip You've already seen routing variables being used in this way in the `page` controller from the SimpleSite tutorial in Chapter 8, and you'll recall from Chapter 3 that you can also retrieve the `controller` name and `action` in the same way. All the routing variables that are passed to the action are also automatically added as attributes to the template context global `c`.

In addition to routing variables, you can also specify both `environ` and `start_response` as arguments in your actions. The `environ` argument will get populated with the same WSGI environment dictionary you can access via the Pylons request global as `request.environ`, and the `start_response()` callable is a WSGI callable you'll learn about in Chapter 16. Both `environ` and `start_response` get added as attributes to the template context global c in the same way as the routing variables do if you use them in an action. To see all these features in action, consider the following example. When the `test()` action is called, the browser will display `True`, `True`, `True`, `True`:

```
def __before__(self, id):
    c.id_set_in_before = id

def test(self, environ, start_response, controller, id):
    w = c.id_set_in_before == id
    x = c.environ == environ == request.environ
    y = c.start_response == start_response
    z = c.controller == controller
    request.content_type = 'text/plain'
    return "%s %s, %s, %s"%(w, x, y, z)
```

After an action is called, Pylons looks for an __after__() method attached to the controller, and if it exists, it is called too. You can use __after__() for performing any cleanup of objects you created in the __before__() method.

Both the __before__() and __after__() methods can also accept any of the routing variable names as arguments in exactly the same way as the controller action can.

Of course, there are occasions where it is useful to be able to access the routing variables outside your controller code. All the routing variables are available in the `request.urlvars` dictionary and are also available in `request.environ["wsgiorg.routing_args"]`.

Routes in Detail

Now that you have seen some examples of routes being matched against URLs and understand how Pylons uses the routing variables to dispatch to your controller actions, it is time to learn the details of how you can construct individual routes.

Route Parts

As you've already seen, a route is specified by arguments to `map.connect()` that include a route path and a number of options. The route path itself can consist of a number of different types of parts between / characters:

Static parts: These are plain-text parts of the URL that don't result in any route variables being defined. In the default Pylons setup, the string error in the route path /error/{action} is a static part.

Dynamic parts: The text in the URL matching the dynamic part is assigned to a routing variable of that name. Dynamic parts are marked in the route path as the routing variable name within curly brackets. In the default Pylons setup, the string {action} in the route path /error/{action} is a dynamic part. Dynamic parts can also be specified by the routing variable name preceded by a colon, which is the style used in earlier versions of Routes. For example, you could change the first error route path from /error/{action} to /error/:action, and it would still work.

Wildcard parts: A wildcard part will match *everything* (including / characters) except the other parts around it. Wildcard parts are marked in the route path by preceding them with the * character. The default Pylons setup doesn't include any routes that use wildcard parts, but you can use them in your own routes if you need to do so.

To demonstrate the different types of route parts, consider the following URL:

```
/wiki/page/view/some/variable/depth/file.html
```

and a route path to match it, which includes a wildcard part:

```
/wiki/{controller}/{action}/*url
```

In this case, wiki is treated as a static part, and page is a dynamic part that is assigned to the controller route variable. In Routes, / characters separating dynamic or wildcard parts are not treated as static parts, so the next / is ignored. view is a dynamic part assigned to the action route variable. The following / is also ignored, and the whole of the rest of the URL is considered a wildcard part and assigned to the url route variable.

Any URL starting with /wiki/ followed by two sets of characters, each followed by a / character, will be matched by this route path as long as the controller exists.

Let's test this with a simple example. Rather than modifying the SimpleSite project, you can set up your own route map directly. You just have to specify a dummy controller_scan function to return a list of valid controllers. In the example, map.minimization is set to False so that the route map is set up in the same way it would be in a Pylons application. The controller_scan() function will just return ['error', 'page'] to simulate that only the page and error controllers exist. Here's what the route map looks like:

```
>>> def controller_scan(directory=None):
>>>     return ['error', 'page']
...
>>> from routes import Mapper
>>> map = Mapper(controller_scan=controller_scan)
>>> map.minimization = False
>>> map.connect('/wiki/{controller}/{action}/*url')
>>> print map.match('/wiki/page/view/some/variable/depth/file.html')
{'action': u'view', 'url': u'some/variable/depth/file.html', 'controller': u'page'}
```

The URL is matched as expected. Let's try to match some different URLs:

```
>>> print map.match('/some/other/url')
None
>>> print map.match('/wiki/folder/view/some/variable/depth/file.html')
None
```

Notice that if the URL doesn't match or if the matched controller doesn't exist, the route is not matched, and the `map.match()` function returns `None`.

The Pylons implementation of Routes doesn't require the dynamic and wildcard portions of the route path to be separated by a / character. Here you're using a . character as a separator. Note that you need to create a new `Mapper` to set this new route because you have already called `map.connect()` on the previous one. Once again, you use the dummy `controller_scan()` function and set `map.minimization = False` to turn off minimization in the same way as the Pylons setup:

```
>>> map = Mapper(controller_scan=controller_scan)
>>> map.minimization = False
>>> map.connect('/blog/{controller}.{action}.*url')
>>> print map.match('/blog/page.view.some/variable/depth/file.html')
{'action': u'view', 'url': u'some/variable/depth/file.html', 'controller': u'page'}
```

As these examples have demonstrated, you can think of wildcard parts as being very much like dynamic parts but also matching / characters.

Although wildcard parts are a powerful tool, they generally aren't used very often and can be a sign that you haven't designed your routes very well. The risk is that because they match any character including /, they will match very many URLs. If you were to have a wildcard route near the top of your route map, it could easily match URLs for which there was a more specific route later in the route map. The vast majority of the time you will just use static and dynamic parts in your route paths, but if you do use wildcard routes, they should always be placed near the bottom of the route map to avoid them accidentally matching URLs when there is a more specific route later in the map.

These are three cases when you might choose to use wildcard routes:

- When an entire portion of the URL is going to be passed to another application (for example, Paste's static file server)

- When you are trying to match a string ID that might include / characters

- When you want to pass the entire request URL to a particular action to handle an error condition, rather than allowing a 404 Not Found error page to be returned

Default Variables

With the knowledge you've already gained, you will be able to create most of the routes you are likely to need, but there is one problem. Every route matched must result in at least the routing variables `controller` and `action` being assigned a value, but URLs such as / don't contain enough characters to be able to deduce the controller and action names from them.

To solve this problem, Routes allows you to specify default values for any routing variables as part of the routing map's `connect()` function. You've already seen default variables in action during the discussion of Pylons' error route, but let's look at another example:

```
>>> map = Mapper(controller_scan=controller_scan)
>>> map.minimization = False
>>> map.connect('/archives/by_eon/{century}', controller='page', action='list')
```

In this example, the `controller` and `action` both have default values, so they are called *default variables*. You'll notice that you can't create a URL that will affect the value of the `controller` and `action` variables since they aren't present in the route path, so their default values of `'archives'` and `'list'` will always be used. Such variables are known as *hard-coded variables*.

The value assigned to the `century` routing variable will depend on the URL with which it is matched:

```
>>> print map.match('/archives/by_eon/')
None
>>> print map.match('/archives/by_eon')
None
>>> print map.match('/archives/by_eon/1800')
{'action': u'aggregate', 'controller': u'page', 'century': u'1800'}
```

■**Caution** One thing you have to be aware of when choosing names for routing arguments is that the `map.connect()` method also accepts certain keyword arguments including `requirement`, `_explicit`, `_encoding`, and `_filter`. If you choose a routing variable with the same name as one of these arguments, then you will not be able to specify a default value because Routes will not interpret the argument as a default value. To prevent this potential problem, future versions of Routes will not allow any routing variable names starting with an `_` character, so you would be wise to avoid starting your routing variables with an `_`.

You should avoid using two other names as routing variables; these are the WSGI objects `environ` and `start_response`. Both can be passed automatically to controller actions when they are called. If you choose routing variables with the same names as these, you won't be able to access the routing variables as arguments to the controller actions because the Pylons dispatch mechanism will assume you want the WSGI objects themselves rather than the routing variables of the same name.

It is possible to take the use of default variables to an extreme. A route where the controller and action are hard-coded is known as an *explicit route*. Here's an example:

```
map.connect('/blog/view/1', controller='blog', action='view', id=1)
```

Here the whole route path is made only from static parts, and all the routing variables are hard-coded as default variables. The benefit of this approach is that only one URL will ever match this route, but the drawback is that defining all your URLs this way requires adding an awful lot of routes to your application.

Generating URLs

Now that you have seen how Pylons uses Routes and you understand the details of how URLs are matched, you can turn your attention once again to how to generate URLs.

Routes includes two functions for use in your web application that you will find yourself using frequently:

- `h.url_for()`
- `redirect_to()`

You've already seen the `h.url_for()` function a few times, and you'll recall that to make it available in your controllers and templates, you need to import it into your project's `lib/helpers.py` file from the `routes` module.

The `redirect_to()` function is automatically imported into your controllers from the `pylons.controllers.util` module. It is used to redirect a controller to a different URL within your application. If you look at the page controller in the SimpleSite project you've been developing, you'll see that up to now redirects have been coded manually by specifying the correct HTTP status code for a redirect and setting a `Location` HTTP header using the `response` global. Here's the `save()` action as an example:

```
@restrict('POST')
@validate(schema=NewPageForm(), form='edit')
def save(self, id=None):
    page_q = meta.Session.query(model.Page)
    page = page_q.filter_by(id=id).first()
    if page is None:
        abort(404)
    for k,v in self.form_result.items():
        if getattr(page, k) != v:
            setattr(page, k, v)
    meta.Session.commit()
    session['flash'] = 'Page successfully updated.'
    session.save()
    # Issue an HTTP redirect
    response.status_int = 302
    response.headers['location'] = h.url_for(controller='page', action='view', I
        id=page.id)
    return "Moved temporarily"
```

You could instead replace the last five lines to use `redirect_to()` like this:

```
# Issue an HTTP redirect
return redirect_to(controller='page', action='view', id=page.id)
```

As you can see, this is much neater, so it is a good idea to use `redirect_to()` in your controllers rather than writing out the long version of the code. `redirect_to()` is commonly used after a form submission to redirect to another URL so that if the user clicks Refresh, the form data isn't sent again.

One of the major benefits of using `h.url_for()` and `redirect_to()` rather than generating your own URLs manually is that Pylons can automatically take account of the URL at which your application is deployed and adjust the URLs automatically.

As an example, imagine you have created a new Pylons project to manage application forms. You might choose to deploy the Pylons application at a URL such as `/forms` so that it appears to be part of an existing site. This means that when a user visits `/forms`, the Pylons application needs to know that they are really requesting a URL, which would be `/` if the Pylons application was running on a stand-alone server. This also means that any time the application creates a URL, it has to start `/forms`; otherwise, the links wouldn't point to the Pylons application. In this setup, the `SCRIPT_NAME` environment variable would be set to `/forms` so Pylons can work out that the URLs needed to be adjusted. Any time you call any of the Pylons URL generation functions, the URL generated is modified to take account of the `SCRIPT_NAME` environment variable, so all the URLs get generated correctly without needing any manual modification.

Named Routes

If you are regularly using the same route in your application, it can quickly become tedious to type all the routing variables every time you want to use `h.url_for()`. This is where *named routes* come in. A named route is like an ordinary route, but you access it directly via a name.

Here's an example:

```
map.connect('category_home', 'category/{section}', controller='blog', action='view',
        section='home')
```

Then in your Pylons application you might use this:

```
h.url_for('category_home')
```

This is equivalent to generating the URL using the routing variables in full, both generate the URL /category/home:

```
h.url_for(controller='blog', action='view', section='home')
```

As you can see, this saves a bit of typing. You can also specify keyword arguments, and it will override defaults associated with the route name. The following:

```
h.url_for('category_home', section='admin')
```

generates the URL /category/admin and is equivalent to this:

```
h.url_for(controller='blog', action='view', section='admin')
```

Static Named Routes

Routes also supports a feature called *static named routes*. These are routes that do not involve actual URL generation but instead allow you to quickly alias common URLs that are external to your site. To make a route static, you add _static=True as an argument. For example, if your route map contained this:

```
map.connect('google_search', 'http://www.google.com/search', _static=True)
```

you could now reference http://www.google.com/search by typing this in your application:

```
h.url_for('google_search')
```

This is especially useful if you are accessing resources throughout your application that you think might change because it means you have to change the URL in only one place. Static named routes are ignored entirely when matching a URL.

Internal Static Routes

You can also use h.url_for() to reference static resources in your project's public directory. Routes will automatically prepend the URL you give it with the proper SCRIPT_NAME so that even if you are running your Pylons application under a different URL, the correct URL will be generated. For example, if your Pylons application was mounted at /forms and you used this in your application, the URL /forms/css/source.css would be correctly generated with this code:

```
h.url_for('/css/source.css')
```

For portable web applications, it's highly encouraged that you use h.url_for() for all your URLs, even those that are static resources and images. This will ensure that the URLs are properly handled in any of the possible deployment setups you could use for your application.

Choosing Good URLs

Now that you've seen some of the ways you can use Routes to match and generate URLs, let's take a look at what actually makes a good URL structure.

First here's a definition of the parts of a URL:

```
http://jimmyg.org:80/some/url#fragment?foo=bar
|--|   |---------|--|--------|--------|------|
 |          |      |    |        |        |
protocol    |     port  |    fragment    |
        domain name  path info      query string
```

Now here are some tips:

Describe the content: An obvious URL is a great URL. If a user can glance at a link in an email and know what it contains, you have done your job. This means choosing URL parts that accurately describe what is contained at that level of the URL structure. It's usually better to use a descriptive word rather than an ID in the URL wherever possible. For example, if you were designing a blog, you should try to use apr instead of 04 to represent April, and you should use the name of a category rather than its ID if that is appropriate. Choosing URLs that describe their content makes your application intuitive to your users and gives search engines a better chance of accurately ranking the page.

Tip Edward Cutrell and Zhiwei Guan from Microsoft Research conducted an eye-tracking study of search engine use that found people spend 24 percent of their "gaze time" looking at the URLs in the search results. If your URLs accurately describe their content, users can make a better guess about whether your content is relevant to them.

Keep it short: Try to keep your URLs as short as possible without breaking any of the other tips here. Short URLs are easier to type or to copy and paste into documents and emails. If possible, keeping URLs to less than 80 characters is ideal so that users can paste URLs into email without having to use URL-shortening tools such as tinyurl.com.

Hyphens separate best: It is best to use single words in each part of a URL, but if you have to use multiple words, such as for the title of a blog post, then hyphens are the best characters to use to separate the words, as in /2008/nov/my-blog-post-title/. The - character cannot be used in Python keywords, so if you intend to use the URL fragments as Python controller names or actions, you might want to convert them to _ characters first. Incidentally, using hyphens to separate words is also the most readable way of separating terms in CSS styles.

Static-looking URLs are best: Regardless of how your content is actually generated, it is worth structuring URLs so that they don't contain lots of &, =, and ? characters that most visitors won't properly understand. If you can write a URL like ?type=food&category=apple as /food/apple, then users can see much more quickly what it is about. Routes makes this sort of transformation easy, so there is no need to make extensive use of variables in query strings when they could form part of the URL.

Keeping URLs lowercase makes your life easier: The protocol and domain name parts of a URL can technically be entered in any case, but the optional fragment part after the # character is case sensitive. How a particular server treats anything between the two depends on the server, operating system, and what the URL resolves to. Since Pylons applications can be deployed on many different servers, you have to be aware of the potential problems. Unix filesystems are usually case sensitive, while Windows ones aren't. Mac OS X systems can be case sensitive or case insensitive depending on the filesystem. This means that if the URL resolves to a file, Windows servers will generally allow any case, while Unix ones won't. Query string parameters are also case sensitive. You can generally save yourself a headache by keeping everything lowercase and issuing a 404 for anything that isn't. Of course, if you are writing a wiki application where the page names depend on the capitalization, then you'll need to make the URLs case sensitive.

Keep the underlying technology out of the URL: Your users aren't likely to care which specific technology you are using to generate your pages or whether they are generated as HTML or XHTML, so the basic rule is don't use a file extension for dynamically generated pages unless you are doing something clever in your application internally like determining the format to represent the content based on the extension. It is generally best to choose names that represent what the URL *is* rather than its technology.

Never change a URL: Otherwise, your users won't be able to find the page they bookmarked, and any page rank you built up in social bookmarking sites or search engines will be lost. If you absolutely have to change a URL, ensure you set up a permanent 301 redirect to the new one so that your users don't get 404 errors. The W3C put it best: "Cool URLs don't change."

Only use disambiguated URLs: Any piece of content should have one and only one definitive URL, with any alternatives acting as a permanent redirect. In the past, features such as Apache's `DirectoryIndex` have meant that if you entered a URL that resolved to a folder, the default document for that folder would be served. This means that two URLs would exist for one resource. To make matters worse, servers are often configured so that `http://www.example.com/someresource` and `http://example.com/someresource` both point to the same resource. This means there can easily be four URLs for the same resource.

There are three good reasons why this is bad:

- Search engines and social bookmarking sites give pages with the most links the highest rank. If you have four different URLs for the same page, different people are likely to link to different versions, so you are effectively dividing your rank by 4.

- Browser or server caches will have to cache four versions of the page. Put another way, this means they can't improve performance if a user visits a different version of the same URL the second time.

- All versions of the page will be treated by web browsers as different resources, so the user's browsing history won't be accurate.

The only time you might want to have more than one URL for the same resource is if all but one of the URLs redirects to the other one so that users of your site who have already bookmarked links can still find them.

Treat the URL as part of the UI: Navigation links, sidebars, and tabs are all well and good, but if you have a good URL structure, your users should be able to navigate your site by changing parts of the URL. There are a few rules about how best to do this:

- Ensure that for every part of the path info part of a URL that a user might remove, a useful page is returned. For example, if the URL `/2007/nov/entry` gives a blog entry, `2007/nov` might list all the November entries, and `/2007` might list all entries from 2007.

- Never have a URL on your domain that gives a 500 error. It doesn't take a genius to realize that you don't want any URL in your web site to crash and cause a server error, but developers don't always think about what will happen if a user starts hacking the URL to contain different values. For example, if you have a URL `/food/apple` and a user changes it to `/food/pizza` when the application is set up only to deal with fruit, it should give a 404 Page Not Found error, not a 500 Internal Server error. Users are much more likely to stop trying to guess URLs if they get a 500 page because they'll be worried either that they might be breaking something or that the site is of low quality. The moment they stop hacking the URL, it has lost its usefulness as a UI component.

The most important tip is that you should use common sense when designing a URL structure. Don't apply any of the tips too rigidly; after all, you know your application and your users' requirements, so you can use your judgment about what will work best for you.

Unnecessary Routes Features

Because Routes was originally ported from the Ruby on Rails version, a few "features" have been added that in hindsight aren't necessary and are best to disable. In the following sections, you'll look at these features, what they do, and how to disable them.

■**Note** It is highly likely that all these features will be completely removed in a future release of Routes.

Route Minimization

Previous versions of Pylons had a feature called *route minimization* enabled by default. Route minimization allowed you to specify optional default variables for a particular route. To demonstrate route minimization, let's look at the previous example again but this time with minimization enabled and with an optional default variable, century:

```
>>> map = Mapper(controller_scan=controller_scan)
>>> map.minimization = True
>>> map.connect('/archives/by_eon/{century}', controller='page',
...      action='aggregate', century=1800)
>>> print map.match('/archives/by_eon/')
{'action': u'aggregate', 'controller': u'page', 'century': u'1800'}
>>> print map.match('/archives/by_eon')
{'action': u'aggregate', 'controller': u'page', 'century': u'1800'}
>>> print map.match('/archives/by_eon/1800')
{'action': u'aggregate', 'controller': u'page', 'century': u'1800'}
```

Notice this time that all three URLs result in a match, even though two of them don't have a part of the URL that could correspond to the century dynamic part. This is because with minimization enabled, Routes assumes you want to use the optional default variables automatically if they aren't specified in the URL.

Here are some of the reasons why route minimization is a bad idea:

- It means multiple URLs serve the same page, which as explained earlier is bad for caches and search engine rankings.

- It makes it difficult to choose which URL should be generated for a particular action when using h.url_for(), so Routes always generates the shortest URL with minimization enabled.

- Complex routes and many defaults can make it hard to predict which route will be matched.

It is recommended that you leave route minimization disabled by keeping map.minimization set to False at the top of your route map.

Route Memory

One feature of Routes that was designed to make your life as a developer easier was called *route memory*. When your controller and action are matched from the URL, the routing variables that are set get remembered for the rest of that request. This means that when you are using h.url_for(), you actually only need to specify routing variables, which are different from the ones matched in the current request.

Consider this route:

```
map.connect('/archives/{year}/{month}/{day}', controller='page', action='view')
```

If the URL /archives/2008/10/4 was entered, this route would match the following variables:

```
{'controller': 'page', 'action': 'view', 'year': '2008', 'month': '10', 'day': '4'}
```

With these routing variables matched, h.url_for() would generate the following results:

```
h.url_for(day=6)        # =>    /page/2008/10/6
h.url_for(month=4)      # =>    /page/2008/4/4
h.url_for(year=2009)    # =>    /page/2009/10/4
```

The majority of times you use h.url_for() will be in view templates. Since the same template is often called from multiple different controllers and actions, you can't always rely on h.url_for() generating the same URL in the same template, and this can introduce unexpected bugs, so it is usually much better to specify all your routing arguments explicitly.

There is another problem with route memory. Consider a route map set up with the following routes:

```
map.connect('/{controller}/{action}')
map.connect('/{controller}/{action}/{id}')
```

With route memory enabled, let's imagine someone visited the URL /page/view/1. Here are the routing variables that would be matched:

```
{'controller': 'page', 'action': 'view', 'id': '1'}
```

Now try to work out which URL would be generated with this code:

```
h.url_for(controller='page', action='new')
```

The result is /page/new/1 even though the new() action might not take an id argument. This means that in order to have this matched by the first route to generate the URL /page/new, you would have to explicitly specify id=None like this:

```
h.url_for(controller='page', action='new', id=None)
```

You may not have noticed, but this is exactly what you did in the footer for the SimpleSite view.html template in Chapter 8. If route memory was disabled globally, you would not have had to specify id=None for the new(), list(), or delete() action routes.

As well as explicitly setting a routing variable to None, you can also disable route memory on a per-call basis by specifying the controller starting with a / character. For example:

```
h.url_for(controller='/page', action='new')
```

This is not ideal either, though. To avoid this complication, it is highly recommended that you disable route memory completely and always specify all arguments to h.url_for() explicitly. You can do this by passing explicit=True to the Mapper() constructor in your project's config/routing.py. This will ensure route memory isn't used, and you will have to explicitly specify each routing variable in every call to h.url_for():

```
map = Mapper(directory=config['pylons.paths']['controllers'],
    always_scan=config['debug'], explicit=True)
```

If you should choose not to disable the route memory feature, you should be aware that it works only with h.url_for() and not with its counterpart redirect_to().

Implicit Defaults

Routes has a surprising legacy feature that means that if you don't specify a controller and an action for a particular route, the *implicit defaults* of `controller='content'` and `action='index'` will be used for you. This can be demonstrated very simply:

```
>>> map = Mapper(controller_scan=controller_scan)
>>> map.minimization = False
>>> map.connect('/archives/')
>>> print map.match('/archives/')
{'action': u'index', 'controller': u'content'}
```

It is highly unlikely you want Routes to make up `action` and `controller` variables for you, so it's strongly recommended that you disable this feature. You can do this by passing `_explicit=True` as an argument to the individual routes you want implicit defaults to be disabled for:

```
>>> map = Mapper(controller_scan=controller_scan)
>>> map.minimization = False
>>> map.connect('/archives/', _explicit=True)
>>> print map.match('/archives/')
None
```

In reality, it is likely you will want these implicit defaults disabled for all your routes. Luckily, the `explicit=True` option you passed to the `Mapper()` object to disable route memory also disables implicit defaults, which is another reason to use it.

Best Practice

With route minimization, route memory, and implicit defaults disabled, the way you use Routes in your application might be quite different from the way you used it in previous versions of Pylons. To demonstrate this, let's look at an old routing structure that you might have used in Pylons 0.9.6:

```
>>> map = Mapper(controller_scan=controller_scan)
>>> map.minimize = True
>>> map.connect(':controller/:action/:id', controller='blog', action='view', id=1)
```

Here minimization is enabled as well as implicit routes and route memory. Look how many different URLs match the same controller, action, and ID. This clearly breaks the URL disambiguation rule listed earlier in the "Choosing Good URLs" section:

```
>>> print map.match('/blog/view/4/')
{'action': u'view', 'controller': u'blog', 'id': u'1'}
>>> print map.match('/blog/view/4')
{'action': u'view', 'controller': u'blog', 'id': u'1'}
>>> print map.match('/blog/view/')
{'action': u'view', 'controller': u'blog', 'id': u'1'}
>>> print map.match('/blog/view')
{'action': u'view', 'controller': u'blog', 'id': u'1'}
>>> print map.match('/blog/')
{'action': u'view', 'controller': u'blog', 'id': u'1'}
>>> print map.match('/blog')
{'action': u'view', 'controller': u'blog', 'id': u'1'}
>>> print map.match('/')
{'action': u'view', 'controller': u'blog', 'id': u'1'}
```

With route minimization, route memory, and implicit defaults disabled, you would have to add the following routes to achieve the same effect:

```
>>> map = Mapper(controller_scan=controller_scan, explicit=True)
>>> map.minimize = False
>>> map.connect('/', controller='blog', action='view', id=1)
>>> map.connect('/{controller}', action='view', id=1)
>>> map.connect('/{controller}/', action='view', id=1)
>>> map.connect('/{controller}/{action}', id=1)
>>> map.connect('/{controller}/{action}/', id=1)
>>> map.connect('/{controller}/{action}/{id}')
>>> map.connect('/{controller}/{action}/{id}/')
```

Of course, as has been mentioned, it is generally a bad idea to have more than one URL map to the same resource, so you are unlikely to want to do this in most applications. Even if you did want to do this, the explicit approach requires a lot more typing, but it is also much clearer what is happening. Although using explicit routes can sometimes mean more typing, being explicit about what you expect to happen makes life much easier when you have more complicated route setups.

Disabling route memory, implicit defaults, and route minimization also requires you to do more work when generating URLs, but once again, this will prevent you from finding obscure URL generation problems later in a project. To generate the URL to view the blog post with ID 1 and with the explicit argument set to True, you would always have to type the following, no matter which routing variables were generated for the request that calls the code:

```
h.url_for(controller='blog', action='view', id=1)
```

This would generate the URL / because this is the first route to match. Since routes are matched from top to bottom, if you wanted this to generate the URL /blog/view/1 instead you could move the second-to-last route to the top so that it was matched first. This would affect the way URLs were generated for other controllers too, though:

```
>>> map = Mapper(controller_scan=controller_scan, explicit=True)
>>> map.minimize = False
>>> map.connect('/{controller}/{action}/{id}')
>>> map.connect('/', controller='blog', action='view', id=1)
>>> map.connect('/{controller}', action='view', id=1)
>>> map.connect('/{controller}/', action='view', id=1)
>>> map.connect('/{controller}/{action}', id=1)
>>> map.connect('/{controller}/{action}/', id=1)
>>> map.connect('/{controller}/{action}/{id}/')
```

Alternatively, you could add an *explicit route* as the first route. You'll remember from the discussion of default variables earlier in the chapter that an explicit route matches only *one* URL:

```
>>> map = Mapper(controller_scan=controller_scan, explicit=True)
>>> map.minimize = False
>>> map.connect('/blog/view/1', controller='blog', action='view', id=1)
>>> map.connect('/', controller='blog', action='view', id=1)
>>> map.connect('/{controller}', action='view', id=1)
>>> map.connect('/{controller}/', action='view', id=1)
>>> map.connect('/{controller}/{action}', id=1)
>>> map.connect('/{controller}/{action}/', id=1)
>>> map.connect('/{controller}/{action}/{id}')
>>> map.connect('/{controller}/{action}/{id}/')
```

Some people would argue that you should always specify the controller and action for *every* URL as hard-coded default variables using an explicit or named route. There are some other advantages to this approach:

- Temporarily blocking access to a particular controller can be difficult with nonexplicit routes because it isn't always obvious whether another route you have specified will also resolve the URL to the controller. If you have named or explicit routes, you can just comment out the routes that point at the controller in question, and you're all set.

- Imagine you have a Pylons application that is a couple of years old and has an established group of users who have bookmarked various parts of your site. If you were to refactor the application, moving controllers around or putting certain actions in different controllers, you would find it difficult to maintain the existing URL structure if you were using implicit routes. With explicit or named routes, you could simply update where the URL pointed to so that the old URLs would still work.

I hope what is clear from the discussion in this section is that you should always set `explicit=True` in your `Mapper` to disable route memory and implicit defaults and that you should disable route minimization with `map.minimization=False`, but it is up to you whether you choose to go further and be even more explicit about your routes with hard-coded defaults for the controller and action or named routes.

Only you can decide whether ordinary, explicit, or named routes are the correct choice for your application. Ordinary routes that use the "convention over configuration" philosophy don't result in disambiguated URLs. Named and explicit routes give you complete control over how your URLs are generated but are more effort to set up. The nice thing about Routes is, of course, that you can use all three techniques together.

Advanced URL Routing

It is now time to learn about some of the really advanced features of Routes that, when used effectively, can very much simplify your route maps or enable your Pylons application to deal with any number of complex legacy URL structures you might have inherited from an old application.

Requirements

Any route you specify can have a `requirement` argument specified as a keyword to the map's `connect()` method. The requirement argument should be a dictionary of routing variable names for any dynamic or wildcard parts and a corresponding regular expression to match their values against. Regular expressions are documented in the Python documentation for the `re` module. Any valid Python regular expression can be used.

Here's an example:

```
map.connect('archives/{year}/{month}/{day}', controller='archives', action='view',
    year=2004,requirements={'year': '\d{2,4}', 'month': '\d{1,2}'})
```

One particularly useful regular expression used in the previous example is \d, which matches a digit. In this case, the year can be either two or four digits long, and the month can be one or two digits long.

Here's another example; this time we are ensuring the theme is one of the allowed themes:

```
theme_map = 'admin|home|members|system'
map.connect('users/{theme}/edit', controller='users',
    requirements={'theme': theme_map})
```

Conditions

Conditions specify a set of special conditions that must be met for the route to be accepted as a valid match for the URL. The conditions argument must always be a dictionary and can accept three different keys:

method: The request must be one of the HTTP methods defined here. This argument must be a list of HTTP methods and should be uppercase.

function: This is a function that will be used to evaluate whether the route is a match. This must return True or False and will be called with environ and match_dict as arguments. The match_dict is a dictionary with all the routing variables for the request. Any modifications your function makes to the match_dict will be picked up by Routes and used as the routing variables from that point on.

sub_domain: If this is present, it should be either True (which will match any subdomain) or a Python list of subdomain strings, one of which must match the subdomain used in the request for the route to match.

These three types of conditions can all be used together in the same route by specifying each argument to the conditions dictionary, but I'll discuss them each in turn.

Let's deal with the method option first. This allows you to match a URL based on the HTTP method the request was made with. One problem with testing examples using the method condition is that the match depends on information from the WSGI environment, which is usually set during a request. Since there isn't a real HTTP request for this test code, you have to emulate it, so in the following examples you set map.environ with fake environment information to test how the matching works. Obviously, you wouldn't do this in your own code. The example also sets up a new controller_scan() function which only accepts the value user for the controller:

```
>>> from routes import Mapper
>>> def controller_scan(directory=None):
>>>     return ['user']
...
>>> map = Mapper(controller_scan=controller_scan)
>>> map.minimization = False
>>> map.connect('/user/new/preview', controller='user', action='preview',
...     conditions=dict(method=['POST']))
>>> # The method to be either GET or HEAD
>>> map.connect('/user/list', controller='user', action='list',
...     conditions=dict(method=['GET', 'HEAD']))
>>> map.environ = {'REQUEST_METHOD':'POST'}
>>> print map.match('/user/new/preview')
{'action': u'preview', 'controller': u'user'}
>>> print map.match('/user/list')
None
>>> map.environ = {'REQUEST_METHOD':'GET'}
>>> print map.match('/user/new/preview')
None
>>> print map.match('/user/list')
{'action': u'list', 'controller': u'user'}
```

As you can see, the method condition works as expected, allowing the routes to match only when the request contains the correct request method.

Now let's look at the function condition. This condition is extremely powerful because it effectively allows you to write custom code to extend Routes' functionality. The function can return True to indicate the route matches or False if it doesn't. The function also has full access to the WSGI environment and the dictionary of routing variables, which have already been matched, so the function is free to modify or add to them as well.

Here's an example of a function that extracts the action to be called from the X-ACTION HTTP header in the request and compares it to allowed values:

```
from webob import Request
def get_action(environ, result):

    # Create a Pylons-style request object from the environment for
    # easier manipulation
    req = Request(environ)

    action = req.GET.get('X-ACTION')
    if action in ['call', 'get', 'view']:
        result['action'] = action
        return True

    return False
```

You wouldn't often design this sort of functionality into your routes if you were creating your own application from scratch, but having such low-level access to the underlying details of the request is very powerful and can be useful when writing a Pylons application to replace legacy code.

Here is another use that might be useful in your application, this time to treat the referrer as an ordinary routing variable:

```
def referals(environ, result):
    result['referer'] = environ.get('HTTP_REFERER')
    return True
```

You could use this function in a route like this to add the referrer to the matched routing variables:

```
map.connect('/{controller}/{action}/{id}', conditions=dict(function=referals))
```

Now let's think about subdomains. These are easiest to demonstrate with examples, and once again you have to create a fake HTTP request environment for your examples to emulate requests coming from different subdomains.

First let's set up the map object. Notice that you specify map.sub_domains=True to enable subdomain support:

```
>>> from routes import Mapper
>>> def controller_scan(directory=None):
...     return ['user']
...
>>> map = Mapper(controller_scan=controller_scan)
>>> map.minimization = False
>>> map.sub_domains = True
```

Now let's set up two routes. The first will accept any subdomain and produce an action routing variable with a value any, and the second will accept only the subdomains foo and bar and will produce an action routing variable certain:

```
>>> map.connect('/user/any', controller='user', action='any',
... conditions={'sub_domain':True})
>>> map.connect('/user/certain', controller='user', action='certain',
... conditions={'sub_domain': ['foo', 'bar']})
```

Now let's attempt some matches, emulating different requests by setting different environ dictionaries. First let's emulate a domain foo.example.com and test two URLs. The first will test what happens when sub_domain is set to True, and the second will test what happens when it is restricted to ['foo', 'bar']:

```
>>> map.environ = {'HTTP_HOST':'foo.example.com'}
>>> print map.match('/user/any')
{'action': u'any', 'controller': u'user', 'sub_domain': 'foo'}
>>> print map.match('/user/certain')
{'action': u'certain', 'controller': u'user', 'sub_domain': 'foo'}
```

As you can see, both the routes match because foo is a valid subdomain for either condition. Notice how 'sub_domain': 'foo' is added to the matched routing variables.

Now let's try the domain not.example.com:

```
>>> map.environ = {'HTTP_HOST':'not.example.com'}
>>> print map.match('/user/any')
{'action': u'any', 'controller': u'user', 'sub_domain': 'not'}
>>> print map.match('/user/certain')
None
```

This time, since not is not one of the allowed domains for the second route, only the first example works. Let's see what happens if no subdomain is specified in the request:

```
>>> map.environ = {'HTTP_HOST':'example.com'}
>>> print map.match('/user/any')
None
>>> print map.match('/user/certain')
None
```

As you can see, neither of the routes matches.

Caution To be able to use matching based on subdomain, you must set the map's sub_domains attribute to True. Otherwise, none of the routes checking the subdomain conditions will match.

To avoid matching common aliases to your main domain like www, the subdomain support can be set to ignore certain specified subdomains. Here's an example:

```
>>> from routes import Mapper
>>> def controller_scan(directory=None):
...     return ['user']
...
>>> map = Mapper(controller_scan=controller_scan)
>>> map.minimization = False
>>> # Remember to turn on sub-domain support
... map.sub_domains = True
>>> # Ignore the ``www`` sub-domain
... map.sub_domains_ignore = ['www']
>>> map.connect('/user/any', controller='user', action='any',
...     conditions=dict(sub_domain=True))
>>> map.connect('/user/certain', controller='user', action='certain',
...     conditions=dict(sub_domain=['www', 'foo']))
>>> map.environ = {'HTTP_HOST':'foo.example.com'}
>>> print map.match('/user/any')
{'action': u'any', 'controller': u'user', 'sub_domain': 'foo'}
```

```
>>> print map.match('/user/certain')
{'action': u'certain', 'controller': u'user', 'sub_domain': 'foo'}
>>> map.environ = {'HTTP_HOST':'www.example.com'}
>>> print map.match('/user/any')
None
>>> print map.match('/user/certain')
None
```

You can see that requests to the www subdomain are not matched even if one of the conditions specifies that the subdomain www should be matched. Now let's look at how h.url_for() handles subdomains.

When subdomain support is on, the h.url_for() function will accept a sub_domain keyword argument. Routes then ensures that the generated URL has the subdomain indicated. For example:

```
h.url_for(controller='user', action='certain', sub_domain='foo')
```

would generate the following URL but it will only work during a Pylons request, not from the interactive Python session we've been using so far in this chapter:

```
http://foo.example.com/user/certain
```

Filter Functions

Named routes can have functions associated with them that will operate on the arguments used during generation. Filter functions don't work with implicit or explicit routes because the filter function itself can affect the route that actually gets chosen, so the only way to be explicit about which route to use is to specify it with a name.

To highlight the problem filter functions solve, consider this route:

```
map.connect('/archives/{year}/{month}/{day}', controller='archives',
        action='view', year=2008,
        requirements=dict(year='\d{2,4}', month='\d{1,2}'))
```

Generating a URL for this will require a month and day argument and a year argument if you don't want to use 2008. Imagine this route links to a story and that your model has a story object with year, month, and day attributes. You could generate a URL for the story like this:

```
h.url_for(year=story.year, month=story.month, day=story.day)
```

This isn't terribly convenient and can be brittle if for some reason you need to change the story object's interface. It would be useful to be able to pass the story object directly to h.url_for() and have Routes extract the information it requires automatically. You can do this with a filter function.

Here's what the filter function for the story object might look like:

```
def story_expand(result):
    # Only alter args if a story keyword arg is present
    if 'story' not in result:
        return result

    story = result.pop('story')
    result['year'] = story.year
    result['month'] = story.month
    result['day'] = story.day

    return result
```

You can then create a named route with a `_filter` argument like this:

```
m.connect('archives', '/archives/{year}/{month}/{day}',
          controller='archives', action='view', year=2004,
          requirements=dict(year='\d{2,4}', month='\d{1,2}'),
          _filter=story_expand)
```

This filter function will be used when using the named route `archives`. If a `story` keyword argument is present, it will use that and alter the keyword arguments used to generate the actual route.

If you have a `story` object with those attributes, you would now be able to generate a URL like this:

```
h.url_for('archives', story=my_story)
```

As well as making it substantially easier to generate the URL, you can also easily change how the arguments are pulled out of the `story` object simply by changing the filter function if the `story` object interface were ever to change.

Although filter functions can be very powerful, you might decide against using them in your application because they can also make it less obvious what is happening to generate your URLs.

Summary

You've now seen all the main features of Routes and how you can take advantage of them to perform some very complex URL mappings as simply as possible or to integrate with legacy systems. You also saw how some of Routes legacy features such as route minimization, route memory, and implicit defaults can cause problems you might not have expected, and you now know how to avoid using these features in your application. Although route minimization is disabled by default in new Pylons applications, route memory and implicit defaults are not, so it is recommended you set `explicit=True` as an argument to `Mapper()` in your project's `config/routing.py` file.

In Chapter 14, you'll look at Routes again to see how you can use its features to improve the SimpleSite application.

CHAPTER 10

■■■

Unicode

If you've ever come across text in a foreign language that contains lots of question mark characters in unexpected positions or if you've written Python code that causes an exception such as the following one to be raised, then chances are you have run into a problem with character sets, encodings, and Unicode:

```
UnicodeDecodeError: 'ascii' codec can't decode byte 0xff in position 6:➥
ordinal not in range(128)
```

Many developers try to avoid getting involved with Unicode because these error messages seem obscure and difficult to fix, but the good news is that Python has great Unicode support, so with a little effort, you will be able to banish these problems from your applications entirely as well as properly support languages other than English. This chapter and the next will show you how.

Note All the libraries that come with Pylons have Unicode support, so it is always best to use Unicode in a Pylons application. The Python 3.0 language will treat all strings as Unicode by default, so Unicode support will become even more standard across all Python libraries in the future.

A Brief History

As I'm sure you are aware, computers operate on binary numbers that can be thought of as a collection of 1s and 0s. For example, the binary number 1110 represents the decimal number 14. Each 1 or 0 in the binary number is called a *bit*. A binary number made up from seven 1s and 0s is called a *7-bit* number and can represent all the decimal numbers from 0 to 127.

In the early days of computers, people wanted to be able to represent characters as well as binary numbers, and at the time, the most important characters were unaccented English letters, numbers, and punctuation, which could all be represented by a number between 0 and 127. These numbers can therefore all be stored in binary with just seven 1s and 0s (in other words, in 7 bits). The character set defined by these numbers eventually became standardized as ASCII. In the ASCII character set, *P* is represented by 80, and *y* is represented by 121. Python understands ASCII, so you can find out the codes for characters with the built-in ord() function like this:

```
>>> print ord("P"), ord("y"), ord("l"), ord("o"), ord("n"), ord("s") ➥
80 121 108 111 110 115
```

You can also find out a character from its ASCII representation with chr() like this:

```
>>> ''.join([chr(80), chr(121), chr(108), chr(111), chr(110), chr(115)]) ➥
'Pylons'
```

Computers of the day used 8-bit bytes in their calculations. These can represent the decimal numbers 0 to 255, so people quickly realized that an extra 128 characters were available. Different people assigned these extra numbers to different characters, and before long, these different collections of extra characters were also standardized into sets known as *code pages*. As an example, code page 857 is for Turkish characters, and code page 861 is for Icelandic characters. The code page system was adequate for representing most Western languages as long as you used the correct code page for the language you wanted to represent and as long as you didn't want to work on a document that contained two different languages at once.

It quickly became apparent, though, that code pages would not be suitable for representing every language. Asian languages in particular can contain many more than 256 characters, so a system was needed that represented a much wider set of characters. This is where Unicode came in.

The origins of Unicode date back to 1987 when Joe Becker, Lee Collins, and Mark Davis started investigating the practicalities of creating a universal character set. In the following year, Joe Becker published a draft proposal for an "international/multilingual text character encoding system, tentatively called Unicode." In this document, entitled "Unicode 88," he outlined a model where every script and character in modern usage could be represented in 16 bits. It soon became clear that people would also want to be able to represent scripts and characters that weren't in modern-day use, and over successive releases of the Unicode standard more scripts and characters were added until the most recent version, Unicode 5.1, was released in April 2008 with more than 100,000 characters. As you can imagine, this requires more than the 16 bits of Joe Becker's original draft of Unicode 88.

Introducing Unicode

Unicode is an industry standard allowing computers to consistently represent and manipulate text expressed in most of the world's writing systems. Unlike ASCII, where each character is represented in 7 bits, Unicode characters are represented by something called a *code point*, which is effectively an abstract integer ID for that character. For example, the characters in *Pylons* could be represented by the Unicode code points U+0050, U+0079, U+006C, U+006F, U+006E, and U+0073.

If you've worked with hexadecimal numbers, you might notice that the last two characters of each code point correspond to the decimal representation of the corresponding character in the ASCII character set for the word *Pylons* shown in the previous paragraph. This is because the first 256 Unicode code points were made identical to the numbers representing the characters in the ISO 8859-1 encoding of the Latin alphabet (less formally known as Latin-1). This in turn shares the first 128 characters and their respective codes with the ASCII character set. I'll return to the significance of this backward compatibility in a moment.

Unicode also has the concept of an *encoding*. One way of encoding Unicode code points into binary numbers on a disk would be to store each code point as a 32-bit (4-byte) number (since a 32-bit number is more than capable of storing every possible Unicode code point). This might seem sensible at first, but representing Unicode code points on disk in this way would take up a lot of space, especially if you used only those characters with low code points such as those also represented in ISO 8859-1 and ASCII because each character would be using 4 bytes when it really needed only one.

Another way of storing the values would be to use a variable number of bytes for each character. Those with low code points such as the unaccented English characters could be stored in 1 byte, and those with much higher code points such as Arabic or Chinese characters would use more than 1 byte. This would mean that all the Unicode characters could be represented if necessary, but the most commonly used ones (the unaccented English characters) could be represented in just 1 byte. This is exactly what happens in the UTF-8 encoding, which you will probably have come across.

UTF-8 is one of the most popular encodings for Python programmers, so much so that Python 3.0 will assume that files you open are encoded in UTF-8 unless you say otherwise.

Encoding Unicode characters with a variable number of bytes for each character as UTF-8 has an interesting side effect. It means that UTF-8 encoded Unicode for the characters represented by the ASCII character set has the same binary representation as ASCII itself. This means computers can treat UTF-8 encoded Unicode as ASCII without any errors being raised as long as characters used are in the first 128 Unicode code points. This explains why your application might already be working perfectly well with certain Unicode strings even though you haven't made a special effort to work with any character set except ASCII. This is also why as soon as a character such as £ or é is entered, the application will break because these are not ASCII characters; therefore, treating their UTF-8 encoded versions as ASCII will cause the kind of `UnicodeDecodeError` shown at the start of the chapter.

Luckily, working properly with Unicode is very straightforward, so you shouldn't need to rely on the backward compatibility of the UTF-8 encoding for the ASCII characters.

Before you look at Unicode in Python, I'll recap the important points:

- Unicode can represent pretty much any character in any writing system in widespread use today as well as some historical characters.

- Unicode uses code points to represent characters, and the way these map to bits on disk depends on the encoding.

- The most popular encoding is UTF-8, which has several convenient properties:

    - It can handle any Unicode code point.

    - A string of ASCII text is also valid UTF-8 encoded Unicode.

    - UTF-8 doesn't use much storage space; the majority of code points are turned into 2 bytes, and values less than 128 occupy only 1 byte.

Unicode in Python 2

In Python 2, Unicode strings are expressed as instances of the built-in `unicode` type. Under the hood, Python represents Unicode strings as either 16-bit or 32-bit integers, depending on the way the Python interpreter was compiled. Python 3 will treat all strings as Unicode automatically, but the discussion in this chapter relates only to the Unicode handling of recent Python 2 releases such as Python 2.4, 2.5, and 2.6.

Unicode Literals

In Python source code, Unicode literals are written as strings prefixed with the u or U character (although you will hardly ever see the uppercase version used).

```
>>> u'abcd'
>>> U'efgh'
```

You can also use ", """, or ''' versions too. For example:

```
>>> u"""This
... is a multiline
... Unicode string"""
```

Individual code points can be written using the escape sequence \u followed by four hex digits specifying the code point. You can also use \U followed by eight hex digits instead of four. Unicode literals can also use the same escape sequences as 8-bit strings including \x, but this takes only two hex digits, so it can't express many of the available code points. You can add characters to Unicode strings using the `unichr()` built-in function, and you can find out what the ordinal is with `ord()`, which you also saw earlier in the chapter when it was used with ASCII characters.

Here is an example demonstrating the different alternatives:

```
>>> s = u"\x66\u0072\u0061\U0000006e" + unichr(231) + u"ais"
>>> for c in s:
...     print ord(c),
...
97 102 114 97 110 231 97 105 115
```

Here `\x66` is a two-digit hex escape, `\u0072` and `\u0061` are four-digit Unicode escapes, and `\u0000006e` is an eight-digit Unicode escape. The example also demonstrates the use of `unichr()`. The word made in this is as follows:

```
>>> print s
français
```

■**Note** If you are working with Unicode in detail, you might be interested in the `unicodedata` module, which can be used to find out Unicode properties such as a character's name, category, numeric value, and the like.

Handling Errors

Now that you have seen how to write Unicode literals, let's look at how you can create Unicode strings with the `unicode()` constructor. Here is an example:

```
>>> cost = unicode('50.00')
>>> cost
u'50.00'
>>> type(cost)
<type 'unicode'>
```

Let's see what happens if you try to concatenate the `cost` Unicode string with a normal ASCII string:

```
>>> '$' + cost
u'$50.00'
```

Python decodes the string `'$'` from ASCII to Unicode, concatenates the two Unicode strings, and returns the result.

Now let's try to use a £ sign instead of a $. The £ character is not an ASCII character, so you have to represent it by its ordinal, which is 163. Let's see what happens:

```
>>> chr(163) + u'50.00'
Traceback (most recent call last):
  File "<stdin>", line 1, in <module>
UnicodeDecodeError: 'ascii' codec can't decode byte 0xa3 in ➥
position 0: ordinal not in range(128)
```

In this case, because £ is not an ASCII character, when Python internally calls `unicode(chr(163))` to try to decode it from ASCII to Unicode, an error occurs.

Python's `unicode()` constructor takes three arguments, including an `errors` argument that determines what should happen in a situation like this:

string: This is the Python string to decode to Unicode.

encoding: This is an optional encoding to specify how the string is currently encoded. If you don't specify an encoding, ASCII will be used, so characters with code points greater than 127 will be treated as errors.

errors: This specifies how to handle any errors. This can be one of the following: the string "strict" (the default), which results in a ValueError being raised if an invalid character is found; "ignore", which simply results in any errors being silently ignored; or "replace", which causes the official Unicode replacement character, U+FFFD (usually displayed ❖), to be inserted instead.

Let's explore what happens if you perform the conversion explicitly and use the errors option:

```
>>> unicode(chr(163), errors='ignore') + u'50.00'
u'50.00'
>>> unicode(chr(163), errors='replace') + u'50.00'
u'\ufffd50.00'
```

As you can see, using 'ignore' silently ignores the problem, and using 'replace' results in the Unicode character U+FFFD being inserted in place of the pound sign. Neither of these is quite what you want. The solution to the problem lies in understanding the encoding option. Let's look at encoding and decoding Unicode data next.

Decoding Unicode

Unicode strings are simply a series of Unicode code points. When you are converting an ASCII or UTF-8 string to Unicode, you are actually *decoding* it; when you are converting from Unicode to UTF-8 or ASCII, you are *encoding* it. This is why the error in the example said that the ASCII codec could not *decode* the byte 0xa3 from ASCII to Unicode. You might be used to thinking of ASCII as the "natural" representation of characters and anything else to be an encoding, but this is not the way you should think with Unicode. You should always think of the Unicode code point as the "natural" representation and anything else as being a particular encoding.

The 0xa3 characters that appeared in the UnicodeDecodeError message are hex for 163, which represents the £ sign. The error occurred because this is outside the ASCII range. However, this character is present in the ISO 8859-1 character set. If you tell Python that the data it is decoding is encoded with the 'iso_8859_1' character set, you get the result you expected:

```
>>> unicode(chr(163), encoding='iso_8859_1') + cost
u'\xa350.00'
```

Notice that because 163 can be represented in just two hex digits, Python chose to use the \x representation rather than its \u or \U representation of Unicode characters.

Let's print the result:

```
>>> print u'\xa350.00'
£50.00
```

Be aware that not all terminals will be able to display all Unicode characters when printed like this; it will depend on the encoding of the terminal and the fonts available on the system.

Encoding Unicode

Now that you've seen how to decode to Unicode, let's see how to encode it. All Python Unicode objects have an encode() method that takes the encoding you want to use as its argument. It is used like this:

```
>>> u'$50.00'.encode('utf-8')
'$50.00'
>>> u'$50.00'.encode('ascii')
'$50.00'
```

As you can see, u'$50.00', when encoded to UTF-8, is the same as the ASCII representation. The same cannot be said for u'£50.00' because this isn't an ASCII character, as I've already explained:

```
>>> u'\xa350.00'.encode('utf-8')
'\xc2\xa350.00'
>>> print '\xc2\xa350.00'
£50.00
>>> u'\xa350.00'.encode('ascii')
Traceback (most recent call last):
  File "<stdin>", line 1, in <module>
UnicodeEncodeError: 'ascii' codec can't encode character u'\xa3' in ➥
position 0: ordinal not in range(128)
```

Once again, you get the familiar UnicodeEncodeError, this time specifying that the encoding failed as you would expect.

Note Python supports many more character encodings besides the ones mentioned in this chapter; you can find the full list at http://docs.python.org/lib/standard-encodings.html.

Python Source Code Encoding

If you are working with non-ASCII characters in your application, you are likely to also want to be able to use them in your Python source code. Although you could manually escape each character you use in a Unicode literal, Python 2.4 and newer let you define the encoding you are using at the top of the source file like this:

```
# -*- coding: utf-8 -*-
```

This special setting tells Python to treat the source code as UTF-8 encoded Unicode. This allows you to use Unicode characters in the source code itself as long as you remember to set your editor to save the file in UTF-8. Windows users who use the SciTE editor can specify the encoding of their file from the menu using the File ➤ Encoding menu option. Vim users can set the encoding with set encoding=utf8.

If you use a non-ASCII character, which is still part of the ISO 8859-1 character set, in your source file (such as the £ character) but fail to specify an encoding, versions of Python newer than 2.4 will assume that you are using the ISO 8859-1 character set but will still issue a warning:

```
sys:1: DeprecationWarning: Non-ASCII character '\xe9' in file testas.py on line
2, but no encoding declared; see http://www.python.org/peps/pep-0263.html for de
tails
```

You can correct this by specifying the correct encoding at the top of your source file. If you use other characters but fail to specify an encoding or if you forget to save the file in the encoding you have specified, Python will give an error.

If you look back at Chapter 8, you'll see that the base template you created for the SimpleSite tutorial starts with this line:

```
## -- coding: utf-8 --
```

When Mako creates a Python version of the template in the Mako cache, the ## characters get converted to a single # character. This results in the Python file having the correct encoding definition at the top, which allows you to use Unicode characters within the template source file as long as your editor encodes the file to UTF-8 when you saves it.

Unicode and Files

To write Unicode data to a file, you will need to encode it first. Likewise, when reading encoded Unicode from a file, it will need to be decoded. The easiest way to handle this in Python is to use the codecs module. Here is an example of how to read Unicode from a UTF-8 encoded file:

```
import codecs
f = codecs.open('unicode.txt', encoding='utf-8', mode='r')
for line in f:
    print repr(line)
```

Each line will have been automatically decoded to a Unicode string. Here's an example of writing Unicode to a file encoded in ISO 8859-1:

```
f = codecs.open('unicode.txt', encoding='latin-1', mode='w')
f.write(u"\x66\u0072\u0061\U0000006e" + unichr(231) + u"ais")
f.close()
```

I've used latin-1 here to demonstrate that Python will accept a number of different descriptions if an encoding has multiple names in common use. Reading/writing files in different encodings is almost as easy as normal Python file operations.

It is also possible to use Unicode strings as file names if the underlying filesystem supports Unicode file names. For example:

```
filename = u"\x66\u0072\u0061\U0000006e" + unichr(231) + u"ais"
f = open(filename, 'w')
f.write('Bonjour!\n')
f.close()
```

Other functions such as os.listdir() will return Unicode if you pass them a Unicode argument and will try to return strings if you pass an ordinary 8-bit string. Add the previous code to a file called test.py, and then add the following afterward:

```
import os
print os.listdir('.')
print os.listdir(u'.')
```

If you ran python test.py, you would see the following output:

```
['Fran\xcc\xa7ais', 'test.py']
[u'Fran\u0327ais', u'test.py']
```

As you can see from the second line, when os.listdir() is given a Unicode argument, it returns Unicode strings.

Unicode Considerations in Pylons Programming

There are three main rules when dealing with using Unicode in a Pylons application:

The main rule is that your application should use Unicode for all strings internally, decoding any input to Unicode as soon as it enters the application and encoding the Unicode to UTF-8 or another encoding only on output. If you perform all the decoding right at the edge of your application, as soon as it is passed any encoded Unicode data, then it will be obvious where any problems are caused. If you fail to do this and some of the data your application receives is badly encoded, it is possible your application will crash in an obscure place or, worse, that the badly encoded data poses a security risk.

The second rule is to always test your application with characters greater than 127 wherever possible. If you fail to do this, you might think your application is working fine, but as soon as your users do put in non-ASCII characters, you will have problems. Using Arabic is always a good test, and http://www.google.ae is a good source of sample text.

The third rule is to always do any checking of a string for illegal characters once it's in the form that will be used or stored; otherwise, the illegal characters might be disguised.

For example, let's say you have a content management system that takes a Unicode file name and you want to disallow paths with a / character. You might write this code:

```
# DO NOT DO THIS
def read_file(filename):
    if '/' in filename:
        raise ValueError("'/' not allowed in filenames")
    unicode_name = filename.decode('base64')
    f = open(unicode_name, 'r')
    # ... return contents of file ...
```

This is incorrect because the check was performed before the actual data to be used was decoded. An attacker could have passed the data L2V0Yy9wYXNzd2Q=, which is the base-64 encoded form of the string '/etc/passwd'. The previous code would have resulted in this file being opened and returned to the browser, which wasn't what you expected. Instead, decode the data first and then perform the check. Although this is obvious advice when using the base-64 encoding where the encoded version looks very different from the original, it is less obvious when using UTF-8 where you could easily forget you are not using a decoded string.

Those are the three basic rules, so now I will cover some of the places you might want to perform Unicode decoding in a Pylons application.

Request Parameters

Pylons automatically decodes incoming form parameters into Unicode objects so that when you access request.POST, request.GET, or request.params in your application, the values are already Unicode strings. Only parameter values (not their associated names) are decoded to Unicode by default. Since parameter names commonly map directly to Python variable names (which are restricted to the ASCII character set), it's usually preferable to handle them as strings.

You can change the encoding used to decode the request information by setting the request.charset attribute.

Templating

Pylons uses Mako as its default templating language. Mako handles all content as Unicode internally. It only deals in raw strings upon the final rendering of the template just before it returns a value from the render() function. The encoding of the rendered string can be configured; Pylons sets the default value to UTF-8. To change this value, edit your project's config/environment.py file, and update the output_encoding argument to TemplateLookup:

```
# Create the Mako TemplateLookup, with the default auto-escaping
config['pylons.app_globals'].mako_lookup = TemplateLookup(
    directories=paths['templates'],
    module_directory=os.path.join(app_conf['cache_dir'], 'templates'),
    input_encoding='utf-8', output_encoding='utf-8',
    imports=['from webhelpers.html import escape'],
    default_filters=['escape'])
```

The input_encoding argument specifies the encoding that Mako expects the templates to have if they don't have an explicit ## -*- coding: utf-8 -*- comment at the top of the file. You can find more information about Unicode in Mako at http://www.makotemplates.org/docs/unicode.html.

Output Encoding

Web pages should always be generated with a specific encoding, most likely UTF-8. At the very least, that means you should specify the following in the <head> section of your HTML:

```
<meta http-equiv="Content-Type" content="text/html; charset=utf-8" />
```

You can specify the character set for the HTTP response from within a controller action using the Pylons response global:

```
response.charset = 'utf8'
```

This will automatically add the character set to the end of the Content-type header, and most browsers will trust this over the value in the <meta> tag. When you return a Unicode string from the controller action, it will be encoded using the character specified by response.charset, but if you return a non-Unicode string, it will be passed directly to the browser without being encoded again because it is assumed you have already encoded it.

The web browser will usually submit form data back to the server using the same character set as that used in the page containing the form. You should therefore try to make sure you are using the same character set in request.charset and response.charset. The defaults of UTF-8 are a good choice, though.

Databases

Another place where you will have to think about encoding and decoding is the database. You should encode to whichever encoding the database expects immediately before executing a query and decode to Unicode immediately after receiving results from the database.

SQLAlchemy has a Unicode column type that you can use to store Unicode characters. If you use this column type, SQLAlchemy will be responsible for handling the encoding and decoding for you so that you don't need to worry about it yourself. If you look back at the model for the SimpleSite application, you'll see that you have already been using Unicode columns. This is good practice because you never know when a user of your application might place a non-ASCII character in a form field, and it is best to be able to handle that situation.

A Complete Request Cycle

Now that you've seen the various places your Pylons applications might have to deal with Unicode, I'll take you through an example request cycle and explain exactly what happens in terms of encoding and decoding Unicode.

Start the SimpleSite application, and edit a page by visiting `http://localhost:5000/page/view/1`. Try copying and pasting some Chinese or Arabic text into the content field. (Just search Google for the words *Arabic* or *Chinese characters*, and some of the results are bound to contain suitable sample text.) When you save the page, the text will be sent to your application as UTF-8 (since this is the encoding of the page). Pylons will then receive the request, and the form fields will be decoded to Unicode in the Pylons `request` global. The code within the `view()` action then retrieves the value of the content field from `request.params` where it has already been decoded to a Unicode string. It then sets the `.content` attribute of the `page` object using the Unicode value. When the session is committed, the page object is automatically flushed. SQLAlchemy takes over and performs the necessary encoding before sending the content to the underlying database engine.

When the saved page is redisplayed, SQLAlchemy will issue a query to fetch the content and decode the results it fetches to Unicode. The page's content data is passed as a Unicode string to a Mako template where it is rendered. The `render()` function will obtain the result from Mako and return the entire template as a UTF-8 encoded string, which is then returned from the `view()` action. Pylons assembles the response using the UTF-8 encoded response from the action and any settings in the `response` global. Because `response.charset` is set to `'utf-8'`, Pylons adds the following header to the response:

```
Content-Type: text/html; charset=utf-8
```

Pylons then returns the response to the browser. The browser knows to expect UTF-8 because of the `charset=utf=8` part of the previous header and decodes the content that follows to its Unicode representation so that it can correctly display the text.

Summary

You should now understand the history of Unicode, how to use it in Python, and where to apply Unicode encoding and decoding in a Pylons application. You should also be able to use Unicode in your web app; remember that the main rule is to use UTF-8 to talk to the world, performing the necessary encoding and decoding at the very edge of your application (or letting Pylons do it for you!).

Now that you know how to handle multiple different characters and scripts, it is time to turn your attention to how to write a Pylons application that is designed to be able to be used by people from different countries at the same time, customizing the language used on each request for each user. You'll learn this in the next chapter.

CHAPTER 11

■■■

Internationalization and Localization

Internationalization and localization are means of adapting software for non-native environments, especially for other nations and cultures.

The following are the parts of an application that might need to be localized:

- Language

- Date/time format

- Numbers such as decimal points, positioning of separators, and characters used as separators

- Time zones (UTC in internationalized environments)

- Currency

- Weights and measures

The distinction between internationalization and localization is subtle but important. *Internationalization* is the adaptation of products for potential use virtually everywhere, while *localization* is the addition of special features for use in a specific locale.

For example, in terms of language used in a Pylons application, internationalization is the process of marking up all strings that might need to be translated, and localization is the process of producing translations for a particular locale.

Pylons provides built-in support to enable you to internationalize language but leaves you to handle for yourself any other aspects of internationalization that might be appropriate for your application. In this chapter, you'll concentrate on how to internationalize and localize the strings used in your Pylons application.

Note Internationalization is often abbreviated as *I18N* (or *i18n* or *I18n*) where the number 18 refers to the number of letters omitted. Localization is often abbreviated *L10n* or *l10n* in the same manner. These abbreviations also avoid picking one spelling (*internationalisation* vs. *internationalization*) over the other.

To represent characters from multiple languages, you will need to utilize Unicode. By now you should have a good idea of what Unicode is, how to use it in Python, and in which areas of your application you need to pay specific attention to decoding and encoding Unicode data. If not, you should read the previous chapter.

Understanding the Process

Internationalizing a Pylons application involves marking every string in your application that needs to be available in more than one language with a function that will perform the necessary translation.

Localizing an application involves the following steps:

1. Running a tool to extract the strings you've marked

2. Creating a translation of the strings for each language your application will support

3. Displaying the correct translation for the current user

Before you learn how this works in a real application, I'll discuss some of the background information you will need to understand.

Marking Strings for Internationalization

Marking the strings that will need to be internationalized is actually very simple. You wrap them in a function to tell Pylons that they need to be translated. For example, if you had a controller action that looked like this:

```
def hello(self):
    return u'Hello!'
```

and you wanted to internationalize the string `Hello!`, you would do so by wrapping it in one of the Pylons translation functions. You import them like this:

```
from pylons.i18n.translation import _, ungettext
```

and use them like this:

```
def hello(self):
    return _(u'Hello!')
```

Strings to be internationalized are known as *messages* in internationalization terminology. The correct translation function to use depends on the situation. Pylons currently provides the following functions in the `pylons.i18n.translation` module:

ugettext() and its alias _(): These mark and translate a Unicode message. Developers usually choose to use _() rather than ugettext() because as well as being a well-understood convention it also saves on keystrokes.

ungettext(): This marks and translates a Unicode message that might have a slightly different form for the singular and the plural. You'll learn about this in the "Plural Forms" section later in the chapter.

Pylons also provides gettext() and ngettext() functions, which are equivalent to ugettext() and ungettext(), respectively, but take an ordinary Python string as their argument rather than a Unicode string. There is really no reason to use the non-Unicode versions if you have read the previous chapter and understand what Unicode is, so I won't cover the non-Unicode versions further.

When wrapping strings in the _() (or ugettext()) function, it is important not to piece sentences together manually because certain languages might need to invert the grammar. Instead, you should try to specify whole strings in one go. For example, you shouldn't do this:

```
# BAD!
msg = _("Starbug was built to last sir; this old baby's crashed ")
msg += _("more times than a ZX81.")
```

But the following is perfectly acceptable because the whole string is passed as an argument to
_():

```
# GOOD
msg = _("Starbug was built to last sir; this old baby's crashed "
    "more times than a ZX81.")
```

Python will automatically concatenate adjacent strings, so having two shorter strings on separate lines like this is a perfectly acceptable way to pass a long string to a function. This is surprising
behavior if you haven't seen it before, but it is quite useful in this situation.

Extracting Messages and Handling Translations

As you might have guessed from the names of the functions you've already seen, Pylons internationalization support is based on GNU gettext (http://www.gnu.org/software/gettext/). The
idea is simple: you run a tool on your source code that searches for times when you have used
any of the Python I18N functions such as _(), ungettext(), and others. The tool extracts the Unicode strings passed as arguments to the functions and places them in a portable object template
(.pot) file.

You would then generate a portable object (.po) file based on the portable object template for
each language you wanted to support. You send these to a translator, and they will return the
portable object file together with the translations of the messages for a particular locale.

Finally, the .po files are compiled by a tool to a machine object (.mo) file, which is an optimized
machine-readable binary file that the Pylons internationalization tools can understand.

You can use a few different tools to extract messages from your source files and to compile
the .mo files, but by far the most popular for use with Pylons applications is Babel (http://babel.
edgewall.org/). Unlike the GNU gettext tool xgettext, Babel supports extracting translatable
strings from Python templating languages (including Mako and Genshi) and has a plug-in architecture to allow it to extract messages from other types of Python source files.

Babel is comprised of two main parts:

- Tools to build and work with gettext message catalogs

- A Python interface to the Common Locale Data Repository (CLDR), providing access to various locale display names, localized number and date formatting, and so on

In the next section, you'll look at a real example that uses Babel to help in the internationaliza-
tion/localization process.

Seeing It in Action

Now that you've seen the theory and understand the process, it's time to see it in action in a Pylons
application. The application you'll write will simply display the greeting "Hello" in three different
languages: English, Spanish, and French. The default language will be English. I'll show how to use
the Pylons translator functions together with Babel to create the application.

Let's call the project TranslateDemo and choose to use Mako but not SQLAlchemy:

```
$ paster create --template=pylons TranslateDemo
```

Now let's add the controller:

```
$ cd TranslateDemo
$ paster controller hello
```

Edit `controllers/hello.py`, and import the `_()` function:

```
from pylons.i18n.translation import _, set_lang
```

Then update the `index()` action to look like this:

```
class HelloController(BaseController):

    def index(self):
        set_lang('es')
        return _(u'Hello!')
```

Notice that the example uses the `_()` function everywhere the string `Hello!` appears. Start the Paste HTTP server with the `--reload` option, and visit `http://localhost:5000/hello/index`:

```
$ paster serve --reload development.ini
```

You will see the following error:

```
LanguageError: IOError: [Errno 2] No translation file found for➥
domain: 'translatedemo'
```

Although the controller has been internationalized, no message catalogs are yet in place. You'll create the necessary translations next.

Using Babel

You'll need to install Babel using Easy Install:

```
$ easy_install "Babel==0.9.4"
```

You'll use Babel to extract messages to a `.pot` file in your project's `i18n` directory. First, the directory needs to be created. Don't forget to add it to your revision control system if you're using one:

```
$ mkdir translatedemo/i18n
```

Be sure to use the number 1 in the word `i18n` and not a lowercase l. Next, extract all the messages from the project with the following command:

```
$ python setup.py extract_messages
 extract_messages
running extract_messages
extracting messages from translatedemo/__init__.py
extracting messages from translatedemo/websetup.py
extracting messages from translatedemo/config/__init__.py
extracting messages from translatedemo/config/environment.py
extracting messages from translatedemo/config/middleware.py
extracting messages from translatedemo/config/routing.py
extracting messages from translatedemo/controllers/__init__.py
extracting messages from translatedemo/controllers/error.py
extracting messages from translatedemo/controllers/hello.py
extracting messages from translatedemo/lib/__init__.py
extracting messages from translatedemo/lib/app_globals.py
extracting messages from translatedemo/lib/base.py
extracting messages from translatedemo/lib/helpers.py
extracting messages from translatedemo/model/__init__.py
extracting messages from translatedemo/tests/__init__.py
```

```
extracting messages from translatedemo/tests/test_models.py
extracting messages from translatedemo/tests/functional/__init__.py
extracting messages from translatedemo/tests/functional/test_hello.py
writing PO template file to translatedemo/i18n/translatedemo.pot
```

As you can see, Babel searches your project for Python files looking for strings marked with the translation functions. The strings are extracted, and a new file is created called translatedemo.pot in your project's translatedemo/i18n directory. It looks like something like this:

```
# Translations template for TranslateDemo.
# Copyright (C) 2008 ORGANIZATION
# This file is distributed under the same license as the TranslateDemo project.
# FIRST AUTHOR <EMAIL@ADDRESS>, 2008.
#
#, fuzzy
msgid ""
msgstr ""
"Project-Id-Version: TranslateDemo 0.1\n"
"Report-Msgid-Bugs-To: EMAIL@ADDRESS\n"
"POT-Creation-Date: 2008-09-26 11:07+0100\n"
"PO-Revision-Date: YEAR-MO-DA HO:MI+ZONE\n"
"Last-Translator: FULL NAME <EMAIL@ADDRESS>\n"
"Language-Team: LANGUAGE <LL@li.org>\n"
"MIME-Version: 1.0\n"
"Content-Type: text/plain; charset=utf-8\n"
"Content-Transfer-Encoding: 8bit\n"
"Generated-By: Babel 0.9.4\n"

#: translatedemo/controllers/hello.py:18
msgid "Hello!"
msgstr ""
```

As you can see, after the heading information, it has found the one internationalized string in the hello.py controller. The :18 means that this string was found on line 18 of the file.

Next you'll need to create a .po file for the Spanish language. You can do so with this command:

```
$ python setup.py init_catalog -l es
running init_catalog
creating catalog 'translatedemo/i18n/es/LC_MESSAGES/translatedemo.po' ➥
based on 'translatedemo/i18n/translatedemo.pot'
```

The new translatedemo.po file looks similar, but some of the content has been updated slightly for the Spanish language:

```
# Spanish translations for TranslateDemo.
# Copyright (C) 2008 ORGANIZATION
# This file is distributed under the same license as the TranslateDemo
# project.
# FIRST AUTHOR <EMAIL@ADDRESS>, 2008.
#
msgid ""
msgstr ""
"Project-Id-Version: TranslateDemo 0.1\n"
"Report-Msgid-Bugs-To: EMAIL@ADDRESS\n"
"POT-Creation-Date: 2008-09-26 10:35+0100\n"
"PO-Revision-Date: 2008-09-26 10:49+0100\n"
"Last-Translator: FULL NAME <EMAIL@ADDRESS>\n"
"Language-Team: es <LL@li.org>\n"
```

```
"Plural-Forms: nplurals=2; plural=(n != 1)\n"
"MIME-Version: 1.0\n"
"Content-Type: text/plain; charset=utf-8\n"
"Content-Transfer-Encoding: 8bit\n"
"Generated-By: Babel 0.9.4\n"

#: translatedemo/controllers/hello.py:18
msgid "Hello!"
msgstr ""
```

Update the .po file with the correct details including your name, your e-mail address, and the revision date.

Edit the last line to specify the Spanish translation for the greeting Hello!, and save the changes, making sure you set the encoding in your editor to UTF-8 if you are using Unicode characters. (Don't worry if you can't find the ¡ character on your keyboard; this is only an example, so you can leave it out if you prefer):

```
#: translatedemo/controllers/hello.py:18
msgid "Hello!"
msgstr "¡Hola!"
```

Now that the translation is in place, you need to compile the .po file to a .mo file. Once again, Babel has a tool to help, and you access it via your project's setup.py file:

```
$ python setup.py compile_catalog
running compile_catalog
1 of 1 messages (100%) translated in ➡
'translatedemo/i18n/es/LC_MESSAGES/translatedemo.po'
compiling catalog ➡
'translatedemo/i18n/es/LC_MESSAGES/translatedemo.po' to ➡
    'translatedemo/i18n/es/LC_MESSAGES/translatedemo.mo'
```

Now is a good time to test the application. Start the server with the following command:

```
$ paster serve --reload development.ini
```

Test your controller by visiting http://localhost:5000/hello/index. You should see the following output:

```
¡Hola!
```

Congratulations, you've internationalized and localized a Pylons application!

Supporting Multiple Languages

Supporting one language is useful, but Pylons can support multiple languages at once. To do so, you simply repeat the process of generating the .po and .mo files for the other languages. You don't need to extract the messages again, though, because the existing .pot file already contains all the information you need.

As an example, let's also create French and English translations:

```
$ python setup.py init_catalog -l fr
running init_catalog
creating catalog 'translatedemo/i18n/fr/LC_MESSAGES/translatedemo.po' ➡
based on 'translatedemo/i18n/translatedemo.pot'
```

```
$ python setup.py init_catalog -l en
running init_catalog
creating catalog 'translatedemo/i18n/en/LC_MESSAGES/translatedemo.po' ➥
based on 'translatedemo/i18n/translatedemo.pot'
```

Modify the last lines of the fr catalog to look like this:

```
#: translatedemo/controllers/hello.py:18
msgid "Hello!"
msgstr "Bonjour!"
```

Since the original messages are already in English, the en catalog msgstr string can stay blank because gettext will fall back to the original.

Once you've edited the two new .po files, compile them to .mo files like this:

```
$ python setup.py compile_catalog
running compile_catalog
0 of 1 messages (0%) translated in ➥
'translatedemo/i18n/en/LC_MESSAGES/translatedemo.po' compiling catalog ➥
'translatedemo/i18n/en/LC_MESSAGES/translatedemo.po' to ➥
'translatedemo/i18n/en/LC_MESSAGES/translatedemo.mo'
1 of 1 messages (100%) translated in ➥
'translatedemo/i18n/es/LC_MESSAGES/translatedemo.po' compiling catalog ➥
'translatedemo/i18n/es/LC_MESSAGES/translatedemo.po' to ➥
'translatedemo/i18n/es/LC_MESSAGES/translatedemo.mo'
1 of 1 messages (100%) translated in ➥
'translatedemo/i18n/fr/LC_MESSAGES/translatedemo.po' compiling catalog ➥
'translatedemo/i18n/fr/LC_MESSAGES/translatedemo.po' to ➥
'translatedemo/i18n/fr/LC_MESSAGES/translatedemo.mo'
```

By the end of the process, your i18n directory will contain these files:

```
i18n/translatedemo.pot
i18n/en/LC_MESSAGES/translatedemo.po
i18n/en/LC_MESSAGES/translatedemo.mo
i18n/es/LC_MESSAGES/translatedemo.po
i18n/es/LC_MESSAGES/translatedemo.mo
i18n/fr/LC_MESSAGES/translatedemo.po
i18n/fr/LC_MESSAGES/translatedemo.mo
```

If you look at your project's setup.py file, you'll see the following line:

```
package_data={'translatedemo': ['i18n/*/LC_MESSAGES/*.mo']},
```

This line ensures that all the binary message catalogs your application relies on are automatically included in any packages or egg files produced from your Pylons project.

With the changes in place, add a new action to the controller to test the different languages. First import the get_lang() function, which retrieves the current language being used:

```
from pylons.i18n.translation import get_lang
```

Now add the following action to the controller:

```
def multiple(self):
    resp = 'Default: %s<br />' % _(u'Hello!')
    for lang in ['fr','en','es']:
        set_lang(lang)
        resp += '%s: %s<br />' % (get_lang(), _(u'Hello!'))
    return resp
```

Start the server, and visit `http://localhost:5000/hello/multiple`. You should see the following output:

```
Default: Hello!
['fr']: Bonjour!
['en']: Hello!
['es']: ¡Hola!
```

This correctly outputs the three different languages you have prepared. The `set_lang()` function is called for each language, this changes the message catalog used so that the correct translation is produced when the `_()` function is called. Now that you know how to set the language used in a controller on the fly, let's look at how to update the message catalogs.

Updating the Catalog

You'll notice that the previous example worked even though `Hello!` is marked for translation in multiple places and not just on the line specified in the `.po` and `.pot` files. The Pylons translation functions don't use the line number a message is defined on, only the message itself, so as long as a translation of the message for the particular language exists somewhere, the message can be translated everywhere. The line numbers are used by Babel to keep track of which strings have been translated.

If you want to add a new message to the catalog, you'll need to update the `.po` and `.pot` files. Once again, Babel provides a tool to help. To demonstrate this, update the original `index()` action to look like this:

```
def index(self):
    set_lang('es')
    return _('Goodbye!')
```

You'll need to run the extract command again (I've omitted some of the output for brevity):

```
$ python setup.py extract_messages
running extract_messages
...
extracting messages from translatedemo/controllers/hello.py
...
writing PO template file to translatedemo/i18n/translatedemo.pot
```

The last lines of the file look like this:

```
#: translatedemo/controllers/hello.py:19
msgid "Goodbye!"
msgstr ""

#: translatedemo/controllers/hello.py:22 translatedemo/controllers/hello.py:25
msgid "Hello!"
msgstr ""
```

Notice that both of the lines the `Hello!` message are found on have been noted and that the `Goodbye!` message is also included.

Now run the command to update the catalogs:

```
$ python setup.py update_catalog
running update_catalog
updating catalog 'translatedemo/i18n/en/LC_MESSAGES/translatedemo.po' ➡
based on 'translatedemo/i18n/translatedemo.pot'
updating catalog 'translatedemo/i18n/es/LC_MESSAGES/translatedemo.po' ➡
based on 'translatedemo/i18n/translatedemo.pot'
updating catalog 'translatedemo/i18n/fr/LC_MESSAGES/translatedemo.po' ➡
based on 'translatedemo/i18n/translatedemo.pot'
```

You'd then update all the .po files and compile them to .mo files again, but since you are using only the Spanish language in the action in this example, you'll just edit the Spanish .po file. Its last few lines now look like this:

```
#: translatedemo/controllers/hello.py:19
msgid "Goodbye!"
msgstr ""

#: translatedemo/controllers/hello.py:22 translatedemo/controllers/hello.py:25
msgid "Hello!"
msgstr "¡Hola!"
```

Notice that Babel added the entry for the Goodbye! message but kept the existing translation for Hello!, updating the line numbers to reflect those in the new .pot file.

Update the msgstr line for Goodbye! to read as follows:

```
msgstr "¡Adiós!"
```

and recompile the catalog:

```
$ python setup.py compile_catalog
running compile_catalog
0 of 2 messages (0%) translated in ➡
'translatedemo/i18n/en/LC_MESSAGES/translatedemo.po'
compiling catalog 'translatedemo/i18n/en/LC_MESSAGES/translatedemo.po' to ➡
'translatedemo/i18n/en/LC_MESSAGES/translatedemo.mo'
2 of 2 messages (100%) translated in ➡
'translatedemo/i18n/es/LC_MESSAGES/translatedemo.po'
compiling catalog 'translatedemo/i18n/es/LC_MESSAGES/translatedemo.po' to ➡
'translatedemo/i18n/es/LC_MESSAGES/translatedemo.mo'
1 of 2 messages (50%) translated in ➡
'translatedemo/i18n/fr/LC_MESSAGES/translatedemo.po'
compiling catalog 'translatedemo/i18n/fr/LC_MESSAGES/translatedemo.po' to ➡
'translatedemo/i18n/fr/LC_MESSAGES/translatedemo.mo'
```

If you start the Paste HTTP server and visit http://localhost:5000/hello/index, you will see the message updated to read ¡Adiós!. You have successfully updated the message catalog without losing any of the existing translated messages.

Translations Within Templates

Although some of the messages you will want to internationalize will appear in controllers, most of them are likely to be found in your project's templates. Luckily, the internationalization and localization tools work in templates too.

Let's change the multiple() action to use a template instead. Update it to look like this:

```
def multiple(self):
    return render('/hello.html')
```

Then create hello.html in your project's template directory with this content:

```
<%!
    from pylons.i18n.translation import set_lang, get_lang
%>
<html>
<head>
    <title>Multiple Translations</title>
</head>
```

```
<body>
    <h1>Multiple Translations</h1>
    <p>
        Default: ${_(u'Hello!')}<br />
        % for lang in ['fr','en','es']:
            <% set_lang(lang) %>
            ${get_lang()}:  ${_(u'Hello!')}<br />
        % endfor
    </p>
</body>
</html>
```

The statement at the top is used to import the get_lang() and set_lang() functions, but Pylons automatically puts the translator, ungettext(), _(), and N_() functions into the template namespace, so you don't need to import the _() function in this case.

If you test the example again, you will see that the same output is produced, only this time in an HTML template with a title.

It turns out that using messages that have already been translated in a template file is easy because the Pylons translation functions are called in the same way they would be from within a controller. What is much harder is extracting the strings that need to be internationalized from a template in the first place because the extraction tools won't necessarily understand the syntax of the templating language.

One approach that was recommended in very early versions of Pylons was to run a standard tool such as xgettext on the Mako (or Myghty as it was then) cache directory, which, after heavy development testing, would contain a cached Python version of every template. The extraction tool will then run on the cached templates in the same way it runs on ordinary Python files. Although this process worked adequately, it was rather cumbersome. Babel provides a much better solution, which you'll learn about next.

Babel Extractors

Babel supports the concepts of extractors. These are custom functions that, when called by Babel, will perform the work of extracting internationalizable messages from a particular source file. Babel currently supports extracting gettext messages from Mako and Genshi templates as well as from Python source files.

If you look at your project's setup.py files, you will see the following lines commented out:

```
#message_extractors = {'translatedemo': [
#        ('**.py', 'python', None),
#        ('templates/**.mako', 'mako', None),
#        ('public/**', 'ignore', None)]},
```

If you uncomment them, Babel will know that any .py files should be treated as Python source code, any .mako files should be treated as Mako templates, and everything in the public directory should be ignored. You'll also want .html files in the templates directory treated as Mako source, so update these lines to look like this:

```
message_extractors = {'translatedemo': [
        ('**.py', 'python', None),
        ('templates/**.mako', 'mako', None),
        ('templates/**.html', 'mako', None),
        ('public/**', 'ignore', None)]},
```

For a project using Genshi instead of Mako, the Mako lines might be replaced with this:

```
('templates/**.html, 'genshi', None),
```

Similar options can also be set in the setup.cfg file if you prefer. See http://babel.edgewall.org/wiki/Documentation/cmdline.html#extract for details.

Once you've changed the setup.py file, you may need to run this command again to reinstall the package in development mode so that the changes are recognized:

```
$ python setup.py develop
```

With the changes made, you can use Babel to extract messages from the templates as well as the Python source files in your project:

```
$ python setup.py extract_messages
running extract_messages
extracting messages from translatedemo/__init__.py
extracting messages from translatedemo/websetup.py
extracting messages from translatedemo/config/__init__.py
extracting messages from translatedemo/config/environment.py
extracting messages from translatedemo/config/middleware.py
extracting messages from translatedemo/config/routing.py
extracting messages from translatedemo/controllers/__init__.py
extracting messages from translatedemo/controllers/error.py
extracting messages from translatedemo/controllers/hello.py
extracting messages from translatedemo/lib/__init__.py
extracting messages from translatedemo/lib/app_globals.py
extracting messages from translatedemo/lib/base.py
extracting messages from translatedemo/lib/helpers.py
extracting messages from translatedemo/model/__init__.py
extracting messages from translatedemo/templates/hello.html
extracting messages from translatedemo/tests/__init__.py
extracting messages from translatedemo/tests/test_models.py
extracting messages from translatedemo/tests/functional/__init__.py
extracting messages from translatedemo/tests/functional/test_hello.py
writing PO template file to translatedemo/i18n/translatedemo.pot
```

Notice this time that the templates/hello.html file is included in the extraction process.

■**Tip** If you want to create a Babel extractor for a template language you use or another source file type, you should read the documentation at http://babel.edgewall.org/wiki/Documentation/messages.html# writing-extraction-methods.

Setting the Language in the Config File

Pylons supports defining the default language to be used in the config file. Set a lang variable to the desired default language in your development.ini file, and Pylons will automatically call set_lang() with that language at the beginning of every request.

For example, to set the default language to French, you would add lang = fr to your development.ini file:

```
[app:main]
use = egg:translatedemo
lang = fr
```

If you are running the server with the `--reload` option, the server will automatically restart if you change the `development.ini` file. Otherwise, restart the server manually, and the output would this time be as follows:

```
Default: Bonjour!
fr: Bonjour!
en: Hello!
es: ¡Hola!
```

Using a Session to Store the User's Language

In a real application, the language to be used is likely to be set on each request so that each user sees pages in their own language. In this section, I'll show you one way of setting this up.

You'll remember from Chapter 9 that each controller can have a `__before__()` method, which is run before each controller action. This is a great place to set the language to be used for that controller. You can also use Pylons' `session` global to store the language to be used when the user signs in. Replace the `index()` action with this:

```
def signin(self):
    # Place your sign in code here
    # Replace this with code to set the language for the signed in user
    session['lang'] = request.params.getone('lang')
    session.save()
    return 'Signed in, language set to %s.'%request.params.getone('lang')

def __before__(self):
    if 'lang' in session:
        set_lang(session['lang'])

def index(self):
    return _(u'Hello!')
```

When a user signs in, their language is set and saved in the session. On each subsequent request, the language is looked up in the session and set automatically before each action is called.

To test this, visit `http://localhost:5000/hello/signin?lang=es`. You'll see the message telling you have been signed in. Now visit `http://localhost:5000/hello/index`, and you'll see the message in the language you signed in with, which in this case is Spanish.

If you want to set the language for each request in every controller rather than dealing with each controller individually, you could write some similar code at the top of the `lib/base.py` BaseController class's `__call__()` method instead of in an individual controller's `__before__()` method:

```
def __call__(self, environ, start_response):
    """Invoke the Controller"""
    # WSGIController.__call__ dispatches to the Controller method
    # the request is routed to. This routing information is
    # available in environ['pylons.routes_dict']

    if 'lang' in session:
        set_lang(session['lang'])

    return WSGIController.__call__(self, environ, start_response)
```

You'll need to import the set_lang() function and the session global into that module, though:

```
from pylons.i18n.translation import set_lang
from pylons import session
```

If you delete the page controller's __before__() method and visit http://localhost:5000/hello/multiple again, notice that the default language is still the language you signed in with.

Advanced Internationalization Techniques

Now that you've seen how internationalization and localization work in practice in a Pylons application, I can show you some of the more advanced techniques that will make your internationalization and localization work easier.

Fallback Languages

You've already seen that if your code calls _() with a string that doesn't exist in the language catalog already being used, then the string itself will be returned. This is how the English version of the Hello! message has been produced in the examples so far despite that the English .po file doesn't contain the translation explicitly. Although this is useful, Pylons also provides a much more sophisticated mechanism that allows you to specify the order in which other message catalogs should be searched for a message if the primary language doesn't have a suitable translation.

If you have been following along with the examples so far, then French will be set as the default language in the config file, and Spanish is set as the default language in the session. Set the default language in the session to be French too by visiting http://localhost:5000/hello/signin?lang=fr. Now change the index() action to use the word 'Goodbye!':

```
def index(self):
    return _('Goodbye!')
```

You'll remember that you didn't add a translation for the Goodbye! message to the French message catalog, but you did add it to the Spanish one.

With the current language set to French, visit http://localhost:5000/hello/index, and you will see Goodbye! as the original text passed to the function is used because no French translation is available.

Now change the example to add Spanish as a fallback language like this (if you are using the __call__() version of the example, you will need to make the change in lib/base.py):

```
def __before__(self):
    add_fallback('es')
    if 'lang' in session:
        set_lang(session['lang'])
```

This tells Pylons to look for messages in the Spanish catalog if there are no translations in the French catalog. You'll need to import the add_fallback()function at the top of the file:

```
from pylons.i18n.translation import add_fallback
```

■**Caution** It is important that the call to add_fallback() happens before the call to set_lang(), or the fallback will not be used.

If you run the example again, you will see the message ¡Adiós!.

You can add as many fallback languages with the add_fallback() function as you like, and they will be tested in the order you add them.

One case where using fallbacks in this way is particularly useful is when you want to display content based on the languages requested by the browser in the HTTP_ACCEPT_LANGUAGE header. Typically the browser may submit a number of languages, so it is useful to add fallbacks in the order specified by the browser so that you always try to display words in the language of preference of the user, searching the other languages in order if a translation cannot be found. The languages defined in the HTTP_ACCEPT_LANGAUGE header are available in Pylons as request.languages and can be used like this:

```
def __before__(self):
    for lang in request.languages:
        add_fallback(lang)
    if 'lang' in session:
        set_lang(session['lang'])
```

You must be sure you have the appropriate languages supported if you are going to use this approach, or you should test their existence before calling add_fallback().

Lazy Translations

Occasionally you might come across a situation when you need to translate a string when it is accessed, not when the _() or other functions are called.

Consider this example:

```
set_lang('en')
text = _(u'Hello!')

class HelloController(BaseController):

    def lazy(self):
        resp = ''
        for lang in ['fr','en','es']:
            set_lang(lang)
            resp += u'%s: %s<br />' % (get_lang(), _(u'Hello!'))
        resp += u'Text: %s<br />' % text
        return resp
```

If you run this, you get the following output:

```
['fr']: Bonjour!
['en']: Hello!
['es']: ¡Hola!
Text: Hello!
```

Notice that the text line shows Hello! even though the current language at the time the text was generated was Spanish. This is because the function _(u'Hello') just before the controller definition and after the imports is called when the default language is en, so the variable text gets the value of the English translation, even though when the string was used, the default language was Spanish.

The rule of thumb in these situations is to try to avoid using the translation functions in situations where they are not executed on each request. For situations where this isn't possible, perhaps because you are working with legacy code or with a library that doesn't support internationalization, you need to use lazy translations.

Modify the code to use lazy translations. Notice that the text variable is assigned its message with the `lazy_ugettext()` function:

```
from pylons.i18n import get_lang, lazy_ugettext, set_lang

set_lang('en')
text = lazy_ugettext(u'Hello!')

class HelloController(BaseController):

    def lazy(self):
        resp = ''
        for lang in ['fr','en','es']:
            set_lang(lang)
            resp += u'%s: %s<br />' % (get_lang(), _(u'Hello!'))
        resp += u'Text: %s<br />' % text
        return resp
```

This time you get the output expected:

```
['fr']: Bonjour!
['en']: Hello!
['es']: ¡Hola!
Text: ¡Hola!
```

There is one drawback to be aware of when using the lazy translation functions: they are not actually strings. This means that if our example had used the following code, it would have failed with the error `cannot concatenate 'str' and 'LazyString' objects`:

```
u'Text: ' + text + u'<br />'
```

For this reason, you should use the lazy translations only where absolutely necessary. Always ensure they are converted to strings by calling `str()` or `repr()` before they are used in operations with real strings.

Plural Forms

One thing to keep in mind when you are internationalizing an application is that other languages don't necessarily have the same plural forms as English. Although English has only two forms, singular and plural, Slovenian, for example, has singular, dual, and plural, which means that in Slovenian one thing, two things, and three things would all be treated differently! That means that the following will not work:

```
# BAD!
if n == 1:
    msg = _("There is one person here")
else:
    msg = _("There are %(num)d people here") % {'num': n}
```

Pylons provides the `ungettext()` function internationalizing plural words. It can be used as follows:

```
translated_string = ungettext(
    u'There is %(num)d person here',
    u'There are %(num)d people here',
    4
)
```

If you use 1 in the call to ugettext(), the first form will be used; if you use 0 or a number greater than 1, then the second form will be used. Table 11-1 lists the options.

Table 11-1. *The Results from the Original Message Catalog*

Number	Result
0	There are %(num)d people here
1	There is %(num)d person here
2	There are %(num)d people here

As you can see, no matter which translation is used, the result still contains the text %(num)d, so you can use standard Python string formatting to substitute the correct value into the translation after the correct form has been chosen for you:

```
final_string = translated_string % {'num': 4}
```

If you added the previous code to the sample project and reran the extract_messages tool, you would find some lines similar to these in your .pot file:

```
#: translatedemo/controllers/hello.py:27
#, python-format
msgid "There is %(num)d person here"
msgid_plural "There are %(num)d people here"
msgstr[0] ""
msgstr[1] ""
```

The msgstr[0] and msgstr[1] lines give you the opportunity to customize the plurals for different languages. You could then run update_catalog to update the .po files. Looking at the Spanish .po file, you would see this (some lines have been omitted for brevity):

```
...
"Plural-Forms: nplurals=2; plural=(n != 1)\n"
...
...
#: translatedemo/controllers/hello.py:27
#, python-format
msgid "There is %(num)d person here"
msgid_plural "There are %(num)d people here"
msgstr[0] ""
msgstr[1] ""
...
```

The Plural-Forms definition at the top describes which plural version to use. In Spanish there are two plurals, and the plural form should be used whenever the number of items isn't 1. The translation for the singular form should go next to msgstr[0], and the translation for plural should go next to msgstr[1]. When you recompile the message catalog, the ungettext() function will return the correct form of the translation for the number passed to it.

You can find further details about how plural forms should be dealt with in the "The Format of PO Files" section of GNU gettext's manual (http://www.gnu.org/software/gettext/manual/html_chapter/gettext_10.html#PO-Files).

Search Engine Considerations

One issue to be aware of when using a session to determine which version of a site to display, and dynamically generating that page based on the language of the user, is that search engines will be able to search the site in the default language only. This can be a problem if you want search engines to be able to index all the pages on your web site, including the foreign-language versions. In these situations, it can be better to use a different URL for each language.

To implement this, you might set up your URLs so that the first part of the URL path represents the language to be used. For example, the English version of your site might be at /en, and the Japanese version might be at /ja. You can then use Routes to extract the first part of the URL and treat the rest of the URL as the page being requested, using the internationalization tools to produce the correct language version based on the language specified as the first part of the URL.

Note The makers of the Opera web browser used a similar technique for the Pylons-based website at `http://widgets.opera.com`. You can read more about the details of this implementation at `http://my.opera.com/WebApplications/blog/2008/03/17/search-engine-friendly`.

Summary

This chapter covered the basics of internationalizing and localizing a web application. GNU gettext is an extensive library, and the GNU gettext manual is highly recommended for more information. Although the Pylons internationalization tools don't support all the features of gettext, they do support the most commonly used ones, as you've seen in this chapter. The Babel package is also improving all the time and includes tools not covered in this chapter for providing access to various locale display names, localized number and date formatting, time zones, and more.

CHAPTER 12

■■■

Testing

Testing is the process of ensuring that the code you write performs in the way it was intended. Testing encompasses many different aspects that are relevant to a Pylons application. For example, it is important the libraries do what they are supposed to, that the controllers return the correct HTML pages for the actions they are performing, and that the application behaves in a way that the users find intuitive.

Here are some of the many reasons why writing effective tests is a very good idea when developing a Pylons application:

Fast refactoring: Over the course of most software development projects you'll find that a lot of the code you wrote at the very start of the project is modified before the final release. This isn't necessarily because the code contains bugs; it could be because requirements have changed or because you've spotted a better way of implementing the same functionality. If you have already written tests for the code you need to refactor and the tests pass after you've updated the code, then you can be confident that the changes you made are unlikely to have introduced any unexpected bugs.

Ensuring simple design: If writing unit tests for a particular set of classes, methods, or functions turns out to be a difficult process, it is likely that the code is too complicated and not adequately exposing the API that another developer interacting with your code might eventually need. The fact you are able to write a unit test for a piece of code goes some way to ensuring it is correctly designed.

Use case documentation: A set of tests serves to define the use cases for the code that is being tested. This means the tests also form very effective documentation of how the code should work.

At its heart, testing is about having confidence in the code you have written. If you have written good tests, you can have a good degree of confidence that your code works as it should. Having confidence is especially important if you are using beta or prerelease code in your application. As long as you write tests to ensure the features of the product you are using behave as you require, then you can have a degree of confidence that it is OK to use those particular features in your application.

Although writing effective tests does take time, it is often better to spend time writing tests early in the project than debugging problems later. If you have written tests, every time you make a change to the code, then you can run the tests to see whether any of them fail. This gives you instant feedback about any unforeseen consequences your code change has had. Without the tests, bugs that are introduced might not be picked up for a long time, allowing for the possibility that new code you write might depend on the code working in the incorrect way. If this happens, fixing the bug would then break the new code you had written. This is why later in a project fixing minor bugs can sometimes create major problems. By failing to write effective tests, you can sometimes end up with a system that is difficult to maintain.

It is worth noting that Pylons and all the components that make up Pylons have their own automated test suites. The Pylons tests are run every night on the latest development source using a tool called Buildbot, and the results are published online. Without these extensive test suites, the Pylons developers would not be able to have the confidence in Pylons that they do.

Types of Testing and the Development Process

In this chapter, I'll describe three types of testing you can use to help avoid introducing bugs into your Pylons project during the course of development:

- Unit testing
- Functional testing
- User testing

If you are interested in reading more about other types of software testing, the Wikipedia page is a good place to start: http://en.wikipedia.org/wiki/Portal:Software_Testing.

The most common form of testing is *unit testing*. A unit test is a procedure used to validate that individual units of your source code produce the expected output given a known input. In Python, the smallest testable parts of a library or application are typically functions or methods. Unit tests are written from a programmer's perspective to ensure that a particular set of methods or functions successfully perform a set of tasks. In the context of a Pylons application, you would usually write unit tests for any helpers or other libraries you have written. You might also use a unit test to ensure your model classes and methods work correctly. Your Pylons project has a test_models.py file in the tests directory for precisely this purpose.

While unit tests are designed to ensure individual units of code work properly, *functional tests* ensure that the higher-level code you have written functions in the way that users of your Pylons application would expect. For example, a functional test might ensure that the correct form was displayed when a user visited a particular URL or that when a user clicked a link, a particular entry was added to the database. Functional tests are usually used in the context of a Pylons application to test controller actions.

Some people would argue that the best time to write unit and functional tests is before you have written the code that they would test, and this might be an approach you could take when developing your Pylons application. The advantages of this approach are the following:

- You can be confident the code you have written fulfils your requirements.
- It is likely the code you have written is not overengineered, because you have concentrated on getting the test suite to pass rather than future-proofing your code against possible later changes.
- You know when the code is finished once the test suite passes.

Another approach that helps you write code that meets your requirements without being overengineered is to write the documentation for your Pylons project first and include code samples. Python comes with a library called doctest that can analyze the documentation and run the code samples to check that they work in the way you have documented. You'll learn more about doctest in Chapter 13.

The final type of testing you should strongly consider integrating into your development process is *user testing*. User testing doesn't involve writing any automated tests at all but instead typically involves getting together a willing and representative group of the intended users of your product and giving them tasks in order to watch how they interact with the system. You then make notes of any tasks they struggle with or any occasions where the software breaks because of their actions and update your Pylons application accordingly, attributing any problems to deficiencies in your software rather than the incompetence of your users.

The end users of your product are often very good people to test your application on because they will have a similar (or greater) knowledge of the business rules for the tasks they are trying to use the system for, but they might not have the technical knowledge you do. This means they are much more likely to do unusual things during the course of their interaction with your application—things you have learned from experience not to do. For example, they might use the Back button after a POST request or copy unusual characters from software such as Microsoft Word that might be in an unexpected encoding. This behavior helps highlight deficiencies in your software that you may not have noticed yourself.

If you are developing a commercial product for a specific set of users, then there is a secondary reason for involving them in the testing of your prototype. It can help familiarize them with the system and give them a chance to highlight any gaps in the software as you are developing it; this in turn vastly reduces the chance of the software not being accepted at the end of the development process because the users have been involved all along the way. Ultimately, if the users of your application are happy with the way your Pylons application works, then it fulfils its goal.

■**Note** Of course, user testing is a topic in its own right, and I won't go into it further here. User testing is also an important part of many software development methodologies that can be used with Pylons.

If you are interested in development methodologies, the Wikipedia articles on agile and iterative development are good places to start and are often useful methodologies to choose for a Pylons project. You might also be interested to read about the Waterfall method, which is a methodology frequently used in larger IT projects but that many people argue often doesn't work in practice.

```
http://en.wikipedia.org/wiki/Agile_software_development
http://en.wikipedia.org/wiki/Iterative_and_incremental_development
http://en.wikipedia.org/wiki/Waterfall_model
```

Unit Testing with nose

Writing unit tests without a testing framework can be a difficult process. The Python community is fortunate to have access to many good quality unit testing libraries including the `unittest` module from the Python standard library, `py.test`, and nose. Pylons uses nose to run the test suite for your Pylons application because it currently has a slightly more advanced feature set than the others. nose is installed automatically when you install Pylons, so it is ready to go.

Before you learn about how to write unit tests specifically for Pylons, let's start by writing some simple tests and using nose to test them.

Introducing nose

Here's what a very simple unit test written using nose might look like:

```
def test_add():
    assert 1+1 == 2

def test_subtract():
    a = 1
    b = a + 1
    c = b-1
    assert b-a == c
```

The example uses the Python keyword `assert` to test whether a particular condition is `True` or `False`. Using the `assert` statement in this way is equivalent to raising an `AssertionError` but is just a little easier to write. You could replace the `test_add()` function with this if you prefer:

```
def test_add():
    if not 1+1 == 2:
        raise AssertionError()
```

nose differentiates between assertion errors and other exceptions. Exceptions as a result of a failed assertion are called *failures*, whereas any other type of exception is treated as an *error*.

To test the example code, save it as `test_maths.py`, and run the following command:

```
$ nosetests test_maths.py
```

You'll see the following output:

```
..
----------------------------------------------------------------------
Ran 2 tests in 0.001s

OK
```

For every test that passes, a `.` character is displayed. In this case, since there are only two tests, there are two `.` characters before the summary. Now if you change the line a = 1 to a = 3 in the `test_subtract()` function and run the test again, the assertion will fail, so nose tells you about the failure and displays `F` instead of the `.` for the second test:

```
.F
======================================================================
FAIL: test_maths.test_subtract
----------------------------------------------------------------------
Traceback (most recent call last):
  File "/home/james/lib/python2.5/site-packages/nose-0.10.3-py2.4.egg/➥
nose/case.py", line 182, in runTest
    self.test(*self.arg)
  File "/home/james/Desktop/test_maths.py", line 8, in test_subtract
    assert b-a == c
AssertionError

----------------------------------------------------------------------
Ran 2 tests in 0.002s

FAILED (failures=1)
```

This isn't too helpful because you can't see the values of a, b, or c from the error message, but you can augment this result by adding a message after the `assert` statement to clarify what you are testing like this:

```
assert b-a == c, "The value of b-a does not equal c"
```

which results in the following:

```
.F
======================================================================
FAIL: test_maths.test_subtract
----------------------------------------------------------------------
Traceback (most recent call last):
  File "/home/james/lib/python2.4/site-packages/nose-0.10.3➥
-py2.5.egg/nose/case.py", line 182, in runTest
    self.test(*self.arg)
  File "/home/james/Desktop/test_maths.py", line 8, in test_subtract
    assert b-a == c
AssertionError: The value of b-a does not equal c


----------------------------------------------------------------------
Ran 2 tests in 0.002s

FAILED (failures=1)
```

This is better but still not particularly helpful because you still can't tell the values of a, b, or c from the output. nose has three different ways to help you solve this problem, covered in the following three sections.

Debug Messages

Any print statements you add to your tests are displayed only if the test fails or results in an error. Try modifying the test_subtract() function so that it looks like this:

```
def test_subtract():
    a = 3
    print "a is %s"%a
    b = a + 1
    print "b is %s"%b
    c = b-1
    print "c is %s"%c
    assert b-a == c
```

If you run the test again, you'll see the following extra information displayed after the AssertionError:

```
-------------------- >> begin captured stdout << ---------------------
a is 3
b is 4
c is 3

-------------------- >> end captured stdout << ----------------------
```

From this you can easily see that 4-3 != 3, but the test output wouldn't be cluttered with these debug messages unless the test failed. If you would prefer nose to always print debug messages like these, you can use the -s option so that it doesn't capture the standard output stream.

Detailed Errors

If you run nose with the -d flag, it will try to display the values of the variables in the assert statement:

```
$ nosetests -d test_maths.py
```

In this case, the output also contains the following line, so you can immediately see the mistake:

```
>>  assert 4-3 == 3
```

Command-Line Debugging

If you want even more flexibility to debug the output from your tests, you can start nose with the --pdb and --pdb-failures options, which drop nose into debugging mode if it encounters any errors or failures, respectively. As the option names suggest, nose invokes pdb (the Python debugger), so you can use the full range of commands supported by the pdb module.

Let's give it a try—start by running the test again with the new flags set:

```
$ nosetests --pdb --pdb-failures test_maths.py
```

Now when the failure occurs, you'll see the pdb prompt:

```
.> /home/james/Desktop/test_maths.py(11)test_subtract()
-> assert b-a == c
(Pdb)
```

You can display a list of commands with h:

```
Documented commands (type help <topic>):
========================================
EOF    break  condition  disable  help    list  q       step      w
a      bt     cont       down     ignore  n     quit    tbreak    whatis
alias  c      continue   enable   j       next  r       u         where
args   cl     d          exit     jump    p     return  unalias
b      clear  debug      h        l       pp    s       up

Miscellaneous help topics:
==========================
exec   pdb

Undocumented commands:
======================
retval  rv
```

Of these, some of the most important are l, which lists the code nearby, and q, which exits the debugger so that the tests can continue. The prompt also works a bit like a Python shell, allowing you to enter commands. Here's an example session where you print some variables, obtain help on the l command, and then exit the debugger with q:

```
(Pdb) print b-a
1
(Pdb) print c
3
(Pdb) h l
l(ist) [first [,last]]
List source code for the current file.
Without arguments, list 11 lines around the current line
or continue the previous listing.
With one argument, list 11 lines starting at that line.
With two arguments, list the given range;
if the second argument is less than the first, it is a count.
(Pdb) l
```

```
 6          print "a is %s"%a
 7          b = a + 1
 8          print "b is %s"%b
 9          c = b-1
10          print "c is %s"%c
11  ->      assert b-a == c
12
[EOF]
(Pdb) q;
```

The pdb module and all its options are documented at http://docs.python.org/lib/module-pdb.html.

Search Locations

nose uses a set of rules to determine which tests it should run. Its behavior is best described by the text from the nose documentation:

> *nose collects tests automatically from python source files, directories and packages found in its working directory (which defaults to the current working directory). Any python source file, directory or package that matches the* testMatch *regular expression (by default:* (?:^|[\b_\.-])[Tt]est) *will be collected as a test (or source for collection of tests). In addition, all other packages found in the working directory will be examined for python source files or directories that match* testMatch*. Package discovery descends all the way down the tree, so* package.tests *and* package.sub.tests *and* package.sub.sub2.tests *will all be collected.*

> *Within a test directory or package, any python source file matching* testMatch *will be examined for test cases. Within a test module, functions and classes whose names match* testMatch *and* TestCase *subclasses with any name will be loaded and executed as tests.*

To specify which tests you want to run, you can pass test names on the command line. Here's an example that will search dir1 and dir2 for test cases and will also run the test_b() function in the module test_a.py in the tests directory. All these tests will be looked for in the some_place directory instead of the current working directory because the code uses the -w flag:

```
$ nosetests -w some_place dir1 dir2 tests/test_a.py:test_b
```

When you are developing a Pylons application, you would normally run nosetests from the Pylons project directory (the directory containing the setup.py file) so that nose can automatically find your tests.

▪Note For more information about nose, see the wiki at http://code.google.com/p/python-nose/wiki/NoseFeatures.

Functional Testing

Pylons provides powerful unit testing capabilities for your web application utilizing `paste.fixture` (documented at `http://pythonpaste.org/testing-applications.html#the-tests-themselves`) to emulate requests to your web application. Pylons integrates `paste.fixture` with nose so that you can test Pylons applications using the same techniques you learned for nose in the previous section.

■**Note** It is likely that at some point Pylons will switch to using the newer WebTest package, but since WebTest is simply an upgrade of `paste.fixture` with some better support for Pylons' newer `request` and `response` objects, the upgrade shouldn't introduce huge changes, and therefore the contents of this section should still largely apply.

To demonstrate functional testing with `paste.fixture`, let's write some tests for the SimpleSite application. If you look at the SimpleSite project, you'll notice the `tests` directory. Within it is a `functional` directory for functional tests that should contain one file for each controller in your application. These are generated automatically when you use the `paster controller` command to add a controller to a Pylons project. To get started, update the `tests/functional/test_page.py` file that was generated when you created the `page` controller so that it looks like this:

```
from simplesite.tests import *

class TestPageController(TestController):

    def test_view(self):
        response = self.app.get(url_for(controller='page', action='view', id=1))
        assert 'Home' in response
```

The page controller doesn't have an `index()` action because you replaced it as part of the tutorial in Chapter 8, so the previous example tests the `view()` action instead.

The `self.app` object is a Web Server Gateway Interface application representing the whole Pylons application, but it is wrapped in a `paste.fixture.TestApp` object (documented at `http://pythonpaste.org/modules/fixture.html`). This means the `self.app` object has the methods `get()`, `post()`, `put()`, `delete()`, `do_request()`, `encode_multipart()`, and `reset()`. Unless you are doing something particularly clever, you would usually just use `get()` and `post()`, which simulate GET and POST requests, respectively.

`get(url, params=None, headers=None, extra_environ=None, status=None, expect_errors=False)`: This gets the URL path specified by `url` using a GET request and returns a response object.

- `params`: A query string, or a dictionary that will be encoded into a query string. You may also include a query string on the `url` argument.

- `headers`: A dictionary of extra headers to send.

- `extra_environ`: A dictionary of environmental variables that should be added to the request.

- status: The integer status code you expect (if not 200 or 3xx). If you expect a 404 response, for instance, you must give status=404, or an exception will be raised. You can also give a wildcard, like '3*' or '*'.

- expect_errors: If this is not True, then if anything is written to wsgi.errors, an exception wlll be raised. You'll learn about wsgi.errors in Chapters 16 and 20. If the value is set to True, then non-200/3xx responses are OK.

post(url, params='', headers=None, extra_environ=None, status=None, upload_files= None, expect_errors=False): This is very similar to the get() method, but it performs a POST request, so params are put in the body of the request rather than the query string. It takes similar arguments and returns a response object.

- upload_files: Should be a list of [(fieldname, filename, file_content)] representing files to upload. You can also use just [(fieldname, filename)], and the file content will be read from disk.

The example you've just added to tests/functional/test_page.py uses the get() method to simulate a GET request to the URL /page/view/1. Because a fully configured Pylons environment is set up in the simplesite.tests module, you are able to use url_for() to generate the URL in the same way you would in a Pylons controller. The get() method returns a paste.fixture response object. You can then use this to check the response returned was the one you expected. In this case, you check that the home page contains the text 'Home' somewhere in the response.

In addition to the methods on the self.app() object, Pylons also gives you access to some of the Pylons globals that have been created during the request. They are assigned as attributes of the paste.fixture response object:

response.session: Session object

response.req: The Pylons request object based on the WebOb Request

response.c: The template context global containing variables passed to templates

response.g: The Pylons app globals object

response.response: The Pylons response global

To use them, just access the attributes of the response *after* you've used a get() or post() method:

```
def test_view(self):
    response = self.app.get(url_for(controller='page', action='view', id=1))
    assert 'Home' in response
    assert 'REQUEST_METHOD' in response.req.environ
```

Note The paste.fixture response object already has its own request object assigned to it as the .request attribute, which is why the Pylons request global is assigned to the .req attribute instead.

For simple cases, it is fine to work with the paste.fixture response object, but for more complicated cases, you will probably prefer to work with the more familiar Pylons response global available as response.response.

Before you test the previous method, you really need to understand exactly how the test setup works because, as it stands, it could damage your development setup. Let's see why in the next section.

How Does the Test Setup Work?

To run the test, you would execute the nosetests command, but before you do, let's consider what this command actually does.

When the nosetests command is executed, it reads some of its configuration from the project's setup.cfg file. This file contains a section that looks like this:

```
[nosetests]
with-pylons=test.ini
```

This tells nose to use the test.ini file to create a Pylons application rather than the development.ini file you've been using so far.

■**Note** You can also choose the config file to use for the tests by specifying the --with-pylons option on the command line. Likewise, you can also put other nosetests command-line options in the setup.cfg file if that is more convenient. Here are some examples of options you could set:

```
[nosetests]
verbose=True
verbosity=2
with-pylons=test.ini
detailed-errors=1
```

The test.ini file is specifically for your testing configuration and (if properly configured) allows you to keep your testing and development setups completely separate. It looks like this:

```
#
# SimpleSite - Pylons testing environment configuration
#
# The %(here)s variable will be replaced with the parent directory of this file
#
[DEFAULT]
debug = true
# Uncomment and replace with the address which should receive any error reports
#email_to = you@yourdomain.com
smtp_server = localhost
error_email_from = paste@localhost

[server:main]
use = egg:Paste#http
host = 0.0.0.0
port = 5000

[app:main]
use = config:development.ini

# Add additional test specific configuration options as necessary.
```

This should seem very familiar, but notice the line marked in bold in the [app:main] section. This causes the test.ini [app:main] section to use *exactly* the same configuration as the development.ini file's [app:main] section. Although this can save you some effort in some circumstances, it can also cause your tests to interfere with your development setup if you are not careful.

Once `nosetests` has correctly parsed the `test.ini` file, it will look for available tests. In doing so, it imports the `tests/__init__.py` module, which executes this line:

```
SetupCommand('setup-app').run([config['__file__']])
```

Although it looks fairly innocuous, this results in the equivalent of this command being executed:

```
$ paster setup-app test.ini
```

You'll recall from Chapter 8 that this will run the project `websetup.py` file's `setup_app()` function with the configuration from `test.ini`, but because the `test.ini` file currently uses the configuration from the `[app:main]` section of the `development.ini` file, it will be called with the same `sqlalchemy.url` as your development setup. If your `websetup.py` was badly written, this could damage the data in your development database.

To make matters worse, the `test.ini` file doesn't come with the `development.ini` file's logging configuration, so you can't even see what is happening behind the scenes. Copy all the logging lines from the `development.ini` file to the end of `test.ini` starting with `# Logging configuration` and ending at the end of the file. If you run `nosetests` again, you will see what has been happening behind the scenes:

```
$ nosetests
20:14:02,807 INFO  [simplesite.websetup] Adding home page...
20:14:02,918 INFO  [simplesite.websetup] Successfully set up.
.
----------------------------------------------------------------------
Ran 1 test in 0.347s

OK
```

As you can see, every time the test suite was run, a new home page was accidentally added to the database. You can confirm this by starting the Paste HTTP server and visiting `http://localhost:5000/page/list` to verify that an extra home page has been added.

Now that you understand what is happening, update the `test.ini` file with its own configuration so the `[app:main]` section looks like this:

```
[app:main]
use = egg:SimpleSite
full_stack = true
cache_dir = %(here)s/data
beaker.session.key = simplesite
beaker.session.secret = somesecret

# SQLAlchemy database URL
sqlalchemy.url = sqlite:///%(here)s/test.db
```

Notice that `sqlalchemy.url` has been changed to use `test.db`. This still doesn't prevent a new home page from being added each time the tests run, so you should update `websetup.py` too. Ideally, you want a completely fresh database each time the tests are run so that they are consistent each time. To achieve this, you need to know which config file is being used to run the tests. The `setup_app()` function takes a `conf` object as its second argument. This object has a `.filename` attribute that contains the name of the file used to invoke the `setup_app()` function.

Update the `setup_app()` function in `websetup.py` to look like this. Notice the import of `os.path` as well as the code to drop existing tables if using the `test.ini` file.

```
"""Setup the SimpleSite application"""
import logging
import os.path
from simplesite import model

from simplesite.config.environment import load_environment

log = logging.getLogger(__name__)

def setup_app(command, conf, vars):
    """Place any commands to setup simplesite here"""
    load_environment(conf.global_conf, conf.local_conf)
    # Load the models
    from simplesite.model import meta
    meta.metadata.bind = meta.engine
    filename = os.path.split(conf.filename)[-1]
    if filename == 'test.ini':
        # Permanently drop any existing tables
        log.info("Dropping existing tables...")
        meta.metadata.drop_all(checkfirst=True)
    # Continue as before
    # Create the tables if they aren't there already
    meta.metadata.create_all(checkfirst=True)
    log.info("Adding home page...")
    page = model.Page()
    page.title=u'Homepage'
    page.content = u'Welcome to the SimpleSite home page.'
    meta.Session.save(page)
    meta.Session.commit()
    log.info("Successfully set up.")
```

With these changes in place, let's run the test again:

```
$ nosetests
14:02:58,646 INFO  [simplesite.websetup] Dropping existing tables...
... some lines of output omitted ...
14:02:59,603 INFO  [simplesite.websetup] Adding homepage...
14:02:59,617 INFO  [sqlalchemy.engine.base.Engine.0x...26ec] BEGIN
14:02:59,622 INFO  [sqlalchemy.engine.base.Engine.0x...26ec] INSERT INTO page ➥
(content, posted, title, heading) VALUES (?, ?, ?, ?)
14:02:59,623 INFO  [sqlalchemy.engine.base.Engine.0x...26ec] [u'Welcome to ➥
the SimpleSite home page.', '2008-11-04 14:02:59.622472', u'Home Page', None]
14:02:59,629 INFO  [sqlalchemy.engine.base.Engine.0x...26ec] COMMIT
14:02:59,775 INFO  [simplesite.websetup] Successfully set up
.
----------------------------------------------------------------------
Ran 1 test in 0.814s

OK
```

This time the setup_app() function can determine that it is being called with the test.ini config setup, so it drops all the tables before performing the normal setup. Because you updated the
test.ini file with a new SQLite database, you'll notice the test database test.db has been created in
the same directory as test.ini.

Testing the save() Action

The page controller's save() action currently looks like this:

```
@restrict('POST')
@validate(schema=NewPageForm(), form='edit')
def save(self, id=None):
    page_q = meta.Session.query(model.Page)
    page = page_q.filter_by(id=id).first()
    if page is None:
        abort(404)
    for k,v in self.form_result.items():
        if getattr(page, k) != v:
            setattr(page, k, v)
    meta.Session.commit()
    session['flash'] = 'Page successfully updated.'
    session.save()
    # Issue an HTTP redirect
    response.status_int = 302
    response.headers['location'] = h.url_for(controller='page', action='view',
        id=page.id)
    return "Moved temporarily"
```

Let's write a test to check that this action behaves in the correct way:

- GET requests are disallowed by the @restrict decorator.
- The action returns a 404 Not Found response if no ID is specified.
- The action returns a 404 Not Found response for IDs that don't exist.
- Invalid data should result in the form being displayed.
- The action saves the updated data in the database.
- The action sets a flash message in the session.
- The action returns a redirect response to redirect to the create action.

You could write the tests for each of these in a single method of the TestPageController class, but if one of the tests failed for any reason, nose would not continue with the rest of the method. On the other hand, some of the tests are dependent on other tests passing, so you cannot write them all as separate methods either. For example, you can't test whether a flash message was set if saving the page failed. To set up the tests correctly, let's create the following methods:

```
def test_save_prohibit_get(self):
    """Tests to ensure that GET requests are prohibited"""

def test_save_404_invalid_id(self):
    """Tests that a 404 response is returned if no ID is specified
    or if the ID doesn't exist"""

def test_save_invalid_form_data(self):
    """Tests that invalid data results in the form being returned with
    error messages"""

def test_save(self):
    """Tests that valid data is saved to the database, that the response redirects
    to the view() action and that a flash message is set in the session"""
```

These tests will require some imports, so add the following lines to the top of tests/functional/test_page.py:

```
from routes import url_for
from simplesite.model import meta
from urlparse import urlparse
```

Now let's implement the test methods starting with test_save_prohibit_get(), which looks like this:

```
class TestPageController(TestController):

    def test_save_prohibit_get(self):
        """Tests to ensure that GET requests are prohibited"""
        response = self.app.get(
            url=url_for(controller='page', action='save', id='1'),
            params={
                'heading': u'Updated Heading',
                'title': u'Updated Title',
                'content': u'Updated Content',
            },
            status = 405
        )
```

As you can see, the example uses the get() method of self.app to simulate a GET request to the save() action with some sample params, which will be sent as part of the query string. By default, the get() and post() methods expect either a 200 response or a response in the 300s and will consider anything else an error. In this case, you expect the request to be denied with a 405 Method Not Allowed response, so to prevent paste.fixture from raising an exception, you have to specify the status parameter explicitly. Because paste.fixture checks that the status will be 405, you don't have to add another check on the response object.

Now let's look at the test_save_404_invalid_id() method:

```
    def test_save_404_invalid_id(self):
        ""Tests that a 404 response is returned if no ID is specified
        or if the ID doesn't exist"""
        response = self.app.post(
            url=url_for(controller='page', action='save', id=''),
            params={
                'heading': u'Updated Heading',
                'title': u'Updated Title',
                'content': u'Updated Content',
            },
            status=404
        )
        response = self.app.post(
            url=url_for(controller='page', action='save', id='2'),
            params={
                'heading': u'Updated Heading',
                'title': u'Updated Title',
                'content': u'Updated Content',
            },
            status=404
        )
```

As you can see, this code is similar but uses the post() method and performs two tests rather than one. In the first, no ID is specified, and in the second the ID specified doesn't exist. In both cases, you expect a 404 HTTP response, so the status parameter is set to 404.

The test_save_invalid_form_data() method is more interesting. Once again a POST request is triggered, but this time the title is empty, so the @validate decorator should cause the page to be redisplayed with the error message Please enter a value:

```
def test_save_invalid_form_data(self):
    """Tests that invalid data results in the form being returned with
    error messages"""
    response = self.app.post(
        url=url_for(controller='page', action='save', id='1'),
        params={
            'heading': u'Updated Heading',
            # title is required so this next entry is invalid
            'title': u'',
            'content': u'Updated Content',
        }
    )
    assert 'Please enter a value' in response
```

As you can see from the last line, the presence of the error message in the response is tested. Because you expect a 200 HTTP response, there is no need to specify the status argument, but you can if you like.

Finally, let's look at the test_save() method:

```
def test_save(self):
    """Tests that valid data is saved to the database, that the response redirects
    to the view() action and that a flash message is set in the session"""

    response = self.app.post(
        url=url_for(controller='page', action='save', id='1'),
        params={
            'heading': u'Updated Heading',
            'title': u'Updated Title',
            'content': u'Updated Content',
        }
    )

    # Test the data is saved in the database (we use the engine API to
    # ensure that all the data really has been saved and isn't being returned
    # from the session)
    connection = meta.engine.connect()
    result = connection.execute(
        """
        SELECT heading, title, content
        FROM page
        WHERE id=?
        """,
        (1,)
    )
    connection.close()
    row = result.fetchone()
    assert row.heading == u'Updated Heading'
    assert row.title == u'Updated Title'
    assert row.content == u'Updated Content'

    # Test the flash message is set in the session
    assert response.session['flash'] == 'Page successfully updated.'
```

```
# Check the respone will redirect to the view action
assert urlparse(response.response.location).path == url_for(
    controller='page', action='view', id=1)
assert response.status == 302
```

The first part of this test generates a paste.fixture response after posting some valid data to the save() action. A SQLAlchemy connection object is then created to perform a SQL SELECT operation directly on the database to check the data really has been updated. Next you check the session contains the flash message. You'll remember from earlier in the chapter that certain Pylons globals including session are available as attributes of the response object. In this example, response.session is tested to ensure the flash message is present. Finally, you want to check the HTTP response headers contain the Location header with the correct URL to redirect the browser to the view() action. Here we are using the Pylons response object because it has a .location attribute specifying the location header rather than the paste.fixture response object. The location header contains the whole URL, so you use urlparse() to just compare that the path component matches the path to the view() action.

Once you've implemented the tests, you can check they pass by running nosetests in your main project directory:

```
$ nosetests simplesite/tests/functional/test_page.py
... log output omitted ...
..
------------------------------------------------------------------------
Ran 4 tests in 0.391s

OK
```

The tests all pass successfully, so you can be confident the save() action functions as it is supposed to function.

■Tip The TestPageController is derived from the TestController class, which itself subclasses the standard Python unittest.TestCase class. This means you can also use its helper methods in your tests. The unittest.TestCase object is documented at http://docs.python.org/lib/testcase-objects.html. This is well worth a read if you plan to write anything more than simple tests.

Testing Your Own Objects

As you saw earlier in the chapter, Pylons adds certain objects to the response object returned by paste.fixture when you call the self.app object with one of the HTTP methods such as get() or post(). You can also set up your own objects to be added to the response object. If a test is being run, Pylons makes available a paste.testing_variables dictionary in the request.environ dictionary. Any objects you add to this dictionary are automatically added as attributes to the paste.fixture response object. For example, if you had a custom Cache object that you wanted to make available in the tests, you might modify the __call__() method in the BaseController in your project's lib/base.py file to look like this:

```
class BaseController(WSGIController):

    def __call__(self, environ, start_response):
        # Add the custom cache object
        if 'paste.testing_variables' in environ:
            environ['paste.testing_variables']['cache'] = CustomCacheObj()
        try:
            return WSGIController.__call__(self, environ, start_response)
        finally:
            meta.Session.remove()
```

In the `TestPageController` you would now find the `response` object has a `.cache` attribute:

```
def test_cache(self):
    response = self.app.get(url(controller='page', action='view', id='1'))
    assert hasattr(response, 'cache') is True
```

For more details on running tests using `paste.fixture`, visit `http://pythonpaste.org/testing-applications.html#the-tests-themselves`.

Interactive Shell

Sometimes it is useful to be able to test your application from the command line. As you saw earlier in the chapter, one method for doing this is to use the `--pdb` and `--pdb-failures` options with nose to debug a failing test, but what if you want to quickly see how a particular part of your Pylons application behaves to help you work out how you should write your test? In that case, you might find the Pylons interactive shell useful.

The Pylons interactive shell enables you to use all the tools you would usually use in your tests but in an interactive way. This is also particularly useful if you can't understand why a particular test is giving you the result it is. The following command starts the interactive shell with the test setup, but you could equally well specify `development.ini` if you wanted to test your development setup:

```
$ paster shell test.ini
```

Here's the output you receive:

```
Pylons Interactive Shell
Python 2.5.1 (r251:54863, Apr 15 2008, 22:57:26)
[GCC 4.0.1 (Apple Inc. build 5465)]

  All objects from simplesite.lib.base are available
  Additional Objects:
  mapper    -  Routes mapper object
  wsgiapp   -  This project's WSGI App instance
  app       -  paste.fixture wrapped around wsgiapp

>>>
```

As you can see, the shell provides access to the same objects as you have access to in the actions of your functional test classes.

You can use the Pylons interactive shell in the same way you would usually use a Python shell. Here are some examples of its use:

```
>>> response = app.get('/page/view/1')
13:24:31,824 INFO  [sqlalchemy.engine.base.Engine.0x..90] BEGIN
13:24:31,828 INFO  [sqlalchemy.engine.base.Engine.0x..90] ➡
SELECT page.id AS page_id, page.content AS page_content, ➡
page.posted AS page_posted, page.title AS page_title,➡
page.heading AS page_heading
FROM page
WHERE page.id = ?
 LIMIT 1 OFFSET 0
13:24:31,828 INFO  [sqlalchemy.engine.base.Engine.0x..90] [1]
>>> assert 'Updated Content' in response
>>> print response.req.environ.has_key('REMOTE_USER')
False
>>>
```

Notice that you receive the same logging output because of the logging configuration you added to `test.ini` earlier in the chapter. Also notice that because you've already run the `nosetests` command, the database currently has the text `Updated Content` for the content rather than the message `Welcome to the SimpleSite home page.`, which was the original value.

Summary

In this chapter, you saw how nose, `paste.fixture`, and the Pylons interactive shell work together to allow you to test Pylons applications. You've seen how to use some of the more common options available to nose to customize the output from the tests and how to debug failures and errors with Python's `pdb` module. You also learned the difference between unit testing, functional testing, and user testing and saw why all of them are important. You also now know exactly how Pylons sets up your tests so that you can customize their behavior by changing the `websetup.py` file or adding new objects to the `paste.fixture response` object.

In the next chapter, you'll look at some of the recommended ways to document a Pylons project, and you'll learn about one more type of testing known as a *doctest*, which allows examples from within the documentation to be tested directly.

CHAPTER 13

■ ■ ■

Documentation

In this chapter, you'll learn about the tools you can use to document your Pylons applications. Documentation can take a number of forms:

- Source code documentation (comments and docstrings)
- API documentation
- User guides
- Developer guides

The combination of approaches you choose to use for your project will depend on who will be using it and in what manner. For example, if you are developing an application on your own for your home page, you might decide that source code documentation is sufficient. If you are writing a library to support a Pylons application and you hope other developers will use it, then API documentation will be important. If you are creating an application like the SimpleSite tutorial application that might eventually be distributed on the Internet, then a user guide explaining how to install the application and what functionality it contains will be important. Finally, if you are developing a Pylons application or library that you hope other developers will contribute to or if you are working in a larger team, you will need developer guides that explain the structure of the code, the conventions being used, and any particular code styles that the application uses.

The tools you'll learn about in this chapter will help you with each of these types of documentation.

Python's Documentation Tools

The Python language has very good support for source code documentation. In the following sections, I'll cover some of the language features that facilitate writing documentation as well as some of the tools available in the Python standard library for extracting documentation from Python source code.

Comments

Source code comments are a great way to leave information about your programs that will be read at a later time by people (possibly yourself) who need to know what you were thinking at the time you wrote them. They should be used anywhere you are doing something nonstandard or anywhere you think someone coming fresh to the code might misunderstand your intentions.

Luckily, Python code is generally fairly easy to read and understand, so a lot of the time you won't need to write detailed comments about the code itself because it should be self-illuminating. Comments like the following one, for example, add no value and are best avoided:

```
# set i to 1
i = 1
```

As you'll see next, a feature of Python known as a *docstring* is ideal for more detailed source code descriptions.

Docstrings

Python treats certain strings as documentation. If a bare string appears immediately at the beginning of a module, class, method, or function definition, with nothing but whitespace or comments before it, it will be considered the object's *docstring*.

Here are some examples of docstrings:

```
>>> def test():
...     "This is a test function"
...
>>> class Test:
...     """
...     This is a test class
...     """
...     def test(self):
...         '''
...         This is a test method
...         which is defined on more than one line.
...         '''
...
...
>>>
```

Internally, Python assigns each docstring to a variable named __doc__ attached to the object being documented, and in fact you can access this directly:

```
>>> print test.__doc__
This is a test function
>>> print Test.__doc__

    This is a test class

>>> print Test().__doc__

    This is a test class

>>> print Test.test.__doc__

        This is a test method
        which is defined on more than one line

>>>
```

Docstrings enable you to write detailed documentation describing the object they represent. That documentation can then be read by anyone looking at the source code to understand what the code does. In addition, thanks to Python's introspection abilities and various tools that can extract the docstring itself, detailed documentation can be produced in a variety of formats. You'll learn about some of these tools in this chapter, starting with the built-in help() function.

The Built-In help() Function

The Python language has built-in support for help messages via the help() function. The best way to see how it works is to load an interactive Python prompt and test it. Let's try to get help on the integer 1:

```
>>> help(1)
Help on int object:

class int(object)
 |  int(x[, base]) -> integer
 |
 |  Convert a string or number to an integer, if possible.  A floating point
 |  argument will be truncated towards zero (this does not include a string
 |  representation of a floating point number!)  When converting a string, use
 |  the optional base.  It is an error to supply a base when converting a
 |  non-string. If the argument is outside the integer range a long object
 |  will be returned instead.
 |
 |  Methods defined here:
 |
 |  __abs__(...)
 |      x.__abs__() <==> abs(x)
 |
 |  __add__(...)
 |      x.__add__(y) <==> x+y
 |
 |  __and__(...)
 |      x.__and__(y) <==> x&y
 |
```

As you can see, detailed help on the behavior of Python integers is returned (I've shown only the first few lines for brevity).

The information help() displays comes from a combination of introspection of the object passed to it and any docstrings associated with the object itself or any related objects. For help() to work effectively, you need to write good docstrings.

The help() function will reformat docstrings to remove whitespace and allow them to be better displayed on the command line. If you look at the example in the previous section, you'll notice that the whitespace in the string was maintained in each of the .__doc__ variables themselves, but as you'll see from the following example, unnecessary whitespace is removed by help():

```
>>> help(Test.test)
Help on method test in module __main__:

test(self) unbound __main__.Test method
    This is a test method
    which is defined on more than one line
```

This allows you to write multiline docstrings with the same indentation as the module, class, function, or method that they describe, which helps keep your source code neater.

■**Note** Many tools that operate on docstrings will treat the first line of a multiline string as having special significance. For example, nose, which you learned about in the previous chapter, will add the first line of the docstring on a test method to the error output if that test fails. You should therefore make sure the first line contains an appropriate summary if you are using a multiline docstring.

The whole Python standard library makes extensive use of docstrings as does Pylons. In fact, all the API documentation for Pylons is currently generated directly from docstrings using a tool called Sphinx, which you'll learn about later in the chapter. Here is an example of the first few lines of output you'll see if you use the `help()` function on the `pylons` module:

```
>>> import pylons
>>> help(pylons)
Help on package pylons:

NAME
    pylons - Base objects to be exported for use in Controllers

FILE
    /Users/james/pylons-dev/pylons/__init__.py

PACKAGE CONTENTS
    commands
    config
    configuration
    controllers (package)
    database
    decorator
    decorators (package)
    error
    helpers
    i18n (package)
    legacy
    log
    middleware
    templates (package)
    templating
    test
    testutil
    util
    wsgiapp
```

Documentation generated by `help()` is very useful at the Python console but less useful if you are coding an application. Luckily, the same docstrings can also be used to generate browseable documentation in HTML.

Doctests

From the previous chapter you'll recall that one method for testing code was to use Python's `doctest` module, which runs the Python code specified in the documentation to check that it works correctly. A *doctest* is simply a piece of sample code within a docstring but written as if it were typed at a Python interactive prompt.

Chapter 5 contained a simple `emphasize()` function in one of the examples that simply wrapped some HTML in `<em>` and `</em>` tags, escaping the HTML if it isn't a literal. Let's add a docstring to the function and add a doctest to the docstring. Save this as `emphasize_helper.py`:

```
from webhelpers.html import literal, HTML

def emphasize(value):
    """\
    Emphasize some text by wrapping it in <em> and </em> tags

    Any value passed to this function is HTML escaped if it is not
    an instance of a webhelpers.html literal().

    Here is an example that demonstrates how the helper works:

        >>> emphasize('Greetings')
        literal(u'<em>Greetings</em>')
        >>> print emphasize('<strong>Greetings</strong>')
        <em>&lt;strong&gt;Greetings&lt;/strong&gt;</em>
    """
    return HTML.em(value)
```

I think you'll agree this is a lot of documentation for such a simple function, but it illustrates the point. The idea is that if you were to start a Python interactive prompt and import everything contained in the file and then if you copied the lines starting with >>> into the interactive prompt, the lines following them would be exactly what was produced. The doctest module can perform this check automatically.

The following Python script could then be used to extract the docstring and run the test. Save it as run_doctest.py:

```
import emphasize_helper
import doctest
doctest.testmod(emphasize_helper)
```

Run the test like this:

```
$ python run_doctest.py
```

If the test passes, no output will be generated. Now try introducing an error, perhaps by removing the final </em> tag from the second example. If you run the test again, you'll get the following output:

```
**********************************************************************
File "/Users/james/emphasize_helper.py", line 13, in emphasize_helper.emphasize
Failed example:
    print emphasize('<strong>Greetings</strong>')
Expected:
    <em>&lt;strong&gt;Greetings&lt;/strong&gt;
Got:
    <em>&lt;strong&gt;Greetings&lt;/strong&gt;</em>
**********************************************************************
1 items had failures:
   1 of   2 in emphasize_helper.emphasize
***Test Failed*** 1 failures.
```

Docstrings aren't the only place you might want to write Python interactive prompt examples. You might also write them in standard documentation. The doctest module can also be used to extract doctests from ordinary text files like this:

```
import doctest
doctest.testfile('docs.txt')
```

Now that you've seen how to use doctests, you might consider incorporating them into the tests you learned about in the previous chapter. Generally speaking, doctests are more appropriate for testing functions and methods without a large number of dependencies. This makes them great for testing helpers but less suited to testing Pylons controller actions where you would also have to find some way of setting up the Pylons globals as part of the test.

For more information on doctests, take a look at the doctest module documentation at `http://docs.python.org/library/doctest.html#module-doctest`.

Introducing reStructuredText

Now that you've learned about doctests, let's return to the business of writing documentation. As you'll recall, tools like the `help()` function can introspect objects and extract docstrings, but one problem with this approach is that it doesn't allow for any formatting. For example, you can't mark code blocks or make certain words bold or italic. To solve this problem, a language called *reStructuredText* has become standard in the Python and Pylons communities, and it can be used within docstrings too.

reStructuredText is a lightweight markup language intended to be highly readable in source format and yet is full featured enough to produce sophisticated documentation. Here's a sample reStructuredText document; save this as `test.txt`, and you'll use it as an example for generating the various output types reStructuredText can be converted to:

```
Hello World
+++++++++++

This is a sample paragraph followed by a bulleted list:

* Item 1
* Item 2
* Item 3
```

reStructuredText documents tend to have file extensions of `.rst` or `.txt`. When you are packaging a Pylons project into egg format, `setuptools` will check for the presence of a `README.txt` file, so for the purposes of documenting a Pylons project, it is usually best to use a `.txt` extension if you want to use reStructruedText in any of the standard files that make up a Pylons project.

The tools to work with reStructuredText are found in a package called `docutils`. You can install `docutils` with Easy Install:

```
$ easy_install "docutils==0.5"
```

To create documentation using reStructuredText, you can use one of the conversion tools that comes with the `docutils` package. These tools are named as follows:

```
rst2html.py        rst2newlatex.py    rst2s5.py
rst2latex.py       rst2pseudoxml.py   rst2xml.py
```

As a Pylons developer, most of the time you'll be interested in HTML output, which can be generated like this:

```
$ ./rst2html.py test.txt > test.html
```

Here's what the `test.html` file contains:

```
<?xml version="1.0" encoding="utf-8" ?>
<!DOCTYPE html PUBLIC "-//W3C//DTD XHTML 1.0 Transitional//EN" ➥
"http://www.w3.org/TR/xhtml1/DTD/xhtml1-transitional.dtd">
<html xmlns="http://www.w3.org/1999/xhtml" xml:lang="en" lang="en">
```

```
<head>
<meta http-equiv="Content-Type" content="text/html; charset=utf-8" />
<meta name="generator" content="Docutils 0.5: http://docutils.sourceforge.net/" />
<title>Hello World</title>
<style type="text/css">
   ... styles excluded for brevity
</style>
</head>
<body>
<div class="document" id="hello-world">
<h1 class="title">Hello World</h1>

<p>This is a sample paragraph followed by a bulleted list:</p>
<ul class="simple">
<li>Item 1</li>
<li>Item 2</li>
<li>Item 3</li>
</ul>
</div>
</body>
</html>
```

Figure 13-1 shows what the HTML looks like in a browser.

Figure 13-1. *The generated HTML displayed in a browser*

Although this might look plain, you are free to apply your own style sheet to the output produced, and because the HTML is well constructed, you can do a lot with the generated output.

▪Tip You might be interested to know that this book is written entirely in reStructuredText and that many of the articles on the Pylons wiki are written in reStructuredText as well.

You can also generate HTML output from reStructuredText source programmatically. The following demonstrates this:

```
from docutils import core

def rstify(string):
    result = core.publish_parts(string)['html_body']
    return result['html_body']
```

To generate HTML from a string containing reStructuredText, you use the `docutils.core.publish_pars()` function. This returns a dictionary containing different parts of the HTML document. In most cases where you are generating HTML programmatically, it is likely you'll want only the `html_body` part because you will make up the rest of the HTML yourself. The previous `rstify()` function does just that. The `docutils` package is actually very modular, and with a little effort you can create some very powerful customizations.

Rather than trying to explain the reStructuredText syntax in the book, I'll refer you to some excellent resources online that will teach you everything you need to know:

reStructuredText primer: This is an excellent introduction to reStructuredText. It forms part of the Sphinx documentation; you can find it at `http://sphinx.pocoo.org/rest.html`.

reStructuredText home page: You can find the authoritative reStructruredText documentation at `http://docutils.sourceforge.net/rst.html`. Of particular value is the Quick reStructuredText guide at `http://docutils.sourceforge.net/docs/user/rst/quickref.html`.

Introducing Sphinx

Although using reStructedText as a stand-alone documentation tool is very useful, reStructuredText can also be used within docstrings to document individual functions, classes, and methods.

This functionality brings with it certain possibilities. Wouldn't it be handy, for example, if there were a tool for extracting module documentation but that also understood reStructuredText for formatting that documentation? Well, there is just such a tool; I've mentioned it a number of times already, and it is called *Sphinx*.

Sphinx is a tool that translates a set of reStructuredText source files into various output formats including HTML and LaTeX (which can then be used to produce a PDF), automatically producing cross-references and indexes. The focus of Sphinx is handwritten documentation, but as you'll see shortly, Sphinx can also be used to automatically generate documentation from source code.

You can install Sphinx with Easy Install like this (it requires Python 2.4 or newer to run):

```
$ easy_install "Sphinx==0.4.2"
```

Sphinx uses Jinja for its templating support, so Easy Install will install Jinja too if you didn't install it in Chapter 5. Jinja currently expects a compiler to be present if you install it from source, so Mac OS X users will need to have Xcode installed (it includes GCC) or use a binary version.

Using Sphinx

Let's use Sphinx to document the SimpleSite project. You'll notice that the source directory already contains a `docs` directory. This is a great place to set up Sphinx. It already contains an `index.txt` file, but you'll replace this with one generated by Sphinx, so delete it because it currently contains instructions about how to generate documentation with a tool called Pudge, which Sphinx supercedes.

Create a new Sphinx build like this, and answer the questions:

```
$ cd SimpleSite/docs
$ rm index.txt
$ sphinx-quickstart
```

Enter `SimpleSite` as the project name, and choose 0.1.0 as the version number. Use `.txt` as the file extension. Accept the defaults for everything else except `autodoc`. You *do* want to use Sphinx's `autodoc` extensions, which will pick up documentation from docstrings in your Pylons project's source code, so enter y to that question.

The `docs` directory will contain these files once the utility has finished:

`Makefile`: Generated on non-Windows platforms if you answered y to the makefile question at the end of the wizard. I won't describe it here because all the functionality it contains can be reached via the command line directly.

`conf.py`: Contains all the Sphinx configuration for your project. There are quite a few options, but they are well commented in the `conf.py` file and documented on the Sphinx web site at http://sphinx.pocoo.org.

`index.txt`: This file represents your entire documentation for the project.

Here's `index.txt`:

```
.. SimpleSite Documentation documentation master file, created by ➥
sphinx-quickstart on Thu Oct  2 14:16:47 2008.
   You can adapt this file completely to your liking, but it should at least
   contain the root `toctree` directive.

Welcome to SimpleSite Documentation's documentation!
=====================================================

Contents:

.. toctree::
   :maxdepth: 2

Indices and tables
==================

* :ref:`genindex`
* :ref:`modindex`
* :ref:`search`
```

Now that Sphinx is configured, let's build the documentation. The `sphinx-build` command takes the source directory and output directory commands. In this case, the source directory is the current directory (docs), and the output directory is a new subdirectory called `.build`. The `-b html` option tells Sphinx you want HTML output (the default). Run the command like this:

```
$ sphinx-build -b html . ./.build
Sphinx v0.4.2, building html
trying to load pickled env... not found
building [html]: targets for 1 source files that are out of date
updating environment: 1 added, 0 changed, 0 removed
reading... index
pickling the env... done
checking consistency...
writing output... index
finishing...
writing additional files... genindex modindex search
copying static files...
dumping search index...
build succeeded.
```

After the build has succeeded, the subdirectories `.build`, `.static`, and `.templates` will be present in the `docs` directory.

Note Unix and Mac OS X users should note that folders beginning with `.` are often hidden in the file browser software, so you may not see these directories unless you use the command line.

The `.build` directory contains the HTML output. Open the `index.html` file in a web browser; Figure 13-2 shows what you'll see.

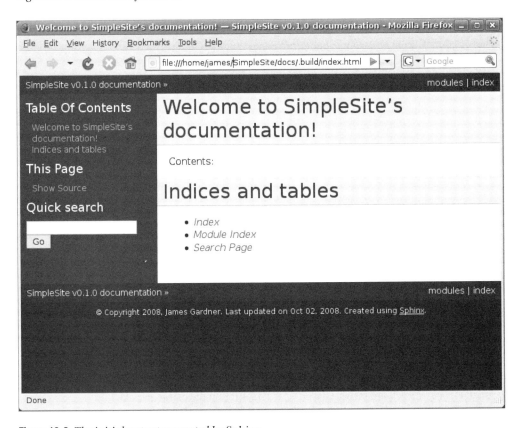

Figure 13-2. *The initial output generated by Sphinx*

You can easily customize the look and feel of the generated documents using templates. See the Sphinx documentation for the details.

Now let's add two files to the `docs` directory. These will form the basis for our user and developer documentation, respectively. Add `user_guide.txt` with this content:

```
User Guide
==========

This will contain instructions for end users of the application.
```

Add `developer_guide.txt` with this content:

```
Developer Guide
===============

This software is documented in detail in the SimpleSite tutorial
chapters of the book *The Definitive Guide to Pylons* available
under an open source license at http://pylonsbook.com. You should
read those chapters to discover how SimpleSite is developed.
```

The reStructuredText format doesn't have any option for linking documents, so Sphinx provides its own called `toctree`. The `toctree` directive should have a list of all the documents you want included in the documentation. Update the `toctree` directive in the `index.txt` file to look like this (notice that the file names shouldn't contain the `.txt` extensions and that there is a blank line before the document list):

```
.. toctree::
   :maxdepth: 2

   user_guide
   developer_guide
```

When choosing names for your documents, you should avoid using `genindex`, `modindex`, and `search` and instead choose names that don't start with an _ character.

Now rebuild the documentation by running the `sphinx-build` command again:

```
$ sphinx-build -b html . ./.build
```

If you add a file to the directory structure but forget to include it in the `toctree`, Sphinx will show you a warning like this when you try to build the documentation:

```
checking consistency...
WARNING: /Users/james/SimpleSite/docs/developer_guide.txt:: document ➡
isn't included in any toctree
```

Once the build completes successfully, you will see that the new `index.html` file has two links in the `Contents` section. Sphinx automatically uses the titles from the documents themselves rather than using their file names. If you click the links, you will see the guides have been correctly generated. What is more, you'll also find the search box to the left side also works. Sphinx compiles a search index in `.build/searchindex.json` as part of the build process, and it uses this to search your documentation.

Documenting Python Source Code

Although being able to write paragraphs of text is very useful a lot of the time, you will want to be able to document Python source code directly. To facilitate this, Sphinx adds a number of markup constructs to the standard ones supported by reStructuredText.

Let's add a new file called `api.txt` to contain some API documentation. You'll also need to add it to the `toctree` directive in `index.txt`.

Let's start by adding a title and a brief summary to the file:

```
API Documentation
=================

This page contains some basic documentation for the SimpleSite project. To
understand the project completely please refer to the documentation on the
Pylons Book website at http://pylonsbook.com or read the source code directly.
```

Now let's add some information about the `simplesite` and `simplesite.controllers` modules. To do this, you might write the following:

```
The :mod:`simplesite` Module
----------------------------

.. module:: simplesite

Contains all the controllers, model and templates as sub-modules.

The :mod:`controllers` Module
-----------------------------

.. module:: simplesite.controllers

Contains all the controllers. The most important of which is
:class:`PageController`.
```

Let's also document the page controller since so far it contains the majority of the application's logic. You might add this:

```
.. class:: PageController

The :class:`PageController` is responsible for displaying pages as well as
allowing users to add, edit, delete and list pages.

.. method:: PageController.view(self[, id=None])

When a user visits a URL such as ``/view/page/1`` the :class:`PageController`
class's :meth:`view` action is called to render the page.
```

If you rebuild the documentation this time, the API documentation page will look like Figure 13-3.

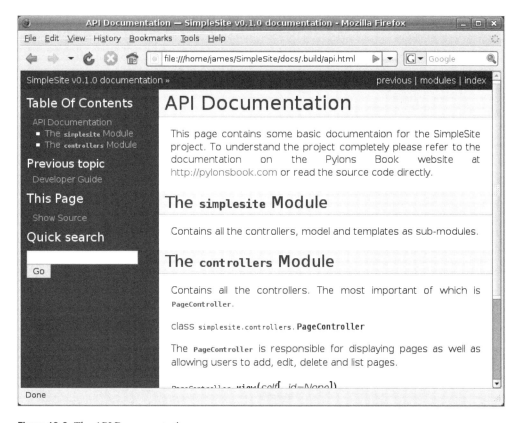

Figure 13-3. *The API Documentation page*

More interestingly, Sphinx has understood that the page documents the `simplesite` and `simplesite.controllers` modules, and it has recognized that `PageController` is in the `simplesite.controllers` module. With this knowledge, it has been able to produce both a Global Module Index and a general Index page. Figure 13-4 shows the Index page.

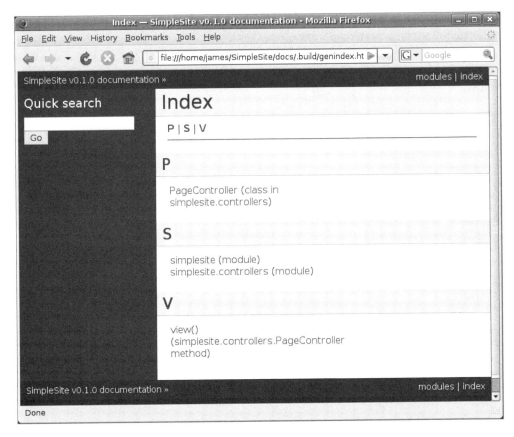

Figure 13-4. *The Index page*

■**Tip** All the current Python documentation is written in reStructuredText and generated in this manner by Sphinx. You can see it online at `http://docs.python.org`.

Automatically Generating Documentation

If you have a lot of modules, classes, methods, and functions to document, it can become very tedious to document them all manually, particularly if you also duplicate much of the documentation in the docstrings themselves. Sphinx provides the `sphinx.ext.autodoc` extensions for this purpose. The `autodoc` extension automatically extracts docstrings from the objects you tell it about and includes them as part of your Sphinx documentation.

Let's use it to extract the docstring from the SimpleSite `lib/helpers.py` module. Add the following to the end of `api.txt`:

```
The :mod:`helpers` Module
-------------------------
```

```
.. automodule:: simplesite.lib.helpers
```

For `autodoc` to work, it must be able to import the `simplesite.lib.helpers` module. This means the SimpleSite application must be installed in the same virtual Python environment you are running Sphinx with. Run this command to install it in develop mode so that any changes you make are immediately available to Sphinx:

```
$ python setup.py develop
```

Now you can build the documentation again:

```
$ sphinx-build -b html . ./.build
```

You'll see that autodoc has found the correct docstring and used it to generate the necessary documentation. In addition to the .. automodule:: construct, there are others to handle classes, functions, and methods. There is also a range of options for each of the constructs.

Syntax Highlighting

Sometimes it is useful to show code examples. In reStructuredText, you would normally just use an empty :: directive to tell reStructuredText to display the following text verbatim, but Sphinx allows you to be slightly more sophisticated. If you install a package called Pygments, Sphinx will be able to automatically highlight source code.

It is usually installed along with Sphinx, but you can also install Pygments directly like this:

```
$ easy_install "Pygments==0.11.1"
```

You then mark blocks of code in your source by using a .. code-block:: directive. The Pygments short name for the type of code the block represents should be added immediately after the :: characters and the code itself in an indented block after that. Pygments can highlight many different types of code including HTML, Mako templates, a Python interactive console, and more. A full list of the different lexers for source code highlighting, as well as their corresponding short names, is available at http://pygments.org/docs/lexers/.

Let's add some documentation about the FormEnocde schema being used in the page controller as an example. Add this to api.txt just before the heading for the helpers module. The Pygments short name for Python code blocks is python, so this is what you add after the .. code-block::` directive:

```
The page controller makes use of a FormEncode schema to validate the page
data it receives. Here is the schema it uses:

.. code-block:: python

    class NewPageForm(formencode.Schema):
        allow_extra_fields = True
        filter_extra_fields = True
        content = formencode.validators.String(
            not_empty=True,
            messages={
                'empty':'Please enter some content for the page. '
            }
        )
        heading = formencode.validators.String()
        title = formencode.validators.String(not_empty=True)

As you can see the schema includes validators for the title, heading
and content.
```

If you save this and rebuild the documentation, you will see the example syntax nicely highlighted (see Figure 13-5).

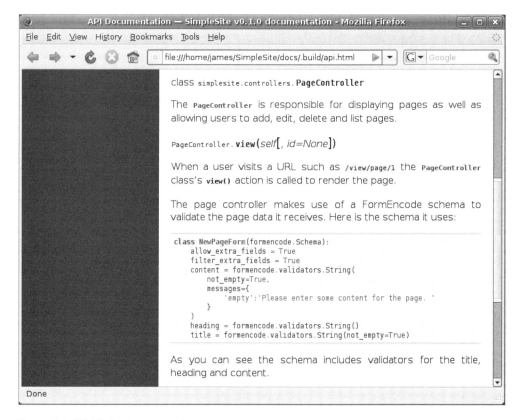

Figure 13-5. *Highlighted source code*

Sometimes the code you are demonstrating will contain a mixture of two different types of source code. For example, it might be Mako syntax that also contains HTML or Mako that also contains CSS. In these cases, Pygments provides lexers that you can use via their short names, which are html+mako and html+css, respectively.

As you can see, Sphinx is a powerful and useful tool. It is well worth reading the documentation at http://sphinx.pocco.org to find out exactly what it can do. Two areas that are beyond the scope of this chapter but are nonetheless worth investigating for yourself are Sphinx's extensive cross-referencing and indexing tools and its ability to generate LaTeX output that can be used to produce high-quality book-style PDF documents.

Summary

In this chapter, you saw every aspect of documenting a Pylons project from using docstrings to learning reStructuredText and building documentation with Sphinx. You've even learned how tests can be integrated into documentation.

Documenting a project properly can really help other users of your code. This chapter has given you the knowledge and tools you need to create really good documentation for your Pylons project.

In the next chapter, you'll return to the SimpleSite tutorial to add a range of new features and learn more about Pylons development as you do.

CHAPTER 14

■ ■ ■

SimpleSite Tutorial Part 2

■Note You can download the source for this chapter from http://www.apress.com.

Now that you've seen a bit more of Pylons and are more familiar with how it works, I'll continue the SimpleSite tutorial. Here are the topics I'll cover in this chapter:

- Adding a comments system to demonstrate how to deal with one-to-many mappings

- Adding a tags system to demonstrate many-to-many mappings as well as how to deal with forms containing multiple check boxes

- Adding a navigation hierarchy involving sections and pages to demonstrate SQLAlchemy's inheritance features as well as a custom Routes setup

Then in Chapter 15, I'll cover JavaScript, Ajax, and YUI to show some improvements that you can make to both the visual appearance of the site and the usability.

There's a lot to cover in this chapter and you might not want to tackle it all in one go. If not feel free to continue with the other chapters and come back to this one later.

Comments System: One-to-Many Mappings

You'd like visitors to the web site to be able to leave comments about each page. The comments will consist of the date they were posted, the name of the poster, their e-mail address, and the comment itself.

I discussed one-to-many mappings in Chapter 7. Situations where one entity (in this case, a page) can have one or more instances of another entity associated with it (in this case, comments) are known as *one-to-many* mappings, and they can all be dealt with in the same way, which in this case is by having a *foreign key* in the comments table represent the ID of the page with which the comment is associated.

Here is the table:

```
comment_table = schema.Table('comment', meta.metadata,
    schema.Column('id', types.Integer,
        schema.Sequence('comment_seq_id', optional=True), primary_key=True),
    schema.Column('pageid', types.Integer,
        schema.ForeignKey('page.id'), nullable=False),
    schema.Column('content', types.Text(), default=u''),
    schema.Column('name', types.Unicode(255)),
    schema.Column('email', types.Unicode(255), nullable=False),
    schema.Column('created', types.TIMESTAMP(), default=now()),
)
```

You'll recall that the table contains an `id` field so that each comment can be uniquely identified and that it contains a `pageid` field, which is a foreign key holding the `id` of the page to which the comment is associated.

The class definition for the comment looks like this:

```
class Comment(object):
    pass
```

The mapper for the page already takes into account that each page could have multiple comments:

```
orm.mapper(Page, page_table, properties={
    'comments':orm.relation(Comment, backref='page'),
    'tags':orm.relation(Tag, secondary=pagetag_table)
})
```

You'll recall that this mapper sets up a `.comments` property on `Page` instances for accessing a list of comments, and it also sets up a `.page` property on `Comment` instances for identifying the page associated with a comment. If you've been following the tutorial, you already added these to your model in Chapter 8.

Planning the Controller

Let's think about the requirements for the controller. You would need the following actions:

`view(self, id)`: Displays a comment for a page

`new(self)`: Displays a form to create a new comment on a page

`create(self)`: Saves the information submitted from `new()` and redirects to `view()`

`edit(self, id)`: Displays a form for editing the comment `id` on a page

`save(self, id)`: Saves the comment `id` and redirects to `view()`

`list(self)`: Displays all comments on a page

`delete(self, id)`: Deletes a comment from a page

The comment controller actions need to know which page the comment is associated with (or will be associated with in the case of `new()` and `create()`) so that they deal with the comments for a particular page only. This means in addition to the ID of the comment the actions are changing, they will also need to know the ID of the page the comment is associated with.

With other frameworks, you might have to use hidden fields in your forms and query parameters in your URLs to keep track of the page ID, but Pylons provides a better method: modifying the routes to keep the page ID as part of the URLs used to route requests to the comment controller's actions.

Modifying the Routes

The URLs you will use will be in this form:

```
/page/1/comment/view/4
```

This URL would result in the comment with ID 4 being viewed on page 1. By setting up Routes to understand this URL and map it to the comment controller you will create in a minute, the issue of how to keep track of the page `id` goes away because it will automatically be added when you use `url_for()` and can always be accessed via `request.urlvars`.

To make this work, you need to add the following routes to `config/routing.py` immediately after `# CUSTOM ROUTES HERE` and before the existing `map.connect('/{controller}/{action}')` route:

```
map.connect(
    '/page/{pageid}/{controller}/{action}',
    requirements=dict(pageid='\d+')
)
map.connect(
    '/page/{pageid}/{controller}/{action}/{id}',
    requirements=dict(pageid='\d+', id='\d+')
)
```

These routes require that both the `pageid` and `id` routing variables are integers. Checking this here saves you from having to perform the check in each of the controller actions.

Now that you've learned about the `explicit=True` option to Routes' `Mapper` object, let's use this option in the SimpleSite project to disable route memory and implicit defaults as recommended in Chapter 9. Change the `Mapper()` lines in `config/routing.py` to look like this, ensuring minimization is also disabled by setting `map.minimization = False`:

```
map = Mapper(directory=config['pylons.paths']['controllers'],
             always_scan=config['debug'], explicit=True)
map.minimization = False
```

With this change in place, you'll also need to update the section links because when using `explicit=True`, you no longer need to override the route memory value for id. Edit `templates/derived/page/view.html` so that the first two links are changed from this:

```
<a href="${h.url_for(controller='page', action='list', id=None)}">All Pages</a>
| <a href="${h.url_for(controller='page', action='new', id=None)}">New Page</a>
```

to the following:

```
<a href="${h.url_for(controller='page', action='list')}">All Pages</a>
| <a href="${h.url_for(controller='page', action='new')}">New Page</a>
```

There's one more subtle place where the change to explicit routing has a consequence: inside the paginator. Luckily, additional keyword arguments passed to the `Page` constructor are also passed to any calls the paginator makes to `h.url_for()`. This means you just have to specify `controller` and `list` explicitly as keyword arguments to the `Page()` constructor. Replace the current `list()` action with this, renaming the `records` variable to `page_q` at the same time to reflect that it is really a query object:

```
def list(self):
    page_q = meta.Session.query(model.Page)
    c.paginator = paginate.Page(
        page_q,
        page=int(request.params.get('page', 1)),
        items_per_page = 2,
        controller='page',
        action='list',
    )
    return render('/derived/page/list.html')
```

Creating the Controller

Rather than creating the controller from scratch, let's reuse the page controller you wrote in Chapter 8. Make a copy of it named `comment.py` in the `controllers` directory, and then replace every instance of the string page with comment and every instance of the string Page with Comment. If you are on a Linux or Unix platform, these commands will do it for you:

```
$ cd simplesite/controllers
$ cp page.py comment.py
$ perl -pi -w -e 's/page/comment/g; s/Page/Comment/g;' comment.py
```

Now let's do the same with the templates:

```
$ cd ../templates/derived
$ cp -r page comment
$ cd comment
$ perl -pi -w -e 's/page/comment/g; s/Page/Comment/g;' *.html
```

You'll need to correct the new comment controller's `list()` action because some of the **variables** will have been accidentally renamed. Change it to look like this:

```
def list(self):
    comments_q = meta.Session.query(model.Comment)
    c.paginator = paginate.Page(
        comments_q,
        page=int(request.params.get('page', 1)),
        items_per_page = 10,
        controller='comment',
        action='list'
    )
    return render('/derived/comment/list.html')
```

You'll actually use this basic controller template again later in the tutorial when you create a controller to handle tags and sections, so take a copy of the comment controller and call it `template.py.txt` so that you can use it later (you are using a `.py.txt` extension so that the template isn't accidentally treated as a controller):

```
cd ../../../
$ cp comment.py template.py.txt
```

Updating the Controller to Handle Comments

Now that the basic structure of the comment controller is in place, it needs to be updated to correctly handle the fields and relationships of the `comment` table. Comment objects have a `.content` property for the comment text itself, a `.name` property to hold the name of the person who left the comment, and an `.email` property for their e-mail address. You'll need fields for each of these so that a user can leave a comment. Let's start by creating a FormEncode schema. Update the `NewCommentForm` schema to look like this:

```
class NewCommentForm(formencode.Schema):
    allow_extra_fields = True
    filter_extra_fields = True
    name = formencode.validators.String(not_empty=True)
    email = formencode.validators.Email(not_empty=True)
    content = formencode.validators.String(
        not_empty=True,
        messages={
            'empty':'Please enter a comment.'
        }
    )
```

The example uses the `allow_extra_fields = True` option so that the form's submit button isn't validated and uses the `filter_extra_fields = True` option so that it isn't included in the results returned when the schema converts the form input to a Python dictionary. A custom error message is used if the user forgets to enter a comment, and the e-mail address uses an `Email` validator to make sure the user enters a string that looks like an e-mail address.

You'll also need to update the `/templates/derived/comment/fields.html` file so it represents the correct fields you'd like users to enter:

```
${h.field(
    "Name",
    h.text(name='name'),
    required=True,
)}
${h.field(
    "Email",
    h.text(name='email'),
    required=True,
    field_desc = 'Use to help prevent spam but will not be published',
)}
${h.field(
    "Comment",
    h.textarea(name='content', rows=7, cols=40),
    required=True,
)}
```

Notice that although the field name is called `content`, it is labeled `Comment`. This is to make it more obvious to the users of the application. After all, they don't need to know that the comment text they enter is actually stored in the `content` column of the table.

Next update the `edit()` action so that the correct values are prepared for the call to `htmlfill.render()`:

```
values = {
    'name': comment.name,
    'email': comment.email,
    'content': comment.content,
}
```

Let's also update the `view.html` template to display the comment information to look more like a comment. Update it to look like this:

```
<%inherit file="/base/index.html"/>

<%def name="title()">Comment</%def>
<%def name="heading()"><h1>Comment</h1></%def>

${c.comment.content}

<p><em>Posted by ${c.comment.name} on ${c.comment.created.strftime('%c')}.</em></p>

<p><a href="${h.url_for(controller='page', action='view', ➥
id=c.comment.pageid)}">Visit the page this comment was posted on.</a></p>
```

Finally, you'll need to update the `list.html` template so that the `pager()` method of the paginator is named `pager()` rather than `commentr()` after the automatic rename and so that the paginator displays information relevant to the comments rather than pages. Here's the updated version:

```
<%inherit file="/base/index.html" />

<%def name="heading()"><h1>Comment List</h1></%def>

<%def name="buildrow(comment, odd=True)">
    <tr class="${odd and 'odd' or 'even'}">
        <td valign="top">
            ${h.link_to(
                comment.id,
                h.url_for(
                    controller=u'comment',
                    action='view',
                    id=unicode(comment.id)
                )
            )}
        </td>
        <td valign="top">
            ${h.link_to(
                comment.name,
                h.url_for(
                    controller=u'comment',
                    action='edit',
                    id=unicode(comment.id)
                )
            )}
        </td>
        <td valign="top">${comment.created.strftime('%c')}</td>
    </tr>
</%def>

% if len(c.paginator):
<p>${ c.paginator.pager('$link_first $link_previous $first_item to $last_item ➥
of $item_count $link_next $link_last') }</p>
<table class="paginator"><tr><th>Comment ID</th><th>Comment Title</th>➥
<th>Posted</th></tr>
<% counter=0 %>
% for item in c.paginator:
    ${buildrow(item, counter%2)}
    <% counter += 1 %>
% endfor
</table>
<p>${ c.paginator.pager('~2~') }</p>
% else:
<p>
    No comments have yet been created.
    <a href="${h.url_for(controller='comment', action='new')}">Add one</a>.
</p>
% endif
```

At this point, you would be able to perform all the usual actions on comments such as add, edit, and remove if it weren't for the fact they also need a pageid.

Now you can start the server and see what you have:

```
$ paster serve --reload development.ini
```

Visit http://localhost:5000/comment/new, and you should see the comment form shown in Figure 14-1.

Figure 14-1. *The create comment form*

Setting the Page ID Automatically

If you try to create a comment at the URL you've just visited, an `IntegrityError` will be raised specifying `comment.pageid may not be NULL` because no page ID has been specified. As I mentioned earlier in the chapter, you'll obtain the page ID from the URL. To set this up, you are going to use the `__before__()` method that gets called before each of the Pylons actions. Add it right at the top of the controller before the `view()` action:

```
class CommentController(BaseController):

    def __before__(self, action, pageid=None):
        page_q = meta.Session.query(model.Page)
        c.page = pageid and page_q.filter_by(id=int(pageid)).first() or None
        if c.page is None:
            abort(404)
```

This code causes the variable `c.page` to be set before any actions are called. If the page ID is not included in the URL or the page doesn't exist, a 404 Not Found response is returned. With this code in place, visiting `http://localhost:5000/comment/new` results in a 404 Not Found response; visiting `http://localhost:5000/page/1/comment/new` correctly displays the new comment form, but the comment will still not save because the form does not yet submit to `http://localhost:5000/page/1/comment/create`. Let's fix that by editing the `new.html` template to change the `h.url_for()` call to include the page ID:

```
<%inherit file="/base/index.html" />
<%namespace file="fields.html" name="fields" import="*"/>

<%def name="heading()">
    <h1 class="main">Create a New Comment</h1>
</%def>
```

```
${h.form_start(h.url_for(pageid=c.page.id, controller='comment', action='create'), ➥
method="post")}
    ${fields.body()}
    ${h.field(field=h.submit(value="Create Comment", name='submit'))}
${h.form_end()}
```

You'll also need to change the edit.html template so that the form also includes the page ID:

```
<%inherit file="/base/index.html" />
<%namespace file="fields.html" name="fields" import="*"/>

<%def name="heading()">
    <h1 class="main">Editing ${c.title}</h1>
</%def>

<p>Editing the source code for the ${c.title} comment:</p>

${h.form_start(h.url_for(pageid=c.page.id, controller='comment', action='save', ➥
id=request.urlvars['id']), method="post")}
    ${fields.body()}
    ${h.field(field=h.submit(value="Save Changes", name='submit'))}
${h.form_end()}
```

Let's consider each of the actions of the comment controller in turn to decide how they should behave and how they will need to be modified:

view(): The view method needs to be updated to ensure that the comment requested is actually a comment from the page specified in the URL. You can do this by updating the query used in the view() action from this:

```
c.comment = comment_q.get(int(id))
```

to the following:

```
c.comment = comment_q.filter_by(pageid=c.page.id, id=int(id)).first()
```

new(): This action needs no change since it is responsible only for displaying the form for adding a new comment.

create(): This action needs to know the page to which the comment is being added. Just before the comment is added to the session, add the following line to set the page ID:

```
comment.pageid = c.page.id
```

You'll also need to include the page ID in the URL to which the browser is redirected. Since you already learned about the redirect_to() function in Chapter 9, let's use it here. Replace the redirect lines with these:

```
# Issue an HTTP redirect
return redirect_to(pageid=c.page.id, controller='comment', action='view', ➥
id=comment.id)
```

edit(): The edit action needs a similar modification to the one made to the view() method. Although you know which page a comment is associated with, you want to make sure the URL requested has the same page ID as the comment. Change the query from this:

```
comment = comment_q.filter_by(id=id).first()
```

to the following:

```
comment = comment_q.filter_by(pageid=c.page.id, id=id).first()
```

save(): Again, you'll want to check that the page ID in the URL is the same as the one in the comment. Since the form doesn't allow you to change the page ID, this can once again be ensured by adding c.page.id to the query:

```
comment = comment_q.filter_by(pageid=c.page.id, id=id).first()
```

Replace the redirect lines with this:

```
# Issue an HTTP redirect
return redirect_to(pageid=c.page.id, controller='comment', action='view', ➥
id=comment.id)
```

list(): Only comments associated with the current page should be listed, so once again the query is modified to include the page ID. In this case, though, we also have to pass the pageid argument, which will in turn get passed to any h.url_for() calls in the paginator.

```
def list(self):
    comments_q = meta.Session.query(model.Comment).filter_by(pageid=c.page.id)
    comments_q = comments_q.order_by(model.comment_table.c.created.asc())
    c.paginator = paginate.Page(
        comments_q,
        page=int(request.params.get('page', 1)),
        items_per_page=10,
        pageid=c.pageid,
        controller='comment',
        action='list'
    )
    return render('/derived/comment/list.html')
```

Notice the use of order_by() to ensure that the earliest comments are displayed first. I've used the comment_table column metadata in the order_by() method just to remind you that you can use table metadata as well as class attributes when specifying query arguments, and I've used the .asc() method to specify that the results should be specified in ascending order.

delete(): Again, this requires only a check that the page ID in the URL is the same as the one in the comment. Since the form doesn't allow you to change the page ID, this can once again be ensured by adding c.page.id to the query:

```
comment = comment_q.filter_by(pageid=c.page.id, id=id).first()
```

Now that all the changes have been made, let's test the new controller. Start by adding a new comment to the home page by visiting http://localhost:5000/page/1/comment/new and filling in the form. When you click Create Comment, you will see Figure 14-2.

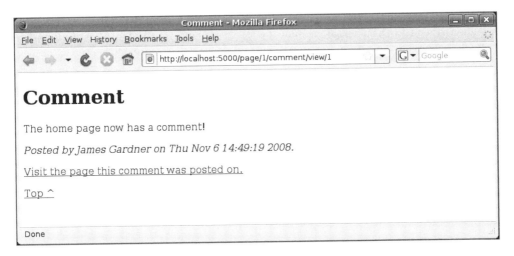

Figure 14-2. *The first comment*

Finally, let's update the comment view template `derived/comment/view.html` so that edit and delete links are added to the footer. Add the following at the end of the template:

```
<%def name="footer()">
## Add our comment links
<p>
  <a href="${h.url_for(pageid=c.page.id, controller='comment', action='edit', ➥
id=c.comment.id)}">Edit Comment</a>
| <a href="${h.url_for(pageid=c.page.id, controller='comment', action='delete', ➥
id=c.comment.id)}">Delete Comment</a>
</p>
## Include the parent footer too
${parent.footer()}
</%def>
```

Make sure you followed the instructions earlier in the chapter to update the `values` variable in the `edit()` action; you will then find you can easily edit or delete comments. There are still no links to display or add comments from the bottom of individual pages. You'll fix that in the next section.

Updating the Page View

SimpleSite will not display a list of comments on the page itself (although you could set it up to do so if you preferred) but will instead display a link at the bottom of each page of the form that says, for example, "Comments (8)" where the number in parentheses is the current number of comments on that page. Users can click this link to view the list of comments. There will also be an Add Comment link so that users can add a comment directly. Figure 14-3 shows what the updated screen will look like.

Figure 14-3. *The updated page view screen*

For this to work, you need to modify both the page controller's view() action and the template. Let's start with the view() action. You need to add a SQLAlchemy query to count the number of pages associated with the page. Add this to the end of the action just before the return statement:

```
c.comment_count = meta.Session.query(model.Comment).filter_by(pageid=id).count()
```

Then modify the templates/derived/page/view.html template so the footer() def looks like this:

```
<%def name="footer()">
## Then add our page links
<p>
  <a href="${h.url_for(controller='page', action='list')}">All Pages</a>
| <a href="${h.url_for(controller='page', action='new')}">New Page</a>
| <a href="${h.url_for(controller='page', action='edit', ➥
id=c.page.id)}">Edit Page</a>
| <a href="${h.url_for(controller='page', action='delete', ➥
id=c.page.id)}">Delete Page</a>
</p>
## Comment links
<p>
  <a href="${h.url_for(pageid=c.page.id, controller='comment', ➥
action='list')}">Comments (${str(c.comment_count)})</a>
| <a href="${h.url_for(pageid=c.page.id, controller='comment', ➥
action='new')}">Add Comment</a>
</p>
## Include the parent footer too
${parent.footer()}
</%def>
```

Now when you view a page, you will also be able to list or add comments, and by viewing comments individually, you can edit or delete them.

Handling Deleted Pages

Now that comments are related to pages, you need to think about what to do with comments once a page is deleted. Since a comment without the page it is commenting on isn't very useful, you can automatically delete all comments associated with a page when the page itself is deleted.

You could program this code manually in the delete() action of the page controller, but there is actually a better way. SQLAlchemy mappers support the concept of configurable cascade behavior on relations so that you can specify how child objects are dealt with on certain actions of the parents. The options are described in detail at http://www.sqlalchemy.org/docs/05/documentation. html#unitofwork_cascades, but we are simply going to use the option all so that the comments are updated if the page ID changes and are deleted if the page they are for is deleted.

Modify the page mapper in model/__init__.py so that the comments relation has cascade='all' specified like this:

```
orm.mapper(Page, page_table, properties={
    'comments':orm.relation(Comment, backref='page', cascade='all'),
    'tags':orm.relation(Tag, secondary=pagetag_table)
})
```

Try creating a page, adding some comments, and then deleting the page. If you looked at the database table, you'd find that the comments are automatically deleted too.

If you are following along with a SQLite database named development.db, you could check this by connecting to the database with the sqlite3 program:

```
$ sqlite3 development.db
```

Then by executing this SQL:

```
SELECT id, pageid FROM comment;
```

you'd find that there were no comments for the page you just deleted because the SQLAlchemy cascade rules you specified led to SQLAlchemy deleting them for you.

Tags: Many-to-Many Mappings

Now that you've seen how to handle a one-to-many mapping (sometimes called a *parent-child* relationship) between pages and comments, you can turn your attention to the many-to-many mapping between tags and pages. Once again, tags can be created, viewed, updated, or deleted. So, the controller that manipulates them would need the same actions as the page and comment controllers you've created so far. In addition, each page can have multiple tags, and each tag can be used on multiple pages so that tags can't be considered children of pages any more than pages can be considered children of tags.

The way you'll implement this is by once again starting with a simple controller and renaming the core variables with the word *tag*. You'll then tweak the controller so that it correctly handles the columns of the tag table.

After you've done this, users will be able to add, edit, remove, and list tags. I'll then cover how to associate tags with pages. Ordinarily, you would need to create a second controller for handling the adding, editing, listing, and deleting of the *associations* between the page table and the tag table. In this case, though, you'll take a shortcut. Rather than having a second controller to handle the interactions, you will simply display a check box group of all the available tags on each page. Users can then select the tags they want associated with the page, and SQAlchemy will handle how to store those associations in the pagetag table for you automatically.

Creating the tag Controller

Let's start by creating the `tag` controller from the template copied earlier:

```
$ cd simplesite/controllers
$ cp template.py.txt tag.py
$ perl -pi -w -e 's/comment/tag/g; s/Comment/Tag/g;' tag.py
```

You'll need to correct the new tag controller's `list()` action too because some of the variables will have been accidentally renamed. Change it to look like this:

```
def list(self):
    tag_q = meta.Session.query(model.Tag)
    c.paginator = paginate.Page(
        tag_q,
        page=int(request.params.get('page', 1)),
        items_per_page = 10,
        controller='tag',
        action='list'
    )
    return render('/derived/tag/list.html')
```

Now let's do the same with the templates, but let's use the page templates as a basis:

```
$ cd ../templates/derived
$ cp -r page tag
$ cd tag
$ perl -pi -w -e 's/page/tag/g; s/Page/Tag/g;' *.html
```

Once again, you'll need to update `list.html` to use `c.paginator.pager()`, not `c.paginator.tagr()`.

Now restart the server if you stopped it to make these changes, and let's get started with the updates:

```
$ cd ../../../../
$ paster serve --reload development.ini
```

Tags have a name only, so update the `NewTagForm` schema to look like this:

```
class NewTagForm(formencode.Schema):
    allow_extra_fields = True
    filter_extra_fields = True
    name = formencode.validators.String(not_empty=True)
```

Change the `edit()` action so that the values passed to `htmlfill.render()` look like this:

```
values = {
    'name': tag.name,
}
```

Next, change the `fields.html` template so that it looks like this:

```
${h.field(
    "Name",
    h.text(name='name'),
    required=True,
)}
```

Update the tag `view.html` template so it looks like this:

```
<%inherit file="/base/index.html"/>

<%def name="title()">Tag</%def>
<%def name="heading()"><h1>Tag</h1></%def>

${c.tag.name}

<%def name="footer()">
## Add our tag links
<p>
  <a href="${h.url_for(controller='tag', action='edit', id=c.tag.id)}">Edit Tag</a>
| <a href="${h.url_for(controller='tag', action='delete', ➥
id=c.tag.id)}">Delete Tag</a>
</p>
## Include the parent footer too
${parent.footer()}
</%def>
```

Finally, update the `tag/list.html` template so it looks like this:

```
<%inherit file="/base/index.html" />

<%def name="heading()"><h1>Tag List</h1></%def>

<%def name="buildrow(tag, odd=True)">
    <tr class="${odd and 'odd' or 'even'}">
        <td valign="top">
            ${h.link_to(
                tag.id,
                h.url_for(
                    controller=u'tag',
                    action='view',
                    id=unicode(tag.id)
                )
            )}
        </td>
        <td valign="top">
            ${tag.name}
        </td>
    </tr>
</%def>

% if len(c.paginator):
<p>${ c.paginator.pager('$link_first $link_previous $first_item to $last_item ➥
of $item_count $link_next $link_last') }</p>
<table class="paginator"><tr><th>Tag ID</th><th>Tag Name</th></tr>
<% counter=0 %>
% for item in c.paginator:
    ${buildrow(item, counter%2)}
    <% counter += 1 %>
% endfor
</table>
```

```
<p>${ c.paginator.pager('~2~') }</p>
% else:
<p>
    No tags have yet been created.
    <a href="${h.url_for(controller='tag', action='new')}">Add one</a>.
</p>
% endif
```

That's it—the tag controller is complete, so you could now start creating tags by visiting http://localhost:5000/tag/new; however, before you do, let's add a few restrictions to what can be used as a tag name.

Constraining Tag Names

You'll put a restriction on tag names to ensure they can be made only from letters, numbers, and the space character and can consist of 20 characters or less. Also, you don't want users to add a tag with a name that already exists. Of course, because of the constraints you set up when defining the model, you know that an exception will be raised if a nonunique tag name is added, but the 500 Internal Server Error page that will be generated doesn't provide a way to let the user fix the error, so you need a FormEncode validator to check for the error before it occurs and to display an appropriate error message if necessary.

First let's create a validator to check for unique tags and update the NewTagForm schema to use it. Add this to the top of the tag controller instead of the current NewTagForm schema:

```
import re

class UniqueTag(formencode.validators.FancyValidator):
    def _to_python(self, value, state):
        # Check we have a valid string first
        value = formencode.validators.String(max=20).to_python(value, state)
        # Check that tags are only letters, numbers, and the space character
        result = re.compile("[^a-zA-Z0-9 ]").search(value)
        if result:
            raise formencode.Invalid("Tags can only contain letters, ➥
numbers and spaces", value, state)
        # Ensure the tag is unique
        tag_q = meta.Session.query(model.Tag).filter_by(name=value)
        if request.urlvars['action'] == 'save':
            # Ignore the existing name when performing the check
            tag_q = tag_q.filter(model.Tag.id != int(request.urlvars['id']))
        first_tag = tag_q.first()
        if first_tag is not None:
            raise formencode.Invalid("This tag name already exists", value, state)
        return value

class NewTagForm(formencode.Schema):
    allow_extra_fields = True
    filter_extra_fields = True
    name = UniqueTag(not_empty=True)
```

There's quite a lot going on in the UniqueTag validator, so let's go through what it does. When the validator is called, the first thing that happens is a check to ensure the tag name is a valid string with 20 characters. If the check passes, a regular expression is used to ensure that only alphanumerics and the space character are used in the name. Next, a SQLAlchemy query object is set up to query any tags with a name equal to the name being validated. What happens next depends on whether the validator is used in the save() action decorator or the create() action decorator. You'll recall that `request.urlvars` contains all the routing variables matched by Routes, so in this case the action is stored in `request.urlvars['action']`. If this is equal to `'save'`, the `save()` action is being called, and the tag query is filtered to exclude the tag with the same ID as the current request. This prevents the tag save from failing when someone saves a tag without changing its name. If a tag with the same name exists after the query has been set up and filtered, then an `Invalid` exception is raised, which results in an error message above the form field.

With these changes in place, you can visit `http://localhost:5000/tag/new` to test the new tag functionality. If you try to create two tags with the same name, you'll see the error message shown in Figure 14-4.

Figure 14-4. *The error message shown when you create two tags with the same name*

That's it! SimpleSite now supports tags, but you can't yet add them to pages. Let's look at this in the next section.

■**Caution** Sharp-eyed readers might not be too happy with the validator I've just described. In this case, the validator uses `model.Session` and `request`, both of which are request-specific and should ordinarily be passed via the `state` argument to a schema's `to_python()` method, as you'll recall from Chapter 6. In this case, though, all the validation happens behind the scenes in Pylons' `@vailidate` decorator, so there isn't an opportunity to specify a `state` argument. Luckily, both `model.Session` and `request` are special objects that Pylons ensures behave correctly during each request, even in a multithreaded environment, so this example is perfectly OK in this case.

If your validator accessed an object that wasn't thread-safe, you could do the following:

- Assign the non-thread-safe object to the template context global `c` in the controller's `__before__()` method to make it available in the validator's `_to_python()` method before the validator is called.

- Handle the entire validation process manually, explicitly passing a state object to the `to_python()` method as demonstrated in the `process()` action of the example in the "Solving the Repeating Fields Problem" section of Chapter 6 where the template context global `c` is itself used as the `state` argument.

- Use a `StackedObjectProxy` object to give Pylons the responsibility of using the correct version of the object for the particular request that is running.

The first two alternatives are the preferred approaches, but see the section "The Registry Manager, StackedObjectProxy, and Pylons Globals" in Chapter 17 if you want to investigate the `StackedObjectProxy` approach.

Adding Tags to Pages

Now that you have a system for adding and editing tags, you need a way of associating tags with pages. As was mentioned earlier, you can choose to do this in two ways. The first is with the `pagetag` controller to provide an interface to allow users to manually add entries to the `pagetag` table to create the associations. If the `tag` table contained more fields or didn't have a column that could be used naturally as a primary key, then this would be a good option. In this case, though, the tag name provides a unique way to specify the tag, so you can simply provide a list of all available tags on each page with a check box next to each, and users can simply select the boxes of the tags they want to use.

Figure 14-5 shows what a page will look like when you've finished this section and saved the tags associated with a page.

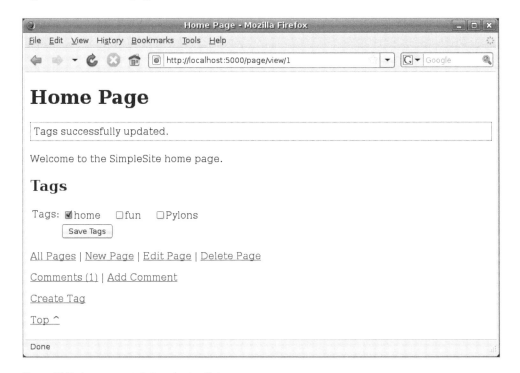

Figure 14-5. *A page containing the tag list*

Let's start by editing the page controller's `view()` action to obtain a list of all the available tag names. Update it to look like this (the lines to add are in bold):

```
def view(self, id=None):
    if id is None:
        abort(404)
    page_q = meta.Session.query(model.Page)
    c.page = page_q.filter_by(id=int(id)).first()
    if c.page is None:
        abort(404)
    c.comment_count = meta.Session.query(model.Comment).filter_by(pageid=id).count()
```

```
tag_q = meta.Session.query(model.Tag)
c.available_tags = [(tag.id, tag.name) for tag in tag_q]
c.selected_tags = {'tags':[str(tag.id) for tag in c.page.tags]}
return render('/derived/page/view.html')
```

In the templates/derived/page/view.html template, add a new form for the tags just before the footer() def. The code is wrapped in a def block because later in the section you'll need to capture its output to use with HTMLFill to populate the fields:

```
<%def name="tags(available_tags)">
    <h2>Tags</h2>
    ${h.form_start(h.url_for(controller='page', action='update_tags', ➡
id=c.page.id), method='post')}
        ${h.field(
            "Tags",
            h.checkbox_group('tags', selected_values=None, align="table", ➡
options=available_tags)
        )}
        ${h.field(field=h.submit(value="Save Tags", name='submit'))}
    ${h.form_end()}
</%def>
```

For this to work, you'll need to add the check box_group() helper to lib/helpers.py:

```
from formbuild.helpers import checkbox_group
```

This form will submit to the page controller's update_tags() action which you'll create in a minute. Once again though, you'll need to validate the result of any form submission. Since the check boxes are effectively a set of repeating fields, you could use a ForEach validator like this:

```
class ValidTagsForm(formencode.Schema):
    allow_extra_fields = True
    filter_extra_fields = True
    tags = formencode.foreach.ForEach(formencode.validators.Int())
```

Although this schema checks that the tags have integer values, it doesn't actually check that the values are actually valid for the tags. To do this, you could derive your own validator from the Int validator and override its _to_python() method to check the value using a similar technique to the one used in UniqueTag, but then a separate database call would need to be made for each tag that needed to be validated. Instead, you'll create a *chained validator* that will take the list of integers and validate them all in one go. It looks like this:

```
class ValidTags(formencode.FancyValidator):
    def _to_python(self, values, state):
        # Because this is a chained validator, values will contain
        # a dictionary with a tags key associated with a list of
        # integer values representing the selected tags.
        all_tag_ids = [tag.id for tag in meta.Session.query(model.Tag)]
        for tag_id in values['tags']:
            if tag_id not in all_tag_ids:
                raise formencode.Invalid(
                    "One or more selected tags could not be found in the database",
                    values,
                    state
                )
        return values
```

Add the ValidTags validator to the top of the page.py controller after the existing schema, then add the the ValidTagsForm schema to look like this:

```
class ValidTagsForm(formencode.Schema):
    allow_extra_fields = True
    filter_extra_fields = True
    tags = formencode.foreach.ForEach(formencode.validators.Int())
    chained_validators = [ValidTags()]
```

Now we can write the update_tags() action. Add this to the page controller:

```
@restrict('POST')
@validate(schema=ValidTagsForm(), form='view')
def update_tags(self, id=None):
    if id is None:
        abort(404)
    page_q = meta.Session.query(model.Page)
    page = page_q.filter_by(id=id).first()
    if page is None:
        abort(404)
    tags_to_add = []
    for i, tag in enumerate(page.tags):
        if tag.id not in self.form_result['tags']:
            del page.tags[i]
    tagids = [tag.id for tag in page.tags]
    for tag in self.form_result['tags']:
        if tag not in tagids:
            t = meta.Session.query(model.Tag).get(tag)
            page.tags.append(t)
    meta.Session.commit()
    session['flash'] = 'Tags successfully updated.'
    session.save()
    return redirect_to(controller='page', action='view', id=page.id)
```

This code iterates over the real tags twice, deleting any unselected boxes first and adding any new associations from boxes that have just been selected.

Now that the tags are correctly saving, you need to ensure that their values are correctly populated when the page is displayed. To do this, you'll call the tags() def with Mako's special capture() function to capture the HTML from the form and then pass the HTML through HTMLFill to populate the tags. This is a lot like the method you've been using for populating forms, but rather than calling htmlfill.render() in the controller with the whole output from the template, you are just calling it in the template with the form output from the tags() def.

Update the page view.html template to call the tags() def you added earlier in this section. Add this just after the tags() def and before the footer() def:

```
<%!
    from formencode import htmlfill
    from webhelpers.html import literal
%>

% if c.available_tags:
${literal(htmlfill.render(capture(self.tags, c.available_tags), c.selected_tags))}
% endif
```

In this case, it should be safe to use literal() here since the output from self.tags will already be escaped and htmlfill.render() correctly escapes the values passed in. Notice that Mako's capture() function takes the def to capture as the first argument and any arguments to pass to that

function as subsequent arguments. If you were to call `capture(self.tags(c.available_tags))`, the
`tags()` def would be called, outputting its content to the buffer, and `capture()` would try to call
the return value from the def instead of the def itself.

There is one last change you need to make. Let's add a link in the footer to enable users to add
new tags:

```
<%def name="footer()">
## Then add our page links
<p>
  <a href="${h.url_for(controller='page', action='list')}">All Pages</a>
| <a href="${h.url_for(controller='page', action='new')}">New Page</a>
| <a href="${h.url_for(controller='page', action='edit', ➡
id=c.page.id)}">Edit Page</a>
| <a href="${h.url_for(controller='page', action='delete', ➡
id=c.page.id)}">Delete Page</a>
</p>
## Comment links
<p>
  <a href="${h.url_for(pageid=c.page.id, controller='comment', ➡
action='list')}">Comments (${str(c.comment_count)})</a>
| <a href="${h.url_for(pageid=c.page.id, controller='comment', ➡
action='new')}">Add Comment</a>
</p>
## Tag links
<p><a href="${h.url_for(controller='tag', action='list')}">All Tags</a>
| <a href="${h.url_for(controller='tag', action='new')}">Add Tag</a></p>
## Include the parent footer too
${parent.footer()}
</%def>
```

Deleting Tags and Pages

When a tag is deleted, it can no longer be used on a page, so all references to that tag need to be
removed from the `pagetag` table. Likewise, when a page is deleted, there is little point in keeping
track of which tags used to be associated with it, so all references to that page should be removed
from the `pagetag` table too.

Add the following line just before `meta.Session.delete(page)` in the `delete()` action in the
page controller:

```
meta.Session.execute(delete(model.pagetag_table, ➡
model.pagetag_table.c.pageid==page.id))
```

Now add this just before `meta.Session.delete(tag)` in the `delete()` action of the tag controller:

```
meta.Session.execute(delete(model.pagetag_table, ➡
model.pagetag_table.c.tagid==tag.id))
```

Both controllers will require the following import:

```
from sqlalchemy import delete
```

If you visit the home page at `http://localhost:5000/page/view/1` and create some tags, you'll
now be able to tag pages. The application should look like it did in Figure 14-5.

Creating a Navigation Hierarchy

Now that the basic functionality of the web site is in place, I'll cover how to add a navigation structure to turn the application into a full (albeit simple) content management system. In this second part of the chapter, you'll learn about table inheritance and how to structure hierarchical data in SQLAlchemy.

Let's start by thinking about how pages are typically structured on web sites. Pages can usually be thought of as being divided into sections, with each section containing pages and other sections. You will need top-level tabs for the top-level sections and then a navigation menu so that the pages within each section can be displayed. You'll also need a breadcrumb trail so that the user can always navigate to a section higher up in the hierarchy.

The URL for each page will be determined by the URL path info part. If a URL resolves to a section rather than to a page, you need to render the index page for that section. The index page will simply be the page in the section named `index`. You'll also set up the URLs such that those with a trailing slash (`/`) at the end always resolve to sections and those without resolve to a page. Thus, `/dev` will display a page, and `/dev/` will display the `index` page in the `dev` section. Some people find it a little strange to have pages without file extensions, but if you would prefer your pages to have URLs that end in `.html`, feel free to update the code as you work through the examples.

The following is the URL structure to create. The first part represents the URL, the second is the name of the page, and the third part explains whether it is a page or a section:

```
/ Home (Section)
    home Home (Page)
    dev/ Development (Section)
        home Development Home (Page)
        SVN Details (Page)
    Contact (Page)
```

The top-level tabs will therefore show the text *Home*, *Development*, and *Contact*.

Using Inheritance in SQLAlchemy

If you think about how pages and sections might work, you'll notice that both pages and sections will need the following attributes:

- Unique ID

- Display name in the navigation structure

- URL path fragment (for example, `/dev` or `dev.html`)

- Parent section ID

- The ID of the sibling node that this node appears before (or `None` if this is the last node in the section)

Because both the pages and the sections share the same attributes, it makes sense to store them both in the same table. This table will also need a Type column to describe whether the record represents a page or a section.

You can also imagine a situation where other content types are supported, perhaps Word documents or PNG images. Although you won't implement them, you can imagine that any such objects would also need these same attributes. The characteristic that pages, sections, and other types of objects share is that they can all be accessed via a URL and should appear in the navigation structure of the site. In effect, they all can be *navigated*, so let's name the table that will store this information `nav`. The new `nav` table looks like this:

```
nav_table = schema.Table('nav', meta.metadata,
    schema.Column('id', types.Integer(),
        schema.Sequence('nav_id_seq', optional=True), primary_key=True),
    schema.Column('name', types.Unicode(255), default=u'Untitled Node'),
    schema.Column('path', types.Unicode(255), default=u''),
    schema.Column('section', types.Integer(), schema.ForeignKey('nav.id')),
    schema.Column('before', types.Integer(), default=None),
    schema.Column('type', types.String(30), nullable=False)
)
```

You will still want to be able to work with page and section objects in the model, so you'll need to use SQLAlchemy's powerful inheritance tools so that the Page and Section classes inherit information from a Nav class. Replace the existing Page class with these three classes:

```
class Nav(object):
    pass

class Page(Nav):
    pass

class Section(Nav):
    pass
```

You'll also need a new mapper for the Nav class, and you'll need to tell SQLAlchemy that Page and Section will inherit from Nav and therefore should also have all the same properties a Nav object would have. Here's what the updated mappers look like:

```
orm.mapper(Comment, comment_table)
orm.mapper(Tag, tag_table)
orm.mapper(Nav, nav_table, polymorphic_on=nav_table.c.type, ➥
polymorphic_identity='nav')
orm.mapper(Section, section_table, inherits=Nav, polymorphic_identity='section')
orm.mapper(Page, page_table, inherits=Nav, polymorphic_identity='page', properties={
    'comments':orm.relation(Comment, backref='page', cascade='all'),
    'tags':orm.relation(Tag, secondary=pagetag_table)
})
```

The important points to notice are that the Nav mapper specifies that Nav is polymorphic on nav_table.c.type, in other words, that the type column will contain a string to specify whether the record is a page or a section. The Section and Page mappers then specify that they inherit from Nav and specify the text to be used in the nav table's type column to identify them. Now would be a good time to make these changes to your model if you haven't already done so.

With the class and mapper changes set up, let's think about how you need to modify the page table and what fields you'd like the section table to contain.

In SimpleSite, the section table doesn't need to hold any data other than an ID because all the attributes it needs are already inherited from the nav table. The ID for a section has to be the same as the corresponding ID in the nav table so that SQLAlchemy knows how sections and navs are related. This means the ID should be a foreign key. Add the section table like this:

```
section_table = sa.Table('section', meta.metadata,
    schema.Column('id', types.Integer,
        schema.ForeignKey('nav.id'), primary_key=True),
)
```

Note In this particular case, the attributes required suggest you could have simply created a Section object and had the Page inherit from it rather than having a separate Nav object and choosing that Section and Page inherit from it. The important point to be aware of is that you should also look at how objects you are modeling relate to each other in the real world as well as looking at how their attributes suggest they could be related. Pages aren't really like sections because they can't contain other pages and sections, so it is not wise to structure your model in a way that assumes they are.

The page table remains unchanged because you still want page-specific data stored in the page table and navigation information about the page stored in the nav table. Once again, though, the page's ID field needs to be a foreign key representing the ID of the record in the nav table from which it inherits. Change the definition for the id column of the page table to this:

```
schema.Column('id', types.Integer, schema.ForeignKey('nav.id'), primary_key=True),
```

With these changes in place, our Page and Section objects will automatically have all the attributes of Nav objects even though the information is physically stored in a different table.

Setting Up Initial Data

Now that the new model structure is in place, you'll need to update the websetup.py file so that the project contains more appropriate initial data. Update websetup.py so that it looks like this (notice that you drop all the tables first if the function is being called with configuration from test.ini as described in Chapter 12):

```
"""Set up the SimpleSite application"""
import logging
import os.path
from simplesite import model

from simplesite.config.environment import load_environment

log = logging.getLogger(__name__)

def setup_app(command, conf, vars):
    """Place any commands to setup simplesite here"""
    load_environment(conf.global_conf, conf.local_conf)

    # Load the models
    from simplesite.model import meta
    meta.metadata.bind = meta.engine
    filename = os.path.split(conf.filename)[-1]
    if filename == 'test.ini':
        # Permanently drop any existing tables
        log.info("Dropping existing tables...")
        meta.metadata.drop_all(checkfirst=True)
# Continue as before
    # Create the tables if they aren't there already
    meta.metadata.create_all(checkfirst=True)

    log.info("Adding home page...")
    section_home = model.Section()
    section_home.path=u''
    section_home.name=u'Home Section'
    meta.Session.add(section_home)
    meta.Session.flush()
```

```
page_contact = model.Page()
page_contact.title=u'Contact Us'
page_contact.path=u'contact'
page_contact.name=u'Contact Us Page'
page_contact.content = u'Contact us page'
page_contact.section=section_home.id
meta.Session.add(page_contact)
meta.Session.flush()

section_dev = model.Section()
section_dev.path=u'dev'
section_dev.name=u'Development Section'
section_dev.section=section_home.id
section_dev.before=page_contact.id
meta.Session.add(section_dev)
meta.Session.flush()

page_svn = model.Page()
page_svn.title=u'SVN Page'
page_svn.path=u'svn'
page_svn.name=u'SVN Page'
page_svn.content = u'This is the SVN page.'
page_svn.section=section_dev.id
meta.Session.add(page_svn)
meta.Session.flush()

page_dev = model.Page()
page_dev.title=u'Development Home'
page_dev.path=u'index'
page_dev.name=u'Development Page'
page_dev.content=u'This is the development home page.'
page_dev.section=section_dev.id
page_dev.before=page_svn.id
meta.Session.add(page_dev)
meta.Session.flush()

page_home = model.Page()
page_home.title=u'Home'
page_home.path=u'index'
page_home.name=u'Home'
page_home.content=u'Welcome to the SimpleSite home page.'
page_home.section=section_home.id
page_home.before=section_dev.id
meta.Session.add(page_home)
meta.Session.flush()

meta.Session.commit()
log.info("Successfully set up.")
```

Now that you have updated the model and written a new websetup.py, you need the changes to be reflected in the underlying database. The easiest way of doing this is to create a new database from scratch. Once you've done this, you'll continue with the tutorial.

```
$ mv development.db development.db.old
$ paster setup-app development.ini
```

With these changes in place, IDs are shared between pages and sections. This means that nav ID 1 represents a section, whereas nav ID 2 represents a page. Visiting `http://localhost:5000/page/view/1` will therefore give a 404 Not Found response because there is no page with an ID of 1. In fact, the home page now has an ID of 6.

Creating the Controllers

Now that the model correctly supports the navigation structure, you'll need to think again about the controllers.

I mentioned before that you generally need a controller for every table in your database, but in this case you might think that there isn't a lot of point in having a controller for the navigation table because the `Section` and `Page` objects in the model handle all the functionality for that table anyway. It turns out that it can be useful to have a navigation controller as long as it can't be accessed directly because both the page and section controllers can inherit any functionality that affects only the nav table, such as the ability to move pages or sections. Create the navigation controller and a directory for its templates:

```
$ paster controller nav
$ cd simplesite/templates/derived
$ mkdir nav
```

Now change the `NavController` class. Delete the `index()` action, and add a `__before__()` method that prevents any of the actions you'll add later being called directly as a result of a URL being entered:

```
def __before__(self):
    abort(404)
```

You'll also need to add the following imports:

```
from simplesite import model
from simplesite.model import meta
```

With the nav controller in place, let's start by thinking about the section controller.

Your users will need to be able to add, edit, and remove sections just as they can with pages, but they probably won't need to list all the sections. Let's use the `template.py.txt` file you created earlier in the chapter as a starting point for the new controller:

```
$ cd simplesite/controllers
$ cp template.py.txt section.py
$ perl -pi -w -e 's/comment/section/g; s/Comment/Section/g;' section.py
```

Now let's also create a set of templates:

```
$ cd ../templates/derived
$ cp -r page section
$ cd section
$ perl -pi -w -e 's/page/section/g; s/Page/Section/g;' *.html
```

Delete the `section/list.html` template because you won't need it. Now restart the server if you stopped it to make these changes:

```
$ cd ../../../../
$ paster serve --reload development.ini
```

As usual, let's start by thinking about the FormEncode schema you're going to need. You'll need validators for each of the columns in the nav table. To validate the value of the `before` column (which is used to determine the order of pages and sections within a subsection), you'll need a custom validator. Since pages also have a value of `before`, they will need the same validator, so rather than defining the custom validator in the section controller, let's create the validators in the nav controller. Add this to the nav controller after the existing imports:

```python
import formencode

class ValidBefore(formencode.FancyValidator):
    """Checks the ID specified in the before field is valid"""
    def _to_python(self, values, state):
        nav_q = meta.Session.query(model.Nav)
        # Check the value for before is in the section
        if values.get('before'):
            valid_ids = [nav.id for nav in nav_q.filter_by(
                section=values['section']).all()]
            if int(values['before']) not in valid_ids:
                raise formencode.Invalid("Please check the section "
                    "and before values", values, state)
        return values

class NewNavForm(formencode.Schema):
    allow_extra_fields = True
    filter_extra_fields = True
    name = formencode.validators.String(not_empty=True)
    path = formencode.validators.Regex(not_empty=True, regex='^[a-zA-Z0-9_-]+$')
    section = formencode.validators.Int(not_empty=True)
    before = formencode.validators.Int()
    chained_validators = [ValidBefore()]
```

The NewNavForm schema handles each of the fields but uses the ValidBefore chained validator to also check that the navigation node specified in before is either None (which means add the new section at the end of the existing section) or is the ID of a navigation node, which does exist in that section. You'll recall that chained validators are run only once after all the individual validators for each of the fields have been checked. The schema also uses a Regex validator to ensure that only allowed characters are used on the path.

Let's now use the NewNavForm schema as a basis for creating a schema for new sections. Add this to the section controller in place of the existing NewSectionForm schema:

```python
from simplesite.controllers.nav import NewNavForm, ValidBefore

class UniqueSectionPath(formencode.validators.FancyValidator):
    "Checks that there isn't already an existing section with the same path"
    def _to_python(self, values, state):
        nav_q = meta.Session.query(model.Nav)
        query = nav_q.filter_by(section=values['section'],
            type='section', path=values['path'])
        if request.urlvars['action'] == 'save':
            # Ignore the existing ID when performing the check
            query = query.filter(model.Nav.id != int(request.urlvars['id']))
        existing = query.first()
        if existing is not None:
            raise formencode.Invalid("There is already a section in this "
                "section with this path", values, state)
        return values

class NewSectionForm(NewNavForm):
    chained_validators = [ValidBefore(), UniqueSectionPath()]
```

The `UniqueSectionPath` validator ensures there isn't another subsection with the same path in the section to which this section is being added. Although this code works well for adding a new section, there are some different constraints when editing a section. Sections cannot be moved to sections that are children of the section being moved. This means you need another validator to ensure that if the section is being edited, the new section is in a valid position. Here's the new validator and an `EditNavForm` that uses it. Add them to the section controller after the `NewSectionForm` you just added:

```
class ValidSectionPosition(formencode.FancyValidator):
    def _to_python(self, values, state):
        nav_q = meta.Session.query(model.Nav)
        if values.get('type', 'section') == 'section':
            # Make sure the section we are moving to is not already
            # a subsection of the current section
            section = nav_q.filter_by(id=int(values['section'])).one()
            current_section = nav_q.filter_by(id=request.urlvars['id']).one()
            while section:
                if section.section == current_section.id:
                    raise formencode.Invalid("You cannot move a section to "
                        "one of its subsections", values, state)
                if section.section == 1:
                    break
                section = nav_q.filter_by(id=section.section).first()
        return values

class EditSectionForm(NewNavForm):
    chained_validators = [
        ValidBefore(),
        UniqueSectionPath(),
        ValidSectionPosition()
    ]
```

The `ValidSectionPosition` validator iterates through each of the parent sections of the section to which you are trying to move the section you are editing. If it reaches the top of the navigation tree without finding the section you are moving, then you are allowed to move the section.

At this point, all the validators that will be shared between pages and sections are in the nav controller, and all the validators that the section needs are in the section controller, but they inherit from those in the navigation controller. You'll make the necessary changes to the page controller later in the chapter, so now let's think about the templates.

Both the page and the section will need the extra fields from the `nav` table, so create a new file called `fields.html` in the `templates/derived/nav/` directory to be shared by the page and section templates. Add the following content:

```
${h.field(
    "Name",
    h.text(name='name'),
    required=True,
)}
${h.field(
    "Path",
    h.text(name='path'),
    required=True,
)}
```

```
${h.field(
    'Section',
    h.select(
        "section",
        id='section',
        selected_values=[],
        options=c.available_sections,
    ),
    required=True
)}
${h.field(
    "Before",
    h.text(
        "before",
        id='before',
    ),
)}
```

These fields will be used by both the page controller and the section controller. Update the derived/section/fields.html file to import and use the fields you've just created:

```
<%namespace file="/derived/nav/fields.html" name="fields" import="*"/>
## Nav fields
${fields.body()}
## Section fields would go here if there were any
```

Because of the way the templates are set up, these fields will be used in both the derived/section/new.html and derived/section/edit.html templates. You'll notice that the section field relies on the value of c.available_sections. You haven't set this up yet, so let's do that now by adding the following __before__() method to the section controller:

```
def __before__(self, id=None):
    nav_q = meta.Session.query(model.Nav)
    if id:
        nav_q=nav_q.filter_by(type='section').filter(model.nav_table.c.id!=int(id))
    else:
        nav_q = nav_q.filter_by(type='section')
    c.available_sections = [(nav.id, nav.name) for nav in nav_q]
```

Notice that you are using a query based on model.Nav here and specifying type='section' in the filter rather than querying model.Section. This is because the nav table contains the name column you need access to, but the section table doesn't.

At this point you'll be able to see the form for creating a new section by visiting http://localhost:5000/section/new. This is shown in Figure 14-6, but the section won't save correctly yet.

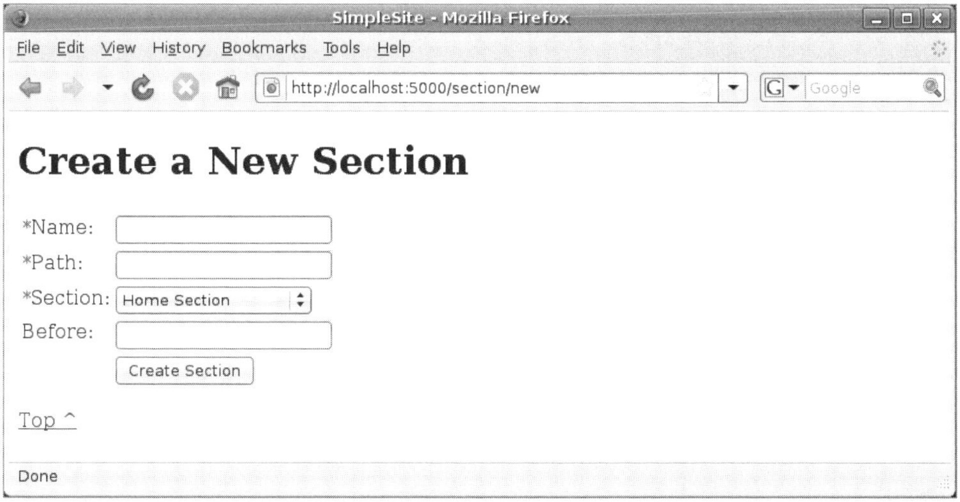

Figure 14-6. *The create section form*

Simply adding the section to the table isn't enough. Because this is a hierarchy, you also need to modify the node this node appears before to update its value of before to point to the ID of the section the user is adding so that the ordering is correct. You could add a function to perform this task as a helper, but in this case the work mainly has to do with the model, so it would be better to add it there.

Rather than simply adding the function to the model module itself, you're going to add it as a static method to the Nav class. A static method in Python is one that is associated with the class itself and not the instance of a class. As such, it doesn't have a self argument. Update the Nav class in model/__init__.py to look like this:

```
class Nav(object):
    @staticmethod
    def add_navigation_node(nav, section, before):
        nav_q = meta.Session.query(Nav)
        new_before = nav_q.filter_by(section=section, before=before).first()
        if new_before is not None and new_before.id != nav.id:
            new_before.before = nav.id
```

You can now access this functionality as model.Nav.add_navigation_node() in your controllers without needing any additional imports, and it is clear what the functionality does. The Section and Page classes will also inherit this method, although you'll use the version attached to Nav to keep what is happening more explicit.

Update the section controller's create() action so that the navigation structure is correctly updated when a section is added by calling model.Nav.add_navigation_node(). Since a section isn't a lot of use on its own, let's also generate an index page for the section. To do this, you need to flush the session so that the section object gets assigned an ID. You can then use the ID to help create the index page. The finished code looks like this with the new lines bold:

```
@restrict('POST')
@validate(schema=NewSectionForm(), form='new')
def create(self):
    # Add the new section to the database
    section = model.Section()
    for k, v in self.form_result.items():
        setattr(section, k, v)
    meta.Session.add(section)
    model.Nav.add_navigation_node(section, self.form_result['section'],
        self.form_result['before'])
    # Flush the data to get the session ID.
    meta.Session.flush()
    index_page = model.Page()
    index_page.section = section.id
    index_page.path = 'index'
    index_page.title = 'Section Index'
    index_page.name = 'Section Index'
    index_page.content = 'This is the index page for this section.'
    meta.Session.add(index_page)
    meta.Session.commit()
    # Issue an HTTP redirect
    return redirect_to(controller='section', action='view', id=section.id)
```

Since you can't actually *see* a section, there isn't a lot of point in having the `create()` action redirect to a view of it. For this reason, delete the `view()` action and the `view.html` template because you won't use them. For the time being, after you create a new section, you'll get the error "`Action u'view' is not implemented`". You'll fix this later in the chapter.

Now that you can create sections, let's think about editing them. First you'll need to update the `edit()` action so that the `values` reflect those of a section. It should look like this:

```
values = {
    'name': section.name,
    'path': section.path,
    'section': section.section,
    'before': section.before,
}
```

When you save a section, there is a chance you are moving it to another section. If this is the case, you need to formally remove it from the node hierarchy before adding it in the new location. You already have an `add_navigation_node()` method, so here's the `remove_navigation_node()` static method. Add this to the `Nav` class in `model/__init__.py` too:

```
@staticmethod
def remove_navigation_node(nav):
    nav_q = meta.Session.query(Nav)
    old_before = nav_q.filter_by(section=nav.section, before=nav.id).first()
    if old_before is not None:
        old_before.before = nav.before
```

Update the section controller's `save()` action to look like this. Make sure you update the redirect code and change the schema in the `@validate` decorator to use the `EditSectionForm` you created earlier.

```
@restrict('POST')
@validate(schema=EditSectionForm(), form='edit')
def save(self, id=None):
    section_q = meta.Session.query(model.Section)
    section = section_q.filter_by(id=id).first()
    if section is None:
        abort(404)
    if not(section.section == self.form_result['section'] and \
        section.before == self.form_result['before']):
        model.Nav.remove_navigation_node(section)
        model.Nav.add_navigation_node(section, self.form_result['section'],
            self.form_result['before'])
    for k,v in self.form_result.items():
        if getattr(section, k) != v:
            setattr(section, k, v)
    meta.Session.commit()
    session['flash'] = 'Section successfully updated.'
    session.save()
    # Issue an HTTP redirect
    return redirect_to(controller='section', action='view', id=section.id)
```

Once again, when you save a section after editing, you will be redirected to the nonexistent view() action. You'll fix this later too.

Next you'll need to look at the delete() action. Ideally you should not be able to delete a section while it still contains pages or subsections. However, if you deleted all the pages a section contained, then there would be no page on which to display a link to delete the section. Instead, you will set things up so that deleting a section also deletes its index page, but you can't delete a section if any other pages or sections exist within the section you're deleting. Update the delete() action so that it looks like this:

```
def delete(self, id=None):
    if id is None:
        abort(404)
    section_q = meta.Session.query(model.Section)
    section = section_q.filter_by(id=id).first()
    if section is None:
        abort(404)
    nav_q = meta.Session.query(model.Nav)
    existing = nav_q.filter_by(section=id, type='section').filter(
        model.Page.path != 'index').first()
    if existing is not None:
        return render('/derived/section/cannot_delete.html')
    index_page = nav_q.filter_by(section=id, path='index', type='page').first()
    if index_page is not None:
        model.Nav.remove_navigation_node(index_page)
        meta.Session.delete(index_page)
    model.Nav.remove_navigation_node(section)
    meta.Session.delete(section)
    meta.Session.commit()
    return render('/derived/section/deleted.html')
```

You'll need to create the derived/section/cannot_delete.html file with this content:

```
<%inherit file="/base/index.html"/>

<%def name="heading()"><h1>Cannot Delete</h1></%def>

<p>You cannot delete a section which still contains pages or subsections
other than the index page. Please delete the pages and subsections
first.</p>
```

That's it—now you can also delete sections, but before we move on, let's add the section links to the page footer so that users can access the functionality you've just implemented without having to type the URL directly. Edit templates/derived/page/view.html so that the footer() def looks like this:

```
<%def name="footer()">
## Then add our page links
<p>
  <a href="${h.url_for(controller='page', action='list')}">All Pages</a>
| <a href="${h.url_for(controller='page', action='new', ➥
section=c.page.section, before=c.page.before)}">New Page</a>
| <a href="${h.url_for(controller='page', action='edit', ➥
id=c.page.id)}">Edit Page</a>
| <a href="${h.url_for(controller='page', action='delete', ➥
id=c.page.id)}">Delete Page</a>
</p>
## Comment links
<p>
  <a href="${h.url_for(pageid=c.page.id, controller='comment', ➥
action='list', id=None)}">Comments (${str(c.comment_count)})</a>
| <a href="${h.url_for(pageid=c.page.id, controller='comment', ➥
action='new', id=None)}">Add Comment</a>
</p>
## Section links
<p>
  <a href="${h.url_for(controller='section', action='new', ➥
section=c.page.section, before=c.page.before)}">New Section</a>
| <a href="${h.url_for(controller='section', action='edit', ➥
id=c.page.section)}">Edit Section</a>
| <a href="${h.url_for(controller='section', action='delete', ➥
id=c.page.section)}">Delete Section and Index Page</a>
</p>
## Tag links
<p><a href="${h.url_for(controller='tag', action='list')}">All Tags</a>
| <a href="${h.url_for(controller='tag', action='new')}">Add Tag</a></p>
## Include the parent footer too
${parent.footer()}
</%def>
```

You'll notice that the call to h.url_for() to the section controller's new() action contains some extra arguments, section and before. When Routes' h.url_for() function gets passed arguments, and it doesn't recognize them; it will simply add them as parameters to the query string. In this case, the arguments represent information about the current page that can be used on the new() action to automatically populate some of the values. The URL generated might look like /section/new?section=1&before=7. To take advantage of these arguments, you will have to update the section controller's new() action to look like this:

```
def new(self):
    values = {}
    values.update(request.params)
    if values.has_key('before') and values['before'] == u'None':
        del values['before']
    return htmlfill.render(render('/derived/section/new.html'), values)
```

The h.url_for() call to create a new page has also had a similar change. It now takes both the section and the before value of the current page as arguments too, so now you can turn your attention to updating the page controller.

The Page Controller

Let's start by updating the page controller's new() action to accept the variables that will be passed to it when a user clicks the New Page link now that you've updated the arguments to h.url_for() in the page view template footer. The new action should look like this:

```
def new(self):
    values = {}
    values.update(request.params)
    if values.has_key('before') and values['before'] == u'None':
        del values['before']
    return htmlfill.render(render('/derived/page/new.html'), values)
```

The page controller also needs the same fields and functionality as the section controller. This is not surprising since both sections and pages inherit from the Nav class. Edit the derived/page/fields.html file to include fields from the derived/nav/fields.html file. Add the following at the top of the before the existing fields:

```
<%namespace file="/derived/nav/fields.html" name="fields" import="*"/>
## Nav fields
${fields.body()}
## Page fields
```

Now that the extra fields are in place, let's change the NewPageForm schema in the page controller to inherit from NewNavForm instead of formencode.Schema so that it has all the validators of NewNavForm as well as its own. You'll also need a UniquePagePath validator to ensure there isn't already a page with the same name in the current section. Add this to the top of page.py replacing the existing NewPageForm schema:

```
from simplesite.controllers.nav import NewNavForm, ValidBefore

class UniquePagePath(formencode.validators.FancyValidator):
    def _to_python(self, values, state):
        nav_q = meta.Session.query(model.Nav)
        query = nav_q.filter_by(section=values['section'],
            type='page', path=values['path'])
        if request.urlvars['action'] == 'save':
            # Ignore the existing id when performing the check
            query = query.filter(model.Nav.id != int(request.urlvars['id']))
        existing = query.first()
        if existing is not None:
            raise formencode.Invalid("There is already a page in this "
                "section with this path", values, state)
        return values
```

```
class NewPageForm(NewNavForm):
    allow_extra_fields = True
    filter_extra_fields = True
    content = formencode.validators.String(
        not_empty=True,
        messages={
            'empty':'Please enter some content for the page. '
        }
    )
    heading = formencode.validators.String()
    title = formencode.validators.String(not_empty=True)
    chained_validators = [ValidBefore(), UniquePagePath()]
```

Notice that the NewPageForm schema also has the same ValidBefore() chained validator as the NewSectionForm.

Now modify the page controller's create() action so that new pages are added in the correct place in the hierarchy and the redirect code is updated.

```
@restrict('POST')
@validate(schema=NewPageForm(), form='new')
def create(self):
    # Add the new page to the database
    page = model.Page()
    for k, v in self.form_result.items():
        setattr(page, k, v)
    meta.Session.add(page)
    model.Nav.add_navigation_node(page, self.form_result['section'],
        self.form_result['before'])
    meta.Session.commit()
    # Issue an HTTP redirect
    return redirect_to(controller='page', action='view', id=page.id)
```

And just as with the section controller, update the redirect code and change the lines in the save() action before the line for k,v in self.form_result.items():

```
@restrict('POST')
@validate(schema=NewPageForm(), form='edit')
def save(self, id=None):
    page_q = meta.Session.query(model.Page)
    page = page_q.filter_by(id=id).first()
    if page is None:
        abort(404)
    if not(page.section == self.form_result['section'] and \
        page.before == self.form_result['before']):
        model.Nav.remove_navigation_node(page)
        model.Nav.add_navigation_node(page, self.form_result['section'],
            self.form_result['before'])
    for k,v in self.form_result.items():
        if getattr(page, k) != v:
            setattr(page, k, v)
    meta.Session.commit()
    session['flash'] = 'Page successfully updated.'
    session.save()
    # Issue an HTTP redirect
    return redirect_to(controller='page', action='view', id=page.id)
```

Now you'll need to update the edit() method so that it also populates all the new values:

```
values = {
    'name': page.name,
    'path': page.path,
    'section': page.section,
    'before': page.before,
    'title': page.title,
    'heading': page.heading,
    'content': page.content,
}
```

For this to work, you'll need a similar __before__() action used in the section controller to set c.available_sections:

```
def __before__(self):
    nav_q = meta.Session.query(model.Nav)
    c.available_sections = [(nav.id, nav.name) for nav in ➥
nav_q.filter_by(type='section')]
```

You'll also need to update the delete() action. This is much easier than it is for sections; simply add the following line:

```
def delete(self, id=None):
    if id is None:
        abort(404)
    page_q = meta.Session.query(model.Page)
    page = page_q.filter_by(id=id).first()
    if page is None:
        abort(404)
    meta.Session.execute(delete(model.pagetag_table,
        model.pagetag_table.c.pageid==page.id))
    model.Nav.remove_navigation_node(page)
    meta.Session.delete(page)
    meta.Session.commit()
    return render('/derived/page/deleted.html')
```

Changing the Routing

At this point you now have all the functionality necessary for a fully working web site. These are the only missing elements:

- The ability to enter a proper URL rather than the ID of the page you want to view

- Navigation controls such as tags, a menu, and breadcrumbs

Before I get into too much detail about the code, I'll discuss exactly how these things will be implemented. You want a setup where the URL appears as if it is mapping to a directory structure of sections and subsections. So, rather than visiting /page/view/4 to view the SVN page in the development section, you will be able to access it as /dev/svn. To do this, you need to get Routes to understand your alternative URL structure. You'll also want some navigation components. You'll use a set of tabs for the main navigation. Any page or section that is in the home section will be displayed on these tabs. For any page that isn't in the home section, a navigation menu will be also generated to display the links in that section. Finally, you'll have a breadcrumb trail so that users can see where they are in the navigation hierarchy. There's a lot to do, so let's get started.

You'll implement both these elements, but you'll start with the routing. Ideally, you want to be able to specify a route that will handle a URL not already matched by the other routes. You can do this by using a wildcard part, as you learned in Chapter 9. One approach could be to add a route like this as the last route in SimpleSite's `config/routing.py` file:

```
map.connect('*url', controller='page', action='nav')
```

This would redirect any URL not already matched by the other routes to the page controller's `nav()` action from where the appropriate dispatch can be performed; however, there is also a slightly neater solution that involves having the page or section ID calculated as part of the matching process. This avoids needing to use a controller action for dispatch.

Create a named route called `path` as the last route in the route map, and specify a function condition on the route called `parse()` and a filter on the route named `build()`. Conditions and filters are advanced Routes functionality that I discussed in Chapter 9. Here's how the route map should look, with the new route shown in bold:

```
def make_map():
    """Create, configure and return the routes Mapper"""
    map = Mapper(directory=config['pylons.paths']['controllers'],
                always_scan=config['debug'], explicit=True)
    map.minimization = False

    # The ErrorController route (handles 404/500 error pages); it should
    # likely stay at the top, ensuring it can always be resolved
    map.connect('/error/{action}', controller='error')
    map.connect('/error/{action}/{id}', controller='error')

    # CUSTOM ROUTES HERE

    map.connect(
        '/page/{pageid}/{controller}/{action}',
        requirements=dict(pageid='\d+'),
    )
    map.connect(
        '/page/{pageid}/{controller}/{action}/{id}',
        requirements=dict(pageid='\d+', id='\d+'),
    )
    map.connect('/{controller}/{action}')
    map.connect('/{controller}/{action}/{id}')
    map.connect('path', '*url', conditions={'function':parse}, _filter=build)
    return map
```

Add the `parse()` and `build()` functions to the top of the `config/routing.py` file before the `make_map()` function:

```
from simplesite import model

def parse(environ, result):
    url = result.pop('url')
    try:
        environ['simplesite.navigation'] = navigation_from_path(url)
    except NoPage, e:
        result['controller'] = 'nav'
        result['action'] = 'nopage'
        result['section'] = e.section
        result['path'] = e.path
```

```
    except NoSection, e:
        result['controller'] = 'nav'
        result['action'] = 'nosection'
        result['section'] = e.section
        result['path'] = e.path
    except NotFound, e:
        # This causes the route to not match
        return False
    else:
        result['controller'] = 'page'
        result['action'] = 'view'
        result['id'] = environ['simplesite.navigation']['page'].id
    return True

def build(routing_variables):
    controller = routing_variables.get('controller')
    action = routing_variables.get('action')
    id = routing_variables.get('id')
    del routing_variables['id']
    routing_variables['url'] = model.Nav.nav_to_path(id)
    return routing_variables
```

When Routes can't match any URL against the other routes, the 'path' named route you've just added gets tested. This causes the parse() condition to be called, which in turn calls the navigation_from_path() function with the current URL as its argument.

I'll show you the navigation_from_path() function in a moment, but let's think about what it has to do. Its main job is to match the URL entered against a section or page that already exists so that the correct routing variables can be set up. If the URL doesn't match an existing section or a page, the function should ideally determine whether it is possible to create a page or section at that URL. If it is possible, you'll need some mechanism to let the user know they can create a section or page. If it isn't, a 404 Not Found response should be returned.

It turns out that performing these checks requires the navigation_from_path() function to look up each part of the URL to check that it exists and to determine whether it is a section or page. Since these checks are already being performed, it makes sense for the same function to also gather the information that will be required to generate the navigation components you'd like to use in the site including top-level tabs, a menu, and breadcrumbs. This is precisely what the function does, returning a dictionary with the following keys:

breadcrumbs: A list of all the sections in the navigation hierarchy up to the current node, followed by the final page or section. Each item in the list has an attribute added called path_info, which is the full URL PATH_INFO to that page or section that can be used to help generate links.

menu: A list of all the pages and sections in the section to which the URL resolves.

tabs: The pages and sections in the topmost section. Used in the main navigation tabs.

page: The page object for the page the URL resolves to or the index page if the URL resolves to a section.

This dictionary returned is then added to the environ dictionary as the simplesite.navigation key so that it can be accessed in the rest of the application.

Note Some people would argue that this sort of functionality is better implemented as Web Server Gateway Interface middleware. You'll learn about middleware in Chapter 16 and are free to reimplement the previous functionality a different way if you prefer.

The navigation_from_path() function is shown here together with the menu() function it relies on and three Exception classes that are used as part of the process. The code looks like this and should be added to the top of config/routing.py after the build() function:

```
class NoPage(Exception):
    pass

class NoSection(Exception):
    pass

class NotFound(Exception):
    pass

def navigation_from_path(path_info):
    result = {}
    nav_q = model.meta.Session.query(model.Nav)
    path_parts = path_info.split('/')
    result['breadcrumbs'] = []
    if path_info.endswith('/'):
        path_info += 'index'
    path_parts = path_info.split('/')
    for path in path_parts[:-1]:
        s = nav_q.filter_by(type='section', path=path).first()
        if s:
            result['breadcrumbs'].append(s)
        else:
            if path_info.endswith('/index') and \
                len(result['breadcrumbs']) == len(path_info.split('/'))-2:
                exception = NoSection('No section exists here')
                exception.section = result['breadcrumbs'][-1].id
                exception.path = path_parts[-2]
                raise exception
            else:
                raise NotFound('No section can be created here')
    result['page'] = nav_q.filter_by(type='page',
        section=result['breadcrumbs'][-1].id, path=path_parts[-1]).first()
    if result['page'] is None:
        if len(result['breadcrumbs']) == len(path_info.split('/'))-1:
            exception = NoPage('No page exists here')
            exception.section = result['breadcrumbs'][-1].id
            exception.path = path_parts[-1]
            raise exception
        else:
            raise NotFound('No page can be created here')
    result['breadcrumbs'].append(result['page'])
    # Add the path_info
    cur_path = ''
    for breadcrumb in result['breadcrumbs']:
        cur_path +=breadcrumb.path
        breadcrumb.path_info = cur_path
        if isinstance(breadcrumb, model.Section):
            breadcrumb.path_info = cur_path + '/'
            cur_path += '/'
```

```
    result['menu'] = menu(nav_q, result['breadcrumbs'][-2].id,
        result['breadcrumbs'][-2].path_info)
    result['tabs'] = menu(nav_q, result['breadcrumbs'][0].id,
        result['breadcrumbs'][0].path_info)
    return result

def menu(nav_q, sectionid, path_info):
    # There might also be child sections
    last = None
    navs = [nav for nav in nav_q.filter_by(section=sectionid).order_by(
        model.nav_table.c.before.desc()).all()]
    for nav in navs:
        if nav.before is None:
            # This is our last node
            last = nav
            break
    menu_dict = dict([[nav.before, nav] for nav in navs])
    if not last:
        raise Exception('No last node found')
    # Iterate over the nodes building them up in the correct order
    menu = [last]
    while len(menu) < len(navs):
        id = menu[0].id
        if not menu_dict.has_key(id):
            raise Exception("This section doesn't have an item %s to go "
                "before %r id %s"%(id, menu[0].name, menu[0].id))
        item = menu_dict[menu[0].id]
        menu.insert(0, item)
    f_menu = []
    for menu_item in menu:
        menu_item.path_info = path_info + menu_item.path
        if isinstance(menu_item, model.Section):
            menu_item.path_info += '/'
        elif menu_item.path_info.endswith('/index'):
            menu_item.path_info = menu_item.path_info[:-5]
        f_menu.append(menu_item)
    return f_menu
```

As you can see, the navigation_to_path() function looks at each part of path to check that it exists, building up a list of breadcrumbs as it does. If it matches a page or section, it will also generate data structures for top-level tabs and a navigation menu containing links to other sections and pages in the same section as the section to which the URL resolves.

If the URL entered can't be matched, the function checks to see whether it could represent a section if that section was created. If it does, a NoSection exception is raised. This is caught in the parse() function and results in the nav controller's nosection() action being called. A similar thing happens if the URL resolves to a page that could exist if it were created, only a NoPage exception is raised, eventually resulting in a call to the nav controller's nopage() action.

If the URL doesn't resolve to a page or section and the component above it doesn't exist either, then a NotFound exception is raised, causing the parse() function to return False, which in turn tells Routes that the 'path' named route hasn't matched. This results in a 404 Not Found page being displayed as normal.

Let's implement the nosection() and nopage() actions. Replace the NavController class with this (you don't need the __before__() method anymore):

```
class NavController(BaseController):

    def nopage(self, section, path):
        return render('/derived/nav/create_page.html')

    def nosection(self, section, path):
        return render('/derived/nav/create_section.html')
```

You'll also need to create the templates on which these actions rely. Create derived/nav/create_page.html like this:

```
<%inherit file="/base/index.html"/>

<%def name="heading()"><h1>Create Page</h1></%def>
<p><a href="${h.url_for(controller='page', action='new',
    section=c.section, path=c.path)}">Create a new page here</a>.</p>
```

and create derived/nav/create_section.html like this:

```
<%inherit file="/base/index.html"/>

<%def name="heading()"><h1>Create Section</h1></%def>
<p><a href="${h.url_for(controller='section', action='new',
    section=c.section, path=c.path)}">Create a new section here</a>.</p>
```

Now when you visit a URL that doesn't exist but for which a page or a section could be created, you will be shown a page with a link allowing you to create it.

To view the page, the attributes c.menu, c.tabs, and c.breadcrumbs must be set. Add the lines in bold to the end of the page controller's view() method to obtain the values calculated during the processing of the routes and set them for use in the template.

```
def view(self, id=None):
    if id is None:
        abort(404)
    page_q = meta.Session.query(model.Page)
    c.page = page_q.filter_by(id=int(id)).first()
    if c.page is None:
        abort(404)
    c.comment_count = meta.Session.query(model.Comment).filter_by(pageid=id).count()
    tag_q = meta.Session.query(model.Tag)
    c.available_tags = [(str(tag.id), tag.name) for tag in tag_q]
    c.selected_tags = {'tags':[tag.id for tag in c.page.tags]}
    c.menu = request.environ['simplesite.navigation']['menu']
    c.tabs = request.environ['simplesite.navigation']['tabs']
    c.breadcrumbs = request.environ['simplesite.navigation']['breadcrumbs']
    return render('/derived/page/view.html')
```

For this to work, you need to use the named route 'path' when generating URLs to the page or section controller's view() actions so that the build() filter function can generate the correct URL.

Update all the calls to redirect_to() in the page controllers to this:

```
return redirect_to('path', id=page.id)
```

Update all the calls to redirect_to() in the section controller to look like this:

```
return redirect_to('path', id=section.id)
```

This build() function relies on a nav_to_path() static method that you should add to the Nav class in your model after the existing static methods:

```
class Nav(object):

    ... existing methods ...

    @staticmethod
    def nav_to_path(id):
        nav_q = meta.Session.query(Nav)
        nav = nav_q.filter_by(id=id).one()
        path = nav.path
        if nav.type=='section':
            path += '/'
        while nav.section is not None:
            nav = nav_q.filter_by(type='section', id=nav.section).one()
            path = nav.path+'/'+path
        return path
```

There are two other places that need updating to use the new route. Edit templates/derived/page/list.html, and replace these lines:

```
h.url_for(
    controller=u'page',
    action='view',
    id=unicode(page.id)
)
```

with the following:

```
h.url_for('path', id=page.id)
```

Then edit templates/derived/comment/view.html, and update the link back to the page the comment was posted on to look like this:

```
<p><a href="${h.url_for('path', id=c.comment.pageid)}">➡
Visit the page this comment was posted on.</a></p>
```

At this point, everything is in place to test the new code, but you are advised to create a new database because the navigation structure is fairly fragile if the validators aren't in place and because it is possible that as you've been building and testing the functionality you may have introduced some errors.

Delete the database and run this:

```
$ paster setup-app development.ini
```

Start the server again, visit http://localhost:5000/, and you should see the home page exactly as if you had visited http://localhost:5000/page/view/6 before making the routing changes.

Adding the Navigation Elements

Now all you need to do is add the navigation elements to the pages. Start by editing templates/base/index.html to add this import to the top:

```
<%namespace name="navigation" file="/component/navigation.html" import="*" />\
```

Then add `templates/component/navigation.html` with the following content:

```
<%!
import simplesite.model as model
%>
<%def name="breadcrumbs()">
    % if c.page and c.page.id != 1:
    <div id="breadcrumbs"><p>${render_breadcrumbs(c.breadcrumbs)}</p></div>
    % endif
</%def>

<%def name="tabs()">
    % if c.tabs:
    <div id="maintabs">
        <ul class="draglist">
            ${render_list(c.tabs, c.breadcrumbs[1].path,
                type_=c.breadcrumbs[1].type, id='li1_', class_='list2')}
        </ul>
    </div>
    % endif
</%def>

<%def name="menu()">
% if len(c.breadcrumbs) > 2:
    <div id="menu">
        <h2>Section Links</h2>
        <ul class="draglist">
                ${render_list(c.menu, c.breadcrumbs[-1].path,
                    type_=c.breadcrumbs[1].type, id='li1_', class_='list2')}
        </ul>
    </div>
% endif
</%def>

<%def name="render_list(items, current, id, class_)">
% for item in items:
    % if item.path == current and item.type == type_:
<li class="${class_} active" id="${id}${str(item.id)}"><span class="current"><a
    href="${item.path_info}" id="current">${item.name}</a></span></li>\
    % else:
<li class="${class_}" id="${id}${str(item.id)}"
    onclick="document.location ='${item.path_info}'"
><span><a href="${item.path_info}">${item.name}</a></span></li>\
    % endif
% endfor
</%def>

<%def name="render_breadcrumbs(breadcrumbs)">
    % for i, item in enumerate(breadcrumbs):
    % if i < len(breadcrumbs) - 1:
        <a href="${item.path_info}">${item.name}</a> &gt;
    % elif isinstance(c.breadcrumbs[-1], model.Section):
        ${item.name} &gt;
    % else:
        ${item.name}
    % endif
    % endfor
</%def>
```

Finally, edit `templates/base/index.html` again to replace the following defs:

```
<%def name="tabs()"></%def>
<%def name="menu()"></%def>
<%def name="heading()"><h1>${c.heading or 'No Title'}</h1></%def>
<%def name="breadcrumbs()"></%def>
```

with the following versions:

```
<%def name="tabs()">${navigation.tabs()}</%def>
<%def name="menu()">${navigation.menu()}</%def>
<%def name="heading()"><h1>${c.heading or 'No Title'}</h1></%def>
<%def name="breadcrumbs()">${navigation.breadcrumbs()}</%def>
```

With these changes in place, as shown in Figure 14-7, you can test the navigation components you've created.

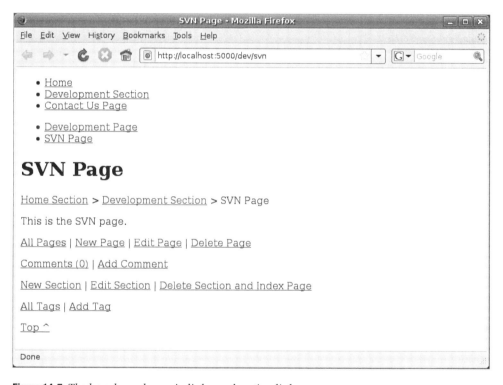

Figure 14-7. *The breadcrumbs, main links, and section links*

Adding Some Style

Now that all the functionality for the SimpleSite is in place, let's add some style to `public/css/main.css`. It would be good if the navigation tabs looked like tabs rather than a bulleted list. These styles will fix this; add them to the end of the file:

```
#maintabs ul {
    margin: 0px;
    padding: 0px;
    height: 23px;
}
#maintabs {
    background: #87AFD7;
    border-bottom: 3px solid #113958;
    margin: 0;
    padding: 10px 0 0px 17px;
}
#maintabs li {
    list-style: none;
    margin: 0;
    display: inline;
}
#maintabs li a {
    padding: 6px 10px;
    margin-left: 3px;
    border-bottom: none;
    text-decoration: none;
}
#maintabs li a:link { color: #113958; }
#maintabs li a:visited { color: #113958; }
#maintabs li a:hover {
    color: #000;
    background: #fff;
    border-color: #227;
}
#maintabs li a#current
{
    background: #113958;
    color: #fff;
    font-weight: bold;
    border-right: 2px solid #468AC7;
}
```

Tip If you find yourself frequently styling bulleted lists in this way, a useful site is listamatic at `http://css.maxdesign.com.au/listamatic/`; it provides quite a few different styles to apply to the same style sheet.

At this point, all the core functionality of SimpleSite is in place. You can add comments, tag pages, create sections and subsections, and move pages and sections around. Now is a good time to test the application to check that it behaves as you expect it to and that you haven't made any mistakes.

Figure 14-8 shows what the application looks like with some tags added.

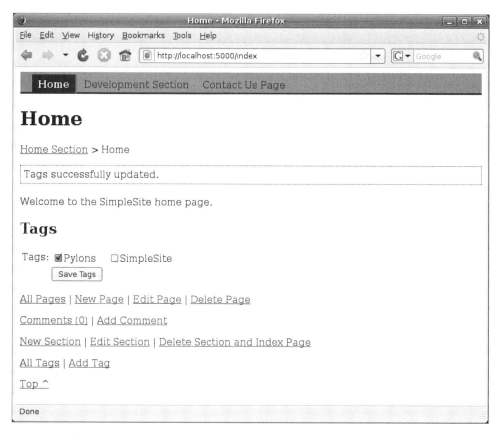

Figure 14-8. *CSS and tags*

Summary

You accomplished an awful lot in this chapter. You implemented a full comment and tag system, used SQLAlchemy's sophisticated inheritance features, shared code between different validators and templates, and built some sophisticated extensions to Routes.

In the next chapter, you'll learn about JavaScript and CSS. You'll then update SimpleSite to use a CSS grid. You'll add some Ajax so that the before text field is implemented as a select field whose values change when you select a different section, and you'll add some animation to the flash message.

CHAPTER 15

■ ■ ■

CSS, JavaScript, and Ajax

One of the definitive technologies of Web 2.0 is Ajax, which means Asynchronous JavaScript and XML and allows the browser to communicate with a server without needing to refresh the page the user is viewing. Interestingly, Ajax doesn't necessarily need to use JavaScript or XML, so it is only the *Asynchronous* part of the name that is the truly important aspect of the technology.

The world of JavaScript web frameworks is changing as fast now as the world of Python web frameworks was five years ago. Early versions of Pylons officially supported the Prototype and Script.aculo.us libraries used by Ruby on Rails, but despite this, Pylons users actually used a range of JavaScript frameworks. Two things quickly became apparent:

- Pylons users choose whichever framework best provides the tools they need, rather than going with the official library.

- JavaScript frameworks for the most part actually operate quite independently from the web framework that is using them. After all, one set of code runs on the server, and the other runs on the client.

The latest versions of Pylons (and in particular, WebHelpers) do not integrate any JavaScript framework, and as a result, you are free to choose whichever framework you prefer.

At the time of writing, the following three JavaScript frameworks are the most popular with Pylons developers:

- JQuery

- YUI

- ExtJS

One of the main benefits of YUI is that it is more than just a JavaScript framework. It also has tools for managing CSS and for creating user interface requirements.

Adding YUI to Your Project

You can use YUI in your project in two ways; the first is to copy the YUI library to your project's `public` directory and have Pylons serve the files, and the second is to use the files that Yahoo serves directly from its content delivery network (CDN).

Because Yahoo has servers all over the world, it is more likely that it will have a server physically near the person using your application, which should mean that users a long way from the server serving your Pylons application might get a small performance improvement.

I don't know about you, but when I'm responsible for a web site, I like to be in control of as many of the dependencies as possible; therefore, despite the possible benefits, I recommend installing YUI into your `public` directory. That way, if someone should trip over a wire and disconnect a server at Yahoo, your application won't be affected.

You can download the latest version of YUI from `http://developer.yahoo.com/yui/download/`. This book describes version 2.6.0.

To add YUI to a Pylons project, unzip the download into the project's `public` directory:

```
$ cd public
$ unzip yui_2.6.0.zip
```

You need to serve files from the `build` directory only, although the other folders contain useful documentation and examples you might want to browse. Remove the files you don't need with this:

```
$ cd yui
$ rm -r as-docs as-src assets docs examples tests index.html README
```

I usually also rename the `build` directory with the version number of the YUI library I'm using so that I can later use a different version alongside the current one:

```
$ mv build 2.6.0
```

The examples in this chapter will assume you have set up YUI in this way.

Resetting the Browser CSS

Anyone who has ever created a web site for one browser only to find that it looks completely different on another will understand this problem: different browsers interpret the same CSS in different ways. Fixing the broken style on one browser then makes it look different in the first, and before long you are tearing your hair out.

YUI has a fairly effective solution to this problem: reset browser styles across all browsers before you start coding your CSS; then, since the styles you add don't rely on the styles the browser implementation has decided to add by default, your styles stand a much greater chance of being consistent across different browsers.

You can add the YUI `reset.css` style sheet by adding the following lines to the `<head>` section of your HTML page:

```
<link rel="stylesheet" type="text/css" href="/yui/2.6.0/reset/reset-min.css">
```

To add the style sheet to a Pylons application with the YUI files in the `public` directory as you added earlier, you would use this in the head of your HTML in your base template:

```
${h.stylesheet_link(h.url_for('/yui/2.6.0/reset/reset-min.css'))}
```

Always make sure the `reset.css` style sheet is defined before any others; otherwise, you might find that your carefully coded styles are reset when you didn't expect them to be. You'll need to add this import to your `lib/helpers.py` file:

```
from webhelpers.html.tags import stylesheet_link
```

Tip It is much easier to use the YUI `reset.css` style at the beginning of a project before you define any styles rather than trying to apply it after other styles are already in place, so I strongly recommend you use it in all your projects from the beginning.

You can find more information about the `reset.css` style sheet at `http://developer.yahoo.com/yui/reset/`.

Once you have reset all the styles, there's a good chance you'll want some common ones back. For example, `<p>` tags usually have a margin, and the various headings should be different sizes.

Once again, the YUI team has thought of this, and common styles are defined in the base.css file. You can add the base.css file by adding this line to the head of your HTML document:

```
${h.stylesheet_link(h.url_for('/yui/2.6.0/base/base-min.css'))}
```

Notice that for both the base and reset style sheets, I have included minimized versions (they have -min added just before the file extension). These have all the unnecessary whitespace removed so that they are faster for a browser to download and parse. If you ever want to take a look at the styles they contain, you can look at the nonminimized versions, which are identical except for the whitespace.

Fonts

Another area developers sometimes struggle with is fonts. Typically you want the fonts to display at a particular size across all browsers, but you don't want to specify those sizes explicitly using px units because that would prevent certain browsers from adjusting the font size based on the size a user has chosen from a browser menu.

Once again, YUI has a style sheet that comes to the rescue, this time named fonts.css, which sets up font families and sizes so that they render consistently across browsers as 13-pixel Arial with 16-pixel line spaces. The <pre> and <code> elements render in monospace.

You can then specify any font sizes you want to use as a percentage of the default sizes, as shown in Table 15-1.

Table 15-1. *Pixels to Percent Translation*

If You Want This Size in Pixels (px)	Declare This Percent (%)
10	77
11	85
12	93
13	100
14	108
15	116
16	123.1
17	131
18	138.5
19	146.5
20	153.9
21	161.6
22	167
23	174
24	182
25	189
26	197

Be sure to always use percentages in your application, not the corresponding pixel size.

You can include fonts support in a Pylons application by adding the following after the reset CSS import in the <head> section of your HTML:

```
${h.stylesheet_link(h.url_for('/yui/2.6.0/fonts/fonts-min.css'))}
```

Tip The sharp-eyed amongst you might have spotted that you could achieve similar font standardization using ems, but the percentage technique described here results in more consistent rendering across browsers.

If you want to change the font family, you need to provide only the specific font you're interested in and not any fallbacks. When your font is missing, YUI provides a fallback for you.

For example, you would write this:

```
font-family: "Times New Roman";
```

and not this:

```
font-family: "Times New Roman", serif;
```

Grids

Another frequent problem in web development is the creation of grid layouts. Of course, you can always use tables to lay out your HTML content, but this is considered bad practice and is heavily frowned upon by CSS experts because table-based designs don't degrade gracefully. For example, with a table layout, if your screen resolution is too small, your users will be forced to scroll. CSS layouts, on the other hand, can cause one column of information to appear below another when the browser width is too small, which is generally considered better.

Sites such as Amazon still use table-based layout for some aspects of their pages, so the importance of always using CSS layouts all the time is debatable. Of course, you could also detect the screen resolution with JavaScript and provide a different layout for small screens, but this requires extra work and will not work if the browser doesn't support JavaScript or has it disabled.

Using a CSS grid framework makes setting up a CSS layout much easier. First you should declare your doctype as HTML 4 strict to force browsers into standards mode for rendering. You can do this by making sure the top of your HTML file looks like this:

```
<!DOCTYPE HTML PUBLIC "-//W3C//DTD HTML 4.01//EN"
    "http://www.w3.org/TR/html4/strict.dtd">
<html>
<head>
```

You also need to include the YUI `grids.css` file, but using grids also requires the reset and fonts CSS files to be used. Rather than including three separate files, YUI also provides a combined and minified file called `reset-fonts-grids.css` that you can use instead like this:

```
<link rel="stylesheet" type="text/css"
    href="/yui/2.6.0/reset-fonts-grids/reset-fonts-grids.css">
```

Although the file doesn't have `-min` as part of the file name, this is a fully minified CSS file.
You could also include this in a template with this line:

```
${h.stylesheet_link(h.rul_for('/yui/2.6.0/reset-fonts-grids/reset-fonts-grids.css))}
```

YUI assumes you will want a header, body, and footer in your HTML page, so to use the YUI grid, you need to set up your page's HTML like this with a `<div>` tag containing three other `<div>` tags:

```
<div id="doc">
   <div id="hd"><!-- header --></div>
   <div id="bd"><!-- body --></div>
   <div id="ft"><!-- footer --></div>
</div>
```

The `id` attribute of the inner `<div>` elements must be as shown earlier, but the `id` of the outer `<div>` element can be customized to determine the width of the page. You have the following options:

```
<!-- #doc = 750px width, centered-->
<div id="doc"></div>

<!-- #doc2 = 950px width, centered -->
<div id="doc2"></div>

<!-- #doc3 = 100% width -->
<div id="doc3"></div>

<!-- #doc4 = 974px width, centered -->
<div id="doc4"></div>
```

It's also possible to create your own page widths, but for the vast majority of cases, the YUI defaults are fine.

As an example, to create a content area with a 100 percent width, you would use an `id` of `doc3` on the outer `<div>` element, as shown here:

```
<div id="doc3">
   <div id="hd"><!-- header --></div>
   <div id="bd"><!-- body --></div>
   <div id="ft"><!-- footer --></div>
</div>
```

Once you've set up your template with the correct ID to specify the width of the content, you can think about how content within the header, body, and footer is arranged. YUI provides three types of grids you can use separately or combine to achieve a huge variety of different layouts:

- Template presets
- Nesting grids
- Special nesting grids

Template presets give you common configurations for two-column layouts with a column on the left or the right, and *nesting grids* and *special nesting grids* give you more control to produce more complex layouts, as you'll see in the following sections.

Template Preset Grids

Template preset grids are used after you have chosen the overall width of the content to subdivide either the header, body, or footer into two columns, one of which has a fixed width. To achieve, this you need to add some extra markup to either the header, body, or footer `<div>`. In this example we are splitting the body into two columns. The extra markup is shown in bold:

```
<div id="bd">
    <!-- body -->
    <div id="yui-main">
       <div class="yui-b"></div>
    </div>
    <div class="yui-b"></div>
</div>
```

You then choose which template preset to use by adding a class to the same outer <div> element that was used earlier to specify the width. Table 15-2 lists the options.

Table 15-2. *Template Class Presets*

Template Class	Preset Description
.yui-t1	160px on left
.yui-t2	180px on left
.yui-t3	300px on left
.yui-t4	180px on right
.yui-t5	240px on right
.yui-t6	300px on right

As an example, to have a 240-pixel column on the right of the same layout that you saw in the previous example with a 100 percent width, you would use this:

```
<div id="doc3" class="yui-t5">
    <div id="hd"><!-- header --></div>
    <div id="bd">
       <!-- body -->
       <div id="yui-main">
          <div class="yui-b"></div>
       </div>
       <div class="yui-b"></div>
    </div>
    <div id="ft"><!-- footer --></div>
</div>
```

This will produce the desired layout. What is more, you can also use a similar structure in the header and footer divs, but because it is the class of the outer div that defines the layout, the header, footer, and body all use the same layout with the template preset approach.

Sometimes you might want the content in the second <div class="yui-b"> element to appear in the HTML before the first, perhaps for search engine optimization reasons or perhaps to put your navigation before your content for accessibility reasons. If you are using a YUI template preset, you can change the order of the two columns in the HTML without changing how they are displayed. For example, this markup will produce the same results:

```
<div id="doc3" class="yui-t5">
    <div id="hd"><!-- header --></div>
    <div id="bd">
       <!-- body -->
       <div class="yui-b"></div>
       <div id="yui-main">
          <div class="yui-b"></div>
```

```
        </div>
    </div>
    <div id="ft"><!-- footer --></div>
</div>
```

Notice that the naked `<div class="yui-b">` element now comes *before* the one wrapped in `<div id="yui-main">`.

Nested Grids

Within the basic templates you can nest further grids so that each grid you nest divides the content area in two, with each area taking up 50 percent of the available space. Here's an example of how to do this:

```
<div class="yui-g">
    <div class="yui-u first"> </div>
    <div class="yui-u"> </div>
</div>
```

The important point to notice is that the first child of the grid has to be marked with the class `first` to ensure the grids work in all the main browsers. You can also nest nested grids within other nested grids to create more complex layouts.

Special Nested Grids

It isn't always particularly useful to subdivide areas in half, so YUI provides five *special nested grids* that subdivide grids in the ratios given in Table 15-3.

Table 15-3. *Grid Class Ratios*

Special Grid Class	Ratios
.yui-gb	1/3, 1/3, 1/3
.yui-gc	2/3, 1/3
.yui-gd	1/3, 2/3
.yui-ge	3/4, 1/4
.yui-gf	1/4, 3/4

Let's extend the example from the "Template Presets" section to use the `yui-gf` class in the header so that you can have a logo on the left taking up 1/4 of the page and the main navigation tabs on the right taking the remaining 3/4 of the space, while the body remains split in two with a 240-pixel column on the right.

Here's what the updated HTML looks like:

```
<div id="doc3" class="yui-t5">
    <div id="hd">
        <div class="yui-gf"> <!-- the "special grid" -->
            <div class="yui-u first"><img src="/image/logo.png" alt="Logo" /></div>
            <div class="yui-u"><!-- Navigation tabs here --></div>
        </div>
    </div>
```

```
<div id="bd">
    <!-- body -->
    <div id="yui-main">
        <div class="yui-b"></div>
    </div>
    <div class="yui-b"></div>
</div>
<div id="ft"><!-- footer --></div>
</div>
```

Notice that although in this example you are using a special nested grid directly in the header, you can also put them within template preset regions and nested grids too.

Updating SimpleSite to Use CSS Grids

Now that you've seen the theory of how to use YUI's CSS reset style sheet, fonts, and grids, you can update the SimpleSite project to use them too.

Start by preparing the YUI source code as described at the beginning of the chapter:

```
$ cd public
$ unzip yui_2.6.0.zip
$ cd yui
$ rm -r as-docs as-src assets docs examples tests index.html README
$ mv build 2.6.0
```

Make sure the first HTML in the `templates/base/index.html` file looks like this:

```
<!DOCTYPE HTML PUBLIC "-//W3C//DTD HTML 4.01//EN"
"http://www.w3.org/TR/html4/strict.dtd">
<html>
<head>
```

Then edit the `head()` def to add the YUI combined `reset-fonts-grids.css` file, which includes the grid styles:

```
<%def name="head()">
    ${h.stylesheet_link(h.url_for➥
('/yui/2.6.0/reset-fonts-grids/reset-fonts-grids.css'))}
    ${h.stylesheet_link(h.url_for('/css/main.css'))}
</%def>
```

For this example, you're going to have a two-column layout with a header and footer. You'd like the right column to be 240-pixels wide and contain the menu navigation and the list of tags that can be used on the page. You'll put the main navigation tabs in the header and style the footer to match it.

Replace the `<body>` part of the `base/index.html` file that currently looks like this:

```
<body>
    ${self.header()}
    ${self.tabs()}
    ${self.menu()}
    ${self.heading()}
    ${self.breadcrumbs()}
    ${self.flash()}
    ${next.body()}
    ${self.footer()}
</body>
```

with the YUI grids version that looks like the following. Notice the id=doc3 attribute on the outer <div> element to make the content use 100 percent of the width. The self.heading() def is now also called in the header, not the body:

```
<body>
    <div id="doc3">
        <div id="hd">
            ${self.heading()}
            ${self.header()}
            ${self.tabs()}
        </div>
        <div id="bd">
            ${self.breadcrumbs()}
            ${self.flash()}
            ${self.menu()}
            ${next.body()}
        </div>
        <div id="ft">
            ${self.footer()}
        </div>
    </div>
</body>
```

Next, add the markup to use a template preset for a 240-pixel column on the right. Notice the class="yui-t5" attribute and the two extra <div class="yui-b"> elements with the content for the two columns:

```
<body>
    <div id="doc3" class="yui-t5">
        <div id="hd">
            ${self.heading()}
            ${self.header()}
            ${self.tabs()}
        </div>
        <div id="bd">
            <div id="yui-main">
                <div class="yui-b">
                    ${self.breadcrumbs()}
                    ${self.flash()}
                    ${next.body()}
                </div>
            </div>
            <div class="yui-b">
                ${self.menu()}
            </div>
        </div>
        <div id="ft">
            ${self.footer()}
        </div>
    </div>
</body>
```

Finally, modify the header to contain a logo or title on the left and space for some additional links on the right using a special nested grid:

```
<body>
    <div id="doc3" class="yui-t5">
        <div id="hd">
            <div class="yui-gc">
                <div class="yui-u first">${self.heading()}</div>
                <div class="yui-u"></div>
            </div>
            ${self.header()}
            ${self.tabs()}
        </div>
        <div id="bd">
            <div id="yui-main">
                <div class="yui-b">
                    ${self.breadcrumbs()}
                    ${self.flash()}
                    ${next.body()}
                </div>
            </div>
            <div class="yui-b">
                ${self.menu()}
            </div>
        </div>
        <div id="ft">
            ${self.footer()}
        </div>
    </div>
</body>
```

You'll use Arial in SimpleSite for the body text, but you'll use Georgia for the headings. Since all the font styles have also been reset, you'll need to specify the heading size too. Add this to the end of the public/css/main.css file:

```
body{
    font-family: Arial;
}
#hd {
    background: #87AFD7;
    border-bottom: 3px solid #113958;
}
h1 {
    font-family: Georgia;
    color: #003;
    font-size: 197%;
    margin: 15px 20px 10px 20px;
}
h2 {
    font-family: Georgia;
    color: #003;
    font-size: 138.5%;
    margin-top: 1.5em;
}
#menu {
    padding-top: 20px;
}
```

```
#breadcrumbs {
    margin-bottom: 20px;
}
#doc3 {margin:auto;}
#bd, #ft {
    padding: 20px;
}
form {
    margin-top: 20px;
}
form table td {
    padding-bottom: 3px;
}
```

This particular grid template has a 10-pixel margin that you don't need. The earlier #doc3 style removes it. You'll also need to tweak two of the #maintabs styles. They should now look like this:

```
#maintabs ul {
    margin: 0px;
    padding: 0px;
    height: 21px;
}
#maintabs {
    margin: 0;
    padding: 10px 0 0px 17px;
}
```

Now that you have two columns, let's move the tags to the right column. Edit the templates/derived/page/view.html file so that the lines relating to the tags look like this:

```
<%def name="tags(available_tags)">
    <h2>Tags</h2>
    ${h.form_start(h.url_for(controller='page', action='update_tags', ➥
id=c.page.id),  method='post')}
        ${h.checkbox_group(name='tags', selected_values=None, align="vert",➥
 options=available_tags)}
        ${h.submit(value="Save Tags", name='submit')}
    ${h.form_end()}
</%def>

<%!
    from formencode import htmlfill
    from webhelpers.html import literal
%>

<%def name="menu()">
${parent.menu()}
% if c.available_tags:
${literal(htmlfill.render(capture(self.tags, c.available_tags), c.selected_tags))}
% endif
</%def>
```

With these changes in place and with one Pylons tag added, the development home page now looks like Figure 15-1. You might need to force a browser refresh before the new styles are noticed. If the section links and tags aren't on the right, check you have added the yui-t5 class to the outer div.

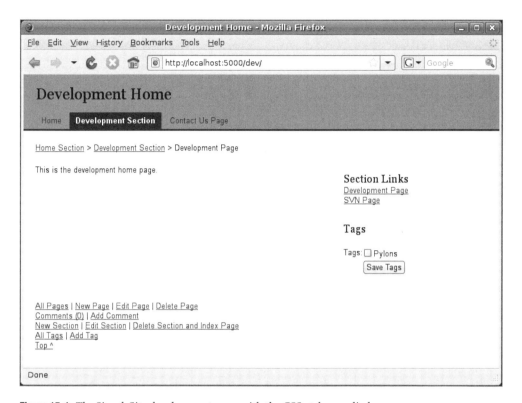

Figure 15-1. *The SimpleSite development page with the CSS styles applied*

Now that you have a good understanding of modern CSS techniques and have seen how they are applied with the YUI framework, it's time to investigate another tool of the modern web developer: JavaScript. Before you do that, though, I'll introduce a very useful plug-in called Firebug that will help you greatly when using JavaScript in the browser.

Introducing Firebug

When you are working with client-side code in the browser, you should consider using a tool that many developers find invaluable called Firebug. If you haven't come across Firebug yet, it is a plug-in for the Firefox browser that contains a range of useful tools for client-side web development, including a JavaScript console, Document Object Model (DOM) inspector, debugger, profiler, CSS display, HTTP request and response analysis tool, and a CSS visualization and manipulation tool.

If you don't have Firebug installed already, you should install it now. First download Firefox from http://www.mozilla.com/firefox, and after installing it, install the Firebug plug-in from http://getfirebug.com/. Firebug is available only for Firefox, but if you aren't already using Firefox for development, the Firebug plug-in is a good reason to consider switching.

Let's use the Firebug console to test some JavaScript. Start the SimpleSite application, and then visit http://localhost:5000/. Open Firefox, and select Tools ➤ Firebug ➤ Open Firebug in New Window from the menu. (Alternatively, you can press Ctrl+F12 or Command+F12 on a Mac to open Firebug from within Firefox.) Select the boxes for Console, Script, and Net, and click the Enable Selected Panels for Localhost button, as shown in Figure 15-2.

Figure 15-2. *Enabling the Firebug add-on*

Once you've enabled Firebug, you will be able to test the JavaScript examples from the previous section in Firebug. Click the red square button on the bottom right of Firebug to put Firebug into multiline input mode. You can then enter JavaScript statements more than one line a time and click the Run button. In Figure 15-3, I've entered `alert('Hello reader!')` and clicked Run. Firebug copies the input to the console on the left and executes the JavaScript as if it were being executed in the scope of the browser window. This means you have access to all the DOM functions you would have if you were writing JavaScript for the browser normally.

Figure 15-3. *Using the JavaScript console*

Firebug has a huge amount of useful functionality, some of which you'll see over the course of this chapter. It's well worth visiting `http://getfirebug.com` and clicking each of the pictures on the home page to get a full idea of what Firebug can do.

Introducing JavaScript

Although Python programmers can typically get a long way by copying and tweaking JavaScript examples, if you want to write any serious code to run on the browser, you need to learn JavaScript properly.

JavaScript is a language in its own right, and although it is frequently used for DOM manipulation (changing HTML within a browser), the JavaScript language shouldn't be confused with the DOM API.

Note JavaScript isn't actually based on Java at all but was given its name for political reasons between Sun and Netscape early in the history of web browsers. Microsoft also had an implementation called JScript, but today the standard is defined as ECMA-262, so JavaScript should really be known as ECMAScript.

At first glance, JavaScript appears fairly familiar to Python programmers; it has functions, hash tables (dictionaries), objects, and arrays as well as string, number, boolean, and date types. It also has all the standard control statements such as if, while, else, try, catch, and so on. Apart from curly braces and semicolons, JavaScript seems very approachable. Once you start using the language, though, you quickly realize that things aren't quite as simple as they seem. Consider this example (I'm using js> here to differentiate a JavaScript prompt from a traditional Python prompt >>>):

```
js> var a = [1,2,3,4];
js> a.length;
4
js> delete a[1];
js> a
[1, undefined, 3, 4]
js> a.length
4
```

As you can see, the Array type doesn't behave much like the Python equivalent. In JavaScript an Array behaves more like a Python dictionary where all the keys are consecutive numbers than a traditional array.

Let's look at functions:

```
js> function b(c, d) {
    alret(c);
    alert(d);
}
js> b(1)
```

This doesn't look a million miles from Python, but when you run it, you are shown two alert boxes with the values 1 and undefined. No error is thrown even though the function appears to take two parameters and you have specified only one. Try calling b() with three parameters, and you'll find it appears to just ignore the third, again without an error. That's not what you would expect from Python, although it's perfectly rational once you understand how JavaScript works. As you'll see later, functions in JavaScript also have a local variable called arguments that behaves a bit like an array of all the arguments passed.

Perhaps the most obvious difference is in the way JavaScript handles inheritance. Unlike Python, JavaScript doesn't have the concept of a class. Instead, it uses something called *prototypal inheritance* where objects inherit directly from other objects. This is quite different from Python and will cause you a good deal of confusion if you don't understand it. As you'll learn shortly, though, it is really rather simple.

Another difference to be aware of is the way variables are defined. Consider this example:

```
js> var a = function() {
    b = 1;
    var c = 2;
}
js> a()
js> b
1
js> c
undefined
```

In this case, the variable c was declared using the var keyword so is considered local to the scope of function a(). Because b wasn't declared using the var keyword, it was assigned to global scope. This is potentially a very bad thing because if a programmer forgot to use var when declaring another variable called b in another library you are using, both would refer to the same global b, which could cause problems that are difficult to track down.

In web browsers you can actually access the global scope directly because it is aliased as window. Continuing with the previous example, because b was declared without the var keyword, you could write this:

```
js> window.b
1
```

All the issues highlighted so far are simply meant to demonstrate that JavaScript is different from Python; it isn't worse, but if you expect it to work like Python without learning its differences, you are likely to quickly get confused, particularly because JavaScript often returns the value undefined in situations where Python would raise an exception. I've seen many Python programmers curse JavaScript when their code doesn't work the way it is supposed to, but if you take the time to learn it properly, you will quickly come to appreciate the language.

JavaScript Essentials

This isn't a book on JavaScript, so I don't intend to go through the whole language in detail; I'll give you enough of an understanding to start writing your own code and to highlight one or two traps Python programmers might fall into.

Tip If you want to learn JavaScript, I highly recommend you invest the time in watching Douglas Crockford's JavaScript videos. In them he talks you through all aspects of the language, inheritance, namespace issues, scope, closures, and more. Although the talks are fairly long, they are by far the most time-effective way to learn JavaScript properly. You'll struggle to understand JavaScript without them. Douglas has also written a book recently called *JavaScript: The Good Parts*, which I can strongly recommend for teaching you the important principles of the JavaScript language while avoiding the traps. It isn't focused on web development, though, but there are plenty of other books that are.

Operators of Interest

The full list of operators is defined in the ECMAScript specification at `http://www.ecma-international.org/publications/standards/Ecma-262.htm`, but certain equality operators, such as the + and / operators, are of particular interest to Python programmers because their behavior is slightly different.

JavaScript has two types of equality operators:

- `===` compares the type *and* value of the object. If they are different types or are the same type but with different values, the comparison will return `false`. Its inverse is `!==`.

- `==` tries to coerce one of the operands into the type of the other in order to make the comparison. Its inverse is `!=`.

If you don't realize that `==` and `!=` could be changing the types of the values you are comparing, you could run into trouble. The vast majority of the time you will want to use `===` and `!==` since they are the conceptual equivalents of `==` and `!=` in Python. Using `==` and `!=` in JavaScript is usually a mistake.

The + operator is used for adding numbers together as you would expect, but it is also used for string concatenation. Python has this behavior too, but the difference between JavaScript and Python is that in JavaScript if any of the operands are not strings, it will silently convert them to strings and then concatenate them:

```
js> 4+"2"
"42"
```

Python would raise a `TypeError` if you try to concatenate objects that aren't strings or Unicode in Python, so it can be slightly unexpected. This also means you can do operations such as this in JavaScript to convert a string to a number:

```
js> +"42"
42
```

In Python the / operator doesn't always mean a traditional divide operation. When the operands are integers, Python performs a floor divide operation. That is, it performs a division and discards the remainder. When one of the operands is a float, it performs a traditional division. For example:

```
# Python:
>>> 10/3
3
>>> 10/3.0
3.3333333333333335
```

In JavaScript, all numbers are 64-bit floating-point numbers (JavaScript doesn't differentiate between floats and integers in the way Python does), so / always behaves like a Python operation on floats:

```
// JavaScript
js> 10/3
3.3333333333333335
```

Types

JavaScript technically has nine types, although you'll only ever use the data types: `Undefined`, `Null`, `Boolean`, `String`, `Number`, and `Object`. You will also come across the value `NaN`, and you will use arrays (which are objects) and functions.

You'll learn about objects a bit later in this chapter, so let's start by looking at booleans. Booleans take the values `true` and `false` and behave as you would expect. In JavaScript, `true==1` is `true`, but `true===1` is `false` because a boolean is not the same as a number type.

Strings consist of 16-bit characters (technically the UCS-2 character set if you are interested), although there is no character type as such. You represent a character as a string of length 1. Strings can be declared with either single or double quotes and are immutable, which means if you want to perform some operation on a string, it will create a new one rather than change the existing one.

There is only one number type in JavaScript, and it is a 64-bit floating-point number. This can cause some problems because it means arithmetic is approximate. For example, 10/3 is not $3\frac{1}{3}$ but is 3.3333333333333335. Normally the small difference won't be a problem, but in some circumstances it might be, so it is worth being aware of. There is a special value `NaN` that means "Not a Number," which is the result of undefined or erroneous operations such as dividing by 0. This is unlike Python, which would raise an exception when an error occurred. Any arithmetic operation with `NaN` as an input will have `NaN` as a result, so it can sometimes be a little tricky to work out where the actual error occurred. `NaN` is not equal to anything, including `NaN`.

`null` is a value that isn't anything, analogous to `None` in Python. Many of the DOM operations such as `document.getElementById()` return `null` when a data structure cannot be found.

The final value you will run into is `undefined`. It's the default value for variables that haven't been assigned a value yet and for parameters that are passed to a function. It is also the value of missing members in objects. Python doesn't have anything equivalent to `undefined` because the same circumstances that would lead to an `undefined` value in JavaScript either aren't possible or would cause an exception to be raised in Python. For example, Python is strict about the arguments passed to a function, and you would get a `KeyError` if you tried to access a member that didn't exist. Python programmers tend to rely on these features of the language and are surprised when errors don't occur in their JavaScript code. Once you understand JavaScript's behavior in this regard, you are much less likely to be confused.

It can sometimes be a bit tricky to remember how to check the type of objects or whether objects are `null` or `undefined`, so the YUI library defines some functions in `YAHOO.lang` that make it easier. Here are some examples from the YUI documentation::

```
// true, an array literal is an array
YAHOO.lang.isArray([1, 2]);

// false, an object literal is not an array
YAHOO.lang.isArray({"one": "two"});

// however, when declared as an array, it is true
function() {
    var a = new Array();
    a["one"] = "two";
    return YAHOO.lang.isArray(a);
}();

// false, a collection of elements is like an array, but isn't
YAHOO.lang.isArray(document.getElementsByTagName("body"));
```

```
// true, false is a boolean
YAHOO.lang.isBoolean(false);

// false, 1 and the string "true" are not booleans
YAHOO.lang.isBoolean(1);
YAHOO.lang.isBoolean("true");

// null is null, but false, undefined and "" are not
YAHOO.lang.isNull(null); // true
YAHOO.lang.isNull(undefined); // false
YAHOO.lang.isNull(""); // false

// a function is a function, but an object is not
YAHOO.lang.isFunction(function(){}); // true
YAHOO.lang.isFunction({foo: "bar"}); // false

// true, ints and floats are numbers
YAHOO.lang.isNumber(0);
YAHOO.lang.isNumber(123.123);

// false, strings that can be cast to numbers aren't really numbers
YAHOO.lang.isNumber("123.123");

// false, undefined numbers and infinity are not numbers we want to use
YAHOO.lang.isNumber(1/0);

// true, objects, functions, and arrays are objects
YAHOO.lang.isObject({});
YAHOO.lang.isObject(function(){});
YAHOO.lang.isObject([1,2]);

// false, primitives are not objects
YAHOO.lang.isObject(1);
YAHOO.lang.isObject(true);
YAHOO.lang.isObject("{}");

// strings
YAHOO.lang.isString("{}"); // true
YAHOO.lang.isString({foo: "bar"}); // false
YAHOO.lang.isString(123); // false
YAHOO.lang.isString(true); // false

// undefined is undefined, but null and false are not
YAHOO.lang.isUndefined(undefined); // true
YAHOO.lang.isUndefined(false); // false
YAHOO.lang.isUndefined(null); // false
```

You might think that the results described here are obvious, but in fact performing the tests yourself can be quite tricky because there are often subtleties that can catch you out. It is much safer to use the YUI library's functions when performing these tests.

Functions

You can declare a function in two ways. The first is to give the function a name when you declare it as was done in the "Introducing JavaScript" section for the function b(). The second is to create an anonymous function and assign it to a variable, as shown here:

```
js> var change = function(a){ a = 2; }
```

Both methods are equivalent, but anonymous functions can be very useful in their own right. There are actually four different ways to invoke functions, but in this chapter you'll stick to the method that is most similar to Python.

As with Python, any objects passed into functions as parameters are passed by reference to functions. This means that if (within a function) you modify an object passed as a parameter to that function, you are actually modifying the object itself, not a copy of it:

```
js> var change = function(a) { a = 2; }
js> var a = 1;
js> change(a);
js> a;
2
```

There is actually a subtlety going on when you call a function. In addition to the parameters you've passed in, you will find two other variables in the function's scope: this and arguments. You'll learn about this later, but arguments is an array-like object mentioned earlier that contains the values of each of the parameters passed to the function regardless of how many parameters the function is defined to accept. It is array-like because although it has a .length property, it is not formally a JavaScript Array. You can use it like this to create a function which multiplies all its arguments together:

```
js> function multiply() {
js>     var i;
js>     var n = arguments.length;
js>     var result = 1;
js>     for (i = 0; i < n; i += 1) {
js>         result *= arguments[i];
js>     }
js>     return result;
js> }
js> multiply(2, 3);
6
```

Function Scope and Closures

In JavaScript, variables exist in the scope of the function in which they were defined. This means that even if you put some variables within a block (using curly braces), the variables will have the same scope as they would before or after the block. For example:

```
function a() {
    var a = 1;
    {
        a = 2;
        var b = 3;
    }
    alert(a); // will have the value 2
    alert(b); // will have the value 3
}
a();
```

Because variables have function scope, it makes sense to just declare them all at the start of the function rather than when you first use them. This helps avoid the problem of assigning a value to a variable that hasn't been declared with the var keyword and then finding it has accidentally been assigned to the global scope.

If a function in JavaScript is defined within another function, the inner function will still have access to the variables in the scope of the outer function, even after the outer function has returned.

As an example, think about how you would add an event handler to a button so that when it was clicked, an alert with a message would appear. Consider the following example where there are two buttons. The msg variable is assigned a value, and this is used as both an argument to the add_alert_handler() function and to show_alert(). Then the value of the message is changed.

```
var add_alert_handler = function (message) {
    return function(e) {
        alert(message);
    };
};

var show_alert(message) {
    alert(message);
};

var msg = 'Alert button clicked';
document.getElementById('alert_button1').onclick = add_alert_handler(msg);
document.getElementById('alert_button2').onclick = show_alert(msg);
msg = 'The message has changed';
```

When alert button 1 is clicked, the message displayed is "Alert button clicked," but when alert button 2 is clicked, the message is "The message has changed." The reason for this is simple. The function show_alert() has access to the msg variable's value directly so that when msg gets changed, so does the value it displays. Alert button 1, on the other hand, uses a closure, so the value of message that the function defined within add_alert_handler() has access to is a copy defined only in the scope of the returned add_alert_handler() function. When the msg variable is changed, the message variable in the closure remains unchanged.

If you are working with event handlers, you should always use closures or use a tool such as the YUI event library.

Objects

In JavaScript, objects are similar to dictionaries in Python. For example, suppose you want an object with two attributes, name and age. You could write this in two ways:

```
var object = new Object();
object.name = 'James';
object.age = 28;


object = {
    name: "James",
    age: 28
};
```

Both of these are identical because in JavaScript objects and dictionaries (or *hash tables* as they are called) are the same thing, but it is generally recommended you use the object literal notation to define objects (the example using the curly brackets) because it is clearer what is happening.

Regardless of how you create your objects, you can add new members or access existing members using either . or [ ].

```
js> object['name'] = 'Mike';
js> object.name;
'Mike'
js> object.name = 'Ben';
js> object['name'];
'Ben'
```

One point to be aware of is that quite a few words in JavaScript are reserved even though they aren't used. You can access object members whose names are not reserved words using the . notation. You can access any member regardless of the name using the [ ] notation.

As well as assigning strings and numbers to objects, you can also assign functions:

```
var simpleMaths = {
    add: function(a,b){
        return a+b;
    },
    subtract: function(a,b){
        return a-b;
    }
};
```

You can now use your object for calculations:

```
js> simpleMaths.add(1+1);
2
```

You can probably already see that this object is beginning to behave a bit like Python objects with methods.

this

`this` is available in any function; its value is bound at runtime, and what it refers to depends on the calling form of the function that was called. For ordinary functions that are not members of an object, `this` refers to the global namespace, that isn't particularly useful but when the function is bound to an object, `this` refers to the object itself. This is useful because it allows you to access the other members of the object from within the function. In the context of a method, `this` behaves like an implicit version of Python's `self`. Here's an example:

```
var simpleMaths = {
    _value: 0
    add: function(a){
        return this._value + a;
    },
    subtract: function(a){
        return this._value - b;
    }
};
```

This time the functions use a member variable to store a value, and then the methods add and subtract from that value. In Python any class member that starts with an _ character is considered private, and although the programmer is asked politely not to modify private members, the language itself doesn't prevent you from doing so.

In JavaScript, you can use closures to create member variables that genuinely are private:

```
var singleton = function () {
    var privateVariable;
    function privateFunction(x) {
        // do something with privateVariable
    }

    return {
        firstMethod: function (a, b) {
            // do something with privateVariable, privateFunction(),
            // this.firstMetod() or this.secondMethod()
        },
        secondMethod: function (c) {
            // do something with privateVariable, privateFunction(),
            // this.firstMetod() or this.secondMethod()
        }
    };
}();
```

In this example, privateVariable and privateFunction() are declared in the scope of the function, so because of closure, firstMethod() and secondMethod() have access to them even after the function returns. The brackets after the final curly brace call the function, so singleton is assigned the object returned by the function, but with each of the methods still having access to the private variable and function. This means you can do this to call firstMethod() or secondMethod():

```
js> singleton.firstMethod();
```

but you can't access singleton.privateVariable or singleton.privateFunction(). They are truly private in this case, unlike in Python.

Namespaces

Because variables in JavaScript are declared in the global namespace if they are not declared with the var keyword inside a function, it is fairly easy for programs that use the same names in the global namespace to change each other's variables accidentally.

One solution to this problem is to set up a single object as global for your application and take special care to create all your application's other objects and variables as members of that object. This is exactly what happens in YUI where all the functionality of the library is contained within the YAHOO namespace.

YUI recommends you choose an all-uppercase name for your namespace to minimize the chance of your name conflicting with an application that is already using that name. Say you wanted to create one called SIMPLESITE. You could do this:

```
var SIMPLESITE = {};
```

Now when you want to create objects global to your application, you can add them as members of the SIMPLESITE object like this:

```
SIMPLESITE['test'] = 1;
```

and access the `test` variable like this:

```
SIMPLESITE.test;
```

If you are writing a YUI component, you might like to use the `YAHOO.namespace()` function that sets up a namespace for you under the `YAHOO` namespace. You can also use it to set up nested namespaces if you specify the namespaces you want separated by a `.` character. For example:

```
// Creates a namespace for "myproduct2", and for "mysubproject1"
YAHOO.namespace("myproduct1.mysubproject1");
YAHOO.myproduct1.mysubproject1.Class1 = function(info) {
    // do something here...
};
```

Closures and anonymous functions can also be used to wrap an entire application in a function, keeping its namespace localized:

```
function() {
// local namespace declarations here.
}()
```

The last () invokes the function.

Inheritance

Inheritance is object-oriented code reuse, which is a useful pattern. In the classical model, objects are instances of classes, and classes inherit from other classes. In the prototypal model, objects inherit directly from other objects, and there are no classes. They do this with a secret link to the object being inherited from. In Mozilla browsers, you can actually access this secret link with __proto__, but this is nonstandard and shouldn't be used.

JavaScript actually has a third way to create an object that I didn't mention earlier: via an `object()` function. The function isn't part of JavaScript, but you can write it easily enough yourself like this:

```
function object(o) {
    function F() {}
    F.prototype = o;
    return new F();
}
```

When you use this function, you can specify which object your object should be linked to:

```
var oldObject = {
    firstMethod: function () {...},
    secondMethod: function () {...}
};

// create a new instance of the object
var newObject = object(oldObject);

// augment it
newObject.thirdMethod = function () {...};
```

```
// create a new instance of the augmented object
var thirdObject = object(newObject);

// this object has all three methods we've defined.
thirdObject.firstMethod();
```

This is very simple and doesn't need traditional classes. If you try to access a property of the object and the object lacks that property, each object in the inheritance chain will be tested, and if it has the property, that property will be used. Finally, if the member can't be found in any of the objects, then `undefined` will be returned. The name for this pattern is *linkage*.

This model has a few interesting consequences. For example, if you were to change the `firstMethod()` of `oldObject`, the change would be immediately visible in `newObject` and `thirdObject`. Changes to `thirdObject` will have no effect on `oldObject` or `newObject` because when their members are accessed, it is only the objects *they* are linked to that are searched.

If you were to change the `thirdMethod()` method of `thirdObject`, then `thirdObject.thirdMethod()` would behave differently from `newObject.thirdMethod()` because they now point to different functions. In this circumstance, deleting `thirdMethod()` from `thirdObject` won't actually delete the method entirely; it will just delete the function assigned to the name `thirdMethod` *for* `thirdObject`, but because `thirdObject` is still linked to `newObject` when you access `thirdObject.thirdMethod()`, the `thirdMethod()` from `newObject` will be called instead. This might surprise you if you don't understand that linkage works in only one direction. Incidentally, JavaScript doesn't impose any limits on the lengths of the inheritance chains you can create, but bear in mind that deep nested object hierarchies require lots of lookups so aren't as efficient as shallow hierarchies.

The process of adding new methods and members to an object is called *augmentation*.

Prototypes

You might be wondering what an object's secret link points to if you create an object that isn't explicitly linked to anything else. The answer is that it points to `Object.prototype` that contains a number of methods that all objects therefore inherit.

Similar prototypes exist for other types:

- `Object.prototype`
- `Array.prototype`
- `Function.prototype`
- `Number.prototype`
- `String.prototype`
- `Boolean.prototype`

and these can be used to modify how all objects of their type behave.

It isn't considered particularly good practice to modify the prototype, though, because it's possible that modifications made by one JavaScript application will affect how another application behaves.

When you iterate over an object in a `for` loop, you get all of its members, all of its parent's members, all of its parent's parent's members, and so on, right down to all the members of `Object.prototype`. This isn't always what you want, so JavaScript has a `hasOwnProperty()` function used like this:

```
for (var name in object) {
    if (object.hasOwnProperty(name)) {
        // within the loop, name is the key of the current member
        // object[name] is the current value

        // only names associated with members of the current object
        // will be available here
    }
}
```

This enables you to distinguish between the object you want to iterate over and its parent members.

JavaScript in HTML

It is generally not a good idea to include too much JavaScript in the body of an HTML document because it is harder to version control, compress, or validate with external tools. A much better way is to write JavaScript in a separate text file and include it in the HTML document like this:

```
<script src="/yourscript.js" />
```

You don't need to use `language="javascript"`; it is a leftover from a time when Microsoft wanted people to be able to use VBScript in browsers, and you don't actually need to use `type="text/javascript"` because the correct MIME type for JavaScript is `application/javascript` or `application/ecmascript` and because the browser trusts the MIME type set by the server that serves the document over what you specify in the `<script>` tag. That being said, if you want your XHTML to be valid, you should add the `type="text/javascript"` attribute.

Another leftover from the past is the way developers use comments to hide JavaScript embedded in HTML from old browsers. They might do this:

```
<script>
<!--
    alert("Script goes here.");
// -->
</script>
```

If browsers come across tags they don't understand, they are supposed to ignore the tag but continue processing other nested tags. This means very old browsers that didn't understand JavaScript would print the JavaScript as text, and the comments would force them to ignore the JavaScript instead. Nowadays, there are so few of these browsers left that you might just as well ignore the comments. If you include your JavaScript from separate files (as advised earlier), you avoid this problem anyway.

The Document Object Model

As well as understanding the basics of the JavaScript language, it is useful to understand a little bit about how browsers work and how they deal with web pages returned from Pylons using the Document Object Model (DOM).

The DOM is an API for HTML and XML documents. It provides a representation of the document, enabling you to modify its structure and content as well as the way the HTML elements are rendered. All the properties, methods, and events from the DOM are organized into objects so that they can be accessed from JavaScript. In fact, some of the functions you might use quite frequently when programming JavaScript actually come from the DOM and not the JavaScript language itself. For example, `setTimeout()`, `alert()`, `confirm()`, and `prompt(text, default)` are all DOM functions.

The vast majority of coding you will do for the web browser will use the DOM APIs, and although the JavaScript language itself is similar across browsers, the DOM APIs that different browsers expose can still be different in some frustrating ways. It is these differences more than anything else that make client-side web development in JavaScript difficult, and it is why you are strongly advised to use a framework such as YUI or JQuery to abstract away the complications.

The basis of the DOM is the parse tree generated when the browser parses the HTML. The top of the parse tree is the `#document` element. Beneath it the individual nodes are available, and any text between HTML tags is stored in a `#text` node. Internet Explorer ignores whitespace, whereas the W3C DOM standard includes it as text nodes. It's worth noting that the HTML elements are named with the uppercase version of their tag name, so `node.tagName` for the `<body>` node will be BODY.

The `#document` node can be accessed from JavaScript as the global `document`. The element representing the `<body>` tag is accessed as `document.body`, and the element representing the `<html>` tag is `document.documentElement`. This arguably isn't the best naming convention, but it is the one we are stuck with. It's worth noting that the browser might add elements such as `<head>` to the DOM tree even if they weren't present in the original HTML, so the DOM tree doesn't always exactly match the HTML source.

Tip Try entering `document.documentElement` into a Firebug console to double-check this. If you click the `<html>` object displayed as the return value in the console, Firebug will open its HTML view at that element. From there you can click the DOM tab to see all properties associated with that element. This is typical of the sort of useful functionality Firebug contains.

Each HTML element in the tree can be given an ID to uniquely identify it, which means the same ID cannot be used by two elements in the page. You can then access the DOM element for that node with this:

```
document.getElementById(id)
```

Notice that the last part of the method is `Id` and not `ID` as you might have expected. You can also access elements that have a `name` attribute like this:

```
document.getElementsByName(name)
```

Because there can be more than one element with the same name in the DOM tree, this function uses the plural `Elements` and returns an array. The `name` attribute should be used for form fields and for the names of windows and frames, and the `id` attribute should be used everywhere else.

You can also access the nodes beneath a particular node by the name of their tags like this:

```
node.getElementsByTagName(tagName)
```

It is also possible to access certain collections of DOM elements as properties of the `document` object, such as `document.forms`, `document.images`, and the Microsoft-specific `document.all`. Generally speaking, it is better to give the elements you are interested in a `name` or `id` attribute and just use the methods mentioned earlier rather than using the collections.

Navigating the DOM

Each element in the DOM beneath #document holds a number of references to other DOM elements so that you can easily navigate the DOM:

.firstChild: The first child element in the DOM structure

.lastChild: The last child element in the DOM structure

If there are no children, these properties will return null. If there is only one child node, they will both reference that child element:

.childNodes: Returns an array of all the child nodes or an empty array [ ] if there are no children

.parentNode: References the parent node

There are also properties for finding the next and previous sibling elements at the same level of the DOM; unsurprisingly, these are as follows:

.nextSibling: The next sibling node at the same level

.previousSibling: The next sibling node at the same level

Once again, these return null if there is no next or previous sibling.

With these properties in place, it is possible to define a function to walk the DOM tree and apply a particular function to each node. This is a handy pattern to use for DOM manipulation:

```
function walkTheDOM(node, func) {
    func(node);
    node = node.firstChild;
    while (node) {
        walkTheDOM(node, func);
        node = node.nextSibling;
    }
}
```

Once you've obtained the DOM element you want to manipulate, you will want to know what you can change. The short answer is that you are likely to be able to set using JavaScript anything that can be set as an HTML attribute. If you have installed Firebug, you can click the Inspect button and select the element you want to inspect with the mouse. Right-clicking the element in the HTML view and clicking Inspect in DOM Tab will show you all the properties available to edit. These include things such as title, alt, value, src, className (which couldn't be called class because it is a reserved word in JavaScript), and others. You can edit them directly in Firebug to see their effect. Rather than learning all the available attributes or trawling through the DOM specifications, it is generally easiest to look up available DOM properties in Firebug in this way, although bear in mind other browsers might be slightly different.

You can also easily change the CSS style of elements by changing the node's .style. This is another JavaScript object whose properties map to CSS styles. The only complication is that although CSS styles have names like font-family or background-color, their DOM counterparts are named in CamelCase, so the two examples become fontFamily and backgroundColor. As an example, here's how you would write a function using the earlier walkTheDOM() function to change the CSS border-style and border-width of all images that have an <a> tag as their parents, starting at the #document node:

```
walkTheDOM(document, function(node) {
    if (node.tagName === 'IMG' && node.parentNode.tagName === 'A'){
node.style.borderStyle = 'dotted';
node.style.borderWidth = '3px';
    }
})
```

Notice that the node names were uppercase; that we used the `===` comparison operator, which is the one that doesn't coerce types; and that the CSS `border-style` was set with the `borderStyle` member and the `border-width` was set with `borderWidth`.

Manipulating the DOM

The DOM also provides methods for manipulating the DOM. If you've ever done any XML DOM work using Python's `xml.dom.minidom` module, these methods will be familiar to you.

These methods create new DOM nodes that won't yet be linked to the DOM:

`document.createElement(tagName)`: Creates a tag of type `tagName`.

`document.createTextNode(text)`: Creates a text node.

`node.cloneNode()`: Clones an individual element on its own.

`node.cloneNode(true)`: Clones an element and all of its descendents.

These methods manipulate the DOM:

`node.appendChild(new)`: Adds the new node or tree of nodes as the last child of `node`

`node.removeChild(child)`: Removes the child node `child` from `node` and returns it

`node.insertBefore(new, sibling)`: Adds the new node or tree of nodes as a child of `node` but before the node `sibling`

`old.parentNode.replaceChild(new, old)`: Replaces the node `old` with the node or node tree `new`

Notice the syntax of the `replaceChild()` method is a little messy because it requires access to the parent node of the node being replaced. This is how the API works, though.

It can be quite cumbersome to programmatically build DOM structures using the methods outlined earlier, so most modern browsers also provide an `.innerHTML` attribute to each node. Any value set as the value of `.innerHTML` is parsed by the browser's HTML parser and converted into DOM nodes, replacing the node's existing children. This is really handy because you can generate complex fragments of HTML using Pylons, fetch them with the browser using Ajax, and then simply set the `.innerHTML` value of the node whose HTML should be changed. This is a technique you'll see later in this chapter.

The Event Model

The final piece of the JavaScript puzzle to learn about is the event model. As with the language itself and the DOM, Python programmers can usually guess what is going on enough to make their code work but then get very frustrated on the odd occasion when the code they've written doesn't behave in the way they expect.

There are two models for event handling in browsers: trickling down and bubbling up. In the *trickling-down* model, when an event occurs, it is passed to the `#document` node, and then it works its way down the DOM tree until finally it gets to the node where something happened. In the *bubbling-up* model, the event is first passed to the node at which something happened and *then* on to each of the parents in turn until the top of the DOM tree is reached. If you have many child nodes for which something might happen (say a load of images that might change in some way as the mouse moves over them), it would be expensive to add a handler to each image. Instead, using the bubbling-up approach, you could add just the one handler to the parent node of all the images, and it could respond to the event instead.

Whether tricking down or bubbling up is the best event model is a somewhat academic discussion because Microsoft supports only bubbling up, so if you want to write portable code, this is the event model you have to use. The differences between the browsers don't stop there. There are three different ways of adding an event to a node:

- `node["on"+type] = function() {}`
- `node.attachEvent("on"+type, f);`
- `node.addEventListener(type, f, false);`

All the browsers support the first method, but only Microsoft supports the second, and the W3C standard suggests the third method. The third method here always takes `false` as the third argument because this specifies that the handler should use the bubbling-up method, which is what you'd need for cross-browser code.

Unfortunately, the differences don't end there. In Microsoft browsers, the event itself is accessed as the global `event` object, whereas in the others it is passed as the first argument to the event handler.

Because of these differences, it is highly recommended you use a third-party JavaScript library for event handling because it will abstract away these differences. Here's a simple example using YUI events to attach a simple `onclick` handler to an element:

```
var elm = document.getElementById("button-1");
function fnCallback(e) {
    alert("Button 1 was clicked.");
}
YAHOO.util.Event.addListener(elm, "click", fnCallback);
```

Once you have written an event handler, you've installed it, and it has been fired, you might want to prevent the event from bubbling up to nodes higher up the DOM tree. Again, the way to do this differs across browsers, so it's best to do it with a framework like YUI. In the YUI case, you'd call `YAHOO.util.Event.stopPropogation(e)` where e is the event passed to the handler.

Despite that the event is no longer bubbling up, you might also want to prevent the default behavior. For example, clicking a link would navigate the user to a different page, and you might like to prevent this too. You can do so with `YAHOO.util.Event.preventDefault(e)` where again e is the event passed to the handler. YUI also provides a convenience method `YAHOO.util.Event.stopEvent(e)`, which stops the bubbling and prevents the default.

■**Caution** One point to be aware of is that in Internet Explorer 6 if you remove a DOM node without removing all the event handlers attached to it, a memory leak might occur, so you should always remove event listeners (by setting them to `null`) before you remove a DOM node so that the garbage collector can clean them up. Better still, use a JavaScript framework to handle this for you.

Same Origin Policy

An important point to be aware of when writing JavaScript code is the same origin policy, which is a security measure implemented by browsers to prevent a document or script loaded from one "origin" from getting or setting properties of a document from a different "origin." This means a script loaded from Example.com can't change variables in a script loaded from Example.org. The purpose of this is to prevent one site maliciously reading or modifying data presented to a user from another domain.

An *origin* in this context is a domain name accessed on a particular port with a particular protocol. If any of these is different, most browsers will treat them as different origins except Internet Explorer, which ignores the port and will thus treat two domain names with the same protocol as the same origin regardless of the port.

You can sometimes work around the same origin policy; one method is this: if the two origins you want to be able to communicate with each other are on the same second-level domain, you can change the JavaScript variable `document.domain` for both documents to that second-level domain. For example, if scripts from some.example.com and other.example.com both set `document.domain='example.com'`, they will be able to communicate. This works only if the two documents have a common sub-domain.

Browser Detection vs. Feature Detection

Because browsers often behave differently, it can be useful to try to work out which browser the user is using to visit a site and to write different JavaScript depending on the browser being used. There is, however, one very serious problem with this approach: browsers lie.

Browser manufacturers have found that lots of old code already exists to try to detect which browser is being used. As a result, when they release new browsers, much of this code wouldn't work correctly if the browser correctly identified itself because it wasn't coded for the new browser. As a result, browser manufacturers frequently identify themselves as other browsers. For example, Internet Explorer 7 identifies itself as `Mozilla/4.0 (compatible; MSIE 7.0b; Windows NT 6.0)`.

A much better approach is to simply test whether a browser has a particular feature you want to use and, if it does, to use it. That way, the code will work for any browser that has the feature, not just ones that pass your browser detection tests.

Of course, by using a JavaScript framework like YUI or JQuery, you isolate yourself from browser differences because they are handled by the framework, so you are less likely to need either browser or feature detection code.

Now that you've seen how JavaScript works in the browser, let's return once more to the SimpleSite application and use some YUI JavaScript to spruce up the application.

Adding Animation to the SimpleSite Flash Message

Although the flash message system you created in Chapter 8 works perfectly well, you can draw the users' attention to it better by adding some animation. In this section, you'll learn how to animate the message so that it appears after the page has loaded and fades away after the user clicks it. To achieve this, you'll need to use YUI's animation facilities.

YUI provides a number of animation classes. You'll need the following:

`YAHOO.util.Anim`: For animating any numeric attributes of an `HTMLElement`

`YAHOO.util.ColorAnim`: For animating attributes related to color

Since the animation appears only on the view pages, you need to add the JavaScript imports to the `derived/pages/view.html` template. Animation functionality requires both the YUI animation JavaScript file and the combined `yahoo-dom-event.js` JavaScript file. Add this def at the end of the `view.html` template:

```
<%def name="js()">
    <script src="/yui/2.6.0/yahoo-dom-event/yahoo-dom-event.js" ➥
type="text/javascript"></script>
    <script src="/yui/2.6.0/animation/animation-min.js" ➥
type="text/javascript"></script>
</%def>
```

You'll also need to update `base/index.html` with a new `js()` def so that this code gets called. At the top of the template, add the line in bold:

```
## -*- coding: utf-8 -*-

<%namespace name="navigation" file="/component/navigation.html" import="*" />\

<!DOCTYPE HTML PUBLIC "-//W3C//DTD HTML 4.01//EN"
"http://www.w3.org/TR/html4/strict.dtd">
<html>
<head>
    <title>${self.title()}</title>
    ${self.head()}
    ${self.js()}
</head>
<body>
```

At the bottom of the template, add this so that child templates that don't have a `js()` def will inherit an empty one:

```
<%def name="js()"></%def>
```

The flash element will start out invisible, so update the styles in `public/css/main.css` so the `#flash` style looks like this:

```
#flash {
    background: #ffc;
    padding: 5px;
    border: 1px dotted #000;
    margin-bottom: 20px;
    height: 0px;
    overflow: hidden; /* so we can animate from zero height */
}
```

Next you need to write the JavaScript function to make the flash message appear. Add this to the bottom of the `js()` def you just created in the view.html template after the `<script>` tags:

```
% if session.has_key('flash'):
<script type="text/javascript">
YAHOO.util.Event.onAvailable(
    'flash',
    function() {
        var a = new YAHOO.util.Anim(
            YAHOO.util.Dom.get('flash'), {
                height: {
                    to: 16
```

```
                    }
                },
                0.4,
                YAHOO.util.Easing.easeIn
            );
            a.animate();
            YAHOO.util.Event.on('flash', 'click', function() {
                    var b = new YAHOO.util.Anim(
                        YAHOO.util.Dom.get('flash'), {
                            opacity: {
                                to: 0
                            },
                        },
                        0.4
                    );
                    b.onComplete.subscribe(function(){
                        YAHOO.util.Dom.setStyle('flash', 'display', 'none');
                    });
                    b.animate();
            }
        )
    }
);
</script>
% endif
```

Notice that you use the `onAvailable` event that is triggered as soon as the HTML element is available to start the animation as soon as possible. As the animation is running, you also install an event handler to make the flash message gracefully disappear by changing the CSS `opacity` until it is 0.

Now that the code is in place, try editing and saving a page. You should see the yellow flash box appear gradually with its height growing until it reaches its full size. Then, when you click the message, it fades out and disappears. Unfortunately, Internet Explorer doesn't understand the CSS `opacity` tag, so the fading out won't work on Internet Explorer.

Ajax

By now you should have a good understanding of JavaScript, the DOM, and event handling and have some understanding of how to use YUI. Turn your attention to one of the most useful JavaScript techniques: Ajax.

Ajax is a technique that allows the browser to communicate asynchronously with the server. This means you can fetch data from the browser and use JavaScript to update part of a web page without needing to refresh the page.

Using Ajax would be useful in one area of the SimpleSite application in particular: the edit form. At the moment when you edit a page or section, it is possible to enter a value into the `before` field for a page that isn't in that section. The FormEncode validation picks up the error, but it would be better if the `before` field was a drop-down list containing values automatically populated with pages or subsections of the section currently selected in the section drop-down list. Figure 15-4 shows how this would look.

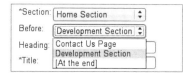

Figure 15-4. *The Before drop-down list, populated using Ajax*

This pattern of populating one drop-down list from the values of another using Ajax applies to any situation where you have hierarchical data. First you need to listen for any onchange events from the parent drop-down list. Then you need to contact the server to fetch the HTML for a new before field and replace the old one.

Let's get started. First you need a function that will return the appropriate values of before for a given section ID. Add this as a static method to model.Nav in model/__init__.py. The exclude option allows you to exclude the current page; after all, it wouldn't make a lot of sense to have a page or section appear before itself:

```
class Nav:

    .. existing methods

    @staticmethod
    def get_before_options(section, exclude=None):
        nav_q = meta.Session.query(Nav)
        query = nav_q.filter_by(section=section)
        if exclude is not None:
            query = query.filter(Nav.id != exclude)
        return [(nav.id, nav.name) for nav in query.all()]
```

In the page controller's edit method, set the value of c.before_options:

```
def edit(self, id=None):
    if id is None:
        abort(404)
    page_q = meta.Session.query(model.Page)
    page = page_q.filter_by(id=id).first()
    if page is None:
        abort(404)
    values = {
        'name': page.name,
        'path': page.path,
        'section': page.section,
        'before': page.before,
        'title': page.title,
        'heading': page.heading,
        'content': page.content
    }
    c.before_options = model.Nav.get_before_options(page.section, page.id)
    c.before_options.append(['', '[At the end]'])
    return htmlfill.render(render('/derived/page/edit.html'), values)
```

Notice the second line in bold where an extra option is added. This allows a user to specify that the page should be at the end of the section.

You'll also need to make a similar change to the section controller's edit() method:

```
def edit(self, id=None):
    if id is None:
        abort(404)
    section_q = meta.Session.query(model.Section)
    section = section_q.filter_by(id=id).first()
    if section is None:
        abort(404)
    values = {
        'name': section.name,
        'path': section.path,
        'section': section.section,
        'before': section.before,
    }
    c.before_options = model.Nav.get_before_options(section.section, section.id)
    c.before_options.append(['', '[At the end]'])
    return htmlfill.render(render('/derived/section/edit.html'), values)
```

Of course, the page and section controller new() actions also require a similar change. Notice that this time the before key isn't deleted from the values dictionary, just set to contain an empty string. Update the page controller's new() action to look like this:

```
def new(self):
    values = {}
    values.update(request.params)
    if values.has_key('before') and values['before'] == u'None':
        values['before'] = ''
    c.before_options = model.Nav.get_before_options(values.get('section', 0))
    c.before_options.append(['', '[At the end]'])
    return htmlfill.render(render('/derived/page/new.html'), values)
```

Update the section controller's new() action to look like this:

```
def new(self):
    values = {}
    values.update(request.params)
    if values.has_key('before') and values['before'] == u'None':
        values['before'] = ''
    c.before_options = model.Nav.get_before_options(values.get('section', 0))
    c.before_options.append(['', '[At the end]'])
    return htmlfill.render(render('/derived/section/new.html'), values)
```

Now update the derived/nav/fields.html template to replace the existing before field with this:

```
${h.field(
    "Before",
    h.select(
        "before",
        id='before',
        options = c.before_options,
        selected_values=[],
    ),
)}
```

The before field now correctly displays the possible options for the section selected when the form is rendered, but you still need to add the JavaScript to detect when the section value changes and trigger the Ajax calls.

You'll write a JavaScript function called `callAjax()` that takes the URL for the Ajax call as the first argument, the ID of the field containing the value you want to submit as the second, and the name of the element to take the result as the third. Add this to the bottom of the `derived/nav/fields.html` file:

```
<%def name="js()">
    <script src="/yui/2.6.0/yahoo-dom-event/yahoo-dom-event.js" ➥
type="text/javascript"></script>
    <script src="/yui/2.6.0/connection/connection-min.js" ➥
type="text/javascript"></script>

    <script type="text/javascript">
    function callAjax(url, field, replace){
        var callback = {
            success: function(o) {
                YAHOO.util.Dom.get(replace).innerHTML = o.responseText;
            },
            failure: function(o) {
                alert("Failed to retrieve required information.");
            }
        }
        url = url +'?selected='+YAHOO.util.Dom.get(field).value;
        var transaction=YAHOO.util.Connect.asyncRequest('GET', url, callback, null);
    }
    </script>
</%def>
```

Notice that this code relies on the connection JavaScript library being in place before it is parsed. It also requires the yahoo-dom-event library. Sometimes you will need to access objects from the calling function's scope in the `success()` and `failure()` callbacks. You can do this in YUI by specifying an `argument` list as a member of the earlier `callback` object, in addition to the `success` and `failure` callbacks used in the previous example. The arguments you specify can then be accessed as `o.argument` in the callback functions. See the YUI Event documentation for an example.

Add an `onchange` argument to the `h.select()` helper for the `section` field in `derived/nav/fields.html` so it looks like this:

```
${h.field(
    'Section',
    h.select(
        "section",
        id='section',
        selected_values=[],
        options=c.available_sections,
        onchange="callAjax('%s', 'section', 'before'); return false;"%(
            h.url_for(controller="nav", action="before_field_options")
        ),
    ),
    required=True
)}
```

This code triggers an Ajax call to the `before_field_options()` action. If the call is successful, the `before` field's options are replaced with the HTML fragment from the Pylons controller; otherwise, a JavaScript alert box displays an error message.

Next you need to add the `before_field_options()` action to the nav controller to return the new options with the correct values for the section ID sent in the Ajax call. The new action requires the following import:

```
from webhelpers.html.tags import HTML
```

and looks like this:

```
def before_field_options(self):
    result = []
    for id, label in model.Nav.get_before_options(request.params.getone➥
('selected')):
        result.append(HTML.option(label, value=id))
    result.append(HTML.option('[At the end]', value=''))
    return u''.join(result)
```

Finally, you need to update the `edit.html` and `new.html` templates for both the section and the page. Update `derived/page/edit.html`, `derived/section/edit.html`, `derived/page/new.html`, and `derived/section/new.html` by adding the following import and def at the end of the files:

```
<%namespace file="/derived/nav/fields.html" name="navfields" import="js"/>

<%def name="js()">
    ${parent.js()}
    ${navfields.js()}
</%def>
```

This pulls in the `js()` def from the `derived/nav/fields.html` file and adds the contents of its `head()` def.

At this point, you are ready to test the updated application. Try to edit a page or section; as you change the section you want the item to appear in, an Ajax call is made, and the correct values of `before` for that section are set automatically.

Debugging Ajax Requests

You can use two tools to debug Ajax requests. The first is the Pylons interactive debugger. If you refer to Chapter 4, you'll recall that any time an error occurs during a request when Pylons is in debug mode, a header called `X-Debug-URL` is added to the response containing a URL. The URL is also printed on the console if you are using the `paster serve` command to serve the Pylons application. If you visit that URL, you will be able to interactively debug the request that caused the error in the same way you debug normal problems in a Pylons application.

On the client side, Firebug is once again the tool of choice. Its console can help you determine any errors that occurred. As an example, the Net tab in Figure 15-5 shows the requests occurring when I edit page 2. The first GET request is to load page 2. The second request is the Ajax request that occurred when I change the `section` select field. It also shows you how long each request took; this can be very useful in determining how to optimize your Pylons applications, as you'll see later in the chapter. When you hover your mouse over a request (as I have done on the second request), Firebug shows you the whole request URL. Clicking the + icon shows you the HTTP headers for the request and response, so if an error occurs on an Ajax call, you can also find out the debug URL from the headers displayed by Firebug.

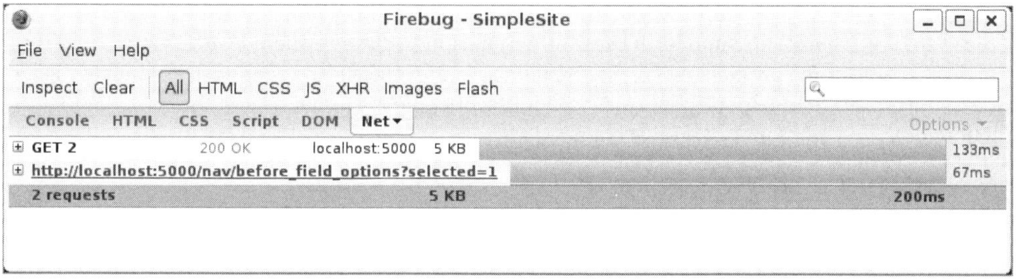

Figure 15-5. *The Net tab in Firebug showing an Ajax request*

JSON

Although returning HTML from a Pylons controller and using a node's `.innerHTML` property to update its content is a perfectly acceptable way of using Ajax, you should be aware of another useful technique.

Instead of taking the approach just described, you could have simply returned the labels and values for the `before` field from the Pylons controller action and assembled the HTML nodes using DOM manipulation with JavaScript in the browser. If you chose to take this approach, you would have to decide what format you are going to use to send the data in, and the most sensible choice would be a format known as JSON.

JSON stands for JavaScript Object Notation and is quite simply just a string of text written in the same way you would define a JavaScript object using the object literal notation you saw earlier. For example, a JSON data structure representing the `before` field's values might look like this:

```
{
    options: [
        {id: 4, value: "SVN Page"},
        {id: 5, value: "Development Page"},
        {id: "", value: "[At the end]"}
    ]
}
```

You'll notice that this looks like the type of data structure you might create in Python, so much so that Pylons provides an `@jsonify` decorator that you can use on a controller action, which will turn an ordinary Python data structure made up of lists, dictionaries, strings, and numbers into a JSON string.

Add a new action to the nav controller to return a JSON data structure for the `before` field. You'll need to import the `@jsonify` decorator at the top of the file:

```
from pylons.decorators import jsonify
```

Now add the controller action like this:

```
@jsonify
def before_field_json(self):
    result = {
        'options': [
            dict(id=id, value=value) for value, id in model.Nav.get_before_options(
                request.params.getone('selected'))
        ]
    }
    result['options'].append({'id': u'[At the end]', 'value': u''})
    return result
```

When the Ajax call is made to this action, the Python dictionary returned is converted to JSON by the @jsonify decorator (which itself uses the simplejson package installed with Pylons), and this is made available in the JavaScript success() callback as o.responseText. Let's use Firebug to log its value to the console. Update the derived/nav/fields.html file's js() def so that the callAjax() function looks like this. Lines that have changed are in bold.

```
function callAjax(url, field, replace){
    var callback = {
        success: function(o) {
            console.log(o.responseText);
         },
        failure: function(o) {
            alert("Failed to retrieve required information.");
        }
    }
    url = url +'?selected='+YAHOO.util.Dom.get(field).value;
    var transaction = YAHOO.util.Connect.asyncRequest('GET', url, callback, null);
}
```

The console object is provided by Firebug so won't be present on browsers without Firebug. This means using the console object is appropriate only for debugging, and you should always remove all references to it in production code.

Also, update the onchange argument for the select field so that when its value changes, it calls the new before_field_json() action:

```
${h.field(
    'Section',
    h.select(
        "section",
        id='section',
        selected_values=[],
        options=c.available_sections,
        onchange="callAjax('%s', 'section', 'before'); return false;"%(
            h.url_for(controller="nav", action="before_field_json")
        ),
    ),
    required=True
)}
```

If you edit a page or section, enable Firebug, and change the section field to Home Section, you should see this in the Firebug console:

```
{"options": [{"id": "Contact Us Page", "value": 2}, {"id": "Development Section",➥
"value": 3}, {"id": "Home", "value": 6}, {"id": "[At the end]", "value": ""}]}
```

This is the string the @jsonify decorator returned, but to be useful, it needs to be turned into a JavaScript object. The safest way to do this is with a JSON parser like the one included with YUI, but since JSON is also valid JavaScript source code, you can also use JavaScript's eval() function to simply evaluate it. As you'll see later, though, using eval() has some potential security implications.

Update the js() def in the derived/nav/fields.html file to look like this:

```
<%def name="js()">
    <script src="/yui/2.6.0/yahoo-dom-event/yahoo-dom-event.js" ➥
type="text/javascript"></script>
    <script src="/yui/2.6.0/connection/connection-min.js" ➥
type="text/javascript"></script>
    <script src="/yui/2.6.0/json/json-min.js" type="text/javascript"></script>
```

```
<script type="text/javascript">
function callAjax(url, field, replace){
    var callback = {
        success: function(o) {
            var parsed_options = YAHOO.lang.JSON.parse(o.responseText);
            var evaluated_options = eval('('+o.responseText+')');
            console.log(parsed_options);
            console.log(evaluated_options);
          },
        failure: function(o) {
            alert("Failed to retrieve required information.");
        }
    }
    url = url +'?selected='+YAHOO.util.Dom.get(field).value;
    var transaction = YAHOO.util.Connect.asyncRequest('GET', url, ➥
callback, null);
    }
    </script>
</%def>
```

Once again, the lines that have changed are in bold. If you refresh the page and change the section, you'll see something like this in the Firebug console:

```
Object id=Contact Us Page value=2
Object id=Contact Us Page value=2
```

Both methods produce the same result.

You might be wondering why when evaluating the JSON string with the eval() function you had to add a bracket to the beginning and end of the string. The answer is that it forces JavaScript to unconditionally treat the string as an expression. If you try to call eval() with an empty object string, as in "{}", it returns undefined, which clearly isn't what you want. Adding the parentheses fixes the problem. As it happens, array literals such as "[]" work fine even without the parentheses, but it is best to use them. Here's an example demonstrating these effects:

```
js> eval("{}")
js> YAHOO.lang.isUndefined(eval("{}"))
true
js> eval("({})")
Object
js> eval("[]")
[]
```

The reason you should always use a JSON parser rather than eval() is that you never quite know whether someone might have found a way to compromise your application to get some illegal characters into the JSON your application has generated. For example, imagine that if instead of the JSON it does generate, the before_field_json() action returned "{options: alert (document.cookies)}". With the eval('('+o.responseText+')') technique, the alert() function gets called, and any cookies the application uses appear in an alert window. Now imagine that rather than calling alert(), a hacker calls a different function. They could potentially get hold of your user's cookies and set up their own browsers with their cookies. The Pylons application would think that the hacker was actually the real user. Of course, lots of other exploits are possible, but the point is that if a hacker can compromise your JSON, an attack is possible.

```
js> eval("({options: alert(document.cookies)})")
[The alert window is displayed]
```

On the other hand, if you use a JSON parser, the JSON will not pass as valid, and a simple JavaScript error will be raised without doing any damage except causing the code that updates the before field not to be called.

```
js> YAHOO.lang.JSON.parse("{options: alert(document.cookies)}")
SyntaxError: parseJSON
```

For this reason, you should *always* use a JSON parser, just to be safe. With this firmly established, let's remove the lines that refer to the Firebug `console` object and finish updating the `js()` def in the `derived/nav/fields.html` file so that it looks like this:

```
<%def name="js()">
    <script src="/yui/2.6.0/yahoo-dom-event/yahoo-dom-event.js" ➥
type="text/javascript"></script>
    <script src="/yui/2.6.0/connection/connection-min.js" ➥
type="text/javascript"></script>
    <script src="/yui/2.6.0/json/json-min.js" type="text/javascript"></script>

    <script type="text/javascript">
    function callAjax(url, field, replace){
        var callback = {
            success: function(o) {
                var parsed_options = YAHOO.lang.JSON.parse(o.responseText);
                var before = document.getElementById(replace);
                // Remove current options
                while(before.hasChildNodes() === true)
                {
                    before.removeChild(before.childNodes[0]);
                }
                // Add new options
                for (var i=0; i<parsed_options.options.length; i++) {
                    var new_option = document.createElement('option');
                    new_option.text = parsed_options.options[i].id;
                    new_option.value =  parsed_options.options[i].value;
                    before.appendChild(new_option);
                }
            },
            failure: function(o) {
                alert("Failed to retrieve required information.");
            }
        }
        url = url +'?selected='+YAHOO.util.Dom.get(field).value;
        var transaction = YAHOO.util.Connect.asyncRequest('GET', url, ➥
callback, null);
    }
    </script>
</%def>
```

If you test the example, you should find it works exactly as it did when you used the `.innerHTML` technique instead. Which technique you choose to use in your own applications is up to you.

Reducing Page Load Time

If you are including a large number of CSS or JavaScript files in your pages, the length of time it takes to load a page can begin to become significant. The vast majority of the time it isn't the speed of your Pylons application that affects how fast your application appears to your users. Much more important usually is the speed with which the browser can pull in and process all the files that will need to be loaded and rendered to display the finished web page.

You can generally reduce page load times fairly easily in the following ways:

Compressing text files: Transmitting less data takes less time. In Chapter 16, I'll show how you can write some middleware to compress text data automatically.

Concatenating text files: An overhead is involved in each HTTP request made, so the fewer requests the browser makes, the better.

Putting multiple icons or image fragments in a single image: You can then use the same image lots of times throughout the page and use CSS to choose which part of the image you display in each place. Again, the fewer images you have to fetch, the fewer HTTP requests are needed, and the faster the page should load.

Cache data: If the browser can fetch a file from its cache, it doesn't have to fetch it from the network, so that will be faster. Pylons automatically supports E-Tag caching for the static files it serves, which means that browsers should fetch a new copy only if the E-Tag changes. This can speed things up a little, but since the browser has to make a request to see whether the E-Tag has changed, this isn't as effective for small files as it is for large ones.

Some other less obvious things can affect page load time too:

Number of DNS queries: The more different domains (or subdomains) that your page loads information from, the more DNS lookups the browser will have to do to discover the IP addresses associated with those domains. Depending on the number of name servers involved, it can take up to a second or more for each DNS lookup. Of course, the browser will cache the DNS information, but it is worth remembering that the first page load will be quicker if all the resources are served from the same domain. This is particularly worth remembering for applications using Routes' subdomain feature because you probably wouldn't want to serve static resources from lots of different subdomains if you could serve them all from the same domain.

Minimizing JavaScript: Writing JavaScript usually involves adding quite a lot of whitespace. If you use a JavaScript minification tool, it can strip whitespace and comments and also rename local variables to ones that use fewer characters. Again, fewer characters means faster transfer time. One JavaScript minifier is the YUI compressor written in Java and available from `http://developer.yahoo.com/yui/compressor/`.

Positioning of CSS and JavaScript within HTML: CSS files should be included with the `<link>` tag as close to the top of the `<head>` as possible. This gives browsers all the information they need about the styles as early as possible, which in turn means they can start rendering the page sooner. By contrast, JavaScript `<script>` tags should go as close to the bottom of the `<body>` as possible because browsers typically won't start downloading other resources like images while script downloads are in place, so it makes sense to have them later.

Knowing which of these problems is affecting your site the most is very tricky without a detailed analysis of how long each component takes to load. Luckily, there are tools to help with this. As you saw earlier in the chapter, Firebug's Net tab displays the time taken for each request as well as the overall page load time, so this will give you a good indication of where files are being requested more than they need to be. If you need detailed information to optimize page load performance, you should download another Firefox plug-in called YSlow which can give you a detailed performance analysis. YSlow relies on Firebug for some of its functionality. You can get YSlow from `http://developer.yahoo.com/yslow/`, and if you plan on using it, the help page at `http://developer.yahoo.com/yslow/help/` is very useful.

Summary

Once again, I covered a lot in this chapter, from CSS grids to prototypal inheritance, DOM manipulation, events, and Ajax. The appropriate use of CSS, JavaScript, and Ajax can really improve your application and allow you to build interfaces that aren't possible with traditional static HTML.

There is plenty more in the YUI library, and I strongly encourage you to investigate it. I hope that the discussion in this chapter goes some way toward giving you the knowledge you'll need to begin reading the YUI documentation in earnest. As well as good documentation and plenty of examples, there are also some very handy A4 cheat sheets for each component. Visit `http://developer.yahoo.com/yui` for more information, but don't forget that Pylons works equally well with other frameworks like JQuery.

That's all for Part 2 of the book. In Part 3, you'll begin looking at expert Pylons topics starting with a discussion of the Web Server Gateway Interface, which is at the core of Pylons' architecture.

PART 3

■■■

Expert Pylons

■ ■ ■

# CHAPTER 16

The Web Server Gateway Interface (WSGI)

The Web Server Gateway Interface is a Python standard created in 2003 by Philip J. Eby and the Python web community. Back in 2003 Python suffered from a very fragmented web framework community where applications written with code from one framework wouldn't run on the server component from a different framework. The Web Server Gateway Interface standard (known as WSGI and pronounced "wizgy" by those in the Python community) was designed to change that and enable a degree of cross-framework interoperability.

In the first part of this chapter, you'll learn how a simple WSGI application works, how you can use WSGI applications as Pylons controllers, how WSGI servers work, and how WSGI leads to new classes of components called *middleware*.

Internally Pylons relies on middleware components to provide some of its core functionality, so in the second part of the chapter, I'll explain the different ways of writing WSGI middleware, and you'll develop your own Gzip middleware (mentioned in the previous chapter) for compressing your Pylons projects' CSS and JavaScript code.

In the normal course of Pylons development, you don't need to write WSGI applications because you will use Pylons controllers and actions instead. You don't need to know how to develop WSGI middleware yourself either because Pylons already provides all the middleware you need as well as specific APIs that are much easier to work with than their underlying WSGI APIs (for example, those exposed by the request and response objects). For these reasons, you might want to skip the "Writing WSGI Middleware" section in the second half of the chapter if it doesn't apply to you yet and move straight onto the next chapter at that point. You should still read "Introducing WSGI" in this chapter, though.

Introducing WSGI

The WSGI standard defines three different classes of component: *applications*, *servers*, and *middleware*. I'll cover each of these types of components in turn and explain how they are relevant to a Pylons application.

■**Tip** If you want to know the details of WSGI programming, there is no substitute for reading its formal specification, which is called Python Enhancement Proposal 333 and is at `http://www.python.org/dev/peps/pep-0333/`.

WSGI Applications

You'll remember from all the way back in Chapter 3 that at its heart Pylons deals with the HTTP protocol, that communication with the browser involves a request and a response, and that all the HTTP request information, together with information about the server, is encapsulated in a CGI-like environment dictionary.

In Pylons, a controller action to handle a request and return some plain text might look like this:

```
def hello(self):
    response.status = '200 OK'
    response.content_type = 'text/plain'
    return "Hello World!"
```

The equivalent WSGI application would look like this:

```
def hello(environ, start_response):
    start_response('200 OK', [('Content-type','text/plain')])
    return ["Hello World!"]
```

Technically speaking, setting the response status to '200 OK' in the Pylons example isn't necessary because it is the default, but I've added it to the example to emphasize the similarity between the two cases. Let's compare each of the examples by their main features:

Request information: In Pylons, all the request information is available as a global object called request. In the WSGI application, the request information is all contained in the environ dictionary passed as the first positional parameter to the WSGI application. In Pylons, request. environ is actually the same dictionary that would be passed to a WSGI application as the environ argument.

HTTP response status: In Pylons, the status is set by changing the status attribute of the global response object. In a WSGI application, it is set by passing a string as the first argument to the start_response() function, which itself is passed into the WSGI application as its second positional parameter.

HTTP headers: In Pylons, common HTTP headers such as Content-Type have their own attributes that you can set on the global response object. Others have to be added to response. headers, as in response.headers['X-Some-Header'] = 'value'. In a WSGI application, the headers are passed as the second argument to start_response() as a list of tuples where the first string in a tuple is a string containing the header name and the second is a string containing the value. Here's an example: [('Content-type', 'text/plain'), ('X-Some-Header', 'value')].

The response: In Pylons, the response is simply the string returned from the action. If you return Unicode from a Pylons controller action, it will be encoded into UTF-8 automatically. In a WSGI application, it is an iterable, which should yield strings when it is iterated over. A list made up of strings is an example of an iterable that fulfils this criterion. The WSGI response cannot contain Unicode. Any Unicode must be encoded to an encoding such as UTF-8 before it is used in an iterable.

On the surface, the WSGI application is really fairly similar to the Pylons controller action except it doesn't use the simplifying global variables request and response that Pylons provides; however, you need to be aware of a couple of complications when writing WSGI applications, which Pylons takes care of for you when you use a controller action:

- The `start_response()` callable that gets passed to the WSGI application as its second argument can be called only *once* (except in rare circumstances when an error occurs, as you'll see in the "Handling Errors" section later in the chapter).

- `start_response()` *must* be called *before* the application returns any response data.

- After being called, `start_response()` returns a writable object that can be used to write response data directly without having to return it as an iterable from a WSGI application.

Here is the same example you saw earlier but written to use the writable object returned from `start_response()`:

```
def hello(environ, start_response):
    writable = start_response('200 OK', [('Content-type','text/html')])
    writable("Hello ")
    return ["World!"]
```

Here the first part of the output was written via the writable returned by `start_response()`, and the rest was returned normally by returning the iterable as before.

■**Caution** This way of returning response data to the browser was included in the specification because some servers weren't capable of buffering data returned in any other way. It is really considered very bad practice to use this approach; in fact, this functionality may be removed in a future version of the WSGI specification because it significantly complicates the writing of middleware components.

Using Instances of Classes

So far, you've seen only how to write WSGI applications as functions, but they can also be written as iterators, as generators, or as class instances. Writing applications as class instances can be useful if you want to write a more complex WSGI application. Take a look at this example:

```
class Hello(object):

    def __call__(self, environ, start_response):
        start_response('200 OK', [('Content-type','text/plain')])
        return ['Hello World!']

hello = Hello()
```

The `Hello` class itself isn't a WSGI application, but if you think about how the `hello` instance will behave, you'll realize that when it is called, it accepts two positional parameters; it calls `start_response()` and returns an iterable, which in this case is just a list with one string. These are exactly the conditions outlined in the previous section to describe how a WSGI application should behave, so the class *instance* is a valid WSGI application. This approach is very handy for two main reasons:

- It provides a way to group related WSGI applications together by having the __call__() dispatch the request to different methods.

- It provides a way to configure an application by passing arguments to the __init__() method.

Let's see an example demonstrating these two uses:

```
class Application(object):
    def __init__(self, name):
        self.name = name

    def __call__(self, environ, start_response):
        if environ['PATH_INFO'] == '/hello':
            return self.hello(environ, start_response)
        elif environ['PATH_INFO'] == '/goodbye':
            return self.goodbye(environ, start_response)
        else:
            start_response('404 Not Found', [('Content-type','text/html')])
            return ['Not found']

    def hello(self, environ, start_response):
        start_response('200 OK', [('Content-type','text/html')])
        return ['Hello %s'%(self.name)]

    def goodbye(self, environ, start_response):
        start_response('200 OK', [('Content-type','text/html')])
        return ['Goodbye %s'%(self.name)]

app = Application('Harry')
```

In this example, you can see that the method that is executed depends on the path in the URL and that the text returned from the two methods depends on the name that was given when the WSGI application was created. You might notice that this is beginning to look like an ordinary Pylons controller, and as you'll find out in the next section, it turns out that Pylons is designed to be able to run WSGI applications like this as Pylons controllers.

■**Caution** It is easy to fall into a trap when using class instances in this way as WSGI applications. You might be tempted to pass variables between the class methods by assigning values to `self` and then calling other methods. This would be fine if you were using the application only outside of a multithreaded environment or if you re-created the application on each request, but in a multithreaded environment there would be no guarantee that the value attached to `self` in one method call would be the same value that was used in the next method call, because another thread of execution might have taken place in between.

If that sounds a bit confusing, just remember the simple rule that you should never set or change a variable assigned to `self` in a WSGI application outside the `__init__()` method.

This isn't a problem in a Pylons controller because Pylons controller instances are re-created on each request.

WSGI in Pylons Controllers

If you look at a Pylons controller, you will see it is derived from `BaseController`, which is defined in your project's `lib/base.py` file. The `BaseController` class is itself derived from `pylons.controllers.WSGIController`, but in fact Pylons is designed so that any valid WSGI application can be used as a controller. This means you don't actually need to use a Pylons controller class in your controller at all; any WSGI application will work as long as you give it the same name your controller would have had so that Pylons can find it.

For example, if you added a `hello` controller to a Pylons application by running the `paster controller hello` command, you could replace the entire contents of the `hello.py` file with this:

```
def HelloController(environ, start_response):
    start_response('200 OK', [('Content-Type','text/plain')])
    return ['Hello World!']
```

Pylons will call your custom WSGI application in the same way as it would call a normal WSGIController instance. To test the example you'll need to visit a URL which will resolve to the controller such as /hello/index or add a new route so that the controller can be accessed as /hello:

```
map.connect('/hello', controller='hello')
```

You will still have all the session, debugging, and error-handling facilities a normal Pylons controller has. The only difference is that although Pylons would instantiate a new WSGIController on each request, it will assume that any WSGI application you use either is a function (such as the HelloController() function earlier) or is already instantiated and ready to handle multiple requests at once. This means if you want to write a WSGI application as a class and want it to be used as a controller, the class *instance* would have to be named HelloController, not the class itself. Here's an example:

```
class HelloControllerApplication:
    def __call__(self, environ, start_response):
        start_response('200 OK', [('Content-Type','text/plain')])
        return ['Hello World!']

HelloController = HelloControllerApplication()
```

Pylons avoids this problem with controllers derived from pylons.controllers.WSGIController because it automatically creates a new controller instance on each request before it calls it.

Being able to mount WSGI applications as Pylons controllers is very useful because it gives you the basis for integrating Pylons applications with third-party WSGI-enabled software such as MoinMoin or Mercurial. As an example, it is perfectly possible to mount an entire Trac instance as a Pylons controller. This has the benefit that Trac will be able to use the same authentication and authorization system that you are using with Pylons and will also benefit from Pylons' automatic error documents and interactive debugger.

There may be occasions where you don't want to replace your entire controller with a WSGI application but simply want to run a WSGI application from within a particular controller action. For example, if you had a WSGI application called wsgi_app, you could call it from the index() controller action like this:

```
# WSGI application
def wsgi_app(environ, start_response):
    start_response('200 OK',[('Content-type','text/html')])
    return ['<html>\n<body>\nHello World!\n</body>\n</html>']

# Pylons controller
class RunwsgiController(BaseController):

    def index(self, environ, start_response):
        return wsgi_app(environ, start_response)
```

Notice that the WSGI objects environ and start_response are automatically passed to the Pylons controller action if it has their names as arguments. This is another feature of the Pylons dispatch designed to make working with WSGI applications easier, but you'll remember from Chapter 9 that this is why you shouldn't choose routing variables with the same names.

Not all WSGI applications can be run as or from Pylons controllers. Some of the problems are as follows:

- Python cannot support more than one version of the same library in the same interpreter at the same time, so the WSGI application cannot use a different version of one of the libraries Pylons is already using.

- Not all WSGI applications are written correctly to be mounted at a URL other than /, so when you use them as part of a Pylons controller at a URL such as /controller/action, they might break.

- Not all WSGI applications are compatible with the WSGI middleware components Pylons uses. For example, they might not expect the presence of error documents middleware that could get in the way of some of their responses.

Despite these potential difficulties, a lot of WSGI applications will run from within Pylons, and this can lead to interesting new ways of using those applications.

WSGI Servers

Now that you've seen what WSGI applications are and how, in many cases, they can be run from a Pylons controller, it is time to turn your attention to what happens with WSGI servers. Luckily, you are very unlikely to have to write a WSGI server yourself because WSGI is now an established standard and almost all the common web servers are now WSGI compatible. Nevertheless, it is still useful to know how they work since their interface forms the basis for WSGI middleware.

A WSGI server must do a few things. First, it must prepare the environ dictionary and start_response() callable and pass them as the first and second positional parameters to a WSGI application. The WSGI application always calls the start_response() callable to set the status and HTTP headers before it starts returning data (as you've seen), so the server has to assemble start_response() in such a way that, when it is called, the status and headers get sent to the web browser. You'll remember that according to the specification, WSGI applications are allowed to use the writable returned from start_response(), so servers must also assemble start_response() to return a compatible object.

It is also the server's responsibility to set certain WSGI-specific variables in the environ dictionary that give the application some information about the type of server they are running on. Table 16-1 lists the variables that are set.

Table 16-1. *The WSGI Variables and Their Meanings According to PEP 333*

Variable	Value
wsgi.version	The tuple (1,0), representing WSGI version 1.0.
wsgi.url_scheme	A string representing the "scheme" portion of the URL at which the application is being invoked. Normally, this will have the value "http" or "https", as appropriate.
wsgi.input	An input stream (file-like object) from which the HTTP request body can be read. (The server or gateway may perform reads on demand as requested by the application, it may preread the client's request body and buffer it in memory or on disk, or it may use any other technique for providing such an input stream, according to its preference.)

Variable	Value
wsgi.errors	An output stream (file-like object) to which error output can be written, for the purpose of recording program or other errors in a standardized and possibly centralized location. This should be a "text mode" stream; that is, applications should use "\n" as a line ending and assume it will be converted to the correct line ending by the server/gateway. For many servers, wsgi.errors will be the server's main error log. Alternatively, this may be sys.stderr or a log file of some sort. The server's documentation should include an explanation of how to configure this or where to find the recorded output. A server or gateway may supply different error streams to different applications, if this is desired.
wsgi.multithread	This value should evaluate true if the application object may be simultaneously invoked by another thread in the same process and should evaluate false otherwise.
wsgi.multiprocess	This value should evaluate true if an equivalent application object may be simultaneously invoked by another process and should evaluate false otherwise.
wsgi.run_once	This value should evaluate true if the server or gateway expects (but does not guarantee!) that the application will be invoked only this one time during the life of its containing process. Normally, this will be true only for a gateway based on CGI (or something similar).

Of particular interest to a Pylons developer are the wsgi.multithread and wsgi.multiprocess variables that tell the WSGI application whether it is being run in a multithreaded or multiprocess environment. You'll learn more about the differences between multithreading and mulitprocess servers in Chapter 21, but for now you just need to know that these variables can be accessed from the environ dictionary to discover what sort of server is being used.

The wsgi.errors variable is also interesting and will become particularly relevant when you look at application logging in Chapter 20. It provides a file-like object that the server provides for you to log error messages to. By using this for your log messages, you can be sure that your Pylons application logs will always be logged in an appropriate manner no matter which server they are running on. There are downsides to this approach too, though, which you'll see in Chapter 20.

■**Tip** Because Pylons is a WSGI framework and runs on WSGI servers, these variables are also available in Pylons through the request.environ dictionary. For example, to find out whether your application is running on a multi-threaded web server, you could do this:

```
if bool(request.environ['wsgi.multithreaded']):
    # Multithreaded
else:
    # Not multithreaded
```

Rather than write a full WSGI HTTP server as an example, let's consider a much simpler case. Imagine you already have a CGI server that was capable of running the CGI script you saw all the way back in Chapter 1. If you wanted to write an adaptor that would be able to run a WSGI application in a CGI environment, you would need to implement the WSGI server API.

Here's the code you would use:

```
import os, sys

def run_with_cgi(application):

    environ = dict(os.environ.items())
    environ['wsgi.input']        = sys.stdin
    environ['wsgi.errors']       = sys.stderr
    environ['wsgi.version']      = (1,0)
    environ['wsgi.multithread']  = False
    environ['wsgi.multiprocess'] = True
    environ['wsgi.run_once']     = True

    if environ.get('HTTPS','off') in ('on','1'):
        environ['wsgi.url_scheme'] = 'https'
    else:
        environ['wsgi.url_scheme'] = 'http'

    headers_set = []
    headers_sent = []

    def write(data):
        if not headers_set:
            raise AssertionError("write() before start_response()")

        elif not headers_sent:
            # Before the first output, send the stored headers
            status, response_headers = headers_sent[:] = headers_set
            sys.stdout.write('Status: %s\r\n' % status)
            for header in response_headers:
                sys.stdout.write('%s: %s\r\n' % header)
            sys.stdout.write('\r\n')

        sys.stdout.write(data)
        sys.stdout.flush()

    def start_response(status,response_headers,exc_info=None):
        if exc_info:
            try:
                if headers_sent:
                    # Re-raise original exception if headers sent
                    raise exc_info[0], exc_info[1], exc_info[2]
            finally:
                exc_info = None     # avoid dangling circular ref
        elif headers_set:
            raise AssertionError("Headers already set!")

        headers_set[:] = [status,response_headers]
        return write
```

```
result = application(environ, start_response)
try:
    for data in result:
        if data:    # don't send headers until body appears
            write(data)
    if not headers_sent:
        write('')   # send headers now if body was empty
finally:
    if hasattr(result,'close'):
        result.close()
```

This example forms part of the WSGI specification in PEP 333, so I won't discuss it in detail, but notice that it sets up an `environ` dictionary and a `start_response()` callable before calling the WSGI application in the line marked in bold. The information returned from the WSGI application forms the body of the response, and the information passed to the `start_response()` callable from the application is used to set the HTTP status and headers. Notice that the example also sets up a `write()` function that is returned from `start_response()` and that the application can also use to output information. As noted earlier, though, the vast majority of WSGI applications should return their data as an iterable. It's also worth drawing your attention to `wsgi.errors`. Here the `wsgi.errors` key simply points to `sys.stderr`, so any log messages your application sends when using `run_with_cgi()` just get sent to the standard error stream.

Let's write a sample CGI script that uses `run_with_cgi()` to run the `hello()` WSGI application from earlier in the chapter. The script would look like the following, but be sure to specify the correct path to the `python` executable. This is likely to be the one in your virtual Python environment:

```
#!/home/james/env/bin/python

import os, sys

def run_with_cgi(application):
    ... same as in the example above ...

def hello(environ, start_response):
    start_response('200 OK', [('Content-type','text/plain')])
    return ["Hello World!"]

if __name__ == '__main__':
    run_with_cgi(hello)
```

You can also run this CGI script from the command line because CGI applications send their output to the standard output. Save the previous example as `wsgi_test.py`, and you can run it like this:

```
$ chmod 755 wsgi_test.py
$ ./wsgi_test.py
Status: 200 OK
Content-type: text/plain

Hello World!
```

This sort of setup can sometimes be useful for debugging problems too because you can customize how the `environ` dictionary is set up in `run_with_cgi()` to simulate different sorts of requests.

■**Caution** Running a WSGI application through a CGI script is generally very inefficient because the WSGI application (along with the Python interpreter and the CGI script itself) has to be re-created on each request. Most WSGI
applications (including your Pylons application) are designed to be loaded into memory once and then executed
lots of times without being re-created, and this is a lot more efficient.

Since Python 2.5, WSGI has been built into the Python standard library in the form of the
wsgiref module, which provides basic WSGI tools including a WSGI server. The server is built using
the same methodology as the other servers that make up the Python Standard Library including
BaseHTTPServer. Here's how you would use it to serve the same hello WSGI application used in the
previous example, although you could use the same code to serve *any* WSGI application just by
changing the argument to httpd.set_app():

```
from wsgiref import simple_server

def hello(environ, start_response):
    start_response('200 OK', [('Content-type','text/plain')])
    return ["Hello World!"]

httpd = simple_server.WSGIServer(
    ('0.0.0.0', 8000),
    simple_server.WSGIRequestHandler,
)
httpd.set_app(hello)
httpd.serve_forever()
```

■**Tip** If you are running a version of Python prior to 2.5, you will need to install the wsgiref package from the
Python Package Index to run the example. You can do that with the following:

```
$ easy_install wsgiref
```

If you run this application, you'll find the server running on port 8000 and available on all IP
addresses. You change which interface or port the WSGI application is served from by changing the
first argument to simple_server.WSGIServer(). Once the server is running, you can visit
http://localhost:8000/ to see the hello application running.

Now you have seen how to write WSGI applications and servers and understand the API for
each, it should be clear that any WSGI application can run on any WSGI server without any modification needed to either the server or the application. In the next chapter, you'll learn how to obtain
a WSGI application object from a Pylons application through its config file. Because Pylons applications are also WSGI applications, it means they can be deployed on a large range of WSGI servers
without modification. You can serve these Pylons WSGI applications in the same ways you saw the
hello application being served in the examples in this chapter. You'd just swap hello for the Pylons
WSGI application. You'll learn about some of the more common deployment setups in Chapter 21.

WSGI Middleware

Now that you've learned about WSGI applications and servers, it is time to learn about another
type of component that sits in the middle between a server and an application and is known as
middleware.

WSGI middleware are components that, from a WSGI application's point of view, appear as though they are a WSGI server because they provide the `environ` dictionary and `start_response()` callable when they call the WSGI application and iterate over the result to return the response in the same way a WSGI server would. The reason middleware components are not WSGI servers, though, is that they look to a server as if they are a WSGI application. They are callables that accept the `environ` dictionary and `start_response()` arguments and return an iterable response.

This dual nature puts middleware components in a unique position to be able to change all the HTTP information an application receives from a server and to change all the HTTP information a server receives from the application. This turns out to be extremely useful and means that middleware can therefore do any of the following things or a combination of them:

- Change any of the request information by modifying the `environ` dictionary

- Change the HTTP status returned from an application

- Intercept an error

- Add, remove, or change HTTP headers returned from an application

- Change a response

Middleware is therefore extremely powerful and can build a broad range of discrete components that can be used with different WSGI servers and applications. For example, a middleware component can do the following:

- Produce error documents when certain status codes are received (typically responding to 404 and 500 codes)

- E-mail error reports to a developer if a problem occurs

- Provide interactive debugging facilities

- Forward requests to other parts of the application

- Test the API compliance of applications and servers to the WSGI standard

- Authenticate a user

- Cache pages

- Provide a session store

- Handle cookies

- Gzip the response

Since a WSGI application wrapped in a piece of WSGI middleware is still a valid WSGI application, you can also wrap the combined middleware+application in another piece of middleware. You can keep adding middleware components until your middleware stack provides all the functionality you need. Doing so is called creating a *middleware chain*. This is exactly what is happening in your Pylons application's `config/middleware.py` file in the `make_app()` function that you'll look at in detail in the next chapter.

Writing WSGI Middleware

Now that you've seen a bit about how WSGI works and how middleware components in particular can be used to change the behavior of a Pylons application, it is time to look in detail at how you can write WSGI middleware yourself. As was noted in the introduction to the chapter, writing your own middleware isn't necessary to develop Pylons applications, so feel free to skip the rest of this chapter if it doesn't interest you at this stage; however, bear in mind that if you have an understanding of how it is done, you will be better able to understand how components such as AuthKit work. If you want to become a Pylons expert or want to contribute to Pylons itself, a good understanding of WSGI applications and middleware is essential.

Let's start off by looking at middleware that does nothing at all so that you can see its constituent parts:

```
class Middleware(object):
    def __init__(self, app):
        self.app = app

    def __call__(self, environ, start_response):
        return self.app(environ, start_response)
```

You can use this middleware like this to wrap the hello WSGI application you saw earlier:

```
app = Middleware(hello)
```

The combined app object is itself a valid WSGI application, and since the middleware doesn't do anything, it would behave in the same way as the hello application on its own. Let's think about what happens when it is called by a WSGI server to handle a request.

When the app object is created, the Middleware object is instantiated with the hello application as its first argument, which gets set as self.app. The app object is a class instance, but since it has a __call__() method, it can be called and therefore can behave as a WSGI application in a similar manner to the way you saw a class instance being used as a WSGI application earlier in the chapter.

When the instance is called, it in turn calls the hello application (self.app) and then returns its result to the server, which will iterate over the result from Middleware.__call__() in the same way as it would have iterated over the result from hello() if Middleware wasn't present.

Now that you've seen the basic API of a middleware component, let's look at an example of each of the things mentioned in the previous section, which you can do with a middleware component starting with modifying the environment.

Modifying the Environment

Let's write some middleware that modifies the environ dictionary to add a key specifying a message. You'll also add a facility allowing the message to be configured when the middleware is instantiated:

```
class Middleware(object):
    def __init__(self, app, message):
        self.app = app
        self.message = message

    def __call__(self, environ, start_response):
        environ['example.message'] = self.message
        return self.app(environ, start_response)
```

This middleware adds a key to the environ called example.message. All WSGI environ keys have to be strings containing just one . character, so here, example.message is a valid key. A WSGI application can now access this modified example. Here's a new version of the hello application that uses this key to display a message and an example of how it is used:

```
def custom_message(environ, start_response):
    start_response('200 OK', [('Content-type', 'text/plain')])
    return [environ['example.message']]

app = Middleware(custom_message, "Hello world again!")
```

This time, the `Middleware` class takes a `message` parameter that is set as `self.message`. When the application is called, the middleware adds this message as a key in the `environ` dictionary, which the application can now extract from the environment.

Changing the Status and Headers

Next I'll cover how to change the status or the headers in a piece of middleware. The WSGI application calls `start_response()` to set the status and headers, so all the middleware has to do is provide its own `start_response()` function that performs any modifications before calling the `start_response()` function it has been passed. This example simply sets a cookie named `name` with the value `value`:

```
class Middleware(object):
    def __init__(self, app):
        self.app = app

    def __call__(self, environ, start_response):

        def custom_start_response(status, headers, exc_info=None):
            headers.append(('Set-Cookie', "name=value"))
            return start_response(status, headers, exc_info)

        return self.app(environ, custom_start_response)
```

Notice that `custom_start_response()` returns the value of calling the original `start_response()`. This is very important so that the writable returned from the application calling the function it receives as `start_response()` can use the writable object returned by the server. It is also important that you remember to pass the custom start response callable as the second argument when calling the WSGI application, rather than the original `start_response()` the middleware receives.

Handling Errors

To be able to deal with errors, you need to know that the `start_response()` callable you have been using throughout this chapter takes an optional third parameter named `exc_info`, which defaults to `None`.

If an error occurs in your application (or even in one of the middleware components), you might want to have that error intercepted so that you could log the error, send an e-mail error report, or display a traceback to the user for debugging. It is possible that the server hasn't actually sent the HTTP headers yet, so the middleware doing the intercepting has an opportunity to call `start_response()` itself with any status or headers it needs in order to display the traceback or indicate an error. Since the error-handling middleware doesn't know whether the server has actually sent the headers, it behaves as if it hasn't and calls the server as usual to generate the required response, but it also specifies the `exc_info` argument to `start_response()` as a Python `sys.exc_info()` tuple representing the error that occurred.

When `start_response()` is called with the `exc_info` argument, the server will check whether the headers have already been sent and raise the exception passed to it via the `exc_info` argument if they have. If they haven't, it can use the new headers specified by the error-handling middleware.

If you refer to the `run_with_cgi()` example from earlier in the chapter, you can see this behavior is implemented in the `start_response()` callable:

```
def start_response(status,response_headers,exc_info=None):
    if exc_info:
        try:
            if headers_sent:
                # Re-raise original exception if headers sent
                raise exc_info[0], exc_info[1], exc_info[2]
        finally:
            exc_info = None     # avoid dangling circular ref
    elif headers_set:
        raise AssertionError("Headers already set!")

    headers_set[:] = [status,response_headers]
    return write
```

In this example, if the headers have already been set and there is no exc_info() argument, an
AssertionError is raised to indicate that it is likely the start_response() callable has been called
twice by mistake.

With a good understanding of how the exc_info argument works, let's go ahead and write an
example that simply displays a traceback using the cgitb module from the Python Standard Library:

```
import cgitb
import sys
from StringIO import StringIO

class Middleware(object):
    def __init__(self, app):
        self.app = app

    def format_exception(self, exc_info):
        dummy_file = StringIO()
        hook = cgitb.Hook(file=dummy_file)
        hook(*exc_info)
        return [dummy_file.getvalue()]

    def __call__(self, environ, start_response):
        try:
            app_iter = self.app(environ, start_response)
            for data in app_iter:
                yield data
        except:
            exc_info = sys.exc_info()
            start_response(
                '500 Internal Server Error',
                [('content-type', 'text/html')],
                exc_info
            )
            for data in self.format_exception(exc_info):
                yield data
        else:
            # Calling .close() could cause an exception too
            # so in a real handler you might test for that too
            if hasattr(app_iter, 'close'):
                app_iter.close()
```

As you can see, the middleware just uses a simple try... except block, and if it encounters an
error, it calls start_response() with the exc_info argument so that the server can raise an exception
if the headers have already been sent. Then it calls its format_exception() method, which uses the
cgitb module to generate an HTML error page that it then returns.

Altering the Response

Another thing you can do with WSGI middleware is alter the response returned from a WSGI application. In Chapter 15, I discussed ways of speeding up the time it takes a browser to render a page from a Pylons application, and one of the recommendations was to compress JavaScript or CSS files using Gzip compression so that they took less time to download from a server. One way of doing this is with middleware, so let's write some middleware to Gzip JavaScript and CSS files before they are sent to the browser.

The example is quite complex, so rather than showing you the final code, let's build up the middleware in steps. First you need to know how to use Gzip compression in Python. Here's an example function that just compresses its input:

```python
import gzip
import StringIO

def compress(string, compresslevel=9):
    # The GZipFile object expects to operate on a file, not a string
    # so we create a file-like buffer for it to write the output to
    buffer = StringIO.StringIO()

    # Now let's create the GzipFile object which compresses any
    # strings written to it and adds the output to the buffer
    output = gzip.GzipFile(
        mode='wb',
        compresslevel=compresslevel,
        fileobj=buffer
    )
    output.write(string)
    output.close()

    # Finally we get the compressed string out of the buffer
    buffer.seek(0)
    result = buffer.getvalue()
    buffer.close()

    return result
```

Let's make a first attempt at applying this technique to some middleware:

```python
import gzip
import StringIO

# CAUTION: This doesn't work correctly yet

class GzipMiddleware(object):
    def __init__(self, app, compresslevel=9):
        self.app = app
        self.compresslevel = compresslevel

    def __call__(self, environ, start_response):
        buffer = StringIO.StringIO()
        output = gzip.GzipFile(
            mode='wb',
            compresslevel=self.compresslevel,
            fileobj=buffer
        )
```

```
        app_iter = self.app(environ, start_response)
        for line in app_iter:
            output.write(line)
        if hasattr(app_iter, 'close'):
            app_iter.close()
        output.close()
        buffer.seek(0)
        result = buffer.getvalue()
        buffer.close()
        return [result]
```

When the middleware is called, the `__call__()` method behaves in a similar way to the `compress()` function from the previous example. A buffer is set up to receive the compressed data, and a `GzipFile` object is created to do the work of compressing any data passed to it via its `write()` method. The WSGI application the middleware wraps is then called, and its result is iterated over, writing each line to the `GzipFile` object `output`. Notice that any time you iterate over the result, you are also responsible for calling the `close()` method on the iterator if it has one. This is to support resource release by the application and is intended to complement PEP 325's generator support and other common iterables with `close()` methods. Once the iterator has been closed, the method returns the compressed contents of the buffer to the middleware beneath it as a list.

The example so far correctly generates a compressed response, but there are some problems with it:

- Not all browsers support Gzip compression, so this middleware would break the application on those browsers.

- Any data written to the writable object returned by `start_response()` wouldn't be compressed.

- If a `Content-Length` was set, it would now be incorrect because the response has changed.

- Not all content should be compressed; only JavaScript and CSS files should be.

Let's start by writing a custom `start_response()` function that returns the `GzipFile` object. This object has a `write()` method which can be returned to fulfil the requirement of the WSGI specification for `start_response()` to return a writable object. At the same time, update the code to check that the browser supports Gzip compression. The new code looks like this with modified lines in bold:

```
import gzip
import StringIO

# CAUTION: This doesn't work correctly yet

class GzipMiddleware(object):
    def __init__(self, app, compresslevel=9):
        self.app = app
        self.compresslevel = compresslevel

    def __call__(self, environ, start_response):
        if 'gzip' not in environ.get('HTTP_ACCEPT_ENCODING', ''):
            return self.app(environ, start_response)
```

```
    buffer = StringIO.StringIO()
    output = gzip.GzipFile(
        mode='wb',
        compresslevel=self.compresslevel,
        fileobj=buffer
    )

    def dummy_start_response(status, headers, exc_info=None):
        return output.write

    app_iter = self.app(environ, dummy_start_response)
    for line in app_iter:
        output.write(line)
    if hasattr(app_iter, 'close'):
        app_iter.close()
    output.close()
    buffer.seek(0)
    result = buffer.getvalue()
    buffer.close()
    return [result]
```

If the browser doesn't support Gzip encoding, the middleware does nothing, returning the application as it stands. If Gzip encoding is supported, a dummy_start_respose() function is returned that, when called by the application, returns the object output. Although this code fixes two of the problems, it introduces a third. The start_response() callable that is passed to the __call__() method isn't called itself, so the headers and status won't actually get passed to the server, which you'll recall is responsible for providing start_response() in the first place. To call the start_response() function, you'll need to know the status and headers it should be called with.

The problem here is that status, headers, and exc_info are only locally available in your dummy_start_response() function, and you need to be able to access them in the scope of the __call__() method in order to call start_response() after the WSGI application is called. If you were to set them as globals, they become globally available, not just available in the scope of the __call__() method, so you definitely don't want to do that. The solution is to create a list variable in the scope of the __call__() method and then append the status, headers, and exc_info to it from the scope of the dummy_start_response() function; then after the application has been called, the variables will have been set, so you can iterate over the result based on the values in the list. Let's update the code to call the real start_response() callable:

```
import gzip
import StringIO

# CAUTION: This doesn't work correctly yet

class GzipMiddleware(object):
    def __init__(self, app, compresslevel=9):
        self.app = app
        self.compresslevel = compresslevel

    def __call__(self, environ, start_response):
        if 'gzip' not in environ.get('HTTP_ACCEPT_ENCODING', ''):
            return self.app(environ, start_response)
```

```
            buffer = StringIO.StringIO()
            output = gzip.GzipFile(
                mode='wb',
                compresslevel=self.compresslevel,
                fileobj=buffer
            )

            start_response_args = []
            def dummy_start_response(status, headers, exc_info=None):
                start_response_args.append(status)
                start_response_args.append(headers)
                start_response_args.append(exc_info)
                return output.write

            app_iter = self.app(environ, dummy_start_response)
            for line in app_iter:
                output.write(line)
            if hasattr(app_iter, 'close'):
                app_iter.close()
            output.close()
            buffer.seek(0)
            result = buffer.getvalue()
            start_response(**start_response_args)
            buffer.close()
            return [result]
```

This version correctly calls `start_response()`, but two problems are left to fix. First you need to update the `Content-Length` header to contain the correct length of the new compressed content, and then you need to ensure that only JavaScript and CSS files are compressed. Since this example will be used in the SimpleSite application, let's enable compression for any URL that ends in `.js` or `.css`. Here's the final version of the code:

```
import gzip
import StringIO

class GzipMiddleware(object):
    def __init__(self, app, compresslevel=9):
        self.app = app
        self.compresslevel = compresslevel

    def __call__(self, environ, start_response):
        if 'gzip' not in environ.get('HTTP_ACCEPT_ENCODING', ''):
            return self.app(environ, start_response)
        if environ['PATH_INFO'][-3:] != '.js' and environ['PATH_INFO'][-4:] != '.css':
            return self.app(environ, start_response)
        buffer = StringIO.StringIO()
        output = gzip.GzipFile(
            mode='wb',
            compresslevel=self.compresslevel,
            fileobj=buffer
        )
```

```
        start_response_args = []
        def dummy_start_response(status, headers, exc_info=None):
            start_response_args.append(status)
            start_response_args.append(headers)
            start_response_args.append(exc_info)
            return output.write

        app_iter = self.app(environ, dummy_start_response)
        for line in app_iter:
            output.write(line)
        if hasattr(app_iter, 'close'):
            app_iter.close()
        output.close()
        buffer.seek(0)
        result = buffer.getvalue()
        headers = []
        for name, value in start_response_args[1]:
            if name.lower() != 'content-length':
                headers.append((name, value))
        headers.append(('Content-Length', str(len(result))))
        headers.append(('Content-Encoding', 'gzip'))
        start_response(start_response_args[0], headers, start_response_args[2])
        buffer.close()
        return [result]
```

As you can see, this version will work correctly, but it wasn't exactly a piece of cake to write. Although changing the response is one of the more difficult things you can do with middleware, it really makes you appreciate all the things Pylons does for you!

Testing the Gzip Middleware

Let's test this middleware. Add the previous code to a new file in the SimpleSite project's `lib` directory called `middleware.py`. Then edit the project's config file to include this import at the top:

```
from simplesite.lib.middleware import GzipMiddleware
```

Then change the code at the end of `config/middleware.py` so that it looks like this:

```
# Static files (If running in production, and Apache or another web
# server is handling this static content, remove the following 2 lines)
static_app = StaticURLParser(config['pylons.paths']['static_files'])
app = Cascade([static_app, app])
app = GzipMiddleware(app, compresslevel=5)
return app
```

If you start the SimpleSite server on your local machine and reload one of the pages that uses JavaScript such as `http://localhost:5000/page/edit/6`, you might find it actually loads more slowly than it did before. Take a look at the Net tab of Firebug to find out. This is because it is running on your local computer, so your machine has to do the extra work of compressing and uncompressing the data. If you were viewing the page over a network, the extra time it takes your browser to uncompress the data should be less than the time saved in sending the file across the network.

Here are the relevant headers from Firebug when the `yahoo-dom-event.js` file is requested before the Gzip middleware is in place:

```
Server           PasteWSGIServer/0.5 Python/2.5.2
Date             Fri, 10 Oct 2008 19:31:22 GMT
Content-Type     application/x-javascript
...
Content-Length   31637
```

Here are the headers with the Gzip middleware:

```
Server             PasteWSGIServer/0.5 Python/2.5.2
Date               Fri, 10 Oct 2008 19:30:44 GMT
Content-Type       application/x-javascript
...
Content-Length     10577
Content-Encoding   gzip
```

As you can see, the Gzip middleware has reduced the file size by about 20KB, which on a very slow connection could save up to half a second in the page load time.

Summary

This chapter has been a whistle-stop tour of the Web Server Gateway Interface. I hope you can see that WSGI is actually a very powerful API. If you managed to follow all the examples in the chapter, you might be keen to start writing WSGI middleware. If you are, that's great. A good place to start is the WSGI specification defined in PEP 333, but WSGI is best learned from examples. The Paste package that is installed with Pylons is particularly rich in WSGI middleware and is a good place to look to see how different situations are handled with WSGI.

Here are some links for further reading:

- PEP 333, `http://www.python.org/dev/peps/pep-0333/`

- The WSGI web site, `http://wsgi.org`

- Introducing WSGI—Python's Secret Web Weapon Part 1,
  `http://www.xml.com/pub/a/2006/09/27/introducing-wsgi-pythons-secret-web-weapon.html`

- Introducing WSGI—Python's Secret Web Weapon Part 2, `http://www.xml.com/pub/a/2006/10/04/introducing-wsgi-pythons-secret-web-weapon-part-two.html`

CHAPTER 17

Pylons' Internal Architecture

Now that you've seen what WSGI is and how it works, in this chapter you'll look at how Pylons' architecture is built around the opportunities WSGI provides. Before getting into too much detail, though, it is helpful to put the Pylons architecture in context by looking at how it came about in the first place.

A Bit of History

All web frameworks are fundamentally involved in the process of responding to HTTP requests and generating HTTP responses using APIs that are convenient for developers. These APIs might provide session handling, cookie handling, E-Tag caching, error reporting, or other features that read information from the HTTP request and affect the HTTP response. It turns out that the vast majority of HTTP services that web frameworks provide are easily implemented as WSGI middleware because, as you've just learned, middleware has the ability to change all aspects of the HTTP request and the HTTP response, which is exactly what most frameworks' internal stacks have to do.

Now, just because it is possible to do something doesn't mean it is always a good idea, but it turns out that building a web framework stack out of WSGI middleware is very useful because once a piece of middleware has been written, it can be used between *any* WSGI-compatible web server and web application. This means it can be used in any web framework, which in turn means that for the first time WSGI allows web developers to reuse components at the web framework stack level. This is really important because it has three implications:

- Developers can easily customize their WSGI frameworks by adding or removing their own middleware components.

- Web framework developers no longer need to constantly reinvent the wheel because they can just use existing middleware components instead of creating their own custom implementations.

- Users can write their own middleware, such as a custom transaction logger to be used with several applications.

These more than any other reasons are why Pylons exists today. Once the WSGI standard was specified and tools such as Paste began to emerge, many people in the Python community were very keen to refactor existing frameworks such as Django and Zope to be built from WSGI middleware. Understandably, these communities were rather reluctant to stop development to refactor code to use WSGI middleware when it already worked perfectly well as it was. Doing so would benefit the wider Python community that could then reuse much of their code, but this was more effort than it was worth to the communities themselves. As a result, WSGI wasn't adopted in any of the major frameworks of the time other than as an adaptor to allow them to run on WSGI servers.

Finally, late in 2005 Ben Bangert and I started Pylons as a wake-up call to the other Python communities to demonstrate that writing a full-stack Python framework using WSGI middleware was not only possible but would also form the very best basis for developers because it put them in complete control of every aspect of their applications. It would also be the best solution for the wider community because it would create, as a side effect of its architecture, a huge variety of reusable Python components. This was the basis on which the Pylons WSGI architecture was born.

At the same time, not every component a web framework provides is appropriate as WSGI middleware. In keeping with Pylons' philosophy of developer choice and reusability, the Pylons developers decided early on not to code an integrated set of components for database access, templating, or form creation in the way Django does but rather to tackle the essence of the workflow and underlying technical requirements that each of these components has and provide APIs and written recommendations for how to use these components together. This loosely coupled architecture has meant that Pylons has been able to easily move from SQLObject to SQLAlchemy and from Myghty to Mako (while still supporting alternatives) and is able to support form generation systems as diverse as HTML Fill, ToscaWidgets, and FormAlchemy.

As communities within Python continue to innovate on individual projects, Pylons will continue to be able to use them because the framework isn't strongly dependent on the other components it recommends, whereas the perceived simplicity of other frameworks, notably Django, comes from its tight integration of components, and this limits that community's ability to respond to changes. It also severely limits a developer's opportunity to do things differently if the solution provided out of the box doesn't quite fit your needs.

So, Pylons' big secret is that actually it isn't really a framework in the traditional sense at all; it favors the creation of reusable middleware components over an integrated framework stack and favors supporting other communities' efforts over writing anything custom and tightly integrated. There are other subtle benefits to this that you might not notice at first. Because most of the components that make up Pylons are actually stand-alone projects in their own right, you will find the following:

- You can generally get very good support because you can go to the component-specific mailing list as well as the Pylons one.

- You can easily use the components (and the code you have written) outside the Pylons web environment because many of the components were designed to run stand-alone in the first place.

- The skills you learn when developing a Pylons application are very transferable because the same tools are used by other companies and organizations in nonweb environments.

With these ideas in mind in this chapter, let's look in detail at how Pylons is really built beneath the surface. You'll learn about the following:

- The Paste Deploy package
- The Pylons config file and how to use it to set up middleware
- The Pylons middleware stack
- The `Cascade`
- What actually happens during a request

But before I can discuss these points, I must discuss one piece of technology that is critical to the way Pylons works: egg entry points.

Egg Entry Points

As you'll remember from Chapter 2, most of the components used by Pylons are distributed as Python eggs. Eggs have a number of useful features for Pylons developers, but one feature called *entry points* is particularly useful.

To understand how entry points work, let's imagine you want to allow the SimpleSite application's pages to support different types of content. At the moment, they support plain text, but you might want to support HTML, reStructuredText, or some other markup type. Let's say you decide to design SimpleSite to use a plug-in architecture so that other people can write plug-ins to support each of the different formats. Each plug-in will need a `display_name()` function so SimpleSite can display a list of available plug-ins in an HTML select field, a `markup_to_html()` function that will be called every time a page was viewed, and a `render_input_field()` function that will return various HTML fragments necessary to display an edit field for the particular type of markup.

A plug-in developer can then create a new project that implements each of these functions and packages them up into another egg, but how does SimpleSite know whether the plug-in is installed? This is where egg entry points come in. The plug-in writer would list the functions SimpleSite needs in the entry points part of its `setup.py` file. The syntax is `entry_point_name=package.module:object`. Others who write similar plug-ins would define similar entry points.

Then a program that wants to use these plug-ins, be it SimpleSite or a different application, can ask for all the entry points in all the packages installed on the system to obtain a list of entry points. It can then select the packages that have the entry points it needs and load the functions pointed to by the entry points, and it can therefore use the plug-in.

Entry points are arranged in groups with names that can include a period (`.`), so the SimpleSite application might define entry points in a `simplesite.content_plugin` group. Each entry point in a group has a name, so the entry point that points to the `render_input_field()` function defined in the HTMLPlugin might just be called `render`. SimpleSite can then access the function by looking for the `render` entry point in the `simplesite.content_plugin` group. It doesn't even need to know what the function's name is in the HTMLPlugin package.

The beauty of the entry points system is that entry points allow packages to expose fixed APIs that other plug-in packages can implement. This system is used a lot within Pylons itself, particularly in relation to the Pylons config files.

Entry Points and websetup.py

If you look at the `setup.py` file for a Pylons project, this is what the entry point definition looks like:

```
setup(
    ...
    entry_points="""
    [paste.app_factory]
    main = simplesite.config.middleware:make_app

    [paste.app_install]
    main = pylons.util:PylonsInstaller
    """,
)
```

This means your Pylons application implements the functionality expected of an application supporting the `main` entry point of a `paste.app_factory` group and the `main` entry point for the `paste.app_install` group. In effect, your Pylons application behaves like a Paste app factory and as a Paste installer.

You'll see how the `main` entry point of a `paste.app_factory` group is used in the next section, so for the moment, let's concentrate on the `main` entry point for the `paste.app_install` group, which is used by the `paster setup-app` command.

When you run the `paster setup-app` command, Paste Script discovers the Pylons application you want to set up by looking at the `use` line in the `[app:main]` section of the config file. It looks like this:

```
[app:main]
use = egg:SimpleSite
```

The Pylons config file is in a special format understood by the `PasteDeploy` package. The `use` line simply tells Paste Deploy which package to use and that the package is an egg. The `use` line can also be written like this:

```
[app:main]
use = egg:SimpleSite#main
```

This tells Paste Deploy that the entry point it is looking for is called `main`, but this is assumed to be the case anyway if the `#main` part is ignored.

Once `paster setup-app` knows the package to look for and the name of the entry point, it looks it up in the `paste.app_install` group with code similar to this:

```
from pkg_resources import load_entry_point
entry_point = load_entry_point(spec, 'paste.app_install', 'main')
installer = entry_point.load()
```

The `load_entry_point()` function can also take a version specification such as `'SimpleSite>=0.1.0'` as its first argument.

Tip The `pkg_resources` package comes with `setuptools`, the same package that provides the `easy_install` script. There are other ways of loading objects using entry points too, which you can learn about in the entry points section of the `pkg_resources` page at http://peak.telecommunity.com/DevCenter/PkgResources#entry-points.

Now, Pylons applications are unusual in the sense that this entry point doesn't point to an object in the Pylons project in which it is defined but in `pylons.util` instead. This means the object that is loaded is always `pylons.util.PylonsInstaller` no matter which Pylons project is being used. The `PylonsInstaller` object itself is responsible for then calling the `setup_app()` function in your project's `websetup.py` file.

Now that you have seen how entry points can be used to set up a Pylons application, you can learn about how they are used when serving an application.

The Pylons Config File

Pylons is designed to be as easy as possible for everyone to use, and this design philosophy also extends to end users of your Pylons application. People configuring your Pylons application might not be confident configuring WSGI applications in Python source code, so the Pylons config file provides a more familiar environment for them to make configuration changes. It also provides an API to allow them to set up some complex combinations of applications and middleware without needing to get involved in Python code.

In this section, you'll look at the different ways a Pylons config file can be used and what is actually going on behind the scenes to convert sections from the config file into real Python objects. Then, later in the chapter, you'll see how you can use the same API as the Pylons tools to construct Python objects directly from the config file.

Note I won't be discussing the logging configuration options in this chapter. Although the logging options look similar, they are actually used in a completely different way behind the scenes, so the techniques in this chapter for the other Pylons config options do not apply in any way to the logging options. Logging options are described in Chapter 20.

When you serve a Pylons application via its config file with the `paster serve` command, these are the steps that take place:

1. The Paste Script package's `serve` plug-in is loaded by `paster`.

2. The `serve` plug-in uses the Paste Deploy package to parse the config file.

3. Paste Deploy uses code in the `[*:main]` section to construct a valid WSGI application, pipeline, or composite application.

4. Paste Deploy uses code in the `[server:main]` section to load and configure a suitable WSGI server with the pipelines, filters, and application object, and then the server is started.

In the following sections, you'll concentrate on the work Paste Deploy does to parse the config file, but if you are interested in how to write Paste Script plug-ins so that you can create your own extensions to the `paster` program, you should read the Paste Script developer documentation at `http://pythonpaste.org/script/developer.html`. You won't be surprised to hear that plug-ins rely on entry points.

Default Config Options

The first section in a Pylons config file is the `[DEFAULT]` section. This contains a set of variables that will make up the global configuration, accessed in a Pylons application as `config.global_conf`. The options are also passed to each of the functions used to construct objects in other sections of the config file. These options are labeled `DEFAULT` rather than `global_conf` because they also work as if they were present in each of the other sections (apart from the logging sections). As an example, consider how the `debug` option works. In the `[DEFAULT]` section, the `debug` option is set to `true`. This means that in the `[app:main]` section, if no `debug` option is specified, `debug` in that section will also be set to `true`. In effect, options in the `[DEFAULT]` section are providing defaults for the other sections. When the `debug` option is set to `false` in the `[app:main]` section, the value in the `[DEFAULT]` section is overridden, and debugging is disabled.

Now that you understand the role of the `[DEFAULT]` section, let's see how Paste Deploy handles the other sections.

Constructing a Server

When Paste Deploy parses a config file, the `[server:main]` section is inspected to find out which server to use. The Pylons config file typically has a section that looks like this:

```
[server:main]
use = egg:Paste#http
host = 127.0.0.1
port = 5000
```

The use line tells the Paste Script package's server plug-in that it should look up an egg entry point in the Paste package named http. Because this is a [server:main] section, Paste Script knows that the entry point will be in the paste.server_runner entry point group.

The host option tells the server specified in the use line which host to serve the application on. You'll remember from Chapter 3 that if you want to serve an application on all interfaces, you will need to change the host option to 0.0.0.0 because it is set by default to 127.0.0.1 to prevent you from accidentally serving an application across a network when it is running in debug mode on your development machine. You can also specify a hostname or domain name as long as they can be correctly resolved on your computer.

The port option simply tells the server which port to serve on. For production use, you would use port 80, but for development use, port 5000 is fine.

Let's take a closer look at how Paste Deploy loads the Paste HTTP server from the use line. First the Paste package has the following as part of its entry point definition:

```
entry_points="""
    ...
    [paste.server_runner]
    http = paste.httpserver:server_runner
    ...
"""
```

The use = egg:Paste#http line therefore points to the server_runner() function in the paste.httpserver module. This function is responsible for taking the arguments Paste Deploy sends it from the information it parsed from the config file and returning a running server. The function looks like this:

```
def server_runner(wsgi_app, global_conf, **kwargs):
    ...
```

The server_runner() function takes a dictionary of all the options in the [DEFAULT] section of the config file as the global_conf argument and all the options specified in [server:main] as keyword arguments that are gathered up by **kwargs into a dictionary. In this case, the global_conf options aren't used, but the port and host options passed as keyword arguments are. The wsgi_app argument is the WSGI application obtained by constructing all the other objects specified in the config file. I'll cover these in the next sections.

Once all the options are in place, the function is called, and this starts the server.

Note In the next chapter, you'll also see some extra options that can be used in the [server:main] section to configure the Paste HTTP server with SSL support.

Constructing an Application

Constructing the application happens using a similar mechanism, except Paste Deploy starts by looking for either an [app:main] section, a [composite:main] section, or a [pipeline:main] section in the config file. Only one section other than [server:main] can have the name :main. I'll cover composite applications and pipelines later in the chapter, so let's concentrate on what happens when your main section is an [app:main] section.

The Pylons config file [app:main] section starts like this:

```
[app:main]
use = egg:SimpleSite
...
```

This tells Paste Deploy to look in the `SimpleSite` package `paste.app_factory` entry point group, and just as was the case earlier in the chapter, because no `#name` is specified after the definition, Paste Deploy will look for an entry point named `main`.

Let's look at SimpleSite's `setup.py` file again to see whether it contains a `paste.app_factory` group:

```
setup(
    ...
    entry_points="""
    [paste.app_factory]
    main = simplesite.config.middleware:make_app

    [paste.app_install]
    main = pylons.util:PylonsInstaller
    """,
)
```

In this case, the `main` entry point in the `paste.app_factory` group points to the `make_app()` function in `simplesite.config.middleware`, so it is this function that is responsible for assembling the Pylons application and middleware that will form the WSGI application that gets served by the server specified in the `[server:main]` section.

The `make_app()` function looks like this:

```
def make_app(global_conf, full_stack=True, **app_conf):
    ...
    return app
```

Once again, the config options from the `[DEFAULT]` section get passed to the function as `global_conf`, just as they did when the server was being called, and once again the section-specific options get passed as named parameters that this time are gathered up into the `app_conf` dictionary.

The WSGI application returned by `make_app()` as app is what PasteScript's `serve` plug-in passes as the first argument to the `server_runner()` function when it serves the function.

We'll take a detailed look at what happens in the `make_app()` function to turn the configuration options into a Pylons application later in the chapter, but there is one point worth noting first. Because the `full_stack` option is specified as an argument to `make_app()`, it doesn't get added to the `app_conf` dictionary in the same way as all the other variables. There isn't really a good reason for this, so it might change in a future version of Pylons to be more like this:

```
def make_app(global_conf, **app_conf):
    full_stack = asbool(app_conf.get('full_stack', 'true'))
    ...
    return app
```

As you've probably realized, the Pylons config file format is slightly more powerful than most frameworks' config files. It turns out that you can actually use the config file to directly assemble a whole range of WSGI (and hence Pylons) applications into one *composite* application, and you can even add middleware to individual WSGI (or Pylons) applications using *filters* and *pipelines*. Let's start with composite applications.

Composite Applications

Composite applications are WSGI applications that are made up of other WSGI applications. A good example of a composite app is a URL mapper that mounts WSGI applications at different paths relative to the base URL. Here's an example that mounts your Pylons application at the path `/pylons` and mounts an application for handling downloads at the path `/downloads`:

```
[composite:main]
use = egg:Paste#urlmap
/pylons = pylons
/downloads = staticapp

[app:staticapp]
use = egg:Paste#static
document_root = /path/to/docroot

[app:pylons]
# The standard [app:main] section goes here
use = egg:SimpleSite
... etc
```

When this config file is loaded, Paste Deploy will look for the [server:main] section and any other main section and find that this time, rather than the second main section being an [app:main] section, it is a [composite:main] section. It will therefore look up the urlmap entry point name in the Paste package and the paste.composite_app group, and this in turn will load the paste.urlmap. urlmap_factory() to load a paste.urlmap.URLMap. The URLMap will be set up with the two WSGI applications (the Pylons app and the staticapp) at the appropriate paths.

Notice that for this to work the Pylons configuration section had to be renamed from [app:main] to [app:pylons]. If you hadn't done this, the two main sections would have conflicted.

One reason for setting up other WSGI applications via a composite section in the config file rather than as a Pylons controller or from a Pylons controller action is that none of the Pylons middleware will be in place. This is useful if you find that the Pylons middleware interferes with some aspect of the behavior of the other WSGI app when it is mounted inside a Pylons application.

It is worth noting that the Paste URLMap in this example will automatically adjust the SCRIPT_NAME and PATH_INFO environment variables so that your WSGI applications mounted under it will be able to work out where they are. This means that as long as the applications you mount use the h.url_for() helper (or their own equivalents), then the URLs generated by the WSGI applications under URLMap will still be correct even though they are mounted at a path other than /.

Pipelines and Filters

Now let's look at pipelines and filters. Filters are just Paste Deploy's name for functions that set up WSGI middleware, and pipelines are just Paste Deploy's name for a middleware chain.

To use filters, instead of specifying the main section to be your Pylons application or a composite application, you specify a pipeline. The pipeline takes just one configuration option, which is a list of the filters to use. The list should always end with the WSGI *application* you want to serve, which is usually your Pylons application.

Let's use a pipeline to add the Gzip middleware you developed in the previous chapter. Remember that you added it to the simplesite.lib.middleware module you created. Here's an example of how the relevant sections of the config file should be set up:

```
[pipeline:main]
pipeline = gzip pylons

[filter:gzip]
use = egg:SimpleSite#gzip

[app:pylons]
# Your normal Pylons [app:main] section
use = egg:SimpleSite
...
```

Once again, because you've named the pipeline `main`, the section holding the configuration for Pylons will have to be renamed from `[app:main]` to something else, and once again this example uses `[app:pylons]` as a sensible name, so the WSGI application at the end of the pipeline list is named `pylons` to point to that section.

■**Note** Pylons config files typically allow you to specify lists, such as the list of filters on the pipeline, on multiple lines. The whitespace will be removed, so you could also write this example like this:

```
[pipeline:main]
pipeline = filter1
           filter2
           filter3
           app
```

This syntax makes it easier for you to comment out particular filters, which can sometimes be useful for debugging.

There is just one problem with this example as it stands: the `gzip` entry point doesn't exist in the SimpleSite application yet, so this example won't be able to actually load your Gzip middleware. You could fix this by using the Paste Gzip middleware instead by using `use = egg:Paste#gzip`, but let's update the SimpleSite project so that your middleware can be used. To do that, you need to know about factories.

Understanding Factories

In the examples so far, the `use` option has been used to specify a named entry point within an entry point group in a package, and that entry point has been used to load a function that, when called with arguments reflecting config file options, results in the construction of a particular object such as a server or WSGI application. In Paste Deploy terminology, the function pointed to by the entry point is known as a *factory* because it produces the desired object.

As you've seen, different types of sections in the config file use different entry point groups, and these point to different types of factories. Server sections point to server factories, app sections point to application factories, composite sections point to composite factories, and filters point to filter factories. Factories effectively translate the config options passed to them into appropriate variables that can be used to construct the objects they create. For the Gzip middleware to be usable directly from the config file, you'll need to create a filter app factory for it. A suitable factory would look like this:

```
def make_gzip_middleware(app, global_conf, **app_conf):
    compresslevel = int(app_conf.get('compresslevel', 9))
    return GzipMiddleware(app, compresslevel)
```

This factory would be passed the options in `[DEFAULT]` as the `global_conf` option and the options in the section for that filter as keyword arguments that can be gathered up into the `app_conf` dictionary. The `app` is a WSGI application that the middleware should wrap. As you can see, the `compresslevel` argument (a number from 0–9 is used to specify how much compression should be applied) is turned into an integer if it is present, and if not, the default value of 9 is used. The WSGI application is then wrapped in the middleware and returned.

Add this factory to the SimpleSite `lib/middleware.py` file you created in the previous chapter if you want to test the example.

Now that the factory is in place, let's set up the entry point. Filter factories are put in the `paste.filter_app_factory` entry point group. Edit the SimpleSite `setup.py` file to update the entry points section:

```
setup(
    ...
    entry_points="""
    [paste.app_factory]
    main = simplesite.config.middleware:make_app

    [paste.app_install]
    main = pylons.util:PylonsInstaller

    [paste.filter_app_factory]
    gzip = simplesite.lib.middleware:make_gzip_middleware
    """,
)
```

You'll need to run `python setup.py develop` again for the entry point change to be noticed; otherwise, you'll see this error:

```
LookupError: Entry point 'gzip' not found in egg 'SimpleSite' (dir: ➡
/home/james/Desktop/SimpleSite2b; protocols: paste.filter_factory, ➡
paste.filter_app_factory; entry_points: )
```

Once you've reinstalled the application, you will be able to test the filter. Be sure to remove the `app = GzipMiddleware(app, 5)` line from `config/middleware.py`; otherwise, you will get a `Content-Encoding` header with `gzip` specified twice. The browser won't understand this and will expect normal CSS or JavaScript instead of compressed content and will therefore most likely complain about illegal characters.

Once the Gzip middleware is disabled in `config/middleware.py`, update the config file. The lines in bold are the ones that have been changed:

```
...
[server:main]
use = egg:Paste#http
host = 127.0.0.1
port = 5000

[pipeline:main]
pipeline = gzip pylons

[filter:gzip]
use = egg:SimpleSite#gzip

[app:pylons]
use = egg:SimpleSite
full_stack = true
cache_dir = %(here)s/data
beaker.session.key = simplesite
beaker.session.secret = somesecret
...
```

With these changes in place, if you test the SimpleSite application and use LiveHTTPHeaders or Firebug to inspect the response at a URL such as `http://localhost:5000/page/edit/6`, you'll see the `.js` and `.css` files are still being Gzipped.

There is also an alternative syntax you can use if you simply want to wrap a WSGI application in one piece of middleware. You can use the `filter-with` option. Here's the config file with the `[pipeline:main]` section removed, the `[app:main]` section reintroduced, and the `filter-with` option being used:

```
...
[server:main]
use = egg:Paste#http
host = 127.0.0.1
port = 5000

[app:main]
use = egg:SimpleSite
filter-with = egg:SimpleSite#gzip
full_stack = true
cache_dir = %(here)s/data
beaker.session.key = simplesite
beaker.session.secret = somesecret
...
```

If you test this setup, you'll find it behaves in the same way as before and that the CSS and JavaScript files are Gzipped correctly.

There is one complication with the setup described so far. Paste Deploy, and hence the Pylons config file, supports two types of filters. The one you are using here is called a *filter-app* because the WSGI application is passed along with the configuration options to the filter-app factory. Another type of factory is one that is passed only the configuration options and that returns a function that, when *called*, returns the WSGI application wrapped in the filter. Such a factory is called a *filter* and would look like this:

```
def make_gzip_middleware_filter(global_conf, **app_conf):
    compresslevel = int(app_conf.get('compresslevel', 9))
    def filter(app):
        return GzipMiddleware(app, compresslevel)
    return filter
```

Add this to the `lib/middleware.py` file too, and update the entry points in `setup.py`:

```
setup(
    ...
    entry_points="""
    [paste.app_factory]
    main = simplesite.config.middleware:make_app

    [paste.app_install]
    main = pylons.util:PylonsInstaller

    [paste.filter_app_factory]
    gzip = simplesite.lib.middleware:make_gzip_middleware

    [paste.filter_factory]
    gzip = simplesite.lib.middleware:make_gzip_middleware_filter
    """,
)
```

If you run `python setup.py develop` again, the new entry points will take effect. When you have both a filter and a filter-app for the same entry point name, Paste Deploy uses the filter, so the new function you've added will be used in preference to the previous one.

Alternative Ways of Specifying Factories

So far in this chapter you've seen two ways to specify a factory. The first is to use an egg URI such as the following one to identify a factory via an entry point:

```
[filter:gzip]
use = egg:SimpleSite#gzip
```

The second approach is to refer to a different section within a config file and have that section be responsible for looking up the factory. You've just seen this in the discussion of pipelines where the items in the pipelines were the names of sections, for example:

```
[pipeline:main]
use = gzip pylons
```

In addition to these techniques, there are two other approaches. The first is to specify a section in an entirely different config file like this:

```
[app:main]
use = config:development.ini#main
```

You've actually seen this technique in Chapter 12 when it was used to ensure the test setup used the same configuration as the development setup. In that particular situation, you'll recall that the approach also had unexpected consequences because the `websetup.py` `setup_app()` function was automatically called each time you ran the tests and this interfered with your development database setup.

The final way to specify a factory is to point to it in some Python code:

```
[filter:gzip]
paste.filter_app_factory = simplesite.lib.middleware:make_gzip_middleware
```

In this last approach, rather than using the word `use`, you have to specify the entry point group name as the option name. This might seem slightly counterintuitive, but it is how the config file format works.

Configuration Inheritance

Paste Deploy also supports a very simple form of inheritance so that if you have to specify multiple sections with similar configuration options, you don't have to write them all out again. Here's how it works:

```
[app:main]
use = egg:AnimalTracker
cat = Tabby
dog = St Bernard

[app:other]
use = main
dog = Jack Russell
```

In this example, the `other` app inherits all the options from the `main` app, including the value for the `cat` option, but it overrides the `dog` option with the value `Jack Russell`.

The Pylons config file is actually a very flexible format. You can learn more about it at `http://pythonpaste.org/deploy/`.

Accessing the Pylons WSGI Application and Other Objects Programmatically

It is all very well for the `paster serve` and `paster setup-app` commands to be able to load WSGI applications and middleware from the config file, but sometimes you might want to be able to access them yourself. You frequently need to do this if you want to serve the application with a tool other than Paste's HTTP server, as you'll see when you learn about deployment in Chapter 19.

Accessing the Server, Application, and Filters

Paste Deploy provides three functions to allow you to access servers, applications (pipeline, composite, and app sections), and filters:

`loadserver(uri, name=None, **kw)`: This function returns a server wrapper function that takes the WSGI application to serve as its first argument. When called, the function uses the options from the `[server:main]` section, together with the WSGI application passed to it, to start the server. If your config file defines multiple servers, you can specify the one to use with `name`. For example, here you load the `alternative` server instead of the `main` one:

```
from paste.deploy import loadserver
server_wrapper = loadserver('config:/path/to/config.ini', name='alternative')
# Serve the application with the options in ``[server:alternative]``
server_wrapper(app)
```

`loadapp(uri, name=None, **kw)`: This is the function you are most likely to use, which returns a WSGI app based on the name of the application section you specify. If you don't specify a section name, it assumes you want the main section so loads the application based on the information in the `[app:main]`, `[composite:main]`, or `[pipeline:main]` section in the config file, depending on which you've used. For example:

```
from paste.deploy import loadapp
app = loadapp('config:/path/to/config.ini')
```

`loadfilter(uri, name=None, **kw)`: This function behaves similarly to `loadserver()` returning a wrapper function that, when called with a WSGI application, returns the application wrapped in the middleware specified in the filter section named `name` and constructed with the options from that section.

This doesn't load filter-app factories, just filter factories.

```
from paste.deploy import loadfilter
filter_wrapper = loadfilter('config:/path/to/config.ini')
# Wrap the application with the middleware specified by ``[filter:main]``
app = filter_wrapper(app)
```

Notice that each of these functions takes a config URI, not simply a path to a config file as you might have expected. Each of these functions also takes a `relative_to` argument that you can use if you want to specify a relative location for the URI; you can use it like this:

```
import os
from paste.deploy import loadserver
server = loadserver('config:config.ini', relative_to=os.getcwd())
# Start the server
server(wsgi_app)
```

If you try to use a relative path without specifying `relative_to`, you will get an error explaining `no context keyword argument given`. This error isn't particularly informative, but specifying `relative_to` resolves this error.

Accessing Configuration Options

There are occasions when even the functions described so far aren't low level enough and you want to get directly at the individual options set. For this circumstance, Paste Deploy provides an `appconfig()` function that returns a config object. Return the application configuration for the app factory specified:

```
appconfig(uri, name=None, relative_to=None, global_conf=None)
```

The config object returned has two attributes, `local_conf` and `global_conf`, both of which are dictionaries. The `.global_conf` dictionary contains all the options from the [DEFAULT] section, and the `.local_conf` dictionary contains all the options from whichever application section you specified as the `name` argument to `appconfig()` defaulting to `main` if no `name` is specified.

The config object itself behaves like a dictionary too. It has all the keys of both the `local_conf` dictionary and the `global_conf` dictionary, but where two keys have different values, the `local_conf` value overrides the global conf value. The config object therefore has the same values you would access as `pylons.config['app_conf']` from a Pylons controller, and the `.global_conf` attribute contains the same values you would access as `pylons.config['app_conf']`.

Here's an example demonstrating this:

```
>>> from paste.deploy import appconfig
>>> config = appconfig('config:/path/to/config.ini')
>>> combined = {}
>>> combined.update(config.global_conf)
>>> combined.update(config.local_conf)
>>> print config.items() == combined.items()
True
```

As you can see, the configuration in the `config` object itself matches that obtained by combining the `global_conf` and `local_conf` dictionaries.

Creating a Pylons Application with Paste Deploy

Using the Paste Deploy `loadapp()` function described earlier is the best way of getting access to the Pylons WSGI application. At the start of this chapter, you learned how to use entry points to access the `make_app()` function in your project's `config/middleware.py` file. This function is a standard Paste Deploy app factory, so although you can create a Pylons WSGI application object by calling it directly with the configuration options you want to create the application with, it is usually much easier to use the `loadapp()` function. This function does both steps at once, looking up the entry point and calling the `make_app()` factory with the configuration options from the config file.

You can get the WSGI application object from your Pylons configuration file like this:

```
from paste.deploy import loadapp
wsgi_app = loadapp('config:/path/to/config.ini')
```

You can then serve the file using a WSGI server. Here is an example using the WSGI Reference Implementation server included in Python 2.5 and newer:

```
from paste.deploy import loadapp
wsgi_app = loadapp('config:/path/to/config.ini')

from wsgiref import simple_server
httpd = simple_server.WSGIServer(('',8000), simple_server.WSGIRequestHandler)
httpd.set_app(wsgi_app)
httpd.serve_forever()
```

The `paster serve` command you are used to using while developing Pylons projects combines these two steps of creating a WSGI app from the config file and serving the resulting file to give the illusion that it is serving the config file directly.

The Pylons Middleware Stack

Let's just recap what you've learned so far about how a Pylons application is constructed:

- A Pylons application is loaded from a config file in a format understood by the Paste Deploy package.

- The Paste Deploy `loadapp()` function is called to parse the config file.

- The `use` option in the main application section (be it an `[app:main]`, `[pipeline:main]`, or `[composite:main]` section) is used to determine the factory to use to create the Pylons application.

- The `make_app()` factory in the project's `config/middleware.py` file is called and returns the configured Pylons app ready to serve requests.

If you open a Pylons project's `config/middleware.py` file and look at the `make_app()` function, you will see that a WSGI application named `app` is created. This is your Pylons application object and is what is ultimately responsible for calling the actions in the controllers you have created. The `make_app()` function looks like this at the time of writing:

```
def make_app(global_conf, full_stack=True, **app_conf):

    # Configure the Pylons environment
    load_environment(global_conf, app_conf)

    # The Pylons WSGI app
    app = PylonsApp()

    # CUSTOM MIDDLEWARE HERE (filtered by error handling middlewares)

    # Routing/Session/Cache Middleware
    app = RoutesMiddleware(app, config['routes.map'])
    app = SessionMiddleware(app, config)
    app = CacheMiddleware(app, config)

    if asbool(full_stack):
        # Handle Python exceptions
        app = ErrorHandler(app, global_conf, **config['pylons.errorware'])
```

```
    # Display error documents for 401, 403, 404 status codes (and
    # 500 when debug is disabled)
    if asbool(config['debug']):
        app = StatusCodeRedirect(app)
    else:
        app = StatusCodeRedirect(app, [400, 401, 403, 404, 500])

# Establish the Registry for this application
app = RegistryManager(app)

# Static files (If running in production, and Apache or another web
# server is handling this static content, remove the following 3 lines)
static_app = StaticURLParser(config['pylons.paths']['static_files'])
app = Cascade([static_app, app])
return app
```

After the app object is created, it is then wrapped in lots of different WSGI middleware components. Each of the components performs a different task:

RoutesMiddleware: This is responsible for matching a URL against the route map you've specified in config/routing.py and setting up the routing variables.

SessionMiddleware: This is responsible for providing the Pylons session global that provides the session functionality you used in Chapter 8 to create the flash message.

CacheMiddleware: This sets up a Beaker CacheManager and provides the caching facility you saw in Chapter 5 when I covered caching templates. The SessionMiddleware is also provided by the Beaker package.

ErrorHandler: This catches any exceptions that have occurred during the processing of a request and, depending on the settings in the config file, either will return a 500 Internal Server Error for the StatusCodeRedirect middleware mentioned next to handle or will start the Pylons interactive debugger you learned about in Chapter 4 to help you track down where the error occurred.

StatusCodeRedirect: This catches responses with certain HTTP status codes such as 401, 403, 404, and sometimes 500 and internally redirects the request to the error controller in your project's controllers/error.py file so that a nice-looking error page can be generated.

RegistryManager: This keeps track of which of the Pylons global variables should be used in each thread of execution so that information from one request doesn't get confused with information from another request being handled by Pylons at the same time.

Cascade: This handles two apps, a StaticURLParser application to serve files from the public directory and the Pylons app itself. On each request the two applications are called in turn until one of them is able to handle the request URL.

The reason this architecture is so powerful is that you are free to add your own middleware to the stack, enabling you to completely change the way Pylons behaves if you want. For example, if you didn't want the error documents support, you could comment out the StatusCodeRedirect middleware. If you wanted all the responses to be Gzip compressed to save bandwidth, you can simply add Gzip middleware, as you've seen already.

Application State vs. Request State

Once the application has been created with all the middleware components correctly set up, it is held in memory by the server, ready to receive a request. The application object, the middleware, and all the other Pylons objects that were configured when make_app() was called will persist between each request. This means the make_app() factory is called only once when the Pylons application is created, but the app object returned from make_app() is called on each request. This makes Pylons very fast because the app object doesn't need to be re-created to handle a request, but it also means that the process of creating a Pylons application is completely separate from the process of handling a request.

In the next sections, you'll see in detail which processes occur when the app object is being set up and which occur before and after a request has been handled by a controller action.

Creating an Application

You've already seen the objects and middleware involved in the creation of an application, but in the following sections, you'll see in detail what happens in each of the components as the application is created.

Loading the Pylons Environment

The first thing that happens in make_app() is a call to load the environment:

```
# Configure the Pylons environment
load_environment(global_conf, app_conf)
```

This function is actually located in your project's config/environment.py file and is responsible for any configuration of your application that you don't want to expose to the end user of an application in the config file. You have to be slightly careful when editing config/environment.py because some aspects of Pylons' behavior rely on the objects that are set up there.

The load_environment() function is responsible for the following:

- Setting up the paths that will be used in your project to access controllers, static files, and templates. By default, the paths are configured to point to your project's controllers, public, and templates directories, respectively.

- Initializing the Pylons config object with information about the project including where the function to set up the routes is, which module should be used as the h object within templates, and which object should be used as the app_globals object. By default, these are set to the config/routing.py file's make_map() function, the project's lib/helpers.py module, and an instance of the Globals class in lib/app_globals.py, respectively.

- Using the config object to indirectly attach a mako_lookup attribute to the app_globals object, which will later be used by the render() function to render Mako templates. The mako_lookup attribute is actually an instance of a Mako TemplateLookup object, and as you'll recall from Chapter 5, this can be customized to change Mako's behavior or replaced if support for a different templating language is required.

- Setting up a SQLAlchemy engine and initializing the model (if you chose a project template that included SQLAlchemy when running the paster create command). The way the engine is created and the role of init_engine() is explained in Chapter 7.

At the end of the load_environment() function are these lines:

```
# CONFIGURATION OPTIONS HERE (note: all config options will override
# any Pylons config options)
```

Any further customization you want to do should usually happen after these lines.

The PylonsApp Instance

After the environment has been loaded to set up the app_globals, h, and config objects as well as the template engine and SQLAlchemy (if necessary), a Pylons application is created. This is done with the following line in make_app():

```
# The Pylons WSGI app
app = PylonsApp()
```

The PylonsApp instance is the very heart of your Pylons application; it is defined in the pylons.wsgiapp module, and its instance (app) is a valid WSGI application. At this stage, all app has to do is initialize itself with the config object, the app_globals object, and the package name and various options that will be used to set up the request and response during a request. This all happens behind the scenes and is not something you would normally have to deal with. You'll hear more about the PylonsApp instance when I discuss how it behaves during a request.

The Middleware Chain

Next, the PylonsApp instance app is wrapped in a series of different middleware components, each of which is initialized:

```
# Routing/Session/Cache Middleware
app = RoutesMiddleware(app, config['routes.map'])
app = SessionMiddleware(app, config)
app = CacheMiddleware(app, config)
```

First the RoutesMiddleware is initialized and is passed the route map it will be expected to deal with via the config['routes.map'] object that was set up in the call to load_environment().

Note You might be wondering how the config object was set up even though it wasn't passed directly to load_environment(). Both config/middleware.py and config/environment.py import the object from the pylons module, which itself imports it from pylons.configuration. The config object is defined as a module global and is an instance of pylons.configuration.PylonsConfig. It isn't an ordinary global, though; it is inherited from a paste.config.DispatchingConifg object, which can keep different configurations separate in different threads. Because both files are accessing the same object, changes made in config/environment.py are reflected in config/middleware.py.

After the RoutesMiddleware is set up, SessionMiddleware and CacheMiddleware are both set up. These use the beaker.* configuration options from the config object in order to initialize themselves. The options specify where the session and cache stores should be set up. By default, this happens in a data directory relative to the config file being used to serve the application.

What happens next depends on whether you've set full_stack to true or false in the configuration file. If it is true, which is the default, then the ErrorHandler and StatusCodeRedirect middleware will be set up; otherwise, they'll be ignored.

```
if asbool(full_stack):
    # Handle Python exceptions
    app = ErrorHandler(app, global_conf, **config['pylons.errorware'])
```

```
# Display error documents for 401, 403, 404 status codes (and
# 500 when debug is disabled)
if asbool(config['debug']):
    app = StatusCodeRedirect(app)
else:
    app = StatusCodeRedirect(app, [400, 401, 403, 404, 500])
```

If the fullstack option is enabled, the ErrorHandler is set up with options from config ['pylons.errorware']. These in turn are set up when the config object's init_app() method is called in config/environment.py and contain the options that will be used in error reporting such as the e-mail address to send error reports to, the SMTP server to use, and who the e-mail should appear to have come from. The values used are all obtained from the [DEFAULT] section of the config file. The subject of the e-mail and the error log to use are also passed to the ErrorHandler in the same dictionary, but these values cannot be configured in the config file.

If debug mode is on, the ErrorHandler middleware sets up the WebError package's EvalException middleware, which provides the Pylons Interactive Debugger you first saw in Chapter 4; otherwise, it sets up the WebError package's ErrorMiddleware to handle the e-mail error reports.

During a request, the StatusCodeRedirect middleware creates a copy of the current request in case it later needs to perform a subrequest to the error controller's document() to generate an error page, but during application initialization, the middleware just wraps itself around the app object.

Next to be wrapped around the app object is the RegistryManager middleware. This doesn't need any configuration as the application is being created, but its importance will become apparent when you look at how Pylons handles a request in the next section.

```
# Establish the Registry for this application
app = RegistryManager(app)
```

The final piece of middleware is the Cascade. This is configured with an instance of a StaticURLParser as its first argument. The StaticURLParser will be responsible for serving static files and is configured with config['pylons.paths']['static_files']), which was set up in config/environment.py to point to your project's public directory. The second item in the list specified as an argument to the Cascade is the app object all the middleware components have been wrapping.

```
# Static files (If running in production, and Apache or another web
# server is handling this static content, remove the following 3 lines)
static_app = StaticURLParser(config['pylons.paths']['static_files'])
app = Cascade([static_app, app])
return app
```

At this point, the application state has been configured. All the middleware has been initialized, and the PylonsApp and StaticURLParser WSGI applications have been initialized. At this point, the app object is ready to handle a request, and this is where the middleware components play an important part.

With the application state successfully configured, make_app() can return the app object to the server, ready to be called to handle a request.

Handling a Request

You'll remember from the previous chapter that when a WSGI application is called (whether wrapped in middleware or not), it is passed two arguments, the environment dictionary and the start_response() callable. Let's assume for the moment that there are no pipelines or composite applications set up in the config file. In that case, because the Cascade middleware was the last middleware that wrapped the `app` object, it will be the first one to be passed the `environ` and `start_response()` arguments.

This means that although the middleware components were set up from top to bottom when they were being initialized, it is actually the middleware at the bottom of the `config/middleware.py` file that receives the request information first, and the request information passes from the bottom of the middleware chain toward the top and eventually to the `PylonsApp` instance, `app`. Figure 17-1 illustrates this request behavior.

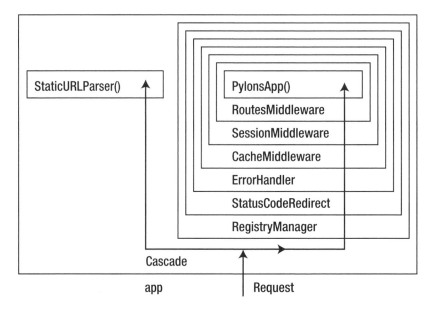

Figure 17-1. *Middleware request architecture*

The Cascade

The first piece of middleware to be called on any request is the `Cascade`. When it is passed `environ` and `start_response()`, it first calls `static_app` to see whether the URL requested matches a file in your project's `public` directory. If `static_app` returns a 404 Not Found response, the `Cascade` will instead call the main Pylons application.

■**Note** This is why you need to delete the `public/index.html` file before the root URL of the site will serve content from a controller. If you changed the order of the applications in the `Cascade`, you would not need to delete the file because the Pylons application would be checked first before the `public` directory, but since more files are likely to be handled by `static_app` than Pylons during each page view, it is usually more efficient to keep the order as it is.

The next middleware in the chain is the `RegistryManager`, which is responsible for managing the Pylons globals in a thread-safe way. Let's look at it in detail before returning to the middleware chain.

The Registry Manager, StackedObjectProxy, and Pylons Globals

Pylons aims to avoid the use of any complex Python code that appears to behave in a "magical" way, but there is one aspect of the Pylons architecture that often appears to be magic to those who haven't seen anything similar before: the Pylons globals. People wonder how a module global such as the Pylons template context c can be available throughout an application and yet take a different value depending on the thread in which it is executing.

The answer is that Pylons globals (such as c, request, and response) are all instances of the paste.registry.StackedObjectProxy class and not the objects they appear to be at all. When you access their properties or methods, they return the result of applying that action to the object they are associated with in the current thread so that they behave as if they were that object. Put another way, they *proxy* attributes to the correct object in a thread-safe way based on the scope of the request in which they run to give the illusion of being the objects themselves.

You can always access the underlying object for a particular global in the current request by calling the _current_obj() method on a StackedObjectProxy. For example, to obtain the *actual* request object being used in a request, rather than the StackedObjectProxy that is *proxying* to it, you could use pylons.request._current_obj().

Now that you know what a StackedObjectProxy is, let's look at the role of the RegistryManager during a request. Here's an example based on the Paste Registry documentation, which demonstrates how the globals are set up and used in a pure-WSGI environment:

```
from paste.registry import RegistryManager, StackedObjectProxy
from pylons.controllers.util import Request

request = StackedObjectProxy()

# WSGI app stack (imagine the middleware stack in config/middleware.py)
app = App()
app = RegistryManager(App)

# WSGI app (imagine the PylonsApp)
class App(object):
    def __call__(self, environ, start_response):
        obj = Request(environ) # The request-like theread-local object you want
                               # to access via pylons.myglobal
        if environ.has_key('paste.registry'):
            environ['paste.registry'].register(request, obj)
```

The RegistryManager adds a new Registry() as environ['paste.registry'] on each request and calls the existing registry's prepare() method to set it up for the new registry context.

The registration process involves telling the registry which objects in the current thread should be attached to which globals. This ensures that during the scope of the request, attributes from the correct real object will be returned any time you access an attribute or method of one of the Pylons global objects, even though the global is really a StackedObjectProxy.

You'll see in the section "The Role of PylonsApp" that the registration happens within the PylonsApp instance app.

▪**Tip** If you ever see StackedProxyObject errors in your Pylons application, it may be because you are trying to access one of the Pylons globals outside the scope of a request and therefore before Pylons has had a chance to set up and register the real object with the particular StackedObjectProxy global it is associated with.

Returning to the Middleware Chain

Now that you have an idea of how the `RegistryManager` middleware works, let's continue looking at how the other middleware components in the chain behave during a request.

If the `full_stack` option is set to `true`, the `StatusCodeRedirect` and `ErrorHandler` middleware are called. The `StatusCodeRedirect` middleware creates a copy of the request information, but it doesn't do anything with it until it deals with the response after a controller action is called. Next, the `CacheMiddleware` and then the `SessionMiddleware` are called, each adding information to the `environ` dictionary that the `PylonsApp` app instance will use when it is eventually called to set up the Pylons cache and session functionality.

Next, the `RoutesMiddleware` is called. This now assembles the request URL from the information in the `environ` dictionary it is passed and works through the route map as you saw in Chapter 9. It adds the routing variables it matches to the `environ` dictionary.

Finally, the `PylonsApp` instance, app, gets called itself.

The Role of PylonsApp

The ultimate responsibility of app is to call a Pylons controller action and return a response, but it has to do a number of things first. Each of these is handled by a different method on the `PylonsApp` class, and they are called in the order described here:

> `PylonsApp.setup_app_env()`: This creates all the global objects for the request including the Pylons `request` and `response` objects, the translator used for internationalization, and the Pylons template context global c. It adds these and other objects to the template context object as attributes and makes it available as `pylons.pylons` in the `environ` dictionary.

> `PylonsApp.register_globals()`: If the `RegistryManager` middleware is present, each of the Pylons globals is registered with the registry. This includes `pylons.response`, `pylons.request`, `pylons.app_globals`, `pylons.config`, `pylons.h`, `pylons.c`, and `pylons.translator`. It will also register `pylons.session` and `pylons.cache` if the `SessionMiddleware` and `CacheMiddleware` are present. Pylons also adds a `pylons.url` object that is simply the current request URL.

> At this point, all of these objects, when imported from the `pylons` module in your application, will proxy the attributes and methods you call on them to the correct underlying objects for the current request thread (that is, the ones created in the `PylonsApp.setup_app_env()` call or as the request passed through the middleware stack).

> `PylonsApp.load_test_env()`: If Pylons is operating in testing mode, this method will be called to add the standard Pylons environment variables described earlier to `environ['paste.testing_variables']` so that they are available as attributes of the `paste.fixture response` object you learned about in Chapter 12. These currently include the attributes req, response, `tmpl_context` and its alias c, `app_globals` and its alias g, h, and config. If the session and cache middleware are present, it also sets up `session` and `cache` attributes.

With all the objects correctly set up and registered, the dispatch to the controller action can begin. The following methods on `PylonsApp` are called in this order:

> `PylonsApp.resolve()`: This uses the routing arguments that the `RoutesMiddleware` added to `environ['wsgiorg.routing_args']` to retrieve a controller name and return the controller instance from the appropriate controller module.

> `PylonsApp.dispatch()`: Finally, once the controller instance has been created, PylonsApp can call its `__call__()` method with `environ` and `start_response()` to begin the dispatch.

Note You can override these last two methods to change how controllers are resolved and dispatched to if you want to customize Pylons' behavior. You just need to use your derived object in `config/middleware.py` instead of `PylonsApp`.

Even though the controller has now been dispatched, there is still some more you need to know about how the controller behaves to call the action.

The Role of WSGIController

You'll remember that your project's controllers are inherited from `BaseController` in your project's `lib/base.py` file and that `BaseController` is inherited from `pylons.controller.core.WSGIController`. This means that when `PylonsApp` instantiates and calls one of your project's controllers, it is actually calling the `WSGIController.__call__()` method.

The `WSGIController.__call__()` method proceeds as follows. First, it checks to see whether the controller has a `__before__()` method. If it does, it calls its `_inspect_call()` method that itself calls `_get_method_args()` to find out which arguments the method expects. The `__before__()` method is then called with those arguments.

Next, the controller action itself needs to be called. This is done with a call to the controller's `_dispatch_call()` method, which finds out which action to call from the routing variables and then calls `__inspect_call()` itself to find out the arguments the action needs and to call the action with those arguments.

Finally, after the action is called, the `__call__()` method checks to see whether an `__after__()` method exists. If it does, it will *always* be run on each request after the action, even if the action raises an exception or issues a redirect. Once again, `__after__()` is run by a call to the `_inspect_call()` method.

If an action is not found to handle the request, the controller will raise an "Action Not Found" error in debug mode; otherwise, a 404 Not Found error will be returned.

Handling the Response

Once the controller action is finally called, it can perform all manner of operations using the Pylons objects that have just been described. The whole of the first two parts of the book were dedicated to some of the ways Pylons could be used, so I won't repeat them here.

The action can do any of the following:

- Call the `abort()` or `redirect_to()` functions to halt the request
- Trigger an unexpected exception
- Return a response that requires an error document
- Return a function to stream content
- Return a Unicode object or UTF-8 encoded string as a result

Let's see how Pylons handles each of these cases.

abort(), redirect_to(), and HTTPException

During each call to WSGIController's _inspect_call() method when the request was being handled, the call to the method being inspected is wrapped in a try...except block. If a certain type of exception known as an HTTPException occurs, Pylons will turn that exception into a normal HTTP response. This might seem like an odd behavior, but you'll recall that Pylons provides the functions abort() and redirect_to() in pylons.controllers.util. These functions work by raising an HTTPException when they are called, so it is the code in the _inspect_call() method that is responsible for making these functions result in the correct HTTP response.

Since the _inspect_call() method is also used to call the __before__ and __after__ actions if they exist, abort() and redirect_to() can also be used in those actions.

Exception Handling

When an exception that isn't an HTTPException is raised, it goes straight through the try...except block in _inspect_call() and isn't caught until another try...except block in the error-handling middleware. If debug mode was enabled, the EvalException middleware would have been set up. If not, the ErrorMiddleware would be in place.

If the EvalException middleware is set up, you will see the familiar Pylons Interactive Debugger. If not, an error report gets e-mailed, and the exception is turned into a 500 Internal Server Error response by the ErrorMiddleware.

The StatusBasedRedirect middleware is below the error-handling middleware, so it receives the response *after* the error handler. At this point, the StatusCodeRedirect middleware can't distinguish between a 500 error triggered by the ErrorMiddleware or a 500 response from a Pylons controller action, so both are treated in the same way. In debug mode 500, responses are ignored by the StatusCodeRedirect middleware; with debug mode disabled, an error document is displayed.

Error Documents

When the StatusCodeRedirect middleware receives a response that it was set up to intercept, it uses a copy of the request information (which it made when the request was passing through it toward the controller action) to start a subrequest to the error controller's document() action to generate the familiar Pylons error page. You'll see more about error documents, how they work, and how to customize them in Chapter 21.

Streaming Content

If you need to stream content, you can always use one of the techniques described in Chapter 16 to mount a WSGI application in a Pylons application and set up the WSGI application to stream the content, but Pylons controller actions support streaming directly too.

You need to turn debug mode off to stream content because the exception middleware needs to have the entire response finished before it will pass on the result farther down the middleware chain.

Turn off debug mode in your INI file by uncommenting the following line:

```
#set debug = false
```

Now that it's disabled, returning an iterator object or a generator is sufficient to start streaming output. Here's an example that sends a new number every two seconds:

```
import time

class StreamingController(object):

    def output(self):
        def output_pause():
            number = 0
            while 1:
                number += 1
                yield number
                time.sleep(2)
        return output_pause()
```

If you were to set this up in a Pylons project and visit
http://localhost:5000/streaming/output, you should now see a number sent every two seconds,
continuing forever.

■**Caution** You have to be slightly careful when using time.sleep() in a production system because it causes
the thread in which the Pylons application is running to simply sleep. If you are running Pylons on a multithreaded
server using a worker pool of ten threads (which is the default setup you will be using when running paster
serve), there is a chance that in busy periods all your threads could just be sleeping rather than serving requests,
and this will adversely affect the performance of your Pylons application.

Returning Unicode from an Action

Now that you've seen some of the less usual cases for controller action responses, let's look at
what happens during a normal response when you return a string, most likely as a result of a call
to render() to render a template.

First the response passes back from the WSGIController.__call__() method and the
PylonsApp.dispatch() method to the middleware chain. The response will start at the middleware
defined at the top of config/middleware.py and end with the ones defined at the bottom. As it
passes through the SessionMiddleware, it will have a session cookie added to it if there was a session
cookie in the request or if you called session.save() during the request to create a session store for
the current user. The response will then pass back through the other middleware without being
altered and eventually be sent back to the server where it is passed to the browser.

Summary

This chapter covered a lot including entry points, the config file format, factories, and the details of
Pylons' request and response architecture. There is a lot going on in Pylons, but I hope this chapter
will have given you a good enough overview for you to be able to explore the Pylons code for yourself.

Pylons was always designed to be highly customizable and to expose all the relevant parts so
that you can change it yourself if you need to do so. Feel free to read the Paste and Pylons source
code to get a better idea of how they work and to experiment with alternative setups in your own
Pylons applications.

# CHAPTER 18

Authentication and Authorization

There comes a point in most projects when you need to be able to restrict access to certain parts of your web site. This might be so that you can create an administration area or because your users are storing private information and want to know their data is password protected. To do this, you will need to implement a security system that can confirm the identity of a user and then restrict the pages each user has access to based on their permissions to each area. These two processes are known as *authentication* and *authorization*.

Authentication is typically performed by asking a visitor for their username and password. If the visitor enters the correct password, you can be fairly sure they are who they claim to be. Once a user has been authenticated, your security system needs some way of remembering who the user is so that they are not asked to enter their username and password the next time they try to access a restricted page. This could be achieved by setting a cookie on the user's browser so that the next time they visit a page, the security system can read a secret code from the cookie and determine which user is accessing the page from the secret code.

Just because the user has been authenticated, it doesn't necessarily mean they should be authorized to access the page they are trying to visit. If, for example, you signed into a Yahoo! Mail account with your username and password, you wouldn't expect to be able to read the e-mails of other users, because you wouldn't be authorized to do so.

Authorization is usually performed by checking the authenticated user has the appropriate permissions to access the page they are trying to visit. The permission check can be as simple as ensuring that a user has in fact signed in but can also be very sophisticated involving checks about the user's roles, group, or even which computer the user is accessing the web site from.

In this chapter, you'll start off by looking at how Pylons handles private data before learning how to implement a basic security system from scratch. You'll then move on to considering an authentication and authorization tool called AuthKit and looking at its main features. In the next chapter, you'll use the knowledge you've gained about AuthKit in this chapter to add a sign-in form and role-based permissions system to the SimpleSite application.

Private Data

The easiest way to prevent *any* user from accessing a controller action is to make that action private. You'll remember from Chapter 9 that Pylons treats any controller method that starts with an underscore (_) character as private and will not dispatch to it as a controller action. This means controller methods beginning with _ are not directly publicly accessible.

Let's create a controller to demonstrate this. Run the following commands to create a test project; you won't need SQLAlchemy or Google App Engine support:

```
$ paster create --template=pylons AuthTest
$ cd AuthTest
$ paster controller example
$ paster serve --reload development.ini
```

Now add the following content to the example controller:

```
class ExampleController(BaseController):

    def hello(self):
        return self._result()

    def _result(self):
        return 'Hello World!'
```

If you start the server and visit http://localhost:5000/example/_result, you will be shown a 404 Not Found error document, but if you visit http://localhost:5000/example/hello, you will see the Hello World! message because the public action hello() is able to return the value from the private method _result().

A Homegrown Solution

Although making certain controller actions private prevents any user from accessing a method, you will often need to restrict access to just certain users. You can do this by using Pylons' __before__() method and session functionality.

Create a new controller for the AuthTest project called homegrown:

```
$ paster controller homegrown
```

You'll recall that on each request the __before__() method of the controller is called before the controller action is called. Let's set up a simple session variable named user that will be used to store the username of the authenticated user. If the user session variable isn't set, you can assume no user is signed in. If it is set, you can set the REMOTE_USER environment variable.

```
class HomegrownController(BaseController):

    def __before__(self, action, **params):
        user = session.get('user')
        if user:
            request.environ['REMOTE_USER'] = user

    def signin(self):
        if len(request.params) > 1 and \
         request.params['password'] == request.params['username']:
            session['user'] = request.params['username']
            session.save()
            return redirect_to(controller='homegrown', action="private")
        else:
            return """\
                <html>
                  <head><title>Please Login!</title></head>
                  <body>
                    <h1>Please Login</h1>
                    <form action="signin" method="post">
```

```
            <dl>
              <dt>Username:</dt>
              <dd><input type="text" name="username"></dd>
              <dt>Password:</dt>
              <dd><input type="password" name="password"></dd>
            </dl>
            <input type="submit" name="authform" />
            <hr />
          </form>
        </body>
      </html>
    """

def public(self):
    return 'This is public'

def private(self):
    if request.environ.get("REMOTE_USER"):
        return 'This is private'
    else:
        return redirect_to(controller='homegrown', action="signin")
```

In this example, you can access `http://localhost:5000/homegrown/public` without signing in, but if you visit `http://localhost:5000/homegrown/private`, you will be redirected to the sign-in form at `http://localhost:5000/homegrown/signin` to sign in. If you enter a username that is the same as the password, you will be shown the private message. You will be able to continue to see the private message until you clear the Pylons session cookie by closing your browser.

This example works perfectly well for the straightforward case described earlier, but when you start dealing with complex permissions and different authentication methods, it quickly becomes preferable to use an authentication and authorization framework.

AuthKit

AuthKit is a complete authentication and authorization framework for WSGI applications and was written specifically to provide Pylons with a flexible approach to authentication and authorization. AuthKit can be used stand-alone with its user management API or integrated with other systems such as a database. You'll see both of these approaches in this chapter and the next.

AuthKit consists of three main components:

Authentication middleware: Intercepts any permission errors or HTTP responses with a 401 status code and presents a user with a way to sign in. Various authentication methods can be used, and the middleware is also responsible for setting the `REMOTE_USER` environ variable once a user has signed in.

Permission objects: Represent a particular permission that a user may or may not have.

Authorization adaptors: Check the permissions, triggering a `PermissionError`, which is intercepted by the authentication middleware if the permission check doesn't pass. If no `PermissionErrors` are raised, the user is considered to be authorized.

In this chapter, you'll learn about each of these components in turn before looking at AuthKit's more advanced features.

Of course, AuthKit is just one of the authentication and authorization tools available for Pylons. There may be occasions when you want to handle all authentication yourself in your application rather than delegating responsibility to AuthKit. Although AuthKit provides a basic platform on which to build, you should also be willing to look at the AuthKit source code and use it as a basis for your own ideas.

Note One toolset that is proving to be particularly popular at the time of writing is `repoze.who`, which is part of the repoze project to help make Zope components available to WSGI projects such as Pylons. If you are interested in `repoze.who`, you should visit the web site at `http://static.repoze.org/whodocs/`.

Authentication Middleware

AuthKit is actually very straightforward to integrate into an existing Pylons project. You'll remember from Chapter 3 that a web browser finds out what type of response has been returned from the server based on the HTTP status code. There are two HTTP status codes that are particularly relevant to authentication and authorization. A 401 status code tells the browser that the user is not authenticated, and a 403 status code tells the browser that the user is not authorized (which you may have seen described in error pages as `Forbidden`). AuthKit's authentication middleware works at the HTTP level by responding to 401 status responses so that the authentication middleware can work with *any* application code that is HTTP compliant, regardless of whether AuthKit is used for the authorization checks.

Let's create a new project to use with AuthKit. Run the following commands to install AuthKit and create a test project; again, you won't need SQLAlchemy support:

```
$ easy_install "AuthKit>=0.4.3,<=0.4.99"
$ paster create --template=pylons AuthDemo
$ cd AuthDemo
$ paster serve --reload development.ini
```

To set up the authentication middleware, edit the AuthTest project's `config/middleware.py` file, and add the following import at the end of the existing imports at the top of the file:

```
import authkit.authenticate
```

Then add this line:

```
app = authkit.authenticate.middleware(app, app_conf)
```

just before these lines and at the same indentation level:

```
# Display error documents for 401, 403, 404 status codes (and
# 500 when debug is disabled)
if asbool(config['debug']):
    app = StatusCodeRedirect(app)
else:
    app = StatusCodeRedirect(app, [400, 401, 403, 404, 500])
```

The authentication middleware has to be set up before the error documents middleware because you don't want any 401 responses from the controllers being changed to error pages before the authentication middleware has a chance to present a sign-in facility to the user.

If you had set the `full_stack` option to `false` in the Pylons config file, you would need to add the AuthKit authenticate middleware before these lines; otherwise, it wouldn't get added:

```
if asbool(full_stack):
    # Handle Python exceptions
    app = ErrorHandler(app, global_conf, **config['pylons.errorware'])
```

■ **Tip** You'll remember from Chapter 16 that middleware is simply a component that sits between the server and the controller action that is being called and has an opportunity to change the response that the controller action returns.

Now that the authentication middleware is set up, you need to configure it. AuthKit is designed to be completely configurable from the Pylons config file and has a number of required options that tell AuthKit which authentication method you want to use and how AuthKit should check whether the username and password that have been entered are correct.

Add the following options to the end of the [`app:main`] section:

```
authkit.setup.method = form, cookie
authkit.form.authenticate.user.data = visitor:open_sesame
authkit.cookie.secret = secret string
```

These options set up AuthKit to use form and cookie-based authentication. This also sets up a user named `visitor` with the password `open_sesame`. These options will be passed to the authentication middleware via the `app_conf` argument.

At this stage, you can test that the middleware is set up and ready to be used. Create a new controller called `auth`:

```
$ paster controller auth
```

and add the following action:

```
def private(self):
    response.status = "401 Not authenticated"
    return "You are not authenticated"
```

If you visit `http://localhost:5000/auth/private`, the 401 status will be returned and intercepted by the AuthKit middleware, and you will see the default sign-in screen for form and cookie authentication displayed at the same URL, as shown in Figure 18-1.

Figure 18-1. *The default sign-in screen when using the form and cookie authentication method*

There is just one more change you need to make in order to properly test your authentication setup. At the moment, the `private` action always returns a 401 HTTP status code, even if a user is authenticated. This means the first time you sign in, you'll see the error document for a 401 response, but on subsequent requests you'll see the sign-in form again.

The authenticate middleware automatically adds a key to the `environ` dictionary named `REMOTE_USER` if a user is authenticated. The value of the key is the username of the authenticated user. Let's use this fact to update the `private()` action so that a user can see the message once they are authenticated:

```
def private(self):
    if request.environ.get("REMOTE_USER"):
        return "You are authenticated!"
    else:
        response.status = "401 Not authenticated"
        return "You are not authenticated"
```

If you start the server and visit `http://localhost:5000/auth/private`, you will now be able to sign in. If you sign in with the username and password you specified in the config file (`visitor` and `open_sesame`), you will see the message `You are authenticated!`. If you refresh the page, you will notice you are still signed in because AuthKit set a cookie to remember you.

To implement a facility for signing out, you will need to add this line to your config file:

```
authkit.cookie.signoutpath = /auth/signout
```

This tells AuthKit that when a user visits the URL `http://localhost:5000/auth/signout`, an HTTP header should be added to the response to remove the cookie. AuthKit doesn't know what else should be included in the response, so you will also need to add a `signout()` action to the controller at that URL so that the visitor is not shown a 404 Not Found page when they sign out:

```
def signout(self):
    return "Successfully signed out!"
```

After you have restarted the server, you can test the sign-out process by visiting `http://localhost:5000/hello/signout`. If you use Firebug to look at the HTTP headers, you'll notice AuthKit has added this to the response headers to sign you out:

```
Set-Cookie    authkit=""; Path=/
```

■**Caution** Setting the header to remove the AuthKit cookie happens in the AuthKit middleware, *after* the response from the controller action. The controller action itself plays no part in the sign-out process, so it could return the text You are still signed in, but the user would still be signed out. More dangerously, if you entered an incorrect path for the authkit.cookie.signoutpath option, the user would still get a message saying they are signed out when they are actually still signed in. It is therefore very important that you enter the correct path in the authkit.cookie.signoutpath option.

Authorization and Permissions

By using the AuthKit middleware, you have been able to quickly implement a fully working authentication system, but so far you have had to perform the authorization by manually checking environ["REMOTE_USER"] to see whether there was a user signed in. AuthKit can help simplify authorization too.

The Authorization Decorator

Let's start by looking at how the @authorize decorator can be used with AuthKit permission objects to protect entire controller actions.

Add the following imports to the top of the auth controller:

```
from authkit.authorize.pylons_adaptors import authorize
from authkit.permissions import RemoteUser, ValidAuthKitUser, UserIn
```

Next change the private() action to look like this:

```
@authorize(RemoteUser())
def private(self):
    return "You are authenticated!"
```

This code is clearly a lot neater than what you had previously. If you sign out or clear your browser's cookies, you'll see it behaves exactly as it did before, allowing you to view the private message You are authenticated, but only after you have signed in.

In this example, the @authorize decorator simply prevents the action from being called if the permission check fails. Instead, it raises a PermissionError, which is derived from an HTTPException and is therefore converted either by Pylons or by AuthKit itself into a response with either a 401 status code or a 403 status code depending on whether the permission failed because of an authentication error or an authorization error. The response is then handled by the authentication middleware triggering a response, resulting in the sign-in screen you've just used.

The RemoteUser permission might not be the best permission to use in this case since it simply checks that a REMOTE_USER is set and could therefore potentially grant permission to someone who wasn't in the list of users specified in the config file if some other part of the system were to set the REMOTE_USER environment variable. Instead, it might be better to use the ValidAuthKitUser permission, which does a similar thing but allows only valid AuthKit users. You imported the ValidAuthKitUser at the same time you imported RemoteUser, so you can use it like this:

```
@authorize(ValidAuthKitUser())
def private(self):
    return "You are authenticated!"
```

You can also use an AuthKit permission object named UserIn to specify that only certain users are allowed. Add another user to the config file like this:

```
authkit.form.authenticate.user.data = visitor:open_sesame
                                       nobody:password
```

Then change the way the permission is used like this:

```
@authorize(UserIn(["visitor"]))
def private(self):
    return "You are authenticated!"
```

This time, even if you signed in as nobody, you would still not be authorized to access the action because the permission check will authorize only the user named visitor.

■**Tip** You don't actually need to instantiate a permission in the decorator itself; you can also create a permission instance elsewhere and use it as many times as you like in different authorize() decorators.

You've now seen how to use the @authorize decorator to check permissions before an action is called, but there are actually two other ways of checking permissions that automatically raise the correct PermissionError if a permission check fails:

- The authorize middleware for protecting a whole WSGI application
- The authorized() function for checking a permission within a code block

Let's look at these next.

The Authorization Middleware

To protect a whole application, you can use AuthKit's authorization middleware. You need to set this up in your project's config/middleware.py file *before* the authentication middleware to use it. If you set it up after the authentication middleware, any PermissionError raised wouldn't get intercepted by the authentication middleware. Let's test this on the AuthDemo project. First import the authorization middleware and ValidAuthKitUser permission at the end of the imports at the top of config/middleware.py:

```
import authkit.authorize
from authkit.permissions import ValidAuthKitUser
```

Then set up the authorization middleware *before* the authentication middleware:

```
permission = ValidAuthKitUser()
app = authkit.authorize.middleware(app, permission)
app = authkit.authenticate.middleware(app, app_conf)
```

Now every request that comes through your Pylons application will require the user to be signed in as a valid AuthKit user. To test this, add a new action to the auth controller, which looks like this:

```
def public(self):
    return "This is still only visible when you are signed in."
```

Even though this doesn't have an @authorize decorator, you still won't be able to access it until you are signed in because of the presence of the authorization middleware. Try visiting http://localhost:5000/auth/public to test it.

> ■**Caution** Using the authorization middleware in this way will protect only the WSGI applications defined above it in `config/middleware.py`. In this case, the middleware is set up above the `Cascade`, so any requests that are served by the `StaticURLParser` application will not be covered. This means that files served from your project's `public` directory won't be protected. You can protect them too by moving all the AuthKit middleware to below the `Cascade` in `config/middleware.py`.

The Authorization Function

Of course, sometimes you will want to be able to check a permission from within an action or a template. AuthKit provides a function for doing this too named `authorized()`. The function returns `True` if the permission check passes or `False` otherwise. If you comment out the authorization middleware you set up in `config/middleware.py` a few moments ago (leaving the authenticate middleware), you will be able to test this function:

```
# permission = ValidAuthKitUser()
# app = authkit.authorize.middleware(app, permission)
app = authkit.authenticate.middleware(app, app_conf)
```

First edit the auth controller to import the `authorized()` function:

```
from authkit.authorize.pylons_adaptors import authorized
```

Then update the `public()` action to look like this:

```
def public(self):
    if authorized(UserIn(["visitor"])):
        return "You are authenticated!"
    else:
        return "You are not authenticated!"
```

Using the `authorized()` function will never actually trigger a sign-in; if you want to trigger a sign-in, you either need to manually return a response with a status code of 401 like this:

```
def public(self):
    if authorized(UserIn(["visitor"])):
        return "You are authenticated!"
    else:
response.status = "401 Not authenticated"
return "You are not authenticated!"
```

or raise the appropriate permission error:

```
def public(self):
    if authorized(UserIn(["visitor"])):
        return "You are authenticated!"
    else:
from authkit.permissions import NotAuthenticatedError
```

You can test this at `http://localhost:5000/auth/public`.

> ■**Caution** Although all the permission objects that come with AuthKit can be used with the `authorized()` function, it is possible to create custom permissions that will not work. This is because permissions can perform checks on both the request and the response, and although the authorization decorator and authorization middleware both have access to the response, the `authorized()` function does not and so is not capable of performing checks on permissions that depend on the response.

Protecting a Controller

Sometimes you might want to protect a controller rather than an individual action or an entire WSGI application. Since all Pylons controllers have a __before__() method, adding an @authorize decorator to __before__() is equivalent to protecting the entire controller.

For example:

```
class AuthController(BaseController):

    @authorize(ValidAuthKitUser())
    def __before__(self):
        pass

    def public(self):
        return "This is still only visible when you are signed in."
```

Groups, Roles, and Permissions

So far, you have seen how to authenticate users and how to use permissions to authorize them, but the permissions you've used haven't been very complicated.

One common and extremely flexible pattern used in many authorization systems is that of groups and roles. Under this pattern, each user can be assigned any number of roles that relate to tasks they might use the system for. They can also be a member of one group, usually a company or organization.

As an example, if you were designing a content management web site, you might choose the following roles:

Writer: Someone tasked with creating new articles

Editor: Someone with permission to update existing articles

Reviewer: Someone who reviews articles before they are published

Admin: Someone who has permission to set the roles of other users

Certain users might have more than one role, and others might not have any roles at all.

An appropriate use for groups would be when you give access to the same web site to users from different companies and each user is either from one company or the other. Of course, you could implement the same functionality by creating a role for each company and checking which role each user had, but using groups is simpler. If you find you need to assign more than one group to the same person, then you should be using roles, not groups.

Tip The groups and roles pattern even works when conceptually you have more than one application to which each person should be assigned roles. You can append application names to the front of the roles so that, for example, intranet_editor is a role for an editor on an intranet application and website_editor is a role for an editor on a public-facing web site application.

You can specify AuthKit groups and roles in the configuration file along with the user information. Here is the configuration to set up roles for four users of our content management system:

```
authkit.form.authenticate.user.data = ben:password1 writer editor reviewer admin
                                       james:password2 writer
                                       graham:password3 writer reviewer
                                       philip:password4 editor reviewer
```

As you can see, user information is specified in the format `username:password role1 role2 role3`, and so on. Each new user is on a new line, and roles are separated by a space character. In this example, Ben and Philip are Editors; Ben, James, and Graham are Writers; Ben, Graham, and Philip are Reviewers; and Ben is the only Admin.

If our imaginary content management system was used by two web framework communities, it might be useful to be able to specify which community each user belonged to. You can do this using AuthKit's group functionality:

```
authkit.form.authenticate.user.data = ➥
    ben:password1:pylons writer editor reviewer admin
    simon:password5:django writer editor reviewer admin
```

As you can see, the group is specified after the password and before the roles by using another colon (`:`) character as a separator.

■**Caution** You have to be a little careful when using groups because your users can never be members of more than one group. In this instance, you would hope that people from both the Django and Pylons communities might contribute to each others' projects, so in this instance it might be more appropriate to create two new roles, `django` and `pylons`, and assign the `pylons` role to Ben and the `django` role to Simon. Then, if at a later date Simon wants to work on Pylons, he can simply be assigned the `pylons` role too.

Groups and roles can be checked in a similar way to other permissions using the authorization middleware, the `@authorize` decorator, or the `authorized()` function.

The two important permissions for checking groups and roles are `HasAuthKitRole` and `HasAuthKitGroup`. They have the following specification:

```
HasAuthKitRole(roles, all=False, error=None)
HasAuthKitGroup(groups, error=None)
```

The roles and groups parameters are a list of the acceptable role or group names. If you specify `all=True` to `HasAuthKitRole`, the permission will require that all the roles specified in `roles` are matched; otherwise, the user will be authorized if they have been assigned any of the roles specified. Here are some examples of using these permission objects:

```
from authkit.permissions import HasAuthKitRole, HasAuthKitRole, And

# User has the 'admin' role:
HasAuthKitRole('admin')

# User has the 'admin' or 'editor' role:
HasAuthKitRole(['admin', 'editor'])

# User has the both 'admin' and 'editor' roles:
HasAuthKitRole(['admin', 'editor'], all=True)

# User has no roles:
HasAuthKitRole(None)

# User in the 'pylons' group:
HasAuthKitGroup('pylons')

# User in the 'pylons' or 'django' groups:
HasAuthKitGroup(['pylons', 'django'])

# User not in a group:
HasAuthKitGroup(None)
```

It is also possible to combine permissions using the And permission class. This example would require that the user was an administrator in the Pylons group:

```
And(HasAuthKitRole('admin'), HasAuthKitGroup('pylons'))
```

In addition to the permissions for roles and groups, AuthKit also comes with permission objects for limiting users to particular IP addresses or for allowing them to access the resource only at particular times of day:

```
# Only allow access from 127.0.0.1 or 10.10.0.1
permission = FromIP(["127.0.0.1", "10.10.0.1"])

# Only allow access between 6pm and 8am
from datetime import time
permission = BetweenTimes(start=time(18), end=time(8))
```

User Management API

All the examples so far have been using the authkit.users.UsersFromString driver to extract all the username, password, group, and role information from the config file for use with the permission objects. If you had lots of users, it could quickly become unmanageable to store all this information in the config file, so AuthKit also comes with a number of other drivers.

The first driver you will learn about is the UsersFromFile driver from the authkit.users module. This driver expects to be given a filename from which to load all the user information. For example, if you stored your user information in the file C:\user_information.txt, you might set up your config file like this:

```
authkit.form.authenticate.user.type = authkit.users:UsersFromFile
authkit.form.authenticate.user.data = C:/users_information.txt
```

The users_information.txt file should have the user data specified in the same format as has been used so far in this chapter with one user per line. For example:

```
ben:password1 writer editor reviewer admin
james:pasword2 writer
graham:password3 writer reviewer
philip:password4 editor reviewer
```

Of course, you may want to perform checks on the users in your application code as well as on permissions. AuthKit allows you to do this too via a key in the environment called authkit.users, which is simply an instance of the particular instance class you are using.

You can use it like this:

```
>>> users = request.environ['authkit.users']
>>> users.user_has_role('ben', 'admin')
True
>>> users.user_has_group('ben', 'django')
False
>>> users.list_roles()
['admin', 'editor', 'reviewer', 'writer']
```

The full API documentation is available on the Pylons web site.

Cookie Options

The AuthKit cookie-handling code supports quite a few options:

> `authkit.cookie.name`: The name of the cookie; the default is `auth_tkt`.
>
> `authkit.cookie.includeip`: Should be `True` or `False`. If `True`, the IP address of the user is also included in the encrypted ticket to prevent the same cookie from being used from a different IP address and hence to try to improve security.
>
> `authkit.cookie.signoutpath`: A path that, when visited, will cause the cookie to be removed and the user to therefore be signed out. The application should still display a page at this path; otherwise, the user will see a 404 page and think there is a problem.
>
> `authkit.cookie.secret`: A string you can set used to make the encryption on the cookie data more random. You should set a secret and make sure it isn't publically available.
>
> `authkit.cookie.enforce`: If a cookie `expires` param is set and this is set to `True`, then there will also be server-side checking of the expire time to ensure the user is signed out even if the browser fails to remove the cookie.
>
> `authkit.cookie.params.*`: The available options are `expires`, `path`, `comment`, `domain`, `max-age`, `secure`, and `version`. These are the values described in RFC 2109, but for convenience `expires` can be set as the number of seconds and will be converted automatically.

So, for example, to have a cookie that expires after 20 seconds with a cookie name `test` and the comment `this is a comment`, you would set these options:

```
authkit.cookie.secret = random string
authkit.cookie.name = test
authkit.cookie.params.expires = 20
authkit.cookie.params.comment = this is a comment
```

If you want a more secure cookie, you can add these options:

```
authkit.cookie.enforce = true
authkit.cookie.includeip = true
```

The first option enforces a server-side check on the cookie expire time as well as trusting the browser to do it. The second checks the IP address too and will work only if the request comes from the same IP address the cookie was created from.

AuthKit's default cookie implementation is based on the Apache `mod_auth_tkt` cookie format. This means the cookie itself contains the username of the signed-in user in plain text. You can set another option called `authkit.cookie.nouserincookie` if you'd prefer AuthKit used a session store to hold the username, but this option breaks compatibility with `mod_auth_tkt` and means you have to move the AuthKit authentication middleware to above the `SessionMiddleware` in your project's `config/middleware.py` file so that AuthKit can use the Beaker session.

```
authkit.cookie.nouserincookie = true
```

Alternative Methods

So far, our discussion about authentication, groups, and roles has centered around AuthKit's User Management API. AuthKit also provides six ways of authenticating users including HTTP basic and digest authentication, and of course, it provides APIs for implementing your own authentication method. To use one of the alternative authentication methods, you just need to change the AuthKit options in your config file.

As an example, to use HTTP digest authentication, you could change the AuthKit options in your config file to look like this:

```
authkit.setup.method = digest
authkit.digest.authenticate.user.data = visitor:open_sesame
authkit.digest.realm = 'Test Realm'
```

Now when you access a controller action that causes a permission check to fail, the browser will display an HTTP digest dialog box prompting you to sign in. Once you are signed in, you will be able to access the controller action as before. The process of handling the sign-in and setting the REMOTE_USER variable is done automatically for you by AuthKit as before, so the rest of your application can remain unchanged.

AuthKit has similar setups for HTTP basic authentication and OpenID authentication and also has other plug-ins that can redirect users to a URL to sign in or forward the request to a controller inside your Pylons application.

Functional Testing

As you'll remember from Chapter 12, creating functional tests for key controllers is highly recommended. If your controller actions are protected by AuthKit, you will need to emulate a user being signed in by setting the REMOTE_USER environment variable when setting up your tests. Here's how to set up a user called james by passing the extra_environ argument when using the get() method to simulate a GET request:

```
from authdemo.tests import *

class TestAuthController(TestController):

    def test_index(self):
        response = self.app.get(
url(controller='auth', action='public'),
            extra_environ={'REMOTE_USER':'james'}
        )
        # Test response...
        assert "you are signed in" in response.body
```

Alternatively, AuthKit 0.4.1 supports two further options for helping you handle tests:

```
authkit.setup.enable = false
authkit.setup.fakeuser = james
```

The first of these options completely disables the AuthKit authenticate middleware and makes all the authorization facilities return that the permission check passed. This enables you to test your controller actions as though AuthKit wasn't in place. Some of your controller actions might expect a REMOTE_USER environment variable, so this is set up with the value of the authkit.setup.fakeuser option, if it is present. Both these options should be used only in test.ini and never on a production site.

How useful the previous options are depends on the complexity of your setup. For more complex setups, you are likely to want to specify environment variables on a test-by-test basis using the extra_environ argument.

▓**Caution** Always remember to set authkit.setup.enable = true on production sites; otherwise, all authentication is ignored and authorization checks always return that the user has the appropriate permission. Although useful for testing, this makes all your controller actions public, so it is not a good idea on a production site.

General Security Considerations

So far, everything we have discussed has been around how to authenticate a user and check their permissions in order to authorize them to perform certain actions. A very important aspect of this is making sure the authentication is secure and that no one can get hold of the usernames and passwords your users use. Security as a whole is a huge topic on which many books have been written, but you can take three steps to greatly reduce the risk of an intruder obtaining a user's username and password:

- Ensure other users of the system cannot read passwords from your Pylons config file. This is especially relevant if you are deploying your Pylons application in a shared hosting environment where other users of the system might be able to read database passwords and other information from your `development.ini` file.

- Ensure a user never sends their password in any form over an unencrypted connection such as via e-mail or over HTTP.

- Never directly store a user's password anywhere in your system.

Secure Sockets Layer

If you are using a form and a cookie or HTTP basic authentication, then the user's password is transmitted in plain text to the server. This means that anyone on the network could potentially monitor the network traffic and simply read the username and password. It's therefore important that on a production site using these authentication methods you set up a secure connection for the authentication using Secure Sockets Layer (SSL) to encrypt the communication between the browser and server during authentication.

Even HTTP digest authentication, which does use some encryption on the password, isn't particularly secure because anyone monitoring the network traffic could simply send the encrypted digest and be able to sign onto the site themselves, so even if you are using digest authentication, it is worth using SSL too.

To set up an SSL certificate, you need two things:

- A private key
- A certificate

The certificate is created from a certificate-signing request that you can create using the private key.

The private key can be encrypted with a password for extra security, but every time you restart the server, you will need to enter the password. The certificate-signing request (CSR) is then sent to a certificate authority (CA) that will check the details in the certificate-signing request and issue a certificate. Anyone can act as a certificate authority, but most browsers will automatically trust certificates only from the main certificate authorities. This means that if you choose a lesser-known certificate authority or you choose to sign the certificate yourself, your users will be shown a warning message asking them whether they trust the certificate.

For production sites, you should always choose one of the major certificate authorities such as VeriSign or Thawte because virtually all browsers will automatically trust certificates issued by them. CAcert.org is an initiative to provide free certificates, but these are not trusted by all commonly used browsers yet.

On a Linux platform with the `openssh` package installed, you can run the following command from a terminal prompt to create the key:

```
$ openssl genrsa -des3 -out server.key 1024
```

You'll see output similar to the following:

```
Generating RSA private key, 1024 bit long modulus
....................++++++
................++++++
unable to write 'random state'
e is 65537 (0x10001)
Enter pass phrase for server.key:
```

If you want to use a key without a passphrase, you can either leave out the -des3 option or create an insecure version from the existing key like this:

```
$ openssl rsa -in server.key -out server.key.insecure
```

You should keep the private key server.key private and not send it to anyone else.

Once you have a key, you can use it to generate a certificate-signing request like this:

```
$ openssl req -new -key server.key -out server.csr
```

The program will prompt you to enter the passphrase if you are using a secure key. If you enter the correct passphrase, it will prompt you to enter your company name, site name, e-mail, and so on. Once you enter all these details, your CSR will be created, and it will be stored in the server.csr file. The common name you enter at this stage must match the full domain name of the site you want to set up the certificate for; otherwise, the browser will display a warning about a domain mismatch. It is worth checking with the certificate authority about the exact details it requires at this stage to ensure the CSR you generate is in the format required by the certificate authority.

Now that you have your certificate-signing request server.csr, you can send it to the certificate authority. The CA will confirm that all the details you've entered are correct and issue you a certificate that you can store as server.crt.

If you want to sign the certificate yourself, you can do so with this command:

```
$ openssl x509 -req -days 365 -in server.csr -signkey server.key -out server.crt
```

Caution If you are planning on using your secure server in a production environment, you probably need a CA-signed certificate. It is not recommended to use self-signed certificates because of the warnings the browser will show the user.

Now that you have your private key and the certificate, you can use them to set up your server. How to set up SSL depends on the server you are using to deploy your Pylons application. You should consult your server's documentation for more information.

Note If you are using Apache, there is a good entry in the Pylons Cookbook describing how to set up SSL. You can find it at http://wiki.pylonshq.com/display/pylonscookbook/Setting+up+Apache+and+SSL+for+Pylons.

The Pylons server (started with the paster serve command) also supports SSL as long as you install the pyOpenSSL package. The Paste HTTP server requires the certificate and the private key to be added to the same file, so if you want to use your certificate and the key you generated earlier, you need to create a server.pem file like this:

```
$ cat server.crt server.key > server.pem
$ chmod 400 server.pem
```

Edit your project's `development.ini` file, and change the `[server:main]` section so it uses the following options marked in bold:

```
[server:main]
host = 127.0.0.1
ssl_pem = server.pem
port = 443
```

Port 443 is the default port for HTTPS. If you restart the server and visit `https://localhost/`, you should be able to access your Pylons application. You'll need the pyOpenSSL package installed though. Make sure the URL starts with `https` and not `http`; otherwise, you won't be able to connect to your Pylons application. Also make sure you change the host to `0.0.0.0` if you want to be able to access the server from a different machine on the network.

Encrypted Passwords

As was mentioned earlier, it is a good idea never to store users' passwords anywhere on your system in case the worst happens and someone breaks in and steals that information. One way to avoid this is to set up a function to encrypt the passwords before they are stored. One drawback to this approach is that if the user forgets their password, you are not able to send them a reminder by e-mail because you do not ever store the original password. Instead, you have to randomly generate a new password for them and send them an e-mail asking them to sign in with the new password and then change the password to something more memorable.

You can set up encrypted passwords with form authentication by adding the following to your AuthKit config:

```
authkit.setup.method = form, cookie
authkit.cookie.secret = secret string
authkit.form.authenticate.user.data = visitor:9406649867375c79247713a7fb81edf0
authkit.form.authenticate.user.encrypt = authkit.users:md5
authkit.form.authenticate.user.encrypt.secret = some secret string
```

The `authkit.form.authenticate.user.encrypt.secret` option allows you to specify a string that will be used to make the password encryption even harder to break.

Once this option is enabled, you will need to manually convert all existing passwords into their encrypted forms. Here is a simple program that converts the passwords you have used so far in this chapter into their encrypted forms using the secret "`some secret string`". As you can see the encrypted password in the previous example corresponds to `password1`:

```
from authkit.users import md5

passwords = [
    'password1',
    'password2',
    'password3',
    'password4',
    'password5',
]

for password in passwords:
    print md5(password, "some secret string")
```

The result is as follows:

9406649867375c79247713a7fb81edf0
4e64aba9f0305efa50396584cfbee89c
aee8149aca17e09b8a741654d2efd899
2bc5a9b5c05bb857237d93610c98c98f
873f0294070311a707b941c6315f71f8

You can try replacing the passwords in the config file with these passwords. As long as you set the config options listed here, everything should still work without the real passwords being stored anywhere. This is more secure because an attacker would still need the original password in order to sign in, even if they knew the encrypted version.

Summary

Although the tools and techniques you've learned about in this chapter will enable you to write fairly advanced authorization and authentication systems that will be adequate for a lot of cases, you may sometimes need to do things slightly differently. AuthKit also supports custom authentication functions and a SQLAlchemy driver for storing the user information.

In the next chapter, you'll apply some of the knowledge you've gained in this chapter to the SimpleSite application you've been working on throughout the book, and you'll see some more techniques involving AuthKit, including how it integrates with SQLAlchemy and how to use a template to give the sign-in screen a theme.

# CHAPTER 19

SimpleSite Tutorial Part 3

In this final part of the SimpleSite tutorial, you'll add authentication and authorization facilities to SimpleSite so that only registered users can edit pages and so that only administrators can move pages or sections around or delete them.

After the authentication and authorization facilities are in place, you'll learn how to customize Pylons' error pages so that they use the same templates as the rest of SimpleSite. At that point, you'll learn how to package up an application and publish it on the Python Package Index. Finally, you'll turn the whole SimpleSite project into a project template (similar to the Pylons template you are used to using to with the `paster create --template` command) so that other people can use it as a basis for their own projects.

There's a lot to do, so let's get started!

Note There is some code in Chapters 15 and 16 related to SimpleSite that handles animating the flash message, includes some extra CSS, and handles populating the `before` field drop-down list with Ajax. You should add this to your project before continuing with the tutorial or download the source code for the beginning of this chapter from the Apress website.

Authentication and Authorization

In the first part of this chapter, you'll use AuthKit to add authentication and authorization facilities to the SimpleSite project. If you haven't already installed AuthKit, you should do so now with this command:

```
$ easy_install "AuthKit>=0.4.3,<=0.4.99"
```

Setting Up the Middleware

You'll remember from Chapter 18 that the first thing you need to do to use AuthKit in a Pylons application is to set up the AuthKit authentication middleware. Edit `config/middleware.py`, and add the following import at the top of the file:

```
import authkit.authenticate
```

Then add the AuthKit middleware immediately before the `StatusCodeRedirect` middleware (it is shown in bold here):

```
app = RoutesMiddleware(app, config['routes.map'])
app = SessionMiddleware(app, config)
app = CacheMiddleware(app, config)

if asbool(full_stack):
    # Handle Python exceptions
    app = ErrorHandler(app, global_conf, **config['pylons.errorware'])

    app = authkit.authenticate.middleware(app, app_conf)

    # Display error documents for 401, 403, 404 status codes (and
    # 500 when debug is disabled)
    if asbool(config['debug']):
        app = StatusCodeRedirect(app)
    else:
        app = StatusCodeRedirect(app, [400, 401, 403, 404, 500])
```

▌Note If you find you have a conflict with the version of Pylons you are using or if you are using a configuration with the `full_stack` option set to `false`, set the AuthKit middleware up after the `Cascade`, just before the `make_app()` function returns `app`.

AuthKit comes with a SQLAlchemy driver that can be used to store AuthKit user information in a relational database. The driver requires slightly more configuration to integrate it into a Pylons project than the file-based `UsersFromFile` driver you saw in the previous chapter but is still fairly straightforward. First you'll need to edit your `development.ini` file so that these lines appear at the end of the `[app:main]` section:

```
authkit.setup.enable = true
authkit.setup.method = form, cookie
authkit.form.authenticate.user.type = ➡
authkit.users.sqlalchemy_driver:UsersFromDatabase
authkit.form.authenticate.user.data = simplesite.model
authkit.cookie.secret = secret string
authkit.cookie.signoutpath = /signout
```

These options tell AuthKit that you are going to be using a SQLAlchemy database to manage the users and that the SQLAlchemy model used by the rest of your Pylons application is defined in the `simplesite.model` module.

AuthKit will expect the model to be set up in the standard way described in Chapter 7 with a `Session` object and the `meta` module present. It will add its own tables and classes to the model automatically during the first request, so you don't need to manually change the model to use the new SQLAlchemy tables.

To make it harder for someone to guess a user's cookie, you should always set a new string for the `authkit.cookie.secret` option. Using the same string as the example (which is `secret string`) isn't very secure.

Adjusting websetup.py

At this point, the middleware is correctly configured, but the database tables AuthKit requires don't exist yet. You'll need to change SimpleSite's `websetup.py` file so that these tables are created at the same time as any other tables used by your model.

First add the following import to the top of the `websetup.py` file:

```
from authkit.users.sqlalchemy_driver import UsersFromDatabase
```

Then after these lines:

```
# Load the models
from simplesite.model import meta
meta.metadata.bind = meta.engine
```

add these lines to add the AuthKit classes and mappers to the model:

```
log.info("Adding the AuthKit model...")
users = UsersFromDatabase(model)
```

Next you'll need to add some users and roles to the application. After these lines:

```
# Create the tables if they aren't there already
meta.metadata.create_all(checkfirst=True)
```

add these:

```
log.info("Adding roles and uses...")

users.role_create("delete")
users.user_create("foo", password="bar")
users.user_create("admin", password="opensesame")
users.user_add_role("admin", role="delete")
```

While you are updating the `websetup.py` file, it also makes sense to add a default set of tags so that users can begin tagging pages. Although it doesn't have anything to do with AuthKit, add these Pylons-related tags by adding these lines after the ones earlier:

```
log.info("Adding tags...")

tag1 = model.Tag()
tag1.name = u'Pylons'
meta.Session.add(tag1)

tag2 = model.Tag()
tag2.name = u'Paste'
meta.Session.add(tag2)

tag3 = model.Tag()
tag3.name = u'Tutorial'
meta.Session.add(tag3)

tag4 = model.Tag()
tag4.name = u'Database'
meta.Session.add(tag4)

tag5 = model.Tag()
tag5.name = u'Recipe'
meta.Session.add(tag5)
```

With the changes in place, you will need to drop the database you've been using so far or change the config file to use a new database so that you can set up the new AuthKit tables. Re-create the database with this command:

```
$ paster setup-app development.ini
Running setup_config() from simplesite.websetup
22:30:49,808 INFO  [simplesite.websetup] Adding the AuthKit model...
... omitted log output for brevity ...
22:30:50,076 INFO  [simplesite.websetup] Successfully set up.
```

If you are using the `filter-with` option in `[app:main]` you'll need to disable it to create the database. If all goes well and you see the `Successfully set up` message, you should find the new tables have been successfully created. If you use a command-line tool to inspect the database, you will notice that there are some new tables used by AuthKit, including `users`, `roles`, `groups`, and `user_roles`:

```
$ sqlite3 development.db
SQLite version 3.4.2
Enter ".help" for instructions
sqlite> .tables
comment    nav      pagetag    section    users
groups     page     roles      tag        users_roles
```

Protecting Controller Actions

Now that AuthKit is set up, let's think about how it should be used in the SimpleSite application. Over the following sections, you'll add functionality that allows anyone to create pages and sections but allows only signed-in users to edit or move them. Only users with the `delete` role should be able to delete pages or sections, edit comments, or rename tags.

Let's start by ensuring only people who are signed in can edit pages. To do this, you need to add a `ValidAuthKitUser()` permission to the `page` controller's `edit` action. Add the following imports at the top of the `page.py` controller:

```
from authkit.permissions import ValidAuthKitUser
from authkit.authorize.pylons_adaptors import authorize
```

Then add an authorize decorator before the `edit()` action so that it looks like this:

```
@authorize(ValidAuthKitUser())
def edit(self, id=None):
    ...
```

Let's start the server and see what happens:

```
$ paster serve --reload development.ini
```

If you are following along from the previous chapter, close your browser to clear any AuthKit session cookies you might still have from the previous application, and visit `http://localhost:5000/`. You will be able to see the front page as usual (albeit with the extra tags), but if you click the Edit Page link at the bottom, you will be shown the AuthKit sign-in page you saw in Figure 18-1. Sign in with the username `foo` and the password `bar`, which were set up in the `websetup.py` file.

Once you are signed in, you can then see the edit page as usual, and because AuthKit automatically sets a cookie, on each subsequent request you will also be able to edit pages too because AuthKit can read the cookie to find out which user is signed in.

So far, you have protected the `edit()` action only, but it is the `save()` action that actually modifies the database, so currently a malicious user could still make changes to pages if they knew that there was a `save()` action. You'd better protect `save()` too:

```
@authorize(ValidAuthKitUser())
@restrict('POST')
@validate(schema=NewPageForm(), form='edit')
def save(self, id=None):
    ...
```

The decorators on both the edit() and save() actions use a different instance of the ValidAuthKitUser permission class, but AuthKit permission objects are designed to be used multiple times; therefore, a better way of organizing permissions is in their own module. Add a new file to the lib directory called auth.py, and add the following code to it:

```
from authkit.permissions import ValidAuthKitUser
is_valid_user = ValidAuthKitUser()
```

In the next section, you'll need to access the is_valid_user permission in the templates as well as the controllers, so it makes sense to import the whole auth module into the lib/helpers.py so that permissions can be easily accessed via h.auth, for example, as h.auth.is_valid_user. Add this to the end of the helper imports:

```
from simplesite.lib import auth
```

Now you can update the @authorize decorators in the page controller to look like this:

```
@authorize(h.auth.is_valid_user)
```

You can also remove the import of the ValidAuthKitUser from the page controller if you like because it isn't needed now, thanks to the addition of the permissions to the helpers module.

Although all signed-in users should be able to create new pages and edit existing ones, only users with the delete role should be able to delete pages. You'll need to create a different permission object to handle this condition. Add the following line to lib/auth.py:

```
has_delete_role = HasAuthKitRole(['delete'])
```

You'll also need to add this import at the top of the file:

```
from authkit.permissions import HasAuthKitRole
```

Now edit the page controller's delete() action so that it looks like this:

```
@authorize(h.auth.has_delete_role)
def delete(self, id=None):
    ...
```

If you try to delete a page while still being signed in as the user foo, you will be shown the Pylons 403 Forbidden page because although you are signed in, you don't have permission to access the resource, so AuthKit triggers a 403 response that the StatusCodeRedirect middleware will intercept to produce the error document (see Figure 19-1).

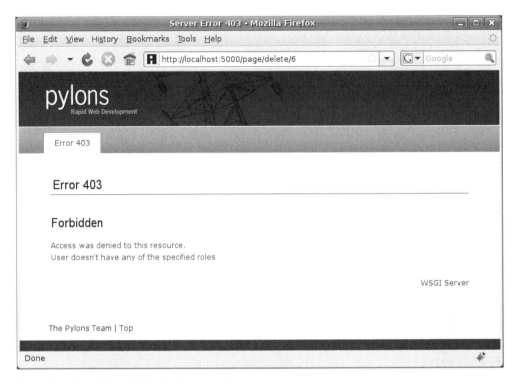

Figure 19-1. *The Pylons 403 Forbidden error document*

Now that you've tested the permissions as user foo, close the browser, and open it again at http://localhost:5000/. This will clear the AuthKit cookie and hence sign out the user foo. Now visit http://localhost:5000/page/edit/6 to edit the home page. Once again, you will be asked to sign in. This time sign in with the username admin and the password opensesame that you also set up in websetup.py. You'll now find you have permission to delete pages because the admin user has the delete role.

Changing Templates Based on Permissions

Now that users who aren't signed in can't edit pages, it isn't sensible to show them the Edit Page link. Once again, you can use AuthKit, but this time, you'll use the authorized() function, which returns True if the user has the permission specified and False otherwise.

Let's add this function to the lib/auth.py file so that it can easily be accessed as h.auth. authorized() from the project's templates:

```
from authkit.authorize.pylons_adaptors import authorized
```

Now you can update the derived/page/view.html template so that the Edit Page link looks like this:

```
% if h.auth.authorized(h.auth.is_valid_user):
| <a href="${h.url_for(controller='page', action='edit', id=c.page.id)}">Edit
Page</a>
% endif
```

When a user is signed in, they will now see the Edit Page link, and when they are not, they won't. This isn't too easy to test yet, so let's add some facilities for signing in and out more easily first.

Signing In and Signing Out

When you added the AuthKit configuration to the config file, you specified the option `authkit.cookie.signoutpath = /signout`. This means that when a user visits the path `/signout`, the AuthKit cookie will be removed, and they will be signed out. Try visiting `http://localhost:5000/signout` now. You'll be shown the standard Create Page screen, but when you try to browse the site again, you'll see that you've been signed out by the AuthKit middleware because the URL you visited matched the value of the `authkit.cookie.signoutpath` option in the config file.

Let's add a new controller to the application to specifically handle signing in and signing out. Call this controller `account` because it could eventually be extended to handle other account functionality. Add it like this:

```
$ paster controller account
```

Edit the skeleton account controller in `controllers/account.py` so that it has the following two actions:

```
class AccountController(BaseController):

    def signin(self):
        if not request.environ.get('REMOTE_USER'):
            # This triggers the AuthKit middleware into displaying the sign-in form
            abort(401)
        else:
            return render('/derived/account/signedin.html')

    def signout(self):
        # The actual removal of the AuthKit cookie occurs when the response passes
        # through the AuthKit middleware, we simply need to display a page
        # confirming the user is signed out
        return render('/derived/account/signedout.html')
```

When a user is signed in, AuthKit sets the environment variable `REMOTE_USER` to contain the user's username. The `signin()` action checks this to see whether it is present. If it isn't, it aborts with a 401 response to trigger AuthKit to prompt the user to sign in.

Once a user is signed in, the `signedin.html` template is rendered. Create the `templates/derived/account` directory, and add the `signedin.html` template to it with the following content:

```
<%inherit file="/base/index.html"/>

<%def name="title()">Signed In</%def>
<%def name="heading()"><h1>Signed In</h1></%def>

<p>You are signed in as ${request.environ['REMOTE_USER']}.
<a href="${h.url_for(controller='account', action='signout')}">Sign out</a></p>
```

Next you'll need to add the `signedout.html` template to the `account` directory too with the following content:

```
<%inherit file="/base/index.html"/>

<%def name="title()">Signed Out</%def>
<%def name="heading()"><h1>Signed Out</h1></%def>

<p>You have been signed out.</p>
```

Now you need to modify the routes so that the path /signin points to the signin() action and the path signout() points to the signout() action. Add the following named routes immediately after the # CUSTOM ROUTES HERE line in config/routing.py:

```
map.connect('signout', '/signout', controller='account', action='signout')
map.connect('signin', '/signin', controller='account', action='signin')
```

Now let's add an extra line to the header so it contains a link to the signin() action when you are not signed in and contains your username and a link to the signout() action when you are signed in. Modify the base/index.html template so that the header has the extra links. The lines in bold are the ones you need to change:

```
<div id="hd">
    <div class="yui-gc">
        <div class="yui-u first">
            ${self.heading()}
        </div>
        <div class="yui-u">
            % if h.auth.authorized(h.auth.is_valid_user) and not ( ➥
    request.urlvars['controller'] == 'account' and ➥
    request.urlvars['action'] == 'signout'):
                <p>Signed in as ${request.environ['REMOTE_USER']},
                    <a href="${h.url_for('signout')}">Sign out</a></p>
            % else:
                <p><a href="${h.url_for('signin')}">Sign in</a></p>
            % endif
        </div>
    </div>
    ${self.header()}
    ${self.tabs()}
</div>
```

Because you don't want the "Signed in as..." message on the signed-out page, you have to test the routing variables to ensure that the user isn't on the signed-out page. The routing variables are always available as the request.urlvars dictionary, which can be useful if you haven't explicitly added them to the template context global c.

Notice also that because you set up named routes for signing in and signing out in the config/routing.py file, you just need to specify the name of the route when using h.url_for(), and not the routing variables as well. This is particularly handy for routes that get used a lot or for ones that don't have any variable parts.

You can also add a style so that the text appears on the right. Add this to public/css/main.css:

```
#hd p {
    text-align: right;
    padding-right: 20px;
    padding-top: 5px;
}
```

With these changes in place, you can test the sign-in and sign-out functionality. Figure 19-2 shows what the home page looks like when you are signed out. Notice the Sign In link in the top right and the fact the Edit Page link isn't visible, because you are not signed in.

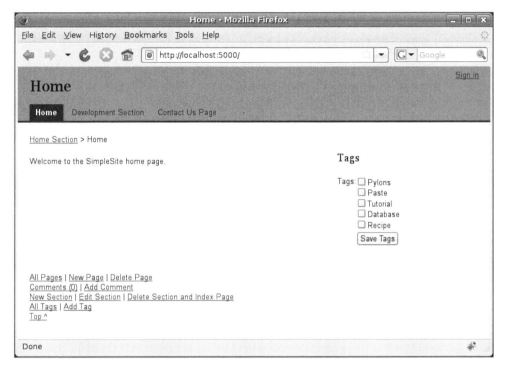

Figure 19-2. *The updated home page*

Styling the Sign-in Screen

You've now seen AuthKit and its user management API in action, but for a production system, you need to style the sign-in screen so that it looks like the rest of the site. AuthKit allows you to do this in two ways. The first is to provide all the HTML for the sign-in screen as a config option. In reality, though, it would be more useful if you could use the template structure you've set up for the rest of the pages so that if the styles in the base template were to change at some point in the future, you wouldn't have to generate a new static version for AuthKit. Luckily, AuthKit also allows you to specify a custom function, which, when called, will generate a template dynamically. Let's create such a function.

First, create a new template in `derived/account/signin.html` with this content:

```
<%inherit file="/base/index.html"/>

<%def name="title()">Sign In</%def>
<%def name="heading()"><h1>Sign In</h1></%def>

${h.form_start('%s', method="post")}
    ${h.field(
        "Username",
        h.text(name='username'),
    )}
```

```
${h.field(
    "Password",
    h.password(name='password'),
)}
${h.field(field=h.submit(value="Sign in", name='submit'))}
${h.form_end()}
```

AuthKit expects the username and password to be submitted as the `username` and `password` fields, respectively, and is designed to handle a POST method. AuthKit will use Python string interpolation to replace the `%s` string with the URL the form needs to submit to. For this to work you'll need to import `password` from the `webhelpers.html.tags` module into `lib/helpers.py`.

Now let's create a new function in `lib/auth.py` to render it:

```
def render_signin():
    return render('/derived/account/signin.html')
```

You'll need to add this import to the top of the file:

```
from pylons.templating import render_mako as render
```

You can then specify in the `development.ini` config file that, instead of using the default template, AuthKit should call the `render_signin()` function you created in `simplesite.lib.auth` to render the `signin.html` page. Add this to the config options:

```
authkit.form.template.obj = simplesite.lib.auth:render_signin
```

■**Caution** One potential problem with this approach is that if the HTML returned from the template contains other % characters, then the string interpolation will fail in AuthKit. In these situations, you can put a string such as FORM_ACTION in the signin.html template and then modify the render_signin() function to escape the % characters like this:

```
def render_signin():
    result = render('/derived/account/signin.html')
    result = result.replace('%', '%%').replace('FORM_ACTION', '%s')
    return result
```

Once the server has restarted, you will be able to test the new sign-in screen (see Figure 19-3), and you should find it now shares the same theme as the rest of the site.

Now that you can sign in and out easily, have a go at signing in as the `admin` user. You'll find you can delete pages as the `admin` user but not as the `foo` user.

■**Note** Previous versions of Pylons required a more complex version of the render_signin() function, so this works only with Pylons 0.9.7 or newer. This is because previous Pylons required the initialization of a component called Buffet before templates could be rendered, and this was not set up by the point in the middleware stack where AuthKit needed to access it to render the sign-in screen. Pylons 0.9.7 and newer replace Buffet with the simple render functions you learned about in Chapter 5 and that have been using throughout the book.

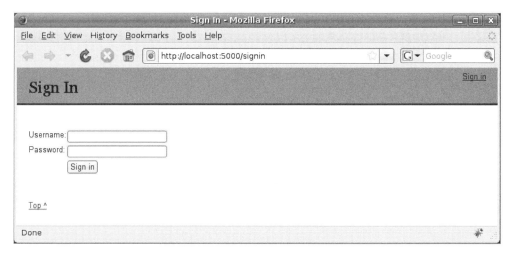

Figure 19-3. *The updated sign-in page*

Protecting the Rest of the Actions

Now that the edit and delete functionality for the page controller is properly protected, you need to protect the actions in the other controllers. Table 19-1 lists the permission objects you need to add to each controller action with an @h.auth.authorize decorator. For this to work you'll need to import the @authorize decorator at the top of the lib/auth.py file. Once these permissions are added, you can continue with the tutorial.

Table 19-1. *The Controller Actions and Their Associated Permissions*

Controller	Permission	Actions
Page	h.auth.is_valid_user	edit(), save()
Page	h.auth.has_delete_role	delete(), list()
Section	h.auth.is_valid_user	edit(), save()
Section	h.auth.has_delete_role	delete()
Tab	h.auth.has_delete_role	delete(), list(), edit(), save()
Comment	h.auth.has_delete_role	delete(), edit(), save()

With this setup and in line with the original requirements, anyone can now create pages and sections, but only signed-in users can edit or move them. Only users with the delete role can delete pages or sections, edit comments, or rename tags.

With this in mind, let's update the page/view.html footer so that people are shown the links only for functionality they are entitled to use. The finished footer looks like this:

```
<%def name="footer()">
## Then add our page links
<p>
% if h.auth.authorized(h.auth.has_delete_role):
  <a href="${h.url_for(controller='page', action='list')}">All Pages</a> |
% endif
```

```
<a href="${h.url_for(controller='page', action='new', section=c.page.section,
before=c.page.before)}">New Page</a>
% if h.auth.authorized(h.auth.is_valid_user):
| <a href="${h.url_for(controller='page', action='edit', id=c.page.id)}">Edit
Page</a>
% endif
% if h.auth.authorized(h.auth.has_delete_role):
| <a href="${h.url_for(controller='page', action='delete', id=c.page.id)}">Delete
Page</a>
% endif
</p>
## Comment links
<p>
  <a href="${h.url_for(pageid=c.page.id, controller='comment', action='list')}"
>Comments (${str(c.comment_count)})</a>
| <a href="${h.url_for(pageid=c.page.id, controller='comment', action='new')}"
>Add Comment</a>
</p>
## Section links
<p>
  <a href="${h.url_for(controller='section', action='new', section=c.page.section,
before=c.page.before)}">New Section</a>
% if h.auth.authorized(h.auth.is_valid_user):
| <a href="${h.url_for(controller='section', action='edit', id=c.page.section)}"
>Edit Section</a>
% endif
% if h.auth.authorized(h.auth.has_delete_role):
| <a href="${h.url_for(controller='section', action='delete', id=c.page.section)}"
>Delete Section and Index Page</a>
% endif
</p>
## Tag links
<p>
% if h.auth.authorized(h.auth.has_delete_role):
<a href="${h.url_for(controller='tag', action='list')}">All Tags</a>
|
% endif
<a href="${h.url_for(controller='tag', action='new')}">Add Tag</a></p>
## Include the parent footer too
${parent.footer()}
</%def>
```

Finally, let's update the `base/index.html` template's footer so that there is always a link back to the home page available:

```
<%def name="footer()">
    <p>
        <a href="${h.url_for('/')}">[Home]</a> |
        <a href="#top">Top ^</a>
    </p>
</%def>
```

Notice the use of the explicit URL in the `href` attribute because you always want the link to point to the root of the site, no matter which page or section that serves. This still takes advantage of Routes' ability to adjust URLs for you if the application is mounted at a nonroot URL.

Using the AuthKit User Management API

At this point, all the permissions are set up, but in real life you might want to add a new user to the system or perhaps change a user's roles. You could do that by altering `websetup.py` and re-creating the database, but that would result in all your data being lost. Another solution would be to manually alter the data in the AuthKit tables using SQL, or you could even create your own interface for managing users. For the moment, though, let's use the Pylons interactive shell.

Start the interactive shell like this:

```
$ paster shell development.ini
```

AuthKit automatically adds a `UsersFromDatabase` instance (like the one you used in `websetup.py` as the `users` object) to the `authkit.users` key in the WSGI `environ` dictionary so you can easily access it from your application, your tests, or the interactive shell. The commands below show you how to give the user `foo` the `delete` role. Don't run them just yet though.

```
>>> from pylons import request
>>> users = request.environ['authkit.users']
>>> users.user_add_role("foo", role="delete")
>>> from simplesite.model import meta
>>> meta.Session.commit()
```

The AuthKit `users` object has a series of different methods for managing users, described in detail at `http://authkit.org/docs/0.4/class-authkit.users.Users.html`. Using this API and the Pylons interactive shell, you can manipulate the AuthKit settings directly without needing to re-create any database tables.

Error Documents

Now that the authentication and authorization facilities are in place, let's pause for a moment to look at how and why Pylons generates error documents such as the 403 error document shown in Figure 19-1.

In certain circumstances, your Pylons application will return a status code that isn't 200. This might be because the URL requested doesn't exist, because the user is not authorized to view a particular URL, or occasionally because there is a bug in your code that caused an exception. Most browsers will understand the status code and display some sort of error message so that the user knows what went wrong, but rather than relying on the browser to inform the user of the problem, it is often preferable for your application to display an error document so that the page contains the same branding as the rest of your site.

As you saw in Chapter 17, whenever a response with a 401, 403, 404, or 500 response is returned down the middleware chain as far as the `StatusCodeRedirect` middleware, it is intercepted, and a request is forwarded to your project's error controller. The exact HTTP response status codes to be intercepted can be customized by changing the arguments to the `StatusCodeRedirect` middleware. The error controller itself is a special controller set up by Pylons specifically for generating error documents.

Your project's `controllers/error.py` will look something like this:

```
import cgi
import os.path
```

```
from paste.urlparser import StaticURLParser
from pylons import request
from pylons.controllers.util import forward
from pylons.middleware import error_document_template, media_path
from webhelpers.html.builder import literal

from simplesite.lib.base import BaseController

class ErrorController(BaseController):

    def document(self):
        """Render the error document"""
        resp = request.environ.get('pylons.original_response')
        content = literal(resp.body) or cgi.escape(request.GET.get('message'))
        page = error_document_template % \
            dict(prefix=request.environ.get('SCRIPT_NAME', ''),
                code=cgi.escape(request.GET.get('code', str(resp.status_int))),
                message=content)
        return page

    def img(self, id):
        """Serve Pylons' stock images"""
        return self._serve_file(os.path.join(media_path, 'img'), id)

    def style(self, id):
        """Serve Pylons' stock stylesheets"""
        return self._serve_file(os.path.join(media_path, 'style'), id)

    def _serve_file(self, root, path):
        """Call Paste's FileApp (a WSGI application) to serve the file
        at the specified path
        """
        static = StaticURLParser(root)
        request.environ['PATH_INFO'] = '/%s' % path
        return static(request.environ, self.start_response)
```

When the StatusCodeRedirect middleware forwards a request, it does so by passing the status code and status message to the document() action of the error controller by modifying the request so that it looks as if it came from a URL such as this: /error/document?code=404&message=Not%20Found. It is the responsibility of the document() action to then return the HTML of the error document with the code and message provided.

For the default implementation, the error document is generated from the Python string error_document_template in the pylons.middleware module, which is used to generate a response after the code, and messages have been substituted in the appropriate places. What is craftier is that to avoid having to add error document static files into your project template, the Pylons developers have added two further actions, img() and style(), that both create a static file server application and serve the static files from the Pylons module directory. (They use the same StaticURLParser WSGI application that is used to serve files from your project directory.) The template then references these actions so that all the images and CSS styles that the default template use are actually served from the Pylons module directory and don't clutter up your application.

Customizing the Error Documents for SimpleSite

Now that you've seen how error documents are generated by default, let's look at how you can customize them to change the theme for the SimpleSite application. The easiest way to do this is to simply replace `error_document_template` with a different string containing the HTML you want returned. The string can contain the variables %(prefix)s, %(code)s, and %(message)s, which get substituted for the URL path where the application is mounted, the HTTP status code that was intercepted, and the default Pylons description of the HTTP status, respectively.

Although this approach works perfectly well, for the SimpleSite application you'll go one step further and use a custom template to generate the error documents. To do this, you need to modify the `document()` action. Update it to look like this:

```
def document(self):
    """Render the error document"""
    resp = request.environ.get('pylons.original_response')
    code = cgi.escape(request.GET.get('code', ''))
    content = cgi.escape(request.GET.get('message', ''))
    if resp:
        content = literal(resp.status)
        code = code or cgi.escape(str(resp.status_int))
    if not code:
        raise Exception('No status code was found')
    c.code = code
    c.message = content
    return render('/derived/error/document.html')
```

The start of the action remains the same, but the lines in bold pass the code and message to a template rather than generating a response based on a string. Notice that you've also changed `resp.body` to `resp.status` because `resp.body` contains some HTML markup you don't need.

For the previous code to work, you need to add imports for the `c` global and Mako `render()` function at the top of the file:

```
from pylons import tmpl_context as c
from simplesite.lib.base import render
```

Create the new `derived/error/document.html` template with the following content:

```
<%inherit file="/base/index.html"/>

<%def name="title()">Server Error ${c.code}</%def>
<%def name="heading()"><h1>Error ${c.code}</h1></%def>

<p>${c.message}</p>
```

With the changes in place, you can test the template by visiting a page that doesn't exist such as http://localhost:5000/no/such/page. The result is shown in Figure 19-4.

Figure 19-4. *The updated error document support showing a 404 Not Found page*

When a user tries to access functionality they don't have access to, they are now shown the styled 403 error document. Although this is a significant improvement over the Pylons default version, it would be even better if the user was given a customized error message explaining that they don't have the appropriate permissions to perform the action they are trying to perform. It would also be a good idea to provide a link so they can sign in as a different user who does have the required permissions.

Let's start by customizing the template to display a custom message for the 403 status code and the link to allow the user to sign in again. Update the template so it looks like this:

```
<%inherit file="/base/index.html"/>

<%def name="title()">Server Error ${c.code}</%def>
<%def name="heading()"><h1>Error ${c.code}</h1></%def>

% if c.code == '403':
<p>You do not have sufficient permissions to access this page. Please
<a href="${h.url_for('signinagain')}">sign in</a> as a different user.</p>
% else:
<p>${c.message}</p>
% endif
```

When a user clicks the link, the action that gets called would need to sign them out before displaying the sign-in screen; otherwise, when they try to sign in, they will find they are still signed in as the original user.

Up until now, the only method you've seen for signing out a user is for them to visit the URL specified in the `authkit.cookie.signoutpath` option in the config file; this isn't the only method you can use, though. The AuthKit cookie plug-in you are using is an extended version of the Paste `paste.auth.auth_tkt` functionality and as such uses the same API for signing out users. This means the AuthKit middleware adds a sign-out function to the `environ` dictionary under the key `'paste.auth_tkt.logout_user'`. If you call this function, the middleware will remove the cookie from the headers after the response is returned. Now that you know this, you can write a new action that signs the user out and displays the sign-in form:

Add this action to the account controller:

```
def signinagain(self):
    request.environ['paste.auth_tkt.logout_user']()
    return render('/derived/account/signin.html').replace('%s', h.url_for('signin'))
```

Remember that the `/derived/account/signin.html` page isn't a normal template. It has to be set up so that it returns a string that AuthKit can use Python string interpolation on to replace the `%s` character with the action. Since you are not using the template with AuthKit this time, you have to add the form action yourself. (If you are using `FORM_ACTION` instead of `%s`, you'll have to adjust the last line accordingly.)

You'll also need another route for the `signinagain()` action in the `config/routing.py` file:

```
map.connect('signinagain', '/signinagain', controller='account', ➥
action='signinagain')
```

Finally, add the import for `h` into the `account` controller:

```
import simplesite.lib.helpers as h
```

This new action is now accessible from `/signinagain` and presents the sign-in form with the action adjusted to point to the sign-in screen.

There's one final change to make. You'll need to update the `base/index.html` template so the "Signed in as..." link isn't shown on the sign-in again page. Make the relevant line look like this:

```
    % if h.auth.authorized(h.auth.is_valid_user) and not ( ➥
request.urlvars['controller'] == 'account' and request.urlvars['action']➥
in ['signout', 'signinagain']):
```

If you sign in as user `foo` and try to access a URL such as `http://localhost:5000/page/list`, you will now be shown the page in Figure 19-5. Clicking the sign-in link will then take you to the sign-in again page, where you can sign in as a different user. With these changes in place, the customization of the error documents support is complete.

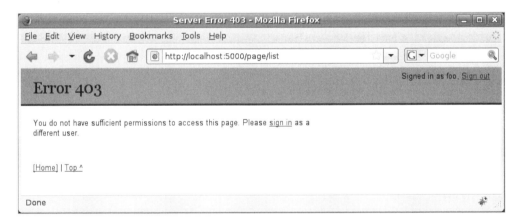

Figure 19-5. *The customized 403 error document*

Adding a WYSIWYG Interface

Even with all the changes you've made so far, SimpleSite is still rather simple. After all, it can be used to edit only plain text, which isn't too helpful for a website. In this section, you'll update the edit page functionality to use the YUI Rich Text Editor, and you'll change the page view template to allow HTML to be rendered.

Let's start by thinking about the JavaScript required to change the content text area on the edit page to use a visual editor. The editor you'll use is the YUI Rich Text Editor and is documented at http://developer.yahoo.com/yui/editor/. To set it up, you need to modify the derived/page/ edit.html template so that the js() def looks like this:

```
<%def name="js()">
    ${parent.js()}
    ${navfields.js()}

    <script type="text/javascript"
        src="/yui/2.6.0/element/element-beta-min.js"></script>
    <script type="text/javascript"
        src="/yui/2.6.0/container/container_core-min.js"></script>
    <script type="text/javascript"
        src="/yui/2.6.0/editor/simpleeditor-min.js"></script>

    <script type="text/javascript">
    (function() {
        // Set up some private variables
var Dom = YAHOO.util.Dom;
var Event = YAHOO.util.Event;

        // The SimpleEditor config
        var myConfig = {
            height: '200px',
            width: '630px',
            dompath: true,
            focusAtStart: true,
            handleSubmit: true
        };

        // Now let's load the SimpleEditor..
        var myEditor = new YAHOO.widget.SimpleEditor('editor', myConfig);
        myEditor._defaultToolbar.buttonType = 'advanced';
        document.e = myEditor;
        myEditor._defaultToolbar.titlebar = 'Rich Text Editor';
        myEditor.render();
    })();
    </script>
</%def>
```

Ordinarily, you would also need the yahoo-dom-event and connection libraries, but you are already using these to support the callAJAX() function used to update the before field, so you don't need to include them again.

For the previous JavaScript to work, you need some more changes. First, you need to add id="editor" to the text area used to edit the content so that the JavaScript you've added is applied to the correct element. Change derived/page/fields.html so the content field definition looks like this:

```
${h.field(
    "Content",
    h.textarea(name='content', rows=7, cols=40, id='editor'),
    required=True,
    field_desc = 'The text which will make up the body of the page'
)}
```

If you were to try to edit the page now, you'd see that although you could correctly edit the text, the Rich Text Editor wouldn't be displayed correctly. This is because you haven't yet chosen a theme for YUI.

YUI's theming system relies on the name of the theme to be used being specified as the class of the <body> tag. The default theme is called *sam skin*, so you'll use this one. Update the <body> tag in base/index.html so that it looks like this:

```
<body class="yui-skin-sam">
```

Finally, add this def to the end of derived/page/edit.html.

```
<%def name="head()">
    ${parent.head()}
    ${h.stylesheet_link(h.url_for('/yui/2.6.0/assets/skins/sam/skin.css'))}
</%def>
```

With these changes in place, try editing a page, and you should see an editor that allows you to add content such as that shown in Figure 19-6.

Figure 19-6. *Adding some HTML and an Image with the YUI Rich Text Editor*

If you try to use the editor to create a complex page, you'll notice that, because you were con-scientious when designing the application, your HTML content is automatically escaped when viewing pages. To prevent the HTML page's content from being escaped, you can edit `derived/page/view.html` and replace this line:

```
${(c.page.content)}
```

with these lines so that content is treated as an HTML literal:

```
<%!
    from webhelpers.html import literal
%>
<div id="page-content">
${literal(c.page.content)}
</div>
```

The final problem is that since you are using the YUI `reset.css` styles in the SimpleSite pages, some of the styles that looked correct in the editor get reset when you view the HTML. To fix this, add the following styles to the end of the `public/css/main.css` file:

```css
#page-content strong {
    font-weight: bold;
}
#page-content em {
    font-style: italic;
}
#page-content p {
    margin-bottom: 20px;
}
#page-content ol, #page-content ul {
    margin: 20px 20px 20px 1em;
    padding-left: 20px;
}
#page-content ol li {
    list-style: decimal;
}
#page-content ul li {
    list-style: disc;
}
```

The pages will now display correctly.

Configuring the setup.py File

At this point, the SimpleSite application is pretty much finished, so it is nearly time to package it up to be distributed. Pylons comes equipped with quite a few tools to help you easily publish your application and to allow other people to easily install it and its dependencies. We'll look at these tools in this section.

Before you can publish the egg, there are a number of changes you need to make including the following:

- Choosing a version number
- Configuring dependencies
- Specifying metadata
- Customizing the production config file template

Choosing a Version Number

The first step in distributing an application is to choose a version number for the project. Ordinarily, the 1.0.0 release is considered to be the first main release of a project. You've made three core sets of revisions to SimpleSite in each of the three chapters, but there are still some changes you might like to make before this is an official product you'd be proud to distribute more widely (notably the lack of documentation), so it probably isn't ready for a 1.0.0 release just yet. Let's set the version number to 0.3.0 to reflect the fact that this is the third minor revision.

The version number is set in `setup.py` and is used by Easy Install when determining which version to install. Update the version number for the SimpleSite project like this:

```
version = '0.3.0',
```

This example uses a simple version number, but Pylons also supports development releases and alpha, beta, and prerelease versions.

Let's start with alpha, beta, and prerelease releases. These are treated by `setuptools` as being before the final version for the purposes of their use in Easy Install conditions. For example, 0.5.0a1 would be considered the first alpha release of the 0.5 version of a particular application. Similarly, 0.5.0pre2 would be the second prerelease, and 0.5.0rc3 would be the third release candidate. This means that if certain software required version 0.5 or greater, none of the releases specified so far would be suitable.

For example, during the process of writing the book, I released the first version of the SimpleSite code as version 0.3.0pre1. As the book went into production, I released the 0.3.0 release, but if there are changes to Pylons before the book is released and these need corresponding changes in SimpleSite, I'd release a 0.3.1 release.

Development versions are slightly more complicated but are an equally useful feature. In development mode, `setuptools` automatically calculates the version revision number from the revision of the Subversion repository you are currently developing the Pylons application in (if indeed you are using Subversion). By default, Pylons applications are set up to be treated as a development version, which means the `.egg` file produced from it will have `dev` as part of the version. For example, if the repository is at revision 68, then the egg produced would be labeled `SimpleSite-0.3.0dev-r68_py2.5.egg`. If you want your release to be treated as a production release, you need to edit `setup.cfg` and comment out these two lines:

```
[egg_info]
#tag_build = dev
#tag_svn_revision = true
```

You should make this change to the SimpleSite project.

At this point, the project is set up to build the egg for the 0.3.0 production release so the egg produced will be named `SimpleSite-0.3.0_py2.5.egg`, but there are still some changes you need to make.

Configuring Dependencies

Now that the version number has been specified, let's update the list of libraries and other Python software the application depends on. This is done by adding the dependencies to the `install_requires` argument of the `setup()` function in your project's `setup.py` file. When you install software with Easy Install, the `easy_install` script automatically installs all the software specified in the `install_requires` line. The SimpleSite `setup.py` file currently has an `install_requires`, which looks like this:

```
install_requires=[
    "Pylons>=0.9.7",
    "SQLAlchemy>=0.4",
    "Mako",
    "FormBuild>=2.0",
],
```

Update this information to use SQLAlchemy 0.5 and to include AuthKit 0.4.3.
Here's what the lines should look like:

```
install_requires=[
    "Pylons>=0.9.7,<=0.9.7.99",
    "SQLAlchemy>=0.5,<=0.5.99",
    "Mako>=0.2.2,<=0.2.99",
    "FormBuild>=2.0.1,<=2.0.99",
    "AuthKit>=0.4.3,<=0.4.99",
],
```

Notice that you've specified all the dependencies with version numbers in a particular range. Package developers should be using the convention that any software release where only the revision has changed (the revision being the very last number making up the version) will be compatible with all previous versions with the same major and minor numbers (the first and second parts of the version, respectively). This means you can be fairly confident that your application should work with more recent versions of the dependencies as long as the major and minor components of the version number haven't changed. By specifying a range of suitable alternatives in your application, if any bug fix releases of the dependencies are made, SimpleSite can use them. It also means that if a user has a slightly different yet still compatible version of a dependency already installed, then Easy Install can use that rather than downloading a new version.

Note You might expect that you would be able to specify dependencies like this:

```
"AuthKit>=0.4,<=0.5"
```

This isn't quite what you want, though, because as has already been discussed, Easy Install would also treat other AuthKit versions including 0.5.0dev, 0.5.0a1, and 0.5.0pre2 as being lower than 0.5, and since these have a different minor version, the APIs might not be backward compatible with the 0.4 release. Instead, the convention is to use <0.4.99 on the basis that it is unlikely that there would be 99 revisions of a minor version of a piece of software.

Extra Dependencies

Sometimes you might want a particular dependency installed only if a user is installing a particular feature. As an example, SimpleSite is designed to work with multiple database engines, each of which require a particular driver. Let's focus on just MySQL and PostgreSQL, though. You wouldn't want to list both the mysql-python and psycopg2 packages in the `install_requires` line as dependencies because your users would only ever need one of the drivers. On the other hand, if you left out the drivers completely, they would not be automatically installed when SimpleSite was installed.

To cater for this situation, Pylons applications can use the `setuptools` optional extra dependency feature. Add the following to the end of the `setup()` function in `setup.py`:

```
extras_require = {
    'MySQL':    ["mysql-python>=1.2"],
    'PostgreSQL': ["psycopg2"],
},
```

Each of the extras is specified as a key and a list of all the dependencies. In this case, both the extras require only one dependency to be installed.

When it comes to installing SimpleSite, the extras required can be specified like this:

```
$ easy_install SimpleSite[MySQL]
```

This will now automatically install the mysql-python package version 1.2 or greater, which provides the MySQLdb module that SQLAlchemy uses for its MySQL support.

Extra Dependency Links

By default, Easy Install installs software only from the Python Package Index unless you use the -f flag to specify extra URLs.

If your application relies on packages hosted at different URLs, you can add them to the setup() function like this:

```
dependency_links = [
    "http://pylonshq.com/download/"
],
```

Easy Install will automatically search these links when trying to resolve the dependencies.

Specifying Metadata

As well as allowing you to specify dependencies, the setup() function takes arguments for specifying metadata about your project. This metadata is used as the basis for the information on the Python Package Index. Update the setup.py with the following metadata:

```
setup(
    name='SimpleSite',
    version='0.3.0',
    description='''A simple website application written as a demonstration of Pylons
for the Definitive Guide to Pylons''',
    author='James Gardner',
author_email='feedback@pylonsbook.com',
    url='http://pylonsbook.com',
    long_description='''\
A simple CMS application allowing WYSIWYG page editing, sections and subsections
and full navigation widgets
    ''',
    ... other options here ...
)
```

The short_description argument is used in the list on the home page of the Python Package Index, and the long_description argument is used in the main page for the project on the Python Package Index. In addition to the author, author_email, and home page url, you can also specify which categories the application should be placed in. The categories are known as *trove classifiers*, and you can find a full list at http://pypi.python.org/pypi?%3Aaction=list_classifiers. Here are the classifiers for Pylons itself:

```
classifiers=[
    "Development Status :: 5 - Production/Stable",
    "Intended Audience :: Developers",
    "License :: OSI Approved :: BSD License",
    "Framework :: Pylons",
    "Programming Language :: Python",
    "Topic :: Internet :: WWW/HTTP",
```

```
        "Topic :: Internet :: WWW/HTTP :: Dynamic Content",
        "Topic :: Internet :: WWW/HTTP :: WSGI",
        "Topic :: Software Development :: Libraries :: Python Modules",
],
```

In addition, it can also be useful to specify keywords related to the application and the license:

```
keywords='pylons simple site book example',
license='BSD, see the simplesite/public/yui/2.6.0/LICENSE.txt file for details.
```

Customizing the Long Description

The long_description argument is used on the main page for the package and also accepts reStructuredText, which you learned about in Chapter 13. This means you can add some quite complex formatting to the long description. You can use something like this, for example:

```
++++++++++
SimpleSite
++++++++++

A simple website application allowing WYSIWYG editing, sections and
subsections and full navigation widgets. The idea is that the application can
form a starting point for your own website projects.


Installation
============

First install Easy Install if you don't have it already by downloading
``ez_setup.py`` from http://peak.telecommunity.com/dist/ez_setup.py and
installing it like this::

    python ez_setup.py

Install SimpleSite like this specifying either MySQL, SQLite or PostgreSQL
as the word within the square brackets depending on the database you intend to
use::

    easy_install SimpleSite["MySQL"]
    paster make-config simplesite.ini

Configure the application by editing ``simplesite.ini`` to specify a database
to use using the format described at
http://www.sqlalchemy.org/docs/05/dbengine.html#dbengine_supported ::

    paster setup-app simplesite.ini
    paster serve simplesite.ini

The running application will now be available at http://localhost/

Files
=====
```

The reason for the Files subheading at the end is that the Python Package Index specifies the files after the long description, so this formatting will result in a nicely structured page on the Python Package Index.

With these changes in place, the Python Package Index page for the project will look eventually look like Figure 19-7 once the package is published.

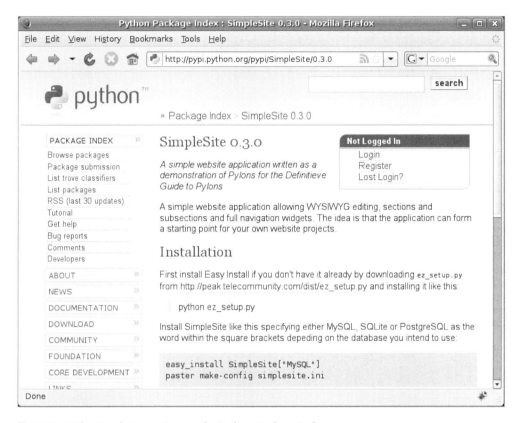

Figure 19-7. *The SimpleSite project on the Python Package Index*

Customizing the Production Config File Template

There is one more customization you need to make before you are ready to publish the egg itself. As you'll see in Chapter 21 about deployment, when a user has installed your `.egg`, they will run the application directly from a config file. To create the config file, they'll use this command:

```
$ paster make-config SimpleSite myconfig.ini
```

The SimpleSite application requires the AuthKit configuration options to be present in the config file that the earlier command generates. To achieve this, you need to customize how Pylons generates the config file. Pylon provides a `deployment.ini_tmpl` file in your project's `config` directory, which will be used as a basis for generating this config file, so you should update it to contain the AuthKit configuration (marked in bold here):

```
#
# SimpleSite - Pylons configuration
#
# The %(here)s variable will be replaced with the parent directory of this file
#
```

```
[DEFAULT]
debug = true
email_to = you@yourdomain.com
smtp_server = localhost
error_email_from = paste@localhost

[server:main]
use = egg:Paste#http
host = 0.0.0.0
port = 5000

[app:main]
use = egg:SimpleSite
full_stack = true
cache_dir = %(here)s/data
beaker.session.key = simplesite
beaker.session.secret = ${app_instance_secret}
app_instance_uuid = ${app_instance_uuid}

authkit.setup.enable = true
authkit.setup.method = form, cookie
authkit.form.authenticate.user.type = ➥
authkit.users.sqlalchemy_driver:UsersFromDatabase
authkit.form.authenticate.user.data = simplesite.model
authkit.cookie.secret = secret string
authkit.cookie.signoutpath = /signout
authkit.form.template.obj = simplesite.lib.auth:render_signin

# If you'd like to fine-tune the individual locations of the cache data dirs
# for the Cache data, or the Session saves, un-comment the desired settings
# here:
#beaker.cache.data_dir = %(here)s/data/cache
#beaker.session.data_dir = %(here)s/data/sessions

# SQLAlchemy database URL
sqlalchemy.url = sqlite:///production.db
sqlalchemy.echo = False

# WARNING: *THE LINE BELOW MUST BE UNCOMMENTED ON A PRODUCTION ENVIRONMENT*
# Debug mode will enable the interactive debugging tool, allowing ANYONE to
# execute malicious code after an exception is raised.
set debug = false

# Logging configuration
[loggers]
keys = root

[handlers]
keys = console

[formatters]
keys = generic

[logger_root]
level = INFO
handlers = console
```

```
[handler_console]
class = StreamHandler
args = (sys.stderr,)
level = NOTSET
formatter = generic

[formatter_generic]
format = %(asctime)s %(levelname)-5.5s [%(name)s] %(message)s
```

You'll notice that this file is slightly different from the default development.ini file. In particular, it has these two extra lines:

```
beaker.session.secret = ${app_instance_secret}
app_instance_uuid = ${app_instance_uuid}
```

The variables ${app_instance_secret} and ${app_instance_uuid} are replaced with appropriate values when the user of the application runs the paster make-config command.

You'll also notice that debugging is automatically set to false to ensure that production deployments don't accidentally have the Pylons interactive debugger enabled.

■**Tip** Pylons 0.9.6 users will be used to using a paste_deploy_config.ini_tmpl in their project's ProjectName.egg-info directory. The config/deployment.ini_tmpl file behaves in the same way but is in a location that is less likely to be deleted accidentally.

Packaging a Pylons Project for Distribution

Now that you know how to customize setup.py, let's look at how to package the SimpleSite application.

Pylons applications are designed to be distributed as .egg files. This is the same format that Pylons itself and all its dependencies are distributed in. You'll remember from Chapter 2 that applications distributed as eggs can be installed with Easy Install. This means that if your Pylons application is published on the Python Package Index, other users will be able to install it with Easy Install too. Let's start by looking at how to build an egg.

Building an Egg File

The first step of building an egg is to remove any unnecessary files that you don't want packaged. In this case, this includes any of the YUI library files the application is not using. By looking at Firebug's Net tab when using the application, you can see that only the following files are being used:

- /css/main.css
- /yui/2.6.0/animation/animation-min.js
- /yui/2.6.0/assets/skins/sam/blankimage.png
- /yui/2.6.0/assets/skins/sam/editor-sprite.gif
- /yui/2.6.0/assets/skins/sam/editor-sprite-active.gif
- /yui/2.6.0/assets/skins/sam/skin.css
- /yui/2.6.0/assets/skins/sam/sprite.png
- /yui/2.6.0/connection/connection-min.js

- /yui/2.6.0/container/container_core-min.js

- /yui/2.6.0/editor/simpleeditor-min.js

- /yui/2.6.0/element/element-beta-min.js

- /yui/2.6.0/json/json-min.js

- /yui/2.6.0/reset-fonts-grids/reset-fonts-grids.css

- /yui/2.6.0/yahoo-dom-event/yahoo-dom-event.js

You should remove all the other files from your project's public directory. Also, because YUI is licensed under a separate license, you should also add the text of the license to /yui/2.6.0/LICENSE.txt. Then you are ready to build the egg. You can do so with this command:

```
$ python setup.py bdist_egg
```

If everything goes smoothly, an .egg file with the correct name and version number appears in a newly created dist directory. The .egg file contains everything anyone needs to run your program. You should probably make eggs for each version of Python your users might require by running the previous command with Python 2.4, 2.5, and 2.6 to create each version of the egg.

At this point, your work as a developer is done. The finished and packaged egg file is now produced and ready to be distributed or deployed. If you emailed the egg to a colleague, they could now install it into their own virtual Python environment just like this:

```
$ easy_install SimpleSite-0.3.0-py2.5.egg
```

You'll learn about how you can deploy eggs like this one in production environments in Chapter 21, but for now let's look at how you can publish eggs on the Python Package Index to make it even easier to share them with the wider Python community.

Publishing an Egg on the Python Package Index

Now that you have successfully created eggs for your application, you can register them on the Python Package Index at http://www.python.org/pypi. Do this by running the following command. *Please do this only with your own projects, though, because SimpleSite has already been registered!*

When you run the command, some processing is done on the project, and then you are given some choices of how to proceed. Here I'm using my existing login details, but you can choose option 2. to register a new account with the system:

```
$ python setup.py register
running register
... some lines omitted ...
We need to know who you are, so please choose either:
 1. use your existing login,
 2. register as a new user,
 3. have the server generate a new password for you (and email it to you), or
 4. quit
Your selection [default 1]:  1
Username: thejimmyg
Password:
Server response (200): OK
I can store your PyPI login so future submissions will be faster.
(the login will be stored in /home/james/.pypirc)
Save your login (y/N)?y
```

The program then asks you whether you want it to save your login details. When I ran the previous example to register SimpleSite, I chose to save them because I knew I'd want to upload the egg files automatically too. This option saved me from having to enter my details again.

___

■**Caution** The Python Package Index authentication is very weak, and passwords are transmitted in plain text. Don't use any sign-in details that you use for important applications because they could be easily intercepted.

___

If you visit `http://pypi.python.org/pypi/SimpleSite/0.3.0`, you'll see the page that was created by the previous command. It was also shown a few pages ago in Figure 19-7. You'll also notice that new projects appear at the top of the list of recent projects on the Python Package Index home page, as shown in Figure 19-8.

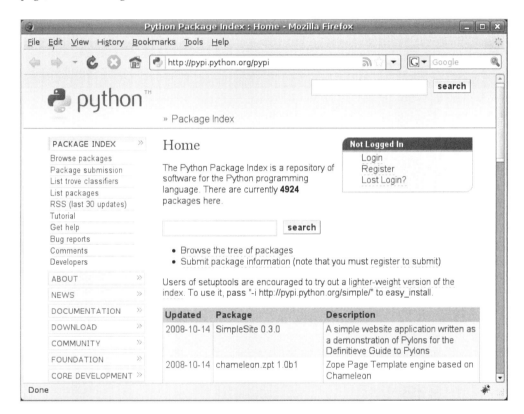

Figure 19-8. *The SimpleSite project on the Python Package Index*

You can now sign in to the Python Package Index with the account details you used when you registered your application and upload the eggs you've created, or if you prefer, you can even have Python do it for you; just enter this command for each version of Python supported to upload the eggs for you:

```
$ python2.4 setup.py bdist_egg register upload
$ python2.5 setup.py bdist_egg register upload
```

If you didn't allow the `register` command to create a `.pypirc` file in your home directory for you, you'll need to create one yourself. It should contain your username and password so that the `upload` command knows who to sign in as, and it should look similar to this:

```
[server-login]
username: james
password: password
```

This works on Windows too, but you will need to set your HOME environment variable first. If your home directory is `C:\Documents and Settings\James`, you would put your `.pypirc` file in that directory and set your HOME environment variable with this command:

```
> SET HOME=C:\Documents and Settings\James
```

You can now use `python setup.py bdist_egg upload` as normal.

At this point, your project has been successfully published. Other Python users can now install it just by entering this command:

```
$ easy_install SimpleSite
```

With the application successfully published, you might think your work is done, but actually, if you have a project you think would make a good starting point for other people's projects, you can package it up as a project template. Let's look at this next.

Making SimpleSite into a Paste Project Template

If you have a Pylons project you think would be useful to other people, it is possible to turn your Pylons *project* into a Paster *project template*, which can then be used to automatically generate a skeleton project based on SimpleSite by running this command:

```
$ paster create --template=SimpleSite MyProject
```

To set this up for SimpleSite, you'll need to create a new project called `SimpleSiteTemplate`, which is just an empty `setuptools`-enabled package (not a Pylons project this time). Run the following command, and enter the appropriate information when prompted:

```
$ paster create SimpleSiteTemplate

Selected and implied templates:
  PasteScript#basic_package  A basic setuptools-enabled package

Variables:
  egg:      SimpleSiteTemplate
  package:  simplesitetemplate
  project:  SimpleSiteTemplate
Enter version (Version (like 0.1)) ['']: 0.1
Enter description (One-line description of the package) ['']: A Paste Template➥
which allows you to create a new Pylons project based on the SimpleSite tutorial➥
described in the Pylons Book
Enter long_description (Multi-line description (in reST)) ['']:
Enter keywords (Space-separated keywords/tags) ['']: Pylons Paste Template ➥
SimpleSite Simple Site Website
Enter author (Author name) ['']: James Gardner
Enter author_email (Author email) ['']: feedback@pylonsbook.com
```

```
Enter url (URL of homepage) ['']: http://pylonsbook.com
Enter license_name (License name) ['']: BSD
Enter zip_safe (True/False: if the package can be distributed as a .zip file) ➥
[False]:
Creating template basic_package
Creating directory ./SimpleSiteTemplate
  Recursing into +package+
    Creating ./SimpleSiteTemplate/simplesitetemplate/
    Copying __init__.py to ./SimpleSiteTemplate/simplesitetemplate/__init__.py
  Copying setup.cfg to ./SimpleSiteTemplate/setup.cfg
  Copying setup.py_tmpl to ./SimpleSiteTemplate/setup.py
Running /Users/james/devenv/bin/python setup.py egg_info
```

This creates a skeleton package with a simple setup.py file built with the settings you entered at the command prompt.

You need a submodule to store the template files that will be used to as a basis for building the Pylons projects. Create a template directory within the SimpleSiteTemplate/simplesitetemplate directory. Next, copy every file and folder underneath the top-level SimpleSite directory into the SimpleSiteTemplate/simplesitetemplate/template directory.

```
$ cd SimpleSiteProject/simplesiteproject/template
$ cp -pr /path/to/SimpleSite/* ./
```

You don't need the data directory, though, because Pylons re-creates this as it is needed based on the settings in the config file of the Pylons package the user eventually creates. You don't need the dist or build directories either because they will get created automatically too if they are needed, and you don't need any of the .pyc files or any of the files in SimpleSite.egg-info because they are all re-created by Paste when a user creates a project from the template. You should also remove any development database files you might have used such as the development.db file because users of your template will create their own database and are unlikely to want your existing content.

One command you can use to delete all .pyc files (tested on Mac OS X Leopard) is as follows:

```
$ find . | grep .pyc | xargs rm
```

Once you have finished, the SimpleSiteTemplate/simplesitetemplate directory should look like this:

```
$ ls
MANIFEST.in             docs                    simplesite
README.txt              ez_setup.py             test.ini
SimpleSite.egg-info     setup.cfg
development.ini         setup.py
```

Next, you'll need to customize the SimpleSiteProject setup.py file so that Paste is automatically installed if a user tries to use the project template (this is not the setup.py file you copied into the template directory):

```
install_requires = [
    "Paste>=1.7",
],
```

At this point, you are ready to start implementing the template part. First, you need to implement the plug-in class, which Paste will use to determine how to create the template. It is very simple. Add this to the SimpleSiteTemplate/simplesitetemplate/__init__.py file:

```
from paste.script.templates import BasicPackage

class SimpleSitePackage(BasicPackage):
    _template_dir = 'template'
    summary = "A Pylons template to create a simple, user-editable website"
    egg_plugins = ['PasteScript', 'Pylons']
```

The _template_dir variable specifies the directory that contains the template files, relative to the Python module the BasicPackage class is defined in (in this case the __init__.py file). The summary variable contains the text that is displayed when a user runs the command paster create --list-templates.

Next you need to use egg entry points so that the paster template program can find your new template. Edit the SimpleSiteProject setup.py file again to update the entry_points argument to the setup() function, to look like this:

```
entry_points="""
    # -*- Entry points: -*-
    [paste.paster_create_template]
    simplesite=simplesitetemplate:SimpleSitePackage
""",
```

The entry point name will be used as the name of the plug-in, which in this case is simplesite. The second part points to the class that Paste will use to create the file structure for the new project. In this case, it is the SimpleSitePackage class you've just created in simplesitetemplate/__init__.py.

At this point, everything is set up and ready to test. Install the package in development mode with the following:

```
$ python setup.py develop
```

You can try to create a sample project somewhere, but there will be some problems:

```
$ cd /path/to/create/new/project
$ paster create --template simplesite MyProject
simplesite MyProject
Selected and implied templates:
  SimpleSiteTemplate#simplesite  A Pylons template to create a simple, ➥
user-editable website

Variables:
  egg:      MyProject
  package:  myproject
  project:  MyProject
Enter version (Version (like 0.1)) ['']:
Enter description (One-line description of the package) ['']:
Enter long_description (Multi-line description (in reST)) ['']:
Enter keywords (Space-separated keywords/tags) ['']:
Enter author (Author name) ['']:
Enter author_email (Author email) ['']:
Enter url (URL of homepage) ['']:
Enter license_name (License name) ['']:
Enter zip_safe (True/False: if the package can be distributed as a .zip file) ➥
[False]:
Creating template simplesite
```

```
Creating directory ./MyProject
  Copying MANIFEST.in to ./MyProject/MANIFEST.in
  Copying README.txt to ./MyProject/README.txt
  Recursing into SimpleSite.egg-info
...
Copying test_models.py to ./MyProject/simplesite/tests/test_models.py
    Copying websetup.py to ./MyProject/simplesite/websetup.py
  Copying test.ini to ./MyProject/test.ini
Running /Users/james/devenv/bin/python setup.py egg_info
Traceback (most recent call last):
...
IOError: No egg-info directory found
...
```

The command created a `SimpleSite.egg-info` directory, not a `MyProject.egg-info` directory, so when the command to set up the `egg-info` directory was run, it failed. You'll need to fix that and also change the files and directories in the `template` directory so that they use variable names that Paste can replace when it creates the template.

It would also be nice if the `paster create` script prompted you for a SQLAlchemy URL so that no manual editing of the `development.ini` file was necessary. You'll learn how do each of these things in the next sections.

Introducing Project Template Variables

Classes derived from `BasicPackage` like the `SimpleSitePackage` class you just created can take a vars member variable. This allows you to ask extra questions just before the project is generated. The answers to those questions can then be assigned to variable names you specify, and those variable names can be used in the filenames, directory names, and file content, and they will be substituted for the options chosen on the command line when someone creates a project using the project template.

As you saw in the previous section, the `BasicPackage` class already asks the person creating a project a number of questions, and it assigns the answers of these questions to the following variables:

```
version
description
long_description
keywords
author
author_email
url
license_name
zip_safe
```

If you look at the output when you run the command, you'll see these variable names in part of the question. For example:

```
Enter author_email (Author email) ['']:
```

Let's modify `SimpleSitePackage` to also ask for a value for `sqlalchemy_url`. Update the `simplesitetemplate/__init__.py` file to look like this:

```
from paste.script.templates import BasicPackage, var

class SimpleSitePackage(BasicPackage):
    _template_dir = 'template'
    summary = "A Pylons template to create a simple, user-editable website"
    egg_plugins = ['PasteScript', 'Pylons']
    vars = [
        var('sqlalchemy_url', 'The SQLAlchemy URL to the database to use',
            default='sqlite:///%(here)s/develpment.db'),
    ]
```

If you run the command again, you'll now be prompted for a SQLAlchemy URL, and if you don't provide one, a default of sqlite:///%(here)s/develpment.db will be used.

```
Enter sqlalchemy_url (The SQLAlchemy URL to the database to use) ➥
['sqlite://%(here)s/develpment.db']:
```

▓**Tip** There are some other options too, but you won't use them in this example. If you want to set up a more complex BasicPackage plug-in, you should have a look at the source code at the following location to understand how everything works: http://pythonpaste.org/script/paste/script/templates.py.html.

Using Project Template Variables

Now that the paster create script is correctly prompting the user for all the information you need, it is time to update the files and directories in simplesitetemplate/template to use these variables.

In addition to the variables described so far, Paste sets up three more variables for you. If you look at the output from running the paster create --template=simplesite MyProject command from the previous section, you'll see them listed near the top:

```
Variables:
  egg:      MyProject
  package:  myproject
  project:  MyProject
```

The egg, package, and project variables represent the name used in the egg file, the Python name of the package, and the project name (which is the name that would be used if you published the package on the Python Package Index), respectively. Now that the variables have values assigned to them, you can begin using them in the files and directories in the template directory. Variables can be used in filenames, in directory names, and in the source code itself, but there are a few rules to follow:

- When a variable is used in a directory name or filename, it must have + characters on either side. For example:

  ```
  +egg+.egg_info
  +project+.py
  ```

- Variables within files should be wrapped in {{ and }} characters. For example:

  ```
  import {{package}}.lib.base
  ```

- Any file that contains variables should be renamed so that its file extension ends in _tmpl. So, foo.ini would become foo.ini_tmpl, and foo would become foo_tmpl.

In fact, you can perform more complex operations too. The paster create template script understands a very simple template language called Tempita documented at http://pythonpaste.org/tempita/, so you can use any constructs supported by Tempita. Now that you know the rules, let's go through and update the files, directories, and code in simplesitetemplate/template to use the variables you now have access too, starting by renaming the SimpleSite.egg-info and simplesite directories:

```
$ cd SimpleSiteTemplate/simplesitetemplate/template
$ rm -r SimpleSite.egg-info
$ mkdir +egg+.egginfo
$ mv simplesite +package+
```

You can delete the +package+/controllers/template.py.txt file you used as a template for other controllers in Chapter 14.

Now let's get a list of all the files that contain the word SimpleSite or simplesite, because you'll need to update them:

```
$ egrep -rl '(simplesite|SimpleSite)' . | grep -v ".pyc"
./+package+/config/deployment.ini_tmpl
./+package+/config/environment.py
./+package+/config/middleware.py
./+package+/config/routing.py
./+package+/controllers/account.py
./+package+/controllers/comment.py
./+package+/controllers/error.py
./+package+/controllers/nav.py
./+package+/controllers/page.py
./+package+/controllers/section.py
./+package+/controllers/tag.py
./+package+/lib/base.py
./+package+/lib/helpers.py
./+package+/model/__init__.py
./+package+/public/yui/2.6.0/LICENSE.txt
./+package+/templates/base/index.html
./+package+/templates/component/navigation.html
./+package+/tests/functional/test_account.py
./+package+/tests/functional/test_nav.py
./+package+/tests/functional/test_page.py
./+package+/websetup.py
./MANIFEST.in
./README.txt
./development.ini
./docs/index.txt
./setup.cfg
./setup.py
./test.ini
```

Rename each of these files so that they all have _tmpl added to the end of the filename. The config/deployment.ini_tmpl will need the extension too so will end up as config/deployment.ini_tmpl_tmpl.

If you don't want to do this manually and are comfortable with a single command that will do this for you in a Bash shell, you could try the following one. The command should be entered on one line, and you are advised to back up your files first in case it behaves slightly differently or your platform:

```
$ for f in `egrep -rl '(simplesite|SimpleSite)' . | grep -v .pyc `; ➥
do mv "$f" "`echo $f`_tmpl"; done
```

Once the files are renamed, you'll need to update the contents of the files. The majority of the work is changing the text `SimpleSite` and `simplesite`, so let's do that first:

```
$ grep -rl simplesite . | xargs perl -pi -w -e 's/simplesite/{{package}}/g;'
$ grep -rl SimpleSite . | xargs perl -pi -w -e 's/SimpleSite/{{project}}/g;'
```

You also need to use the `sqlalchemy_url` variable the user has specified to fill in the value of the `sqlalchemy.url` option in `development.ini`.

Update `development.ini_tmpl` so that the `sqlalchemy.url` option looks like this:

```
sqlalchemy.url = {{sqlalchemy_url}}
```

■**Note** You might be tempted to think that it would be a good idea to use the `sqlalchemy_url` variable in the `config/deployment.ini_tmpl_tmpl` file too, but just because users of your application are using a particular SQLAlchemy URL for their development doesn't mean they will use the same in production.

You should also ensure that none of the files you are about to package contain any usernames, passwords or any other information you don't want distributed. In particular you should check the `development.ini` and `test.ini` files.

Now that everything is set up correctly, let's give the new template a test run. First let's check that the template has been found:

```
$ paster create --list-templates
Available templates:
  authenticate_plugin:  An AuthKit authenticate middleware plugin
  basic_package:        A basic setuptools-enabled package
  paste_deploy:         A web application deployed through paste.deploy
  pylons:               Pylons application template
  pylons_minimal:       Pylons minimal application template
  simplesite:           A Pylons template to create a simple, user-editable website
```

The `simplesite` project template is correctly listed, so let's try to create the `MyProject` application again. Remove the old `MyProject` directory if you tried to create the project earlier in the chapter, and then run the following command:

```
$ paster create --template=simplesite MyProject
```

If everything worked correctly, you can now test the application:

```
$ cd MyProject
$ python setup.py develop
$ paster setup-app development.ini
$ paster serve --reload development.ini
```

If you visit `http://localhost:5000`, you will see the new project correctly serving pages. You've successfully created a new project with the same functionality as SimpleSite with just a few commands. At this point, you are ready to start customizing the MyProject application for your own requirements and needs.

Completing the Cycle

If you've been following along with the tutorial chapters of the book, you'll actually have achieved something quite remarkable by this point. You'll have created a useful product and packaged it up in such a way that other developers can use it as a project template for their own projects without having to re-solve all the problems you've already solved.

To complete the cycle, I'd like to show you how I packaged up and released the SimpleSiteTemplate on the Python Package Index so that other developers can use it as a basis for their projects. First I edited `setup.cfg` to comment out the `tag_build` and `tag_svn_revision` options. Then I created a `MANIFEST.in` file. This tells Python which files need to be included in the package. It looks like this and includes all the files in the `template` directory:

```
recursive-include simplesitetemplate/template *
```

Finally, I ran this command to create and upload the package:

```
$ python setup.py bdist_egg sdist register upload
```

Now any user can create a Pylons project based on SimpleSite, just by entering the following commands:

```
$ easy_install SimpleSiteTemplate
$ paster create --template=simplesite MyProject
```

I hope you consider packaging any projects you frequently use as a basis for your own projects into Paste Templates in a similar way so that other people can use them as starting points. In this way, members of the Pylons community can quickly and easily build on the success of other Pylons users' projects.

Summary

You learned a lot in this chapter, from adding authentication and authorization facilities to SimpleSite to customizing Pylons' error pages. You also saw how to add metadata to projects and how the egg format and Pylons metadata integrate with the Python Package Index so that you can easily publish projects online and automatically create a page containing basic information. You also saw what a project template really is, and you turned the SimpleSite application into a reusable project template so that other people can use it as a basis for their own projects.

That's the end of the SimpleSite tutorial, but I hope many of the techniques and tools you've used to create the SimpleSite application will be useful in your own applications. If you are building a wiki, you might even be able to use the project template as a starting point for your code.

In the next chapter, you'll look at Pylons' logging support before moving on to see how to deploy Pylons applications in production environments.

CHAPTER 20

■ ■ ■

Logging

A useful way of working out what is happening during a request is to write log statements at various points in your code. These log statements can output log messages to multiple places such as the console or a file to help you follow how your code is working.

Tip If you don't want to know the details of how logging works but are just desperate to log a message to the console from within a controller action, you can do so like this:

```
log.debug('Your message goes here')
```

Getting Started with Pylons Logging

Conceptually, it' helpful to think about Pylons applications as having two completely different types of logs:

- Server logs
- Application logs

Server logs are generated by the server running the Pylons application and will typically include information such as the URL that was requested and the time the request was made. The server might also log information such as the IP address of the user visiting the site.

The application logs are generated by your Pylons application and the packages it uses. Application log messages can come from your controllers, model, helpers, templates, or any other part of your application as well as from third-party packages your application uses such as SQLAlchemy or AuthKit. Application log messages are sometimes also sent to the server for logging, and this results in the application log messages being intermingled with the server log messages. As you can imagine, logging can quickly get quite complicated unless you keep the concept of a server log very separate from the concept of an application log in your own mind.

To demonstrate the difference between the two types of logs and how they interact in development mode with the Paste HTTP server, let's create a new project called LogTest with a controller named log. Choose Mako as the templating language, and you won't need SQLAlchemy or Google App Engine support:

```
$ paster create --template=pylons LogTest
$ cd LogTest
$ paster controller log
```

Now edit `logtest/controllers/log.py` so that the `index()` action looks like this:

```
def index(self):
    log.debug('My first Pylons log message!\n')
    return 'Check the logs!'
```

Start the server with the `--reload` and `--log-file` options like this:

```
$ paster serve --reload development.ini --log-file test.log
```

The `--log-file` option specifies the file that the log messages should be written to. Now visit `http://localhost:5000/log/index` in your browser. You should see the message `Check the logs!` in the browser, and you will see the message `My first Pylons log message!` has been written to `test.log`.

Now, with the server still running, add a new action to the `log` controller called `newlog()` that looks like this:

```
def newlog(self, action):
    log.debug("Logged from the 'newlog' action")
    return 'Check the logs again!'
```

The server will restart because you changed the file. Visit `http://localhost:5000/log/newlog`, and then stop the server. Once again, the message returned from the controller will be shown in the browser, and the log message will be written to `test.log`.

After having visited just these two URLs, the Paste HTTP server log file (`test.log`) will contain these lines:

```
serving on http://127.0.0.1:5000
12:49:46,347 DEBUG [logtest.controllers.log] My first Pylons log message!

/home/james/LogTest/logtest/controllers/log.pyc changed; reloading...
Starting server in PID 533.
serving on http://127.0.0.1:5000
12:50:29,567 DEBUG [logtest.controllers.log] Logged from the 'newlog' action
```

As you can see, the log file has two types of messages: the debug messages from the controller and the messages from the server. The server logs (in normal font) and the application logs (in bold) are combined into one file. So, let's discuss exactly what is happening in this example.

When the `log.debug()` function is called, a message is logged, but what happens to that message depends on the configuration you have set up with the logging options in the `development.ini` config file. The default settings cause all log messages of `INFO` level or above to be sent to the standard error stream.

Now, it just so happens that the Paste HTTP server captures all the information sent to the standard error stream to its server logs, so in this example both the server logs and the application logs end up combined in the same file. This is handy for development use, but not all servers will behave in the same way, so you can't guarantee application log output will always end up in the server logs with the default Pylons configuration, although it often will.

In the section "Logging to a File" later in the chapter, you'll learn how to redirect the application logs to a separate file, but before I go into too much detail, you need to learn a little bit more about the `logging` module used to produce the application logs.

Understanding the logging Module

Pylons uses Python's `logging` module to provide its application logging. The basic concept behind the `logging` module is that each message is logged to a particular logger and that each logger has a name. Each controller therefore has the following lines at the top to set up a logger to be used for logging messages related to each controller:

```
import logging
...
log = logging.getLogger(__name__)
```

Python's special __name__ variable refers to the current module's fully qualified name, which in this case is `logtest.controllers.log`. This means that the `log` variable is set up to log messages to a logger named `logtest.controllers.log`.

The named loggers exist in a hierarchy where parent loggers can respond to the log messages of child loggers, and each . character in the name separates a level in the hierarchy. If, for example, you created a second logger in the controller specifically for logging the `index()` action and you named it `logtest.controller.log.index`, the `logtest.controller.log` logger would also receive its messages. This behavior is called *propagation* and can be overridden, as you'll see when it is discussed in more detail later in this chapter.

■**Tip** The loggers don't need to have the names of the modules they are created in; they can have any names as long as you understand that they will be treated as part of a logger hierarchy with . characters separating parents from children. Most of the time, using the full name of the module in which the loggers are defined is a good idea, though.

In addition to ordinary loggers, there is also a *root logger* at the very top of the logging hierarchy. In the default Pylons setup, the individual loggers are not configured to handle their own log messages, so they get propagated to the root logger, which handles them instead. You'll learn more about this behavior later in this chapter.

Understanding Log Levels

Each message logged to a specific logger must also have a log level. Table 20-1 shows the main log levels and their corresponding numeric values.

Table 20-1. *Levels of Importance and Their Corresponding Numeric Values*

Level	Numeric Value
CRITICAL	50
ERROR	40
WARNING	30
INFO	20
DEBUG	10
NOTSET	0

Messages that you want to be displayed only during debugging might be assigned to the DEBUG level, whereas critical error messages should be logged to the CRITICAL level.

To log messages, you simply use one of the methods corresponding to the levels in Table 20-1, which are available on the `log` object you want to log messages for. Here's an example:

```
def index(self):
    log.error('My third Pylons log message!')
    return 'Check the logs!'
```

When this action is executed, the following will be logged:

```
16:20:20,440 ERROR [logtest.controllers.log] My third Pylons log message!
```

Notice that because you called `log.error()`, the message was logged with the `ERROR` level. Let's also try to log a simple warning message. Change the action you were editing earlier to look like this:

```
def index(self):
    log.warning('My third Pylons log message!')
    return 'Check the logs!'
```

If you restart the Paste HTTP server and visit the `http://localhost:5000/log/index` URL again, you will see that the message is displayed on the console with the `WARNING` level:

```
16:21:30,410 WARNI [logtest.controllers.log] My third Pylons log message!
```

It is also possible to log messages by their output number rather than by their level; you can specify any number from 0–50, not just numbers corresponding to a level. This is useful if you want to set your own fine-grained log levels. You can log a message at a particular numeric value like this:

```
def index(self):
    log.log(10, 'Another log message')
    return 'Check the logs!'
```

Logging Variables

Each of the logging methods `debug()`, `info()`, `warning()`, `error()`, `critical()`, and `log()` also accepts an optional set of variable names that will be substituted into the log message itself using standard Python string formatting. This means you can log variables like this:

```
def index(self):
    error = 'Wrong Number'
    value = 5
    log.error('The error %r occurred with a value of %s.', error, value)
    return 'Check the logs!'
```

When this action is executed, the following output will be logged:

```
16:20:20,440 ERROR [logtest.controllers.log] The error 'Wrong Number' occurred ➡
with a value of 5.
```

Logging in Templates

The `logging` module's `getLogger()` function always returns the same logger instance for the name it is given. This means that if you wanted to log to the `logtest.controllers.log` logger from within a template, you could access the same logger like this:

```
<%!
    import logging
    log = logging.getLogger('logtest.controllers.log')
%>
```

Then later in your code you could write a log message like this:

```
<% log.debug('This is a debug message') %>
```

Both the `log` object in the template and the `log` object in the controller log messages to the same log. Of course, you could also attach the controller's `log` object to `c.log` and access that directly in the template instead if you prefer.

Now that you've seen the basics of how the `logging` module works and you understand the difference between server logs and application logs in the context of a Pylons application, let's take a look at how logging is configured.

Introducing Logging Configuration

Pylons logging is configured through the Pylons config file and is used to change how the *application logs* are handled. The format used is the same as that used by the `logging` module, as described at `http://docs.python.org/lib/logging-config-fileformat.html`. Although it looks similar to the Paste Deploy configuration you learned about in Chapter 17, it is actually completely different.

Logging configuration consists of three types of section: *loggers*, *handlers*, and *formatters*. Broadly speaking, the formatters take a message and format it together with extra information available such as the time or the process ID of the running application. The handlers take the formatted messages and handle them in some way, perhaps by writing them to a file or sending them to the standard error stream, and the logger sections override the default setting of each of the loggers that are used to output log messages, either discarding them or passing them onto the appropriate handler depending on the severity level of the message. Each logger, handler, and formatter requires its own section in the config file, but to keep track of the names being used for each section, every config file must also contain sections called [loggers], [handlers], and [formatters] that identify the name and the type of each section in the file through the use of keys.

Here are the first sections defined in the `LogTest` project's `development.ini` file:

```
# Logging configuration
[loggers]
keys = root, routes, logtest

[handlers]
keys = console

[formatters]
keys = generic
```

This means the `logging` module will also expect to see sections named [logger_root], [logger_routes], [logger_logtest], [handler_console], and [formatter_generic]. The [logger_logtest] section is named according to the package name of your Pylons application, so the section name in your own project would reflect its package name instead of `LogTest`'s.

▓**Tip** If you want to supplement the logging configuration supplied by the `development.ini` file, you can also configure logging in Python code. You might want to do this if you have written your own handler or formatter. A good place to add your extra configuration would be your project's `environment.py` file.

Let's take a look at the options you can use with each of the different types of section.

Logger Sections

Logger sections specify how to log messages to a particular logger, such as the `logtest.controllers.log` logger used earlier. Loggers take four configuration options. The `level` option specifies the log level below which log messages should be ignored. The `handlers` option takes a comma-separated list of the names of handlers to which the messages should be sent. The `qualname` option is the name of the logger to log messages for; and the `propagate` option determines whether messages sent to this logger should also be sent to its parent logger.

As an example, here's what the `routes` logger from the `LogTest` project's `development.ini` file looks like:

```
[logger_routes]
level = INFO
handlers =
qualname = routes.middleware
# "level = DEBUG" logs the route matched and routing variables.
```

This logger doesn't have any handlers of its own, but its messages propagate to the root logger, where they are handled instead.

Handler Sections

Handlers are used to handle the log messages passed to them from the loggers you have configured. Here's the console handler as an example:

```
[handler_console]
class = StreamHandler
args = (sys.stderr,)
level = NOTSET
formatter = generic
```

The `class` option indicates the handler's class (as determined by executing Python's `eval()` function in the `logging` package's namespace). The `args` argument is a list of arguments to pass to the handler specified by `class`. It's important to remember to add a comma at the end of the args list if there is just one argument; otherwise, the brackets are treated as parentheses rather than marking the start and end of a tuple.

You can use many handlers besides `StreamHandler` including `FileHandler`, `RotatingFileHandler`, `TimedRotatingFileHandler`, `SocketHandler`, `DatagramHandler`, `SysLogHandler`, `NTEventLogHandler`, `SMTPHandler`, `MemoryHandler`, and `HTTPHandler`. They are all documented in detail at http://docs.python.org/lib/node409.html.

The `level` option determines which level of messages are passed to the formatter and can be any one of the levels mentioned earlier: `CRITICAL`, `ERROR`, `WARNING`, `INFO`, `DEBUG`, and `NOTSET`. Setting the level to `NOTSET` results in everything being logged, setting the level to `INFO` results in messages of `INFO` level and above being logged. Finally, the `formatter` option should be the name of a formatter section that will specify how the log message should be formatted.

Formatter Sections

Formatters are responsible for converting a log record passed from a handler to a format suitable for output, usually a string with certain extra data about when and where the message was logged.

Here is an example:

```
[formatter_form01]
format=F1 %(asctime)s %(levelname)s %(message)s
datefmt=
class=logging.Formatter
```

The `format` option is the overall format string, and the `datefmt` option is the `strftime()`-compatible date/time format string. If it is empty, the `logging` package substitutes ISO8601 format dates and times.

The `class` entry is optional. It indicates the name of the formatter's class (as a dotted module and class name) and is useful if you have created your own `Formatter` subclass you want to use.

Most of the time, the only line in formatter sections that you'll want to change is the `format` line. You can use the variables in Table 20-2 to configure how the log messages will be formatted.

Table 20-2. *Format Codes and Their Descriptions*

Format	Description
%(name)s	Name of the logger.
%(levelno)s	Numeric logging level for the message (DEBUG, INFO, WARNING, ERROR, CRITICAL).
%(levelname)s	Text logging level for the message ('DEBUG', 'INFO', 'WARNING', 'ERROR', 'CRITICAL').
%(pathname)s	Full path name of the source file where the logging call was issued (if available).
%(filename)s	File name portion of path name.
%(module)s	Module (name portion of file name).
%(funcName)s	Name of function containing the logging call. Added in Python 2.5.
%(lineno)d	Source line number where the logging call was issued (if available).
%(created)f	Time when the LogRecord was created (as returned by time.time()).
%(relativeCreated)d	Time in milliseconds when the LogRecord was created, relative to the time the logging module was loaded.
%(asctime)s	Human-readable time when the LogRecord was created. By default, this is of the form 2003-07-08 16:49:45,896 (the numbers after the comma are millisecond portion of the time).
%(msecs)d	Millisecond portion of the time when the LogRecord was created.
%(thread)d	Thread ID (if available).
%(threadName)s	Thread name (if available).
%(process)d	Process ID (if available).
%(message)s	The logged message, computed as msg % args.

The formatter section used by LogTest looks like this:

```
[formatter_generic]
format = %(asctime)s,%(msecs)03d %(levelname)-5.5s [%(name)s] %(message)s
datefmt = %H:%M:%S
```

You can work out what each of the variables in the format option does from Table 20-2.

Over the next sections, you'll learn how to tweak the settings in each of the types of sections to solve common logging problems, so don't worry if you don't understand all the options just yet.

■**Tip** If you want to understand logging in detail, it is well worth reading the logging documentation at http://docs.python.org/lib/module-logging.html.

Redirecting Log Output Using Handlers

Now that you have seen the options for each of the different types of logging configuration sections, let's look at some of the common ways of handling log messages.

One of the most useful things to do with application log messages is to write them directly to a file. In fact, if you are new to logging or are setting up a Pylons applications on a new server, it is highly recommended you start by logging messages to a file because there is a lot less that can go wrong compared with logging either to the standard output stream, the standard error stream, or the WSGI errors stream.

Logging to a File

Although it is helpful to see application log messages in the console when you are developing a Pylons application, for production use the messages often need to be logged to a file.

To capture log output to a separate file, you can use a `FileHandler` or a `RotatingFileHandler`. The following is the configuration to set up a `FileHandler` called `file`. Add it to the end of the `development.ini` file from the `LogTest` project you created at the start of the chapter:

```
[handler_file]
class = FileHandler
args = ('application.log', 'a')
level = INFO
formatter = generic
```

The options here are similar to those used for the `console` handler that already exists in the `development.ini` file. The `args` option specifies the file name of the log file and that it should be opened in *append mode* so that new information is added to the end of the file and doesn't over-write existing data. The new handler will use the same formatter as the console handler.

For Pylons to know this section represents a new log handler, you also have to add the `file` handler to the `[handlers]` section. Update it to look like this:

```
[handlers]
keys = console, file
```

Now that the new handler is set up, you can customize the `root` logger to use the `file` handler rather than the existing `console` handler. Change the `[logger_root]` section to look like this:

```
[logger_root]
level = INFO
handlers = file
```

Now all the root logger's messages will be directed to the `application.log` file instead of the `sys.stderr` error stream.

With the new handler in place, start the Paste HTTP server again, this time using the file name `server.log` for the output log:

```
$ paster serve --reload development.ini --log-file=server.log
```

If you visit `http://localhost:5000/log/index`, you will see that the application log is not sent to `server.log` but instead appears in `application.log`. The server messages continue to appear in `server.log`, though. You have successfully redirected the application logs to a file.

Tip If you are using log files, it can often be useful to see the output that is logged as it is written, without having to constantly close and reopen the file. On Unix platforms you can use this command:

```
$ tail -f server.log
```

With this command running, any messages will be automatically copied to the console as they are written to `server.log` so that you can see the messages appear as you interact with the server.

Logging to wsgi.errors

You'll remember from Chapter 16 that one of the responsibilities of a WSGI server is to provide a suitable writable object as environ['wsgi.errors'] to be used for logging errors. Because of this, any messages written to wsgi.errors are guaranteed to go to the server's error log no matter which server you are using and no matter what format that error log takes (as long as the server conforms to the WSGI specification, of course).

You can test the behavior of wsgi.errors with the Paste HTTP server by adding a new action to the log controller:

```
def wsgi_errors(self):
    request.environ['wsgi.errors'].write(
        'This is sent directly to the wsgi.errors stream')
    return 'Message logged to wsgi.errors'
```

Check that the server is still running and has the --log-file server.log option set. Now visit http://localhost:5000/log/wsgi_errors, and you will see Message logged to wsgi.errors returned to the browser. If you look at server.log, you will see the last line looks like this:

```
This is sent directly to the wsgi.errors stream
```

As you can see, sending messages to the wsgi.errors stream sends messages directly to the *server* log, not the *application* log and so bypasses all the standard logging configuration. As a result, the extra information added by a formatter such as the time or log level has not been added.

Now that you know how the wsgi.errors stream logs messages, you might decide you want to be able to use it via a handler in the configuration file using the existing logging infrastructure. Pylons provides a custom logging handler class specifically for this purpose called WSGIErrorsHandler, which you can use to automatically send log messages to the wsgi.errors stream. It is documented at http://docs.pylonshq.com/modules/log.html. The advantage of using WSGIErrorsHandler is that all application logs get mixed in with the server logs, so you have only one log file to deal with, and you can quickly see the order that particular server and application events occurred in without having to compare their time stamps.

■**Caution** Although using the wsgi.errors stream can be useful, there is one big problem with using the Pylons WSGIErrorsHandler: all messages logged outside of a Pylons request will be silently lost.

The wsgi.errors stream is available only during a request because it has to be accessed via the WSGI environ dictionary, which itself is available only during a request. This means log messages created during application startup, shutdown, or before and after a request are silently lost.

This silent loss of messages may be something you can tolerate in your application, but generally speaking it is better to handle the application logs via a FileHandler (described in the previous section) or a RotatingFileHandler, so you can be sure all the messages are logged.

If you still want to use the WSGIErrorsHandler, this is how you do it. First add the handler name wsgierrors to the [handlers] section of the configuration file so that Pylons knows it is a handler:

```
[handlers]
keys = console, file, wsgierrors
```

Then add a new handler section specifying pylons.log.WSGIErrorsHandler as the class and an empty tuple for args. In this example, only messages with the DEBUG level or higher are logged, and you are using the same generic formatter you used for the console and file handlers.

```
[handler_wsgierrors]
class = pylons.log.WSGIErrorsHandler
args = ()
level = DEBUG
format = generic
```

You could now update the root logger's handler to use the `wsgierrors` handler on its own, but it is safer to use both the `file` handler and the `wsgierrors` handlers together so that any messages ignored by the `wsgierrors` handler are at least captured by the `file` handler. Change the `[logger_root]` section to look like this:

```
[logger_root]
level = INFO
handlers = file, wsgierrors
```

If you try this, notice that application messages are logged both to the Paste HTTP server log (via `wsgierrors`) as well as directly to `application.log`. If you log any messages outside a request, they will appear only in the `application.log` file via the `file` handler.

Configuring Which Messages Are Logged

Now that you've seen a couple of examples of how to use different handlers, it's time to see how you can use handlers to control which messages are logged. The golden rule is that the level that eventually gets logged is the higher of the level specified in the logger and the level specified in the handler.

This means that if you want only `ERROR`-level messages and above going to the `wsgi.errors` stream, you can change its handler definition to look like this:

```
[handler_wsgierrors]
class = pylons.log.WSGIErrorsHandler
args = ()
level = ERROR
format = generic
```

Now only the messages that are logged at the `ERROR` level or above get sent to the `wsgi.errors` stream by the `pylons.log.WSGIErrorsHandler` handler.

Controlling Propagation with Loggers

Now that you've seen some of the things that you can do with handlers, let's look in more detail at loggers.

By default, three loggers are configured for your `development.ini` configuration. In the case of `LogTest`, the relevant lines look like this:

```
[loggers]
keys = root, routes, logtest

...

[logger_root]
level = INFO
handlers =

[logger_routes]
level = INFO
handlers =
qualname = routes.middleware
# "level = DEBUG" logs the route matched and routing variables.
```

```
[logger_logtest]
level = DEBUG
handlers =
qualname = logtest
```

`...`

As you can see, loggers are configured for the following:

- All messages (`logger_root`)
- Routes middleware messages (`logger_routes`)
- Messages from the LogTest project (`logger_logtest`)

If you look at the [`logger_logtest`] section, you'll see that no handler is defined, so you might be wondering how the test messages you wrote in the `log` controller at the beginning of the chapter were logged to the application log. The answer is via *propagation*.

If you don't explicitly set a value for the `propagate` option, it is assumed to be set to 1. This means that any messages sent to the logger are *also* propagated to its parent logger. In this case, the parent logger is the root logger, and this does have a handler specified, so all messages to the `logtest` logger are actually handled by the root logger.

▌Caution You have to be very careful when spelling `propagate` because Pylons won't give you a warning if you misspell it. I've spent quite a long time wondering why propagation wasn't working only to realize I'd made a typo, and I wouldn't want you to make the same mistake!

You can test this behavior by setting `propagate` to 0 in the configuration section for [`logger_logtest`] and restarting the server. If you do this and then visit the `http://localhost:5000/log/index` URL, you'll see the following error message instead of the log message you might have expected:

`No handlers could be found for logger "logtest.controllers.log"`

This is because the messages are no longer propagated to the root logger and no handlers are specified for the `logtest.controllers.log` logger. The logging system is warning you that you might have made a mistake.

You might be wondering how the messages were sent to the `logtest` logger in the first place when the logger the messages were sent to is actually called `logtest.controller.log`. Once again, this occurs via propagation. Because the `qualname` option is specified with the value `logtest`, the [`logger_logtest`] configuration will apply to any logger whose name starts with `logtest.`. To test this, you could create a new logger in the log controller, which looks like this:

`other_log = logging.getLogger('logtest.controllers.log.other')`

Then in the `index()` action you could choose to use the new logger like this:

```
def index(self):
    other_log.info("Logged with the 'logtest.controllers.log.other' logger")
    log.info("Logged with the %r log", __name__)
    return 'Check the logs!'
```

If you tested the example, you'd see that messages to both loggers are output:

```
21:30:43,621 INFO [logtest.controllers.log.other] Logged with the ➡
'logtest.controllers.log.other' logger
21:30:43,622 INFO [logtest.controllers.log] Logged with the ➡
'logtest.controllers.log' log
```

Since both the loggers in this example are children of the logtest logger, both get logged. Remember to change the propagate option back to 1 if you test this example so that the messages are propagated onto the root logger and then onto the handler.

■Tip Remember that the logger name used in controllers is related to the qualname specified in the configuration for the logger section, not to the name of the config file section. This means you could rename the [logger_logtest] section to something completely different such as [logger_foo] as long as you kept the qualname as logtest and updated other references within the config file to use the foo name.

Using Propagation to Filter Messages

You can also use propagation to filter log messages. For example, say you wanted only WARNING messages or above from the logtest.controllers.log.other logger but still wanted DEBUG messages or above for all other children of the logtest logger. You could update the config file like this (changes are in bold):

```
[loggers]
keys = root, routes, logtest, logtest_controllers_log_other

...

[logger_logtest]
level = DEBUG
handlers =
qualname = logtest
propagate = 1

[logger_logtest_controllers_log_other]
level = WARNING
handlers =
qualname = logtest.controllers.log.other
propagate = 1
```

Now if you tested the previous example again so that an INFO message is logged to both the logtest.controllers.log.other logger and the logtest.controllers.log logger, you'd just see the message that was logged to logtest.controllers.log. This is because logtest.controllers.log.other is only accepting messages of WARNING level or above, so the INFO message it receives is ignored. Here is the output logged:

```
21:30:53,422 INFO  [logtest.controllers.log] Logged with the ➡
'logtest.controllers.log' log
```

If you updated the action to use a warning or error message like this, the log message would appear again, this time as a WARNING.

```
def index(self):
    other_log.warning("Logged with the 'logtest.controllers.log.other' logger")
    log.info("Logged with the %r log", __name__)
    return 'Check the logs!'
```

If you tested the example, you'd see the following output:

```
21:31:48,531 WARN  [logtest.controllers.log.other] Logged with the ➡
'logtest.controllers.log.other' logger
21:31:48,532 INFO  [logtest.controllers.log] Logged with the ➡
'logtest.controllers.log' log
```

A logger's `level` option does not affect messages which it receives via propagation from a child logger. This means the `level` option can only be used to filter messages which are received directly. To test this, update the config file so that the level for `logtest.controllers.log.other` is set to DEBUG and the level for `logtest.controllers.log` is set to WARNING. If you call `other_log.info` (`'This message will be logged'`) in the controller you will see the message is logged because it isn't filtered by the `level` = WARNING option in the [`log_logtest`] section.

This is why the very first example in the chapter worked even though it logged a debug message and the root logger level was specified as INFO.

Summarizing Propagation Options

In practical terms, you can use propagation in three main ways:

- Set up nonroot loggers that have no handlers but do propagate. The non-root loggers can then be used to adjust the verbosity of their logging output by changing their level.

- You could also set up nonroot loggers that have handlers but that *do not* propagate. These produce output only in the handlers they specify and not in the root handler. If a handler has a level higher than the underlying message, the output is suppressed. You'll see an example of this setup next when you add SQLAlchemy output to a new log file.

- Some nonroot loggers have handlers and do propagate. The message will appear in both places. This can be useful if you are using the WSGIErrorsHandler to ensure that all messages get logged.

Capturing Log Output from Other Software

When you are trying to debug a problem in a particular controller, or perhaps a particular module from, say, SQLAlchemy, then you might find that setting the root logger to DEBUG or NOTSET will produce too many messages for you to easily deal with, most of which will be generated by modules you aren't interested in. Instead, you want to be able to adjust only the verbosity of output from one logger or set of loggers.

To do this, you need to add logging configuration for the logger you want to add log messages for. You can then choose to have them handled by the root logger using propagation, configure them to use a separate handler, or do both. Let's look at these approaches.

Capturing SQLAlchemy Log Messages Using Propagation

As an example, let's set up a logger to log a SQLAlchemy engine. To do this, you need to set up a new logger in the configuration file; name it `sqlalchemy`:

```
[loggers]
keys = root, routes, logtest, sqlalchemy
```

Now you need to add the configuration for that logger:

```
[logger_sqlalchemy]
level = DEBUG
handlers =
qualname = sqlalchemy.engine
propagate = 1
```

The `qualname` option here specifies that this logger will handle any messages sent to a logger named `sqlalchemy.engine` or any children it might have. Because the `propagate` option is set to 1, this logger's messages get propagated up to the root logger where they are handled by the root logger's handler.

Even if you set the root logger's level to something higher such as `ERROR`, the `sqlalchemy.engine` debug messages logged at the `INFO` and `DEBUG` levels would still be logged because, as you've seen, the `level` option on the root logger doesn't apply to log messages propagated from configured loggers.

If you chose to enable SQLAlchemy support when you used `paster create` to create your Pylons project, you'd see that your config file already has the following configuration set up:

```
[logger_sqlalchemy]
level = INFO
handlers =
qualname = sqlalchemy.engine
# "level = INFO" logs SQL queries.
# "level = DEBUG" logs SQL queries and results.
# "level = WARNING" logs neither.  (Recommended for production systems.)
```

By changing the `qualname` option, you can adjust which parts of SQLAlchemy are logged. By changing the log `level` of the `sqlalchemy` logger, you can adjust which SQLAlchemy messages are propagated to the root logger to be handled. The `INFO` level results in SQL queries being logged, and the `DEBUG` level causes both queries and results to be logged. You may decide that you want to turn off SQLAlchemy log messages temporarily. If so, you can leave the root logger set to `INFO` and set the `sqlalchemy` logger's level to `WARNING`, and then the usual `INFO` log messages will be suppressed.

Capturing AuthKit Messages Using a Handler

Another piece of software that uses log messages is AuthKit. Some of what AuthKit does behind the scenes is rather complicated, so if you are trying to debug a particular behavior, logging can help.

Let's configure AuthKit so that its messages are sent straight to `application.log` via the `file` handler. First add the logger to the `[loggers]` section and change the `[logger_root]` section so that it is no longer using the `file` handler itself:

```
[loggers]
keys = root, routes, logtest, authkit
[logger_root]
level = INFO
handlers = wsgierrors
```

Then add the configuration for the new logger:

```
[logger_authkit]
level = DEBUG
handlers = file
qualname = authkit
propagate = 0
```

In this case, the `qualname` is `authkit` to capture all AuthKit log messages. The `handler` is set to `file` to use the same file handler section you set up earlier, and `propagate` is set to 0 so that the log messages aren't propagated to the root logger.

In this configuration, the AuthKit messages get sent directly to the file handler where they are logged to the `application.log` file. Of course, nothing is stopping you from using a handler and propagating a message to the root logger. To do this, just set `propagate` to 1 and you'll see the message is passed to the root logger which passes it to the `wsgierrors` handler so that it gets logged there too.

Production Configuration

So far in this chapter I've been discussing the logging configuration for a development setup, but Pylons uses a different default configuration for production setups.

If you install the `LogTest` project you can create a production configuration file like this:

```
$ paster make-config LogTest production.ini
Distribution already installed:
  LogTest 0.1dev from /home/james/Desktop/LogTest
Creating production.ini
Now you should edit the config files
  production.ini
```

The logging part of the generated `production.ini` file looks like this:

```
# Logging configuration
[loggers]
keys = root

[handlers]
keys = console

[formatters]
keys = generic

[logger_root]
level = INFO
handlers = console

[handler_console]
class = StreamHandler
args = (sys.stderr,)
level = NOTSET
formatter = generic

[formatter_generic]
format = %(asctime)s %(levelname)-5.5s [%(name)s] %(message)s
```

As you can see, this defines just one logger, the root logger. The console handler is the same for the development setup, and the formatter is only slightly different (it doesn't include the millisecond part of the time).

This means that any messages of `INFO` level or above will be logged to the standard error stream. As you've seen, this is likely to send log messages generated by the application to the server log, so you might prefer to set up a file handler instead. You saw how to do this in the "Logging to a File" section.

Summary

In this chapter, you saw how to use logging within a Pylons controller and template and took a brief tour of some of the features of Python's `logging` module. You also saw how logging configuration is divided into sections for loggers, handlers, and formatters, and you saw the options each of these different sections can take and what the options do.

You also saw how to control log messages, filtering them by changing the log levels in a handler or using propagation to control which levels of messages get propagated. You saw how to direct certain messages to different handlers such as an external file, and you know how to configure logging to have messages from other software included in the logs.

With the knowledge you've gained, you should be able to take control of the Pylons log messages and make them work for you. When used correctly, logging can be a very powerful tool.

CHAPTER 21

■ ■ ■

Deployment

Pylons is designed to be extremely flexible when it comes to deployment. The upside of this is that you will be able to deploy a Pylons application virtually anywhere—on any platform including Linux, Mac, BSD, and Windows; using any popular server including Nginx, Apache, Lighttpd, and IIS; and using most popular protocols or techniques including CGI, FastCGI, and others. The downside is that it is impossible to document all the options in one chapter.

The approach I'll take in this chapter is to first explain the main steps in the deployment process before getting into some of the details of the different architectures that different deployment strategies rely on. Then I'll end with two complete examples. The first explains how to use Apache to proxy to a Pylons application served by Paste and monitored by a cron job. The second is an embedded solution using mod_wsgi and Apache. Of course, I could have used any of the other available servers for the examples, but Apache is the most well known amongst open source developers.

■**Tip** You can find specific information about how to deploy Pylons on different servers and in different ways in the Pylons Cookbook at `http://wiki.pylonshq.com/display/pylonscookbook/Deployment`.

Setting up and deploying a Pylons application involves the following steps:

1. Choosing or setting up a Python environment
2. Installing the required software into the environment
3. Creating a config file for the application
4. Setting up the application instance
5. Serving the application from the installed environment

Let's look at each in turn.

Choosing or Setting Up a Python Environment

Throughout the book so far, I have recommended using a virtual Python environment to isolate the software libraries your particular Pylons application will use from other Python software on the system while developing your Pylons application.

Using a virtual environment is an extremely good way to deploy a Pylons application in a production environment too, but there are alternatives, and it is worth being aware of them.

Using the System Python Environment

The most obvious option is to install your Pylons applications into the system Python environment. If you want to have only one Pylons application running on the server, this is a great option. Because there is only one Python environment, you avoid the need to worry about setting up the appropriate paths, and you can be sure your Pylons application is always using the same libraries as every other Python application on your system.

The disadvantages are that you need to have root access to install libraries and that any changes to the system Python environment (such as platform security updates or another user upgrading software) will also affect your Pylons application.

Platform Packages or Easy Install?

If you do decide to use the system Python environment, you are faced with another choice. Should you use the versions of libraries packaged for your operating system or install them manually? As an example, Pylons itself is available as a `.deb` file for Debian-based systems such as Ubuntu Hardy Heron, which was used to generate the screenshots in this book. This means it can be installed to the system Python environment with `apt-get install python-pylons`. By installing Pylons in this way, you get certain benefits:

- Confidence that the software will be installed correctly for your platform

- Automatic installation of the dependencies

- The ability to easily uninstall

- An assurance from the particular platform package maintainer that if a security flaw is found, an updated package will provided

- Binary versions of any dependencies with C or C++ extensions so that no compilation is required

The big disadvantage is this:

- Your platform probably has a much slower release cycle than the packages your Pylons applications depend on, so it is likely most of the software available is out-of-date. For example, Hardy Heron uses Pylons 0.9.6.1, whereas this book already covers Pylons 0.9.7.

For this reason, it is usually better to install software to the system Python installation using Easy Install and get the latest version of the software on which your application depends. If you need to use Easy Install, you are probably much better off also using a virtual Python environment anyway so that you can keep complete control over the software your application needs. This is why for the vast majority of cases you should use a virtual Python environment.

Using Buildout

The `virtualenv.py` tool for setting up a virtual Python environment isn't the only way to set up an isolated Python sandbox. Another option is to use Buildout.

Buildout does a number of things:

- Creates a sandbox for your application

- Provides various recipes for managing common deployment tasks

- Manages the eggs your application depends on

Buildout is interesting because it provides more than just an isolated Python environment. In fact, it also replaces Easy Install, so you can't easily use Buildout and Easy Install together.

Buildout comes from the Zope world and can be used for setting up any sort of environment via plug-ins called *recipes*. This means Buildout can compile and install Apache, fetch your Python dependencies, run a test suite, and start your application running. Buildout can also cache the eggs it downloads, which can be handy if multiple applications share the same eggs or if you want to provide some resilience against a particular egg dependency not being available the next time you try to install your Pylons application.

The drawback of Buildout from a Pylons user perspective is that you already know how to do all the things Buildout does but in other ways. For example, you can already isolate your Python environment using a virtual Python environment, you can already install dependant packages using Easy Install, and you can easily write your own shell scripts or Python programs to handle more complex deployment or testing requirements. You can even download the required eggs to a cache. Just use this command:

```
$ easy_install -zmaxd . "SimpleSite==0.3.0"
```

This will connect to the Internet and download SimpleSite and all of its dependencies to the current directory, without installing anything. The -a option used here is short for --always-copy, but this command does not copy eggs that are created in development mode (ones that have tag_build=true set in the setup.cfg file), so you'll still need to manually download any development eggs your application requires.

If you are willing to invest some time learning Buildout and the recipes it uses, you'll find it works well, but since most Pylons developers use a virtual Python environment, you might find Pylons-oriented Buildout documentation a bit thin on the ground. Having said that, you can always read the main Buildout documentation at http://pypi.python.org/pypi/zc.buildout/1.1.1.

Setting Up a Virtual Python Environment

Although using the system Python environment has its benefits and Buildout is a useful tool, I'll assume you have decided to create a virtual Python environment. When deploying an application, it is also usually a good idea to create a user for the application. In this chapter, you'll deploy the SimpleSite application you've been developing, so I'll assume you've created a user called simplesite with a home directory in /home/simplesite. To set up a virtual Python environment from scratch in an env directory in the simplesite user's home directory, you would use the following commands as the simplesite user. I like to keep any files I download in a directory called download, so you'll save the virtualenv-1.1.tar.gz file there:

```
$ mkdir /home/simplesite/download
$ cd /home/simplesite/download
$ wget http://pypi.python.org/packages/source/v/virtualenv/virtualenv-1.1.tar.gz
$ tar zxfv virtualenv-1.1.tar.gz
$ cp virtualenv-1.1/virtualenv.py ./
```

You can now remove the old files if you like:

```
$ rm -r virtualenv-1.1
```

Now create the virtual Python environment, ignoring packages installed in the system Python:

```
$ cd /home/simplesite/
$ python2.5 download/virtualenv.py --no-site-packages env
```

The virtual Python environment is now in /home/simplesite/env.

Tip You should always check the virtual Python page on the Python Package Index to see whether there is a more recent release. In particular, virtualenv 1.1 doesn't support Python 2.6 properly, so if you want to use Python 2.6, keep a lookout for a more recent version.

Dealing with Activate

You'll recall from Chapter 2 that one way of using a virtual Python environment is to use the `activate` script (or `activate.bat` on Windows) to automatically modify the `PATH` environment variables in the shell you are working in. This setup means the commands you type such as `paster`, `python`, and `easy_install` will result in the virtual Python environment copies being executed rather than the system Python environment's versions. If you are used to working in an activated virtual Python environment like this, it is easy to forget that the scripts in the virtual Python environment's `bin` directory can be executed equally well outside the activated shell just by specifying their full paths.

For example, if you had set up a virtual Python environment in `/home/simplesite/env`, the following commands would work perfectly well from anywhere:

```
$ /home/simplesite/env/bin/python
$ /home/simplesite/env/bin/easy_install "SimpleSite==0.3.0"
```

When you are deploying an application, you frequently need to run the previous scripts and programs from cron jobs, CGI scripts, or other locations. In such situations, rather than trying to run `activate` first or modify the `PATH`, just specify the full path to the executable you are trying to execute, and everything will work as easily as it would if you were running commands from the system Python's installation.

Installing the Required Software into the Environment

Now that you have a fresh, clean virtual Python environment, you need to install the software you want to deploy into it. You can do this in a number of ways that you have already been using throughout the book:

```
$ /home/simplesite/env/bin/easy_install "SimpleSite==0.3.0"
$ /home/simplesite/env/bin/easy_install SimpleSite-0.3.0-py2.5.egg -f /path/to/eggs
$ cd /path/to/SimpleSite; ~/env/bin/python setup.py develop
```

In the first example, the SimpleSite egg and all its dependencies would be fetched and installed from the Python Package Index (or any of the links you specified as metadata in the `setup.py` file, as you learned in Chapter 19). The second example demonstrates how to install a specific egg that you have created yourself. Once again, the dependencies will be matched from the Python Package Index, the links in the egg's `setup.py` file, or, this time, the eggs in the `/path/to/eggs` directory. The second approach is useful if your project uses some custom modules that aren't publicly distributed. The final example demonstrates how to set up the source code in develop mode, as you have done throughout most of the book. Once again, the dependencies will be matched from the Python Package Index or any of the links in the project's `setup.py` file.

Which method you choose is entirely up to you, but bear in mind that for a production deployment you probably want to be absolutely sure of the version you are using, so you will probably want to use one of the first two methods. If you were to use the third method, you might be tempted to modify the code in the SimpleSite directory in the event of a problem when really you should fix the problem, change the version number, make a release, and deploy the new version to the virtual Python environment.

Creating a Config File for the Application

Once the application and all its dependencies are installed, you'll need to create a config file for your application. Ideally, you will have designed your application in such a way that any configuration that needs to be done to deploy the application happens in the config file. The user shouldn't have to edit any Python code within your application since it is now packaged up into the egg and not easily accessible.

You'll remember from the "Customizing the Production Config File Template" section of Chapter 19 that Pylons has a tool to automatically generate a config file for an application from the deployment.ini_tmpl template in the project's config directory. That tool is the paster make-config command.

Create a skeleton config file for your application instance called production.ini:

```
$ /home/simplesite/env/bin/paster make-config "SimpleSite==0.3.0" production.ini
```

Once the production.ini file is created, you can customize it for your particular deployment. In particular, you'll want to ensure the debug option in [app:main] is set to false. You should also customize the secret for the AuthKit cookie, specify an appropriate DSN in the sqlalchemy_url, and change any other options you need to configure such as the error-reporting options.

One thing to bear in mind is that with the debug option set to false and the error reporting configured correctly, Pylons will e-mail an error report for every request during which an error occurs. If you have a very busy site and a serious problem occurs, your e-mail address could be swamped by e-mails. If you choose an address you don't check very often, you might miss important error reports, so choose an appropriate e-mail address, but be aware of the risks.

■**Tip** The paster make-config command doesn't actually require the software you are creating a config file for to be installed. As long as a recent version of Paste is installed, the command will automatically install all the software you require from the Python Package Index before creating the config file.

Setting Up the Application Instance

Once you have installed the Pylons application and created a config file with the paster make-app command, you can set up the configured application. You've seen how to do this quite a few times now. You simply run the following command, specifying the config file you want to set up, which in this case is production.ini:

```
$ /home/simplesite/env/bin/paster setup-app production.ini
```

This will run the code in the application's websetup.py file using the configuration options you've specified in the config file. In this case, it will set up all the tables and data you need for an empty website in the database specified by the sqlalchemy_url configuration option. You can then access the Pylons interactive shell with this command:

```
$ /home/simplesite/env/bin/paster --plugin=pylons shell production.ini
```

Serving the Application from the Installed Environment

Once the application and all its dependencies are installed into the environment and the application has been set up, you are ready to serve the application.

Once again, there are many options for how to serve your application. Because a configured Pylons application is also a WSGI application, Pylons applications will run on *any* WSGI server, as you learned in Chapter 16.

Deploying a Pylons application involves obtaining a WSGI application based on the configuration in the config file. You learned how to do this manually with the Paste Deploy `loadapp()` function in Chapter 17.

Rather than discuss all the options here, I'll first show how to choose a deployment option and then show two examples of different techniques for deploying a Pylons application via Apache—one as an example of embedding a Pylons application with mod_wsgi and the other an example of using the Paste HTTP server proxied to by an Apache web server and monitored with a simple cron script.

As a test, though, you can run your application using the Paste HTTP server you are used to using for serving development instances of your application:

```
$ /home/simplesite/env/bin/paster serve production.ini
```

Notice that you didn't use the `--reload` option this time.

■**Caution** As was explained in Chapter 4, it is important that you remember to disable the interactive debugger for production deployment. If it is enabled and an error occurs, the visitor will be presented with the same debugging interface you have used and may be able to cause serious harm to your application by doing things such as deleting files, changing data in your database, or worse.

Deployment Options

Pylons applications are designed to be run in a multithreaded environment. This means they are loaded into memory once when the server is started, and on each request a new thread is started. Simply put, threading allows the same code to be executed in parallel to handle different requests, with each thread in turn getting a portion of the CPU time until it has finished executing.

The advantage of the threaded approach is clear. Since most requests take at least a few milliseconds, there is no point in waiting for one request to finish before starting the next because most of the time the Pylons application will be waiting for data, either from the network, the filesystem, the database, or elsewhere; so, handling multiple requests at the same time using threads is much more efficient because while one thread is waiting for network or database information, the others can be performing useful processing. Handling multiple threads at once in this way is called *multithreading*.

An alternative approach is to have multiple Pylons applications running at once as different processes and then pass each new request to one of the running Pylons processes. This approach is called a *multiprocess* approach. Although this takes a lot more memory (since you are running more copies of Pylons), it is arguably more reliable because if one Pylons application has a serious crash, the others will still be available to serve requests. In a multithreaded environment, if one Pylons application were to crash badly, no more requests could be served. Luckily, Pylons is designed to handle problems within individual threads so is highly unlikely to fail in such a way as to prevent other threads from serving requests; therefore, most people stick with a multi-threaded environment.

One drawback of the multiprocess approach is that you can't directly share information between requests. For example, if your application used the counter example from Chapter 3 where the number of requests was stored in the `app_globals` object and you were to run the application as two separate processes, each would have their own counter. You can't share data via the `app_globals` object in a multiprocess environment, but you can in a multithreaded environment.

Of course, nothing is stopping you from setting up multiple Pylons processes, each of which can handle multiple threads, as long as you haven't written any complex code that relies on information in the Pylons `app_globals` object being available.

You could also deploy your Pylons application as a CGI script using the `run_with_cgi()` example you saw in Chapter 16. As was mentioned in that chapter, though, doing so is very inefficient because handling each request would involve loading the entire app into memory including Python itself and all the required libraries, setting up the middleware stack, handling the one request, and then unloading everything again. For this reason, deploying a Pylons application as a CGI script is not recommended.

It is also possible to run Pylons on an asynchronous server, although I've never done so. In practice, this would offer few advantages over multithreading because Pylons itself is not set up for asynchronous use.

The different ways of getting a Pylons application integrated into another server broadly fall into two camps: embedding and proxying.

Embedding

By using a tool such as mod_wsgi or mod_python, you can directly embed a Python interpreter running your Pylons application into the server. If you are used to a particular server architecture, this can be very useful because the Pylons application effectively becomes part of the server itself. The drawback of this approach is that it can be difficult to debug problems because it isn't always clear whether the problem is with a Pylons application, the server setup, or the way the WSGI adaptor is working.

To embed the Pylons application into a server, you usually need to gain access to the actual WSGI object. You can do so like this:

```
#!/home/simplesite/env/bin/python
```

```
from paste.deploy import loadapp
wsgi_app = loadapp('config:/home/simplesite/production.ini')
```

Because you aren't serving the application directly, you don't need to specify any settings in the `[server:main]` section of the config file because servers other than the Paste HTTP server don't currently understand them. Instead, you would configure settings such as the port and the host in your server's configuration.

Another issue when embedding a Pylons application into another server is that you have to ensure that the Python interpreter that serves the application has access to all the libraries in your virtual Python environment. How this is configured would depend on your server. Later in the chapter you'll look at the specific case of using mod_wsgi to embed a Pylons application in Apache.

Proxying

An alternative approach is to serve the Pylons application with a Python server such as the Paste HTTP server and then proxy requests from your main server to the server running the Pylons application. Paste supports a variety of protocols including HTTP and FastCGI, and has a range of threading options. The advantage of this approach is that you have complete control over your Pylons application but get the added security of using a more security-hardened server such as Apache for the Internet-facing side of the setup.

To set this up, you simply specify the settings you want to use in the [server:main] section of the config file and start the paster server as usual with the paster serve command, making sure to use the paster script from the virtual environment you want to serve the application from. You would ordinarily also change the port to one that was not already in use, such as 8080.

You would then configure the main server to proxy requests from port 80 on the public-facing Internet to port 8080 on the local machine where the Paste HTTP server will handle the request. You'll see how to do this with Apache later in the chapter, although you can also easily use Lighttpd or Nginx, both of which are good choices.

Using Apache to Proxy Requests to Pylons

Let's start by looking at a proxying setup. This is a very good way of setting up a Pylons application because it puts you in complete control of the process.

First you'll need to install Apache 2, mod_proxy, and mod_proxy_http. Most platforms will automatically have mod_proxy and mod_proxy_http with the standard Apache installation, but you may need to enable them:

```
$ sudo a2enmod proxy
$ sudo a2enmod proxy_http
```

Once Apache is installed, you can add a new virtual host. A suitable configuration for the SimpleSite application you've been developing might look like this:

```
<VirtualHost *>
    ServerName www.pylonsbook.com
    ServerAlias pylonsbook.com

    # Logfiles
    ErrorLog  /home/simplesite/log/error.log
    CustomLog /home/simplesite/log/access.log combined

    # Proxy
    ProxyPass / http://localhost:8080/ retry=5
    ProxyPassReverse / http://localhost:8080/
    ProxyPreserveHost On
    <Proxy *>
        Order deny,allow
        Allow from all
    </Proxy>
</VirtualHost>
```

You'll need to replace pylonsbook.com with the domain name that will host your Pylons project, create the directory you would like the error logs to be held in, and then save the config file as /etc/apache2/sites-available/simplesite or in the equivalent location for your platform.

The ProxyPass directive tells Apache to forward any requests that have a URL starting with / (that is, all requests) to a server running on port 8080 on the local machine. Notice that you've set the retry timeout to 5 seconds so that Apache tries to connect every 5 seconds if the Pylons application is restarted rather than the default of 60 seconds.

■Tip Retry timeout customization is particularly useful because the default is 60 seconds, which means that Apache will show an error page for 60 seconds if any connection to the Paste HTTP server failed, including when you restart the server. This issue is easily avoided by setting the retry option to a smaller number, but you can do this only on versions of Apache newer than 2.2.

Next, you need to start the Pylons application. Apache is set up to proxy to a server on port 8080, so check that the production.ini config file sets the port to 8080 in the [server:main] section and that the debug setting is false.

Because you want the Pylons server to remain running after you have exited from the shell you started it in, you use a slightly different version of the paster serve command, which looks like this:

```
$ /home/simplesite/env/bin/paster serve --daemon production.ini start
```

You'll see the message Entering daemon mode, and then you'll be returned to the shell.

■Tip Daemon mode isn't supported on Windows, but instead you can run your Pylons application as a Windows service. The "Deployment on Windows" section later in the chapter contains a link that will show you how.

Now that the Pylons application is running in production mode, you are ready to enable the virtual host in Apache, disable the default configuration and enable simplesite:

```
$ sudo a2dissite default
$ sudo a2ensite simplesite
```

You will need to restart Apache for the changes to take effect:

```
$ sudo /etc/init.d/apache2 restart
```

Now you are ready to test your application. Make sure you have created the log directory and then if you visit the external domain for your application, http://pylonsbook.com in the example, you should see your application running. If not, check the Apache error logs and check that the paster server is actually running by visiting the application running on port 8080; in our example, this would be http://pylonsbook.com:8080 but on your local machine this would be http://localhost:8080. If the application doesn't appear on port 8080 either, check that you have set the correct port in your production.ini file, and check that you are serving the production.ini file and not a different file by mistake. Finally, you can check the paster server is running with the following command, which lists all running processes on your system and then displays only those with paster somewhere in the results:

```
$ ps aux | grep paster
```

Once the application is running correctly, you should consider setting up a firewall so that the Paste HTTP server cannot be accessed directly on the Internet on port 8080 because your application expects to have requests proxied from port 80.

Although the example here uses only one Paste HTTP server, you could also set up a whole range of them, each running on different ports. You can then set up Apache to proxy different requests to different servers so that the load can be shared between the different processes. If you are running on a multicode processor, this is one way to ensure all the cores are used effectively.

Setting Up Log Files

For running a Pylons application in a production environment, you might also want the `paster serve` script to log error messages. You can specify a file to log to using the `--log-file` option. You might also want to store the process ID of the running server in a file so that other tools know which server is running; this is done with the `--pid-file` option. Here's what the full command might look like:

```
$ /home/simplesite/env/bin/paster serve --daemon ➡
--pid-file=/home/simplesite/simplesite.pid ➡
--log-file=/home/simplesite/log/paster-simplesite.log production.ini start
```

As well as specifying `start`, you can use a similar command with `stop` or `restart` to stop or restart the running daemon, respectively.

Of course, as well as relying on the Apache and Paste HTTP server logs, you can also use any of the techniques you learned about in Chapter 20 to set up application logs to log messages to files in the `log` directory.

Creating init Scripts

Now that the Pylons application is successfully running, you might want to add a script to ensure the Pylons application is correctly started and stopped when the server is turned on, rebooted, or shut down. Here's a simple script named `simplesite` to achieve this:

```
#!/bin/sh -e

cd /home/simplesite/
case "$1" in
  start)
    /home/simplesite/env/bin/paster serve --daemon ➡
--pid-file=/home/simplesite/simplesite.pid ➡
--log-file=/home/simplesite/simplesite.log /home/simplesite/production.ini start
    ;;
  stop)
    /home/simplesite/env/bin/paster serve --daemon ➡
--pid-file=/home/simplesite/simplesite.pid ➡
--log-file=/home/simplesite/simplesite.log /home/simplesite/production.ini stop
    ;;
  restart)
    /home/simplesite/env/bin/paster serve --daemon ➡
--pid-file=/home/simplesite/simplesite.pid ➡
--log-file=/home/simplesite/simplesite.log /home/simplesite/production.ini restart
    ;;
  force-reload)
    /home/simplesite/env/bin/paster serve --daemon ➡
--pid-file=/home/simplesite/simplesite.pid ➡
--log-file=/home/simplesite/simplesite.log /home/simplesite/production.ini restart
    /etc/init.d/apache2 restart
    ;;
  *)
    echo $"Usage: $0 {start|stop|restart|force-reload}"
    exit 1
esac

exit 0
```

Notice that the force-reload option also restarts Apache. The way you would install this script varies from platform to platform. On Debian-based systems, you would install it like this:

```
$ sudo cp simplesite /etc/init.d/simplesite
$ sudo chmod o+x /etc/init.d/simplesite
$ sudo /usr/sbin/update-rc.d -f simplesite defaults
 Adding system startup for /etc/init.d/simplesite ...
   /etc/rc0.d/K20simplesite -> ../init.d/simplesite
   /etc/rc1.d/K20simplesite -> ../init.d/simplesite
   /etc/rc6.d/K20simplesite -> ../init.d/simplesite
   /etc/rc2.d/S20simplesite -> ../init.d/simplesite
   /etc/rc3.d/S20simplesite -> ../init.d/simplesite
   /etc/rc4.d/S20simplesite -> ../init.d/simplesite
   /etc/rc5.d/S20simplesite -> ../init.d/simplesite
```

This adds the simplesite script to the different run levels so that it will be started automatically when the system starts.

You can now start, restart, and stop the Pylons application with the following commands:

```
$ sudo /etc/init.d/simplesite start
$ sudo /etc/init.d/simplesite restart
$ sudo /etc/init.d/simplesite stop
```

Restarting Stopped Applications

If for any reason the Paste HTTP server daemon running your Pylons application should unexpectedly die (not that it ever should), you will want a way to restart it. Many tools are available to monitor and restart processes including daemontools (http://cr.yp.to/daemontools.html) and Supervisor (http://supervisord.org/). These are documented in the Pylons Cookbook.

For many situations, the simplest approach is simply to use a cron job to attempt to start the Paste HTTP server daemon every couple of minutes. If it is already running, the request is ignored; otherwise, the server is started. Edit the root crontab like this:

```
$ sudo crontab -e
```

Then add this line to check every two minutes:

```
# m h  dom mon dow   command
*/2 * * * * /etc/init.d/simplesite start
```

Although this isn't the most elegant approach, it does work surprisingly well and is a lot less hassle to set up than more advanced monitoring tools. Of course, for more sophisticated setups, a more sophisticated monitoring and restart strategy is required.

Embedding Pylons in Apache with mod_wsgi

Now that you've seen an example of how to proxy to the Paste HTTP server to run a Pylons application, I'll show you an example of a different approach. In this section, you'll embed the Pylons application directly into Apache with mod_wsgi, which is well documented at http://code.google.com/p/modwsgi/. There is also a user group at http://groups.google.com/group/modwsgi if you have any problems.

Since mod_wsgi is relatively new, not all platforms will have a binary package that can be easily installed, so in this section you'll learn how to compile it from scratch. The mod_wsgi package can be compiled for and used with either Apache 1.3, 2.0, or 2.2 on Unix systems (including Linux), as well as with Windows. Either the single-threaded prefork or multithreaded worker Apache MPMs can be used when running on Unix and Linux; in this section, you'll use the worker MPM. If you are using Windows, you can skip the compilation steps and download the appropriate binary for your version of Python from `http://code.google.com/p/modwsgi/wiki/InstallationOnWindows`.

First make sure you have all the required packages. On Ubuntu Hardy Heron you will need at least the following:

```
$ sudo apt-get install build-essential python2.5-dev
$ sudo apt-get install apache2 apache2-mpm-worker apache2-utils apache2-threaded-dev
```

Whichever way you've installed Apache, check it has the `worker`:

```
$ apache2 -l
Compiled in modules:
  core.c
  mod_log_config.c
  mod_logio.c
  worker.c
  http_core.c
  mod_so.c
```

You are now ready to download and build mod_wsgi. At the time of writing, the latest version is 2.3, which you can download and build on Unix-based systems like this. Here I'm using Python 2.5, but you can create a version for a different version of Python if you prefer:

```
$ wget http://modwsgi.googlecode.com/files/mod_wsgi-2.3.tar.gz
$ tar zxfv mod_wsgi-2.3.tar.gz
$ cd mod_wsgi-2.3
$ ./configure --with-python=/usr/bin/python2.5
$ make
```

Check that it can share the Python library by looking for `libpython2.5.so` in the output from the following commands:

```
$ cd .libs
$ ldd mod_wsgi.so | grep python2.5
    libpython2.5.so.1.0 => /usr/lib/libpython2.5.so.1.0 (0x00002b081a2e1000)
```

You can then install it:

```
$ cd ../
$ sudo make install
```

With mod_wsgi installed, you'll need to enable it so that Apache can use it. Create an `/etc/apache2/mods-available/wsgi.load` file with the following content:

```
LoadModule wsgi_module /usr/lib/apache2/modules/mod_wsgi.so
```

Now enable the mod_wsgi module:

```
$ sudo a2enmod wsgi
```

At this point, mod_wsgi is installed. To make debugging Apache easier, it is useful to set the log level to `info` so that you get all the mod_wsgi information. You do this by adding the following line to Apache's `httpd.conf`:

```
LogLevel info
```

You'll need to restart Apache:

```
$ sudo /etc/init.d/apache2 restart
```

Check the error logs to ensure mod_wsgi has loaded:

```
$ cat /var/log/apache2/error.log | grep wsgi
```

Then when you restart, you see the following:

```
[Sun Jun 29 04:54:44 2008] [info] mod_wsgi: Initializing Python.
[Sun Jun 29 04:54:44 2008] [info] mod_wsgi (pid=4237): Attach interpreter ''.
[Sun Jun 29 04:54:44 2008] [info] mod_wsgi (pid=4239): Attach interpreter ''.
[Sun Jun 29 04:54:44 2008] [notice] Apache/2.2.8 (Ubuntu) ➡
mod_wsgi/2.3 Python/2.5.2 configured -- resuming normal operations
```

Setting Up a Virtual Host

Now that mod_wsgi is installed, you'll need to create a virtual host. Create a new file called /etc/apache2/sites-available/simplesite_mod_wsgi with the following content:

```
<VirtualHost *>
    ServerName www.pylonsbook.com
    ServerAlias pylonsbook.com

    # Logfiles
    ErrorLog  /home/simplesite/log/error.log
    CustomLog /home/simplesite/log/access.log combined

    # Setup mod_wsgi
    WSGIScriptAlias / /home/simplesite/mod_wsgi/dispatch.wsgi

    <Directory /home/simplesite/mod_wsgi>
    Order deny,allow
    Allow from all
    </Directory>

</VirtualHost>
```

Once again, you'll need to replace pylonsbook.com with the domain name that will host your Pylons project. In the example, you are using the same log directory as for the proxy example, but you can change that if you want.

The WSGIScriptAlias directive tells mod_wsgi that all requests to the root of your application should be handled by the /home/simplesite/mod_wsgi/dispatch.wsgi script. Create the /home/simplesite/mod_wsgi directory, and add the dispatch.wsgi file with the following content:

```
# Add the virtual Python environment site-packages directory to the path
import site
site.addsitedir('/home/simplesite/env/lib/python2.5/site-packages')

# Avoid ``[Errno 13] Permission denied: '/var/www/.python-eggs'`` messages
import os
os.environ['PYTHON_EGG_CACHE'] = '/home/simplesite/egg-cache'

# Load the Pylons application
from paste.deploy import loadapp
application = loadapp('config:/home/simplesite/production.ini')
```

A few things are going on in this script. The virtual Python environment's site-packages directory is added to the Pylons path so that mod_wsgi can find all the libraries you need. You used site.addsitedir() rather than the more usual sys.path.append() so that eggs listed in the .pth files set up by Easy Install are also added to the path.

Your Pylons application will actually be run as the Apache user, and occasionally mod_wsgi will need to unpack some of the eggs your Pylons application uses. The location it should unpack them to can be customized by setting the PYTHON_EGG_CACHE environment variable, which you first saw in Chapter 2. In this case, the example uses the directory /home/simplesite/egg-cache, so you should create that directory and ensure that the Apache user has permission to read and write to it. If you see a pkg_resources.ExtractionError, which starts with "Can't extract file(s) to egg cache", it means that you haven't specified your egg cache directory correctly or that Apache doesn't have the appropriate permissions to that directory. Apache will also need access to your data directory. The easiest way of setting up the appropriate permissions is to add the Apache user to the simplesite group and then grant group write permission to the egg-cache and data directories so that Apache can write to them. On Ubuntu Hardy you do so like this:

```
$ sudo usermod -a -G simplesite www-data
$ mkdir /home/simplesite/egg-cache
$ chmod g+w /home/simplesite/egg-cache
$ chmod g+w /home/simplesite/data
```

Most developers would choose MySQL or PostgreSQL for a production system but if you are using SQLite as a database bear in mind that mod_wsgi will require write access to the directory containing the database. This means you will have to create a new directory for SQLite, give the Apache user access to it and modify the path in the production.ini file.

The final part of the dispatch.wsgi script uses Paste Deploy to load the Pylons WSGI application object from the config file in the way you learned about in Chapter 17. mod_wsgi knows to look for an object called application in the dispatch script, and it uses this (the Pylons application) to serve the requests.

Now that the virtual host configuration is in place and you've written dispatch.wsgi, you can test the application. First you'll need to enable the virtual host:

```
$ sudo a2dissite simplesite
$ sudo a2ensite simplesite_mod_wsgi
```

Then you will need to restart Apache for the changes to take effect:

```
$ sudo /etc/init.d/apache2 restart
```

If you visit your web site, you should now see the finished SimpleSite application being correctly served by mod_wsgi, as shown in Figure 21-1.

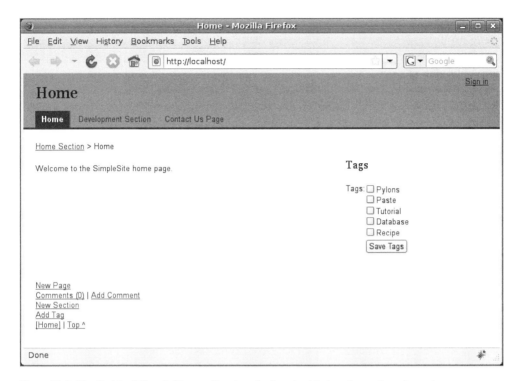

Figure 21-1. *The finished SimpleSite application deployed with Apache and mod_wsgi*

Troubleshooting

If you have problems with mod_wsgi, the first thing you should do is look at the error logs in both the /home/simplesite/log directory and the main Apache error log. Messages from mod_wsgi should be logged. If the problem isn't obvious, try replacing the dispatch.wsgi script with this test script, and make sure it works properly:

```
def application(environ, start_response):
    status = '200 OK'
    output = 'Hello World!'

    response_headers = [('Content-type', 'text/plain'),
                        ('Content-Length', str(len(output)))]
    start_response(status, response_headers)

    return [output]
```

You will need to restart Apache any time you make a change to any code or to the production.ini or dispatch.wsgi files. This is because once an application is loaded into memory, mod_wsgi uses the same application to serve each request so you need to force Apache to recreate the application before your changes will take effect. If you replace the dispatch.wsgi file, restart Apache and visit the site, you should be greeted with "Hello World!" Once this works correctly, you can try with Pylons once again.

One thing that often catches people out when using mod_wsgi with Pylons is that the Pylons interactive debugger cannot be used with mod_wsgi. If you try to use it, you will get an error like this:

```
AssertionError: The EvalException middleware is not usable in a multi-process ➥
environment
```

You should set the `debug` option to `false` to disable the interactive debugger, and then your Pylons application will work.

If you still have problems, you should read the detailed documentation on the `http://code.google.com/p/modwsgi/` site or ask a question on the mailing list.

Deployment on Windows

Pylons can also be deployed on Windows systems. The easiest approach is simply to use the Windows ports of all the software you would usually use with Pylons under Linux. For example, Apache, MySQL, and PostgreSQL all have good-quality versions available for the Windows platform. Pylons and its dependencies run equally well on Windows as on other platforms as long as you use Python 2.4 or newer.

If you want to do things in a more Windows-specific way, you can use one of two approaches that Pylons users have used in the past. The first involves setting up the Paste HTTP server as a Windows service. This is documented in the Pylons Cookbook at `http://wiki.pylonshq.com/display/pylonscookbook/How+to+run+Pylons+as+a+Windows+service`. You will need to install `pywin32` from `https://sourceforge.net/projects/pywin32/` to use this approach.

The second approach is to serve a Pylons application from IIS, and although this is significantly more complicated, the process is fully documented at `http://wiki.pylonshq.com/display/pylonscookbook/Serving+a+Pylons+app+with+IIS`.

A final approach is a bit of a compromise, but if you are installing Pylons on a Windows machine purely because your company's infrastructure is Windows-based, you could consider using a virtualization technology such as VMware to run an entire Linux instance on a Windows server.

Summary

You should now have a solid understanding of how to deploy your Pylons applications. With the information you have gathered throughout this entire book, you should now be ready to design, develop, and deploy your own Pylon applications! I hope you've found this book to be useful guide to web development with Pylons. I'd encourage you to get involved in the Pylons community by contributing to the discussions on the mailing list or on IRC or by writing new articles for the Pylons cookbook. Whatever you intend to use Pylons for, whether it is a simple site like the one developed in the book or a popular service like `http://reddit.com`, I wish you all the very best in your endeavors.

■ ■ ■

Licenses

This appendix gives the full text of each license that applies to the content in this book. The GNU Free Documentation License applies to all content. The Pylons License applies to the examples that are based on ones in the Pylons documentation. The YUI license applies to the YUI source files you will include as part of the SimpleSite example code and YUI documentation quoted in Chapter 15.

GNU Free Documentation License

sourcecode:: text

GNU Free Documentation License

Version 1.2, November 2002

Copyright (C) 2000, 2001, 2002 Free Software Foundation, Inc.

51 Franklin St, Fifth Floor, Boston, MA 02110-1301 USA

Everyone is permitted to copy and distribute verbatim copies of this license document, but changing it is not allowed.

0. PREAMBLE

The purpose of this License is to make a manual, textbook, or other functional and useful document "free" in the sense of freedom: to assure everyone the effective freedom to copy and redistribute it, with or without modifying it, either commercially or noncommercially. Secondarily, this License preserves for the author and publisher a way to get credit for their work, while not being considered responsible for modifications made by others.

This License is a kind of "copyleft", which means that derivative works of the document must themselves be free in the same sense. It complements the GNU General Public License, which is a copyleft license designed for free software.

We have designed this License in order to use it for manuals for free software, because free software needs free documentation: a free program should come with manuals providing the same freedoms that the software does. But this License is not limited to software manuals; it can be used for any textual work, regardless of subject matter or whether it is published as a printed book. We recommend this License principally for works whose purpose is instruction or reference.

1. APPLICABILITY AND DEFINITIONS

This License applies to any manual or other work, in any medium, that contains a notice placed by the copyright holder saying it can be distributed under the terms of this License. Such a notice grants a world-wide, royalty-free license, unlimited in duration, to use that work under the conditions stated herein. The "Document", below, refers to any such manual or work. Any member of the public is a licensee, and is addressed as "you". You accept the license if you copy, modify or distribute the work in a way requiring permission under copyright law.

A "Modified Version" of the Document means any work containing the Document or a portion of it, either copied verbatim, or with modifications and/or translated into another language.

A "Secondary Section" is a named appendix or a front-matter section of the Document that deals exclusively with the relationship of the publishers or authors of the Document to the Document's overall subject (or to related matters) and contains nothing that could fall directly within that overall subject. (Thus, if the Document is in part a textbook of mathematics, a Secondary Section may not explain any mathematics.) The relationship could be a matter of historical connection with the subject or with related matters, or of legal, commercial, philosophical, ethical or political position regarding them.

The "Invariant Sections" are certain Secondary Sections whose titles are designated, as being those of Invariant Sections, in the notice that says that the Document is released under this License. If a section does not fit the above definition of Secondary then it is not allowed to be designated as Invariant. The Document may contain zero Invariant Sections. If the Document does not identify any Invariant Sections then there are none.

The "Cover Texts" are certain short passages of text that are listed, as Front-Cover Texts or Back-Cover Texts, in the notice that says that the Document is released under this License. A Front-Cover Text may be at most 5 words, and a Back-Cover Text may be at most 25 words.

A "Transparent" copy of the Document means a machine-readable copy, represented in a format whose specification is available to the general public, that is suitable for revising the document straightforwardly with generic text editors or (for images composed of pixels) generic paint programs or (for drawings) some widely available drawing editor, and that is suitable for input to text formatters or for automatic translation to a variety of formats suitable for input to text formatters. A copy made in an otherwise Transparent file format whose markup, or absence of markup, has been arranged to thwart or discourage subsequent modification by readers is not Transparent. An image format is not Transparent if used for any substantial amount of text. A copy that is not "Transparent" is called "Opaque".

Examples of suitable formats for Transparent copies include plain ASCII without markup, Texinfo input format, LaTeX input format, SGML or XML using a publicly available DTD, and standard-conforming simple HTML, PostScript or PDF designed for human modification. Examples of transparent image formats include PNG, XCF and JPG. Opaque formats include proprietary formats that can be read and edited only by proprietary word processors, SGML or XML for which the DTD and/or processing tools are not generally available, and the machine-generated HTML, PostScript or PDF produced by some word processors for output purposes only.

The "Title Page" means, for a printed book, the title page itself, plus such following pages as are needed to hold, legibly, the material this License requires to appear in the title page. For works in formats which do not have any title page as such, "Title Page" means the text near the most prominent appearance of the work's title, preceding the beginning of the body of the text.

A section "Entitled XYZ" means a named subunit of the Document whose title either is precisely XYZ or contains XYZ in parentheses following text that translates XYZ in another language. (Here XYZ stands for a specific section name mentioned below, such as "Acknowledgements", "Dedications", "Endorsements", or "History".) To "Preserve the Title" of such a section when you modify the Document means that it remains a section "Entitled XYZ" according to this definition.

The Document may include Warranty Disclaimers next to the notice which states that this License applies to the Document. These Warranty Disclaimers are considered to be included by reference in this License, but only as regards disclaiming warranties: any other implication that these Warranty Disclaimers may have is void and has no effect on the meaning of this License.

2. VERBATIM COPYING

You may copy and distribute the Document in any medium, either commercially or noncommercially, provided that this License, the copyright notices, and the license notice saying this License applies to the Document are reproduced in all copies, and that you add no other conditions whatsoever to those of this License. You may not use technical measures to obstruct or control the reading or further copying of the copies you make or distribute. However, you may accept compensation in exchange for copies. If you distribute a large enough number of copies you must also follow the conditions in section 3.

You may also lend copies, under the same conditions stated above, and you may publicly display copies.

3. COPYING IN QUANTITY

If you publish printed copies (or copies in media that commonly have printed covers) of the Document, numbering more than 100, and the Document's license notice requires Cover Texts, you must enclose the copies in covers that carry, clearly and legibly, all these Cover Texts: Front-Cover Texts on the front cover, and Back-Cover Texts on the back cover. Both covers must also clearly and legibly identify you as the publisher of these copies. The front cover must present the full title with all words of the title equally prominent and visible. You may add other material on the covers in addition. Copying with changes limited to the covers, as long as they preserve the title of the Document and satisfy these conditions, can be treated as verbatim copying in other respects.

If the required texts for either cover are too voluminous to fit legibly, you should put the first ones listed (as many as fit reasonably) on the actual cover, and continue the rest onto adjacent pages.

If you publish or distribute Opaque copies of the Document numbering more than 100, you must either include a machine-readable Transparent copy along with each Opaque copy, or state in or with each Opaque copy a computer-network location from which the general network-using public has access to download using public-standard network protocols a complete Transparent copy of the Document, free of added material. If you use the latter option, you must take reasonably prudent steps, when you begin distribution of Opaque copies in quantity, to ensure that this Transparent copy will remain thus accessible at the stated location until at least one year after the last time you distribute an Opaque copy (directly or through your agents or retailers) of that edition to the public.

It is requested, but not required, that you contact the authors of the Document well before redistributing any large number of copies, to give them a chance to provide you with an updated version of the Document.

4. MODIFICATIONS

You may copy and distribute a Modified Version of the Document under the conditions of sections 2 and 3 above, provided that you release the Modified Version under precisely this License, with the Modified Version filling the role of the Document, thus licensing distribution and modification of the Modified Version to whoever possesses a copy of it. In addition, you must do these things in the Modified Version:

A. Use in the Title Page (and on the covers, if any) a title distinct from that of the Document, and from those of previous versions (which should, if there were any, be listed in the History section of the Document). You may use the same title as a previous version if the original publisher of that version gives permission.

B. List on the Title Page, as authors, one or more persons or entities responsible for authorship of the modifications in the Modified Version, together with at least five of the principal authors of the Document (all of its principal authors, if it has fewer than five), unless they release you from this requirement.

C. State on the Title page the name of the publisher of the Modified Version, as the publisher.

D. Preserve all the copyright notices of the Document.

E. Add an appropriate copyright notice for your modifications adjacent to the other copyright notices.

F. Include, immediately after the copyright notices, a license notice giving the public permission to use the Modified Version under the terms of this License, in the form shown in the Addendum below.

G. Preserve in that license notice the full lists of Invariant Sections and required Cover Texts given in the Document's license notice.

H. Include an unaltered copy of this License.

I. Preserve the section Entitled "History", Preserve its Title, and add to it an item stating at least the title, year, new authors, and publisher of the Modified Version as given on the Title Page. If there is no section Entitled "History" in the Document, create one stating the title, year, authors, and publisher of the Document as given on its Title Page, then add an item describing the Modified Version as stated in the previous sentence.

J. Preserve the network location, if any, given in the Document for public access to a Transparent copy of the Document, and likewise the network locations given in the Document for previous versions it was based on. These may be placed in the "History" section. You may omit a network location for a work that was published at least four years before the Document itself, or if the original publisher of the version it refers to gives permission.

K. For any section Entitled "Acknowledgements" or "Dedications", Preserve the Title of the section, and preserve in the section all the substance and tone of each of the contributor acknowledgements and/or dedications given therein.

L. Preserve all the Invariant Sections of the Document, unaltered in their text and in their titles. Section numbers or the equivalent are not considered part of the section titles.

M. Delete any section Entitled "Endorsements". Such a section may not be included in the Modified Version.

N. Do not retitle any existing section to be Entitled "Endorsements" or to conflict in title with any Invariant Section.

O. Preserve any Warranty Disclaimers.

If the Modified Version includes new front-matter sections or appendices that qualify as Secondary Sections and contain no material copied from the Document, you may at your option designate some or all of these sections as invariant. To do this, add their titles to the list of Invariant Sections in the Modified Version's license notice. These titles must be distinct from any other section titles.

You may add a section Entitled "Endorsements", provided it contains nothing but endorsements of your Modified Version by various parties—for example, statements of peer review or that the text has been approved by an organization as the authoritative definition of a standard.

You may add a passage of up to five words as a Front-Cover Text, and a passage of up to 25 words as a Back-Cover Text, to the end of the list of Cover Texts in the Modified Version. Only one passage of Front-Cover Text and one of Back-Cover Text may be added by (or through arrangements made by) any one entity. If the Document already includes a cover text for the same cover, previously added by you or by arrangement made by the same entity you are acting on behalf of, you may not add another; but you may replace the old one, on explicit permission from the previous publisher that added the old one.

The author(s) and publisher(s) of the Document do not by this License give permission to use their names for publicity for or to assert or imply endorsement of any Modified Version.

5. COMBINING DOCUMENTS

You may combine the Document with other documents released under this License, under the terms defined in section 4 above for modified versions, provided that you include in the combination all of the Invariant Sections of all of the original documents, unmodified, and list them all as Invariant Sections of your combined work in its license notice, and that you preserve all their Warranty Disclaimers.

The combined work need only contain one copy of this License, and multiple identical Invariant Sections may be replaced with a single copy. If there are multiple Invariant Sections with the same name but different contents, make the title of each such section unique by adding at the end of it, in parentheses, the name of the original author or publisher of that section if known, or else a unique number. Make the same adjustment to the section titles in the list of Invariant Sections in the license notice of the combined work.

In the combination, you must combine any sections Entitled "History" in the various original documents, forming one section Entitled "History"; likewise combine any sections Entitled "Acknowledgements", and any sections Entitled "Dedications". You must delete all sections Entitled "Endorsements".

6. COLLECTIONS OF DOCUMENTS

You may make a collection consisting of the Document and other documents released under this License, and replace the individual copies of this License in the various documents with a single copy that is included in the collection, provided that you follow the rules of this License for verbatim copying of each of the documents in all other respects.

You may extract a single document from such a collection, and distribute it individually under this License, provided you insert a copy of this License into the extracted document, and follow this License in all other respects regarding verbatim copying of that document.

7. AGGREGATION WITH INDEPENDENT WORKS

A compilation of the Document or its derivatives with other separate and independent documents or works, in or on a volume of a storage or distribution medium, is called an "aggregate" if the copyright resulting from the compilation is not used to limit the legal rights of the compilation's users beyond what the individual works permit. When the Document is included in an aggregate, this License does not apply to the other works in the aggregate which are not themselves derivative works of the Document.

If the Cover Text requirement of section 3 is applicable to these copies of the Document, then if the Document is less than one half of the entire aggregate, the Document's Cover Texts may be placed on covers that bracket the Document within the aggregate, or the electronic equivalent of covers if the Document is in electronic form. Otherwise they must appear on printed covers that bracket the whole aggregate.

8. TRANSLATION

Translation is considered a kind of modification, so you may distribute translations of the Document under the terms of section 4. Replacing Invariant Sections with translations requires special permission from their copyright holders, but you may include translations of some or all Invariant Sections in addition to the original versions of these Invariant Sections. You may include a translation of this License, and all the license notices in the Document, and any Warranty Disclaimers, provided that you also include the original English version of this License and the original versions of those notices and disclaimers. In case of a disagreement between the translation and the original version of this License or a notice or disclaimer, the original version will prevail.

If a section in the Document is Entitled "Acknowledgements", "Dedications", or "History", the requirement (section 4) to Preserve its Title (section 1) will typically require changing the actual title.

9. TERMINATION

You may not copy, modify, sublicense, or distribute the Document except as expressly provided for under this License. Any other attempt to copy, modify, sublicense or distribute the Document is void, and will automatically terminate your rights under this License. However, parties who have received copies, or rights, from you under this License will not have their licenses terminated so long as such parties remain in full compliance.

10. FUTURE REVISIONS OF THIS LICENSE

The Free Software Foundation may publish new, revised versions of the GNU Free Documentation License from time to time. Such new versions will be similar in spirit to the present version, but may differ in detail to address new problems or concerns. See http://www.gnu.org/copyleft/.

Each version of the License is given a distinguishing version number. If the Document specifies that a particular numbered version of this License "or any later version" applies to it, you have the option of following the terms and conditions either of that specified version or of any later version that has been published (not as a draft) by the Free Software Foundation. If the Document does not specify a version number of this License, you may choose any version ever published (not as a draft) by the Free Software Foundation.

ADDENDUM: How to use this License for your documents

To use this License in a document you have written, include a copy of the License in the document and put the following copyright and license notices just after the title page:

Copyright (c) YEAR YOUR NAME.

Permission is granted to copy, distribute and/or modify this document under the terms of the GNU Free Documentation License, Version 1.2 or any later version published by the Free Software Foundation; with no Invariant Sections, no Front-Cover Texts, and no Back-Cover Texts. A copy of the license is included in the section entitled "GNU Free Documentation License".

If you have Invariant Sections, Front-Cover Texts and Back-Cover Texts, replace the "with...Texts." line with this:

with the Invariant Sections being LIST THEIR TITLES, with the Front-Cover Texts being LIST, and with the Back-Cover Texts being LIST.

If you have Invariant Sections without Cover Texts, or some other combination of the three, merge those two alternatives to suit the situation.

If your document contains nontrivial examples of program code, we recommend releasing these examples in parallel under your choice of free software license, such as the GNU General Public License, to permit their use in free software.

Pylons License

Note: This license applies to Pylons itself, not to its dependencies. Please check the licenses of the dependencies separately.

Copyright (c) 2005-2008 Ben Bangert, James Gardner, Philip Jenvey and contributors.

All rights reserved.

Redistribution and use in source and binary forms, with or without modification, are permitted provided that the following conditions are met:

1. Redistributions of source code must retain the above copyright notice, this list of conditions and the following disclaimer.

2. Redistributions in binary form must reproduce the above copyright notice, this list of conditions and the following disclaimer in the documentation and/or other materials provided with the distribution.

3. The name of the author or contributors may not be used to endorse or promote products derived from this software without specific prior written permission.

THIS SOFTWARE IS PROVIDED BY THE AUTHOR AND CONTRIBUTORS ``AS IS" AND ANY EXPRESS OR IMPLIED WARRANTIES, INCLUDING, BUT NOT LIMITED TO, THE IMPLIED WARRANTIES OF MERCHANTABILITY AND FITNESS FOR A PARTICULAR PURPOSE ARE DISCLAIMED. IN NO EVENT SHALL THE AUTHOR OR CONTRIBUTORS BE LIABLE FOR ANY DIRECT, INDIRECT, INCIDENTAL, SPECIAL, EXEMPLARY, OR CONSEQUENTIAL DAMAGES (INCLUDING, BUT NOT LIMITED TO, PROCUREMENT OF SUBSTITUTE GOODS OR SERVICES; LOSS OF USE, DATA, OR PROFITS; OR BUSINESS INTERRUPTION) HOWEVER CAUSED AND ON ANY THEORY OF LIABILITY, WHETHER IN CONTRACT, STRICT LIABILITY, OR TORT (INCLUDING NEGLIGENCE OR OTHERWISE) ARISING

IN ANY WAY OUT OF THE USE OF THIS SOFTWARE, EVEN IF ADVISED OF THE POSSIBILITY OF SUCH DAMAGE.

ALL TEMPLATES GENERATED ARE COVERED UNDER THE FOLLOWING LICENSE:

Copyright (c) 2005-2008 Ben Bangert, James Gardner, Philip Jenvey and contributors. All rights reserved.

Redistribution and use in source and binary forms, with or without modification, are permitted provided that the following condition is met:

The name of the author or contributors may not be used to endorse or promote products derived from this software without specific prior written permission.

THIS SOFTWARE IS PROVIDED BY THE AUTHOR AND CONTRIBUTORS ``AS IS'' AND ANY EXPRESS OR IMPLIED WARRANTIES, INCLUDING, BUT NOT LIMITED TO, THE IMPLIED WARRANTIES OF MERCHANTABILITY AND FITNESS FOR A PARTICULAR PURPOSE ARE DISCLAIMED. IN NO EVENT SHALL THE AUTHOR OR CONTRIBUTORS BE LIABLE FOR ANY DIRECT, INDIRECT, INCIDENTAL, SPECIAL, EXEMPLARY, OR CONSEQUENTIAL DAMAGES (INCLUDING, BUT NOT LIMITED TO, PROCUREMENT OF SUBSTITUTE GOODS OR SERVICES; LOSS OF USE, DATA, OR PROFITS; OR BUSINESS INTERRUPTION) HOWEVER CAUSED AND ON ANY THEORY OF LIABILITY, WHETHER IN CONTRACT, STRICT LIABILITY, OR TORT (INCLUDING NEGLIGENCE OR OTHERWISE) ARISING IN ANY WAY OUT OF THE USE OF THIS SOFTWARE, EVEN IF ADVISED OF THE POSSIBILITY OF SUCH DAMAGE.

YUI License

Software License Agreement (BSD License)

Copyright (c) 2008, Yahoo! Inc.

All rights reserved.

Redistribution and use of this software in source and binary forms, with or without modification, are permitted provided that the following conditions are met:

- Redistributions of source code must retain the above copyright notice, this list of conditions and the following disclaimer.

- Redistributions in binary form must reproduce the above copyright notice, this list of conditions and the following disclaimer in the documentation and/or other materials provided with the distribution.

- Neither the name of Yahoo! Inc. nor the names of its contributors may be used to endorse or promote products derived from this software without specific prior written permission of Yahoo! Inc.

THIS SOFTWARE IS PROVIDED BY THE COPYRIGHT HOLDERS AND CONTRIBUTORS "AS IS" AND ANY EXPRESS OR IMPLIED WARRANTIES, INCLUDING, BUT NOT LIMITED TO, THE IMPLIED WARRANTIES OF MERCHANTABILITY AND FITNESS FOR A PARTICULAR PURPOSE ARE DISCLAIMED. IN NO EVENT SHALL THE COPYRIGHT OWNER OR CONTRIBUTORS BE LIABLE FOR ANY DIRECT, INDIRECT, INCIDENTAL, SPECIAL, EXEMPLARY, OR CONSEQUENTIAL DAMAGES (INCLUDING, BUT NOT LIMITED TO, PROCUREMENT OF SUBSTITUTE GOODS OR

SERVICES; LOSS OF USE, DATA, OR PROFITS; OR BUSINESS INTERRUPTION) HOWEVER CAUSED AND ON ANY THEORY OF LIABILITY, WHETHER IN CONTRACT, STRICT LIABILITY, OR TORT (INCLUDING NEGLIGENCE OR OTHERWISE) ARISING IN ANY WAY OUT OF THE USE OF THIS SOFTWARE, EVEN IF ADVISED OF THE POSSIBILITY OF SUCH DAMAGE.

Sources of Intellectual Property Included in the YUI Library

YUI is issued by Yahoo! under the BSD license above. Below is a list of certain publicly available software that is the source of intellectual property in YUI, along with the licensing terms that pertain to thosesources of IP. This list is for informational purposes only and is not intended to represent an exhaustive list of third party contributions to the YUI.

- Douglas Crockford's JSON parsing and stringifying methods: In the JSON Utility, Douglas Crockford's JSON parsing and stringifying methods are adapted from work published at JSON.org. The adapted work is in the public domain.

- Robert Penner's animation-easing algorithms: In the Animation Utility, YUI makes use of Robert Penner's algorithms for easing.

- Geoff Stearns's SWFObject: In the Charts Control and the Uploader, YUI makes use of Geoff Stearns's SWFObject v1.5 for Flash Player detection and embedding. More information on SWFObject can be found here (http://blog.deconcept.com/swfobject/). SWFObject is (c) 2007 Geoff Stearns and is released under the MIT License (http://www.opensource.org/licenses/mit-license.php).

Index

You Need the Companion eBook

Your purchase of this book entitles you to buy the companion PDF-version eBook for only $10. Take the weightless companion with you anywhere.

We believe this Apress title will prove so indispensable that you'll want to carry it with you everywhere, which is why we are offering the companion eBook (in PDF format) for $10 to customers who purchase this book now. Convenient and fully searchable, the PDF version of any content-rich, page-heavy Apress book makes a valuable addition to your programming library. You can easily find and copy code—or perform examples by quickly toggling between instructions and the application. Even simultaneously tackling a donut, diet soda, and complex code becomes simplified with hands-free eBooks!

Once you purchase your book, getting the $10 companion eBook is simple:

❶ Visit **www.apress.com/promo/tendollars/**.

❷ Complete a basic registration form to receive a randomly generated question about this title.

❸ Answer the question correctly in 60 seconds, and you will receive a promotional code to redeem for the $10.00 eBook.

Apress®
THE EXPERT'S VOICE™

2855 TELEGRAPH AVENUE | SUITE 600 | BERKELEY, CA 94705

Offer valid through 6/09.